Contemplating Minds

Contemplating Minds

A Forum for Artificial Intelligence

edited by
William J. Clancey, Stephen W. Smoliar, and Mark J. Stefik

The MIT Press
Cambridge, Massachusetts
London, England

Printed and bound in the United States of America.

Library of Congress Cataloging-in-Publication Data

Contemplating minds: a forum for artificial intelligence / edited by William J. Clancey,
  Stephen W. Smoliar, and Mark J. Stefik.
    p. cm. — (Artificial intelligence)
  Includes bibliographical references and index.
  ISBN 0-262-53119-4 (pbk.)
    1. Artificial intelligence—Book reviews. 2. Cognition—Book reviews. I. Clancey, William J.
  II. Smoliar, Stephen W. III. Stefik, Mark. IV. Series: Artificial intelligence (Cambridge, Mass.)
  Q335.C582 1994
  153'.01'1—dc20   93-35759
                                                                                      CIP

Contents

Series Foreword

Artificial intelligence is the study of intelligence using the ideas and methods of computation. Unfortunately, a definition of intelligence seems impossible at the moment because intelligence appears to be an amalgam of so many information-processing and information-representation abilities.

Of course psychology, philosophy, linguistics, and related disciplines offer various perspectives and methodologies for studying intelligence. For the most part, however, the theories proposed in these fields are too incomplete and too vaguely stated to be realized in computational terms. Something more is needed, even though valuable ideas, relationships, and constraints can be gleaned from traditional studies of what are, after all, impressive existence proofs that intelligence is in fact possible.

Artificial intelligence offers a new perspective and a new methodology. Its central goal is to make computers intelligent, both to make them more useful and to understand the principles that make intelligence possible. That intelligent computers will be extremely useful is obvious. The more profound point is that artificial intelligence aims to understand intelligence using the ideas and methods of computation, thus offering a radically new and different basis for theory formation. Most of the people doing work in artificial intelligence believe that these theories will apply to any intelligent information processor, whether biological or solid state.

There are side effects that deserve attention, too. Any program that will successfully model even a small part of intelligence will be inherently massive and complex. Consequently, artificial intelligence continually confronts the limits of computer-science technology. The problems encountered have been hard enough and interesting enough to seduce artificial intelligence people into working on them with enthusiasm. It is natural, then, that there has been a steady flow of ideas from artificial intelligence to computer science, and the flow shows no sign of abating.

The purpose of this series in artificial intelligence is to provide people in many areas, both professionals and students, with timely, detailed information about what is happening on the frontiers in research centers all over the world.

J. Michael Brady
Daniel Bobrow
Randall Davis

Preface

People enjoy reading book reviews. In this time of multidisciplinary collaboration, reviews of a book are sometimes read by more people than the book itself.
The book reviews in the journal *Artificial Intelligence* have become essays, even
tutorial presentations. In many cases multiple reviews of a book are published
together with a response by the author. In this arrangement they constitute a
multidisciplinary forum on the scientific themes of the field. Yet the readership
of the journal is small compared to the community of psychologists, social scientists, engineers, and educators interested in the progress of artificial intelligence
(AI) research. Thus was born the idea of collecting and ordering the reviews into
a form suitable for the general scientific reader, seminar organizer, or student
wanting a critical introduction to the current ideas of the leading thinkers in AI.

The title of this book, *Contemplating Minds*, was chosen because it has two
appropriate meanings. The first refers to an important activity that takes place in
all kinds of forums—people contemplate and debate. The second meaning refers
to the specific theme of this book—contemplating minds themselves, that is,
making theories about how we think.

Since its inception, AI has had the lofty goal of giving an account of thinking.
The first approaches are debated in the first part of this book, which discusses
symbolic models of mind. Part I includes a critical examination of *Unified
Theories of Cognition*, the final book by Alan Newell, which summarizes his
life's work on the development of symbolic models of intelligence. This
exchange is preceded by reviews of an earlier book by Zenon Pylyshyn, which
presents what we might call the "conservative's view" of the relation between
computer programs and human knowledge. Part II addresses an alternative to the
symbolic approach in the form of situated action theory. Four reviews are presented of *Understanding Computers and Cognition*, by Terry Winograd and
Fernando Flores, a book that has provoked much discussion by people interested
and engaged in the design of computer systems. Architectures of Interaction
(part III) concerns the interactions among large numbers of agents (or elements)
in social, economic, and neural contexts. Here the emphasis shifts to considerations for the engineering of intelligent systems: from simple distribution of
agents to interactive processes epitomized by Minsky's *Society of Mind*. The
volume concludes with a reconsideration of the basic issues of memory and consciousness (part IV) that brings together the philosophical arguments and new

ideas of mechanism in Edelman's alternative model of the brain, *Neural Darwinism.*

Paralleling their models of intelligence, Newell, Winograd, Minsky, and Edelman have different points of view concerning what it means to test a theory. Newell synthesizes, attempting to subsume all data under a given theory. Minsky tends more toward constructive criticism, taking a given theory, finding data that disconfirm it, and suggesting an alternative theory. Winograd favors logical, humanistic arguments making new philosophical and linguistic distinctions. Edelman combines these points of view, grounding model building on a philosophical position, supported by neurobiological and psychological data.

Although this volume is restricted to book reviews originally published in *Artificial Intelligence,* we believe that, for this time and this topic, this collection is as good and useful as any we might have deliberately planned. We in fact left behind many other reviews, some for another volume (particularly those concerning connectionism), some because of space constraints, and others because of topic. Our selections meet the following criteria:

- The book or review discusses models of mind.
- The review explains the content of the book sufficiently, so the reader can grasp the essential arguments without reading the book.
- The review attempts to explain difficult ideas, offering bridges, rather than dismissing what is controversial.
- The review informs the reader about seminal work or an interesting book outside the AI field.
- The review will stimulate conversation in a seminar.

Book reviews would be relatively easy to write if they involved merely a summary and a comment on why anyone should care to read the book. The reviews in this volume are essays that explore the multidisciplinary nature of artificial intelligence and give a sense of the landscape of alternative theories and their development. They offer not just opinions or complaints but elaborations and links to philosophy, linguistics, sociology, biology, and psychology.

This collection constitutes a forum, a place for synthesizing and comparing points of view. Multiple reviews, comparative reviews, and reviews of edited collections offer the reader alternative perspectives, different explanations, and chances to understand sometimes difficult, counterintuitive ideas. Single book reviews appear only when they fit within the context provided by multiple and comparative reviews. We have added brief introductions to each part, to bring out thematic relationships among the reviews and books presented there, but the reviews themselves appear as originally published.

We believe that this collection is essential reading for anyone interested in the nature of the human mind. Readers familiar with formal AI research publications will no doubt be surprised by the broad, scientific range of issues discussed here. We believe the student and experienced researcher alike will come away with a thorough and useful understanding for orienting future work.

Perhaps most of all, we intend for these introspective essays to provide a common background that will enable us all to better converse with each other about people and computers. These timely reviews speak enthusiastically, with candor, clarity, scientific professionalism, and breadth. Some are long and thoughtful, others very short. Responses from authors round out the forum, often constituting major contributions to the scientific literature.

We believe that a lively book review process is essential to the health of any scientific community. In this forum about and by contemplating minds, we hope to stir your enthusiasm for AI research and challenge you to absorb the force of unexpected ideas.

Acknowledgments

We wish to acknowledge the crucial support of Daniel G. Bobrow, Editor-in-Chief of *Artificial Intelligence*. He encouraged us to expand the scope of the book review column of that journal, and to include the multiple reviews and author responses that give the column its character as a forum.

We thank Mimi Gardner for assistance in the running of the review column for many years, and for her assistance in collecting the materials for this book. We thank Anne Tourney for helping to prepare the index.

Funding for preparing this collection has been provided in part for Bill Clancey at the Institute for Research on Learning by the Xerox Foundation; the NSF Information, Robotics and Intelligent Systems Program; and Nynex Science & Technology, Inc.

Stephen Smoliar and Mark Stefik acknowledge their research institutes for supporting their work as review editors of *Artificial Intelligence,* and for supporting the preparation of this book. Smoliar is supported by the Institute of Systems Science at the National University of Singapore. Stefik is supported by the Xerox Palo Alto Research Center.

I *Symbolic Models of Mind*

Introduction

The General Problem Solver (GPS) is one of the earliest and most influential examples of using computer systems to model human problem solving. In their classic AI paper (Newell, Shaw, and Simon 1959) and in the more elaborate book that followed (Newell and Simon 1972), Allen Newell and Herbert A. Simon present theory, methodology, and experimental results that explain human problem-solving behavior as the product of laws involving symbol manipulation. In these accounts of mind, symbols are not merely the stuff of external human communication in our written language. They are the internal tokens that govern how our minds work.

Although nonsymbolic models based on cybernetic and neural network ideas were also developed early in AI (see for example Minsky and Papert 1988), symbolic models dominated because they had no rivals for explaining higher-level behavior. When AI researchers debated mental models in the 1970s, the discussion was usually about the best kinds of symbolic models rather than any nonsymbolic alternatives. Symbolic models gained further stature from their use in mathematics and logic, thus fostering a sense that logic is what the mind does.

In the 1980s, there were several challenges to the dominance of symbolic models. The best known of these is connectionism. Connectionist models are akin to nervous systems. They are computational systems made from many (millions or more) simple, interconnected computational elements that exchange signals. Connectionism was used to describe perceptual processing in terms of parallel computation. It gained advocates because of its success in explaining how slow computational elements can compute so fast. See Michael Dyer's review in part III of this book for a discussion of the relation between connectionist and symbolic models.

In 1992 Newell raised the stakes for symbolic models with his book *Unified Theories of Cognition* (henceforth designated as UTC). Here Newell gives a much more comprehensive and richly detailed account than in his earlier books, especially in his attention to timing data and his description of mind in terms of distinct levels. He challenges his colleagues in cognitive science, declaring that enough is now known to attempt a daunting scientific enterprise: putting together comprehensive theories that explain the major mental phenomena. His book offers one such theory, centered on symbolic approaches. In doing this, he also gives his view of just which mental phenomena should be explained. Much of the book reports on the Soar project, a multi-university project founded by Newell, Paul S. Rosenbloom, and John E. Laird. In this way, his book connects his earlier work with an ongoing scientific project that extends the questions and methods of the symbolic approach to explaining human intelligence.

Models of minds are complex. The quest for unified models is analogous to a well-known quest of twentieth-century physics. Throughout this century, there have been increasing efforts to unify theories of physical phenomena that are otherwise explained by separate theories about electricity, magnetism, gravity, and strong nuclear forces. Physics has not yet found its grand unified model or "theory of everything," but the scientific enterprise of constructing such a unification has been quite active. UTC calls for a similar effort for understanding minds.

Most of the contributions to the first part of this book are critiques of UTC written by various members of the AI and cognitive science communities. The reviewers are articulate representatives of different schools of thought in these communities.

In his review of UTC Michael A. Arbib offers a competitive model based on schemas rather than symbols. He wants theories to account for more kinds of experimental data, especially brain lesion data. Daniel C. Dennett is a philosopher of mind, and a long-time commenter on AI and computational models. His own book on consciousness (Dennett 1991) is reviewed in part IV of this volume. Michael R. Fehling criticizes Newell's focus on timing data, and argues that Soar could be used profitably just to model competence rather than performance. Loosely affiliated with the Soar community and trained as a cognitive psychologist, Barbara Hayes-Roth can be viewed as an insider. She argues that the selection of tasks used to evaluate Soar is too artificial. She offers harder challenges that stress the model. Marvin Minsky is often credited, along with Newell, as being one of the fathers of AI and one of its most inventive people. Newell's criticism of Minsky was that he does no empirical experiments. Minsky's criticism of Newell, roughly, is that his attention is focused too narrowly. Minsky's own approach is presented in his book *The Society of Mind* (Minsky 1985), reviewed in part III of this volume. Jordan B. Pollack is an articulate connectionist. Starting with the name "Soar," he reexamines an old AI mantra that "airplanes are to birds as smart machines will be to brains." The resulting review is both a penetrating analysis of fundamental assumptions in Newell's approach and a delight to read. Dale Purves, more than the other reviewers, is an outsider to the AI community. Chairman of the Department of Neurobiology at Duke University Medical Center, he finds UTC to be of little relevance to biologists. Finally, Roger C. Schank and Menachem Y. Jona are positioned similarly to Hayes-Roth—insiders in both AI and cognitive psychology. Their critique of

Soar is technical, concerned with indexing of memory and scaling phenomena. They are interested in how theories of cognition apply to education.

All of the reviewers of UTC wrote these reviews with the expectation of a response by Newell. Tragically, Newell died just as the reviews were completed. His colleagues, co-founders of the Soar project, and former students— Rosenbloom and Laird—agreed to respond to the reviews in his stead. Their essay is a model of careful argument, laying out their best understanding of Newell's attitude about the various criticisms, their own positions as they differ from Newell's, and areas where further work is needed to resolve a question.

The other two reviews in this section are of Zenon Pylyshyn's *Computation and Cognition* (1984). This book was written between Newell's two major books on symbolic models. Given the diversity of models of cognition throughout cognitive science, Pylyshyn's approach has much in common with UTC. The reviews of it and Pylyshyn's response serve as an introduction to basic concepts of representation and cognition in symbolic models.

References

D.C. Dennett. 1991. *Consciousness Explained.* Boston: Little Brown.

M.L. Minsky. 1985. *The Society of Mind.* New York: Simon & Schuster.

M.L. Minsky and S.A. Papert. 1988. *Perceptrons* (expanded edition). Cambridge, Mass.: MIT Press. (Expanded from an earlier version published in 1969.)

A. Newell, J.C. Shaw, and H.A. Simon. 1959. Report on a General Problem-Solving Program. In *Proceedings International Conference on Information Processing*, UNESCO House, 256–264.

A. Newell and H.A. Simon. 1972. *Human Problem Solving.* Englewood Cliffs, NJ: Prentice-Hall.

Z.W. Pylyshyn. 1984. *Computation and Cognition.* Cambridge, Mass.: MIT Press.

Z.W. Pylyshyn, *Computation and Cognition*: *Toward a Foundation of Cognitive Science* **(MIT Press, Cambridge, MA, 1986); 292 pages, $33.75 (hardcover), $9.95 (paperback).**

Reviewed by: Mark Stefik
　　　　　　System Sciences Laboratory, *Xerox Palo Alto Research Center*, *Palo Alto, CA 94304, U.S.A.*

Foundations for Understanding Cognizers

Pylyshyn's book is about foundations. His ambitions for this at first appear modest. As he says,

> A more realistic way to put it might be to say that the material contained here is to the foundations of cognitive science what a hole in the ground is to the foundation of a house. It may not seem like what you eventually hope to have, but you do have to start some place.

Pylyshyn is interested in phenomena of cognition. He proposes to study entities that exhibit intelligent behavior.

> Just as the domain of biology includes something like all living things so the domain of cognitive science may be something like "knowing things," or as George Miller (1984) colorfully dubbed it, the "informavores."

Pylyshyn himself re-dubs these things "cognizers" which gives us cognitive science as the study of cognizers. This sounds somewhat circular; it shifts the matter from a question about the central properties of cognitive science to the central properties of cognizers. Speaking like a philosopher of science, Pylyshyn notices that although cognizers have mass, gravity is already well-covered by physics; similarly phenomena involving sound, or physical hardness, or chemical reactions are already explained by established and separate disciplines. So which properties are central? Pylyshyn doesn't address that question right away. But he sets a direction, arguing that the natural category "cognizer" encompasses a populatiuon of objects such as people and computers.

In part Pylyshyn defines his position in opposition to others. For example, he observes that the philosophical discussions of cognitivism are

> concerned with certain issues, such as the proper understanding of "meaning" or the role of consciousness... While these questions may be fascinating... they may well be precisely the kind of questions that are irrelevant to making scientific progress. Indeed,

they may be like the question, how it is possible to have action at a distance . . . debated with much acrimony in the eighteenth century. The question remains unresolved today; people may have decided that the question is not worth pursuing . . . .

Cognizers act on the basis of representations. Pylyshyn identifies this as their central property. He identifies these representations as rich structures of significance; not only are they "state" in a computational sense, they are about the environment and they correspond to things we call beliefs and goals. His central thesis is that cognizers.

> instantiate such representations physically as cognitive codes and . . . their behaviour is a causal consequence of operations carried out on these codes.

To this reviewer that sounds very much like the physical symbols system hypothesis, rephrased in computerese. One can ask whether this idea explains enough. Pylyshyn sets out to show a range of implications of the idea. Pylyshyn identifies his approach as a "representational theory of mind."

From Philosophy to Computation

Pylyshyn illustrates his points with brilliantly simple, concrete examples. One such example that is extended several times concerns a pedestrian who sees a car skid and crash into a pole. He runs across the street, looks into the wreckage, races off to a telephone, and dials 911. Pylyshyn wants to know what kind of theory would be appropriate for explaining this sequence of events. He first notes that the activities of the Cognizer are not usefully explained by the laws of energy and momentum from physics. Those principles describe the skidding of the car, but the racing of the pedestrian is not connected to the accident by transfer of energy or momentum.

Pylyshyn raises several variations of this story, where the pedestrian dials 91 instead of 911, or in which the pedestrian uses a pushbutton phone instead of a dial phone. Pylyshyn recognizes that it is a weak staw man, indeed, who argues that cognition might be a simple extrapolation of physics. The core of his concern is with explanations that can account for computational quandaries of mind, more than the physical.

What is needed, he argues, is that a computer program should "actually perform at a sufficiently fine and theoretically motivated level of resolution." The early GPS papers (Newell and Simon [1]) are a model of this approach.

The Parts of the Case

Pylyshyn's argument goes through several stages. He argues that one needs to decide which kinds of regularities need explaining. He recommends starting with phenomena similar to those explained by what he calls folk psychology or "grandmother's psychology," that is, stories that account for human behavior in terms of what a person is expected to know or feel. Here, he connects action with stored representation. People do the things they do because of what they know and believe. If they knew or believed different things, they would act differently. A theory that doesn't do some of this starts off on the wrong foot.

Representations are encoded. Pylyshyn describes the nature of encoding and action by analogy with the programming of computers. For many AIers, this set of assumptions at this level of generality passes with neither question nor examination. How could it be wrong? Pylyshyn is interested in understanding cases where it could be wrong, and his sequence of points builds to some problematic examples.

Pylyshyn aruges that mind is understood in levels. He discusses (1) a biological or physical level, (2) a symbolic or functional level, and (3) an intentional or semantic level. The biological level corresponds to the physical substrate of memory. The functional level reflects the situation that many different physical configurations can mean the same thing. Within this level, Pylyshyn wants to define classes of representations according to their equivalent roles in explaining behavior. He wants to be able to assign "symbolic codes" to these classes so as to explain how actions connect with behavior. Pylyshyn equates his semantic level with Newell's knowledge level.

By describing these levels he is trying to establish what he calls a functional architecture. It is worth noting that a description at this level of generality encompasses many possible models of mind. For example, it includes GPS-like models from [1]. It also includes, for example, models of scripts and plans, or say, any of John Anderson's models. The computational framework doesn't rule much out.

Pylyshyn then goes on to develop equivalence criteria, for deciding whether a computational model explains a process. He demands not only a kind of similarity in possible behavior, but also a close complexity equivalence. By this he means more than measures of time and space as in the complexity of computer algorithms. He wants a close correspondence in the actual steps and processes. Two factors make this prescription challenging in practice: limited theory and difficulties in observation. Theories of complexity for parallel algorithms are at a very early stage of development. The combinations of parallel, serial, and distributed processes and systems that are studied systematically in computer science are much simpler than those that arise in biological systems. Secondly, these processes are difficult to observe in biological systems. This combination makes the prescription difficult and limiting. For this reviewer it was not made sufficiently clear just how much leverage Pylyshyn expects from these concepts and techniques because he did not acknowledge the practical impediments.

Pylyshyn is particularly interested in understanding how to tell which behaviors are alterable by changes in knowledge or belief. He characterizes the ones that can be changed as being "cognitively penetrable."

Pylyshyn then applies this development to approach the question of how and whether the processes of perception and mental imagery are cognitively penetrable. In this he wants to contrast his theory with other notions of "imaginal thinking," because as he says, other investigators have felt that a computational view might have to give way to something different. He argues that experiments that illustrate cognitive penetrability support the relevance of a representation theory of mind for partially explaining these phenomena.

Whose Foundations? A Closing Parable

Laying foundations is a challenging task. There is recurring debate in cognitive science about foundations. Frameworks for understanding the mind are as different as the proverbial accounts from a group of blind men, each describing an elephant from where he stands. "It's a hose." "It's a rope." "It's a tree." "It's a hill."

A recent example of this occurred in the opening session of the Symposium "How can slow components think so fast?" organized by the American Association for Artificial Intelligence at Stanford in March 1988. Allen Newell gave the opening presentation describing some general constraints on architectures for cognition.

Beginning with the biological puzzle suggested by the title of the session, Newell developed a set of levels of organization building up from "organelles" which perform operations in 10^{-4} seconds through neurons, neural networks, on up to brain-sized organizations and beyond. At each successive level of organization the larger operations require approximately ten times as long to carry out.

Newell then observed that there is almost no time available for a neural system to produce cognitive behavior. He defined cognitive behavior in terms of "deliberate actions," that is, actions that require bringing knowledge to bear, such as making an appropriate move in chess. In many examples, an interval of about one second (say 150 milliseconds to 10 seconds) is long enough for humans to take deliberate actions. After accounting for time necessary for nondeliberative processes being observed, Newell concludes that deliberation itself requires as little as 100 msecs. From this he surmises that cognitive brain architectures must usually employ learning mechanisms that enable most deliberation to be carried out by recognition.

Following Newell's presentation three speakers were invited to comment on it. This was where the "blind men" phenomenon became apparent. Jack Byrne did not comment on Newell's presentation directly, but rather reported on detailed mechanisms for learning and memory in the nerve "circuitry" for one portion of the simple nervous system of a sea mollusk. Bernardo Huberman gave a whirlwind presentation of results on dynamical systems and how dynamical models can make useful predictions about chaotic behavior, learning, and interactions of agents in an environment.

Only the last speaker, Steve Kosslyn, addressed Newell's presentation directly and this started a debate. Kosslyn argued that while Newell's level analysis provides limits and sanity checks on theories of mind, he doubted its utility for understanding the architecture of the mind. He went on to discuss experimental techniques for mapping human and animal behavior to active areas of brain structure.

To this observer and reviewer the most striking point in the discussion was not any contradiction between Newell's predictions and the mapping of brain activity. Rather, there was a large gap between the phenomena of interest to the different parties. Newell's arguments said nothing about the organization of learning across large areas of a brain; Kosslyn's arguments did not give a fine enough grain to localize behavior and provided essentially no insights into dynamics. Neither gave predictions that would bear on the nerve mechanisms of Bryne's sea mollusk nerve networks; Huberman's theories and equations could apply as well to large networks of many kinds, whether they be computers, nerves, or astronomical bodies.

So where in all of this is cognitive science, and what has this to do with Pylyshyn's book?

To take the second question first, we note that Pylyshyn acknowledges an intellectual debt to Newell, and spent time with him during some of the writing of the book. If Pylyshyn had given an address on this at the Symposium, this reviewer predicts that his claims of foundations would provoke a similar debate.

Pylyshyn's book brings order to the debate by proposing to carve cognitive science "at its natural joints." Thus, he argues that a human mind operates at different levels and can be understood best by recognizing those levels: the physical, the symbolic, and the intentional.

A framework like Pylyshyn's can be challenged by raising different kinds of questions. Are there natural joints for understanding the mind? If yes, are Pylyshyn's and Newell's joints the right ones? Do we know enough about nerves, brain organization, and cognition to adequately evaluate the proposal?

Pylyshyn himself acknowledges this issue in the introduction by his analogy about house foundations and a hole in the ground. Carving nature at joints helps to sort out the kinds of questions we ask. However, we know very little about either mental phenomena or brain structure and the theories and data we have explain a small subset of the range of phenomena.

To be too satisfied with the explanations can preclude attention to other questions. Furthermore, it's not enough that joints separate phenomena into levels. It is better if they also suggest how we can understand the connections between levels.

In the context of this young and active field, any synthesis is incomplete. Cognitive scientists must still contend with the issues of determining which kinds of questions are crucial, and which have answers within their grasp. Controversy arises when claims about foundations are seen as implicitly determining the main questions to be investigated, the methods to be used, and the scientific disciplines said to be central. If the debaters in the AAAI symposium were to offer recommendations for how to understand the organized complexity of the mind, we could imagine very different recommendations. "Study nerve networks." "Study learning and chaotic networks." "Study brain areas and function."

Recommendations

Even given that there are other approaches and foundations for understanding the mind, *Computation and Cognition* is a worthwhile book.

I have two main complaints. The first is that the prose is often dense and wordy. (If I said that it was not cognitively penetrable, I would be misusing that phrase.) The book needs a crisp summary of the definitions of levels and a crisp summary of the cases for perception and mental imagery. So many of Pylyshyn's words were about the stance of his theory relative to others (in terms of the philosophy of science) that it was hard to find out what his position was.

My other complaint is that I wanted a more detailed theory of some aspects of mind. For that, one must turn to other authors. Pylyshyn's book stays at the abstract level. For example, his concern with perception is mainly with whether a representational theory of mind is relevant to explaining it. There are no diagrams of the eye or statements of any detail about how human vision might work. Similarly, although Pylyshyn is interested in drawing from folk psychology, there is a very large gap between grandma's prediction of what cousin Fred might do and a predictive model for any aspect of Fred's mind. Pylyshyn eschews details.

My main praise of Pylyshyn's book is that he provides compelling, short, and clear examples for the points he chooses to make. For students of AI the book shows how phenomena that might seem quite ordinary can be quite remarkable when seen through a psychological perspective informed by computing.

In reviews [1] of an earlier version fo Pylyshyn's work, reviewers of both theoretical and experimental persuasions picked at various aspects of Pylyshyn's approach. They discussed ambiguities in the application of the cognitive-penetrability criterion. They gave examples of computational activities in various kinds of nerve and brain cells that challenged the neat separation Pylyshyn's levels seem to propose between neuroscience and cognitive psychology. The examples show systems affected by information infusion that are not thought of as being cognitive (e.g., the digestive system) and specialized systems of parallel and distributed computation that make crucial use of representations other than beliefs and goals. In responding to these earlier criticisms, Pylyshyn has tightened up his definitions a bit.

If Pylyshyn decides to give us an updated edition of this book, this reviewer would like to see a presentation that reaches into more experimental examples. At this stage of our understanding, it seems more fruitful and illuminating to attend to observations than arguments about philosophy. It is not that the computational perspective is wrong. Rather, the programming and system examples from nature are richer than the ones we have invented ourselves. Thus, it's not that we need to export computer science to psychology and neuroscience; rather, some more traffic in both directions is needed. Making the examples accessible to an AI audience would energize that field at just the right time, as its computational options are becoming more interesting. In the absence of a new edition, this reviewer suggests that AI readers augment the book with its earlier reviews [2, 3].

REFERENCES

1. Newell, A. and Simon, H.A., *Human Problem Solving* (Prentice-Hall, Englewood Cliffs, NJ, 1972).
2. Open Peer Commentary on Cognition and Computation, *Behavioral and Brain Sci.* **3** (1) (1980) 1133–1153.
3. Haugeland, J., Review of Computation and Cognition, *Philosophy of Science* **54** (2) (1987) 309–311.

Z.W. Pylyshyn, *Computation and Cognition: Toward a Foundation for Cognitive Science* (MIT Press, Cambridge, MA, 1986); 292 pages, \$33.75 (hardcover), \$9.95 (paperback).

Reviewed by: Alan K. Mackworth
   Department of Computer Science, University of British Columbia, Vancouver, BC, Canada V6T 1W5

The prototypical working scientist may often safely ignore foundational treatises and debates. Smugly ensconced in the enfolding security of a received framework, he (typically, he is a "he") twiddles symbols or knobs, enjoying the simple pleasures of puzzling out nature's secrets. Tempting as that idyll may be, the prototypical researcher in AI or cognitive science should renounce it. For us, it's premature—both illusive and elusive.

Pylyshyn's goal is to show that cognition, taken broadly to include perception, problem solving, planning, language use and action, is a natural scientific domain. He argues that an autonomous science of cognitive systems must have a unified vocabulary and a coherent set of principles with a range of established theoretical and experimental methods. The principles must be as parsimonious, exact and constraining as possible to allow explanation and prediction of a wide range of cognitive phenomena as well as falsification and revision of the theory. Although this is commonly accepted, most cognitive experimenting and theorizing, by psychologists and computer scientists, is radically underconstrained and thereby flawed. Pylyshyn puts forward a strong testable hypothesis: cognition is computation. This is risky. The popular tactic of seeing computation as a *metaphor* for cognition is much safer. Unfortunately, metaphors are not scientific hypotheses: they cannot be wrong.

Pylyshyn goes further. Even if the computation hypothesis is adopted, he does not allow the claim that any program that simulates some behavior stands as an explanatory theory. A theory must explain and predict behavior by exhibiting a computational embodiment that is "strongly equivalent" to the cognitive process. "Strong equivalence" means isomorphism at the descriptive level of representation-based algorithms and "functional architecture". The operational test of "cognitive penetrability" is one way to determine independently whether a capability is to be modelled by rule-governed computation or embedded directly in the functional architecture. In summary, the hypothesis is that cognition is representation-based computation on a specific functional architecture. The process-architecture interface is system-dependent but task-independent; various methods are proposed for determining it. Computational cognitive theories that presuppose an architectural primitive which is demonstrably cognitively penetrable are, under this view, simply inadequate.

When Pylyshyn's thesis is baldly summarized in this impoverished way, the reader may come to hold one of two incompatible negative views of it. The first is, put crudely, "So what? It's obvious. We all know that." The second is, "No. It's all wrong. It doesn't explain emotion, learning, connectionism, or my grandmother." A reader holding the first view should realize that most of it may feel obvious in hindsight and it is not, of course, entirely original but by summing it up and spelling it out so clearly, Pylyshyn has moved us closer to a science of cognition. A reader holding the second view should carefully consider the importance of focussing a fledgling, sometimes floundering if not foundering, science on the proper questions. Pylyshyn provides a coherent foundational framework for mainstream cognitive science. Sceptics and critics of the mainstream orthodoxy have here a set of clear targets. Other foundational frameworks must address the same issues although the answers could be quite different.

Having built the framework, Pylyshyn then uses the tools it provides to study a range of philosophical, theoretical and experimental approaches to the design and analysis of cognitive systems. For practitioners of AI the key conclusion is that implemented code is only a necessary component of a useful contribution to cognitive science. He outlines a sufficient set of such components.

Some sections of the book are hard to read. They are simply more obscure and discursive than they need be, even granting the intrinsic difficulty of these matters. For the reader with the necessary time, patience, energy and motivation, I recommend reading the book in its entirety. In fairness, I warn the gentle reader that those resources are required in good measure. The faint of heart should start with the excellent epilogue and summary in Chapter 9 and then read the Preface and Chapters 1–5 until any one of the requisite resources is exhausted. As with any complex detective story, with a plot entangled in clues and cues, it can be more rewarding to read the *denouement* first. Much of the material in Chapters 6, 7 and 8 could be skimmed lightly by AI researchers not much interested in private psychological turf wars over behaviorism, direct perception, analogues and mental imagery, although the material there follows coherently from, and supports, the foundational thesis.

In short, *Computation and Cognition* is recommended as an effective, if occasionally indigestible, antidote for methodological smugness.

On *Computation and Cognition*: *Toward a Foundation of Cognitive Science*, a response to the reviews by A.K. Mackworth and M.J. Stefik.

Response by: Zenon Pylyshyn
Centre for Cognitive Science, University of Western Ontario,
London, Ontario, Canada N6A 5C2

Why Foundations, and Where Next?

The two reviews of my book that appear in this issue raise a number of questions that prompt this brief commentary. As to the particular evaluations that are contained in the reviews, I have scarcely any disagreements. I agree with Stefik that there are many perspectives one can take on the major foundational issues, and that there is much room for maneuvering at this stage in the development of the science. I also agree with Mackworth's comments— including his recommendations for how the book might be read. I take the opportunity provided by the editor to comment on these reviews as an invitation to suggest how the book might have been written, now that I have had the advantage of hindsight, a large number of published reviews, and the intervening approximately five years during which a great deal of discussion has taken place concerning the foundations of cognitive science.

It will come as no surprise that I believe the main proposals contained in *Computation and Cognition* still hold. In fact, I am distressed to find them being referred to as the *orthodoxy* [1]. However, if the book were being written now, the arguments in support of these proposals would have to be expanded in several directions in response to recent advances. Despite the fact that the basic assumptions laid out in *C & C* appear to many (e.g., apparently to both Mackworth and Stefik) to be nearly truisms, vigorous opposition to the tri-level view of computation and cognition continues. This is the view, familiar to computer scientists, that both processes have a stable level of organization at the semantic, syntactic, and physical levels; or as Allen Newell puts it, the knowledge level, the symbol level, and the physical level. Opposition to it comes from the same sources discussed in *C & C*: from philosophers who accept intentional (or knowledge level) explanations but do not accept the symbolic level as a genuine level of explanation; from those (including both philosophers and biologists) who eschew both intentional and symbolic explanations, from psychologists who believe that most cognitive processing (e.g. that involving mental imagery) will have to be modeled in terms of processes which do not manipulates discrete symbols—perhaps ones that use an "analogue" medium; and even from some who accept the symbol level but object to the use of knowledge ascriptions (all of these are referenced in *C &*

C). However, by far the most influential recent source of objection has come from the connectionist or PDP movement [2]—a movement whose acceptance, particularly by psychologists and by the popular science press, threatened for a time to undermine the current computational approach in cognitive science.

This is not the proper forum for a discussion of the general issues raised by these objectors, especially since Jerry Fodor and I have just published a rather long analysis of the shortcomings of the connectionist "alternative" [3], and I have also summarized some of my recent views on these issues [4, 5]. But throughout such debates one should not lose sight of the point of trying to illuminate the foundational assumptions and roots of our present "orthodoxy". The reason, as has been said in connection with the study of history more generally, is that otherwise we may be doomed to repeat our mistakes. Indeed, there is every reason to believe that we are in the midst of repeating many of the major errors of the first "cybernetic revolution" as well as the first 50 years of behaviorist psychology.

Two failures have combined to make this new attack on the orthodoxy popular, both of which illustrate the relevance of understanding the foundational assumptions of one's science. The first is the failure to understand what the traditional view, which has come down to us from Turing and other early theorists, is committed to and, even more importantly *why*. The second is the failure to understand the reasons why the first round of cybernetic models were inadequate, and consequently the loss of an opportunity to learn from their failures.

While the differences between the connectionist models and those of the first series of "neural-like" models (e.g., the first *perceptron*, or Uttley's early *conditional probability computer*) may appear to be technically significant, the two approaches are in fact very similar in spirit and in their underlying epistemology. Both are motivated by the same intuitively appealing idea, namely the idea of building a cognizing system from elementary ("neural-like") elements that become organized by virtue of the statistical properties of events occurring at their inputs. In the meantime the lessons learned from the deep discoveries of Turing, mathematicians studying the foundations of mathematics and computing, logicians, and other theorists, are misunderstood and dismissed as "old fashioned". These discoveries include the need for a sufficiently rich symbolic representational system, in order to encode the semantic domains over which the systems are computing, and the need for a system of transformations that preserve the semantic interpretations of the codes (e.g., numerals and operations which mirror the functions of number theory, in the case of Turing's original machine; logical forms for encoding propositional contents and transformations that preserve semantic coherence, in the case of the various systems designed to carry out both logical and heuristic inferences).

The fundamental set of assumptions embodied in the classical view of computing has been discussed by many people, probably most effectively in the

AI tradittion by Allen Newell, who refers to the *Physical Symbol System Hypothesis*, and in the philosophy of mind tradition by Jerry Fodor, who refers to it as the *Language of Thought Hypothesis*. However, instead of focusing on these hypotheses and the elaborate reasons that have been given for adopting them, the connectionism movement has focused on *current implementations* of classical architectures and has dismissed the entire set of ideas on the basis of such irrelevancies as the speed, damage resistance, determinism, lack of parallelism, etc of many of the current models, as well as the apparent differences between present-day computers and the nervous system. These are all properties that, however true they may be of many contemporary models, are irrelevant to the architectural ideas discussed in *C & C*, and certainly do not provide arguments that favor connectionism over the classical ideas about computation, such as those that derive from the insights of von Neumann and Turing.

Mackworth correctly points out that scientists working within an accepted paradigm feel that they can safely ignore foundational questions. As if to illustrate this premise, Stefik asserts that "At this stage of our understanding, it seems more fruitful and illuminating to attend to observations than arguments about philosophy." These are among the most common criticisms I have heard of the enterprise attempted in *C & C*. To the extent that this is a plea for further research, good ideas, and more solid results, then one can scarcely disagree. Yet in cognitive science, unlike, say, in solid state physics, every result comes wrapped in a great number of contentious methodological and philosophical commitments, typically unacknowledged. That's partly because the field is young and diffuse and in the process of defining itself. It's also partly because the questions that are being asked typically have had a long history in philosophical inquiry. Because of this, one cannot begin the process of *scientific* inquiry in cognitive science without taking a stand on a dozen different classical philosophical issues, most of which represent positions that are deeply ingrained in our culture. One of these is a belief in the doctrine that behavioral capacities of organisms can be traced directly to the record of causal events in their immediate environment, particularly to statistical properties of this record. Another is a deep skepticism of mentalism and of related notions such as "meaning", and a consequent belief in the primacy of biological facts over other sorts of facts and considerations for understanding intelligent behavior (e.g., facts about the systematicity of both actual and potential behaviors, the systematicity of cognitive capacities, the nature of the information available in an organism's past experience in relation to the organism's current capacities, as well as considerations of the descriptive adequacy, generality, and sufficiency of models).

There is no question that we badly need results, and that students need detailed expositions of the best current work. I can understand Stefik's wish that there might be more of this sort of exposition in *C & C*. But *C & C* is not intended to be that kind of book (however, see [6] for some attempts at a more expository book). It is a book which, to be sure, purports to be thoroughly informed by results of current work in several fields, but which does not present an exposition of the details of that work. Rather it attempts to map out the territory where work is progressing, abstracted from particular models— except where the latter are needed to illustrate a point (the book does, after all, make most of its points through a very large number of references to empirical results and to particular models). It attempts to lay bare the assumptions that the most sophisticated practitioners have implicitly adopted.

While it would be counterproductive for a large part of the field of cognitive science (or AI) to spend its time engaged in foundational analysis, it is also an illusion that foundational assumptions can be avoided by rolling up one's sleeves and getting down to work—say by proving statistical convergence theorems for some randomly connected network of entities, whose ultimate explanatory capacity has known shortcomings. We need results, but we also need to be nudged now and then into an awareness of the implicit assumptions within which we are working, and with their entailments. And that was the purpose of *C & C*, a purpose which I believe it can fill in a modest way with a certain amount of patient squeezing and shoving, along the lines recommended by Alan Mackworth.

REFERENCES

1. Cummins, R., Critical notice: Review of Compution and Cognition, *Can. J. Phil.* **18** (1988) 147–162.
2. Rumelhart, D. and McClelland, J. (Eds.) *Parallel Distributed Processing* (MIT Press, (Bradford Books), Cambridge, MA, 1986).
3. Fodor, J.A. and Pylyshyn, Z.W., Connectionism and cognitive architecture: A critical analysis, *Cognition* **28** (1988) 3-71; also in: S. Pinker and J. Mehler (Eds.), *Connections and Symbols* (MIT Press (Bradford Books), Cambridge, MA, 1988).
4. Pylyshyn, Z.W., Computing in cognitive science, in: M. Posner (Ed.), *Foundations of Cognitive Science* (MIT Press, Cambridge, MA, 1989).
5. Pylyshyn, Z.W., The role of cognitive architecture in theories of cognition, in: K. VanLehn (Ed.), *Architectures for Intelligence*: The Twenty-Second Carnegie Symposium on Cognition (Erlbaum, Hillsdale, NJ, 1989).
6. Posner, M. (Ed.), *Foundations of Cognitive Science* (MIT Press (Bradford Books), Cambridge, MA, 1989).

Artificial Intelligence 59 (1993) 265–283
Elsevier

ARTINT 1009

Allen Newell, *Unified Theories of Cognition**

Michael A. Arbib

*Center for Neural Engineering, University of Southern California, Los Angeles,
CA 90089-2520, USA*

Received September 1991
Revised September 1992

1. Soar: a general cognitive architecture

Among the classics of AI is GPS, the General Problem Solver (Newell, Shaw and Simon [17] in 1959). Its key notion was that solving a problem consisted in finding a sequence of operators for transforming the present state into some goal state. A given problem area would be characterized by a finite set of *differences* and an *operator-difference table*. Given two states, one would compute the differences to be reduced between them, and then, for each difference, consult the table to find an operator that had proven fairly reliable for reducing that difference in a variety of situations. However, the given operator was not guaranteed to reduce the difference in all circumstances. GPS then proceeds with search by a process called *means–end analysis*: pick a difference, apply an operator, look at the new goal and the new state, look at the new difference and so on until the goal is attained. The challenge is to keep track of these states, operators, and differences to extract a "good" path, i.e., a relatively economical sequence of operators which will carry out the desired transformation.

More than a decade after developing GPS, Newell and Simon (1972) published a huge book called *Human Problem Solving* [18] in which they

---

Correspondence to: M.A. Arbib, Center for Neural Engineering, University of Southern California, Los Angeles, CA 90089-2520, USA. E-mail: arbib@pollux.usc.edu.
* (Harvard University Press, Cambridge, MA, 1990); xvi + 549 pages.

looked at protocols showing how people solve numerical puzzles or word problems. They used such studies to develop means–end analysis into a psychological model of how people solve problems. In this way, GPS contributed to work in both classic AI and cognitive psychology, with each state represented as a small structure of symbols, and with operators providing explicit ways of manipulating symbols in some serial fashion to search a space to find an answer.

Another two decades have passed and, in *Unified Theories of Cognition*, Allen Newell offers us a specific symbolic processing architecture called Soar which may be seen as the culmination of the GPS paradigm. Instead of just measuring a difference and reducing it, Soar can consult a *long-term memory* that has many productions of the form: "if X is the problem, then try Y". It also has a *working memory* containing the current set of goals, the relationships between them, and information about what means have already been tried. Rather than relying on a single operator-difference table as in GPS, Soar can invoke a variety of *problem spaces*, each providing a set of tools appropriate for some subclass of problems (Fig. 1). Rather than always applying an operator to reduce a difference, Soar may recognize that attaining a particular goal suggests a specific problem space which then invokes a particular set of methods to be used. *Subgoal generation* remains a key issue. After applying an operator or using the methods in a particular space, Soar has either solved the problem or it has not—in which case further subgoals must be generated in the attempt to move towards the overall goal. Soar also offers a simple learning mechanism called *chunking*. In trying to achieve a goal, Soar may generate many subgoals and subsubgoals to yield a large tree of different subgoals. Eventually, Soar will grow the tree to the point where it can find a path leading from the present state to the goal state by applying a sequence of operators—at which stage the rest of the search tree can be discarded. Soar can then store this successful "chunk" of the search tree in memory so that when it next encounters a similar problem it can immediately use that sequence of subgoals without getting into extensive search. Soar can have multiple goals and these need not agree, and the system can be set either to pick any one goal and try to achieve it or to take some numerical measure and come up with the best possible result even if it must ignore some of the goals in the process.

I plan to address Newell's bold claim (see especially his Chapter 2, "Foundations of Cognitive Science") that the specific choices which he and his colleagues made in developing Soar are central to the study of cognitive science in general and of human cognitive architecture in particular. I will argue that those choices are so heavily rooted in the classic serial symbol-processing approach to computation that they lead to an architecture which, whatever its merits within AI, is ill-suited to serve as a model for human cognitive architecture. This critique will be grounded in the view that cognitive science is to be conducted in terms of a vocabulary of interacting functional units called

LONG-TERM KNOWLEDGE

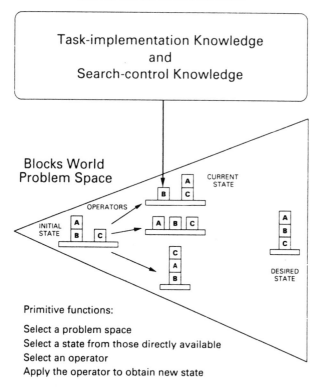

Fig. 1. In Soar, the basic unit of processing is a problem space, as shown here. For different problem domains, different problem spaces may be invoked, each with its own representations and appropriate set of operators to carry out *problem search.* Part of Soar's knowledge is used to determine which is the appropriate knowledge to apply to attack a specific problem—this is *knowledge search.* Acting on a problem in one problem space may create subgoals which require the instantiation of new spaces for their attainment. (Figure 2-16 of Newell's *Unified Theories of Cognition.*)

schemas whose functional definition can in many (but not all) cases be constrained by neurological data. The review will then question the utility of Newell's use of a notion of knowledge akin to Chomsky's notion of competence by asserting that cognitive science must address data on human performance. However, the review closes on a more positive note, suggesting a research plan which links the schema-based approach to intelligence with some of Newell's key insights into the nature of problem solving. In particular, we will pay specific attention to Newell's notion of the "Great Move" from using specialized materials to support different schemas to using a medium in which it is possible to compose copies of whatever schemas are needed to form novel representations.

2. Differing criteria for a human cognitive architecture

What is an appropriate general framework for human cognitive architecture? Newell's approach to cognitive science is close to the following "extreme AI" position:

Position (a). Cognitive tasks rest on a set of basic processes, such as pattern recognition, search, memory, and inference, whose properties and interactions can be characterized in an abstract way independent of implementation. In particular, properties and interactions that we understand by implementing them on serial symbol processors are equally valid for the human mind.

Newell feels that problem spaces and the mechanisms that Soar provides to control them (Fig. 1) underlie any cognitive architecture. However, data may be employed to help constrain the specific problem spaces employed in any specific cognitive system. For a variety of human problem-solving tasks, Newell offers models which not only simulate *what* a human can do, but also have their structure constrained by data on the timing and errors of human performance. As such, these models certainly contribute to cognitive psychology, but in no way meet the demands of *cognitive neuroscience* which seeks to link cognitive capability to the brain mechanisms which subserve it. Timing data is not enough. In particular, Newell fails to make appropriate use of a wealth of data (experimental and clinical) about the effects of brain lesions on human and animal behavior. His approach also fails to connect gracefully with data and theories about instinctual behavior and the basis these provide for cognitive functions. Obviously, much useful work, including Newell's, can be done at a level of aggregation above that requiring the distribution of function over brain regions. I am not making the false claim that no good cognitive science can be done within the Soar framework. Rather, I am claiming that it is an approach that seems ill-suited to unify cognitive science if it is conceded that cognitive science must address, amongst other things, the data of clinical neurology.

Unfortunately, Newell's discussion of the "Foundations of Cognitive Science" (Chapter 2) offers neither an adequate concept of mind nor a well thought out characterization of cognitive science. He offers no "place to stand" from which to evaluate Soar, and takes no account of observations which suggest the importance of neurological data in dissecting cognitive processes. Newell takes "*mind* to be the control system that guides the behaving organism in its interactions with the dynamic real world" (p. 43). However, such a definition does not distinguish mind from brain, for it seems more correct to state that the *brain* is the control system that guides the behaving organism in its interactions with the dynamic real world. Again, he fails to address the notion that much of the control of such interactions is not mental, and that much of what is mental is subsymbolic and/or unconscious. Without offering a precise definition of "mental", let me just say that many people can agree on examples of mental activity (reading, thinking, etc.) even if they take the diametrically opposite philosophical positions of dualism (mind and brain are separate) or monism (mind is a function of brain). They would then agree that some mental activity (e.g., contemplation) need not result in overt "interactions with the dynamic real world", and that much of the brain's activity (e.g., controlling automatic breathing) is not mental. Face recognition seems to be a mental activity which we do not carry out through conscious symbol manipulation. And since Freud, even psychologists who reject his particular psychosexual theories accept his notion that much of our mental behavior is shaped by unconscious forces. (For an assessment of Freud and a schema-theoretic account of consciousness, see [5].)

Newell sees mind as providing *"response functions*. That is, the organism takes actions as a function of the environment. . . . However, many different response functions occur as the organism goes through time . . . such as one when you get yourself out of bed, one when you reach for your clothes, one when you face yourself in the mirror . . ." (p. 43). He then claims that "cognitive science needs a concept of knowledge that is used simply to describe and predict the response functions of a system" (p. 46). This ignores the issue of which response functions are cognitive and which are not. It also ignores the crucial distinction between being able to do something and having knowledge about it, a distinction related to "knowing how" versus "knowing that" which some (e.g., Squire [19]) take to underlie two kinds of human memory ("procedural" and "declarative") dissociable by brain lesions.

Despite his all too inclusive definition of "mind", when Newell (p. 61) charts the *Great Move* in evolution that distinguishes rational behavior from instinctive behavior, he gives the impression that he views rational behavior as the proper province of cognitive science, to the exclusion of instinctive behavior. By contrast, I believe it more fruitful to place human cognition in an evolutionary context rooted in mechanisms for instinctive behavior [1]. A famous example of this is provided by Humphrey's study [14] of "What the Frog's Eye Tells the Monkey's Brain". It had long been known that the role of tectum (the largest visual area in the midbrain) in directing whole body moments in frog is analogous to the role of superior colliculus (the mammalian homolog of tectum) in directing orienting movements in cat and monkey. It had also been believed by neurologists that a monkey (or human) without a visual cortex was blind. However, Humphrey argued that a monkey without visual cortex should have at least as much visual ability as a frog, but that such monkeys had not been taught to pay attention to available visual cues. After two years of attention training, the monkey without visual cortex that he worked with was able to use visual cues to grab at moving objects, and to use changes in luminance—such as an open door—for navigation, even though delicate processes of pattern recognition were never regained. Moreover, it was discovered that humans without visual cortex could also "see" in this sense—but, remarkably, they were not conscious that they could see. This phenomenon is referred to as *blindsight* (see Weiskrantz [21]). Clearly, blindsight is not in itself a rational behavior, being closely linked to the instinctive visually guided behavior of the frog. Yet, it seems to me that the above data are a crucial part of any theory of vision, and that anything that claims to be a "human cognitive architecture" must be able to address such data. This a Soar-based architecture does not do.

Many AI workers have used the slogan "aeroplanes don't flap their wings" to justify the claim that AI may be developed without reference to the study of biological systems. The same slogan equally justifies our skepticism that AI *per se* is adequate to address the needs of cognitive neuroscience. But if we reject Position (a) above (even for an AI informed by data on human performance but not on human neurology) must we go to the other extreme of what might be called "neurochemical reductionism"?:

Position (b). Any human cognitive architecture must take account of the way in which mood, emotion, and motivation affect human performance. We know that drugs can alter mood, and we know that the action of many of these drugs involves the way in which they bind to receptors in the cell membranes of neurons. Thus, no human cognitive architecture can be complete unless it incorporates the relevant specificities of neurochemistry.

Rather than discuss Position (b) explicitly, I will develop an intermediate position which encourages an interchange between *distributed* AI and cognitive neuroscience. To continue with the aeroplanes versus birds analogy, the bridging science of aerodynamics develops key concepts like lift, and then explains the different strategies of planes and birds in terms of the surface properties of the two kinds of wings and the way air is moved across them. Another discipline, materials science, has the task of understanding the surface properties. In the same way, we may hope (it is a research strategy which is yielding results but is by no means universally established) that the following approach may provide the right intermediate between Positions (a) and (b) above:

Position (c). Cognitive science is to be conducted in terms of a vocabulary of interacting functional units called *schemas*. Neuroscience then has the task of explaining the properties of these schemas in terms of neural circuitry or even the underlying neurochemistry and molecular biology. However, the functional definition of the schemas will in many cases be constrained by the data of clinical neurology and observations on modulation of behavior by variations in mood, emotion, and motivation.

To develop this argument, we must first turn to a brief exposition of schema theory, based on Arbib's [4].

3. Schema theory

Schema theory is an approach to knowledge representation that has been explicitly shaped by the need to understand how cognitive and instinctive functions can be implemented in a distributed fashion such as that involving the interaction of a multitude of brain regions. However, many of the concepts have been abstracted from biology to serve as "bringing" concepts which can be used in both distributed (DAI) and brain theory and thus can serve cognitive science whether or not the particular study addresses neurological or neurophysiological data:

(i) Schemas are ultimately defined by the execution of tasks within a physical environment. A set of *basic motor schemas* is hypothesized to provide simple, prototypical patterns of movement. These combine with *perceptual schemas* to form *assemblages* or *coordinated control programs* which interweave their activations in accordance with the current task and sensory environment to mediate more complex behaviors. Many schemas, however, may be abstracted from the perceptual-motor interface. Schema activations are largely task-driven, reflecting the goals of the organism and the physical and functional requirements of the task.

(ii) A schema is both a store of knowledge and the description of a process for applying that knowledge. As such, a schema may be instantiated to form multiple schema *instances* as active copies of the process to apply that knowledge. E.g., given a schema that represents generic knowledge about some object, we may need several active instances of the schema, each suitably tuned, to subserve our perception of a different instance of the object. Schemas can become *instantiated* in response to certain patterns of input from sensory stimuli or other schema instances that are already active.

(iii) Each instance of a schema has an associated *activity level*. That of a perceptual schema represents a "confidence level" that the object represented by the schema is indeed present; while that of a motor schema may signal its "degree of readiness" to control some course of action. The activity level of a schema instance may be but one of many parameters that characterize it. Thus the perceptual schema for "ball" might include parameters to represent size, color, and velocity.

(iv) The use, representation, and recall of knowledge is mediated through the activity of a network of interacting computing agents, the schema instances, which between them provide processes for going from a particular situation and a particular structure of goals and tasks to a suitable course of action (which may be overt or covert, as when learning occurs without action or the animal changes its state of readiness). This activity may involve passing of messages, changes of state (including activity level), instantiation to add new schema instances to the network, and deinstantiation to remove instances. Moreover, such activity may involve self-modification and self-organization.

(v) The key question is to understand how local schema interactions can integrate themselves to yield some overall result without explicit executive control, but rather through *cooperative computation*, a shorthand for "computation based on the competition and cooperation of concurrently active agents". For example, in VISIONS, a schema-based system for interpretation of visual scenes (Draper et al. [13]), schema instances represent hypotheses that particular objects occur at particular positions in a scene, so that instances may either represent conflicting hypotheses or offer mutual support. Cooperation yields a pattern of "strengthened alliances" between mutually consistent schema instances that allows them to achieve high activity levels to constitute the overall solution of a problem; competition ensures that instances which do not meet the evolving consensus lose activity, and thus are not part of this solution (though their continuing subthreshold activity may well affect later behavior). In this way, a schema network does not, in general, need a top-level executor, since schema instances can combine their effects by distributed processes of competition and cooperation, rather than the operation of an inference engine on a passive store of knowledge. This may lead to apparently emergent behavior, due to the absence of global control.

(vi) Learning is necessary because schemas are fallible. Schemas, and their connections within the schema network, must change so that over time they may well be able to handle a certain range of situations in a more adaptive way. In a general setting, there is no fixed repertoire of basic schemas. New schemas may be formed as assemblages of old schemas; but once formed a schema may be tuned by some adaptive mechanism. This tunability of schema assemblages allows them to become "primitive", much as a skill is honed into a unified whole from constituent pieces. Such tuning may be expressed at the level of schema theory itself, or may be driven by the dynamics of modification of unit interactions in some specific implementation of the schemas.

The words "brain" and "neural" do not appear in criteria (i)–(vi). We next spell out just what makes a schema-theoretical model part of brain theory:

(BTi) In brain theory, a given schema, defined functionally, may be distributed across more than one brain region; conversely, a given brain region may be involved in many schemas. A top-down analysis may advance specific hypotheses about the localization of (sub)-schemas in the brain and these may be tested by lesion experiments, with possible modification of the model (e.g., replacing one schema by several interacting schemas with different localizations) and further testing.

(BTii) Once a schema-theoretic model of some animal behavior has been refined to the point of hypotheses about the localization of schemas, we may then model a brain region by seeing if its known neural circuitry can indeed be shown to implement the posited schema. In some cases the model will involve properties of the circuitry that have not yet been tested, thus laying the ground for new experiments. In DAI, individual schemas may be implemented by artificial neural networks, or in some programming language on a "standard" (possibly distributed) computer.

Schema theory is far removed from serial symbol-based computation. Increasingly, work in AI now contributes to schema theory, even when it does not use this term. For example, Minsky [16] espouses a *Society of Mind* analogy in which "members of society", the agents, are analogous to schemas. Brooks [9] controls robots with layers of asynchronous modules that can be considered as a version of schemas (more of this later). Their work shares with schema theory, with its mediation of action through a network of schemas, the point that no single, central, logical representation of the world need link perception and action—the representation of the world is *the pattern of relationships between all its partial representations*. Another common theme, shared with Walter [20], Braitenberg [8], and Arbib [2], is the study of the "evolution" of simple "creatures" with increasingly sophisticated sensorimotor capacities.

We may now return to the claim of Position (c) that cognitive science is to be conducted in terms of a vocabulary of interacting schemas (or schema instances), and that neuroscience then has the task of explaining the properties of these schemas in terms of neural networks. Even though cognitive science itself is thus relieved of responsibility for explaining how schemas are implemented, it must still (a feathered flexible wing is different from a rigid metallic wing) be based, at least in part, on schemas which represent the functioning of hundreds of simultaneously active regions of the human brain. But there is nothing in the GPS tradition, or in Newell's book, that looks at distributed processing in any detail, let alone neurological data which constrains how the different parts of the computation might be located in the different parts of the brain. The point is *not* that all good cognitive science *must be* cognitive neuroscience. It is rather that a general framework for cognitive science must *include* cognitive neuroscience. In fact, given the current state of scientific knowledge, any current schema-level model of a cognitive system must be heterogeneous in that some schemas can be modeled in terms of detailed neural circuitry, some can be related to brain regions for which few details of circuitry are known, while others represent hypotheses about functional components for which little or no constraining neural data are available.

4. A cognitive architecture rooted in computer architecture

To understand why Newell's approach to cognitive science is so little adapted to the needs of cognitive neuroscience, we must see how his view of *cognitive architecture* is rooted in his 1971 work in *computer architecture* (Bell and Newell [6]), and in particular shaped by the hierarchy of computer systems in which the levels are (p. 47):

> *Bell–Newell computer hierarchy*
> program-level systems
> register-transfer systems
> logic circuits
> electrical circuits
> electronic devices

Newell states (p. 87) that such architectures emerged in the 1960s as the complexity of computer systems increased and that the enabling key was the development of the register-transfer level as an abstract description of the processing of bit vectors as a bridge between programs and the circuits that implement them. In developing his views of cognitive architecture, Newell makes three changes: he adds the knowledge level as an AI-motivated addition above the Bell–Newell hierarchy, he equates the symbol system level with the program level, and he does not specify the downward elaboration from the register-transfer level:

> *Newell cognitive hierarchy*
> knowledge-level systems
> symbol-level systems ($\approx$ programs)
> register-transfer systems

The knowledge level "abstracts completely from the internal processing and the internal representation. Thus, all that is left is the *content* of the representations and the *goals* toward which that content will be used" (p. 48). The program level in the Bell–Newell hierarchy is based on sequential operation of programs, and this feature of 1971-style computers (namely, seriality) has colored Newell's view of cognition:

> A knowledge system is embedded in an external environment, with which it interacts by a set of possible actions. The behavior of the system is the *sequence* of actions taken in the environment over time. . . . Its body of knowledge is about its environment, its goals, its actions, and the relations between them. It has a single law of behavior: the system takes actions to attain its goals, using *all* the knowledge that it has. . . . The system can obtain new knowledge from external knowledge sources via some of its actions. . . . Once knowledge is acquired, it is available *forever* after. The system is a single *homogeneous* body of knowledge, *all* of which is brought to bear on the determination of its actions. (p. 50, my italics)

The italicized *forever* and *all* stress the point that the knowledge level is an unattainable ideal, unconstrained by implementation limits of computing space or time (as in Chomsky's preference for theories of "competence" rather than "performance"). Newell's claim that "all the person's knowledge is always used to attain the goals of that person" (p. 50) is not even approximately true of normal human behavior—or even of highly aberrant behavior such as seeking to complete this review. The words *sequence* and *homogeneous* already predispose the theory against a distributed view of AI (coordinated problem solving by a network of heterogeneous schemas) let alone providing a conception of knowledge that can be related to the functioning of human brains. Moreover, Newell carries over from computer science the view that function at each level can be studied without attention to its implementation at lower levels:

> [Behavior at each level is] determined by the behavior laws, as formulated for that level, applying to its state as described at that level. The claim is that abstraction to the particular level involved still preserves all that is relevant for future behavior described at that level of abstraction. . . . Thus, to claim that humans can be described at the knowledge level is to claim there is a way of formulating them as agents that have knowledge and goals, such that their behavior is successfully predicted by the law that says: all the person's knowledge is always used to attain the goals of the person . . . no details of the actual internal processing are required. This behavior of an existing system can be calculated if you know the system's goals and what the system knows about its environment. (pp. 49–50)

My point is not to throw away the idea of a level of abstract specifications (call it the knowledge level, if you will). Rather, it is my point that for cognitive science we need specifications which take timing and real-world interaction into account. Thus "hit the ball" is far removed from the level of retinal activity and muscle contractions, but the task imposes a concreteness of interaction that is far removed from the mere abstract knowledge that, e.g., a bat would serve the task better than a hand. The latter "knowledge" provides a useful annotation, but cannot provide a complete specification that can be refined level by level with logical exactness and without revision of the initial specification.

In Newell's cognitive science, symbol systems play the role of the program level. Newell (pp. 80–81) then defines an *architecture* as the fixed structure that realizes a symbol system. In the computer systems hierarchy it is the description of the system at the register-transfer level, below the symbol level, that provides the architecture. The architecture is the description of the system in whatever system description scheme exists next below the symbol level. This raises the question of what system description scheme exists next below the symbol level (i.e., what is the "register-transfer systems" level of the mind?). The "pure AI" approach of Position (a) would accept any system convenient for mapping symbol systems onto serial computers. However, the move towards brain function takes us away from seriality. We focus on competition and cooperation of concurrently active schema instances. More boldly, I claim that the schema level in the Position (c) approach to cognitive science replaces the symbol-system level in Newell's Position (a) approach, but I add that the Position (c) approach also dispenses with a knowledge level that is distinct from the schema level. The schema theorist may still want a "level" in which to talk about generic properties of schemas without reference to their particular specifications, but I view this as talk *about* cognitive systems, rather than a level of representation *of* those systems. On this account, symbols are replaced by schemas which, by combining representation and execution, are far richer than symbols are often taken to be.

Research in the neurophysiology of vision, memory, and action gives information a non-symbolic representation distributed in patterns that do not lend themselves immediately to a crisp description with a few symbols. It is thus a daunting, but exciting, challenge to show how the insights of Newell's approach can make contact with the study of neural networks and issues in cognitive neuroscience. Some members of the Soar community have begun to look at implementations on parallel computers, or at the use of artificial neural networks to implement Soar's memory functions (Cho, Rosenbloom, and Dolan [10]), but I know of no attempt to make extended contact between Soar and neuroscience.

5. Connectionism ≠ brain theory

In developing Soar and the various cognitive models in his book, Newell ignores the biological substrate save for some timing constraints in Chapter 3, and he emphasizes a serial symbol-computation perspective throughout. However, he does offer a few hints of possible changes. He states that "One of the major challenges in the development of massively parallel connectionist systems is whether they will find a different hierarchical organization. In any event, the computer-systems hierarchy is an important invariant structural characteristic, although its [*sic*] seems to be the only one" (p. 88); and he devotes Section 8.3 to some comparisons of Soar with connectionism. However, Section 8.3, "The Biological Band", is misnamed since the comparisons are with the artificial networks of connectionism, not with biological data on the (human) brain. The "neural networks" of connectionism are nets of abstract computing elements, rather than models of the actual circuitry of the brain.

Since our present focus is to determine the extent to which Soar can provide a framework for cognitive science broad enough to encompass cognitive neuroscience, it is thus important to know how relevant Newell's views are to this extension, and in particular to assess the extent to which the organization of "massively parallel connectionist systems" is the same as that of the brain. The connectionist comparison is, in fact, so undernourished and underconstrained by comparison with what is needed for a cognitive neuroscience that I need to emphasize the claim of the section title: *connectionism ≠ brain theory*.

For some "connectionists", all connectionist systems have the same structure, namely large randomly connected neural-like networks which become increasingly adapted to solve some problem through training and/or self-organization. In such an approach, there seem to be only two levels, the specification of what a network is to do (akin to the knowledge level?) and the tuned neural network itself (akin to the logic-circuit level), with nothing in between. However, brain theory is not connectionism, even though progress in connectionism may enrich our vocabulary of the computations that neural networks, viewed abstractly, can perform. Analysis of animal behavior or human cognition should yield a model of how that behavior is achieved through the *cooperative computation* of concurrently active regions or schemas of the brain (the two analyses are not equivalent: regions are structural units; schemas are functional units), rather than in terms of any simple one-way flow of information in a hierarchically organized system.

Items (BTi) and (BTii) of Section 3 embody the eventual goal of cognitive *neuro*science—that functional and structural analyses be rendered congruent. However, experience with brain modeling shows that a distribution of function across schemas that may seem psychologically plausible may not survive the test of neurological data which demand that the schemas be structured in such a way that their subschemas are allocatable across brain regions to yield a model that predicts the effects of various brain lesions.

For example, a model of our ability to make saccadic eye movements to one or more targets even after they are no longer visible requires a schema to inhibit reflex responses, as well as schemas for working memory (holding a "plan of action") and dynamic remapping (updating the "plan" as action proceeds). But this does not imply that a distinct *region* of the brain has evolved for each functionally distinct *schema*. More specifically, a neural refinement of the model (Dominey and Arbib [12]) distributes these three schemas across a variety of brain regions (parietal cortex, frontal eye fields, basal ganglia, and superior colliculus) in a way that responds to and explains a variety of neurophysiological data. (The reader may recall the data on blindsight, showing how the superior colliculus of monkeys can support a range of subconscious visual functions, but that these nonetheless seem to provide a basis for the totality, dependent on cerebral cortex, of our visual repertoire.)

To summarize, functions that appear well separated in an initial top-down analysis of some behavior or cognitive function may exhibit intriguing interdependencies as a result of shared circuitry in the neural model whose construction was guided by, but which also modifies, that initial analysis. I am thus sceptical of Newell's view (pp. 49–50, cited earlier) that each of the levels in his cognitive hierarchy can be operationally complete with no details of the actual internal processing being required. In particular, schema change may be driven by the dynamics of modification of unit interactions in some specific implementation of the schemas. The learning curve of two different neural networks may be dramatically different even though they come under the same symbolic description of their initial behavior.

As noted earlier, Newell's idea of architecture is rooted in the conceptually serial register-transfer level, and does not really come to terms with the possibility of a framework (cooperative computation) that *drastically* expands the concept of computation to embrace the style of the brain. Although Newell notes that massive parallelism can result in *qualitatively* different computations since real-time constraints reveal the effective amount of computation available within specified time limits, I do not find this issue returned to in the attempt to understand the nature of information processing in the human cognitive system, or in the brain that underlies it. By contrast, schema theory emphasizes the distributed, cooperative computation of multiple schema instances distributed across distinctive brain regions; it is delegation of schema functionality to neural networks that brings in massive parallelism. The hierarchy then becomes:

> *Schema-based cognitive hierarchy*
> descriptions of behaviors
> schemas ($\approx$ programs)
> interacting brain regions
> neural circuitry
> neurons
> sub-neural components (synapses, etc.)

We map schemas onto brain regions where possible, though accepting computer programs as a "default" when constraining neuroscience data are unavailable or inappropriate. In the brain, we might view successive refinements of the overall architecture as involving (i) the segregation into anatomically distinct regions, (ii) the classifications of different circuits and cell types in each region, and (iii) the overall specification of which cell type synapses on what other cell types and with what transmitter. Changes in the detailed pattern of, e.g., cell-by-cell synaptic weighting could then give the architecture its adaptability. The bulk of these changes will be seen as the dynamics of the "software", with changes in "architecture" corresponding only to overall shifts in "computing style" resulting from cooperative effects of myriad small changes.

6. The Great Move: searching for a conclusion

The tone of this review has been negative, in that it has emphasized the problems posed to those of us interested in the role of the brain in cognition by the use of a serial symbol-processing approach, or the use of the knowledge level as providing a performance-independent characterization of cognitive competence. I have not reviewed the many substantial contributions that Newell has made to AI and cognitive psychology, and which are well documented in his book. To somewhat redress the balance, this final section suggests a viable research plan which links the schema-based approach to intelligence with some of Newell's key insights into the nature of problem solving. We may start with Newell's discussion of ethology which sets the stage for his discussion of what he properly calls *the Great Move*:

> Finding feasible representations gets increasingly difficult with a richer and richer variety of things to be represented and richer and richer kinds of operational transformations that they undergo. More and more interlocking representation laws need to be satisfied. . . . [E]thologists have [studied] the adaptive character of lower organisms. . . . Unfortunately, not all adaptations require representations, and the examples, from the digger wasp to the stickleback, are not sorted out to make it easy to see exactly what is representation and what is not. . . . Instead of moving toward more and more specialized materials with specialized dynamics to support an increasingly great variety and intricacy of representational demands, an entirely different turn is possible. This is the move [the Great Move] to using a neutral, stable medium that is capable of registering variety and then *composing* whatever transformations are needed to satisfy the requisite representation law. Far from representational constriction, this path opens up the whole world of indefinitely rich representations. (p. 61)

The line between representation and non-representation is a sticky one. Does the stickleback lack a representation of males with which it is to compete, or is the representation too inclusive to discriminate the experimentalist's simulacrum from the actual opponent? Perhaps the key point is that the stickleback lacks the ability to recognize when it is mistaken and change its ways accordingly (and this is only the beginning of the necessary refinements— cf. Bennett [7] for all the ingredients that a bee would have to exhibit for its "language" to be a true index of rationality).

We may note here a controversy about the nature of AI fomented, e.g., by Brooks [9] which sets an ethologically inspired hierarchy of levels of control (mentioned earlier as being in the spirit of schema theory), each biasing rather than replacing the one below it, in opposition to the "classical" view of abstract operators applied to uniform representations. Newell offers a somewhat broader version of classical AI, since he allows a variety of problem spaces— but nonetheless sees these each as being implemented in some uniform medium, like that offered by the register-transfer level in the Bell–Newell hierarchy. However, it seems mistaken to see this as a sharp dichotomy in which one school or the other must prove triumphant. The schema theorist (as in our discussion of blindsight) explains a complex cognitive function through the interaction of "instinctive" schemas, implemented in specifically evolved circuitry, and "abstract" schemas that are developed through learning and experience in "general-purpose" (highly adaptive, post-Great-Move) circuitry. An intelligent system needs to combine the ability to react rapidly (jumping out of the way of an unexpected vehicle when crossing the street) with the ability to abstractly weigh alternatives (deciding on the best route to get to the next appointment).

In summary, a satisfactory account of Newell's "Great Move" should not seek a complete break from using specialized materials to support different schemas to using a medium in which it is possible to compose copies of whatever schemas are needed to form novel representations. Rather, we should provide—in the manner of schema theory—insight into how instinctive behavior provides a basis for, and is intertwined with, rational behavior. When I study frogs [2], I see the animal's behavior mediated by the dynamic interaction of multiple special-purpose schemas implemented in dedicated neural circuitry. But when I seek to understand human vision, I combine a model of low-level vision implemented across a set of dedicated brain regions (DeYoe and Van Essen [11]) with a general-purpose medium in which copies of schemas (schema instances) can be assembled, parameterized, and bound to regions of the image as they compete and cooperate in a process of distributed planning which creates an interpretation of a visual scene (recall item (v) of Section 3; cf. Arbib [3, esp. Sections 5.1, 5.2, 7.3, and 7.4]). The contrast between frog visuomotor coordination and the flexibility of human visual perception makes explicit the contrast between those schema assemblages that are "evolutionarily hardwired" into patterns of competition and cooperation between specific brain regions, and those which can, through multiple in- stantiations (both data- and hypothesis-driven), yield totally novel forms to develop new skills and represent novel situations. It is this latter form of "creative" representation that Newell espouses:

> The great move has forged a link between representations and composable response functions. If a system can compose functions and if it can do it internally in an arena under its own control, then that system can represent. How well it can represent depends on how flexible is its ability to compose functions that obey the needed representation laws—there can be limits to composability. How- ever, representation and composability are not inherently linked together. If the representations are realized in a special medium with appropriate . . . transformations, there need be no com- posability at all. (p. 63)

Such flexibility of composition, of being able to link in new problem spaces (recall Fig. 1) as the need arises to provide a complex problem-solving structure, is one of the great strengths of Soar. Even though I remain sceptical of Newell's sharp division between knowledge and its application, I feel that he advances our understanding when he makes the key distinction between *problem search* and *knowledge search*:

> There are two separate searches going on in intelligence. One is *problem search* which is the search of [a] problem space. . . . The other is *knowledge search*, which is the search in the memory of the system for the knowledge to guide the problem search. . . . [For] a special purpose intelligent system [only problem search need occur]. [For] agents that work on a wide range of tasks. . . [w]hen a new task arises, [their] body of knowledge must be searched for knowledge that is relevant to the task. . . . [K]nowledge search goes on continually—and the more problematical the situation, the more continuous is the need for it. (pp. 98–99)

All this suggests a rapprochement in which future work explores the integration of key insights from Soar with the distributed approach in which action is mediated through a network of schema instances in which no single, central, logical representation of the world need link perception and action. This would add to Newell's scheme the distinction between *off-line planning* which finds a sequence of operators to go all the way to the goal and *then* applies them in the world, and *dynamic planning* which chooses the next few (possibly concurrent) actions which may help achieve the goal, applies them, and then factors new sensory input into continued activity (cf. the "reactive planning" of Lyons and Hendriks [15]).

Perhaps a starting point is to regard a problem space as the analog of a schema, and the creation of a new problem space to meet a subgoal as the analog of schema instantiation. The key question then becomes: How do we restructure Soar when many problem spaces/schema instances can be simultaneously active, continually passing messages, both modulatory and symbolic, to one another? When this question is answered, the seriality that dominates Newell's book will be sundered, and the full-throated dialog between the Soar community and workers in cognitive neuroscience and distributed AI can truly begin.

References

[1] M.A. Arbib, Perceptual motor processes and the neural basis of language, in: M.A. Arbib, D. Caplan and J.C. Marshall, eds., *Neural Models of Language Processes* (Academic Press, New York, 1982) 531–551.

[2] M.A. Arbib, Levels of modeling of mechanisms of visually guided behavior (with commentaries and author's response), *Behav. Brain Sci.* **10** (1987) 407–465.

[3] M.A. Arbib, *The Metaphorical Brain 2: Neural Networks and Beyond* (Wiley Interscience, New York, 1989).

[4] M.A. Arbib, Schema theory, in: S.C. Shapiro, ed., *The Encyclopedia of Artificial Intelligence* (Wiley Interscience, New York, 2nd ed., 1992).

[5] M.A. Arbib and M.B. Hesse, *The Construction of Reality* (Cambridge University Press, Cambridge, England, 1986).

[6] C.G. Bell and A. Newell, *Computer Structures: Readings and Examples* (McGraw-Hill, New York, 1971).

[7] J. Bennett, *Rationality: An Essay towards an Analysis* (Routledge & Kegan Paul, London, 1964).

[8] V. Braitenberg, *Vehicles: Experiments in Synthetic Psychology* (Bradford Books/MIT Press, Cambridge, MA, 1984).

[9] R.A. Brooks, A robust layered control system for a mobile robot, *IEEE J. Rob. Autom.* **2** (1986) 14–23.

[10] B. Cho, P.S. Rosenbloom and C.P. Dolan, Neuro-Soar: a neural-network architecture for goal-oriented behavior, in: *Proceedings 13th Annual Conference of the Cognitive Science Society*, Chicago, IL (1991).

[11] E.A. DeYoe and D.C. Van Essen, Concurrent processing streams in monkey visual cortex, *Trends Neurosci.* **11** (5) (1988) 219–226.

[12] P.F. Dominey and M.A. Arbib, A cortico-subcortical model for generation of spatially accurate sequential saccades, *Cerebral Cortex* **2** (1992) 153–175.

[13] B.A. Draper, R.T. Collins, J. Brolio, A.R. Hanson and E.M. Riseman, The schema system, *Int. J. Comput. Vision* **2** (1989) 209–250.

[14] N.K. Humphrey, What the frog's eye tells the monkey's brain, *Brain Behav. Evol.* **3** (1970) 324–337.

[15] D.M. Lyons and A.J. Hendriks, Planning, reactive, in: S.C. Shapiro, ed., *The Encyclopedia of Artificial Intelligence* (Wiley Interscience, New York, 2nd ed., 1992) 1171–1181.

[16] M.L. Minsky, *The Society of Mind* (Simon and Schuster, New York, 1985).

[17] A. Newell, J.C. Shaw and H.A. Simon, Report on a general problem-solving program, in: *Proceedings International Conference on Information Processing*, UNESCO House (1959) 256–264.

[18] A. Newell and H.A. Simon, *Human Problem Solving* (Prentice-Hall, Englewood Cliffs, NJ, 1972).

[19] L.R. Squire, *Memory and Brain* (Oxford University Press, Oxford, 1987).
[20] W.G. Walter, *The Living Brain* (Penguin Books, Harmondsworth, England, 1953).
[21] L. Weiskrantz, The interaction between occipital and temporal cortex in vision: an overview, in: F.O. Schmitt and F.G. Worden, eds., *The Neurosciences Third Study Program* (MIT Press, Cambridge, MA, 1974) 189–204.

Artificial Intelligence 59 (1993) 285–294
Elsevier

ARTINT 1010

Allen Newell, *Unified Theories of Cognition* *

Daniel C. Dennett

Center for Cognitive Studies, Tufts University, Medford, MA 02155-7068, USA

Received August 1991
Revised September 1992

The time for unification in cognitive science has arrived, but who should lead the charge? The immunologist-turned–neuroscientist Gerald Edelman [6] thinks that neuroscientists should lead—or more precisely that he should (he seems to have a low opinion of everyone else in cognitive science). Someone might think that I had made a symmetrically opposite claim in *Consciousness Explained* [4]: philosophers (or more precisely, those that agree with me!) are in the best position to see how to tie all the loose ends together. But in fact I acknowledged that unifying efforts such as mine are proto- theories, explorations that are too metaphorical and impressionistic to serve as the model for a unified theory. Perhaps Newell had me in mind when he wrote in his introduction (p.16) that a unified theory "can't be just a pastiche, in which disparate formulations are strung together with some sort of conceptual bailing wire", but in any case the shoe more or less fits, with some pinching. Such a "pastiche" theory can be a good staging ground, however, and a place to stand while considering the strengths and weaknesses of better built theories. So I agree with him.

> It is not just philosophers' theories that need to be made honest by modeling at this level; neuroscientists' theories are in the same boat. For instance, Gerald Edelman's (1989) elaborate theory of

Correspondence to: D.C. Dennett, Center for Cognitive Studies, Tufts University, Medford, MA 02155-7068, USA. E-mail: ddennett@pearl.tufts.edu.
* (Harvard University Press, Cambridge, MA, 1990); xvi+549 pages.

"re-entrant" circuits in the brain makes many claims about how such re-entrants can accomplish the discriminations, build the memory structures, coordinate the sequential steps of problem solving, and in general execute the activities of a human mind, but in spite of a wealth of neuroanatomical detail, and enthusiastic and often plausible assertions from Edelman, we won't know what his re-entrants can do—we won't know that re-entrants are the *right* way to conceive of the functional neuroanatomy—until they are fashioned into a whole cognitive architecture at the grain-level of Act* or Soar and put through their paces. [4, p. 268]

So I begin with a ringing affirmation of the central claim of Newell's book. Let's hear it for models like Soar. Exploring whole cognitive systems at roughly that grain-level is the main highway to unification. I agree, moreover, with the reasons he offers for his proposal. But in my book I also alluded to two reservations I have with Newell's program without spelling out or defending either of them. This is obviously the time to make good on those promissory notes or recant them. "My own hunch", I said, "is that, for various reasons that need not concern us here, the underlying medium of production systems is *still* too idealized and oversimplified in its constraints" [4, p. 267]. And a little further along I expressed my discomfort with Newell's support for the traditional division between working memory and long-term memory, and the accompanying notion of *distal access* via symbols, since it encourages a vision of "movable symbols" being transported here and there in the nervous system—an image that slides almost irresistibly into the incoherent image of the Cartesian Theater, the place in the brain where "it all comes together" for consciousness.

Preparing for this review, I re-read *Unified Theories of Cognition*, and read several old and recent Newell papers, and I'm no longer confident that my reservations weren't based on misunderstandings. The examples that Newell gives of *apparently* alternative visions that can readily enough be accommodated within Soar—semantic and episodic memory within the single, unified LTM, Koler's proceduralism, Johnson-Laird's mental models, for instance—make me wonder. It's not that Soar can be all things to all people (that would make it vacuous), but that it is easy to lose sight of the fact that Soar's level is a *low* or foundational architectural level, upon which quasi- architectural or firmware levels can be established, at which to render the features and distinctions that at first Soar seems to deny. But let's put my reservations on the table and see what we make of them.

On the first charge, that Soar (and production systems in general) are still too idealized and oversimplified, Newell might simply agree, noting that we must begin with oversimplifications and use our experience with them to uncover the complications that matter. Is Soar *the* way to organize cognitive science, or is it "just" a valiant attempt to impose order (via a decomposition) on an incredibly heterogeneous and hard-to-analyze tangle? There's a whole messy world of individualized and unrepeatable mental phenomena out there, and the right question to ask is not: "Does Soar idealize away from these?"—because the answer is obvious: "Yes, so what?" The right question is: "Can the *important* complications be reintroduced gracefully as elaborations of Soar?" And the answer to that question depends on figuring out which complications are really important and why. Experience has taught me that nothing short of considerable mucking about with an actual implementation of Soar, something I still have not done, would really tell me what I should think about it, so I won't issue any verdicts here at all, just questions.

First, to put it crudely, what about pleasure and pain? I'm not just thinking of high-urgency interrupts (which are easy enough to add, presumably), but a more subtle and encompassing focusing role. Newell recognizes the problem of focusing, and even points out—correctly, in my view—that the fact that this can be a problem for Soar is a positive mark of verisimilitude. "Thus the issue for the standard computer is how to be interrupted, whereas the issue for Soar and Act* (and presumably for human cognition) is how to keep focused" (Newell, Rosenbloom and Laird [10]). But the Soar we are shown in the book is presented as hyperfunctional.

> Soar's mechanisms are dictated by the functions required of a general cognitive agent. We have not posited detailed technological limitations to Soar mechanisms. There is nothing inappropriate or wrong with such constraints. They may well exist, and if they do, they must show up in any valid theory. (p. 354)

Doesn't this extreme functionalism lead to a seriously distorted foundational architecture? Newell provides an alphabetized list (Fig. 8.1, p. 434) of some mental phenomena Soar has not yet tackled, and among these are daydreaming, emotion and affect, imagery, and play. Soar is all business. Soar is either working or sound asleep, always learning-by-chunking, always solving problems, never idling. There are no profligate expenditures on dubious digressions, no along-for-the-ride productions cluttering up the problem spaces, and Soar is never too tired and cranky to take on yet another impasse. Or so it seems. Perhaps if we put just the right new menagerie of operators on stage, or the right items of supplementary knowledge in memory, a sprinkling of sub-optimal goals, etc., a lazy, mathophobic, lust-obsessed Soar could stand forth for all to see. That is what I mean about how easy it is to misplace the level of Soar; perhaps all this brisk, efficient problem solving should be viewed as the biological (rather than psychological) activities of elements too small to be visible to the naked eye of the folk-psychological observer.

But if so, then there is a large element of misdirection in Newell's advertising about his functionalism. "How very functional your teeth are, Grandma!" said Red Riding Hood. "The better to model dysfunctionality when the time comes, my dear!" replied the wolf. Moreover, even when Soar deals with "intendedly rational behavior" of the sort we engage in when we are good experimental subjects—comfortable, well-paid, and highly motivated—I am skeptical about the realism of the model. Newell acknowledges that it leaves out the "feelings and considerations" that "float around the periphery" (p. 369), but isn't there also lots of *non*-peripheral waste motion in human cognition? (There certainly seems to me to be a lot of it when I think hard—but maybe Newell's own mental life is as brisk and no-nonsense as his book!)

Besides, the hyperfunctionality is *biologically* implausible (as I argue in my book). Newell grants that Soar *did* not arise through evolution (Fig. 8.1), but I am suggesting that perhaps it *could* not. The Spock-like rationality of Soar is a very fundamental feature of the architecture; there is no room *at the architectural level* for some thoughts to be harder to think *because they hurt*, to put it crudely. But isn't that a fact just as secure as any discovered in the psychological laboratory? Shouldn't it be a primary constraint? Ever since Hume got associationism under way with his quasi-mechanical metaphors of combination and attraction between ideas, we have had the task of describing the dynamics of thought: what makes the next thought follow in the heels of the current thought? Newell has provided us, in Soar, with a wonderfully deep and articulated answer—the best ever—but it is an answer that leaves out what I would have thought was a massive factor in the dynamics of thought: pain and pleasure. Solving some problems is a joy; solving others is a bore and a headache, and there are still others that you would go mad trying to solve, so painful would it be to contemplate the problem space. Now it *may just be* that these facts are emergent properties at a higher level, to be discerned in special instances of Soar chugging along imperturbably, but that seems rather unlikely to me. Alternatively, it may be that the *Sturm und Drang* of affect can be piped in as a later low-level embellishment without substantially modifying the basic architecture, but that seems just as unlikely.

David Joslin has pointed out to me that the business-like efficiency we see in the book is largely due to the fact that the various implementations of Soar that we are shown are all special-purpose, truncated versions, with tailor-made sets of operators and productions. In a fully general-purpose Soar, with a vastly enlarged set of productions, we would probably see more hapless wandering than we would want, and have to cast about for ways to focus Soar's energies. And it is here, plausibly, that an affective dimension might be just what is needed, and it has been suggested by various people (Sloman and Croucher [13], de Sousa [5]) that it cannot be packaged within the contents of further knowledge, but must make a contribution orthogonal to the contribution of knowledge.

That was what I had in mind in my first reservation, and as one can see, I'm not sure how sharply it cuts. As I said in my book, we've come a long way from the original von Neumann architecture, and the path taken so far can be extrapolated to still brainier and more biological architectures. The way to find out how much idealization we can afford is not to engage in philosophical debates.

My second reservation, about symbols and distal access, opens some different cans of worms. First, there is a communication problem I want to warn other philosophers about, because it has bedeviled me up to the time of revising the draft of this review. I think I now understand Newell's line on symbols and semantics, and will try to explain it. (If I still don't get it, no harm done—other readers will set me straight.) When he introduces symbols he seems almost to go out of his way to commit what we philosophers call use–mention errors. He gives examples of symbol tokens in Fig. 2-9 (p. 73). He begins with words in sentences (and that's fine), but goes on to *numbers* in equations. We philosophers would say that the symbols were *numerals*—names for numbers. Numbers aren't symbols. He goes on: atoms in formulas. No. Atom-symbols in formulas; formulas are composed of symbols, not atoms; molecules are composed of atoms. Then objects in pictures. No. Object-depictions in pictures. I am sure Newell knows exactly what philosophers mean by a use–mention error, so what is his message supposed to be? "For the purposes of AI it doesn't matter"? Or "We AI-types never get confused about such an obvious distinction, so we can go on speaking loosely"? I don't believe it. There is a sort of willful *semantic descent* (the opposite of Quine's semantic ascent, in which we decide to talk about talk about things) that flavors many AI discussions. It arises, I think, largely because in computer science the expressions up for semantic evaluation do in fact refer very often to things inside the computer—to subroutines that can be called, to memory addresses, to data structures, etc. Moreover, because of the centrality of the domain of arithmetic in computers, the topic of "discussion" is often numbers, and arithmetical expressions for them. So it is easy to lose sight of the fact that when you ask the computer to "evaluate" an expression, and it outputs "3", it isn't *giving* you a number; it's *telling* you a number. But that's all right, since all we ever want from numbers is to have them identified—you can't eat 'em or ride 'em. (Compare "Gimme all your money!" "OK. $42.60, including the change in my pocket.") Can it be that this confusion of symbols and numbers is also abetted by a misappreciation of the fact that, for instance, the binary ASCII code for the *numeral* "9" is not the binary expression of the number 9?

Whatever its causes—or even its justifications—this way of speaking creates the impression that, for people in AI, semantics is something entirely internal to the system. This impression is presumably what led Jerry Fodor into such paroxysms in "Tom Swift and his Procedural Grandmother" [7]. It is too bad he didn't know how to put his misgivings constructively. I tried once:

> We get the idea [from Newell [9]] that a symbol designates if it gives access to a certain object or if it can affect a certain object. And this almost looks all right as long as what we're talking about is internal states .... But of course the real problem is that that isn't what reference is all about. If that were what reference was all about, then what would we say about what you might call my Julie Christie problem? I have a very good physically instantiated symbol for Julie Christie. I know it refers to her, I know it really designates her, but it doesn't seem to have either of the conditions that Professor Newell describes, alas. [2, p. 53] (See also Smith [14].)

Newell's answer:

> The criticisms seemed to me to be a little odd because to say that one has access to something does not mean that one has access to *all* of that thing; having some information about Julie Christie certainly doesn't give one complete access to Julie Christie. That is what polite society is all about .... The first stage is that there are symbols *which lead to internal structures*. I don't think this is obscure, and it is important in understanding where the aboutness comes from ... the data structures *contain knowledge about things in the outside world*. So you then build up further symbols which access things that you can think of as knowledge about something—knowledge about Julie Christie for instance. If you want to ask why a certain symbol says something about Julie Christie, you have to ask why the symbolic expression that contains the symbol says something about Julie Christie. And the answer may be ... because of processes that put it together which themselves have knowledge about Julie Christie .... Ultimately it may turn out to depend upon history, it may depend on some point in the history of the system when it came in contact with something in the world which provided it with that knowledge. ([2, p. 171], emphasis mine)

What we have here, I finally realize, is simply a two-stage (or *n*-stage) functional role semantics: *in the end* the semantics of symbols is anchored to the world via the knowledge that can be attributed to the whole system *at the knowledge level* in virtue of its capacity, exercised or not, for perspicuous

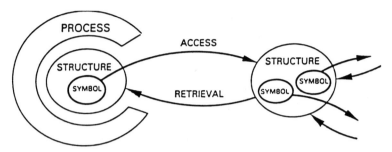

Fig. 1. Symbols provide distal access. (Originally, Fig. 2.10 (p. 75) in *Unified Theories of Cognition.*)

behavior vis-a-vis the items in the world its knowledge is about. And that's my view, too. What makes a data structure about Julie Christie is that it's the part of the system the presence of which explains my capacity to pick her out of a crowd, answer questions about her in quiz shows, etc., etc. That's all there is to it. But it is certainly misleading to say that the symbol gives one *any* "access" (partial access, in polite society!) to the object itself. (It turns out that Julie Christie and I have a mutual friend, who sent her an offprint of [2]. And what do you know, she ... sent me a Christmas card. "Getting closer", I thought. "Maybe Newell's right after all! You just have to be patient. Porsche, Porsche, Porsche.")

Newell's diagram in Fig. 1 makes it all clear (in retrospect) as long as you realize that it is not just that he concentrates (in his book and in his earlier writing) on the semantic link-arrows in the middle of the diagram—the access links tying symbols to their distal knowledge-stores—but that he simply *assumes* there is a solution to any problems that might arise about the interpretation of the arrows on the right-hand side of the diagram: those arrows, as I understand him now, lead one *either* to more data structures or eventually to something in the external world—but he is close to silent about this final, anchoring step. This is fine by me, but then I'm one of the few philosophers who thinks Twin-Earth and narrow content are artifactual philosophical conundrums of no importance to cognitive science [1,3]. Make no mistake, though: serious or not, Newell sweeps them under the rug right here. [1]

---

[1] In a more recent paper, he goes a bit further in defense of this interpretation: "The agent's knowledge is embodied in the knowledge of the four problem space components. However, this latter knowledge is about the problem space, states and operators; hence it cannot of itself be the knowledge of the agent, which is about the goal, actions and environment. It becomes the agent's knowledge by means of the relationships just described. That is, states are about the external world because of KL perception; operators are about the external world because of KL actions; the desired states are about the goal of the KL agent because of formulate-task; and the means-ends knowledge of select-operator is about performing tasks in the environment because it links environment-referring operators on environment-referring states to descriptions of environment-referring desired states." (Newell et al. [11, p. 23])

What concerns him is rather the interesting question of Plato's aviary: how does an intelligent agent with more knowledge than it can "contemplate" all at once get the right birds to come when it calls? (Dennett [4, p. 222–225]). And how do you do this without relying on a dubious *transportation* metaphor, which would require shipping symbol-tokens here and there in the system? I'm not sure I understand his answer entirely, but the crucial elements are given on p. 355:

> Functionally, working memory must be a short-term memory. It is used to hold the coded knowledge that is to be processed for the current task. It is necessary to replace that knowledge when the task changes. That replacement can be achieved in many ways, by moving the data [bad idea!—DCD], by moving the processes [better!—DCD], or by changing the access path [best!—DCD] .... Working memory for cognition has no continued functional existence outside these limits, however, since elements that are no longer linked to the goal stack become unavailable. Furthermore, problem spaces themselves have no existence independent of the impasses they are created to resolve.

I find these ideas some of the most difficult to understand in cognitive science, for they require setting aside, for once, what we might call the concrete crutch: the lazy picture of places (with boxes around them) and things moving to and fro. *That* vision, for all its utility at the symbol level, is a dangerous companion when we turn to the question of mapping computational processes onto brain processes. When Newell says "Search leads to the view that an intelligent agent is always operating within a *problem space*." (p. 98) we should recognize that this is really being presented as an *a priori* constraint on how we shall interpret intelligent agents. Show me an intelligent agent, and whatever it does, I'll show you a way of interpreting it as setting up a problem space. Since the key term "distal" is defined relative to *that* space—that logical space—we should be cautious of interpreting it too concretely (cf. Fodor and Pylyshyn [8]).

So my second reservation is blunted as well. Two strikes, or maybe foul balls. There is one more issue I want to take a swing at as long as I'm up at bat. Newell's silence on the issue of natural language as a symbolic medium of cognition in human beings is uncanny. We know that Soar can (in principle) learn from taking *advice* (e.g., p. 312), and Newell sketches out the way Soar would or might handle language acquisition and comprehension (pp. 440–449; see especially his discussion of redundant encoding, p. 453), but I cannot figure out from these brief passages what Newell thinks happens to the overall shape of the competence of a cognitive system when it acquires a natural language, and I think his reticence on this score hides major issues. Early on he gives an eloquent survey of what he calls the "efflorescence of adaptation" by the human (and only the human) species (pp. 114–115), but does this paean to productive versatility proclaim that the symbols of an *internalized natural language* are necessary, or is it rather that one needs a pre-linguistic language of thought—in which case we may wonder why the human language of thought gives us such an edge over the other species, if it does not get most of its power from the external language we learn to speak. For instance, Newell's discussion of annotated models (pp. 393ff) is a fine perspective on the mental models debates, but I am left wondering: can a non-human intelligent agent—a dog or dolphin or ape, for instance—avail itself of an annotated model, or is that level of cognitive sophistication reserved for language-users? This is just one instance of a sort of empirical question that is left curiously burked by Newell's reticence.

This gap is all the more frustrating since in other regards I find Newell's treatment in Chapters 1 and 2 of the standard debating topics in the philosophy of cognitive science a refreshing challenge. These chapters are simply required reading henceforth for any philosophers of cognitive science.[2] Newell doesn't waste time surveying the wreckage; he gets down to business. He says, in effect: "Sit down and listen; I'll show you how to think about these topics." He simply *makes moves* in all the games we play, and largely leaves it to us to object or play along. This should be a model for all non-philosopher scientists who aspire (correctly!) to philosophical probity. Don't try to play the philosophers' games. Just make your moves, clearly and explicitly, and see if you can get away with them.

I very largely agree with his moves, and it will be a pity if philosophers who disagree with him don't rise to the bait. They may not, alas. At times Newell underestimates how ingrown his jargon is. I have pushed portions of his text on some very smart philosophers and neuroscientists, and they are often completely at sea. (These issues are awfully hard to communicate about, and I am well aware that the alternative expository tactics I have tried in my own writing run their own risks of massive misconstrual.)

It might seem odd, finally, for me not to comment at all on Newell's deliberate postponement of consideration of consciousness, which gets just a brief apology on p. 434. Is this not unconscionable? Not at all. Newell's

---

[2]Philosophers will find important material throughout the book, not just in the foundational chapters at the beginning. For instance, the discussion of the discovery of the data-chunking problem in Soar and its handling (pp. 326–345) can be interpreted as a sort of inverse version of Meno's paradox of inquiry. The problem is not how can I search for something if I don't already know what it is, but how can I set myself up so that when I confront a real Meno-problem, there will be a way I can solve it? (Alternatively, if Soar couldn't solve the data-chunking problem, Meno's claim would not be paradoxical when applied to Soar, but simply true.) I think the memory-management search control strategies that are adopted can be read as part of an explicit answer—much more explicit than any philosopher's answer—to Meno's challenge.

project is highly compatible with mine in *Consciousness Explained* [4]. For instance, I endorse without reservation his list of multiple constraints on mind in Fig. 1-7 (p. 19). How can he achieve this divorce of consciousness? Just look! The enabling insight, for Newell and for me, is that handsome is as handsome does; you don't need any *extra witnesses* in order to explain cognition. Newell modestly denies that he has yet touched on consciousness; I disagree. He's made a big dent.

References

[1] D.C. Dennett, Beyond belief, in: A. Woodfield, ed., *Thought and Object* (Clarendon Press, Oxford, 1982).

[2] D.C. Dennett, Is there an autonomous "Knowledge Level"? in: Z.W. Pylyshyn and W. Demopoulos, eds., *Meaning and Cognitive Structure* (Ablex, Norwood, NJ, 1986) 51–54.

[3] D.C. Dennett, *The Intentional Stance* (MIT Press/Bradford Books, Cambridge, MA, 1987).

[4] D.C. Dennett, *Consciousness Explained* (Little Brown, Boston, 1991).

[5] R. de Sousa, *The Rationality of Emotion* (MIT Press, Cambridge, MA, 1987).

[6] G.M. Edelman, *The Remembered Present: A Biological Theory of Consciousness* (Basic Books, New York, 1989).

[7] J.A. Fodor, Tom Swift and his Procedural Grandmother, *Cognition* **6** (1978) 229–247.

[8] J.A. Fodor and Z.W. Pylyshyn, Connectionism and cognitive architecture: a critical analysis, *Cognition* **28** (1988) 3–71; also in: S. Pinker and J. Mehler, eds., *Connectionism and Symbol Systems* (MIT Press, Cambridge, MA, 1988) 3–71.

[9] A. Newell, The symbol level and the knowledge level, in: Z.W. Pylyshyn and W. Demopoulos, eds., *Meaning and Cognitive Structure* (Ablex, Norwood, NJ, 1986) 169–193.

[10] A. Newell, P.S. Rosenbloom and J.E. Laird, Symbolic architectures for cognition, in: M. Posner, ed., *Foundations of Cognitive Science* (MIT Press, Cambridge, MA, 1989).

[11] A. Newell, G. Yost, J.E. Laird, P.S. Rosenbloom and E. Altmann, Formulating the problem-space computational model, in: R. Rashid, ed., *Carnegie Mellon Computer Science: A 25-Year Commemorative* (ACM Press/Addison-Wesley, Reading, MA, 1992).

[12] Z.W. Pylyshyn and W. Demopoulos, eds., *Meaning and Cognitive Structure* (Ablex, Norwood, NJ, 1986).

[13] A. Sloman and M. Croucher, Why robots will have emotions, in: *Proceedings IJCAI-81*, Vancouver, BC (1981).

[14] B.C. Smith, The link from symbol to knowledge, in: Z.W. Pylyshyn and W. Demopoulos, eds., *Meaning and Cognitive Structure* (Ablex, Norwood, NJ, 1986) 40–50.

Artificial Intelligence 59 (1993) 295–328
Elsevier

ARTINT 1011

Unified theories of cognition: modeling cognitive competence *

Michael R. Fehling

Laboratory for Intelligent Systems, Stanford University, Stanford, CA, USA

Abstract

Fehling, M., Unified theories of cognition: modeling cognitive competence, Artificial Intelligence 59 (1993) 295–328.

In his recent text, *Unified Theories of Cognition,* Allen Newell offers an exciting mixture of theoretical and methodological advice to cognitive scientists on how to begin developing more comprehensive accounts of human problem solving. Newell's perspective is at once both exciting and frustrating. His concept of a unified theory of cognition (UTC), and his attempt to illustrate a UTC with his Soar problem solving architecture, is exciting because it suggests how scientists might use the computational methods of cognitive science and artificial intelligence to formulate and explore both broader and deeper aspects of intelligence in people and in machines. Newell's perspective is equally frustrating because it dictates a behaviorist methodology for evaluating cognitive models. Newell views a UTC as a simulation of behavior. I explore the surprising similarity of Newell's approach to theory to the approaches of classical behaviorists such as John Watson and Edward Chace Tolman. I suggest that Newell's behaviorist methodology is incompatible with his commitment to building theories in terms of complex computational systems. I offer a modification to Newell's approach in which a UTC provides an architecture in which to explore the nature of competence—the requisite body of knowledge—that underlies an intelligent agent's ability to perform tasks in a particular domain. I compare this normative perspective to Newell's commitment to performance modeling. I conclude that his key theoretical concepts, such as the problem space hypothesis, knowledge level systems, and intelligence as approximation to the knowledge level are fundamentally competence constructs. I raise specific concerns about the indeterminacy of evaluating a UTC like Soar against performance data. Finally, I suggest that competence modeling more thoroughly exploits the insights of cognitive scientists like Newell and reduces the gap between the aims of cognitive science and artificial intelligence.

Correspondence to: M. Fehling, Laboratory for Intelligent Systems, Stanford University, CA, USA. E-mail: fehling@bayes.stanford.edu.
* (Harvard University Press, Cambridge, MA, 1990); xvi + 549 pages.

1. Introduction

A great many psychologists, linguists, and other students of human behavior have expressed the hope that their studies might eventually be embedded within a comprehensive theory of human information processing. Over the last twenty years or so this hope has given rise to the research discipline known as cognitive science (Stillings et al. [46]). According to Herbert Simon (Simon and Kaplan [43]) "[c]ognitive science is the study of intelligence and intelligent systems, with particular reference to intelligent behavior as computation". The focus on computational models of cognition establishes a strong and direct relationship between cognitive science and the field of artificial intelligence (AI).

In *Unified Theories of Cognition*, Allen Newell presents cognitive scientists with a bold and exciting challenge, one that should also interest many AI scientists. Newell is very enthusiastic about progress made by cognitive scientists in measuring diverse types of human problem solving behavior. However, his enthusiasm is tempered by the observation that no overarching theory has yet been developed to explain the broad range of data describing human behavior.

Newell proclaims that the time has come to build such a comprehensive theory:

> Psychology has arrived at the possibility of unified theories of cognition—theories that gain their power by positing *a single system* of mechanisms that operate together to produce the *full range* of human cognition .... Such *[comprehensive theories] are within reach and we should strive to attain them.* (p. 1) [emphasis added]

1.1. Toward unified theories of cognition

Newell's primary objective is, therefore, to persuade cognitive scientists to build unified theories of cognition (UTCs). He perceives some urgency in this matter. He declares that "it is time to get going on producing unified theories of cognition" before the body of facts to be explained grows even larger (p. 25). This remark, despite its rather curious logic, illustrates Newell's commitment to developing UTCs. He explicitly distinguishes this goal from that of espousing one particular UTC:

> I am not asserting that there is a unique unified theory and we should all get together on it. ... [M]ultiple theories are the best we can do. The task at hand is to get *some* candidate theories ... to show ... that they are real. The task is somehow to cajole

ourselves into putting it all together, even though we don't know
many of the mechanisms that are operating. (p. 17)

One might reasonably expect Newell to pursue his ambitious objective by
comprehensively surveying and comparing a broad range of candidate UTCs,
or even partial UTCs. Instead, he focuses his attention exclusively on his
own work. Newell's candidate UTC is *Soar*, a problem solving architecture
he and his students have been developing over much of the last decade (cf.,
Laird et al. [28]). Although he worries that Soar's more contentious features
"may detract a little from using Soar simply as an exemplar for a unified
theory of cognition" (p. 39), Newell is satisfied that Soar will illustrate his
proposal for building UTCs. For Newell, research on Soar typifies what a
UTC is, how to build one, and how to assess its adequacy as a theory of
human behavior.

At the least, Newell's monograph contributes significantly by integrating
many of his most important theoretical concepts about human cognition.
Over his long career, Newell has formulated a powerful set of fundamental concepts for describing human cognition as knowledge-based, heuristic
search (Newell et al. [5,39,40]). His concepts have influenced the thinking
of most cognitive scientists as well as many in AI. Newell brings these ideas
together in this work and describes their role in building a solid foundation
for theory in cognitive science.

However, I suggest in this commentary that, on balance, *Unified Theories
of Cognition* will fall somewhat short of achieving its major objective.
This is not because cognitive scientists will reject Newell's counsel to build
UTCs. In fact, many of them have been at this task for quite some time
(e.g. Anderson [1,2], Holland et al. [24], MacKay [29]). Nor is it due,
as Newell fears, to Soar's "contentious" claims. I can think of no better
stimulus to the development of competing UTCs than offering a contentious
or unconvincing theory.

The fundamental problem that I see with Newell's book stems from
his insistence that UTCs accurately describe and predict human behavior.
This commitment is a cornerstone of his methodology for interpreting and
evaluating UTCs. For Newell a good theory, whatever its scope, is one that
"you can really make predictions with" ... (p. 5). And, a UTC simply
extends this commitment more broadly. A UTC embodies "a single set of
mechanisms for all of cognitive behavior" (p. 15). Of course, Newell shares
this commitment to performance prediction with most cognitive scientists as
well as many other theorists who choose not to formulate their psychological
theories in computational terms.

Newell's discussion of theory as behavior simulation and the role of
Soar as such a model illustrates this doctrine with revealing clarity. This
provides an important reason for examining Newell's proposal so carefully.

A number of cognitive scientists (e.g., Anderson [1], Townsend and Ashby [48]) claim that it is impossible to distinguish competing predictive models using performance data alone. Cognitive theorists accepting this argument will be far less inclined to concern themselves with Newell's proposal and to expend enormous effort to develop and compare UTCs. In contrast, Newell seeks to convince us that competing UTCs can be distinguished on the basis of performance prediction. If he can do so then his approach will be interesting. I argue below that he fails in his attempts to overcome the limitations of predictive modeling.

I offer an alternative approach to evaluating and exploring cognitive theories such as Newell's UTCs. I argue that the distinct value of a computational model of cognition emanates from its ability to rigorously depict the knowledge that enables intelligent problem solvers to adequately perform specific tasks. I refer to such embodied knowledge as a *cognitive competence.* A UTC such as Newell's Soar serves as a framework within which to interpret and explore models of cognitive competence.

Although my alternative approach differs radically from Newell's on methodological grounds, it seems to me to be quite consistent with many of his more fundamental theoretical pronouncements about cognition. In this light, I also suggest that this alternative approach to cognitive theory is more consistent with Newell's fundamental theoretical distinctions than is his commitment to performance simulation.

1.2. Modeling cognitive competence

The notion of cognitive competence may be unfamiliar to some readers. I now briefly review some of the central features of competence theories before continuing my commentary on Newell.

Noam Chomsky [6] is perhaps the best known proponent of this approach to cognitive theory. Chomsky revolutionized the study of language by suggesting that a grammar be viewed as a description of the knowledge tacitly or implicitly held by an idealized speaker-listener. An idealized linguistic agent is not subject to errors while generating or comprehending well-formed linguistic utterances. So, a grammar does not make predictions about *actual* performance. Rather, it provides a set of *ideal* performances, here, the set of acceptable sentences of some language. Chomsky proposed that linguistic competence be represented as a collection of recursive production rules. An adequate set of rules must generate all and only the acceptable sentences of the idealized speaker-listener's language. He called such a collection of rules a *generative grammar.*

Moravcsik [33] discusses some important features of a competence account. First, a competence account postulates a *disposition toward a structured class of behaviors.* By "disposition" I mean here a capacity to act in certain restricted ways, and perhaps an inclination toward these actions under certain abstract conditions. For example, a complete theory of an English speaker's competence accounts for her ability to utter syntactically, semantically, and pragmatically acceptable sentences in that language and perhaps her propensity to utter them under hypothesized conditions of intent (e.g., to convey meaning or accomplish a speech act). A disposition embodies knowledge about the structure of these idealized action. For example, an English speaker's competence also manifests itself in the agent's capacity to acknowledge (Chomsky would say to have intuitions about) structural relations among sentences. In particular, a complete competence theory must also account for the English speaker's ability to recognize that one sentence in the passive voice paraphrases (i.e., conveys the same meaning as) another sentence in the active voice, or that one sentence is the negation of another.

Second, although the disposition embodies knowledge of a structured class of behaviors, the competent agent need not be able to directly articulate that knowledge. For example, while competent English speakers can be expected to follow the rules of subject–verb agreement, they may not be able to state those rules. Chomsky labeled this kind of knowledge as "tacit". For example, Chomsky's generative grammar embodies this kind of tacit knowledge by specifying "what the speaker actually knows, not what he may report about his knowledge" (Chomsky [7, p. 8]).

Third, theorists can distinguish a competent agent's disposition toward a set of behaviors from the concrete manifestations of that disposition. A competence theory focuses on *ideal* performance as distinguished from actual, possibly erroneous, performance. A theory of English-speaking competence does not predict when or whether an agent will utter a particular sentence. Nor does it predict that an utterance will or will not be grammatically correct. However, it does claim that, under ideal circumstances, competent English speakers can agree on whether any given construction is acceptable in English, is related to other constructions, etc. Competence is described in a form that is abstracted away from factors idiosyncratically influencing real performance.

Finally, and most importantly for this paper, theories can be developed and explored that characterize competences other than linguistic competence. Moravcsik [33] proposes that cognitive theorists "can characterize grammatical, logical, mathematical, etc. competences, and add ... later characterizations of several other competences or in some cases ... psychological or environmental factors that influence actual performance or occurrence" (p. 86).

In sum, a cognitive theory of competence focuses on describing dispositional knowledge, embodied as generative processes, underlying idealized performance. This outlook on cognitive theory contrasts sharply with Newell's commitment to cognitive theory as a basis for predicting or simulating behavior. Having reviewed this alternative approach to cognitive theory, I am now ready to consider Newell's proposal in more detail.

2. The elements of Newell's approach

This section outlines four central features of Newell's approach—his stance on the goals of cognitive theory, his biologically inspired view of the human cognitive architecture, his view of UTCs as knowledge systems, and his exemplar UTC, the Soar problem solving architecture.

2.1. Theories of cognition

Newell believes that a cognitive theory is concerned above all else with describing human behavior, especially in chronometric terms. He points to the impressive body of experimental data amassed by experimental psychologists and cognitive scientists and in need of explanation. Newell illustrates his view of commendable psychological theory by reviewing such "microtheories" as Fitts' Law [17] and the Power Law of Practice (Snoddy [44]). Fitts' Law predicts the time it will take a subject to move a finger or pointer to a target location. This time varies in proportion to the logarithm of the ratio of the distance moved to the size of the target region. According to the Power Law, the logarithm of some measure of performance, e.g, performance time, is linearly related to the logarithm of the number of practice trials (Fitts and Posner [18]). These chronometric laws illustrate Newell's concern with predicting the time-dependent course of behavior. He also offers information processing mechanisms as hypotheses of the cognitive processes that produce these behavioral regularities.

Newell offers yet another illustration of acceptable theorizing. This example, a model of search in problem solving, differs somewhat from the examples of chronometric laws in being a bit more abstract. The observations in this case take the form of a detailed record of a chess player's verbal report of the sequence of candidate moves (s)he considers at a point in a game. For Newell, these verbal reports, called a *protocol* (Ericsson and Simon [11]), provide observable manifestations of the subject's mental search among possible moves. Unlike the two previous cases, the regularities that Newell observes are qualitative. He finds that the subject engages in a specific pattern of search that he calls "progressive deepening". Here, as in the two previous examples, Newell seeks to illustrate how one can construct an information processing mechanism capable of simulating these behavioral regularities.

Newell also wants to diverge from the strictest approaches to behavior modeling in which a single predictive failure suffices to falsify an entire theory. Newell argues that "theories are … like graduate students" (p. 14). That is, once a theory is adopted one aims to "nurture" it, to find ways to tune or adapt it in the face of contradictory evidence rather than simply reject it. This decidedly non-Popperian view of theorizing is an important aspect of Newell's approach. A UTC approximates a complete or exact account of all the evidence. Theorists strive to refine and modify the UTC to better account for the evidence and to gradually expand the theory's scope. Nevertheless, simulation or prediction of physically measurable performance data comprises the core of Newell's approach regardless of the diversity of types of data or the degree of approximation that he is willing to accept.

2.2. The human cognitive architecture

Newell carries his theme of simulating physical events to the biological level. He presents his picture of the neural system that produces intelligent behavior, the "human cognitive architecture". His architecture is a hierarchy that is built, as he puts it, out of "neural technology". He begins by composing basic neuronal units hierarchically out of even more elemental biophysical units. He then constructs a hierarchy of ever more complex combinations of neuronal units. Newell identifies "levels" in this hierarchy in terms of compositional complexity. He further aggregates adjacent levels in the hierarchy into what he calls "bands". Newell focuses particularly on postulating relationships between bounds on performance capabilities of structures at a particular level (of complexity) and bounds on the performance times required by those units to carry out their functions.

Individual neural elements form a low level of this hierarchy. The first level of composition, in which neural elements are connected, Newell calls the "lowest level of the cognitive band" (p. 132). These element-to-element connections allow information stored at one location to be accessed at another. Distal access is, for Newell, the defining capability for producing and using symbols. Newell postulates that simple distal access takes place within approximately 10 milliseconds. This fixes the functional or processing capability of this level of the hierarchy and associates with it a bound on performance time. Newell emphasizes the inherent inflexibility of this level of processing. Assuming fixed connections, an element's response is entirely determined by the contents of the fixed locations to which it is connected and which may be accessed.

At the next higher level, combinations of these basic connections are hypothesized to produce the simplest forms of what Newell calls "deliberation" (p. 133). Essentially, circuits at this level are composed of a selection element having distal access to some set of remote units. The selection element distally accesses information stored in the remote units, computes over it, and produces a response on the basis of that fixed computation. So, the response of a deliberative unit reflects a comparison of the content of multiple, distal sources of information during one or more cycles of access. Newell estimates the processing time at this level to be on the order of 1/10 of a second. This increase in processing time accompanies the increase in functionality. However, Newell emphasizes the inflexibility of circuits at this basic level of deliberation. The response produced by such a circuit depends upon the information from fixed connections and a fixed choice function.

The next level of circuits provides more flexibility in response. Newell posits that this level provides the minimum flexibility to produce "characteristic interactions with the environment which ... evoke cognitive considerations" (p. 129). Circuits at this level select among the alternatives at the next lower level. Thus, these circuits realize "operations" that give more cognitive flexibility by allowing choices or compositions among alternative basic deliberation mechanisms. Alternative deliberation methods can be distally accessed, selected among, or composed. Newell proposes that these operations take on the order of 1 second to occur. Newell suggests that behaviors resulting from operations at this level of the human cognitive architecture correspond to highly practiced responses such as pushing the appropriate button in a reaction time task.

Newell adds yet another level, the "unit task" level. Circuits at this level are composed from combinations of the "operations" at the immediately preceding level. Accordingly, he calls this the "first level of composed operations". Newell postulates another order-of-magnitude increase in performance times at this level, to approximately 10 seconds. This increase in performance time, of course, corresponds to a further increase in the flexibility and processing power that can be achieved at this level. Newell associates the responses produced by the unit task level with elementary, reportable problem solving steps such as the reportable elements of task performance by skilled computer users (Card et al. [5]) or moves selected in a chess game (Newell and Simon [40]).

Newell names these four levels the "cognitive band". The cognitive band is built hierarchically from the more basic constituents of the "neural technology" in the subordinate "biological band". Newell suggests that the cognitive band constitutes the lowest level of the human cognitive architecture that can manifest the essential functions of problem solving—*symbolic representation, composed representation, knowledge as response capacities, and search.*

Newell extends his hierarchy to higher composed levels. He describes the "intendedly rational band" as immediately superior to the cognitive band. Three levels comprise this band. The functions defined there are, of course, selected and composed from lower level circuits. Rational band functions search even more thoroughly and flexibly among distally accessed alternatives. The rational band's most distinctive feature is, according to

Newell, the ability to perform functions enabling the cognitive system to adapt its responses to attain goals. Newell says little about how goals arise or how they are encoded except to indicate that goals represent a cognitive system's limited "knowledge of [its] environment" (p. 150). He suggests that search in this band, implemented by compositions of composed functions from lower levels provides the flexibility to operate in a goal-driven manner. Of course, these flexible operations also consume more time, taking anywhere from a couple of minutes at the lowest level of this band to a couple of hours at the rational band's highest level.

Still higher level bands are hierarchically composed from the rational, cognitive, and biological bands. Newell calls these the "social, historical, and evolutionary bands". He has even less to say about these bands. Here again, Newell seems primarily concerned to show how structural complexity leads to greater functional capacity and adaptivity, on the one hand, and longer required operating times, on the other.

This brief summary should provide a general feel for Newell's "human cognitive architecture". It illustrates his predominant concern for identifying physical events whose chronometric and other properties provide cognition with a basis in physical reality. By including this architecture as part of his monograph's presentation, Newell seems to be telling us specifically that a UTC's mechanisms must be reducible to measurable biophysical phenomena. Moreover, he makes a concerted (and, in this case, heroic) effort to use performance timings to shed light on other aspects of cognition. He is quite willing, as he freely admits, to construct highly speculative hypotheses of neurophysiological architecture in order to "get some general guidelines for the cognitive architecture regardless of any specific proposal" (p. 157).

2.3. UTCs as knowledge systems

Other than this speculative foray into neurophysiological modeling, Newell focuses most of his discussion on computational rather than neurophysiological mechanisms from which to build UTCs. He develops a comprehensive theory depicting "the symbol processing required for intelligence" (p. 158). Newell presents his AI architecture, Soar, as both the embodiment of this cognitive theory and as a guiding example of UTCs in general. As an exemplar UTC, Soar embodies some constructs that Newell believes are fundamental to any UTC. This section reviews these foundational UTC constructs.

For Newell, a UTC is a theory taking "*mind* to be the control system that guides the behaving organism in its complex interactions with the dynamic real world" (p. 43). Although mind is a control system, Newell rejects the language of control science (Wiener [50]). He chooses instead to describe this control system as "having knowledge and behaving in light of it" (p. 45).

A UTC explains the performance produced by a *knowledge system*. Newell also rejects the analyses of knowledge produced by epistemologists and other philosophers. He presents a concept of knowledge "that is used simply to describe and predict the *response functions* of a system ... to predict (with varying degrees of success) the behavior of the system" (p. 46). The knowledge that a cognitive system embodies provides its capacity to behave—perform tasks, solve problems, and enact decisions—under various conditions.

Newell's presentation of knowledge systems recapitulates ideas he has published previously over more than thirty years. This includes his well-known discussions of physical symbol systems [36], the knowledge level [38] and the problem space hypothesis [37]. His contribution in his current monograph is to integrate these ideas in a common framework, an *architecture*. In fact, Newell believes that the knowledge system specified by a UTC must be embodied in an architecture. He proclaims that "to specify a unified theory of cognition is to specify an architecture" (p. 158). The architecture specified by a UTC constitutes basic mechanisms that realize and manage a knowledge system's most fundamental functions. Furthermore, he suggests that the functions carried out by this architecture itself contribute substantively to the behavioral predictions of the UTC. The architecture's properties show up in what Newell terms "the commonalties ... in behavior" (p. 159).

Newell's list of fundamental knowledge system functions include the use of *symbols, structured and composible representations, knowledge, and problem solving as search*. Because Newell has already written extensively about these things I can be very brief in reviewing them.

- *Symbols.* As already noted, Newell's basic idea of symbolic representation turns upon what he calls "distal access". A symbol is an object providing a cognitive system with the ability to gain access to some remote body of information. A UTC stipulates how symbols are constructed and used within an architecture to establish the laws of information availability and access.
- *Representation.* Symbol structures act as representations insofar as they obey Newell's basic representation law

  $$Decode[Encode[T](Encode[X])] = T(X).$$

  To explain this law, suppose that X is some actual situation in an agent's task environment. Let T be some transformation that can occur in that environment. T maps the situation, X, into another situation, $T(X)$. Newell's representation law says that application of a proper representation of T to a proper representation of X produces a proper representation of $T(X)$. This law specifies how composite representations are built up from simpler representations.

- *Knowledge.* A UTC specifies how knowledge engenders action. The dispositional quality of knowledge is its most fundamental characteristic to Newell. UTCs describe how a cognitive system's knowledge provides its capacity "to take actions to attain goals" (p. 50). Newell does not hold that knowledge must be encoded in some declarative form such as predicate calculus (cf., Genesereth and Nilsson [19]). For example, the knowledge in Newell's UTC, Soar, is encoded in procedural form, as productions, and in its architecture's functions such as the decision cycle that manages operations on Soar's goal stack. Newell does not arbitrarily rule out UTCs that hypothesize declarative encoding of knowledge such as Anderson's [2] ACT* architecture. He does, however, hold that one would need to understand how these declarations are interpreted and converted to action before one could confidently assert the knowledge specified by such a theory.

  Newell uses his dispositional definition of knowledge to show how UTCs can depict the overall capability, or *intelligence*, of a cognitive system. Newell defines a *knowledge level* system as one that uses all of its knowledge or beliefs in performing its tasks. This includes knowledge that is logically entailed by explicitly embodied knowledge. The *intelligence* of a knowledge system is the degree to which it makes complete use of its knowledge. That is, a cognitive system's intelligence is its degree of approximation to being a knowledge level system.

- *Search.* In Newell's view problem solving is fundamentally search. A UTC specifies problem solving amounts to search of a *problem space* for a solution state. The proposition that problem solving may be viewed as state space search is a predominant assumption in both AI and cognitive science. The most unique feature of Newell's version of this well-worn search hypothesis is his stipulation that problem spaces may be generated to solve problems arising from the incomplete or otherwise flawed character of a given problem space representation. For example, if an agent is searching a given problem space, she might find herself in a state for which no operators exist to enable further search. Newell calls this kind of problem solving event an *impasse.* Impasses define new problems which require search in their own associated problem spaces. In the present example, a problem space must be selected and searched to find new operators to add to the original problem space in order to resolve the "no operator" impasse. This hierarchical and generative view of search contrasts with most discussion of problem solving as search in AI and cognitive science that implicitly assume search in a single complete space.

Newell distinguishes between *knowledge search* and *problem search*. Problem search explores a given problem space. Knowledge search seeks information to guide or control problem search. For example, the result of knowledge search can initiate problem search as when the perceived occurrence—i.e., the encoding—of a problematic environmental condition triggers the selection of a particular state space to be searched to resolve that problematic condition. Knowledge search can constrain the steps taken in this problem search. The reaction to an impasse illustrates this case. In my previous example, impasse detection triggers a knowledge search that sets up the problem space to be searched for finding new operators.

2.4. Soar

Newell's problem solving architecture, Soar, embodies his vision of UTCs. I touch lightly those aspects of Soar that I refer to in subsequent discussion.

Soar is a production system architecture. It implements Newell's problem space hypothesis. Soar's key elements include a single *long-term* or *recognition memory*. Recognition memory is populated entirely by production rules. Thus, Soar's knowledge is procedurally encoded. This commitment distinguishes Soar from other UTCs, such as Anderson's ACT*, which encode some or all of the contents of long-term memory as declarative structures such as logic assertions, semantic network structures, or frames. As in any production system, Soar's *working memory* is another key component. The contents of Soar's working memory are object–attribute–value data structures. Working memory's specific contents cause appropriate production rules to execute. The left-hand side of each production rule in long-term memory describes a pattern of object–attribute–value combinations (with variables allowed) that can occur in Soar's working memory. Of course, working memory contents that trigger productions on a given cycle are the result of previous production rule firings (or possibly direct by sensor input, although Newell says little about this).

The *context stack* is a very important structure within working memory. It is an architectural feature of Soar. The context stack encodes a hierarchy of problem solving contexts. Each level in the stack represents a commitment to search a specific problem space, the goal (state) being sought in that space, the current state in the problem space which search has reached, and an operator to apply next to generate successors of the current state. These four items in each level of the context stack represent the current problem solving context. Since the context stack is in working memory, productions can respond to its contents. Among other things, productions may suggest how to complete or change the contents of the context stack. For example, a particular level of the stack may happen to specify only a problem space, goal, and current state. In this case, productions might fire that "propose" operators to fill out this context level. Once an operator has been proposed, accepted, and inserted into the proper level of context, long-term memory productions may then fire that propose the successor state to use to replace the current state entry.

Conflicts can occur in this process. For example, productions may propose multiple candidate operators to complete a level, or multiple candidate successor states in the problem space. So, certain productions insert *preferences* into working memory. These preferences order selection among competing proposals to change the context stack. These preferences will, hopefully, resolve to a single choice. If they do not, an impasse is created that triggers long-term memory productions to set up a new problem space with the goal of resolving the impasse. Thus, the principles that guide conflict resolution in Soar are largely driven by information in long-term memory rather than being defined strictly as part of the overall architecture.

Soar's *decision procedure* is the fixed component of the architecture that manages changes to working memory and resolves competition using the preferences just mentioned. Each cycle of Soar's operation begins with an elaboration phase. In this phase the current contents of working memory trigger concurrent firings of production rules. Rules that fire insert new items in working memory. This may cause more production rules to fire. This continues until no new working memory elements are created and, hence, no more rules fire. This ends the *elaboration phase*. Up to now the multiple, possibly competing proposals created by firing of production rules have not been incorporated in the context stack. This is done next, during the *decision phase*. Soar's *decision procedure* examines the proposals for changes to the context stack and the preferences that have been asserted to resolve conflicts. If the proposals and preferences combine to uniquely stipulate modifications to the context stack, then the indicated modifications are made and Soar moves to the elaboration phase of the next cycle of Soar's operation. An *impasse* may occur, however, if no changes are made or if the preferences in working memory do not specify a unique choice among competing proposals. If this occurs the decision procedure creates data elements encoding the specific type of impasse before a new cycle of rule firing begins. Production rules firing in response to impasse detection create a new level in the context stack. It is subordinate to the level in which the impasse occurs. This new level will identify a problem space to be searched with the goal of resolving the current impasse.

When an impasse is resolved, Soar invokes another important component of its architecture, the *chunking* mechanism. Chunking is Soar's single mechanism for learning. As I have just sketched, Soar resolves an impasse by creating and searching a problem space. Soar keeps a record of the elements of working memory that were involved in the creation of the impasse. When the impasse is resolved, a new rule is created that encodes the search result as the response to make in the future if the conditions leading to the impasse recur.

Soar is a very direct and elegant implementation of Newell's problem space hypothesis [37]. Soar encodes problem spaces implicitly. A problem space is generated by the sequence of production rule firings and the changes that they produce in working memory's context stack. Problem spaces can be created and searched by productions that respond to various working memory contents such as goals, impasses, and other data. So, one may conceptually group subsets of productions in Soar's long-term memory according to the problem space descriptors (problem space identity, goal, state, operator, or other assertions in the context stack) that are a prerequisite to their firing.

3. Critical appraisal

The previous section reviewed four elements of Newell's approach to cognitive theory. His general remarks on theories of cognition show him to be committed to simulation or prediction of specific performance, frequently emphasizing the time-dependent properties of behavior. His description of the human cognitive architecture suggests that a UTC must be reducible to biophysical processes and structures as well as concrete behavior. In contrast, the foundational elements of Newell's theory of knowledge systems emphasize dispositional knowledge as a generative capacity for intelligent behavior. Finally, Soar embodies this theory and provides a direct and elegant implementation of Newell's ideas about problem solving as search in a hierarchy of problem spaces.

As I stated in the introduction, my critical remarks about Newell's proposal focus mostly on problems caused by his view of UTCs, and Soar in particular, in terms of their ability to simulate or predict behavior.

3.1. Cognitive theory as behavior simulation

My most fundamental concern with Newell's approach is prompted by the similarity of Newell's proposal to classical behaviorism. This is surprising because behaviorism is the paradigm that he and others deem to have been displaced in a "paradigm shift" to cognitive science. Newell asserts that the theories and methods of cognitive science have "established a new paradigm" (p. 24). Newell sees the dominance of cognitive science reflected in the critical attention being given to it by recent challenges from such competing paradigms as ecological realism (Gibson [20,21]) and connectionism (McClelland et al. [30,41]). Newell thinks that it is high time that cognitive science has a theoretical manifesto to replace those provided by leading behaviorists such as Watson [49], Tolman [47] or Hull [25].

However, as I carefully studied Newell's exposition of UTCs, I found it increasingly difficult to distinguish his view as a cognitive scientist from the fundamental principles of the behaviorist paradigm. Many aspects of Newell's approach invite comparison to the behaviorist doctrine prescribed by John Watson, typically considered the founding expositor of behaviorism. Other aspects of Newell's approach seem similar to Tolman's version of behaviorism.

John Watson advocated a very rigorous version of behaviorism [49]. He sought to reduce the science of psychology in its entirety to the objective measurement of repeatable, observable performance. He felt that, to be properly scientific, psychologists must provide a physical, mechanistic explanation of psychological phenomena. For Watson, the mechanism was clearly the organisms neurophysiological system. He felt that, to be psychological, laws must describe the observable behavior produced by this neurophysiological system. Such behavioral descriptions would be objective and they would be expressed in physical terms that would be consistent with the physical reductionist language of biology as Watson understood it.

So, Watson wanted to unequivocally ban explanations in terms of purely mental objects and events such as consciousness, concepts, memory, etc. Psychological explanations could not be scientific unless their terms were merely shorthand for, or abstractions of, observable behavior patterns. For example, reference to a subject's "memory" of a set of stimuli must describe the measurable properties of some set of observable responses such as the subject's *verbal reports* of these stimuli at some time following their presentation. Watson felt that constructs defined in terms of behavior could ultimately be reduced to descriptions of neurophysiological structure and function; descriptions containing mental constructs could not. In sum, unlike many inaccurate accounts, Watsonian behaviorism did *not* eschew talk about a mechanism responsible for producing behaviors. Watson merely insisted that such talk either describe this mechanism's biophysical properties directly or else describe other observable physical events, behaviors, that could be reduced to descriptions of biophysical processes. One must interpret theoretical constructs entirely in terms of their relation to observed performance. And, all such constructs must be directly reducible to physical properties of an underlying neurophysiological system.

Newell's approach seems quite compatible with the behaviorist doctrine in its absolute commitment to a UTC as a system for simulating human performance. Newell, like Watson before him, seems to feel that a psychological theory is meaningful only in terms of its ability to describe or predict human performance. To illustrate what a psychological theory ought to be, Newell described two examples of chronometric performance models—Fitts' Law and the Power Law of Practice. The methodological and theoretical commitments of scientists who investigated those laws were, and for the most part still are, very much to mainstream behaviorism.

But, one might say, Newell also espouses using protocol analysis to investigate problem solving. Is that not a paradigmatic departure from behaviorism? It turns out not to be a departure at all, even from John Watson's rigorous version of behaviorism. Watson did *not* eschew the study of so-called cognition—e.g., language, problem solving, memory—as long as such phenomena are reducible to behaviors or to physiological operations. As long as a UTC is interpreted in terms of its capacity for predicting performance, then Newell's program seems to be challenging none of behaviorism's methodological preconceptions.

My conclusion is reinforced by Newell's reductionist account of the human cognitive architecture. It is quite reminiscent of Watson's concern for biophysical reduction. Unhappily, Newell's exposition is also all too reminiscent of the problems that behaviorists encountered in pursuing their reductionist goals. They found the gap between behavior and physiological processes to be much broader than they initially suspected. Attempts to bridge that gap turned out to be oversimplified and highly speculative.

So too with Newell's reductionist account. Newell's human cognitive architecture espouses a number of highly speculative and overly simplified reductions of psychological functions to neurophysiological processes. He builds up his picture of neural cognition from some admittedly controversial assumptions about (a) the complexity of neural activity required for specific classes of cognitive operations, and (b) implied bounds on these performance times. He provides only the most casual evidence for these very strong assumptions. Of course, given the current state of understanding of the relationship between brain function and cognition, he can do little more. Unfortunately, he feels compelled to press ahead. Perhaps Newell believes that he must provide this sort of reduction to provide an "objective" basis for his functional model. In this sense, his perspective seems remarkably similar to that of Watson and other psychologists who argue that psychology can only be scientific if the contents of its theories reduce directly to those of biology and ultimately those of physics. At the least, Newell's proposed human cognitive architecture suggests just how strongly he is committed to the psycho-physical reductionism of the behaviorists that he otherwise decries.

Perhaps one should look past Newell's talk about "neural technology" and regard his account from a purely functional viewpoint. Unfortunately, the functional content of Newell's human cognitive architecture is an old story. Newell basically says that

(a) simple, fast neural circuits manifest simple, inflexible responses,
(b) compositions of these circuits manifest more complex responses, including "cognitive behaviors" (sic), and
(c) the operation times of neural structures are proportionate to the complexity of the cognitive operations that they manifest.

From a functional standpoint, this sort of proposal is hardly new. For example, Miller and his colleagues [31] proposed a similarly hierarchical architecture of cognitive functions. Their architecture is composed of elemental functional units called "TOTEs" (for Test–Operate–Test–Exit). These seem quite similar to Newell's basic deliberative units. Miller et al.'s TOTEs can be composed to produce higher level units capable of more complex goal-oriented activities such as planning. In a concluding chapter these authors even speculate on the reduction of their functional, computational constructs to more basic neurophysiological mechanisms and their interconnections.

I wish to make two more points about Newell's commitment to performance prediction. First, even if one stresses Newell's emphasis on information processing functions that produce intelligent behavior, its contrast with behaviorism again seems minimal at best. Second, and more importantly, the problem of choosing among competing theories seems hopeless, in spite of Newell's claims to the contrary.

The UTCs envisaged by Newell present information processing mechanisms that emit the same behaviors as humans. To put it as Newell does at other places in his book, these information processing mechanisms mediate a system's response to stimuli. Perhaps this focus on mediating processes distinguishes Newell's brand of cognitive science from previous paradigms and their defects. Interestingly, many behaviorists such as E.C. Tolman have been as willing as Newell to postulate mediating processes in their accounts of human behavior. Tolman, like Newell, aimed to describe phenomena such as cognition, goal-directed or "purposive" behavior, and learning as fundamental psychological constructs. Tolman [47] referred to a general learning capability as "docility". Tolman sought what he called "intervening variables" that would explain how an organism's responses to specific stimuli could differ across occasions. Tolman believed that combinations of intervening variables could account for the way that cognition mediates an organism's responses. This, of course, is strikingly similar to Newell's conception of cognition as the control system for intelligent behavior. Tolman proposed that mediating variables could be identified and their effects estimated by abstracting over behavior episodes. For example, a rat that found its way blocked to a food dispenser on one trial might find another path on subsequent trials. This sequence of behaviors, said Tolman, would define a "goal" to get to the dispenser as an intervening variable in the rat's cognitive system. Tolman hoped to extend behaviorism beyond Watson's rather strict boundaries by devising methods to study and predict these mediating effects. For example, the rat's goal to reach the food dispenser might be a function of its level of hunger—another intervening variable—that could be predicted in turn by an objective measurement such as hours of food deprivation. Tolman hoped that his introduction of intervening variables could enable the objective investigation of many cognitive phenomena.

The fundamental differences between Tolman's and Newell's accounts of cognition seem to reside mainly in Newell's use of a computational language to describe mediating cognitive processes and objects such as the memory contents. However, for both Tolman and Newell, the validity of a mediating construct, whether it be computational or a quantitative intervening variable, derives from objective measurement of observable behaviors. Tolman [47, pp. 235–245] even anticipated Newell's use of verbal protocols (Ericsson and Simon [11]). Finally, Tolman, like Newell, stressed the need for unified theories by emphasizing how psychological theorists should build unified *systems* of cognitive mechanisms mediating the transition from stimulus to response.

Recognizing that an information processing model of performance is just a fancier system of intervening variables leads one to a rather serious problem with Newell's proposal. A theory must be *identifiable*. That is, one must be able to compare the predictions of one UTC with another and, eventually, determine which UTC does a better job of predicting human behavior. Unfortunately, psychologists have now experienced many cases in which multiple, competing models or theories predict identical behaviors (e.g., Townsend and Ashby [48]). It turns out that the problem of nonidentifiability of competing theories haunts any paradigm that proposes to uniquely identify complex mediating processes as the causal basis of observable behaviors.

Surprisingly, Newell treats the problem of nonidentifiability rather lightly. According to Newell, nonidentifiability "... is a methodological artifact. It shows up when attention is focused on one specific task, one specific type of data, and one specific inference situation" (p. 244). He asserts that the problem simply vanishes as one uses a UTC to predict the performance regularities of a sufficiently broad range of tasks. He suggests that data already collected on human performance contains "... enough constraining regularities ... to identify the architecture to all extents and purposes" (p. 243).

Newell does not attempt to prove this point. He defends it by describing the success of his own UTC, Soar, in predicting behavioral regularities produced by human subjects across a broad range of tasks. Soar's ability to simulate human performance is indeed impressive, especially given the diverse collection of tasks that Soar must perform. In addition, Soar's chunking mechanism evidently provides it with an equally impressive ability to mimic performance improvements, again on a wide range of tasks.

However, a demonstration of Soar's plausibility does not prove that another, distinct theory could not do as well. In this light, I feel that it is particularly unfortunate that Newell has chosen to focus his exposition on Soar alone. It is highly unlikely that cognitive scientists will be persuaded to endorse *any* single theory, whether that theory is Soar or not. Consequently, Newell's pleas to develop UTCs risk being overshadowed by speculative arguments about Soar's shortcomings. Had Newell compared Soar to other UTCs such as ACT* (Anderson [1]) or the theory offered by John Holland and his colleagues [24], he would have been better able to illustrate how UTCs could be compared. For example, how would Newell compare the implications of Soar's uniform long-term (production) memory with ACT*'s division of long-term memory into procedural and declarative components? How does Soar's chunking mechanism compare to *knowledge compilation* in ACT* (Neves and Anderson [34]) in which declarative information is translated into production rules? In general, the plausibility of Newell's proposal to build UTCs would be greatly enhanced if he had shown how to make such comparisons and illustrate how they could lead to the selection of one UTC over another, competing theory.

Even without comparing one UTC to another, questions about theory validation remain unanswered in Newell's discussion. For example, how would one determine whether to provisionally accept Soar, or under what conditions would it be proper to reject Soar as a UTC?Newell specifically discards the idea that a UTC should be rejected because it fails to predict some specific aspect of human performance. He supplants the Popperian notion of theory falsification with the idea of accumulation or approximation. The scientific community should not reject Soar just because it falsely makes certain specific predictions. Instead, it should alter the theory to bring its predictions in closer correspondence to existing data. Of course, as it does so, it must strive to maintain Soar's ability to emulate performance on other tasks. In this way Soar will simulate an ever-increasing range of intelligent behavior. Problems also arise from the broad coverage of a UTC. For example, one predictive failure might lead the theorist to make a repair that degrades the UTC's ability to predict other types of performance. What should the theorist do in this case? Newell provides no overall guidance on the degree of correspondence needed before one can comfortably accept a UTC's predictions as adequate. Does a required level of predictive adequacy depend on whether Soar is being used to simulate individual behavior or as a simulation of aggregate performance of many subjects? How massive a degradation would be required before Soar were rejected altogether?

All these questions reflect the problem of nonidentifiability. Such questions must go unanswered for Newell because he is embracing an experimental methodology that corresponds to a very different and far simpler form of theorizing. Performance prediction was the forte of behaviorism. Watsonian behaviorism assumed minimal complexity of processes intervening between stimulus and response. Tolman's version admitted complex mediating variables but suffered from the very problems of nonidentifiability I have been discussing. Modern information processing models of cognition, especially

UTCs like Soar, postulate even more complex mediation between stimulus and response. Indeterminacy arises because of the enormous number of degrees of freedom in a UTC's process model. When faced with an error of prediction, the theorist just has too many ways to change the model. Newell claims, but does not demonstrate, that this problem goes away when the theory gets larger. I conclude that a UTC can be neither refuted unambiguously nor validated as a cognitive simulation/prediction model.

3.2. *Architectures versus frameworks*

UTCs as Newell envisions them describe how intelligent behavior arises from the operation of multiple, diverse cognitive mechanisms. An encapsulating *architecture* manages the execution of these mechanisms. I sketched the essential components of Soar's architecture at the end of Section 2. Basic Soar provides this general framework. The actual cognitive theory that Soar embodies depends on its substantive contents—namely, the production rules in long-term memory—that this framework encapsulates.

However, Newell makes it quite clear that the architecture's features also contribute substantively to the claims of a UTC. As Newell asserts, "There is no alternative for a [UTC] based on information processing but to be a theory of the architecture" (p. 431). The properties of the architecture influence the effects of the cognitive subsystems encapsulated within it: "[T]he total theory is an amalgam of information spread over ... the *general principles* and the *simulation details*" (p. 10) [emphasis added]. From a methodological perspective, an implemented architecture provides a framework for generating and exploring the complex and often subtle implications of the UTC it embodies. Or as Newell says, "An important aspect of each architecture-embodied unified theory of cognition is its capacity for generating ... possibilities" (p. 306). For example, Soar's architecture makes no structural or functional distinction between so-called semantic and episodic long-term memory. However, Newell asserts that the semantic–episodic distinction, and many others not yet foreseen, arise as distinctions in Soar's functions. These functional distinctions are due to the content of specific groups of productions that Soar creates together with the way these productions are created and managed by the architecture. Thus, Newell seems very clear in his conviction that an architecture like Soar comprises an information processing framework the design of which makes a substantive theoretical contribution over and above its specific contents.

Newell repeatedly stresses another important way in which a UTC serves as a theoretical or exploratory framework. At various times he emphasizes that a UTC like Soar must be capable of incorporating the full range of more specific models or "microtheories". These smaller scale theories represent theorists' best accounts of specific classes of intelligent behavior. A UTC must smoothly incorporate these microtheories. In this sense, a UTC is not a theory that proposes a new and distinct paradigm. Rather it provides a framework within which "to integrate and synthesize knowledge within the existing paradigm [of cognitive science], not to propose new questions and radically different answers .... The function of a unified theory is to precipitate and consolidate ... the saturated solutions of empirical results and successful microtheories that currently exist" (p. 395). In keeping with this principle, Newell presents numerous examples of Soar's ability to embody the predictive substance of many "microtheories", from chronometric performance models to the use of mental models in syllogistic reasoning.

In spite of his enthusiasm for Soar as an architectural framework in both the preceding senses, Newell seems curiously pessimistic about the work of others to develop general problem solving architectures. Although he briefly acknowledges AI's contribution to the "theoretical infrastructure for the study of human cognition" (p. 40), he summarily dismisses work in that field on what he calls "*frameworks* which are conceptual structures (frequently computational systems) *reputed to be relatively content free* that permit specific cognitive theories to be inserted in them in some fashion" (p. 16) [emphasis added]. Newell gives no examples of these "content free frameworks", nor does he say more beyond this cursory dismissal. However, I can suggest a number of problem solving architectures worthy of consideration, whose features have been substantively influenced by psychological theory. One very prominent example is, of course, the so-called blackboard architecture of the Hearsay-II speech understanding system (Erman et al. [12]). Hearsay-II, and blackboard systems in general, have provided a substantive architectural framework for many modeling efforts in cognitive science (e.g., Hayes-Roth and Hayes-Roth [23]). Does Newell really wish to dismiss such systems as "content free" frameworks? If Soar's properties *as an architecture* have substantive theoretical implications, then why do not these architectures?

I think that Newell misses an important opportunity to clarify and defend his thesis with this rather parochial dismissal of other work on problem solving frameworks. If cognitive scientists are to receive clear guidance on building and exploring UTCs, then clear comparisons are needed among competing hypotheses. And, if one accepts Newell's claims regarding the central theoretical significance of the information processing architecture that a UTC specifies, then sharp comparisons among competing architectures are imperative. Newell's exposition would have benefited significantly by comparing Soar directly with other information processing frameworks, even if they are, as Newell claims, lacking Soar's broad scope (cf., Hayes-Roth's BB1 architecture [22] or my own [13] real-time problem solving architecture, called Schemer). In sum, I find this aspect of Newell's expository strategy to be a major barrier to understanding and accepting his recommendations.

3.3. Cognition and intelligence

Newell believes that a successful UTC should tell us how humans exhibit *intelligence* (e.g., p. 429). Section 2 of this commentary presented his definition of intelligence—the degree of a cognitive system's approximation to the knowledge level. Unfortunately, I find this definition inadequate. More importantly, it seems to contradict other views that Newell expresses on the nature of intelligence and its relationship to cognition.

Newell's definition aims to decouple the knowledge embodied in a cognitive system from its intelligence. A system is intelligent to the extent that it makes full use of whatever knowledge it has. Recall that Newell defines knowledge as a disposition. A system's knowledge is whatever underlies its capacity to perform. A knowledge level system makes full use of its knowledge. It always produces the most appropriate performance up to the limitations of its knowledge. It is the gold standard in terms of which the intelligence of humans and UTCs must be measured.

These commitments force Newell to the rather curious conclusion that a very simple system, such as a thermostat, is more intelligent than a human. In contrast to human problem solvers, the thermostat has an extremely limited body of dispositional knowledge (e.g. a small, closed set of "rules" for starting and stopping the furnace). It uses this knowledge fully in performing its task. A thermostat is, thus, a knowledge level system. Humans possessing far more complex knowledge can only approximate this ideal level of performance, and probably not very closely at that. Newell tries to dismiss this *reductio ad absurdum* critique by asserting that "knowledge-level [systems] cannot be graded by intelligence ..." (p. 90). One is just not allowed to compare the capabilities of knowledge level systems to human performance. Unfortunately, with this move the scale for measuring intelligence seems to suffer a rather serious discontinuity.

More generally, Newell's definition rests upon a hopelessly subjective criterion. One must assess a system's intelligence strictly in terms of that system's knowledge. So, the intelligence of two cognitive systems cannot be compared. I doubt the utility of a concept of intelligence that does not admit comparisons. At the very least, such a subjective definition directly conflicts with Newell's manifest concern for objective theory validation that I discussed earlier in this section.

3.4. Conclusions

Many of these criticisms could have as easily been directed at positions taken by other cognitive scientists. Allen Newell's extensive contributions, on which his monograph is based, have had a powerful and positive impact on psychology and cognitive science. As a consequence, many elements of his bold proposal have already been enthusiastically embraced by the cognitive science community. In particular, Newell's commitment to behaviorist methods and modeling typify assumptions made by most cognitive scientists about the experimental validation of computational, information processing theories of human cognition. His materialist and reductionist perspective of the human cognitive architecture typifies a current trend among many cognitive scientists toward materialist and functionalist reductions of psychological phenomena to biological processes (e.g., Dennett [10], Churchland [8]). As a consequence, the criticisms that I have raised, and the alternative view that I offer below as a response, really address difficulties in the mainstream paradigm (it can be called such) of cognitive science as much as any limitations of Newell's presentation.

On the other hand, Newell's position on the Soar architecture versus other information processing frameworks, and his curiously subjective definition of intelligence seem to articulate less commonly held views. My critical interest in them is tied to the alternative view of cognitive theory that I present in the next section.

4. Theories of cognitive competence

Newell's interest in measuring, simulating, and predicting of concrete performance contrasts sharply with the focus of competence theories as described in the introduction. The criticisms I advanced in the previous section were meant to draw out the weaknesses of Newell's focus on predictive modeling. I now develop my proposal that UTCs be viewed as competence models, a view that better exploits the significant strengths of Newell's theories of knowledge systems and intelligent cognition.

4.1. Cognitive competence

UTC should identify and elucidate the *idealized competences of an intelligent agent*. This statement entails a number of commitments that are worth spelling out.

First, a competence theory is a theory of *knowledge-based agency* (Fehling and Shachter [16]). It explains intelligent agents' interaction with their environment the knowledge that these agents possess. A competence theory also accounts for agents' knowledge of structural relations among these potential actions. For language this includes intuitions about such structural relations as paraphrase, negation among potentially expressible linguistic acts (utterances), and the ability to embed one utterance as a component in another. The importance of structural relations holds for other types of cognitive competence as well. Consider, for example, a competence explanation of agents' ability to construct, execute, monitor, and revise plans. Plans, like linguistic constructions, may stand in "paraphrase" relations as when distinct plans achieve the same objectives with different courses of action. One plan may be "structurally embedded" in another if it may be used as a component to achieve a subgoal, say. A pair of plans may differ only in that one honors a particular constraint while the other relaxes or "negates" that constraint. In general, a psychological (or AI) theory of planning competence would explain how agents synthesize (i.e., learn) and exploit such structural knowledge as well as their ability to construct individual plans from first principles. Newell's concept of a knowledge system and knowledge as a capacity for effective action seem particularly congenial to this aspect of competence theories.

Second, a unified theory of cognitive competence would depict intelligent agents as possessing multiple, distinct competences. Each particular competence would represent the knowledge (tacit or otherwise) sufficient to accomplish a specific set of tasks. In addition, each competence would account for agents' abilities to meet certain criteria of acceptable task performance. For example, a theory of linguistic competence usually takes the task to be the production or comprehension of linguistic expressions in a particular dialect (or even idiolect) of a specific language. In general, competence theory depicts the knowledge required to produce only those expressions having acceptable grammatical form, semantic content, and pragmatic force as components of a conversation. Identification of the defining tasks and acceptance criteria circumscribe the theorist's search for a particular body of knowledge. Change the task definition or criteria and the competence being sought also changes. Here again, non-linguistic cognitive skills, such as planning, decision making, or playing a game like chess, seem equally amenable to this approach. Theorists building unified competence theories would strive to identify bodies of knowledge that are sufficient to generate acceptable completion of an ever-increasing range of tasks. Here again, Newell's knowledge systems would seem to provide a very congenial framework in which to explore candidate competence accounts.

Third, a competence account describes the logical form of generative processes that can produce the potential actions of competent agents. The competence is a disposition. It does not predict that the actions will be taken, it explains how they could be. Furthermore, the agent's knowledge of her competence may be tacit. Though she will act in accordance with the disposition, she may or may not be able to articulate its logical content. For example, a competent English speaker can recognize that an utterance violates a rule of subject–verb agreement whether or not she is capable of describing that rule. The tacit nature of the relevant knowledge may hold for many other types of competence, too. The potentially tacit nature of knowledge embodied in a competence implies that a competence theory is fundamentally neutral on whether agents encode explicit descriptions of the distinctions they are able to manifest. If one expresses that competence theory in computational terms, then this means that a competence theory is essentially neutral regarding the controversy in AI over whether knowledge in a computational agent should be entirely procedural or entirely declarative (Winograd [51]). The far more important commitment is to describe the logical form of knowledge entailed by the disposition (Chomsky [6,7]). This aspect of a competence seems to me to be similar to Rosenschein's concept of "grand strategy" in an AI theory of agency (cited in Genesereth and Nilsson [19]. With the grand strategy a declarative formalism like predicate calculus may be used "to describe the knowledge of an agent, but may or may not be used in the implementation" [19, p. 327].

My fourth point generalizes the previous one. A competence theory may remain essentially neutral to reductionist versus non-reductionist explanations of the generated behavior. A competence theory is an epistemic theory, a theory about knowledge. It focuses on the structural and functional properties of knowledge giving rise to particular cognitive skills. One may explore the epistemological commitments of a particular competence theory without ever being concerned with the ontological status of the embodiment of that knowledge.

Fifth, and perhaps most significantly, while a competence theory is still a theory of behavior, it offers an idealized account. As Moravcsik puts it

> It is reasonable for the study of cognition to borrow a page from the books of the other successful sciences, and conceive of the study of cognition as the study of [cognition and action] abstracted from the real everyday context, and described under idealizations. [33, p. 85]

In sum, a cognitive theory of competence focuses on describing knowledge embodied as generative processes or dispositions that give rise to idealized performance. It does not attempt to predict situation-specific behaviors. Specific deviations in performance are abstracted away from the descriptive content of the theory. If the theory does focus on errors, it does so by showing how they arise systematically and again as idealized performance from a body of knowledge whose content is inadequate (cf., Brown and VanLehn [4]). In this way, the problems of identifiability in predictive modeling are bypassed. On the other hand, this type of theory still provides substantive explanations. It can tell why an agent is or is not capable of acting intelligently in some task context. This alone establishes the value of competence accounts. What I now hope to establish is that this type of theory is quite compatible with Newell's most fundamental theoretical concepts.

4.2. Knowledge systems as competence models

While I remain sharply critical of Newell's commitment to performance prediction and his reductionist account of the human cognitive architecture, I find his theoretical foundations for knowledge systems to be quite compatible with my proposal to use UTCs for exploring cognitive competences. The elements of his theory seem to provide a valuable and powerful vocabulary for articulating the content of a competence.

Newell proposes that one view the goal of UTCs as showing how intelligent systems build and manage structured symbolic representations encoding knowledge that is used to achieve similarly represented goals by a process of knowledge-based search. I am particularly taken by his focus on knowledge as the *abstract capacity to act* to achieve goals, and his lack of emphasis on parametric features of such knowledge or how such features would arise. Knowledge for Newell is abstract in that it is "abstracted from representations and processing" (p. 108). It seems clear that, using Newell's suggested theoretical terms, one is no longer talking about performance, but rather about tacit knowledge embodying performance dispositions. In Newell's own UTC such tacit knowledge is embodied as procedural rules and, he claims, in the architecture's ability to create them and manage their operation. In all these ways, Newell's fundamental terms for cognitive science correspond remarkably well to fundamental commitments of a competence theory.

In addition, Newell offers a dispositional and agent-oriented definition of knowledge that closely matches these aspects of competence theory. For Newell, knowledge is the logical form of the capacity to "select actions to attain goals" (p. 108). Agents employ this knowledge to react to, and interact with, their perceived environment. Or, in Newell's words, agents must use this knowledge to "operate in a rich, complex, detailed environment" (p. 233). Newell's notion of a symbol system is equally dispositional—a symbol embodies the *function* of distal access. One may readily interpret his description of human memory (Chapter 6) as specific competence for the tasks of recognition, recall, or savings in relearning based on the function of distal access.

The problem space hypothesis is a very important element of Newell's view of human cognition that seems to be quite central to competence accounts. Search is a very powerful model of deliberation—successively generating or selecting alternatives and evaluating them until one or some combination provides a solution to the problem being deliberated. Newell's profound contribution has been to extend this abstract model to account for the circumscribed nature of any search space, on the one hand, and the necessary capacity of an agent to cope with incompleteness and other limitations of a given search process by defining a new search to resolve the impasse. The formalism of a problem space hierarchy is likely to provide a basis for describing the collection of competences that an intelligent agent possesses and important relationships among these competences. In particular, each problem space (more properly, the dispositions for selecting and searching it) represent one particular deliberative competence of the agent.

Recasting Newell's UTCs as competence theories also helps to sort out some of my concerns regarding his concept of intelligence. Recall that Newell defines intelligence as the degree to which a cognitive system can approximate a knowledge level system, one that uses all of its knowledge. Of course, if there were no constraints on a cognitive system's use of its knowledge, then all such systems could be knowledge level systems. Unfortunately, constraints introduced by the task environment, such as limitations of time or task-critical information, limit a knowledge system's ability to use its full knowledge. In addition, the system's own capacities determine how constraining these limitations become. So, is the ability to approximate the knowledge level a fixed capacity, independent of knowledge as Newell proposes? Or, is intelligence itself reflective of some form of knowledge? I agree with Newell's description of central cognition as a knowledge-based control system that mediates between perception and motor actions. To intelligently adapt to conditions in its environment, such a control system must augment its basic knowledge for completing tasks with knowledge that allow it to use the most appropriate quality and quantity of that knowledge in the face of contextual constraints. In other words, cognitive scientists must also account for a cognitive system's competence in adapting its deliberations and actions in the face of encountered constraints.

Recently, a great deal of attention has come to be focused on these issues of constrained rationality (Russell [42], Fehling and Shachter [16]). This recent literature suggests significant value in using UTCs based on Newell's concept of a knowledge system to explore the competence required for constrained rationality. In particular, the notion of competence as dispositional knowledge can be used to elucidate a system's idealized ability to adapt its problem solving performance. A number of specific techniques have been proposed that could be incorporated in such a theory and examined for adaptive adequacy. For example, since search takes time, a system may benefit from learning and using decision procedures that trade solution quality for speed of solution construction (Fehling and Breese [15]). Alternatively, a system could exploit knowledge of special methods such as "anytime algorithms" that provide solutions of steadily increasing quality until time runs out (Dean and Boddy [9]). In Newell's terms, these two approaches could enhance a system's manifest intelligence by improving either knowledge search or problem search, respectively.[1] Such knowledge enables the cognitive system to cope with the constraints that specified conditions impose on its ability to approximate its knowledge level competence.

The concept of constrained rationality suggests that intelligence as the degree of approximation to the knowledge level is a knowledge-relative measure. This contrasts sharply with Newell's aim to decouple knowledge and intelligence. However, it has the virtue that one is now free to explore hypotheses that intelligence can be affected by environment or experience. This is not a possibility if the degree of intelligence is independent of the knowledge content of a cognitive system. (Embracing Newell's idea strictly, one must conclude that intelligence reflects fixed properties of the cognitive architecture.) This modification of Newell's definition of intelligence also addresses my concerns about the subjective nature of his definition. A useful measure of intelligence must now include some objective specification of the effectiveness of the agent's actions that are engendered by the portion of its knowledge that it can effectively use.

Finally, I note that, under this view of a UTC as a competence account, a system's intelligence would not be depicted as a monolithic or uniform capacity. Rather, the extent of a system's knowledge can differ widely with respect to different task domains. So too can its ability to approximate the full use of its knowledge for distinct task domains. A UTC specifies a system's intelligence as a collection of competences and the capacity to integrate and situationally adapt them. This non-monolithic view of intelligence corresponds reasonably well to recently developed theories in psychology (Sternberg [45]).

4.3. Methodology—constructing and evaluating competence theories of cognition

UTCs as competence models help cognitive scientists to undertake an important form of theory development that, for the most part, has been restricted to investigations of linguistic behavior. Newell's conception of a knowledge system is happily compatible with this perspective on theory and allows theorists to sidestep the drawbacks of UTCs as behavioral simulations discussed earlier. A few words are in order about the overall methodology that competence theorists would follow.

Moravcsik [32,33] has articulated the general methodology for exploring competence. The following questions paraphrase his exposition of this methodology:

---

[1]The use of a decision procedure differs from assumptions that Newell makes about knowledge search being simply the retrieval of fixed rules for problem search. However, we see no reason to preclude a more constructive process, such as decision modeling, as another, more flexible form of knowledge search. This generalization does no damage to Newell's distinction of these two forms of search.

(1) What does the possessor of a competence need to accomplish to have successfully completed a task?
(2) What are the varying conditions under which the problem solver must possess and exercise the competence?
(3) What are the essential cognitive processes that are required?
(4) How are these processes organized to cope with
    (i) variations in the task requirements or
    (ii) task conditions?

A UTC like Newell's Soar could be used as a framework for answering these questions. Answers to the first two questions would be represented in the goals that Soar encodes and the conditions that trigger assertion of those goals into working memory (in the context stack). Answers to the last two questions come from an analysis of the content of Soar's recognition memory when it has been shown to be adequate for meeting the requirements defined by (1) and (2). There are three salient facts in this regard. First, this methodology aims to populate Soar with a collection of rules that enable it to succeed in completing some specified tasks of interest under a plausibly complete range of expected conditions. Competence theorists have no direct concern for predicting the idiosyncratic details of actual human performance. In particular, they have no concern for modeling error, *per se*. Second, once such a version of Soar has been formulated, investigators will focus primarily on elucidating the basic elements of this competence and the *structural relations* among these elements. Third, in contrast to Newell's assertion, the properties of the framework itself will probably turn out to be theory-neutral. Such a framework is, after all, equivalent to a universal Turing machine. What counts is the substantive content of the knowledge encapsulated in the system. Theorists will focus their attention on the encapsulated knowledge and its sufficiency for producing task performance that meets specified criteria. They can defer concern with most architectural distinctions. Competence explanations focus on the logical content of the architecture and the adequacy of this content for completing specific tasks. Or, as Newell would say, one focuses on characterizing claims about the required knowledge content of the system that may be abstracted from its encoded productions and other processes.

The existence of criteria for defining successful task completion gives a competence theory a normative flavor. The normative aspects of UTCs as competence theories mark a radical shift in focus from the predictive/descriptive focus of Newell's methodology for performance prediction. Because a competence account seeks to elucidate knowledge that enables a system to meet task performance criteria, this type of theory may be of interest to AI investigators who do not share the cognitive scientists concern for explaining human cognition.

5. Conclusions

My commentary has stressed a contrast between Newell's view of UTCs as predictive performance models and the notion of UTCs as providing competence characterizations. Predictive models fall prey to the problems of identifiability, regardless of their scope. If one examines proofs of nonidentifiability in formal logic and automata theory, one sees that the problem really has to do with insufficient density of observation states compared to the functional state sequences in the hypothesized system. This problem can arise regardless of the absolute size of the system. Newell could only make a convincing case by showing formally that the set of distinct observable behaviors grows much more rapidly than the complexity of the internal structure of the formal systems generating such behaviors. Although I have not completed a formal proof, this seems to me to be unlikely in general.

In contrast, a competence account focuses theorists primarily on the job of articulating knowledge embodied by an agent in order to adequately perform some range of tasks. Performance considerations are raised only in the idealized context provided by the competence account. This form of theory has dramatically improved our understanding of important phenomena in cognitive science such as language comprehension and production. Newell's proposal to build UTCs would be dramatically improved by adopting this competence perspective. As Newell himself pointed out many years ago (1973), performance modeling leads to a game of "twenty questions with nature" [35]. It is a game that theorists cannot win. I am persuaded by Newell's profound insight into the problems of validating performance models. I disagree with him in believing that the limitations of performance modeling are resolved simply by building much larger models.

Although I have focused specifically on Allen Newell's proposals, the concerns raised here apply more broadly to the theoretical and methodological presumptions of most cognitive scientists (e.g., Anderson [2]). Newell's proposal illustrates a tension that has existed in cognitive science and, in fact in psychology and other related disciplines, for at least two centuries—a tense self-consciousness over the scientific status of investigations of mental phenomena.

The recent emergence of cognitive science as a discipline has been both exciting and frustrating. It has been exciting because it has turned scientific attention toward things truly psychological, viz., mental or cognitive phenomena. Cognitive science has broadened our perspective on the range of phenomena that may be studied, methodologies for collecting them, and—most importantly here—the use of computational methods to describe and explain these phenomena. Cognitive scientists have reestablished the legitimacy of subjective phenomena such as thinking (Johnson-Laird [26]), imagery (Kosslyn [27]), and the nature of conscious awareness (e.g., Dennett [10], Baars [3], Fehling et al. [14]).

But, the emergence of this cognitive science as a discipline has also been frustrating. Many cognitive scientists seem as engaged as psychologists ever were in a perpetual struggle to reduce cognitive phenomena to either behavioral or biophysical measurement (e.g., Churchland [8]). Accordingly, controversies over dualist, functionalist, or materialist interpretations of cognitive phenomena arise frequently. Sometimes these controversies shed new light on cognition. More often, they simply distract attention from the substantive issues of the nature of thought and, as Newell would have it, thought's role as the control system for a behaving agent. Progress in cognitive science has sometimes been frustrated because cognitive scientists have struggled to adapt their studies to satisfy the methodological and conceptual biases of behaviorism and biophysical reductionism.

The perspective offered by Newell in *Unified Theories of Cognition* is similarly frustrating. It is exciting because Newell offers a carefully worked out conceptual framework that provides a rich and powerful set of distinctions for describing cognition. However, his methodological commitments fail to be equally satisfying. So, is the glass half empty or half full? If one fixates on Newell's idea of cognitive simulation, one will probably conclude that it is half empty. If, on the other hand, one adopts the perspective of a UTC as a theory of cognitive competence, a theory of knowledge in service of effective action, then Newell's contribution is profound. From this perspective, his work has for a long time contributed significantly to our understanding of human cognition. I hope that cognitive scientists will carefully explore his proposal that one view intelligence as the degree of approximation to the knowledge level. They should be able to largely ignore his preoccupation with performance prediction. It is far more interesting and important to focus on Newell's suggested framework—yes, that is what it is—for modeling cognitive competences. From this perspective, Newell gives us the beginnings of a methodology for discovering the knowledge required by humans and machines to manifest important problem solving skills.

I would like to add a final word about the relevance of all this to AI scientists who are not compelled by the excitement of theories of human cognition. As long as cognitive scientists continue to engage in purely *descriptive* modeling, their results will be of only passing interest to many AI practitioners. However, cognitive modeling is a *normative* exercise. This type of model, with its emphasis on task analysis and analysis of knowledge requirements, increases the overlap in the objectives of AI researchers and cognitive scientists. A cognitive scientist's explanation of required competence for a given task domain may well be useful to the designer of an AI system intended for use in that domain. Whether or not the AI designer is willing to model the performance of humans performing her target task, she will benefit from a description of the task and its knowledge requirements. Conversely, a cognitive scientist can extract useful guidance from the analysis and design of AI systems that reflect rigorous consideration of their intended task domain. I hope that this commentary encourages those interested in other forms of human or machine problem solving to take advantage of this communality. If they do, they are likely to find that many of the theoretical constructs discussed by Newell in *Unified Theories of Cognition* will help them in their efforts.

References

[1] J.R. Anderson, *Language, Memory, and Thought* (Lawrence Erlbaum, Hillsdale, NJ, 1976).

[2] J.R. Anderson, *The Architecture of Cognition* (Harvard University Press, Cambridge, MA, 1983).

[3] B.J. Baars, *A Cognitive Theory of Consciousness* (Cambridge University Press, Cambridge, England, 1988).

[4] J.S. Brown and K. VanLehn, Repair theory: a generative theory of bugs in procedural skills, *Cogn. Sci.* **4** (1980) 397–426.

[5] S.T. Card, P. Moran and A. Newell, *The Psychology of Human-Computer Interaction* (Lawrence Erlbaum, Hillsdale, NJ, 1983).

[6] N. Chomsky, *Syntactic Structures* (Mouton, The Hague, Netherlands, 1957).

[7] N. Chomsky, *Aspects of a Theory of Syntax* (MIT Press, Cambridge, MA, 1965).

[8] P.S. Churchland, *Neurophilosophy: Toward a Unified Science of the Mind/Brain* (MIT Press/Bradford Books, Cambridge, MA, 1986).

[9] T. Dean and M. Boddy, An analysis of time-dependent planning, in: *Proceedings AAAI-88*, St. Paul, MN (1988).

[10] D.C. Dennett, *Consciousness Explained* (Little, Brown, and Co., Boston, MA, 1991).

[11] K.A. Ericsson and H.A. Simon, *Protocol Analysis: Verbal Reports as Data* (MIT Press, Cambridge, MA, 1984).

[12] L.D. Erman, F. Hayes-Roth, V.R. Lesser and D.R. Reddy, The Hearsay-II speech understanding system: integrating knowledge to resolve uncertainty, *ACM Comput. Surv.* **12** (2) (1980) 213–253.

[13] M.R. Fehling, A. Altman and B.M. Wilber, The heuristic control virtual machine: an implementation of the Schemer computational model of reflective, real-time problem solving, in: V. Jagannathan, R. Dodhiawala and L. Baum, eds., *Blackboard Architectures and Applications* (Academic Press, Boston, MA, 1989).

[14] M.R. Fehling, B.J. Baars and C. Fisher, A functional role for repression, in: *Proceedings 12th Annual Conference of the Cognitive Science Society*, Cambridge, MA (1990).

[15] M.R. Fehling and J.S. Breese, Decision theoretic control of problem solving under uncertainty, Tech. Rept. 329-88-5, Rockwell International Science Center, Palo Alto Laboratory, Palo Alto, CA (1988).

[16] M.R. Fehling and R. Shachter, Constrained rational agency: foundations for an interactionist theory of intelligent systems, Tech. Rept. No. 92-7, Laboratory for Intelligent Systems, Stanford University, Stanford, CA (1992) (Manuscript currently being revised).

[17] P.M. Fitts, The information capacity of the human motor system in controlling the amplitude of movement, *J. Experimental Psychol.* **47** (1954) 381–391.

[18] P.M. Fitts and M.I. Posner, *Human Performance* (Books/Cole, Belmont, CA, 1969).

[19] M.R. Genesereth and N.J. Nilsson, *Logical Foundations of Artificial Intelligence* (Morgan Kaufmann, Los Altos, CA, 1987).

[20] J.J. Gibson, *The Senses Considered as Perceptual Systems* (Houghton Mifflin, Boston, MA, 1966).

[21] J.J. Gibson, *The Ecological Approach to Visual Perception* (Houghton Mifflin, Boston, MA, 1979)

[22] B. Hayes-Roth, A blackboard architecture for control, *Artif. Intell.* **26** (2) (1985) 251–321.

[23] B. Hayes-Roth and F. Hayes-Roth, A cognitive model of planning, *Cogn. Sci.* **3** (1979) 275–310.

[24] J.H. Holland, K.J. Holyoak, R.E. Nisbett and P.R. Thagard, *Induction: Processes of Inference, Learning, and Discovery* (MIT Press, Cambridge, MA, 1986).

[25] C.L. Hull, *Principles of Behavior: An Introduction to Behavior Theory* (Appleton-Century-Crofts, New York, 1943).

[26] P. Johnson-Laird, *Mental Models: Towards a Cognitive Science of Language, Inference, and Consciousness* (Cambridge University Press, Cambridge, England, 1983).

[27] S. Kosslyn, *Imagery and Mind* (Harvard University Press, Cambridge, MA, 1980).

[28] J.E. Laird, A. Newell and P.S. Rosenbloom, Soar: an architecture for general intelligence, *Artif. Intell.* **33** (1987) 1–64.

[29] D.G. Mackay, *The Organization of Perception and Action* (Springer, New York, 1987).

[30] J.L. McClelland, D.E. Rummelhart and the PDP Research Group, eds., *Parallel Distributed Processing: Explorations in the Micro-Structure of Cognition*, Vol. 2: *Psychological and Biological Models* (MIT Press, Cambridge, MA, 1986).

[31] G.A. Miller, E. Galanter and K.H. Pribram, *Plans and the Structure of Behavior* (Holt, Rinehart and Winston, New York, 1960).

[32] J.M. Moravcsik, Competence, creativity, and innateness, *Philos. Forum* **1** (1969) 407–437.

[33] J.M. Moravcsik, *Thought and Language* (Routledge, London, 1990).

[34] D.M. Neves and J.R. Anderson, Knowledge compilation: mechanisms for the automatization of cognitive skills, in: J.R. Anderson, ed., *Cognitive Skills and Their Acquisition* (Lawrence Erlbaum, Hillsdale, NJ, 1981) 57–84.

[35] A. Newell, You can't play twenty questions with nature and win: projective comments on the papers of this symposium, in: W.G. Chase, ed., *Visual Information Processing* (Academic Press, New York, 1973).

[36] A. Newell, Physical symbol systems, *Cogn. Sci.* **4** (1980) 135–183.

[37] A. Newell, Reasoning, problem solving, and decision processes: the problem space as a fundamental category, in: R. Nickerson, ed., *Attention and Performance* VIII (Lawrence Erlbaum, Hillsdale, NJ, 1980).

[38] A. Newell, The knowledge level, *Artif. Intell.* **18** (1982) 87–127.

[39] A. Newell, J.C. Shaw and H.A. Simon, Elements of a theory of human problem solving, *Psychol. Rev.* **65** (1958) 151–166.

[40] A. Newell and H.A. Simon, *Human Problem Solving* (Prentice-Hall, Englewood Cliffs, NJ, 1972).

[41] D.E. Rumelhart, J.L. McClelland and the PDP Research Group, eds., *Parallel Distributed Processing: Explorations in the Micro-Structure of Cognition*, Vol. 1: *Foundations* (MIT Press, Cambridge, MA, 1986).

[42] S. Russell and E. Wefald, *Do the Right Thing: Studies in Limited Rationality* (MIT Press, Cambridge, MA, 1991).

[43] H.A. Simon and C.A. Kaplan, Foundations of cognitive science, in: M.I. Posner, ed., *Foundations of Cognitive Science* (MIT Press/Bradford Books, Cambridge, MA, 1989) 1–47.

[44] G.S. Snoddy, Learning and stability, *J. Appl. Psychol.* **10** (1926) 1–36.

[45] R.J. Sternberg, *Handbook of Human Intelligence* (Cambridge University Press, Cambridge, England, 1982).

[46] N.A. Stillings, M.H. Feinstein, J.L. Garfield, E.L. Rissland, D.A. Rosenbaum, S.E. Weisler and L. Baker-Ward, *Cognitive Science: An Introduction* (MIT Press/Bradford Books, Cambridge, MA, 1987).

[47] E.C. Tolman, *Purposive Behavior in Animals and Men* (Appleton-Century-Crofts, New York, 1932).

[48] J.T. Townsend and F.G. Ashby, *Stochastic Modeling of Elementary Psychological Processes* (Cambridge University Press, Cambridge, England, 1983).

[49] J.B. Watson, *Behaviorism* (Norton, New York, 1930).

[50] N. Wiener, *Cybernetics: Or Control and Communication in the Animal and the Machine* (MIT Press, Cambridge, MA, 1948).

[51] T. Winograd, Frame representations and the declarative/procedural controversy, in: D.G. Bobrow and A. Collins, eds., *Representation and Understanding: Studies in Cognitive Science* (Academic Press, New York, 1975) 185–210.

Artificial Intelligence 59 (1993) 329–341
Elsevier

ARTINT 1012

On building integrated cognitive agents: a review of Allen Newell's *Unified Theories of Cognition* *

Barbara Hayes-Roth

Department of Computer Science, Stanford University, 701 Welch Road, Bldg. C., Palo Alto, CA 94304, USA

1. Introduction

Twenty years ago, Allen Newell and Herbert Simon gave us a land-mark book, *Human Problem Solving*, in which they introduced the method of protocol analysis, reported the parameters of human cognition, and set the stage for the emerging field of cognitive science. It is only fitting that, with his new book, *Unified Theories of Cognition*, Newell should set our course for the next twenty years. Once again he challenges us to shift paradigms, in this case to leave behind our focus on isolated cognitive tasks and to aim instead for the development of unified theories that account for the full range of cognitive function.

The book retains the easy conversational style of Newell's 1987 William James Lectures at Harvard University, on which it is based. It reflects his characteristic comprehension of the issues, attention to detail, and intellectual honesty. It is spiced with casual metaphors, witty asides, and wry ripostes to colleagues who hold different opinions. Reading it,

---

Correspondence to: B. Hayes-Roth, Department of Computer Science, Stanford University, 701 Welch Road, Bldg. C., Palo Alto, CA 94304, USA. E-mail: bhr@camis.stanford.edu.
* (Harvard University Press, Cambridge, MA, 1990); xiv + 549 pages.

one can easily imagine Newell's intent gaze and, behind it, his passion for the quest. In short, except for being entirely one-sided, reading *Unified Theories of Cognition* is very much like having a conversation with Allen Newell—stimulating, enlightening, and very pleasurable, indeed.

Newell reminds us repeatedly that his "book argues for unified theories of cognition—the plural, not the singular ... I am much more concerned with figuring out how a theory could put it all together, and what could be the plausible yield from doing so, than I am for arguing that Soar is the best or even the favored choice" (p. 234). Nonetheless, he has chosen to deliver his message by example with Soar, the particular theory of human cognition on which he, Paul Rosenbloom, John Laird, and their students have been working for the last ten years. Indeed, after three introductory chapters that explain the objective and give brief tutorials in cognitive science and human cognition, the remainder of the book tells us in great detail what requirements Soar is designed to meet, how it works in general, how it performs a number of specific tasks, and how it might perform others. This progress report is extremely important. A great deal of research has been done on Soar, perhaps more than on any other cognitive theory, and the whole is truly greater than the sum of its parts. We need to have all of the parts in this one place so that we can appreciate the very large picture Newell has begun to paint for us.

To preview the discussion below, my response to *Unified Theories of Cognition* is generally positive. I endorse Newell's goal of developing comprehensive cognitive theories, his research paradigm of empirical evaluation of mechanistic theories, his efforts to identify functional requirements of intelligence as a basis for theory formation, and his demand for generality of candidate theories over many tasks. However, within each of these areas of agreement, I disagree with some of Newell's specific claims. While sharing his long-term goal of developing unified cognitive theories, I would establish more measured intermediate-term research objectives. While advocating empirical evaluation of mechanistic theories, I would develop a more rigorous empirical methodology. While advocating the identification of functional requirements of intelligence, I would emphasize a different set of requirements to drive early theory development. While recognizing the need for generality, I would propose integration as the ultimate evaluation criterion for candidate theories and, with that in mind, I would impose a particular programmatic structure on the research effort. These issues are discussed in Sections 2–5 below. Finally, I disagree with Newell about candidate architectures—but I will save the comparison of Soar and BB1 (my candidate) for another paper.

2. The goal: unified theories of cognition

Newell begins by making his case for the new research goal, unified theories of cognition. "Divide-and-conquer" is a good strategy for coping with complexity; cognition is such a complex system of phenomena that both psychologists and AI researchers have divided and conquered with abandon. As Newell observes, we now have an extensive literature on diverse phenomena, such as how people remember lists of words, how they do syllogistic reasoning, how a computer could learn to recognize a conjunctive concept, how it could diagnose infectious diseases. For each phenomenon, we have competing micro-theories and earnest efforts to support or demolish them. But identifying and discriminating among competing micro-theories is not an end in itself. The ultimate goal is a comprehensive theory that explains all of the phenomena. Ironically, as Newell points out, we face a growing complexity of our own making in the unbounded accumulation of observations to be explained in a comprehensive theory. If we wish to incorporate our observations and micro-theories as elements of a comprehensive theory, we have enough of them to begin the work of theory construction now.

I would add to Newell's arguments that, by studying phenomena in isolation, we virtually guarantee that our most successful micro-theories will be incorrect—they will not survive as elements of a comprehensive theory and may divert us from the path to one. Why? Individual phenomena offer so little constraint that it is easy to generate micro-theories and easy for them to perform well against local optimality criteria. Moreover, it is easy to carry this strategy too far, oversimplifying phenomena so that they will be amenable to careful analysis, but perhaps of limited relevance to the original question. A comprehensive theory is unlikely to comprise a complete set of locally optimal micro-theories. It is one of the commonest and costliest lessons of computer science (and engineering in general) that independently developed software components resist subsequent integration in a smoothly functioning whole. Components need to be designed for integration right from the start. We can expect this lesson to hold as well when the components represent micro-theories of cognitive function. Indeed, in the case of human intelligence, full integration has been the prevailing "design constraint". Nature has had no alternative but to mold diverse cognitive functions around one another within the architectural confines of a single, extremely versatile individual. Newell's quote from Voltaire (p. 16), "The best is the enemy of the good", is apt here. If the goal is a unified theory, we had better strive for integration right from the start even if that means sacrificing optimal micro-theories to achieve a graceful integration of merely good ones.

On the other hand, should we really aim for complete unified theories of all cognition? At this point in time, we can't even agree on what that would mean. Newell will be criticized for the grandiosity and patent unrealizability of his goal. Critics will claim that unified theories are impossible or at least premature. They will riddle his candidate, Soar, with its own faults and limitations. Although these criticisms are probably correct in a literal sense, I believe they are misguided in spirit. We probably never will have a unified theory of cognition. But that is an empirical question, which the Soar team is trying to answer. It almost certainly is premature to think of having one now. But it is not premature to begin working toward one, as the Soar team is doing. In fact, Newell acknowledges that his objective is ambitious, controversial, even presumptuous. He acknowledges that Soar is only a partial theory of selected phenomena. Newell might have avoided criticism by calling for more measured intermediate objectives. For example, I would advocate two such objectives: "multi-faceted systems" that integrate several (not all) individually challenging cognitive capabilities in a graceful, synergistic manner; and "adaptive intelligent systems" that integrate cognition with perception and action in dynamic real-time environments. Pursuit of these kinds of objectives requires a paradigm shift, but not a leap of faith.

Perhaps Newell's call for unified theories of cognition is, in part, a public relations strategy; he certainly has got our attention! But more than that, Newell is sending a fundamental message to the AI and cognitive science communities. He is reminding us what the long-term goal is, where we should be going as a scientific enterprise, and how to insure that short-term and intermediate-term research leads to long-term progress. He is tutoring us in the new paradigm by showing us what he and his colleagues have accomplished with Soar. And, far from being guilty of his "sin of presumption" (p. 37), Newell is urging us to give Soar some serious competition.

3. The paradigm: mechanistic theories and empirical evaluation

Newell's commitment to theory as mechanism is another important message. In the AI community, the term "theory" has been specialized to refer to formal descriptions of computational techniques, accompanied by mathematical or logical analysis of their soundness, completeness, and complexity. By default, mechanistic theories, especially if they are implemented in computer programs, are disparaged as "engineering" or "applications", with the implication of lesser scientific significance. In psychology, the concept of theory is less idiosyncratic and less exalted. With few exceptions, psychological theories abstract only the gross features of observed cognitive phenomena; they typically have neither the rigor of formal AI theories nor the explanatory power of mechanistic AI theories. Newell claims to hold an "unexceptional—even old-fashioned" view: a theory is any "body of explicit knowledge, from which answers can be obtained to questions by inquiries" (p. 13). Whether a theory is cast as a set of facts, axioms, or mechanisms is less important than that it explicitly represent a body of knowledge from which predictions, explanations, prescriptions, etc. can be derived objectively. A good theory is not necessarily formal or elegant or parsimonious—although these might be pleasing attributes, other things being equal. Quite simply, a good theory is one that gives good answers to the questions of interest. In the present context, a good theory is one that correctly accounts for the cognitive behavior of human beings or intelligent computer programs.

Despite this ostensibly catholic view, Newell's own theoretical work is almost exclusively mechanistic. For him, a theory of cognition is an architecture—a fixed computational structure that can process variable content to produce the desired cognitive behavior. In the tension between necessity and sufficiency, Newell is unambiguous: "*Necessary* characteristics are well and good, but they are substantially less than half the story. *Sufficiency* is all-important" (p. 158). Only by actually producing the behaviors in question can a theory claim to explain them. As with other complex systems, a sufficient theory of cognition will not comprise a small number of elegant laws, but rather a carefully designed and coordinated system of mechanisms working in concert. Thus, although Newell accords formal theories a place in the enterprise, for him "God is in the details".

To evaluate whether a theory explains cognitive behavior, Newell advises us to implement the theory in a computer program and evaluate its performance. The objective of a given evaluation is not to confirm or disconfirm the theory—any plausible cognitive theory would be too complex for binary decisions. Rather, the objective is to accumulate evidence that supports the theory and to identify aspects of the theory that need amendment. Thus, we approach the ultimate goal, a unified theory of cognition, by a Lakatosian process of successive approximation; in the meantime, we have a partial theory to use. Most AI researchers will feel comfortable with Newell's frank rejection of Popperian refutation (p. 14); there may be several theories that explain the phenomena of interest and any one will do. Most psychologists will object; their goal is to identify the one psychologically correct theory. Because Newell shares this goal, Soar eventually must undergo the test of necessity. However, he is right to insist on first constructing a more comprehensive and, therefore, more interesting and promising theory that meets the sufficiency test for a diverse set of observations.

Even accepting Newell's empirical approach, however, we are left with tough methodological issues.

First, the concept of "sufficiency" needs definition. Is an implemented theory sufficient if it produces a particular response? If it follows a particular line of reasoning? If its reasoning or behavior follows a particular time course? If it makes particular kinds of errors? Is sufficiency all-or-none or are there degrees of sufficiency? Which is more sufficient: a theory that perfectly models the designated line of reasoning or a theory that imperfectly models both the line of reasoning and its time course? We need measures that allow us to reliably evaluate different aspects of the sufficiency of an implemented theory. Given the goal to unify an array of behaviors within a single theory, we need measures that compare the sufficiency of competing theories that account for overlapping subsets of the full array. Finally, we need measures that evaluate the sufficiency of a theory with respect to unification *per se*, as well as for component behaviors.

Second, what is the relationship between a theory and its implementation? Newell acknowledges that, in his own case, "Soar, like any computer system, is a system always in a state of becoming something else. Many aspects are not yet operational, or only operational in some limited way" (p. 231). For purely practical reasons, a computer implementation must lag behind the theory it represents and it must contain many extra-theoretical hacks. It inevitably reflects the skill and style of its programmers. When instantiated for a particular task, it also reflects the skill and style of the application developers. As a result, given the performance of an implemented theory on a particular task, it is not a pure theory, but this hybrid that we are evaluating. We must distinguish the theory and non-theory in a computer implementation and correctly assign credit between them for important aspects of performance. One approach would be to experimentally manipulate an implementation in order to test predictions about the effects of excising or replacing (non-)theoretical code segments. Another approach would be to lift the theory out of its implementation and replicate its performance in a completely different implementation.

Third, given the complexity of our theories, we must look inside them and understand why they take the shape they do. Which aspects of the theory influence which aspects of behavior? Perhaps, as Newell says, all of the theory influences even apparently simple behaviors. We need to have some evidence that this is so and we need to understand how and why it is so. As our theories evolve, we must determine whether old elements still play their original roles or have become vestigial in the presence of new elements. We need measures of how theoretical complexity increases with the scope of the phenomena being explained. We must assess whether a repeatedly improved theory should be overhauled and streamlined or reconceived anew.

Finally, I would suggest that the proper companion to empirical development of sufficient theories is analysis. Many of the ambiguities inherent in particular implementations of complex theories can be resolved by abstracting theoretical constructs out of the implementation and analyzing the formal relationships among them.

At this time we do not have a rigorous methodology for describing, analyzing, and empirically evaluating complex cognitive theories. Developing that methodology should be a first-order goal of the research community. Implementing and evaluating experimental applications of a complex theory is hard, resource-intensive, and time-consuming. But it is the only way we really come to understand and believe in an architecture.

4. Requirements for intelligence

Newell evaluates the sufficiency of his own theory, Soar, against two categories of requirements for intelligence. First, it must replicate the behavior of two ostensibly intelligent creatures: human beings and AI programs. Second, it must exhibit the characteristics of behavior entailed in a definition of intelligence formulated by Newell himself.

4.1. Replicating the behavior of intelligent creatures

Psychological data are the objective facts that Soar, as a theory of human cognition, is bound to replicate. Newell devotes three of his eight chapters to showing how Soar models three kinds of psychological data. "Immediate behavior" (Chapter 5) refers to simple perceptual-motor reactions, for example pressing a button when a light comes on or pressing one of two buttons depending on which of two lights comes on. "Memory, learning, and skill" (Chapter 6) refers to verbal learning tasks, for example studying and then recalling a list of items or studying a list of cue–item pairs and then recalling the items, given the cues. "Intendedly rational behavior" (Chapter 7) refers to simple verbal puzzles, for example solving cryptarithmetic problems, syllogisms. I am impressed by Newell's discipline and perseverance in working through the details of Soar's treatment of these tasks.

On the other hand, I have reservations about Newell's choice of tasks. Most of them represent low-level cognitive functions, perhaps artifacts of biological hardware that we may never model successfully in a computer program. Put in a positive light, I think we can take this as a measure of Newell's seriousness about Soar as a true psychological theory. What is more problematic, the tasks seem artificial. Who but a cognitive psychologist would find the performance of choice reaction tasks (at which pigeons excel) or cryptarithmetic tasks (which leave most people cold) to be hallmark manifestations of human intelligence? Psychological experiments are notorious for oversimplifying the phenomena of interest—and for good reason: that is the only way to control enough variables to get reliable and interpretable results. I can accept Newell's determination that Soar, as a psychological theory, must explain these carefully documented data. However, I do not think the data offer much in the way of constraint on a comprehensive theory or that they give us insight into other cognitive functions—especially for those who are concerned primarily with producing intelligent computer programs, rather than with modeling psychological truths *per se*.

Newell also reports Soar's replication of the performance of AI programs on four classes of tasks: toy problems and weak methods (e.g., Eight Puzzle, Towers of Hanoi, hill climbing), expert systems applications (e.g., R1, Neomycin), learning programs (e.g., explanation-based generalization), and programs that interact with the external world (e.g., control of a Puma arm with a vision system). Again, I applaud Newell for his determination to "put [Soar] through its paces" (p. 159).

But again, I also have reservations about Newell's choice of these tasks and his implicit rationale. Newell seems to be inferring that these tasks require intelligence simply because researchers have decided to build AI programs to perform them. Somehow, it is incumbent upon Soar to follow in the footsteps of AI programs: "Thus, the demonstration that Soar can exhibit intelligence is only as good as the current state of the art. Indeed, this question must be re-asked continually as AI advances—Soar must keep up with the art, if we are to be able to assert that it predicts that humans are intelligent, according to an increasingly improving view of the nature of intelligence" (p. 220). I disagree. Given the rudimentary state of AI as a discipline, our current view of the nature of intelligence can hardly be bound by its limits. We learn at least as much from the other cognitive sciences. Conversely, it is obviously possible that special-purpose AI systems might perform in a "super-intelligent" manner that cannot be replicated by a unified cognitive theory because of the other constraints a unified theory must meet. This leaves open the question of how we know which AI programs' performances a unified theory must replicate and which we can simply admire.

In addition to the abstract tasks Newell and his colleagues have studied, I would like to see candidate cognitive theories perform important real tasks that intelligent human beings perform in their real lives. These could include everyday tasks familiar to all, such as maneuvering a car through traffic while looking for a parking place close to a destination. They could include esoteric instances of familiar classes of tasks, such as planning and executing a sequence of therapeutic interventions under uncertain conditions in a medical context. Real tasks have several attractive properties. They have "ecological validity"; we do not risk modeling phenomena that occur only in the laboratory. They present important cognitive demands in the context of messy incidental details; we do not risk modeling phenomena that occur only under extraordinarily austere conditions. And they carry extra-theoretical requirements that stimulate theory expansion. In my opinion, as discussed below, one of the most important such requirements is the integration of knowledge and reasoning for several "tasks" within a larger mission. Certainly, the Soar research team has investigated some "real" tasks, notably in R1-Soar. I would like to see more in this category.

4.2. Meeting a definition of intelligence

If we are in the business of building theoretical architectures to support "intelligence", the logical first step would be to define intelligence. How better to know when we have succeeded or failed? However, while many psychologists and AI researchers play fast and loose with the term "intelligence", few have been forthcoming with a definition. Some have declared the very idea misguided—which may be true if we aim immediately for a single universal definition.

Indeed, even informal reflection reveals our fundamental ambivalence about the nature of intelligence. Are all (any?) non-human animals intelligent? What about human neonates? Which is more intelligent: a dog that has a repertoire of 20 command-driven tricks and can fend for itself in the world or a human neonate? Is computer vision a core element of AI? If so, are congenitally blind humans less intelligent than the normally sighted? Do humans who lose their sight lose some of their intelligence? Are eagles more intelligent, in visual matters, than humans? Who was more intelligent: Albert Einstein or Virginia Woolf? Pablo Picasso or Virginia Woolf? Albert Einstein or Marilyn Vos Savant (who reputedly has the highest IQ ever recorded and currently writes the "Ask Marilyn" column for *Parade* magazine)? It quickly becomes obvious that there is no single property that we intuitively call intelligence and no simple rule by which we intuitively determine how intelligent particular individuals are. Rather, there exists a multitude of factors whose differential contributions make an individual appear to be more or less intelligent in particular ways.

Nonetheless, I agree with Newell that we should start by identifying some of the important components of intelligence. If we turn out to be mistaken in the end, at least in the meantime, our colleagues will understand what it is we are trying to achieve with our theories and they will be able to argue with us about that as well as about the theories themselves. Newell distinguishes himself by giving us both a universal definition and an array of component requirements for intelligence.

First, consider Newell's universal definition: "A system is *intelligent* to the degree that it approximates a knowledge-level system." More specifically: "1. If a system uses all of the knowledge that it has [to achieve its goals], it must be perfectly intelligent .... 2. If a system does not have some knowledge, failure to use it cannot be a failure of intelligence .... 3. If a system has some knowledge and fails to use it, then there is certainly a failure of some internal ability ..." (p. 90). This definition is impressive in its simplicity, but it doesn't tell us enough about how to distinguish between "knowledge" and "intelligence", which I take to be the use of knowledge. Can't the ability to use knowledge be viewed as a kind of knowledge? To avoid tautology, the definition must operationalize this distinction. To illustrate, a meta-level exercise of Newell's definition leads to paradox. Assume a system has failed to solve a problem requiring knowledge k1. Is this is a failure of knowledge or intelligence? If the system knows k1, it's a failure of intelligence. But, if the system lacks k2, the knowledge that it ought to use k1 for this problem, it's only a failure of knowledge. Moving up a level, if the system knows k2, but fails to use it, it's a failure of intelligence. But if it lacks k3, the knowledge that it ought to use k2, it's only a failure of knowledge. The continuing regression of meta-levels is obvious—can't we recast every apparent failure of intelligence as a failure of the next meta-level of knowledge? For us to use Newell's definition well—that is, to determine whether a system is or is not behaving intelligently, we need an operational definition of what counts as knowledge, a way to assess the system's current knowledge and goals, and a way to determine what part of the system's knowledge it ought to apply in a given situation.

The universal definition also leads to some conclusions I find unintuitive. A simple computer program that knows the rules of addition and has a single goal to solve addition problems is perfectly intelligent, while a human being who can do a lot of things imperfectly, including arithmetic, is imperfectly (less) intelligent. A system that uses all available reasoning methods to insure a reliably correct answer is more intelligent than one that chooses to use only one of them—even though both get the same answer. A system that solves 100 of 100 problems by retrieving solutions from a table is more intelligent than a system that solves only 10 of them by reasoning imperfectly from a sufficient set of first principles. A system that always uses all of a fixed knowledge base is as intelligent as one that always uses all of a growing knowledge base. I think Newell should extend his universal definition to account for the amount of knowledge a system has, its tendency to use the most effective knowledge, and its ability to acquire knowledge.

Finally, the universal definition ignores several cognitive phenomena I consider fundamental: a system's allocation of limited cognitive resources, its ability to focus attention, its efforts to meet real-time constraints, its balancing of competing demands and opportunities for action, its considered decisions not to apply knowledge that is available, its inclination to satisfice. How can these phenomena be accounted for in a knowledge-level definition?

To complement his universal definition, Newell gives us several lists of component requirements for a unified theory of cognition: "areas to be covered by a unified theory of cognition" (p. 15), "multiple constraints that shape mind" (p. 19), "characteristics of Soar that agree with the basic shape of human cognition" (p. 227), and "potpourri of things Soar has not done" (p. 434). Together, these lists comprise a long, heterogeneous collection of requirements, such as: "Behave flexibly as a function of the environment".

"Be self-aware and have a sense of self." "Be realizable as a neural system." "Operate in real time." "Use language." "Use an indefinitely large body of knowledge."

I find all of Newell's proposed requirements interesting and worth examining in more detail. For example, the constraint that a system operate in real time is fundamental. Because it potentially affects every element of a cognitive architecture and all of their interactions, it can be used to prune severely the space of possible architectures. Given his commitment to model the biological details of human cognition, Newell operationalizes the real-time requirement in terms of constraints imposed by the underlying biological hardware: "There are available only ~ 100 operation times (two minimum system levels) to attain cognitive behavior out of neural-circuit technology" (p. 130). Because Soar's component computations meet these constraints, Newell reports that it has been shown to operate in real time. By contrast, I would operationalize the real-time requirement in terms of constraints imposed by the environment: The utility of the agent's behavior depends on its timing with respect to exogenous events. To show that Soar meets this definition of real time, we need a different kind of evidence. Soar must produce goal-effective behavior within externally imposed time constraints and degrade the quality of its behavior gracefully when necessary. Newell's and my operationalizations of the real-time requirement are not incompatible. In fact, there is a potential bridge between them if we can show how the biological constraints adapt human beings to their particular environmental constraints and, similarly, how the corresponding constraints restrict the environments in which AI programs can function effectively. But the two definitions are separable and individually important.

Critics will object that Newell's combined list of requirements is arbitrary, incomplete, and vulnerable to exceptions. But I think that is a natural consequence of trying to characterize this multi-dimensional thing we call intelligence. The problem is not specific to Newell's effort to build unified theories; anyone who is trying to model intelligence must communicate and establish the significance of whatever requirement(s) they have chosen to address. Mapping out the space of requirements, uncovering their relationships to one another, identifying the constraints they impose on our theories—these are necessary precursors to understanding the nature of the complete problem and the significance of individual research results within that larger context.

5. Generality, integration, and the structure of the research program

Newell's overall argument on behalf of Soar is one of generality: "We are interested in coverage—in whether a single theory, as an integrated conceptual structure, can address many different cognitive phenomena, ranging in time scale and task" (p. 303). So he and his collaborators have given us a proliferation of different versions of Soar—R1-Soar, Designer-Soar, Robo-Soar, etc.—each of which performs a different task. It's an impressive accomplishment, but ambiguous. How much of what we see reflects the theoretical principles embodied in Soar and how much reflects the skill of accomplished AI system builders? Newell recognizes and guards against the weakness in his argument: "It is important that Soar be seen to be a theory and not a framework of some kind. For example, it is not a loose verbal framework, which guides the form of invented explanations but does not itself provide them. ...Soar is a specific theory by means of which one calculates, simulates, and reasons from its fixed structure" (p. 433).

I think that a stronger argument could be made for Soar's (or any theory's) generality if we combined the sufficiency criterion with a "constraint" criterion. A would-be theory has theoretical content to the degree that it constrains the appropriate form in which to model each new demonstration task. Of course, this poses a new construct to be operationalized and measured, but there is a straightforward (if labor-intensive) empirical method for measuring degree of constraint. Ask 10–20 people (Soar experts presumably), working independently, to apply Soar to each of several tasks. Ask another group of people to apply architecture X (a standard of comparison) to the same tasks. If Soar offers a lot of theoretical constraint, there should be substantial agreement among the designs produced by the Soar experts, more than among the designs produced by the architecture X experts. Other things being equal, we prefer a more constraining theory over a less constraining one.

Even with the additional requirement for constraint, generality over many individual tasks in a series of localized demonstrations is a weak test for a unified cognitive theory. The hard test is integration. Acknowledging this, Newell claims: "One should think of [R1-Soar and Designer-Soar] being added together to make a single Soar system with the knowledge of the two tasks. They are kept separate simply because they are worked on by separate investigators at different times" (p. 216). But the assertion that R1-Soar and Designer-Soar are separate for purely logistical reasons is glib and the phrase "added together" is mysterious. What would it mean to integrate these two applications in a substantive way and what difference would it make? Would the integrated knowledge base be smaller (non-redundant) and more interconnected than a simple composite of the original two? What about the problem spaces? Would performance quality or speed on the original tasks be improved or hindered in any way? Would any new capabilities be potentiated? Would Soar be able to combine elements of independently acquired knowledge bases to perform new tasks? Newell does report integration of two algorithm domains (sorting and sets) within

Designer-Soar, with some sharing of problem spaces but no transfer of learning. He also reports integration of an instruction-taking capability with performance of a sentence-verification task. These are promising steps, but I would like to see more of a concerted effort to integrate knowledge and reasoning capabilities that interact in multiple ways—not all of them fully anticipated—and to extend those capabilities in an incremental fashion. In other words, I propose a more programmatic structure to the research effort, in which we incrementally develop an increasingly sophisticated, integrated "cognitive agent".

Let me presume to offer a friendly challenge to the Soar team. Give us "Agent-Soar", integrating all of the "content" of the existing Soar applications in a graceful, principled fashion within a single instance of the Soar architecture. Show us the resulting economies of storage and Agent-Soar's global perspective on its knowledge. Show us how Agent-Soar can exploit all of its content to meet several of the component requirements for intelligence simultaneously. For example, show us Agent-Soar operating continuously, selectively perceiving a complex unpredictable environment, noticing situations of interest, setting and modifying its own goals, and going about achieving them. Show us how it integrates concurrent tasks and coordinates their interacting needs for knowledge, inferences, perceptual information, computational resources, and real time. Show us synergy—unplanned desirable capabilities arising from interactions among independently acquired contents. Show us Agent-Soar learning in the natural course of these activities to produce incremental growth in unanticipated areas of its knowledge. Show us that Agent-Soar is self-aware, possessing and applying knowledge of itself as an agent that possesses and applies knowledge. Show us how it modifies its knowledge based on experience and makes the best use of dynamic, but limited resources under real-time constraints. Finally, show us how Agent-Soar grows and develops and successively approximates the ideal knowledge-level agent.

Acknowledgement

Preparation of this paper was supported by NASA contract NAG 2-581 under DARPA Order 6822.

Artificial Intelligence 59 (1993) 343–354
Elsevier

ARTINT 1013

Allen Newell, *Unified Theories of Cognition* *

Marvin Minsky

Media Lab, Room E-15-489, Massachusetts Institute of Technology, Cambridge, MA 02139, USA

1. Introduction

This book can be seen as at least four different books—about Soar, about the prospects of psychology, about AI, and about philosophy of mind. Its range and depth make it a landmark in our understanding of how minds must work. I found it hard to write this review because whenever I found something to argue about I would soon discover another page in which Newell either answered it or explained why Soar was not ready to attack that issue. Soar itself appears to be a wonderfully economical yet powerful way both for using knowledge to solve problems, and for learning from that experience. But as for the thesis of this book—the search for a Unified Theory of Mind, I'm not sure that this is a good idea.

The Introduction tries to justify that search:

> ... a single system (mind) produces all aspects of behavior. It is one mind that minds them all. Even if the mind has parts, modules, components, or whatever, they all mesh together to produce behavior. (p. 17)

This might be true in some simple sense, but it can lead to bad philosophy. Whatever one may think of Freud, we owe to him the insight that the parts

Correspondence to: M. Minsky, Media Lab, Room E15-489, Massachusetts Institute of Technology, Cambridge, MA 02139, USA. E-mail: minsky@ai.mit.edu.
* (Harvard University Press, Cambridge, MA, 1990); xvi + 549 pages.

of the mind don't always mesh, and that there need be *nothing* to mind them all. When Newell adds, "Unification is always an aim of science" (p. 18), one might reply that new ideas were often made by first disunifying older ones. Chemistry's hundred-odd elements came from the ashes of an older theory based on only four. To be sure, the properties of the new elements were subsequently derived from many fewer principles—but in this review I'll try to show why we can't expect this to happen in regard to the brain. Chapters 5–8 of *Unified Theories of Cognition* (*UTC*) show that Soar can be made to simulate the outcomes of a variety of psychological experiments. A critic might fear that that's not enough, because the mind can do so many things that *any* theory could be made to look good by selecting which tasks to simulate. The list of domains (Fig. 8-1) unexplored by Soar includes some very important ones, such as understanding stories, and reasoning by analogy. But mainly I'll be less concerned with what Soar can do than with how much it could do concurrently.

2. The organic brain

In earlier times, physical science was split into separate "branches" that focused on different phenomena, such as mechanics, optics, electricity, heat, and chemistry. Then heat became part of mechanics, light turned out to be electrical, and then these (and virtually everything else) were "reduced" to a few quantum principles. The term "unified theory" celebrates this discovery that the laws of the universe are few. But we know that this can't happen in biology—because we know too much about the nature of an animal. The trouble is that the structures and functions of an animal's organs are not much constrained by those basic physical laws. This is because the functional details of each organ are determined by the activities of great numbers of specialized genes. Recent research (Sutcliffe [7]) appears to show that in this respect, the brain is unique, because as much as half of the entire mammalian genome is involved in coding for the nervous system.

What is an animal, anyway? Essentially, its body consists of a bizarre collection of organs, each specialized to do only certain jobs. In order for "higher" such forms to survive, those complex assemblies had to evolve along with networks of systems to regulate them; some of these are chemically distributed, while others take the form of additional organs—most notably the brain. The brain itself resulted from several hundreds of megayears of adapting to different environments, and now consists of hundreds of specialized sub-organs called brain centers, each one linked by more-or-less specific connections to several others, to form a huge system of what clearly must be a myriad of mechanisms for synchronizing, managing, and arbitrating among different functions. Newell recognizes this complexity in

Section 4.1 and proposes, at least for the time being, to seek a unified theory only for what he calls central cognition.

> ... the total system is too complex to handle all at once, and the sorts of considerations that go into perception and motor action seem too disparate to integrate. So the strategy is divide and conquer. (p. 160)

My question is, has Newell divided enough? In Section 3.5 he explains with great clarity how each theory in psychology must be applied only at the right level, lest its claims become too strong to be true or too weak to be useful. At the lowest level,

> ... the neural-circuit level remains a realm governed by natural science. The types of laws are those of physics and chemistry. (p. 129)

But because those individual cells could be assembled into unlimited varieties of computational circuitry, the properties of the neurons themselves do not constrain cognition much. Theories based on high-level models of computation provide no guidance for psychology, because it is so easy to design such machines to do whatever we can describe. If we ignore the issue of speed, this applies almost as well to people, too: disciplined humans can instruct themselves to do virtually anything, by combining symbolic thinking and long-term memory. In this regard we differ from all other animals.

Accordingly, in Section 3.3 Newell argues that we'll need different kinds of psychological theories for dealing with the scales of time that he calls biological, cognitive, rational, and social. For Soar he reserves the "cognitive band" of activities that take place over intervals between 0.1 and 10 seconds. The slow and deliberate "rational band", which works on time scales of minutes and hours, will be built over that—whereas Soar itself will be built upon the biological band of events shorter than 0.01 seconds in duration. One could hardly object to any of this—except to note that some low-level events may have longer durations. For example, such attachment events as bonding, infatuation, and mourning take place on scales of weeks and months. Is this because our social relationships are involved with certain synapses that are peculiarly slow to forget? Or is it merely because it takes a long time to rearrange certain large and complex mental structures?

3. The speed of thought

All the things that Soar can do are accomplished by selecting and executing productions—that is, IF–THEN rules—one at a time. The body of Chapter 5 shows that if cognitive activities are indeed production-based, then those productions cannot execute in less than the order of 20-odd milliseconds. Newell's accumulation of evidence for this is as strong as anything of that sort I've ever seen in psychology. He then applies these time-constraints quite forcefully. Whatever we do in that "cognitive band"—that is, any psychological function that can be accomplished in one second or so—Soar must accomplish by executing no more than a few dozen productions. No theory would be acceptable that demands thousands of such steps per second.

This neatly prevents Soar from exploiting its computation potentiality to simulate other theories. Newell's ferocious time-constraint precludes any such trick: Soar cannot appear to succeed because of any "Turing leak". It cannot admit even a single level of "interpreting" of one language in terms of another because, in practice, such simulations expand time scales by factors of hundreds. Then, despite this constraint, almost half of the volume of *UTC* describes ways in which Soar is able to do (and learn to do) significant tasks. This is truly a remarkable claim, for in many of those one-second instances, the human subjects routinely make not merely a recognition, but also a knowledge-based inference and an action decision. It is surely a significant accomplishment to have shown that so many significant things can be done in so few steps.

On second thought, we must ask *which* things. Yes, Soar can indeed do surprising things with just one production at a time. But do there remain important things that Soar can*not* so do? I faced the same question twenty years ago when I first read *Human Problem Solving* [6]. Some simulations worked very well for minutes at a time—until the system would suddenly fail as the human problem solver switched to a different strategy or "changed the subject". Some of those "episodes" could be explained in terms of switching to another pre-established problem space. But other times it seemed to me that the subject must have switched over to a new representation of the problem that was *already adapted* to the situation. To do this so quickly, it seemed to me that the system would need to have been updating that other representation all along—and that would require more productions. Thus, Soar's simulation (Fig. 7-5) of cryptarithmetic gave me a sense of *déjà vu*. Although the system was able to simulate the interiors of each episode, again there was the question of whether Soar could be made to handle more of those impasse-escaping jumps, still using only one production at a time? Surely so, when it is merely a matter of switching to another pre-constructed problem space. But if the new scheme needs extensive updating, then that would need too many productions—and Soar would require more concurrent processes. Humans often change their viewpoints in less than a single second of time—for example, at the punch-line of a joke in which a complex description that first seemed strange (or commonplace) suddenly becomes more meaningful (or the opposite), when one trait of a person is replaced by another, or when a physical interpretation is abruptly replaced by a sexual one. Were both of them running in parallel?

For another perspective, contrast the sorts of problems discussed in *UTC* with the more prosaic kinds of contexts considered in *The Society of Mind* [2, 1.3]. Imagine yourself sipping a drink at a party while moving about and talking with friends. How many streams of processing are involved in shaping your hand to keep the cup level, while choosing where to place your feet? How many processes help choose the words that say what you mean while arranging those words into suitable strings? What keeps track of what you've said to whom; what takes into account what you know of your friends so as not to hurt their feelings? What about those other thoughts that clearly go on in parallel, as one part of your mind keeps humming a tune while another sub-mind plans a path that escapes from this person and approaches that one. Perhaps Soar could be trained to do any of those, but to do them all concurrently would seem to require an order of magnitude more productions per second. If this is correct, then either (1) we could raise the level of Soar up into that rational band, or (2) we might consider using several Soars at once, or (3) we could try to maintain the basic idea while replacing the single-production idea by some more active type of memory. It seems to me that the very rigor of Newell's analysis comes close to showing that a single Soar cannot by itself account for enough of what goes on in each second of human thinking-time.

If a mind consisted of several Soars, what could bind them together? A programmer might instantly say, "Let's put yet one more Soar in charge". A Freudian might counter with, "you must install some set of long-range values into an almost-read-only memory, to serve as a superego to keep the system from drifting away. You must also supply some Censors, too, for the child to learn what *not* to do." A Piagetian might insist that you'll need some more machinery to sequence certain stages of development, to ensure that certain things be learned. A disciple of Warren McCulloch might say that no single processor could suffice: you'll need "redundancy of potential command" to keep the thing from going mad.

4. A framework for representing knowledge?

AI researchers have found many problems that seemed intractable when described in one way but became easy in another representation. Some domains seem well suited to logical expressions, others work well with production systems, yet others prosper when frames are employed—or scripts, semantic nets, fuzzy logic, or neural nets. Perhaps the most radical aspect of Soar is that it employs only a single, universally accessible workspace that supports nothing but the pairs of sets of symbol strings that constitute productions. An obvious alternative would be to use a variety of different, more specialized representations. Newell opposes this idea because, as he says in Section 2.3, using several representations in concert, each along with its own operational procedures, might lead to a combinatorial explosion. In my view, that concern is misplaced. It would indeed apply to an *arbitrary* collection of representation schemes—but might not if we searched for centuries to find some much more compatible set! Now consider that for millions of years our ancestors were doing precisely that! Among the known results of this are those hardware schemes found in the sensory and motor areas that constitute much of our brains. Newell explicitly places these beyond the scope of present-day Soar, because he considers them more likely to be less uniform. But why would evolution have changed its ways, only within the cognitive realm? Ironically, Newell's ideas about processing speed led me in the other direction. For example, human thought seems so proficient at making "chains of reasoning" that one would expect to find that our brains contain special structures for doing this—perhaps in the form of script-like representation schemes. Then because we're very quick at hierarchical reasoning, perhaps we should look for hardware trees. Language-like kinds of reasoning might best be supported by hardware designed to deal with case-frames or semantic nets.

Shortly I'll discuss the processes that I suspect are most vital of all— the ones that deal with *differences*. To manipulate these as fast as we do, we might need hardware for pairs of frames. Much of Newell's previous work emphasized the importance of finding good representations. The position of *UTC* seems to be that we need not provide for these in advance. This faces us with two alternatives. One way would be to simulate such structures at least one level above the productions—thus challenging real-time Soar's potential speed. The other way is to remain at the base level, and "non-simulate" the required functions by building huge look-up tables. But while this could be done at a constant speed, it exposes us to another risk—of exponential growth of memory size and of learning time. Such systems might appear to work on small-sample problems, but then rapidly fail when we try to export them to reality. I myself am more inclined to look for good representations at some lower level of neurology. But going that way would not escape the question of how the mind could so quickly switch between different representation schemes. My conjecture is that this must be the end result of *forcing the different representations to learn to work together from the stages of development.* We must cross-link them by making them "grow up" together.

5. Society of Mind theories

Perhaps the most novel aspect of Soar is the idea of dealing with impasses—and this is why I've dwelt so much on multiple representations. This is based on my belief that *metaphors may constitute our most powerful ways to escape from cognitive impasses—and a multiplicity of representations could systematically support our most pervasive metaphors.* With metaphor, when one type of representation fails, you can quickly switch to another one without the need to start over. It seems to me that, in this regard, *UTC* has tried to avoid a crucial aspect of psychology: how peculiarly good we humans are at exploiting the uses of metaphor in the temporal, spatial, and social realms. Theory: to move among these so fluently, our systems must have learned to assign the same symbols to analogous links of representations in different realms. I see no basic reason why we could not make Soar do such things—but could it do this at lifelike speeds, in ways that infants are likely to learn?

A major goal in designing what Seymour Papert and I called the "Society of Mind" (SOM) theory was to facilitate thinking by analogy. Evidently Newell never read *The Society of Mind* [2] in detail; its only citation in *UTC* is this single remark: "The society-of-mind metaphor is built around relatively small communication channels, but inside each mind it is not that way at all." This seems intended to contrast *SOM*'s assumption that the interiors of agencies are generally opaque to one another against Soar's assumption that all memories share the same uniform space. But that distinction might end up with little effect because Soar productions of different sorts will tend to become insulated from one another. In another respect the two theories might seem strongly opposed in regard to the idea of "unified"; Soar has very few basic mechanisms and a single representation, whereas SOM assumes quite a few different kinds of representations and machinery for employing them. Still, the two theories also have so many common aspects that I think they could serve as alternative ways to interpret the same psychological data. In Soar, everything is learned by forming new "chunks" (which are simply new productions) whereas in SOM almost everything that is learned is ultimately composed of K-lines [1;2, 8.2]. (K-lines are agents that, when activated, arouse sets of other agents, including other K-lines.) The two schemes are rather similar in that both chunks and K-lines serve as ways to reify the "net" effects of recent input-output activity; as such, they are also learned in much the same way. Newell emphasizes (p. 140) that chunk-memories have the property that, once activated, they can then interact to form "reconstructed memories". The same is true of K-lines as well; indeed, they reconstruct (albeit by interacting in parallel) not only declarative, but also procedural and dispositional memories. Both Soar's "objects" and my "polynemes" are little more than attribute–value sets, and most of the "frames" described in [2, 24.8] could be represented in Soar as sets of objects appearing as elements of productions. However, the more complex structures called "frame-arrays" incorporate more innate structure. Some of their terminals (i.e., attributes) are indexed by special activation lines called "pronomes" (which resemble the role-markers of case grammars) that enable the system to quickly switch between frames without recomputing their value-assignments. If the same kinds of role-symbols are applied more globally, they can be used to bridge between corresponding slots in the other representations used in grossly different realms of knowledge— and that would automatically yield some capabilities to reason by analogy. (This is different from the more general, higher-level idea of being able to construct correspondences between different things. Here it is a matter of evolving innate hardware preparations for a small and pre-selected group of "pervasive" metaphors, e.g., between events in time and space, or between spatial and social proximity.)

The discussion of impasse resolution in *UTC* seems somewhat vague:

> Soar responds to an impasse by creating a subgoal to resolve it. What resolves an impasse is knowledge that would lead Soar not to make that impasse at that decision point. There are many ways in which this might happen. (Section 4.1.5)

We're told that one way Soar can accomplish this is by inserting a new entry on a subgoal stack. In *SOM* as well, impasses are recognized and then engaged in various ways. One scheme that pervades the whole system is the idea I called Papert's Principle: throughout child development, knowledge becomes organized through the construction of new agents that serve as "middle level managers". (Some of these manager agents may correspond roughly to Newell's "problem spaces," but I'm not really sure about that.) The managers themselves are installed as consequences of impasse-resolving episodes. One typical function of a manager agent is to resolve conflicts by making other agents "resign". That is, whenever related agents disagree, if they have a common manager, its activation is weakened so that its competitors can "take over". Of course, this will be helpful only if some more competent agent is lying in wait. Another assumption I made in *SOM* is that a typical agency is equipped with provisions for dealing with the most common kinds of impasses. For example, each agent at a certain level could operate under the supervision of some impasse-detecting specialists at another level. (The text of *SOM* calls these the A-Brain and the B-Brain.) These "B-brain" specialists are particularly suited for detecting looping, meandering, and other forms of lack of progress. Of course, the extent to which such functions could be made innate depends on the extent to which they can be done in content-free ways. I presume that such "quasi-reflective" functions could be programmed into Soar, presumably in the form of recursive activations of the same system. But the critical question is, I think, *would enough such structures evolve by themselves if a Soar were raised as a human child?* Eventually, at higher knowledge levels, all normal humans eventually acquire some serial-conscious reflective-memory systems. We could ask of both SOM and Soar how likely such things are to come about without any pre-arranged help. In [2, 10.9 and 31.4] I assume that infants start out with a substantial endowment of pre-constructed machinery or the staging of infant development. This appears to be another domain unexplored by Soar.

6. Reformulation and natural language understanding

"Something seems to have gone wrong here. Just what was I trying to do?" In this typical rational mental scene, you notice that you've got stuck and try to re-describe the situation to yourself. Almost instantly, then, you hear yourself think things like this: *"Gosh that was stupid! The '5' in the third column has nothing at all to do with the 'M' in the first column. What could I have been thinking of?"* This sort of "reformulation" process could be our most powerful impasse-resolving technique—at least in Newell's rational band. But how might reformulation work? I'll argue that from the Society of Mind viewpoint, reformulation needs machinery that must be a lot like GPS. But my reasons may seem wrong from the viewpoint of Soar. This is because in Soar all knowledge is assumed to be uniformly accessible, so there is nothing to bar the central processor from accessing anything—including the current situation-description. However, in a SOM-type theory, higher-level processes will often have to build their own representations of other agencies' plans and goals, because they have such poor access to what happens inside other parts of the brain.

How could one closed agency examine a structure inside another? In [2, 22.10], I proposed a way of doing this, and called it the "re-duplication" method. This scheme is actually nothing more than a variant of Newell and Simon's GPS. Suppose you were given an opaque box that contains an unknown symbol-tree, and you want to find out what's inside? Assume that (1) you're allowed to use list-processing operations to build new things inside the box and (2) that you have a way to detect the "highest-level differences" between two things in the box. Then you can solve the problem in the following way: the goal is to make a *copy* (inside that box) of the unknown tree inside that box. Simply begin with an empty copy—that is, a blank representation. Then continue top-down recursively, to build up the copy by detecting and removing the differences between it and the original; at every step performing whichever operation promises to remove or reduce the last-noticed difference. You need never see the trees themselves because—if everything works—the stream of operations that you have performed is a serial description of that hidden tree.

If this mechanism is invoked when you're stuck in an impasse, the result may be to produce a different and perhaps more suitable representation of the situation or goal because the copying process will be affected by your current choice of GPS-type difference priorities—which in turn you'll adjust to represent your current goals and concerns. Elements that your current copier considers to be irrelevant to the current goal will be considered unworthy of notice and will automatically be stripped out of the copy. This editing could make that impasse disappear—or at least make the problem seem simpler, more abstract, or more easy to match to available knowledge.

How is this related to that "What was I trying to do?" Simply, I think, because language itself may use something like this. Suppose that Mary has a certain idea and wants to explain it to Jack. What might ensue, mechanically? Well, let's assume that somewhere in the Broca region of Mary's brain is a pointer to a certain knowledge representation. The latter might be a complex semantic network that includes pointers to other sorts of trans-frames and scripts, but let's assume for simplicity that Mary's "idea" is merely a tree. Then as that copy-duplication activity proceeds, the resulting stream of operations could be used by Mary's Broca region to produce a serial stream of verbal sounds. If Jack "understands" that language stream (and this is as good a way as any to explain what "understand" means), then the Wernicke region of Jack's brain will interpret that phonemic stream to construct a copy of Mary's tree somewhere in Jack's brain. To do such things, each typical agency should be equipped with at least a pair of high-speed, temporary K-line memories. Let's assume that typical agents (like typical neurons) can serve as temporal change-detecting agents. Then any agency could easily compare two descriptions simply by first activating one description, then the other, and responding to the differences. Cognition constantly involves comparisons. Accordingly I would expect to find pervasive systems in the brain for efficiently comparing things (including ideas) and then reacting to detected differences. The concept of "difference" itself seems notably absent in *UTC*. It does not even occur in the index. In contrast, I predict that the most useful of all the representations proposed in *SOM* will be the trans-frames introduced in [2, 21.3]. A trans-frame is a type of frame that includes a pair of "before–after" frames, along with additional slots to describe their differences and pointers to the operations or "trajectories" that one might use to change one into the other. Trans-frames (which are modeled on older ideas of Roger Schank) are almost perfectly suited, not only to represent knowledge in forms well suited for scripting, chaining, and reasoning, but also for generating verb-centered sentences. If I hadn't rejected that thought from the start, I could have presented SOM as a "unified theory of cognition" based on representing all knowledge in trans-frame form.

Speaking of language, should not a unified theory try to explain why every language has nouns and verbs? I don't know quite how to obtain these from Soar, but it's easy as pie to derive them from SOM, because among our most basic representations are "polynemes" for describing "things" and trans-frames for describing changes and actions. Our ancestors must have evolved those object-nouns at some very early stage, and the action-verbs then later evolved so that they could think one more step ahead. So in spite of some language theorists' view that language is a separate thing, I claim that our brains must first have evolved representations to serve as nouns and verbs. Without having something resembling these, Soar might find it hard to speak.

This leads us into another area. Any unified theory in biology must eventually address the question of how it could have evolved. For example, how could my re-duplication scheme evolve? Perhaps the original function of that machinery was less for social communication and more for communication between different domains of the brain! This, in turn, most likely evolved for an even more critical function: to enable good communication from a mental agency to itself! How could an animal use such a thing? So far as I can see, neuro-cognitive theorists seemed to have overlooked this important problem: *how to produce new copies of the functions embodied in neural nets.* This appears to be a deficiency, for example, in what I understand of Edelman's "Neural Darwinism", which proposes an Ashby-like way to learn by selection—but lacks any way to produce new versions for further development. To be sure, Soar would have no problem *doing* this, either directly or by simulating a recursive re-duplicator—but how long would it take for Soar to *learn* such a thing?

7. Conclusions

We certainly need better "large-scale" theories for psychology, and Soar is a powerful stimulus. But we must also take care not to overshoot. It is always important to discover that a system can do more than we thought it would do—but that should not be our only goal. In this regard, it seems to me, the AI community has turned away from an equally important opportunity. Today, if you wanted to build a machine that used several different representations, you'd find that we have virtually no good ideas about how to do this. I would hope that now, future work will be aimed toward finding ways to synthesize and manage systems that can exploit that diversity. From the moment I met him in 1956, Allen Newell was one of my heroes. At least five times his ideas transformed mine; I was never the same person after understanding LT, GPS, HPS, or MERLIN, and now Soar in the context of *UTC*. This latest work will surely stand as a basic advance in AI's theories of knowledge machines. Reading this monumental book recalled to me my sense of awe in seeing the power of GPS, first in its original form [4] and then in the version with learning [5]. I hope others who read it carefully will have the same experience.

References

[1] M. Minsky, K-lines: a theory of memory, *Cogn. Sci.* **4** (1980) 117–133.

[2] M. Minsky, *The Society of Mind* (Simon and Schuster, New York, 1986).

[3] A. Newell, J.C. Shaw and H.A. Simon, Empirical explorations of the logic theory machine, in: *Proceedings Western Joint Computer Conference* (1955) 218–230.

[4] A. Newell, J.C. Shaw and H.A. Simon, Report on a general problem-solving program, in: *Proceedings International Conference on Information Processing*, Paris, France (1959).

[5] A. Newell, J.C. Shaw and H.A. Simon, A variety of intelligent learning in a general problem solver, in: M.T. Yovitts and S. Cameron, eds., *Self-Organizing Systems* (Pergamon Press, New York, 1960).

[6] A. Newell and H.A. Simon, *Human Problem Solving* (Prentice-Hall, Englewood Cliffs, NJ, 1972).

[7] J.G. Sutcliffe, mRNA in the mammalian central nervous system, *Am. Rev. Neurosci.* **2** (1988) 157–198.

Artificial Intelligence 59 (1993) 355–369
Elsevier

ARTINT 1014

On wings of knowledge: a review of Allen Newell's *Unified Theories of Cognition* *

Jordan B. Pollack

Laboratory for AI Research, The Ohio State University, 2036 Neil Avenue, Columbus, OH 43210, USA

Received January 1992
Revised July 1992

1. Introduction

Besides being a status report on the Soar project, *Unified Theories of Cognition* is Allen Newell's attempt at directing the field of cognitive science by example. Newell argues that his approach to "unification", which involves the programmed extension of a single piece of software-architecture-as-theory to as many psychological domains as possible, is the proper research methodology for cognitive science today:

> In this book I'm not proposing Soar as *the* unified theory of cognition. Soar is, of course, an interesting candidate. With a number of colleagues I am intent on pushing Soar as hard as I can to make it into a viable unified theory. But my concern here is that cognitive scientists consider working with *some* unified theory of cognition. Work with ACT*, with CAPS, with Soar, with CUTC, a connectionist unified theory of cognition. Just work with some UTC. (p. 430)

Correspondence to: J.B. Pollack, Laboratory for AI Research, The Ohio State University, 2036 Neil Avenue, Columbus, OH 43210, USA. E-mail: pollack@cis.ohio-state.edu
* (Harvard University Press, Cambridge, MA, 1990); 549 pages

Over the past decade, Newell and his colleagues at numerous universities (including my own) have applied Soar to a number of different domains, and have adopted a goal of making it toe the line on psychological results. This is a very ambitious goal, and Newell knows it:

> The next risk is to be found guilty of the sin of presumption. Who am I, Allen Newell, to propose a unified theory of cognition ... Psychology must wait for its Newton. (p. 37)

Newell is clearly entitled by a life of good scientific works to write a book at such a level and, in my opinion, it is the most substantial and impressive, by far, of recent offerings on the grand unified mind. My entitlement to review his book is less self-evident, however—who am I to stand in judgement over one of the founding fathers of the field? And so I fear I am about to commit the sin of presumption as well, and to compound it, moreover, with the sin of obliqueness: Because my argument is not with the quality of Newell's book, but with the direction he is advocating for cognitive science, I will not review his theory in detail. Rather, I will adopt a bird's eye view and engage only the methodological proposal. I will, however, belabor one small detail of Newell's theory, its name, and only to use as my symbolic launching pad.

2. Artificial intelligence and mechanical flight

The origin of the name Soar, according to high-level sources within the project, was originally an acronym for three primitive components of the problem-space method. But shortly, these components were forgotten, leaving the proper noun in their stead, a name which evokes "grand and glorious things", and also puts us in mind of the achievement of mechanical flight, AI's historical *doppelgänger.*

> Among those who had worked on the problem [of mechanical flight] I may mention [da Vinci, Cayley, Maxim, Parsons, Bell, Phillips, Lilienthal, Edison, Langley] and a great number of other men of ability. But the subject had been brought into disrepute by a number of men of lesser ability who had hoped to solve the problem through devices of their own invention, which had all of themselves failed, until finally the public was lead to believe that flying was as impossible as perpetual motion. In fact, scientists of the standing of Guy Lussac ... and Simon Newcomb ... had attempted to prove it would be impossible to build a flying machine that would carry a man. (Wright [25, p. 12] [1]

[1] This book is a reissued collection of essays and photographs about the Wright's research and development process. It includes three essays by Orville Wright, and two interpretive essays by Fred C. Kelly. Subsequent citations are to this edition.

I will leave the substitution of contemporary scientists to the reader. Simply put, the analogy "Airplanes are to birds as smart machines will be to brains", is a widely repeated AI mantra with several uses. One is to entice consumers by reminding them of the revolution in warfare, transportation, commerce, etc. brought about by mechanical flight. Another is to encourage patience in those same consumers by pointing to the hundreds of years of experimental work conducted before the success of mechanical flight! A third is to chant it, eyes closed, ignoring the complex reality of biological mechanism.

Although it is quite likely that the analogy between AI and mechanical flight arose spontaneously in the community of AI pioneers, its earliest written appearance seems to be in a "cold war for AI" essay by Paul Armer, then of the Rand Corporation, in the classic collection *Computers and Thought*:

> While it is true that Man wasted a good deal of time and effort trying to build a flying machine that flapped its wings like a bird, the important point is that it was the understanding of the law of aerodynamic lift (even though the understanding was quite imperfect at first) over an airfoil which enabled Man to build flying machines. A bird isn't sustained in the air by the hand of God—natural laws govern its flight. Similarly, natural laws govern what [goes on inside the head]. Thus I see no reason why we won't be able to duplicate in hardware the very powerful processes of association which the human brain has, once we understand them. (Armer [1, p.398])

We all agree that once we understand how natural law governs what goes on in the head, we will be able to mechanize thought, and will then have the best scientific theory of cognition, which could be refined into the technology for "general intelligence". But our field has basically ignored natural law, and settled comfortably upon methodologies and models which involve only the perfect simulation of arbitrary "software" laws. I believe that we are failing to integrate several key principles which govern cognition and action in biological and physical systems, and that the incorporation of these should be the priority of cognitive science rather than of the writing of large programs.

3. Deconstructing the myths of mechanical flight

There are two myths in Armer's analogy which are important to correct. The first is that flight is based mainly upon the principle of the airfoil. The second is that the mechanical means by which nature solved the problem are irrelevant. Translating through the analogy, these two myths are equivalent to believing that cognition is based mainly upon the principle of universal computation, and that the mechanical means by which nature solved the problem are irrelevant.

Although my favorite sections of Newell's book are those in which he emphasizes the importance of constraints from biology and physics, he conducts his research in a way which is consistent with the myths. Indeed the myths are principally supported by his arguments, both the Physical Symbol System Hypothesis [17], which is the assertion that Universal Computation is enough, and the Knowledge Level Hypothesis [16], which legitimizes theories involving only software laws, even though their very existence is based only upon introspection.

In order to see why these myths are a stumbling block to the achievement of mechanical cognition, I will examine several aspects of the solution to mechanical flight, using the reports by Orville Wright.

3.1. The airfoil principle

The principle of aerodynamic lift over an airfoil was around for hundreds of years before the advent of mechanical flight. The Wright brothers just tuned the shape to optimize lift:

> The pressures on squares are different from those on rectangles, circles, triangles or ellipses; arched surfaces differ from planes, and vary among themselves according to the depth of curvature; true arcs differ from parabolas, and the latter differ among themselves; thick surfaces from thin ... the shape of an edge also makes a difference, so thousands of combinations are possible in so simple a thing as a wing .... Two testing machines were built [and] we began systematic measurements of standard surfaces, so varied in design as to bring out the underlying causes of differences noted in their pressures (Wright [25, p. 84])

Assume that the principle of Universal Computation is to AI what the principle of aerodynamic lift is to mechanical flight. In Chapter 2 of this book, Newell reiterates, in some detail, the standard argument for the status quo view of cognition as symbolic computation:

- Mind is flexible, gaining power from the formation of "indefinitely rich representations" and an ability to compose transformations of these representations. (pp. 59–63).
- Therefore mind must be a universal symbol processing machine (pp. 70–71).
- It is believed that most universal machines are equivalent (p. 72).

If one holds that the flexibility of the mind places it in the same class as the other universal machines (subject to physical limits, of course), then the mathematics tells us we can use any universal computational model for describing mind or its subparts (and the biological path is irrelevant). So, for example, any of the four major theories of computation developed (and unified) this century—Church's lambda calculus, Post's production system, Von Neumann's stored program machine, and universal automata (e.g. Turing's Machine)—could be used as a basis for a theory of mind. Of course, these theories were too raw and difficult to program, but have evolved through human ingenuity into their modern equivalents, each of which is a "Universal Programming Language" (UPL): LISP, OPS5, C, and ATN's, respectively.

If we plan to express our UTCs in UPLs, however, we must have a way to distinguish between these UPLs in order to put some constraints on our UTCs, so that they aren't so general as to be vacuous. There are at least five general strategies to add constraints to a universal system: architecture, tradition, extra-disciplinary goals, parsimony, and ergonomics.

The first way to constrain a UPL is to build something, anything, on top of it, which constrains either what it can compute, how well it can compute it, or how it behaves while computing it. This is called architecture, and Newell spends pages 82–88 discussing architecture in some detail. In a universal system, one can build architecture on top of architecture and shift attention away from the basic components of the system to arbitrary levels of abstraction.

The second method of constraining a universal theory is by sticking to "tradition", the practices whose success elevates them to beliefs handed down orally though the generations of researchers. Even though any other programming language would serve, the tradition in American AI is to build systems from scratch, using LISP, or to build knowledge into production systems. Newell is happy to represent the "symbolic cognitive psychology" tradition (p. 24) against the paradigmatic revolutions like Gibsonianism [10] or PDPism [21].

A third way we can distinguish between competing universals is to appeal to scientific goals outside of building a working program. We can stipulate, for example, that the "most natural" way to model a phenomenon in the UPL must support extra-disciplinary goals. Algorithmic efficiency, a goal of mainstream computer science, can be used to discriminate between competing models for particular tasks. Robust data from psychological experiments can be used to discriminate among universal theories on the basis of matching an implemented system's natural behavior with the observed data from humans performing the task. Finally, as a subset of neural network researchers often argue, the model supporting the theory must be "biologically correct". Newell, of course, relies very heavily on the psychological goals to justify his particular UPL.

Fourth, parsimony can be called into play. Two theories can be compared as to the number of elements, parameters, and assumptions needed to explain certain phenomena, and the shorter one wins. Newell makes a good point that the more phenomena one wishes to explain, the more benefit is gained from a unified theory, which ends up being shorter than the sum of many independent theories. This is called "amortization of theoretical constructs" (p. 22) and is one of Newell's main arguments for why psychologists ought to adopt his unified theory paradigm for research. However, such a unification can be politically difficult to pull off when different subdisciplines of a field are already organized by the parsimony of their own subtheories.

Fifth, we might be able to choose between alternatives on the basis of ergonomics. We can ask the question of programmability. How easy is it to extend a theory by programming? How much work is it for humans to understand what a system is doing? The Turing Machine model "lost" to the stored program machine due to the difficulty of programming in quintuples. Systems which use explicit rules rather than implicit knowledge-as-code are certainly easier to understand and debug, but may yield no more explanatory power.

However, unless the constraints specifically strip away the universality, such that the cognitive theory becomes *an application of* rather than *an extension to* the programming language, the problem of theoretical under-constraint remains. Following Newell's basic argument, one could embark on a project of extensively crafting a set of cognitive models in any programming language, say C++, matching psychological regularities, and reusing subroutines as much as possible, and the resultant theory would be as predictive as Soar:

> Soar does not automatically provide an explanation for anything just because it is a universal computational engine. There are two aspects to this assertion. First from the perspective of cognitive theory, Soar has to be universal, because humans themselves are universal. To put this the right way around—Soar is a universal computational architecture; therefore it predicts that the human cognitive architecture is likewise universal. (p. 248)

Thus, just as the Wright brothers discovered different lift behaviors in differently shaped airfoils, cognitive modelers will find different behavioral effects from different universal language architectures. The principle of the airfoil was around for hundreds of years, and yet the key to mechanical flight did not lie in optimizing lift. Using a UPL which optimizes "cognitive lift" is not enough either, as practical issues of scale and control will still assert themselves.

3.2. Scaling laws

> Our first interest [in the problem of flight] began when we were children. Father brought home to us a small toy actuated by a rubber [band] which would lift itself into the air. We built a number of copies of this toy, which flew successfully, but when we undertook to build a toy on a much larger scale it failed to work so well. (Wright [25, p. 11])

The youthful engineers did not know that doubling the size of a model would require eight times as much power. This is the common feeling of every novice computer programmer hitting a polynomial or exponential scaling problem with an algorithm. But there were many other scaling problems which were uncovered during the Wrights' mature R&D effort, beyond mere engine size:

> We discovered in 1901 that tables of air pressures prepared by our predecessors were not accurate or dependable. (Wright [25, p. 55])

> We saw that the calculations upon which all flying-machines had been based were unreliable, and that all were simply groping in the dark. Having set out with absolute faith in the existing scientific data, we were driven to doubt one thing after another .... Truth and error were everywhere so intimately mixed as to be indistinguishable. (Wright [25, p. 84])

Thus it is not unheard of for estimates of scaling before the fact to be way off, especially the first time through based upon incomplete scientific understanding of the important variables. Estimates of memory size [12,13] for example, or the performance capacity of a brain [15,24] may be way off, depending on whether memory is "stored" in neurons, synapses, or in modes of behaviors of those units. So the number of psychological regularities we need to account for in a UTC may be off:

> Thus we arrive at about a third of a hundred regularities about [typing] alone. Any candidate architecture must deal with most of these if it's going to explain typing .... Of course there is no reason to focus on typing. It is just one of a hundred specialized areas of cognitive behavior. It takes only a hundred areas at thirty regularities per area to reach the ~~3000 total regularities cited at the beginning of this chapter .... Any architecture, especially a candidate for a unified theory of cognition, must deal with them all—hence with thousands of regularities. (p. 243)

There is a serious question about whether thousands of regularities are enough, and Newell recognizes this:

> In my view its it time to get going on producing unified theories of cognition—before the data base doubles again and the number of visible clashes increases by the square or cube. (p. 25)

While Newell estimates 3000 regularities, my estimate is that the number of regularities is unbounded. The "psychological data" industry is a generative system, linked to the fecundity of human culture, which Newell also writes about lucidly:

> What would impress [The Martian Biologist] most is the efflorescence of adaptation. Humans appear to go around simply creating opportunities of all kinds to build different response functions. Look at the variety of jobs in the world. Each one has humans using different kinds of response functions. Humans invent games. They no sooner invent one game than they invent new ones. They not only invent card games, but they collect them in a book and publish them .... Humans do not only eat, as do all other animals, they prepare their food ... inventing [hundreds and thousands of] recipes. (p. 114)

Every time human industry pops forth with a new tool or artifact, like written language, the bicycle, the typewriter, Rubik's cube, or rollerblades, another 30 regularities will pop out, especially if there is a cost justification to do the psychological studies, as clearly was the case for typing and for reading. This is not a good situation, especially if programmers have to be involved for each new domain. There will be a never-ending software battle just to keep up:

> Mostly, then, the theorist will load into Soar a program (a collection of productions organized into problem spaces) of his or her own devising...The obligation is on the theorist to cope with the flexibility of human behavior in responsible ways. (Newell, p. 249)

If the road to unified cognition is through very large software efforts, such as Soar, then we need to focus on scalable control laws for software.

3.3. Control in high winds

Although we might initially focus on the scaling of static elements like wing span and engine power, *to duplicate the success of mechanical flight, we should focus more on the scaling of control.* For the principal contribution of the Wright brothers was not the propulsive engine, which had its own economic logic (like the computer), nor the airfoil, a universal device they merely tuned through experiments, but their insight about how to control a glider when scaled up enough to carry an operator:

> Lilienthal had been killed through his inability to properly balance his machine in the air. Pilcher, an English experimenter had met with a like fate. We found that both experimenters had attempted to maintain balance merely by the shifting of the weight of their bodies. Chanute and all the experimenters before 1900, used this same method of maintaining the equilibrium in gliding flight. We at once set to work to devise a more efficient means of maintaining the equilibrium .... It was apparent that the [left and right] wings of a machine of the Chanute double-deck type, with the fore-and-aft trussing removed, could be warped ... in flying ... so as to present their surfaces to the air at different angles of incidences and thus secure unequal lifts .... (Wright [25, p. 12])

What they devised, and were granted a monopoly on, was the *Aileron principle*, the general method of maintaining dynamical equilibrium in a glider by modifying the shapes of the individual wings, using cables, to provide different amounts of lift to each side. (It is not surprising that the Wright brothers were bicycle engineers, as this control principle is the same one used to control two wheeled vehicles—iterated over-correction towards the center.)

Translating back through our analogy, extending a generally intelligent system for a new application by human intervention in the form of programming is "seat of the pants" control, the same method that Lilienthal applied to maintaining equilibrium by shifting the weight of his body.

Just as the source of difficulty for mechanical flight was that scaling the airfoil large enough to carry a human overwhelmed that human's ability to maintain stability, the source of difficulty in the software engineering approach to unified cognition is that scaling software large enough to explain cognition overwhelms the programming teams' ability to maintain stability.

It is well known that there are limiting factors to software engineering [5], and these limits could be orders of magnitude below the number of "lines of code" necessary to account for thousands of psychological regularities or to achieve a "general intelligence". Since software engineers haven't figured out how to build and maintain programs bigger than 10–100 million lines of code, why should people in AI presume that it can be done as a matter of course? [7].

What is missing is some control principle for maintaining dynamical coherence of an ever-growing piece of software in the face of powerful winds of change. While I don't pretend to have the key to resolving the software engineering crisis, I believe its solution may rest with building systems from the bottom up using robust and stable cooperatives of goal-driven modules locked into long-term prisoner's dilemmas [2], instead of through the centralized planning of top-down design. The order of acquisition of stable behaviors can be very important to the solution of hard problems.

3.4. On the irrelevancy of flapping

> Learning the secret of flight from a bird was a good deal like learning the secret of magic from a magician. After you know the trick and know what to look for, you see things that you did not notice when you did not know exactly what to look for. (Wright (attributed) [25, p. 5])

When you look at a bird flying, the first thing you see is all the flapping. Does the flapping explain how the bird flies? Is it reasonable to theorize that flapping came first, as some sort of cooling system which was recruited when flying became a necessity for survival? Not really, for a simpler explanation is that most of the problem of flying is in finding a place within the weight/size dimension where gliding is possible, and getting the control system for dynamical equilibrium right. Flapping is the last piece, the propulsive engine, but in all its furiousness, it blocks our perception that the bird first evolved the aileron principle. When the Wrights figured it out, they saw it quite clearly in a hovering bird.

Similarly, when you look at cognition, the first thing you see is the culture and the institutions of society, human language, problem solving, and political skills. Just like flapping, symbolic thought is the last piece, the engine of social selection, but in all its furiousness it obscures our perception of cognition as an exquisite control system competing for survival while governing a very complicated real-time physical system.

Once you get a flapping object, it becomes nearly impossible to hold it still enough to retrofit the control system for equilibrium. Studying problem solving and decision making first because they happen to be the first thing on the list (p. 16) is dangerous, because perception and motor control may be nearly impossible to retrofit into the design.

This retrofit question permits a dissection of the "biological correctness" issue which has confounded the relationship between AI and connectionism. The naive form, which applied to work in computational neuroscience but not to AI, is "ontogenetic correctness", the goal of constructing one's model with as much neural realism as possible. The much deeper form, which could be a principle someday, is "phylogenetic correctness", building a model which could have evolved bottom up, without large amounts of arbitrary top-down design. Phylogenetically correct systems acquire their behaviors in a bottom-up order that could, theoretically, recapitulate evolution or be "reconverged" upon by artificial evolution. Thus, while the airplane does not flap or have feathers, the Wrights' success certainly involved "recapitulation" of the phylogenetic order of the biological invention of flight: the airfoil, dynamical balance, and then propulsion.

4. Physical law versus software law

By restricting ourselves to software theories only, cognitive scientists might be expending energy on mental ornithopters. We spin software and logic webs endlessly, forgetting every day that there is no essential difference between Fortran programs and LISP programs, between sequential programs and production systems, or ultimately, between logics and grammars. All such theories rely on "software law" rather than the natural law of how mechanisms behave in the universe.

Software laws, such as rules of predicate logic, may or may not have existed before humans dreamed them up. And they may or may not have been "implemented" by minds or by evolution. What is clear is that such laws can be created *ad infinitum*, and then simulated and tested on our physical symbol systems: The computer simulation is the sole guaranteed realm of their existence.

An alternative form of unification research would be to *unify cognition with nature*. In other words, to be able to use the same kind of natural laws to explain the complexity of form and behavior in cognition, the complexity of form and behavior in biology, and the complexity of form and behavior in inanimate mechanisms.

I realize this is not currently a widely shared goal, but by applying Occam's razor to "behaving systems" on all time scales (p. 152) why not use the ordinary equations of physical systems to describe and explain the complexity and control of all behavior? In an illuminating passage, Newell discusses control theory:

> To speak of the mind as a controller suggests immediately the language of control systems—of feedback, gain, oscillation, damping, and so on. It is a language that allows us to describe systems as purposive. But we are interested in the full range of human behavior, not only walking down a road or tracking a flying bird, but reading bird books, planning the walk, taking instruction to get to the place, identifying distinct species, counting the new

additions to the life list of birds seen, and holding conversations about it all afterward. When the scope of behavior extends this broadly, it becomes evident that the language of control systems is really locked to a specific environment and class of tasks—to continuous motor movement with the aim of pointing or following. For the rest it becomes metaphorical. (p. 45)

I think Newell has it backwards. It is the language of symbol manipulation which is locked to a specific environment of human language and deliberative problem solving. Knowledge level explanations only metaphorically apply to complex control systems such as insect and animal behavior [4,6], systems of the body such as the immune or circulatory systems, the genetic control of fetal development, the evolutionary control of populations of species, cooperative control in social systems, or even the autopoetic control system for maintaining the planet. Certainly these systems are large and complex and have some means of self-control while allowing extreme creativity of behavior, but the other sciences do not consider them as instances of universal computing systems running software laws, divorced from the physical reality of their existence!

We have been led up the garden path of theories expressed in rules and representations because simple mathematical models, using ordinary differential equations, neural networks, feedback control systems, stochastic processes, etc. have for the most part been unable to describe or explain the generativity of structured behavior with unbounded dependencies, especially with respect to language [8]. This gulf between what is needed for the explanation of animal and human cognitive behavior and what is offered by ordinary scientific theories is really quite an anomaly and indicates that our understanding of the principles governing what goes on in the head have been very incomplete.

But where might governing principles for cognition come from besides computation? The alternative approach I have been following over the past several years has emerged from a simple goal to develop neural network computational theories which gracefully admit the generative and representational competance of symbolic models. This approach has resulted in two models [18,19] with novel and interesting behaviors. In each of these cases, when pressed to the point of providing the same theoretical capacity as a formal symbol system, I was forced to interpret these connectionist networks from a new point of view, involving fractals and chaos—a dynamical view of cognition, more extreme than that proposed by Smolensky [23]. I have thus been lead to a very different theoretical basis for understanding cognition, which I will call the "Dynamical Cognition Hypothesis", that:

The recursive representational and generative capacities required for cognition arise directly out of the complex behavior of nonlinear dynamical systems.

In other words, neural networks are merely the biological implementation level for a computation theory not based upon symbol manipulation, but upon complex and fluid patterns of physical state. A survey of cognitive models based upon nonlinear dynamics is beyond this review [20], however, I can briefly point to certain results which will play an important role in this alternative unification effort.

Research in nonlinear systems theory over the past few decades has developed an alternative explanation for the growth and control of complexity [11]. Hidden within the concept of deterministic "chaotic" systems which are extremely sensitive to small changes in parameters is the surprise that precise tuning of these parameters can lead to the generation of structures of enormous apparent complexity, such as the famous Mandelbrot set [14].

There is a clear link between simple fractals, like Cantor dust, and rewriting systems ("remove the middle third of each line segment"), and Barnsley has shown how such recursive structures can be found in the limit behavior of very simple dynamical systems [3]. The very notion of a system having a "fractional dimension" is in fact the recognition that its apparent complexity is governed by a "power law" [22].

The equations of motion of nonlinear systems are not different in kind from those of simpler physical systems, but the evoked behavior can be very complicated, to the point of appearing completely random. Even so, there are "universal" laws which govern these systems at all scales, involving where and when phase transitions occur and how systems change from simple to complex modes, passing through "critical" states, which admit long-distance dependencies between components.

The logistic map $x_{t+1} = kx_t(1 - x_t)$ is a well-studied example of a simple function iterated over the unit line where changes in k (between 0 and 4) lead to wildly different behaviors, including convergence, oscillation, and chaos. In a fundamental result, Crutchfield and Young have exhaustively analyzed sequences of most significant bits generated by this map[2] and have shown that at critical values of k, such as 3.5699, these bit sequences have unbounded dependencies, and are not describable by a regular grammar, but by an indexed context-free grammar [9].

Without knowing where complex behavior comes from, in the logistic map, in critically tuned collections of neural oscillators, or in the Mandelbrot set, one could certainly postulate a very large rule-based software system,

---

[2]They analyzed the bit string $y_t = floor(0.5 + x_t)$.

operating omnipotently behind the scenes, like a deity whose hand governs the fate of every particle in the universe.

5. Conclusion

I want to conclude this review with a reminder to the reader to keep in mind the "altitude" of my criticism, which is about the research methodology Newell is proposing based upon the status quo of myths in AI, and not about the detailed contents of the book. These are mature and illuminated writings, and Newell does an excellent job of setting his work and goals into perspective and recognizing the limitations of his theory, especially with respect to the puzzles of development and language.

Despite my disagreement with Newell's direction, I was educated and challenged by the book, and endorse it as an elevator for the mind of all students of cognition. But still, I would warn the aspiring cognitive scientist not to climb aboard any massive software engineering efforts, expecting to fly:

> You take your seat at the center of the machine beside the operator. He slips the cable, and you shoot forward .... The operator moves the front rudder and the machine lifts from the rail like a kite supported by the pressure of the air underneath it. The ground is first a blur, but as you rise the objects become clearer. At a height of 100 feet you feel hardly any motion at all, except for the wind which strikes your face. If you did not take the precaution to fasten your hat before starting, you have probably lost it by this time .... (Wright, [25, p. 86])

References

[1] P. Armer, Attitudes towards artificial intelligence, in: E.A. Feigenbaum and J.A. Feldman, eds., *Computers and Thought* (McGraw Hill, New York, 1963) 389–405.

[2] R. Axelrod, *The Evolution of Cooperation* (Basic Books, New York, 1984).

[3] M.F. Barnsley, *Fractals Everywhere* (Academic Press, San Diego, CA, 1988).

[4] R. Beer, *Intelligence as Adaptive Behavior: An Experiment in Computational Neuroethology* (Academic Press, New York, 1990).

[5] F.P. Brooks, *The Mythical Man-Month* (Addison-Wesley, Reading, MA, 1975).

[6] R. Brooks, Intelligence without representation, *Artif. Intell.* **47** (1–3) (1991) 139–160.

[7] C. Cherniak, Undebuggability and cognitive science, *Commun. ACM* **31** (4) (1988) 402–412.

[8] N. Chomsky, *Syntactic Structures* (Mouton, The Hague, Netherlands, 1957).

[9] J.P. Crutchfield and K. Young, Computation at the onset of chaos, in: W. Zurek, ed., *Complexity, Entropy and the Physics of Information* (Addison-Wesley, Reading, MA, 1989).

[10] J.J. Gibson, *The Ecological Approach to Visual Perception* (Houghton-Mifflin, Boston, MA).

[11] J. Gleick, *Chaos: Making a New Science* (Viking, New York, 1987).

[12] W.D. Hillis, Intelligence as emergent behavior; or, the songs of eden, *Daedelus* **117** (1988) 175–190.

[13] T.K. Landauer, How much do people remember? Some estimates on the quantity of learned information in long-term memory, *Cogn. Sci.* **10** (1986) 477–494.

[14] B. Mandelbrot, *The Fractal Geometry of Nature* (Freeman, San Francisco, CA, 1982).

[15] H. Moravec, *Mind Children* (Harvard University Press, Cambridge, MA, 1988).

[16] A. Newell, The knowledge level, *Artif. Intell.* **18** (1982) 87–127.

[17] A. Newell and H.A. Simon, Computer science as empirical inquiry: symbols and search, *Comm. ACM* **19** (3) (1976) 113–126.

[18] J.B. Pollack, Recursive distributed representation, *Artif. Intell.* **46** (1990) 77–105.

[19] J.B. Pollack, The induction of dynamical recognizers, *Mach. Learn.* **7** (1991) 227–252.

[20] R. Port and T. Van Gelder, Mind as motion (in preparation).

[21] D.E. Rumelhart, J.L. McClelland and the PDP Research Group, eds., *Parallel Distributed Processing: Experiments in the Microstructure of Cognition* (MIT Press, Cambridge, MA, 1986).

[22] M. Schroeder, *Fractals, Chaos, Power Laws* (Freeman, New York, 1991).

[23] P. Smolensky, Information processing in dynamical systems: foundations of harmony theory, in: D.E. Rumelhart, J.L. McClelland and the PDP Research Group, eds., *Parallel Distributed Processing: Experiments in the Microstructure of Cognition*, Vol. 1 (MIT Press, Cambridge, MA, 1986) 194–281.

[24] J. Von Neumann, *The Computer and the Brain* (Yale University Press, New Haven, CT, 1958).

[25] O. Wright, *How we Invented the Airplane* (Dover, New York, 1988).

Artificial Intelligence 59 (1993) 371–373
Elsevier

ARTINT 1015

Brain or mind?
A review of Allen Newell's
Unified Theories of Cognition *

Dale Purves

*Department of Neurobiology, Duke University Medical Center, Box 3209, Durham,
NC 27710, USA*

Received August 1991
Revised September 1992

Cognitive sciences, as defined by its practitioners, seeks to understand a variety of "higher" brain functions, examples of which are thinking, memory, perception, and language. The purpose of Newell's book, based on the William James Lectures he delivered at Harvard in 1987, is to bring together the various aspects of this complex field under the intellectual scepter of a single theory. Not surprisingly, Newell finds the unifying catalyst to be his own Soar program developed over the last three decades. Soar is a computer architecture for artificial intelligence that has been the object of considerable interest (and some controversy) among those interested in AI (see Waldrop [2,3]). Newell argues that the entire spectrum of cognitive functions is subsumed in—and can be explained by—this architecture.

Whatever the value of Newell's program to those interested in artificial intelligence, neurobiologists—that is, reductionists who take it as axiomatic that cognition must be understood in terms of the brain and its component parts—will find this book wanting. The tenor of the discourse is foreshadowed on page 17 of the Introduction where Newell states that his aim is to understand cognition in the context of *mind*, rather than *brain*. Indeed,

---

Correspondence to: D. Purves, Department of Neurobiology, Duke University Medical Center, Box 3209, Durham, NC 27710, USA. Telephone: (919) 684-6122.
* (Harvard University Press, Cambridge, MA, 1990); xiv + 549 pages.

there is no entry in the index of this nearly-five-hundred page book of the word "brain", a surprising omission in a decade dedicated to this singular organ. Newell does pay some attention to the neurobiology of cognition, but this is scant; only a few pages in the middle of the book are devoted to nerve cells, neural circuits, and their role in cognition. The biological part of Newell's argument rests on two facts: that the generation of an action potential takes about a millisecond, and that the conduction of impulses along nerve fibers is quite slow (p. 124). According to Newell, the time consumed by the generation of an action potential, plus the conduction time within local circuits (more milliseconds), allow only about a hundred steps in a minimal cognitive event (which empirically requires about a second). This temporal restriction is considered of basic importance in Soar's design and its relevance to human cognition. "There is no way to put a collection of neurons together", says Newell, "and get them to operate in the $\sim\sim 1$ msec range" (p. 127). For Newell, the "neuron is a statistical engine in which nothing occurs with precise timing" (p. 128).

Although Newell's reasoning is logical enough, the brain has developed strategies that allow it to calculate faster and more precisely than he imagines. A good example is found in the auditory system. Many animals, including man, accurately localize sound in space. This feat is based on the ability of the brain to detect differences in the time of arrival and intensity of a sound at the two ears. Given the velocity of sound (340 m/sec) and the width of the head (about 25 cm), the differences that can be resolved are on the order of tens of microseconds. How the brain can make such precise temporal analyses was suggested in principle, ironically enough, by a cognitive psychologist about forty years ago (Jeffress [1]). Recent studies in cats, owls, and chickens have provided good evidence that Jeffress' hypothesis of how neurons compute tiny differences in binaural sounds with high precision is correct. Evidently, the brain can encode cognitive information with a temporal efficiency that transcends the limitations of its elements. To his credit, Newell does deduce that human cognition must involve a computational system that is "massively parallel", but this conclusion was reached by neurobiologists years ago based on brain structure and function.

From the perspective of a neuroscientist, the basic problem in this book is its consistent failure to deal with the essence of cognition, that is, the brain and what is presently known about it. Achieving (and maintaining) literacy in neuroscience is, to be sure, a daunting prospect for the cognitive scientist (or anyone else). This dilemma has been made more profound by the explosion of information about the brain in the last 25 years. Nonetheless, there is a corpus of principles and important facts about brain structure, function and development that can be assimilated by anyone determined to make the effort.

This criticism of Newell's book should not be taken to mean that neuroscience has no place for those disposed to consider cognition in terms of strategies, goals, and algorithms. Quite the contrary. But ignoring the machinery in which these abstractions must be embedded is no longer an option. Reading Newell's book brings an analogy to mind—a distant race of intelligent beings limited to observing automobiles on the surface of the earth by some primitive telemetry. Having no means to appreciate cars and their purposes other than observation from afar, their speculation would be wide-ranging (and legitimate). If, however, such aliens developed a spacecraft and retrieved a 1973 Dodge, they would no doubt hasten to get inside it, take it apart, and see what, in fact, a car is all about. The opinions of Newell and others who continue to speculate about cognition without considering the wealth of relevant information about the brain now available will not generate much interest outside of their own circle. After reading this book, one can only exhort Newell and any like-minded colleagues to put on their overalls, open the hood, and take a look.

References

[1] L.A. Jeffress, A place theory of sound localization, *J. Comput. Physiol. Psychol.* **41** (1948) 35–39.
[2] M.M. Waldrop, Toward a unified theory of cognition, *Science* **241** (1988) 27–30.
[3] M.M. Waldrop, Soar: a unified theory of cognition?, *Science* **241** (1988) 296–298.

Artificial Intelligence 59 (1993) 375–388
Elsevier

ARTINT 1016

Issues for psychology, AI, and education: a review of Newell's *Unified Theories of Cognition* *

Roger C. Schank and Menachem Y. Jona

*The Institute for the Learning Sciences, Northwestern University, Evanston, IL 60201,
USA*

Received August 1991
Revised September 1992

1. Introduction

With *Unified Theories of Cognition,* Newell has presented us with ideas developed over a twenty-year period. The book touches on so much of both psychology and AI that it provides an opportunity to discuss some important problems currently facing both fields. In fact, it is specifically because it covers so much ground that many real problems that are ignored, overlooked, or simply never discovered in less ambitious bodies of work come to the fore and demand to be addressed.

Newell has had a strong influence on our views of both psychology and AI. As AI researchers, we share many of the same opinions about the field of psychology. Our views on AI, however, while initially quite similar, have diverged. Despite this divergence, we still concur on many points and, as one would expect, people with similar viewpoints tend to find themselves disagreeing on small matters. It is important that this type of disagreement not be mistaken for acrimony, however.

Correspondence to: R.C. Schank, The Institute for the Learning Sciences, Northwestern University, Evanston, IL 60201, USA. E-mail: schank@ils.nwu.edu.
* (Harvard University Press, Cambridge, MA, 1990); xvi+549 pages.

Unified Theories of Cognition raises interesting issues about three fields, psychology, AI, and education, the first two being fields close to Newell's heart and the third being a field close to ours. The structure of this review is organized around the issues raised for each of these fields.

In preview, we find ourselves in agreement with his criticisms of psychology's methodology, particularly his opposition to the obsession with falsifiability. We also agree with him on the importance of studying natural tasks, but feel that he has sometimes violated his own principle and used an unnatural task as a basis for constructing his theory.

In terms of AI, we also find ourselves in agreement with Newell on fundamental issues such as the importance and nature of learning. Yet there are a number of areas of disagreement as well. The work on Soar fails to provide what, in our opinion, is a realistic model of memory organization and access, and nearly completely ignores the importance of knowledge. Finally, while providing lip-service to the necessity of building non-brittle systems, Soar does not address the issue of scale-up in a satisfactory way.

While the book has little to say explicitly about education, there are some elements of it that are implicitly relevant and that raise important issues pertaining to education. In particular, the applicability of a unified theory of cognition, such as the one proposed in the book, should not end at the borders of the research labs of psychology and AI. Rather, it should also be put to practical use by informing the educational system. Researchers in cognitive science need to realize that, by virtue of their work, they have a role to play in educational reform.

2. On psychology

If one could take away only one thing from reading the book, it should be Newell's criticisms of the field of psychology. It is on this point that we are in strongest agreement. Psychology, perhaps in a quest for legitimacy, adopted the "physics model" of science, an obsession with theory falsifiability and an attraction to studying phenomena describable in mathematically rigorous ways. AI too, in spasms of angst over its scientific legitimacy compared to the "hard sciences", is now becoming threatened by this trend. But psychology, the older of the two fields, has been the more affected.

2.1. Psychology's malediction: a crippling methodology

Sadly enough, as Newell himself notes, many of the points he makes about the state of psychology in this book, he made nearly twenty years ago in his "twenty questions" paper [13]. We can only hope that this time someone will listen. In that paper, reflecting on the state of psychological theories at the time, he argued for three methodological changes that are as needed today in the field of psychology as they were then. We repeat them here because of their importance. They are:

- Psychology should construct complete processing models.
- Psychology should take particular tasks and analyze all the psychological phenomena involved in them.
- Psychology should apply a model of a single phenomenon to diverse situations where that phenomenon arises.

Newell has taken these three principles to heart and they have evolved into the main theses of the book, specifically that psychology is ready for unified theories of cognition and that it is scientifically worthwhile to attempt to formulate such unified theories. Following from the above principles, a unified theory of cognition is defined as one that, with a single system of mechanisms, can account for significantly more phenomena than previous theories have.

The research goal here is straightforward. The theory needs to have sufficient scope so that it will be possible to bring to bear a large number of constraints on the shape of the overall theory. This is a very important lesson that AI can provide psychology. By focusing on small, well-defined, and easily testable tasks, psychology has painted itself into a methodological corner. It has expended so much effort in pursuit of clean results, whittling away cognitive tasks until they bear little or no resemblance to anything real, that the important constraints imposed on any plausible theory of cognitive architecture have been lost. AI, having not yet succumbed to the restrictive methodology of the "physics model" of science, has used the power of bringing many diverse constraints to bear to be, in our opinion, much more successful in generating interesting theories of cognition and cognitive architectures.

That psychology is too limited by its own methods is one of the important points of the book. Newell points this out quite explicitly. He argues, and we agree, that psychological theorizing is too discriminating and should be more approximating instead. He also rejects the traditional approach that, as he puts it, "falsifiability is next to godliness" (p. 23). If psychology is to begin to contribute seriously to theories of cognition, it must throw off the methodological shackles that it has placed on itself. To do this, along with Newell's suggestions, it must begin to look at larger, more realistic tasks so that it can bring to bear the constraints that this approach provides.

2.2. The importance of studying realistic cognitive tasks: a case study

Despite Newell's criticisms of psychology's methodologies, he nevertheless goes on to use Soar to explain the results of several experiments that studied unrealistic cognitive tasks. This is a bad idea for at least two reasons. First, AI programs should worry more about examining phenomena that can't be studied in psychology, that is, until psychology's methodology can be changed so that interesting things can be studied. Second, the danger of studying artificial tasks as a basis for cognitive theories is as real in AI as it is in psychology.

What do we mean when we say that AI programs should worry more about examining phenomena that can't be studied in psychology? Newell's position to the contrary, we believe that it is a mistake to attempt to fit an AI program to data gathered from unrealistic and unnatural tasks.[1] It is very debatable whether fitting an AI program to data gathered from an unrealistic, unnatural task helps to build a system that will perform well in a realistic, natural task. Furthermore, advising this as a methodology not only serves to distract research attention from more profitable areas, but also invites the danger of reducing AI models to curve-fitting. AI researchers should not limit the topics they choose to study because of the overly restrictive methodology that another field has chosen to constrain itself with, nor should they try to make their programs conform to data that has been compromised by those same methodological constraints.

A good example of the danger of studying artificial tasks as a basis for cognitive theories and its unfortunate results is the use of the cryptarithmetic task described in Chapter 7. The cryptarithmetic task is used as evidence that people search problem spaces when solving problems. Of course, given the task, what else is there to do but search and backtrack through a space of possible solutions? One can easily imagine how the choice of this unnatural task shaped the early formulations of Soar in such a way that the notions of search and problem spaces became the cornerstones of the Soar architecture. What would have the theory looked like if the task chosen had been more naturalistic, for example, summarizing a newspaper article or explaining why the U.S. should or shouldn't have got involved in the Persian Gulf war? Here is a clear case of Newell falling into the same trap that has plagued psychological theorizing for so long: a bad choice of task leading to a bad choice of theory.

Lest we come across as being too critical of psychology, let us look at an example of the value of psychological studies when they are grounded in an overarching theory and when the task chosen to study is a reasonably natural one. Schank and Abelson [21] developed a theory of memory structures and processing based on the notion of a script. This theory proved not only quite popular, but also quite fruitful as it led to the development of many

---

[1]This is not to say that it is unprofitable to study human performance on a particular task when building an AI program to do that task. Rather, we are focusing on data at the level of, for example, reaction time.

interesting computer models of natural language parsing and understanding (DeJong [4,5], Schank and Riesbeck [23]).

As development continued on these models, problems with script theory began to emerge (see Schank [18], for a discussion). What really put the nail in the coffin, so to speak, and forced a radical rethinking of the theory was a study by Bower, Black and Turner [3]. In that study, subjects confused events from stories about visits to doctor and dentist offices in a way that could not be accounted for by script theory. This forced a reformulation of script theory that eventually became the theory of dynamic memory detailed by Schank [18]. The two points of this case study are first, the importance of grounding empirical studies in sound theory and second, that studying natural tasks like story understanding and recall, as opposed to artificial ones like cryptarithmetic, is the best way to insure having a sound theory to start with.

3. On AI

While Newell's arguments about the state of psychology in general, and psychological theorizing in particular, explicitly point out the problems with the field of psychology and the need for a (more) unified theory of cognition, his exemplar of one such unified theory, Soar, implicitly illustrates several important issues about AI. In fact, the scope of the work forces us to examine what AI is really about and whether and how Soar deals with the important issues.

3.1. What is AI?

To understand the value of *Unified Theories of Cognition's* contribution from the perspective of AI, we need to think about what AI is about. For the purpose of the present discussion, we can categorize AI as being primarily concerned with four things:[2]

- AI is learning.
- AI is memory organization and access.
- AI is functional constraints + knowledge analysis.
- AI is scale-up.

We have always believed that to build an intelligent system, one must build a system that learns. Intelligence means adapting to the environment and improving performance over time. Thus, if the goal of AI is to build intelligent systems, one of the things that AI has to be about is the study

---

[2]There are obviously other ways one might carve up the field as well.

of learning. The second thing that AI is about is memory organization and access. How a system gains access to its knowledge, and how it organizes its memory to facilitate that access, provide fundamental functional constraints on the nature of cognitive architectures. This brings us to the third thing that AI is about and the thing that sets it apart from other fields. The discovery and application of functional constraints imposed on cognitive processing and the analysis of the knowledge used in that processing form the bread-and-butter of AI research. Psychology's tools are experiments and t-tests and AI's are functional constraints and knowledge analysis.

The final thing that AI is about is scale-up. What does scale-up mean? An intelligent system that can only behave intelligently in two or three carefully selected situations is not really intelligent. AI is about building systems that can handle hundreds or even thousands of examples, not just two or three. The process of scaling up a system from handling two or three examples to handling hundreds provides so many functional constraints on the nature of the system that without it one has to be skeptical of the system's architecture and its ability to really perform the task it was designed to do.

How does Soar address these four aspects of AI? What lessons does the Soar project have for us as AI researchers?

3.2. The fundamental nature of learning

One of the points on which we find ourselves in strong agreement with Newell and his work on Soar is on the importance of learning and memory in cognition. As he puts it, "The ubiquity of learning is clearly a phenomenon that characterizes human behavior, and one that a unified theory of cognition should explain" (p. 313). This echoes the arguments about the fundamental importance of learning that we have been making for years, starting with the work on dynamic memory [18]. Real AI entails building systems that learn [20]. We would not consider a human who failed to learn from experience very intelligent and any AI system that has any hope of being "intelligent" that doesn't learn from its experiences and interactions is doomed to failure as an intelligent system. The integration of learning with every phase of cognitive processing is one of the most important lessons AI researchers can take from Soar.

There are two other points about learning made by Soar that we feel strongly about as well. The first is that chunking, the mechanism of learning in Soar, is impasse-driven. That is, chunking, or learning, occurs when there is a failure of some sort. Another way of putting this is that learning is failure-driven [18]. While we may disagree with some of the particulars of how learning takes place in Soar, we share the belief that nearly all learning is prompted by failures in processing. People have all sorts of expectations about what will happen next, and these expectations are continuously being violated. When an expectation fails, we are curious about why it failed, and we try to construct an explanation for why it did [18,22]. If we encounter a situation where none of our expectations are violated, we are often bored and tend not to learn much. It is primarily when our expectations fail, and trigger the construction of an explanation, that learning takes place. The importance of learning being driven by processing failures is that the system can be more efficient by allowing it to focus its cognitive effort on only those areas that caused the failure and hence are in need of modification (see, e.g., Birnbaum, Collins, Freed and Krulwich [1], Hammond [7], Simmons [24] and Sussman [26]).

The second point of value that Soar points out about learning is that it is always goal-oriented. While it is possible for a system to "learn" without being oriented towards a particular goal (e.g., inductive category learning), that is not the way people learn in natural situations (see, e.g., Schank, Collins and Hunter [22]). This is an important point. Not only is learning goal-oriented, meaning that learning occurs in pursuit of a goal, but *what* is learned in a given situation can change dramatically depending on what goal or goals the learner has. Many cognitive theories fail to include goals in their descriptions of learning, and many psychology experiments are designed without regard for the goals the subject may have and how they influence cognitive processing. This is a big mistake and Soar's position on goal-oriented learning should be taken seriously.

3.3. Memory organization and access

Inseparable from the importance of learning, however, is the importance of memory organization and access [18]. Both of these form the cornerstone of any theory of cognition. Newell seems to concur, saying "learning and memory can not be separated from the rest of Soar" (p. 310). Yet while this statement may be true in a limited sense, Newell seems to ignore the important functional constraints that can be obtained from examining memory access and organization. How do we become reminded of X when we see Y? How do we organize the millions of items we have stored in memory and gain access to them at just the moment when we need them?

A good example of the constraints that arise from considering the issues surrounding memory organization and access and their effect on the development of cognitive processing theories is recent work by our colleagues on natural language understanding. Our work in this area has changed from being focused primarily on word-based expectation-driven parsing (see, e.g., Birnbaum and Selfridge [2], Riesbeck and Schank [15])—the technique implemented in Soar (Section 7.3)—to a new style of natural language understanding called Direct Memory Access Parsing (DMAP) (Martin [12], Riesbeck and Martin [16]). Why have we changed our tune? Because of the constraints that come from looking at how people understand natural language and how they use and organize their memory when doing so.

We were forced to move beyond straight word-based expectation-driven parsing because when we compared how our systems read stories and how people read them in real life we saw that there was a significant difference. For all practical purposes, the systems we built had no memory of having read a particular story. They could have read it repeatedly, doing the same work over and over and never get bored. This stands in strong contrast to how people operate. For example, if you read something in a newspaper that you have already seen, you quickly recognize this fact and skip to the next article. What this means is that, like all other experience, reading text alters the state of the understander's memory. DMAP operates in just this way, altering its memory structures each time it reads a new text, and recognizing when it is reading something it has seen before. On the other hand, despite the fact that Soar uses its memory to improve its reading performance by storing new chunks, it is not clear how or whether Soar would have any recollection of having read a story it had already seen.

How memory is altered, and how it is used to understand natural language has provided important constraints on the development of our theory of natural language understanding. Newell seems to concur in principle, asserting that Soar is a system in which "... the language mechanisms can be related to the mechanisms used for all other cognition and in which all these mechanisms mutually constrain each other" (p. 418). Yet, on closer analysis, the theory of language understanding described in the book suffers some serious shortcomings as an even moderately realistic model of how humans perform this task.[3] An important reason for this is the lack of attention to the constraints that arise when language understanding is integrated with a real model of memory. One of Soar's major weaknesses as an AI program, and as a candidate unified theory of cognition, is its lack of attention to memory organization and access. The functional constraints that can be derived from the careful consideration of how memory is used and organized are too important to ignore when building a theory of any type of cognitive process.

The dynamic nature of memory is a fundamental characteristic of an intelligent system [18]. Memory is constantly changing as a result of experience. This seems almost a truism, and if you believe in the ubiquity of learning as Newell does (and we do), it has to be. But having a dynamic memory means more than simply having a bigger list of productions after processing an experience than before, as is the case in Soar. It means, among other

---

[3]For example, the chunking mechanism used by Soar in the natural language processing task essentially caches inferences at the lexical level. This is really a zeroth-order theory of how memory is used when understanding language.

things, organizing and reorganizing the elements of memory so that they can be easily retrieved when they are needed to understand new experiences (see, e.g., Kolodner [11]).

Knowledge in Soar is atomized in productions, and learning means simply aggregating more of these atomic units. There is no notion that the elements of memory cohere in any real sense. To build larger concepts in memory, one must specify how the component concepts relate to each other, that is, how they are structured. The essence of the problem with Soar's model of memory, and a possible explanation for why knowledge in Soar is just aggregates of atomic productions, is that one can't talk about memory organization without also talking about memory contents. This leads us directly to our next point.

3.4. Architecture versus content

Earlier, we said that one of the things that AI is about is the analysis of knowledge. This is one of the most basic tools of AI research, and one that sets it apart from related disciplines. The reason we bring it up here is its glaring absence from the work on Soar. This is unfortunate in our view, because Soar could be used to make valuable contributions in this area. The analysis and careful description of the knowledge needed to get Soar to perform various tasks, if done in a systematic way, would be immensely valuable. It is puzzling, then, that most of the work described in the book seems to be dancing around the need to tackle the hard problem of knowledge analysis. This is especially surprising given that Newell's important "knowledge level" paper [14] was a central voice in arguing for the importance of knowledge.

Newell carves Soar up into two pieces, architecture and content, and asks the obvious question: "... What is embodied in the architecture and what is moved out into the content?" (p. 82). Unfortunately, he focuses on the former to the exclusion of the latter, despite asserting later that "... the architecture itself does not exhibit intelligence. It must be augmented with knowledge ..." (p. 216). This statement seems to reflect the view that, while the architecture is interesting, the factor that provides the bulk of intelligent behavior is the knowledge the system has and how it is used. What follows from this is that the important thing to study, if one wants to understand the nature of intelligence and build intelligent systems, is content not architecture. [4] Or, as Guha and Lenat [6] put it, "[a]lthough issues such as architecture are important, no powerful formalism can obviate the need for a lot of knowledge" (p. 33).

---

[4]See Hayes [8] for a more detailed argument about the importance of tackling the problem of knowledge analysis and representation.

Why does the Soar project seem to shy away from knowledge analysis and stick to the architecture instead? There are at least two answers. One possible answer is that the difficulty of doing a careful analysis of knowledge tends to lead away from unified theories and towards separate micro-theories. Doing knowledge analysis right is hard. Developing a deep content theory for even a single domain requires a great deal of effort. Doing a more superficial analysis is easier, but tends to yield content theories that appear too disparate to unify. Getting such a theory of one domain to interface with one in another domain usually requires radical revision of both theories. Thus, it is usually safer (for the longevity of the theories) to avoid attempts to unify content theories and they tend to get left as separate micro-theories.

One attempt to bite the bullet and face this problem head-on is, of course, the Cyc project (see, e.g., [6]). That project can be seen as both similar to and opposite of Soar. The two projects are similar in that they both are attempting to elucidate functional constraints by trying to do very large tasks. They are opposite in that Soar, as just mentioned, concerns itself primarily with architecture issues, while Cyc is addressing content issues. Both Soar and Cyc are ambitious, interesting projects; yet, because of our perspective on what is important in AI, given a choice of one or the other we would pick Cyc.

A second, and more likely, answer is that Soar has fallen prey to the same misconception that plagues expert system shells, what we call the "I'll build the architecture so all you have to do is put in the knowledge" fallacy. This view is just plain wrong. Knowledge is what determines the architecture. What power expert systems have comes not from their architecture, which is really fairly simple, but from the analysis, organization, and encoding of the important knowledge about a certain domain. The recent hype over connectionism is similar in that there exists a belief among many people both in and outside the field that it is possible to discover a general connectionist architecture, and all that will be required to get intelligent behavior from it will be to "put in the knowledge".

3.5. Why think? Preparation, deliberation, and case-based reasoning

Another facet of the architecture versus content dichotomy is reflected in what Newell calls the preparation and deliberation components of cognition. When facing a given problem, a system can either have a solution already prepared by retrieving and adapting one that worked before, or it can deliberate to find one. In Soar preparation means knowledge search and deliberation means problem search.

The relative contributions of preparation and deliberation to human cognition is another area that we disagree with Newell's work on Soar. Soar's emphasis is obviously on deliberation, or search, while our work (and others) on case-based reasoning (CBR) emphasizes the importance of preparation, that is, of retrieving and adapting old solutions (see, e.g., Hammond [7], Kass [10], Riesbeck and Schank [17], Slade [25], or Jona and Kolodner [9]) for an overview). Most people prefer not to have to think hard if they can help it. They will try to get by with whatever worked before, even if it is less than optimal. We believe that, roughly speaking, people's everyday cognition consists of about 90% retrieving of past solutions and only about 10% or less of actual novel problem solving. Because of our belief about the relative importance of retrieval, it follows that if one wants to understand what it takes to model human intelligence one should focus on the type of processing that contributes the most to people's everyday behavior, namely retrieval and adaptation of old solutions. Even Newell seems to admit that the locus of intelligence resides more with retrieval than it does with constructing a solution from scratch, saying that "... for a given system, with its fixed architecture, improvement comes from adding knowledge, not adding search volume" (p. 106).

This is not so much a right versus wrong issue but rather a focus of research attention issue. Studying processes that account for only a small proportion of human cognition is not wrong, but it makes more sense to focus one's effort where most of the action is, so to speak. In addition, thinking seriously about what it means to retrieve the most relevant past solutions from a very large memory when they are most needed to solve a new problem raises numerous interesting and difficult issues for how all those past solutions are organized and retrieved. For example, one of the most difficult issues that must be faced is how past solutions are labeled, or indexed. This problem is known to CBR researchers as the *indexing* problem (see, e.g., Jona and Kolodner [9] for an overview). It is not clear how Soar could be extended to handle the kinds of memory-intensive tasks typically studied in the CBR community, and especially, as we discuss next, how it could handle very large memories consisting of thousands or tens of thousands of items.

3.6. The scale-up problem

The touchstone of real AI systems is whether they can scale up to handle a large number (i.e., hundreds or thousands) of examples. Even Newell seems to concur on this point, at least in principle, saying that one goal of AI is to build "nonbrittle systems" (p. 231). He believes that Soar architecture will permit it to be scaled up, but unfortunately has not given us much evidence that this has even been attempted. He even admits this explicitly:

> Soar is structured to have a very large knowledge base. That is what the production system provides and the design is for Soar to have a large number of productions ($\sim\sim106$ or more). However,

none of the tasks explored with Soar has dealt with such large memory, so we can only project that Soar would behave plausibly under such conditions (p. 230).

This is a serious flaw, especially for a system aiming to be a large, general architecture for intelligence. The process of scaling up a system may fundamentally alter its architecture, in fact it seems almost certain that it will [8]. This is a lesson we have learned mostly from personal experience, however [20].

Even if we were to suspend disbelief at Soar's ability to scale up to a large memory size, the evidence presented in the book points directly against the likelihood of this happening. When Designer-Soar, a system that designs algorithms, was given two different algorithm design tasks, the transfer of learning from one task to the other was only 1% (p. 216). And this is for two tasks in exactly the same domain! What should we project from this in terms of scaling up to more general cross-contextual learning?

This points to another problem that is related to the issue of memory organization and access described above. The implicit claim made by Soar is that all the productions (knowledge) used in all the different tasks for which Soar has been programmed could all be eventually loaded into the system at one time producing a system that was somehow more than the sum of its parts (that is, it would produce some type of general intelligent behavior by transferring learning from one domain to another). The problem is that loading separate sets of productions into Soar at the same time does not produce a unified system any more than does loading many separate Lisp programs into core memory at once produce a unified program. In addition, what will happen to Soar's constraint of operating in real time when it has to search and match not 100 or 1000 productions, but 100,000 or 1 million? This is why facing the scale-up problem is essential. You can get away with too many insupportable assumptions if you don't.

4. On education

Newell devotes almost no attention at all to education in the book. This is at the same time both surprising and not surprising. It is not surprising because the focus of the book is on theories of cognition, not education. He certainly has enough to talk about trying to unify the field of psychology without trying to tie in education as well. Nonetheless, we strongly believe that a unified theory of cognition should bear some relation to education:

After all, both cognition and education are concerned with how people learn, and what we know about how people learn should inform how they are taught. Moreover, how people can be best taught will likely provide invaluable insights into the underlying cognitive processes of learning.

What Newell says explicitly about education, and what follows from it, is worth noting and thinking about. He says, "The notion of intelligence as a scientific construct defined entirely by a technology for creating tests is set in opposition to a notion of defining it by cognitive theories and experiment" (p. 89). If it is time for psychology to pursue unified theories of cognition, then it is also time for psychology, AI, and the rest of the cognitive sciences to realize that their work is really about the nature of intelligence. We may not have a full-blown, proven theory of all of cognition yet (although this book has started us down that road), but what we do know now about how people think, and how they learn, puts us in a much better position to define intelligence and what it takes to create it in both people and machines than those who are currently in the business of creating tests that measure, and therefore define, intelligence in our children.

Newell argues that it is time for psychologists to come out of their experimental laboratories and put their heads together to build more unified theories of cognition. That is a step in the right direction, but it does not go far enough. More importantly, it is time for all cognitive scientists to realize that, by virtue of their work on learning, memory, and cognition, they have a voice in the debate on education. Good theories of cognition have a practical and important role to play in restructuring the process of education. [5] The separation of the fields of education and cognitive science is both artificial and harmful. A unified theory of cognition must, now more than ever, be put into practical use as the cornerstone of the educational system.

Acknowledgement

The authors thank Jerry Faries, Gregg Collins, Chris Riesbeck, and especially Larry Birnbaum for their insights and comments during the preparation of this review. The Institute for the Learning Sciences was established in 1989 with the support of Andersen Consulting, part of The Arthur Andersen Worldwide Organization. The Institute receives additional support from Ameritech, an Institute Partner, and from IBM.

---

[5]Newell, in Section 8.5, discusses the need for a theory to have practical applications. What we are arguing for here could be restated in Newellæs terms by saying that restructuring the educational system is a useful and necessary practical application for good theories of cognition. In fact, we would argue that it is currently the most important possible application.

References

[1] L. Birnbaum, G. Collins, M. Freed and B. Krulwich, Model-based diagnosis of planning failures, in: *Proceedings AAAI-90*, Boston, MA (1990) 318–323.

[2] L. Birnbaum and M. Selfridge, Problems in conceptual analysis of natural language, Tech. Rept. No. 168, Computer Science Department, Yale University, New Haven, CT (1979).

[3] G.H. Bower, J.B. Black and T.J. Turner, Scripts in text comprehension and memory, *Cogn. Psychol.* **11** (1979) 177–220.

[4] G.F. DeJong, Skimming stories in real time: An experiment in integrated understanding, Ph.D. Dissertation, Yale University, New Haven, CT (1979).

[5] G.F. DeJong, An overview of the FRUMP system, in: W.G. Lehnert and M.H. Ringle, eds., *Strategies for Natural Language Processing* (Lawrence Erlbaum, Hillsdale, NJ, 1982) 149–176.

[6] R.V. Guha and D. Lenat, Cyc: a midterm report, *AI Mag.* **11** (3) (1990) 33–59.

[7] K.J. Hammond, *Case-Based Planning: Viewing Planning as a Memory Task* (Academic Press, Boston, MA, 1989).

[8] P.J. Hayes, The second naive physics manifesto, in: J.R. Hobbs and R. Moore, eds., *Formal Theories of the Commonsense World* (Ablex, Norwood, NJ, 1985) 1–36.

[9] M.Y. Jona and J.L. Kolodner, Case-based reasoning, in: S.C. Shapiro, ed., *Encyclopedia of Artificial Intelligence* (Wiley, New York, 2nd ed., 1992) 1265–1279.

[10] A.M. Kass, Developing creative hypothesis by adapting explanations, Ph.D. Dissertation, Computer Science Department, Yale University, New Haven, CT (1990).

[11] J.L. Kolodner, *Retrieval and Organization Strategies in Conceptual Memory: A Computer Model* (Lawrence Erlbaum, Hillsdale, NJ, 1984).

[12] C.E. Martin, Direct memory access parsing, Ph.D. Dissertation, Yale University, New Haven, CT (1990).

[13] A. Newell, You can't play twenty questions with nature and win: projective comments on the papers at this symposium, in: W.G. Chase, ed., *Visual Information Processing* (Academic Press, New York, 1973) 283–308.

[14] A. Newell, The knowledge level, *Artif. Intell.* **18** (1) (1982) 87–127.

[15] C. Riesbeck and R.C. Schank, Comprehension by computer: expectation-based analysis of sentences in context, in: W.J.M. Levelt and G.B.F. d'Arcais, eds., *Studies in the Perception of Language* (Wiley, Chichester, England, 1976) 247–294.

[16] C.K. Riesbeck and C.E. Martin, Direct memory access parsing, in: J.L. Kolodner and C.K. Riesbeck, eds., *Experience, Memory and Reasoning* (Lawrence Erlbaum, Hillsdale, NJ, 1986) 209–226.

[17] C.K. Riesbeck and R.C. Schank, *Inside Case-Based Reasoning* (Lawrence Erlbaum, Hillsdale, NJ, 1989).

[18] R.C. Schank, *Dynamic Memory* (Cambridge University Press, Cambridge, England, 1982).

[19] R.C. Schank, *Explanation Patterns: Understanding Mechanically and Creatively* (Lawrence Erlbaum, Hillsdale, NJ, 1986).

[20] R.C. Schank, Where's the AI? *AI Mag.* **12** (4) (1991) 38–49.

[21] R.C. Schank and R. Abelson, *Scripts, Plans, Goals, and Understanding* (Lawrence Erlbaum, Hillsdale, NJ, 1977).

[22] R.C. Schank, G.C. Collins and L.E. Hunter, Transcending inductive category formation in learning, *Behav. Brain Sci.* **9** (1986) 639–686.

[23] R.C. Schank and C.K. Riesbeck, *Inside Computer Understanding* (Lawrence Erlbaum, Hillsdale, NJ, 1981).

[24] R.G. Simmons, A theory of debugging plans and interpretations, in: *Proceedings AAAI-88*, St. Paul, MN (1988) 94–99.

[25] S. Slade, Case-based reasoning: a research paradigm, *AI Mag.* **12** (1) (1991) 42–55.

[26] G.J. Sussman, *A Computer Model of Skill Acquisition* (American Elsevier, New York, NY, 1975).

Artificial Intelligence 59 (1993) 389–413
Elsevier

ARTINT 1017

On *Unified Theories of Cognition*: a response to the reviews

Paul S. Rosenbloom

Information Sciences Institute & Department of Computer Science, University of Southern California, 4676 Admiralty Way, Marina del Rey, CA 90292, USA

John E. Laird

Artificial Intelligence Laboratory, 1101 Beal Street, The University of Michigan, Ann Arbor, MI 48109, USA

Received August 1991
Revised September 1992

1. Introduction

This is a tough one. Clearly, neither of us is Allen Newell, and there is no way that we can do the job he would have liked to have done in responding to these thought-provoking reviews of *Unified Theories of Cognition* (henceforth, *UTC*). However, it was very important to Allen— and is very important to us—that the work on Soar and unified theories of cognition carry on. So, here we will do what we can based on our combined understanding of Soar, cognitive science, Allen, and how he would have likely responded to the issues raised by these reviews. In this latter, we have been greatly aided by a prepublication print of [12] that was graciously provided to us by the editors of Behavioral and Brain Sciences, and by Newell's follow-on paper to *UTC* [13]. In general, we will try to be clear about when we are conveying how we think Allen would have responded, and when we are just giving our own views.

Correspondence to: P.S. Rosenbloom, Information Sciences Institute & Department of Computer Science, University of Southern California, 4676 Admiralty Way, Marina del Rey, CA 90292, USA. E-mail: rosenblo@isi.edu. Telephone: (310) 822-1511.

UTC has three principal themes:

(1) "Psychology has arrived at the possibility of unified theories of cognition—theories that gain their power by positing a single system of mechanisms that operate together to produce the full range of human cognition. I do not say they are here. But they are within reach and we should strive to attain them" (p. 1).

(2) There is a common foundation underlying cognitive science.

(3) Soar is a candidate unified theory of cognition that is useful as an exemplar of the concepts introduced in the book.

The first theme is most contentious among traditional experimental psychologists. As none of the present reviewers fit this mold, it is not too surprising that this issue is not a major source of concern for them. Most of the reviewers range from neutral (i.e., they don't mention it) to strong support. The one exception is Minsky, who is "not sure that this is a good idea". However, our impression is that Minsky is really disagreeing with a stronger form of this theme than Newell actually intended. By "unified theory" Newell was referring to any theory that integrates together a set of mechanisms that are intended to model a broad swath of human cognition. Newell's (and our) approach to building such a theory is biased towards having a small set of mechanisms that produce most of the action through their interactions (an issue that we will get back to later). However, the call for the development of unified theories is not limited to just this form of unification. In particular, an integrated architecture built out of a, possibly large, set of specialized modules—such as the Society of Mind theory might ultimately lead to—seems well within the scope of the call.

Though the first theme was clearly the central one in *UTC*, Minsky's comments were the only ones about it, so we won't say anything more about it in the remainder of this response.

The second theme covers basic material on behaving systems, knowledge systems, representation, machines and computation, symbols, architectures, intelligence, search and problem spaces, preparation and deliberation, system levels, and the time scale of human action. Much of this material is common knowledge by now in cognitive science, though still by no means universally accepted (in particular by those more closely tied to the structure of the brain). The new material that might be expected to raise the most controversy comprises:

(1) *The refinement of the notion of symbol and the resulting distinction between symbols and representation.* In Newell's usage, a symbol is a pattern that provides access to distal structures (so that local processing can make use of structures which are initially not localized).

Symbols are involved whenever such distal access occurs. A representation, on the other hand, is defined by encoding and decoding functions, such that if you decode the situation that results from applying an encoded transformation to an encoded situation, then you have exactly the situation that would have been generated if the original transformation had been applied to the original situation; that is:

Decode (Encode (*Transformation*) [Encode (*Situation*)])

= *Transformation* [*Situation*].

Using a representation need not involve distal access, nor must distal access involve representation. Thus our interpretation of this distinction is that it should be possible to have representation without symbols and symbols without representation.

(2) *The definition of intelligence in terms of approximation to a knowledge-level system.* This definition distinguishes the concept of intelligence from the concepts of knowledge, level of performance, and generality by defining intelligence *with respect to a goal* to be how well the *extant knowledge* is used in selecting actions for the goal. So, lack of knowledge implies ignorance, but not lack of intelligence. Failure to perform at a high level could result from a lack of intelligence, but could just as well arise from a lack of either the appropriate knowledge or goals. Generality, rather than being an inherent attribute of intelligence, becomes the scope of goals and knowledge possessed; and general intelligence becomes the ability to exhibit intelligence across a wide range of goals and knowledge. Note that though intelligence is defined in a universal manner, the intelligence exhibited by an agent need not be unitary, and can in fact be quite domain-specific because the ability to use knowledge effectively may not be the same across different ranges of goals and knowledge.

(3) *Describing human action in terms of a hierarchy of system levels which are characterized by time scales roughly an order of magnitude apart.* For example, at 1 ms is the neuron level, at 10 ms is the neural circuit level, and at 100 ms is the deliberate-act level. These levels then aggregate into bands that share a phenomenal world. The biological band consists of three levels concerned with the physical structure of the brain: the neuron and neural-circuit levels, plus one lower level. The cognitive band consists of three levels concerned with symbol processing: the deliberate-act level plus two higher ones. The rational band consists of three levels concerned with intendedly rational behavior; that is, humans at these levels approach knowledge-level systems.

Many of the reviewers comments are focused on foundational topics, though not limited to just these novel contributions.

The third theme, not surprisingly, engenders a large number of comments from the reviewers. Even those who share the same assumptions on unified theories and foundations generally have quite different notions about what the right architecture is for cognition, and about how one ought to go about developing and studying it (including, in particular, what data should drive its development). This is in fact one of the major messages of *UTC*—that Soar is not being proposed as *the* right answer, but as an exemplar (both Purves and Arbib appear to overinterpret the claim being made about Soar), and that others should take up the challenge from their own perspectives (and with their own driving data) and develop alternative unified theories of cognition. However, it is also clear that with all of Soar laid out in *UTC*, it becomes an irresistible target for comment (and that this isn't really inappropriate). So, given that the reviewers go beyond the book's use of Soar, to fundamental comments on its nature, we will feel free to also go beyond the book in responding; in particular, we will refer to results generated since the book's completion wherever they seem relevant to discussions of the architecture and of how it is being developed and studied. In general, we will only provide references for work not already cited in *UTC*.

In the body of this response we focus on the principal comments on both of these latter two themes—foundations and Soar. Related analyses of some of these same issues, along with analyses of some additional issues, can be found in [8,16].

2. Foundations

Two of the three foundational themes that were expected to be controversial—(2) defining intelligence and (3) the bands (and levels) of human cognition—did indeed provoke the lion's share of comments, along with one topic that surprised us, though perhaps it shouldn't have: theories. These three topics are discussed in this section, along with two other topics that had fewer, but still significant, comments: natural language and evolution.

2.1. Defining intelligence

Fehling and Hayes-Roth have several questions about Newell's proposed definition of intelligence. We've already commented on the question of whether intelligence is a unitary quantity or whether intelligence can vary by domain. A second question is the extent to which intelligence is really independent of knowledge. Newell clearly meant that adding a new piece of knowledge relating goals to actions doesn't increase intelligence. However, we don't think he also meant that there is no way to increase intelligence by adding meta-knowledge. It seems quite consistent with the basic definition to say that adding a body of meta-knowledge, M, that makes the system better able to use another body of knowledge, B, can make the system more intelligent *with respect to the uses of B*.

A third question about the definition of intelligence is whether a system that performs perfectly within a very narrow region (such as a thermostat) is more intelligent than a system that performs less perfectly over a wide region (such as a person); or, similarly, whether a system that performs perfectly via a trivial method (such as table look-up) is more intelligent than one that performs less perfectly via a more sophisticated method (such as reasoning from first principles). This is an interesting question that seems to reduce to three fundamental components: ignorance, generality, and complexity. First, if an agent doesn't know the first principles, then it may certainly be ignorant, but not necessarily unintelligent. Likewise, if it knows both a perfect table and an imperfect set of first principles, it is more intelligent with respect to those goals to use the perfect table in answering rather than the first principles. Second, what should make the first principles advantageous is not their substandard use for goals where the table is applicable, but their use for other goals where the table is inapplicable. Thus this is an issue of generality rather than intelligence. Third, there appears to be an implicit appeal to the notion that something that is more complex (or sophisticated) is more intelligent. It is often assumed that complexity is a sign of intelligence, but what must really be meant is the ability to cope with complexity when needed (we've all seen too many complex descriptions that could really have been expressed quite simply). Using the first principles where the table is applicable would be inappropriate complexity. However, if the system knew the principles, but could not use them when they might help with other goals, that would indeed be a failure of intelligence.

A fourth question about the definition of intelligence is whether it ignores important phenomena such as: "a system's allocation of limited cognitive resources, its ability to focus attention, its efforts to meet real-time constraints, its balancing competing demands and opportunities for action, ..." (Hayes-Roth). The answer to this question is that intelligence is about how closely a physical system can approximate the knowledge level; that is, the issue is how the lower levels can provide a rational band. The phenomena Hayes-Roth mentions are precisely about how a physical system can best reflect its knowledge and abilities in resource-limited situations. Thus, systems exhibiting these phenomena are likely to be judged more intelligent by the knowledge-level definition than systems that do not.

Rather than being directly concerned about the definition of intelligence, Schank and Jona are concerned about the definition of AI. They take an eclectic approach that has more in common with Newell's list of constraints that shape the mind (p. 19) than with his proposed definition of intelligence. In Schank and Jona's view AI consists of four topics: learning, memory organization and access, functional constraints + knowledge analysis, and scale-up. All of these topics, except for knowledge analysis (which is discussed in Section 2.2.2), do appear to be covered in Newell's list. Schank and Jona also appear to leave important topics out, such as performance, reasoning, problem solving, planning, and natural language, but without a more detailed description of what they had in mind, it is hard to say much concrete about this apparent lack.

2.2. Bands and levels

Arbib has a general concern that the bands and levels described by Newell are too influenced by their roots in serial 1971-style computers, and thus generally inappropriate for describing human cognition. However, we don't see how a careful reading of the relevant figures in *UTC* could be taken as supporting this concern. Instead, it appears that Arbib is confusing the hierarchy of computer systems (Fig. 2-3, p. 47) with the time scales of human action (Fig. 3-3, p. 122). For example, though a register-transfer level appears in the former figure, there is no sign of it in the latter figure. Likewise, the symbol level in the latter figure—which occurs at ~~10 msec and is identified with the biological level of neural circuits—is in no way inherently serial (see, for example, how this level is mapped onto Soar in Fig. 4-23 on p. 224). We thus don't see how Arbib's concerns are relevant to the levels Newell describes in Fig. 3-3.

2.2.1. The cognitive band

The remaining concerns tend to be about Newell's focus in *UTC* on the cognitive band, with only limited attention being paid to the rational and biological bands (and even less to the others). This focus comes in for some sharp criticism from the reviewers who think it is either too restricted or completely misplaced.

In terms of the focus being too restricted, Arbib is concerned that an attempt is being made to restrict the scope of cognitive science to rational behavior, to the exclusion of everything else; and, in particular, to the exclusion of subjects such as instinctive behavior. However, this seems to us to be a misreading of *UTC* in several ways. First, Newell clearly recognized that models of all of the bands were necessary for a complete model of human behavior. Second, the rational band is the home of rationality, not the cognitive band. In the cognitive band there can easily be procedures which can be executed, but not examined, thus providing "knowing how" without "knowing that". For example, Soar is "aware" of the contents of its working memory, but it has no way to directly examine its productions—indeed, it can only execute them. Instinctive behavior could thus be represented at the cognitive band as unexaminable proceduralized content (such as productions) that is innate and fixed, or indeed simply as part of the architecture.

In terms of the focus being misplaced, Schank and Jona, and Arbib, are concerned that too much attention is being paid to the cognitive band and too little to the rational or biological bands (respectively). Fehling and Purves appear to go beyond this concern to a claim that only one band matters, though they are in complete disagreement as to whether it is the rational (Fehling) or biological (Purves) band. These concerns and claims about the misplacement of the focus are considered in more detail next.

2.2.2. The rational band

Fehling believes that the utility in models of cognition comes from competence theories, and that one key aspect of this is the utility of modeling knowledge rather than mechanism. This aspect is clearly a variation on the expert-system slogan that "Knowledge is Power", as are Schank and Jona's comments that "... the important thing to study, if one wants to understand the nature of intelligence and build intelligent systems, is content not architecture." and "Knowledge is what determines the architecture." We can't disagree with the importance of explicitly studying knowledge, nor with the claim that this has not so far been a central scientific component of the Soar research enterprise. There has been some focus on knowledge, particularly in situations where the functionality being provided is both particularly important and provided in a non-obvious manner (such as when it provides a new form of learning behavior). There has also clearly been a significant amount of informal study of knowledge in the context of applying Soar in various domains. Nonetheless, these activities have not been a large part of the overall enterprise.

Though we do expect the explicit study of knowledge to be a continually growing component of the Soar research effort, this should not be thought of as taking away from the central importance of studying the architecture. The human cognitive architecture is the fixed structure that makes the human mind what it is. It distinguishes people from other animals, and enables people to acquire and effectively use the wide range of knowledge that then lets them perform effectively in such a diversity of domains. In natural systems, at least, the architecture (plus the world and the already extant knowledge) determines what knowledge the agent can and does have, not the other way around. In general, without an architecture, knowledge is nothing more than useless scribbles, and without an appropriate architecture, intelligence (and thus performance) can be severely degraded.

Fehling also believes that a clean separation should be maintained between mind and brain (rather than attempting to ground mental constructs in the physical structures of the brain). He is therefore concerned that Newell is requiring all cognitive theory to be grounded in the physical structure of the brain, and that this is unworkable, unnecessary, and inappropriate. However, here we can only assume that Fehling has radically misunderstood *UTC*. The notion of a system level implies that it is possible to build theories at various levels of the hierarchy without attending to the details of lower levels. Such theories can, in fact, be extremely useful in their own right; a fact that Newell was well aware of, and himself took advantage of throughout his career. Thus there is definitely no intent in *UTC* to claim that all cognitive theories must be so grounded. However, to the extent that the desire is to get an understanding of human cognition at all levels and/or the extent to which the level boundaries are not hard, a one-level (or one-band) model is insufficient. This is not particularly pernicious nor behaviorist—it freely allows the use of "mental" terms—it just hopes to eventually understand how they are grounded, no matter how indirectly or complexly, in the lower levels/bands. What Chapter 3 of *UTC* represents is an initial attempt by Newell to help lay some of the groundwork for bridging the gap between the cognitive and biological bands (see [1] for a small additional step in this direction). There is a very long way to go here still, but the problem has to rank as one of the most important and challenging problems in modern science.

2.2.3. The biological band

Purves' primary concern with *UTC* is "its consistent failure to deal with the essence of cognition, that is, the brain and what is presently known about it." The strong version of this claim is that neurobiological evidence is primary, and that nothing of true importance can be done without it. We find such a claim hard to take seriously, for two reasons. The first reason is that equivalent claims can be made by all bands with respect to those above them; for example, physicists could just as easily claim that chemists should stop speculating about how the world works, and "put on their overalls, open the hood, and take a look"; and chemists could make the same claim about biologists. The fallacy, of course, in all of this is that each band talks about different phenomena and captures different regularities, and thus has its own appropriate technical languages and models. Understanding the relationships between the bands is ultimately of central importance to science; however, it can't replace studying each of the bands in its own right. The second reason is that ultimately the proof is not in such argumentation, but in what research paths lead to understanding cognition. To take one example from *UTC*, is Purves ready to claim that neurobiology can, any time in the near (or even relatively distant) future, make zero-parameter predictions about the amount of time it will take a human to execute a computer command as a function of how the command is abbreviated? Or, to take an important example from elsewhere, can it tell us anything about how students learn, and fail to learn, subjects like mathematics? These two tasks stand in for a whole class of results from the cognitive (and, indeed, rational) band that have both increased our understanding of human cognition and have had significant practical impact. On practical impact, though the command-abbreviation result has not itself had significant economic impact, closely related results have— just one such result saved NYNEX $2.4M per year [4]. More broadly, the whole area of expert systems is a spin-off from the study of the cognitive and rational bands.

The weak version of Purves' comment is that *UTC* is weaker than it would have been had it taken neurobiological data into account (a view which appears to match Arbib's). We are quite willing to believe that this might be true, as it is also likely true with respect to linguistic data and a variety of other bodies of data about human behavior. However, a significant breakthrough in bridging the gap between Soar and neurobiology will probably need to wait for the development of individual researchers who are sufficiently proficient in both of these topics.

Beyond Purves' general concern, he also has a more specific concern about the timings assigned to particular levels. He discusses how the brain can actually make discriminations based on time differences much smaller than the ~~1 msec rate suggested for the neuron level; in fact, it seems to be able to discriminate intervals as short as ~~10 μsec. While we are impressed with the cleverness of how the brain appears to accomplish this, it is hard to see how it bears on the issue of the time scale(s) on which the brain functions. The leading model of auditory localization appears to be that the brain can respond differentially as a function of the correlation between the signals from the two ears [17]. The problem is that there need be no relationship between the time to compute this correlation and the size of the temporal interval that the correlation then implies. Thus, it is quite consistent for the brain to take milliseconds to compute these microsecond differences (though we have not actually seen any data on the exact time course).

2.3. Theories

Concerns about Newell's usage of theories includes the (lack of) methodology for studying and evaluating them, the question of their identifiability, the nature of theoretical form and content, and competence theories.

2.3.1. Methodology

Hayes-Roth is concerned with the development of a "rigorous methodology for describing, analyzing, and empirically evaluating complex cognitive theories". We agree with her general call to arms, though realize that developing such a methodology will be a difficult and extended process. One subpoint worth additional comment is the relationship between a theory and its implementation. Based on the notion of theory development that Newell expressed, this issue, along with the related issue of when a theory should be adopted or rejected (Fehling), loses some of its force. To Newell, the implemented architecture was the theory, implementation hacks and all. The hacks are just part of the approximate nature of the theory. Since incorrectness of one part of a theory is not to be grounds for rejecting the whole theory, this amount of approximation is quite consistent. However, this doesn't preclude having part of the theory stated outside of the context of the implementation. It merely says that all of the implementation is part of it. It also doesn't obviate the development of a meta-theory; that is, an understanding of what parts of the theory are accurate, trustworthy, and significant. Such a meta-theory can be quite important in generating acceptance for the theory.

However, in general, Newell felt that a theory is adopted by an individual or community if it is useful to them. If it is not useful—because it is wrong in some way that matters to them, or because they do not trust or understand it, or because there is some other theory that is more attractive—then they will abandon it (or never even pick it up). He did believe that there should be a minimal threshold a theory should meet before being taken seriously, and that the threshold should evolve over time as the standards set by existing theories climb. But among the contenders, the ultimate success of a particular theory was more to be determined by how far you could get with the theory than by careful comparisons between it and other theories (though, of course, he did pay careful attention to a broad range of other theories, and particularly to whether they offered leverage in expanding the scope of extant unified theories). In the process, unsuccessful theories would just naturally be left by the wayside. He was thus much more concerned with extending his theories to cover new data than in detailed comparisons with other theories. In contrast, comparing his theories to data was always of central concern.

2.3.2. Identifiability

Fehling (along with Pollack) is concerned with the issue of theory identifiability, whether it ever really goes away, and whether it makes the modeling of behavior (rather than competence) impossible. It may be that in some fundamental manner the identifiability problem can never go away. However, what Newell probably meant here is not that the problem isn't still there in at least a technical sense, but that as the body of data gets larger, the issue of identifiability fades in significance because of the increasing constraints under which all of the theories must exist. If the total set of constraints on mind is finite, then ultimately any theory which satisfies them all is as good as any other. Even if there is an unbounded set of constraints—as Pollack might suggest—as long as the significance of the newly discovered constraints eventually follows a predominantly decreasing trend, the significance of the identifiability problem will also decrease correspondingly.

Even if you accept that the identifiability problem will always matter, the conclusion Fehling draws from this—that it is therefore only possible to focus on competence theories—just seems plain wrong. All scientific endeavors have identifiability problems, including the endeavor of developing competence theories—at best a competence theory provides one body of knowledge that is sufficient for generating some class of behaviors, but it does not show that it is the only such body of knowledge. What scientists in general must do is first find at least one theory that works, and then as other theories arrive, understand in what ways they are equivalent, and what the differences (if any) mean. In the area of unified theories of cognition we are still very much in the phase of trying to find just one theory that meets all of the relevant constraints. With respect to Pollack's concerns about basing a theory on a "Universal Programming Language", he is correct in surmising that Newell relies heavily on constraints derived from robust psychological results to distinguish among possible theories; however, these constraints are in no sense extra-disciplinary, as *UTC* is all about modeling the human mind.

2.3.3. Form and content

Pollack is concerned about the use of "natural law" versus "software law". However, it appears to us that he is conflating two distinct issues here—one of form and one of content—neither of which makes his point about *UTC*. The first issue is whether a theory is expressed in terms of mathematical equations versus process descriptions (i.e., what most programming languages provide). Neither form has an a priori claim to appropriateness as a basis for theory expression. What matters is whether a theory of the domain can be represented appropriately in the form—for example, whether a system's knowledge, goals, and processes can adequately be expressed—and whether the theory as so expressed supports answering the key questions we have about the domain. The second issue is whether or not a "theoretical" structure is *about* anything. Both mathematics and computer languages can be used to create arbitrary abstract structures that, while possibly quite beautiful, may have nothing to do with how the world (or the mind works). When AI engages in such activities, it has much in common with pure mathematics (in both the positive and negative senses). However, when the structures are used to model natural activities—such as the phenomena people exhibit when behaving in the world (or in a lab)—what is being talked about is as much natural law as are theories expressed as equations. Even such rational-band theories as competence models are statements of natural law to the extent that they model, at some level of abstraction, classes of activities that do (or can) occur in the world.

Fehling is concerned that Newell is relegating all AI theories other than Soar to the ashbin of "content-free" frameworks. However, it looks to us like Fehling has misinterpreted two parts of Newell's original statement. First, "content-free" is intended to refer to the fact that the frameworks make no content commitments that would keep them from being a neutral (but convenient) language for implementing any theory. It is *not* intended to imply that these frameworks are themselves vacuous in any way. Second, by saying that a unified theory of cognition is not a framework, Newell meant that it should really be a theory—that is, it should make commitments about how things work—rather than being a theoretically neutral (but expressive) framework or programming language within which anything could be encoded. Neither of these points was intended to denigrate existing frameworks, nor to say that other AI architectures could not be considered as possible unified theories of cognition.

2.3.4. Competence theories

Fehling believes that theories of competence are more useful than theories of behavior. However, utility clearly depends on application. If you actually do want to predict human behavior—so that you can teach effectively, or counterplan, or design an aircraft cockpit that minimizes the number of pilot errors, or any number of other important applications—a competence theory is not enough. Likewise, if you actually want to build a working system that can exhibit a behavior (or competence), a competence theory is not close to being enough. Being concerned with performance is clearly shared with the behaviorists—as in fact, it is shared with nearly all other approaches in cognitive psychology, AI, and cognitive science—but this certainly does not make the approach behaviorist. The behaviorists did get some things right.

2.4. Natural language

Dennett is concerned about the role natural language plays in providing a representational medium, and the extent to which this distinguishes humans from other animals. We'll have to be quite speculative here, as we don't know what Newell thought about this, and we are not ourselves experts in this area.

So, what we will do is use Soar as a stand-in for Newell. The most natural prediction from Soar here is that the key difference between human and other animal cognition is in the architecture, and that natural language is based on the basic efflorescence of adaptation provided by the human architecture, rather than itself being the primary source (see, for example, [9] for thoughts on natural language in Soar). However, this prediction doesn't rule out there being specialized problem spaces (and representations within these spaces) for natural language, and their providing general capabilities that can be recruited for use in arbitrary tasks. For example, recent work on *Linguistic Task Operators* in Soar is examining how natural-language representations, along with the operations defined on these representations, can be used in solving parts (or all) of specific problems [10].

Minsky wonders about the origins of nouns and verbs in Soar. This issue can also be dealt with only in a rather speculative fashion. However, it should not be too much of a stretch to imagine them as arising as the linguistic correlates of states (or parts of states) and operators, respectively. These are Soar's primitive notions of objects and actions.

2.5. Evolution

Understanding the evolutionary path by which the human mind evolved is a fascinating scientific problem, and one in which Pollack, Arbib, and Minsky are all deeply interested. Newell clearly understood the importance of the evolutionary constraint on the architecture—as evidenced by its presence in Fig. 1-7 (p. 19) as one of the core constraints on the shape of the mind— but was also just as clearly not ready to deal with it. We are also not ready to deal with this constraint in any detail, other than to notice, with respect to Minsky's comments, that evolution is constrained by both the material it has to start with—that is, the initial organism—and the environment in which the organism must exist (that is, the task environment). Only by understanding the interactions among these two constraints will we be able to get a true sense of the extent to which evolution prefers bizarre over elegant solutions and complex over simple solutions.

Despite the admitted importance of the evolutionary constraint, no one should be misled into believing that the ordering evolution imposes on cognitive functioning need provide the best—or even a particularly good— ordering in which to go about studying and modeling the mind. To use a problem-space metaphor, this would be equivalent to claiming that the best way to understand a state in a space is to understand its parts in the order they were generated by the sequence of operators that led to the state. What this neglects is that states (and organisms) tend to be structures with stable interactions among their parts—if organisms were not, they probably could not survive—and which can often best be understood directly in terms of these interactions, rather than through the possibly convoluted means by which the stability was reached.

3. Soar

The following discussion of Soar is organized around whether the comments being responded to are about memory, scaling up (including integration), task domains, seriality, emotion, or comparisons with other architectures.

3.1. Memory

Schank and Jona are concerned about a lack of organization of Soar's productions into higher-level units, a lack of attention to how memory should be accessed, and a lack of emphasis on preparation (that is, use of memory) rather than deliberation (that is, search). Minsky is also concerned about memory access and about whether Soar can have specialized representations (and whether they can be learned, or must be innate).

3.1.1. Organization

We surmise that Schank and Jona are being misled by the surface syntax of the memory structures and are thus missing the deeper semantic organization that does exist. Soar's productions do not simply comprise a flat memory structure. Instead, they are semantically organized around the objects— i.e., the goals, problem spaces, states, operators, and other miscellaneous subobjects—to which they are relevant. For example, each problem space has a cluster of productions that define it. Likewise, each operator has a cluster of productions that define how it should be applied (as well as when it should be considered and when it should be selected). Such clusters of productions are only eligible for execution when their corresponding objects are active in working memory. When examining Soar's productions it is easy to miss this structure, as it is buried in the conditions of the productions. However, one of the main advantages of this approach is that a large variety of objects can be dynamically (and flexibly) constructed during execution—according to the cluster of productions whose conditions make them relevant—rather than being limited to only instantiations of those object classes predefined in something like a long-term frame hierarchy.

In addition to the organization provided simply by having these objects, we have recently come to realize that the objects themselves are organized into a full-blown new processing level, called the *problem space computational model* [14]. At this level, Soar is appropriately described as consisting of a set of interacting problem spaces, where each problem space effectively realizes a constrained micro-world. Languages defined at the problem-space level, such as TAQL [21], specify systems directly in terms of problem-space components (and can be compiled automatically into Soar productions).

3.1.2. Specialized representations and innateness

Minsky is concerned about whether Soar has specialized representations. Soar definitely can utilize specialized representations because individual problem spaces may have their own representations that are constructed in terms of the uniform low-level attribute–value structure. This has proven adequate for the tasks so far investigated, but we do not yet know whether it will remain so in the future, or whether we will need to add new representations—for example, for spatial information—to the architecture.

Minsky also wonders about the knowledge-genesis issue of whether Soar would be able to acquire specialized representations, along with the ability to convert rapidly among them, or whether it really needs to be born with them. Soar currently doesn't come born with specialized representations—except for the limited way in which they are provided by the "default" rules that are always loaded into Soar on start-up—and though we don't currently know whether or not they could be learned in general, a two-pronged approach to resolving this issue does seem clear. One prong is to investigate in some detail whether (or how) such knowledge could indeed be learned by Soar. The other prong is to continue accumulating evidence about the capabilities humans have at birth. If the conclusion is that the representation and conversion capabilities must all be there at birth, there would then still be the question as to whether it exists as innate content (that is, as productions or whole problem spaces), or as architecture. Either could appear physically in the brain as "specialized sub-organs".

3.1.3. Access

Schank and Jona are concerned that the issue of how memory should be accessed has received insufficient attention in Soar. However, the problem really appears to be not that it hasn't been dealt with in Soar, but that it has been dealt with in a different manner than in, for example, case-based reasoning. In case-based reasoning, the usual assumption is that memory consists of large-grained declarative structures that are processed little at storage time, except for some work on indexing. The understanding and adaptation of the case happen later, at retrieval time. In Soar, much more of the processing occurs at storage time. In fact, storage effectively occurs as a side-effect of the understanding process, resulting in the information usually being proceduralized with respect to the current context into a set of small-grain rules, each of which becomes indexed by those aspects of the situation that determined its consequences. The only form of automatic (that is, architecturally driven) adaptation that occurs at retrieval time is instantiation and combination (of object fragments from multiple rules). More intensive adaptation of retrieved structures is possible, but must be driven by knowledge (i.e., productions) or by more deliberative processing in further problem spaces. It would be quite easy to get into an extended debate about the relative merits of these two approaches to memory access—and of whether phenomena such as *encoding specificity* (p. 321) favor one approach over the other—however, the important message to be taken from here is that significant attention has been paid to the indexing of knowledge in Soar. In fact, indexing is most of what the learning mechanism spends its time doing (i.e., figuring out what conditions to place on a production).

Minsky expresses related concerns about Soar having too easy a time in accessing arbitrary pieces of knowledge: "... in Soar all knowledge is assumed to be uniformly accessible, so there is nothing to bar the central processor from accessing anything ...". However, two factors make such accessing more difficult than it appeared to Minsky. The first factor is that, though the working-memory contents of one problem space can be examined by other problem spaces, the productions cannot be. Productions can only be executed, and then only in the context in which they match. The second factor is that the specialized representations which get built up within individual problem spaces can make it impossible for one problem space to understand the working-memory contents of another space without solving the kinds of integration problems that are discussed in Section 3.2.

3.1.4. Preparation versus deliberation

Here we can only surmise that our propensity to talk about how flexible Soar is as a searcher has misled Schank and Jona into believing that Soar favors deliberation (search) over preparation (use of memory). It was hopefully clear from *UTC* that Soar uses memory (encoded as productions) whenever it has it—and we usually try to make sure it does have it, or can learn it. Search only arises as a response to uncertainty and as a court of last resort when the available knowledge is insufficient (pp. 96–97). One of the things we have learned over the years is that problem spaces are about much more than search—they also provide a deferred-commitment control strategy that allows decisions to be postponed until run time (and which also turns out to make room for the kind of "dynamic planning" that Arbib is concerned about), constrained microworlds for focused deliberation, a forum for error recovery, and a means of bootstrapping into task formulation [14]. We thus have no strong quarrel with the claim that cognition is 90% preparation and 10% deliberation, though the exact numbers must be confirmed with good data.

3.2. Scaling up

Schank and Jona, Hayes-Roth, and Pollack are all concerned about scaling up, which is, of course, a major issue for any proposed intelligent system. Three subissues are raised by Schank and Jona:

(1) *Size*: Whether the architecture can cope with large numbers of productions.
(2) *Integration*: Whether you can scale the knowledge just by adding in the productions from a bunch of independent tasks.
(3) *Transfer*: The amount of cross-contextual transfer of learning that will occur.

Pollack's concerns about the construction of large-scale systems and Hayes-Roth's programmatic suggestions both fit in well with Schank and Jona's concern about integration, and are therefore discussed in that context.

3.2.1. Size

Recent evidence shows that, for at least one significant task—message dispatching—Soar can scale up to over 10,000 productions without a significant loss of speed [3], and more recent results extend this to over 100,000 productions [2]. More clearly needs to be done here—and will be—however, these results should at least allay some of the scale-up fears.

3.2.2. Integration

None of us believe that you can build an integrated large-scale system by just adding together a bunch of productions created for different tasks. Because problem spaces provide Soar with an approximation to a modular structure, you often can just throw the problem spaces from multiple tasks together. However, what you get then is a system which can do the tasks individually, but not particularly a system that understands how to combine them in any effective way. There is integration that needs to go on with knowledge—i.e., among the problem spaces—just as there is for the architecture.

What we do know about knowledge integration in Soar is that problem spaces interact through impasses; that is, when a problem space gets stuck, additional problem spaces can be brought in to discover the information that will allow the original one to proceed. Chunking then provides a permanent transfer of the knowledge integrated together from the additional spaces to the original space. The integration of the chunked rules into their new space is relatively straightforward, as the nature of chunking automatically ensures that the new rules are already in the language of the space for which they are learned—the chunks' conditions and actions are all derived from existing working-memory elements in this space—and the decision cycle provides an openness of knowledge access that enables new rules to contribute their preferences to whichever decisions they are relevant.

Problem-space interactions are normally modulated by hand-coded productions that:

(1) determine which spaces are considered and selected for which impasses;

(2) create initial and desired states in the new problem spaces as a function of the structure and content of the existing context hierarchy (particularly including the immediately preceding impasse and problem space); and

(3) return results to the original problem space.

This approach has worked fine as long as it is possible to predefine the classes of interactions that will arise. However, it falls short of the ideal, which would be to provide the potential for any problem-space to be used for any impasse for which it might be relevant—and to thus enable knowledge from arbitrary spaces to migrate, via chunking, into other spaces as appropriate. Soar does provide a framework that may make this ultimate integration possible, in that it allows the activities of problem-space generation and selection, initial and desired state creation, and result returning to become first-class tasks for the system to work on. However, the super-analogical problem of how, in general, two previously-unrelated problem spaces can be brought into correspondence, so that one can aid the other, is a question that we are only now beginning to seriously address within Soar. It is a great problem though (and clearly not just for us).

Hayes-Roth recommends a program of research that is focused on the cumulation and integration of knowledge (probably from much the same intuition that underlies the CYC project). That seems like a fine idea to us, though clearly a very difficult enterprise, as Hayes-Roth acknowledges. In our own judgement we have so far been reasonably successful in following her recommendation with respect to the architecture, but much less so with respect to the content within the architecture. The reasons are several, including:

(1) the architecture is tightly controlled by a small group of people, whereas the content is developed diffusely over a large loosely-coupled distributed community; and

(2) the architecture contains a relatively small number of reasonably robust algorithms, whereas the content houses a large amount of fragmentary, ill-specified, heuristic knowledge (as it should).

The research effort mentioned above, as well as some of the new tasks we are going after (partly described in Section 3.3), are intended to help drive us further in the direction of knowledge integration. Even so, it can still frequently be useful to back off from the ideal Hayes-Roth presents, and to look at independent integrations of partial capabilities in specific tasks. When it is not possible to see a straight-line path to the integration of a complete new robust capability—which is, in fact, frequently the case—such partial integrations can be a great way to build the scientific base that should eventually support the full integration required (and can also be an easy way to incorporate many loosely coupled researchers).

Pollack proposes "building systems from the bottom up using robust and stable cooperatives of goal-driven modules locked into long-term prisoner's dilemmas" (presumably based on nonlinear dynamical systems). There is a lot of general common sense in this prescription—creating stable, robust modules and developing a stable organization of them—though the effectiveness of the particular approaches he advocates (such as long-term prisoner's dilemmas) is much less clear, as is the relationship of these approaches to existing large-scale system-construction methodologies that attempt to resolve the same basic issues. Specifically with respect to Soar, we see that problem spaces provide "goal-driven modules" that interact through the relationship of impasse resolution. Within problem spaces there are semi-independent objects (states, operators, etc.) each constructed out of productions (or more problem spaces). The productions themselves tend to be significantly more independent than those in most systems because of the lack of conflict resolution—productions fire in parallel, with behavioral arbitration occurring outside of the production system, via preferences and the decision procedure. All of this gives Soar a form of modularity that should help in the construction of large-scale systems. However, it is impossible to tell at this time whether this is enough—even when combined with the growth potential provided by chunking—or whether it is any better or worse than the approach Pollack describes.

3.2.3. Transfer

We do currently see a lot of transfer within and across problems from the same class of tasks; however, we do not yet see a great amount of cross-contextual transfer. Since such transfer is likely to be a direct function of the amount of commonality among the processing across different contexts, it is also probably related to the degree to which particular problem spaces can be used in different contexts, and thus a function of the amount of integration that can be achieved (as just discussed). Additional integration will thus probably help, but we would never expect to see a huge amount of cross-contextual transfer. The evidence on analogy and encoding specificity suggest that such transfer is actually quite limited in humans.

3.3. Task domains

Both Hayes-Roth and Schank and Jona are concerned about the set of tasks used in driving the development of Soar. Hayes-Roth is concerned that the psychological tasks are too low-level and artificial to be informative—and may just "reflect artifacts of biological hardware"—and that the AI tasks may have nothing to do with intelligent behavior (or might reflect super-intelligent behavior). Schank and Jona are concerned that paying attention to "unrealistic and unnatural" psychological tasks—as opposed to the more realistic tasks that AI can study but that psychology has more trouble studying—will both lead to a distortion in the resulting theory and distract effort away from the more important realistic tasks. Let's divide this issue up into two parts: (1) whether there is a right set of tasks to be working on; and (2) if so, what they are, and where Soar stands with respect to them.

On the first part, we are pretty sure we know what Newell would have said: There is no right set of tasks. People are not special-purpose devices that can only work on one type of task. Indeed, any single task can lead to a micro-theory that is overoptimized with respect to its own narrow domain, and that is thus severely distorted with respect to the full complexity and richness of human cognition. So, what really matters is not what task is covered, but what diversity of tasks are covered.

On the second part, we sympathize with the call for AI to study more realistic and naturalistic tasks. A key feature of such tasks is that they often contain within themselves enough essential diversity to keep the resulting micro-theory from being extremely narrow to begin with. The Soar community has put a fair amount of energy into understanding how Soar can perform in reasonably complex knowledge-intensive domains, both in terms of replicating existing systems and in terms of constructing novel ones. The domains range over such areas as computer configuration, medical diagnosis, algorithm design, blood banking [7], message dispatching [3], factory scheduling [5], browsing [15], and playing video games [6]. These are realistic tasks that people do perform, but they may seem to fall somewhat short on the scale of "naturalism". We have not yet looked much at performing everyday tasks, and that would be a useful addendum to the classes of tasks that we have examined. Perhaps the closest we have come is nascent work on how Soar can be used as the basis for developing human-like intelligent agents in large-scale, simulated, physical environments. This is a "real" task in the sense that the simulation environments are developed by groups outside of the Soar community, the environments have significant value for those groups, and they have a direct need for intelligent agents in these environments. This is also a reasonably naturalistic task, as it deals with multiple intelligent agents—some human-controlled and some computer-controlled—in realistic physical situations; however, they do not quite tend to be "everyday" situations.

Despite our general sympathy with the reviewers' calls to more realistic and naturalistic tasks, we also believe that controlled experimentation with more limited tasks can provide valuable information that can be difficult-to-impossible to derive from more complex tasks; for example, the rich bodies of data on controlled versus automatized performance, on memory, and on practice. Newell has already stated the rationale for this better than we could have, but the basic idea is that these short time-scale tasks—i.e., tasks requiring hundreds of milliseconds up to small numbers of seconds—are the ones that get close to the architecture, by eliminating much of the flexibility that humans have at longer time scales. To date, Hayes-Roth's concern about these phenomena being mostly artifacts of the biology (or in Newell's terms, phenomena of the biological band) have not been realized. We have been successful in modeling a number of tasks at this level—such as visual attention [20] and transcription typing—with functional models based on ~~50 msec operator-execution times. In general, as long as you don't restrict yourself to the micro-theory developed from a single such task, and in fact strive for coverage across a broad range of both realistic and controlled tasks, the danger of getting a fundamentally distorted view can be reduced greatly, while the amount of useful information available can be increased greatly.

3.4. Seriality

Minsky is concerned about Soar's "selecting and executing productions—that is, IF–THEN rules—one at a time". However, here Minsky seems to have fundamentally misunderstood the parallel nature of Soar. It is serial at the level of problem-space operations, but quite parallel below that: productions match and execute in parallel, and preferences are generated and decisions made in parallel. (Of course, when we implement Soar on a serial machine, this parallelism can only be simulated, but parallel implementations have also been investigated [19]. Because Soar does embody this parallelism, many of Minsky's arguments about what would be difficult to do quickly enough in Soar don't go through. To take just one specific example, recent work on garden-path sentences in Soar shows precisely the kind of rapid shift of interpretation about which Minsky is concerned. In this work, an ambiguous sentence is not a garden-path sentence precisely when it is possible to repair, in real time, from the incorrect interpretation of the sentence to the correct one [11].

Arbib is also concerned about the seriality of computers (and Soar) versus the parallel/distributed nature of brains. Part of the problem with this concern is that, as with Minsky, Arbib appears to have missed Soar's inherently parallel nature. However, a further problem with this claim is that there is strong evidence for something like serial processing in human cognition; for example, the large body of results on (parallel) automatized processes versus (serial) controlled/attentive processes [18]. In his final remarks, Shiffrin summarizes as follows: "Behavior in general is accomplished by limited, perhaps serial, attentive processes operating in parallel with numerous automatic processes, with the two systems passing information back and forth at all levels of analysis." (p. 805). Soar is, at least at a gross level, consistent with these results, as the productions produce (parallel) automatized behavior while the problem spaces produce (serial) controlled behavior.

3.5. Emotion

Dennett's primary concern about Soar is its being all business, with no pain, pleasure, playfulness, laziness, etc. There is no question that this is a rather large gap with respect to Soar's coverage of human cognition. Even if you abstract away from the purely biological aspects of emotion, there are large and well-documented effects of emotion on cognition—in many ways the issues are not unlike those concerning the interactions between cognition and perceptual-motor systems. So it is an important constraint, but not one that we yet know how to deal with. It will clearly need to be addressed some day and, when it is, it will almost certainly have an impact on the architecture.

3.6. Comparisons with other architectures

One of the things Minsky does in his review is to compare Soar directly with the Society of Mind. On the whole, we think he did an excellent job. The comparison helped us both to understand the Society of Mind better, and to understand some of the ways in which it does map quite nicely onto Soar (and vice versa). However, there are two aspects of the comparison to which we would like to add.

The first addition is that, rather than mapping the Society of Mind's management function onto Soar's problem spaces, we would map it onto Soar's decision procedure, along with the knowledge and processing that generates the preferences used by the decision procedure. This knowledge may consist simply of productions that directly generate preferences upon execution, or it may consist of problem spaces that require arbitrary amounts of processing before being able to generate the appropriate preferences. When management is by the former, it doesn't require impasses or deliberate processing, and can proceed in parallel for many activities. This would also be quite compatible with Minsky's notion that "The managers themselves are installed as consequences of impasse-resolving episodes", as these are exactly the circumstances under which chunking installs new productions in Soar.

The second addition concerns Soar's apparent lack of the concept of a "difference", which is so central to the Society of Mind. Soar does indeed not have a large-grained, architectural, difference-detection mechanism that compares arbitrary pairs of structures. However, it does have at its very core a fairly general match capability that provides a small-grained difference-detection mechanism; that is, it can detect situations where a value bound in one condition of a production is not the same as the value bound in another condition. This capability supports, but does not mandate, large-scale structure comparisons. An important part of the philosophy underlying this choice is that difference detection is not a purely syntactic operation that can be applied to two arbitrary structures and yield meaningful answers. Instead it must be a knowledge-guided process that can be based on which differences really matter in particular contexts. The selective use of difference detection in the matcher is one way of accomplishing this. This choice is also consistent with the overall philosophy underlying Soar's approach to problem solving. In contrast to systems such as GPS, Soar is not locked into a single problem solving method such as means–ends analysis (MEA). Instead it is to be free to use whatever methods are supported by the knowledge it has about the task. Thus, if it has difference information, something like MEA is possible; when it doesn't have such knowledge, other methods should be appropriate; and when it has such knowledge plus additional knowledge, more powerful, possibly hybrid, methods should be usable.

Arbib also compares schema theory with Soar, and generates similar conclusions. In particular, he proposes to map schemata onto problem spaces, but is then concerned about the resulting seriality. However, as with the Society of Mind's management function, it is not at all clear why the mapping shouldn't be extended to, at least, include Soar's productions as schemata.

4. Summary

If we pull up from all of the details, there are three major themes that we hope the reader takes away from this response. The first theme is that studying the architecture is important. No matter how much domain-specific power comes from the knowledge, there is no way to build a unified and effective theory of cognition without significant study of, and effort on, the architecture.

The second theme is that no band of phenomena is special. Each band has its own data, methods, regularities, and applications. A complete model of human behavior requires understanding all of them. Newell focused primarily on the cognitive band in his career, and *UTC* represents his attempt to build a comprehensive theory of the architecture—that is, the fixed structure—that gives this band its distinct shape. Unified theories of the other bands may take on quite different shapes, as might unified theories of cognition that are based on other phenomena within the cognitive band.

The third theme is that there is plenty of room—in fact, Newell tried to explicitly encourage it—for others to develop their own unified theories of the cognitive (or any other) band. As the theories grow, and the set of phenomena covered by them begins to converge, we expect that some of the theories will die (from an inability to grow further), while others will themselves start to converge, if not in their surface structure, then at least in their essence. Be warned though, that the development of such theories can be an immense undertaking, requiring the integration of a rather vast amount of both expertise and manpower. And even then, there will always be significant gaps and inconsistencies that can be criticized. Nonetheless, there are few research paths more exhilarating than trying to put it all together.

References

[1] B. Cho, P.S. Rosenbloom and C.P. Dolan, Neuro-Soar: a neural-network architecture for goal-oriented behavior, in: *Proceedings Thirteenth Annual Conference of the Cognitive Science Society*, Chicago, IL (1991).

[2] B. Doorenbos, *Personal communication* (1992).

[3] B. Doorenbos, M. Tambe and A. Newell, Learning 10,000 chunks: what's it like out there? in: *Proceedings AAAI-92*, San Jose, CA (1992).

[4] W.D. Gray, B.E. John and M.E. Atwood, Project Ernestine: validating GOMS for predicting and explaining real-world task performance, NYNEX Science and Technology Center and School of Computer Science, Carnegie Mellon University, Pittsburgh, PA (1991).

[5] W. Hsu, M. Prietula and D. Steier, Merl-Soar: scheduling within a general architecture for intelligence, in: *Proceedings Third International Conference on Expert Systems and the Leading Edge in Production and Operations Management* (1989).

[6] B.E. John, A.H. Vera and A. Newell, Towards real-time GOMS, Tech. Rept. CMU-CS-90-195, School of Computer Science, Carnegie Mellon University, Pittsburgh, PA (1990).

[7] T.R. Johnson, J.W. Smith, K. Johnson, N. Amra and M. DeJongh, Diagrammatic reasoning of tabular data, Tech. Rept. OSU-LKBMS-92-101, Laboratory for Knowledge-based Medical Systems, Ohio State University, Columbus, OH (1992).

[8] J.E. Laird, M. Hucka, S.B. Huffman and P.S. Rosenbloom, An analysis of Soar as an integrated architecture, *SIGART Bull.* 2 (1991) 98–103.

[9] J.F. Lehman, R.L. Lewis and A. Newell, Integrating knowledge sources in language comprehension, in: *Proceedings Thirteenth Annual Conference of the Cognitive Science Society*, Chicago, IL (1991).

[10] J.F. Lehman, A. Newell, T.A. Polk and R.L. Lewis, The role of language in cognition, in: G. Harman, ed., *Conceptions of the Human Mind* (Erlbaum, Hillsdale, NJ, to appear).

[11] R.L. Lewis, Recent developments in the NL-Soar garden path theory, Tech. Rept. CMU-CS-92-141, School of Computer Science, Carnegie Mellon University, Pittsburgh, PA (1992).

[12] A. Newell, SOAR as a unified theory of cognition: issues and explanations, *Behav. Brain Sci.* **15** (1992) 464–488.

[13] A. Newell, Unified theories of cognition and the role of Soar, in: J.A. Michon and A. Akyürek, eds., *Soar: A Cognitive Architecture in Perspective* (Kluwer Academic Publishers, Dordrecht, Netherlands, 1992).

[14] A. Newell, G.R. Yost, J.E. Laird, P.S. Rosenbloom and E. Altmann, Formulating the problem space computational model, in: R.F. Rashid, ed., *CMU Computer Science: A 25th Anniversary Commemorative* (ACM Press/Addison-Wesley, New York, 1991).

[15] V.A. Peck and B.E. John, Browser-Soar: A computational model of a highly interactive task, in: *Proceedings CHI'92* (ACM Press, New York, 1992).

[16] P.S. Rosenbloom, J.E. Laird, A. Newell and R. McCarl, A preliminary analysis of the Soar architecture as a basis for general intelligence, *Artif. Intell.* **47** 289–325 (1991).

[17] B. Scharf and A.J.M. Houtsma, Audition II: loudness, pitch, localization, aural distortion, pathology, in: K.R. Boff, L. Kaufman, and J.P. Thomas, eds., *Handbook of Perception and Human Performance*, Vol. I: *Sensory Processes and Perception* (Wiley, New York, 1986).

[18] R.M. Shiffrin, Attention, in: R.C. Atkinson, R.J. Herrnstein, G. Lindzey and R.D. Luce, eds., *Steven's Handbook of Experimental Psychology*, Vol. 2: *Learning and Cognition* (Wiley, New York, 2nd ed., 1988).

[19] M. Tambe, D. Kalp, A. Gupta, C.L. Forgy, B. Milnes and A. Newell, Soar/PSM-E: investigating match parallelism in a learning production system, in: *Proceedings ACM/SIGPLAN Symposium on Parallel Programming: Experience with Applications, Languages, and Systems* (1988).

[20] M. Wiesmeyer and J.E. Laird, A computer model of 2D visual attention, in: *Proceedings Twelfth Annual Conference of the Cognitive Science Society*, Cambridge, MA (1990).

[21] G.R. Yost and E. Altmann, TAQL 3.1.3: Soar Task Acquisition Language user manual, School of Computer Science, Carnegie Mellon University, Pittsburgh, PA (1991).

II *Situated Action*

Introduction

The theory of situated action claims that human behavior is, at its core, inherently improvisatory and nondeliberated. Past attempts to model human behavior by plan representations have produced computer programs that can usefully replicate mechanical, highly regular actions (as in rule-based expert systems). Obviously, people use such plans for orienting what they do, but the open nature of comprehension (as in reading and following instructions) is not captured by such models. Indeed, two fundamental claims intricately interweave in this argument: People are more adaptable than any existing computer program, and situations are more dense and changing than any models of objects and properties could capture a priori. Neural processes and processes in the world in general are more dynamic, unique, and intermingled than a model of stored descriptions of beliefs, plans, and causal relations suggests. Perceiving and acting interpenetrate; what we perceive about the world and what we do arise together in our already coordinated activity. These social and philosophical analyses of situated action theory ultimately develop into the broader theories of situated cognition, providing an integrated view of neurobiology, psychology, learning, and linguistic evolution.

Terry Winograd and Fernando Flores's book *Understanding Computers and Cognition*, which anchors this forum on situated action, marks a turning point in the debate about the nature of intelligence and computer programs. Before the appearance of this book, Weizenbaum's *Computer Power and Human Reason* was the most well-known book by an AI insider to question the direction of the field. Winograd's 1971 Ph.D. thesis on natural language understanding is likely to be one of the most memorable products of the MIT AI Lab, as well as the first such document to appear as a book almost immediately after its completion. Perhaps because his work on natural language understanding was so central, his critiques are stinging and difficult to ignore. Winograd and Flores's book effectively legitimized critical discussion in the AI community, stimulating a new generation of researchers to investigate alternative methods.

These books and reviews become a dialogue in print extended over several years. Lucy A. Suchman, an anthropologist, reviews Winograd and Flores's work and then elaborates in her own book, *Plans and Situated Actions*. In his review of Suchman's book, Philip E. Agre tells us how the term "plan" has consequently taken on new meanings and explains the new methods and challenges her work brings to artificial intelligence.

To say that the reviewers and authors are merely arguing would be to miss the point of the books themselves. Winograd, Flores, Suchman, and George Lakoff are exposing the socially constructed nature of knowledge, meaning, and designs. They wish to reveal how engaging in such dialogues is engaging in a kind of interaction. Indeed, as pointed out by Winograd and Flores, the act of writing a review is such an interaction. Speaking itself is a process of creating representations. New ways of describing things are produced in activity, as interactive, perceptual experience, not as something deliberated subconsciously and only brought out later in words. Deliberation doesn't join perception and action, but occurs as sequences of conscious representing behaviors (speaking, drawing, or writing) in which perception and action arise together. Learning occurs with every movement—not just as descriptive reflection after the fact—so every perception and action is adjusted and recoordinated in the course of interaction itself. Unlike rational models of thought based on matching and retrieving stored beliefs and plans, with separately operable perception, reasoning, and motor modules, human behavior is inherently situated in its environment as a tightly coupled, integrated whole. (And crucially, this behavioral environment can be mostly inside the head itself when we dream, imagine conversations, or visualize remote places.)

With Winograd and Flores's book, we depart from the concern in Soar (and many related modeling approaches) for finding "the right representations" to store in the program's memory. Situated action researchers claim a different problem: No objective representations of reality are possible; indeed, intelligence is not based exclusively on manipulating representations (stored or otherwise). Getting the balance between these views right is difficult. Readers will observe the confusion that can result when Winograd and Flores use representations to explain that representations are not needed, and then propose "The Coordinator," which makes representations a central part of collaborative social action! Even sympathetic reviewers such as Suchman become confused. The authors' response carefully separates the issues and attempts another synthesis. Readers might want to reexamine Winograd and Flores's response after reviewing the presentation of alternative architectures and models of mind (parts III and IV).

Following the reviews of *Understanding Computers and Cognition* and *Plans and Situated Actions,* there are three short pieces about plans, language, and design. First, writing some years before the public debate about plans and the environment, Stefik reminds us about Simon's ant on the beach, and his views of social institutions and bounded rationality. Simon's response can be read as supporting the argument of situated action that memory and reasoning are grounded in interaction. The behavior we observe is always a product of interaction between the agent's environment and the mechanism inside. This "inside vs. outside" argument pervades the discussion of situated action. Is serial search of the environment a good metaphor for neural processes involved in trying to remember something? "Searching memory" describes a person's experience of trying to remember, as well as a computer program's examination of places where things are stored. Is the language for describing sequences of conscious experience (matching, searching, planning, deliberating) appropriate for characterizing the inner mechanism that makes these actions possible? Is memory inside or outside the agent?

In the books *Women, Fire, and Dangerous Things* and *The Psychology of Everyday Things*, Lakoff and Donald A. Norman pursue the relation of cognitive models, designs, and everyday human experience. Lakoff's analysis of categorization distinguishes nicely between human knowledge and today's cognitive models. His critique of objectivism and almost encyclopedic review of the interaction-grounded nature of concepts constitutes the philosophical and psychological foundation of Edelman's model of language, learning, and memory (in part IV). Norman's book (later reissued as *The Design of Everyday Things*) engagingly grounds these issues of coordination, representation, and activity in simple examples we encounter every day (such as Suchman's workers struggling with photocopiers). The story of Mr. Tanaka's mnemonic for his motorcycle turn signal (moving the switch forward on the left handle parallels turning the handlebars to the right) clearly demonstrates the embodied, action-oriented aspect of conceptualization described by Lakoff. Daniel S. Weld's reviews may be a good starting point for those who are unfamiliar with philosophical discussions. We find an ironic contrast in styles between the haunting, Promethean seriousness of Winograd and Flores's *Understanding Computers and Cognition* and Norman's playful illustrations.

Perhaps one lesson to be learned in reading this part is that forums for reflecting on research can be fun. Stefik and Weld conclude that the books they reviewed are enjoyable. Clancey ends his review of Winograd and Flores with a joke. In a sense, the very topic lends itself to familiarity and play, for this forum itself is a chance to stop and reflect, How do these theories relate to my personal experience? What do today's computer models leave out about my everyday concerns? What can I do that an expert system such as Mycin cannot? It is this direct investigation of everyday experience that theories of situated action encourage us to pursue.

T. Winograd and F. Flores, *Understanding Computers and Cognition*: *A New Foundation for Design* **(Ablex, Norwood, NJ, 1986); 207 pages, $24.95.**

Reviewed by: André Vellino
                Advanced Computational Methods Center, University of
                Georgia, Athens, GA 30602, U.S.A.

Introduction

The aim of *Understanding Computers and Cognition* is extremely ambitious. In this book Winograd and Flores attempt to outline a new foundation for the design of computer systems, including, but not limited to AI systems. "The alternative we pose," they write in the introduction, "is an attempt to create a new understanding of how to design computer tools suited to human use and human purposes" (p. 8). A theory of how computers systems should be

Artificial Intelligence **31** (1987) 213–261
0004-3702/87/$3.50 © 1987, Elsevier Science Publishers B.V. (North-Holland)

understood in our social context implies, ultimately, ". . . seeking a better understanding of what it means to be human" (p. 13). One cannot fail, therefore, to be sympathetic toward the main thrust of this book.

But if they claim we need a new foundation for design, it is because the old one, what they call the "rationalistic" (read "analytic" or "rationalist") tradition is fatally flawed. Consequently, a major portion of the book (Parts I and II) is devoted to highlighting the deficiencies of this tradition as it pertains to philosophy, cognitive science, and AI. For this critique, they draw on ideas from the hermeneutic school of philosophy, from the biological writings of Maturana, and from the philosophy of language defended by Austin and Searle. The final two chapters advance their views about a "new" design philosophy for understanding the interaction of people and computers. This philosophy eschews specifics in favor of a broader understanding of how computers ought to fit in the fabric of organizations and businesses and everyday life.

Language

Their critique of the "rationalistic" theory of language is central to all the claims Winograd and Flores want to defend. For this analysis, they borrow from philosophical notions belonging squarely to the phenomenological (or hermeneutic) school of philosophy (Heidegger, Gadamer, and Habermass primarily). Sometimes this makes for difficult reading as the following passage on the role of language (admittedly taken out of context) illustrates:

> . . . the world is encountered as something always already lived in, worked in, and acted upon. World as the background of obvious-ness is manifest in our everyday dealings as the familiarity that pervades our situation, and every possible utterance presupposes this. Listening for our possibilities in a world in which we already dwell allows us to speak and to elicit the cooperation of others. That which is not obvious is manifest through language. What is unspoken is as much part of the meaning as what is spoken. (p. 58)

While a greater part of the book avoids this obtuse use of English, the fact that they rely on Heideggerian terminology at all betrays the mistaken belief that the language of the analytic tradition is not sufficient to express ideas that are critical of its own presuppositions. According to them it takes nothing less than a hermeneutic understanding of language to "reveal the blindness" generated by the rationalistic orientation. In their view, the presuppositions or background assumptions that are built into the very language used by propo-nents of this tradition (or any tradition for that matter) can be revealed only by observing where language "breaks down." Often, this requires either inventing a new language or inventing new uses for an old language. As it turns out, the authors chose to use the language of hermeneutics and its accompanying conceptual schemes. But, as the book itself demonstrates in some sections, it is perfectly possible to express whatever they believe are the shortcomings of the "rationalistic" point of view without recourse to phenomenology.

My emphasis on their use of language is no accident. Most of the criticisms of mainstream cognitive science and AI put forth by Winograd and Flores rely heavily on their analysis of the analytic or "rationalistic" theories of language. The importance of this analysis is apparent in the light of their later conclusions concerning AI. They write,

> Our position in accord with the preceding chapters, is that computers cannot understand language. (p. 107)

They do not make it completely clear that they mean it is not possible for computers to understand language rather than the weaker claim that no existing so-called "natural language understanding" computer system is adequate to the task. Nevertheless, they do want to maintain both these claims.

I shall return to these claims about AI below. First, I want to focus on their characterization of the analytical view of language:

> The rationalistic tradition regards language as a system of symbols that are composed into patterns that stand for things in the world. Sentences can represent the world truly or falsely, coherently or incoherently, but their ultimate grounding is in their *correspondence* with the states of affairs they represent. (p. 17)

The authors correctly point out that the analytic literature is apprised of the complexities involved in a correspondence theory of language, problems such as deciding on what exists (ontology) and how words refer. But, they conclude, "it is typically assumed that no formal answers can be given to the general problem of semantic correspondence" (p. 18). It is left to the reader to infer erroneously that analytic philosophers of language have admitted the failure of their enterprise from the outset.

Granted, though, that something like a semantic theory of correspondence is possible, the notion of *meaning* the rationalists have adopted is "truth-theoretic," or, in other words, that the meaning of a sentence is given by the conditions which make it true. These are given by a system of rules that transform the sentences of natural language into formulas of a formal language, that in turn obey explicit rules governing the semantics of their composition. Thus far, the account Winograd and Flores give of truth-theoretic semantics is essentially correct. However, they go on to say:

> In addition to these assumptions, there is a general understanding that in order for the compositional rules to be of interest, the meanings of the items being composed should be fixed *without reference to the context in which they appear*. (p. 19, italics in the original)

The authors go to some length to refute the assertion that the meanings of sentences can be determined independently of context. They give us many examples of ambiguous sentences that might have different meanings in different contexts or that change meanings as further sentences are uttered.

If they did not make this point so crucial to their criticisms of the "rationalistic" tradition, I would have simply noted that this was a misrepresentation of "the general understanding" and that the "rationalistic" tradition has room for other accounts of language, and left it at that. But the force of their alternative analysis of language relies almost exclusively on the belief that analytic theories cannot handle context dependency in natural language. The truth is that there is a significant body of literature in the philosophy of language and linguistics dealing with this problem, and it is neither mentioned nor referenced.[1]

For example, David Lewis [8] has given a truth-theoretic interpretation of J.L. Austin's "performatives"—sentences like "I hereby name this ship the Generalissimo Stalin." These kinds of sentences are taken by Flores and Winograd as typical examples of meaningful sentences that have no truth-value. However, using the notion of a "conversational score" governed by a "rule of accommodation," Lewis shows that these apparently truth-valueless sentences can be attributed a truth-value. Bearing a "truth-value," of course, doesn't necessarily mean bearing a direct "correspondence" to things in the world. All it means is that there are conditions, which can be made explicit and specific, that verify the felicity—to use Austin's term—or the appropriateness of the utterance.

Lewis' conversational scores are intended to capture the intuition that there is a whole host of beliefs, propositions, and actions to which one is committed in the course of a conversation. Contrary to the claim by Flores and Winograd, the fact that these commitments have a social and not merely a mental or linguistic dimension, has been well recognized in the "rationalistic" tradition. Lewis, for example, concludes that ". . . the lesson of performatives, on any theory, is that the use of language blends into other social practices" [8, p. 248]. Willard van Orman Quine, the Eminence Grise of the rationalistic tradition, opens his book *Word and Object* with the sentence "Language is a social art." The rationalistic tradition is not as naive about either the subtlety of natural language or the social nature of its practice as the authors make out.

While it is certainly true that no "rationalistic" theory adequately captures the capacity of language to express all the varieties of possible meanings,

---

[1]There is, however, a footnote to the effect that the problems of indexical and anaphoric pronouns have been discussed in the technical literature of linguistics. Actually, the problems involved in understanding anaphoric pronouns are very intricate and their solution is a substantial step forward in the understanding of the context dependency of discourse in general—see Kamp [7] and Partee [11]. In addition to this literature in linguistics, there are papers by Lewis [8], Nute [10] on conversational scorekeeping, and by Stalnaker [13, 14] on presuppositions to mention only a few.

neither the hermeneutics of Heidegger and Gadamar nor the theories of Austin and Searle fare any better. On more than one occasion they quote John Searle approvingly, often as both the expositor and the critic of the analytic tradition (despite the fact that he belongs to it himself). In this passage, we are led to understand the limitations of the truth-theoretic account:

> ... "The truth conditions of the sentence will vary with variations in these background assumptions; and given the absence or presence of some background assumptions the sentence does not have determinate truth conditions. These variations have nothing to do with indexicality, vagueness or presupposition as these notions are standardly discussed in the philosophical and linguistic literature." Searle, "Literal meaning" (1979) p. 125. (p. 57)

What is it then, we are anxious to know, that these variations *do* have to do with? What are these background assumptions, if not presuppositions? The authors do not answer this question for us, but instead delve deeper into muddier waters. For Searle, at least, "background assumptions" can be formulated linguistically. But for Winograd and Flores,

> ... background is a pervasive and fundamental phenomenon. Background is the space of possibilities that allows us to listen to both what is spoken and what is unspoken. Meaning is created by an active listening, in which the linguistic form triggers interpretation, rather than conveying information. The background is not a set of propositions, but is our basic orientation of "care" for the world. (p. 57)

Frankly, I do not understand what this passage says that cannot be stated more simply by the following sentence: "meaning depends on a set of background beliefs, desires, and dispositions." Surely "interpretation" means bringing the information of context, as expressed by intentions, attitudes, and vested interest, to bear on what is said.[2] No doubt a fuller grasp of Chapter 3, "Understanding and Being," is necessary for an adequate understanding of the hermeneutic notion of "interpretation" and I confess having only a superficial handle on the required notions: *throwness, presence-at-hand, readiness-to-hand*, and *breaking down*.

If the author's claim is simply that no rationalistic theory of language has, as yet, adequately explained natural language discourse, I have no quarrel with them. If they want to infer that such a theory is impossible, they have yet to make their case: each of the limitations they point to in the existing theories of language is also a limitation on a hermeneutic theory. This not suprising; the problems of language are *difficult* and their solutions elusive.

---

[2] See Stalnaker [14] for a "rationalistic" account of beliefs and context.

Science

The misrepresentations of the "rationalistic" viewpoint are not confined to their discussion of language. In their cursory overview of the rationalistic methodology in science they write:

> The scientist first notes some regularity in the phenomena of interest—some recurring pattern of observations. He or she proposes a conceptual or concrete system that can be set into correspondence with the observations and that can be manipulated to make predictions about other potential observations. (p. 16)

This picture of scientific method is more than just naive, it has been abandoned by scientists and philosophers of science since the demise of logical positivism. It is quite certain that no major philosopher of science holds a view even remotely similar [3, 9, 15]. It is widely recognized that scientists approach their enquiry with substantial theoretical presumptions, guiding the course of their experiments and the form of their conclusions. They do not proceed to invent theories that explain "raw" experimental data: the observational data itself is to a greater or lesser extent colored by the theoretical background which suggested the experimentation in the first place.

Their picture of scientific method is taken from the biologist Maturana, whose theory of cognition as a biological phenomenon is the subject of Chapter 4. This theory according to which biological systems, and by extension cognitive systems, are understood to be in constant interaction with the world—making up "coupled systems" sharing a "consensual domain"—gives credence to the notion that the subject/object distinction is falacious (or at least that the boundary is indeterminate). But for the purpose of disputing the view that there is a sharp distinction between "the world" and our theories about it, they need not have looked any further than to the epistemological anarchist Paul Feyerabend [2].

Artificial Intelligence

Chapter 7 on "Computers and Representation," written mostly, I suspect, by Winograd, is a lucid description of what is involved in programming a computer to manipulate "knowledge." The point is made here, that the representation for the information a computer manipulates is determined by the programmer and cannot be thought of as "created" by the computer. This point is made again in Chapter 9 "AI and Language Understanding." "Frames," "scripts," "perspectives" are all examples of conceptual scaffolding into which information is categorized; the computer cannot be thought of as *understanding* information thus represented. The computer "understands" this kind of information in the same way, perhaps, as a television appreciates the humor of a comedy show just because it produces canned laughter at what we consider to be the appropriate places.

At the end of Chapter 8, "Computation and Intelligence," the authors touch on a topic that deserved greater attention. They criticize Dennett for failing to distinguish between

> ... treating a system as though it were rational (in the formalized sense of rationality) ... [and] treating it as though it had beliefs and desires ...

But, they go on to observe,

> we treat other people not merely as "rational beings," but as "responsible beings." An essential part of being human is the ability to enter into commitments and be responsible for the courses of action that they anticipate. A computer can never enter into a commitment ... (p. 106)

There is, indeed, something appealing about the statement that a computer cannot be considered a moral agent. If there is a conceptual distinction between man and machine, the capacity to be morally responsible and the possession of personhood are likely demarcation lines [1, Chapters 12 and 14].

Conclusion

Winograd and Flores have attempted to do for cognitive science what Ivan Illich did for education and medicine: to expose the inadequacy of the profession to its task and lead it in a new direction.[3] Yet many of the statements in their book bring to mind a cartoon I once saw: it features a sheep in wolf's clothing. Their conclusions promise to be devastating, but they are in fact quite meek. For example, they boldly assert "*Nothing exists except through language*" (p. 68, italics in the original). But they equivocate on the meaning of "exists." What they intended, I think, is to say that one cannot *say* that something exists without saying it in a language, and thereby imparting the statement with the concepts that are presupposed by the language. This thought is quite consistent with the view that things exist independently of their being given a linguistic counterpart.

All in all, *Understanding Computers and Cognition* promises more than it delivers. It does not really open new horizons hitherto unexplored and the "new design" for understanding computers in relation to people is sketchy at best. The greatest value of this book is in pointing to the importance of language and its philosophical theories. A correct understanding of the semantics for natural language is undoubtedly necessary for AI and cognitive science to succeed if it is possible at all.

---

[3]See Illich's *Deschooling Society* [5] and *Medical Nemesis* [6]. The strategies in their arguments are different, however. Illich assumes the legitimacy of the task (education, health) but criticizes the institutions purporting to perform them. Winegrad and Flores, on the other hand, criticize the legitimacy of the task (cognitive science, AI), not the adequacy of the individuals or institutions devoted to making it happen.

REFERENCES

1. Dennett, D., *Brainstorms* (Bradford Books, Montgomery, VT, 1978).
2. Feyerabend, P., *Against Method* (Verso, London, 1975).
3. Glymour, C., *Theory and Evidence* (Princeton University Press, Princeton, NJ, 1980).
4. Guentner, F., Lehmann, H. and Shonfeld, W., A theory for the representation of knowledge, *IBM J. Res. Dev.* **30** (1) (1986) 39–56.
5. Illich, I., *Deschooling Society* (Harper and Row, New York, 1971).
6. Illich, I., *Medical Nemisis* (Pantheon Books, New York, 1976).
7. Kamp, H., A theory of truth and semantic representation, in: J.A. Groenendijk, T.M.V. Janssen and M.B.J. Stokhof (Eds.), *Formal Methods in the Study of Language*, MC TRACT 135 (University of Amsterdam, Amsterdam, 1981).
8. Lewis, D., Scorekeeping in a language game, *J. Philos. Logic* **8** (1979) 339–359; reprinted in: Lewis, D., *Philosophical Papers* (Oxford University Press, Oxford, 1983).
9. Newton-Smith, W.H., *The Rationality of Science* (Routledge & Kegan Paul, London, 1981).
10. Nute, D., Conversational scorekeeping and conditionals, *J. Philos. Logic* **9** (1980) 153–166.
11. Partee, B., Bound variables and other anaphors, in: D. Waltz (Ed.), *TINLAP-2: Theoretical Issues in Natural Language Processing* (ACM, New York, 1978) 248–280.
12. Quine, W.O., *Word and Object* (MIT Press, Cambridge, MA, 1960).
13. Stalnaker, R., Presuppositions, *J. Philos. Logic* **2** (1973) 447–457.
14. Stalnaker, R., *Inquiry* (MIT Press, Cambridge, MA, 1984).
15. Van Fraassen, B., *The Scientific Image* (Oxford University Press, Oxford, 1980).

T. Winograd and F. Flores, *Understanding Computers and Cognition*: *A New Foundation for Design* (Ablex, Norwood, NJ, 1986); 207 pages, $24.95.

Reviewed by: Mark J. Stefik and Daniel G. Bobrow
*Xerox Palo Alto Research Center, Palo Alto, CA 94304,
U.S.A.*

In their new book, Winograd and Flores consider computers, their possible uses, and the ways people think about them. The book is an uneven blend of rhetoric and insight; provocative but disappointing both for those who expect a carefully reasoned position, and those who seek an articulate account of the way things should be. It is strongest in its descriptions of philosophical issues that must be considered as part of the problem of understanding understanding.

This review is in two parts. It begins with a short review, which considers briefly the major themes of the book and how it succeeds with them. That is followed by a more leisurely review, which explores some of the interesting controversies in more depth.

The short review

The position articulated by Winograd and Flores begins with the observation that many of the claims and predictions that we read about computers and AI systems are greatly exaggerated in advertisements and in the popular press. They feel problems evident in the advertisements actually go much deeper. These problems are characteristic of common notions about computers in our society that are both widely perceived and deeply rooted in our scientific ("rationalistic") tradition. To understand computers and the essence of cognition we should look to human communication and consider the ways that people interact. Social activity is the ultimate foundation of cognition. Finally, Winograd and Flores conclude, the appropriate roles for computers are in supporting people in the complex conversational structures generated within human organizations.

These reviewers resonate with much of this argument, for example that the likely near-term capabilities of computers have been misunderstood and over-estimated by major institutions [8], that projects for developing AI and computer technology should be focused more on creating knowledge media [9] and technology for collaboration [10] rather than on creating autonomous, intelligent agents. However, the book fails by confusing fragments of argument and rhetoric for substance. This is discussed further with examples in the next section.

We have problems however, with the description by Winograd and Flores of what they call the rationalistic tradition. This is important to their story, because they hold this tradition responsible for many wrong attitudes and misperceptions about computers. In this, the authors take bits and pieces from much longer unrelated works, and provide such an oversimplified account that it weakens the effect of their criticisms of the elements of this "tradition." Examples from philosophy and linguistics showing real language in action are used to decry the pretensions of early AI works, such as Winograd's own SHRDLU program, and are used to point out difficulties in building "intelligent" computers that can "understand." However, the authors neither review recent work that tries to deal with some of these problems, nor do they elaborate an alternative basis for understanding computers and cognition. They conclude that computer systems should *only* be designed as facilitators of communication, based partly on utility, and partly on what they espouse as the ultimate limits of computer capabilities.

What they have to say about limits is appropriate for current methods and technology, but we feel has little enduring value in understanding where symbolic computation will eventually fail. Projections of the ultimate scope of a technology should be argued from carefully defined assumptions, and sources of fundamental limits, as found for example in Drexler's excellent discussion of the possibilities for "nano-technology" [2]. Without these, the arguments about why we should *always* treat and understand computers as different from people are not convincing. Certainly this is reasonable now, but that is a much weaker point.

The long review

Winograd and Flores begin their account of computers and cognition with a discussion of what they call the rationalistic tradition. This is an inauspicious beginning, and perhaps the weakest part of the whole book.

Burning straw men

Apparently the rationalistic tradition isn't any one thing. It is a strange composite that includes one rendition of the scientific method, some out-of-favor notions about how sentences convey meaning, the physical symbol system hypothesis in AI, and various kinds of reductionism. The authors offer a caveat that these elements do not constitute a tradition that is "uniformly accepted in carefully reasoned work of analytic philosophers," and so it is not clear to whom they might ascribe this mess. In addition, they make little attempt to present a balanced or representative account of the relevant ideas.

An example of this is their myopic attention to Searle's position that sentences have a literal meaning, derived from the meanings of the words of which they are composed. Such an account of language is incomplete and misleading because it fails to account for the context and purposes of conversation. As the authors show, the whole gamut of "speech act theory" is full of examples of sentences that convey information other than their apparent literal meaning.

Winograd and Flores are secure in their use of Searle as a strawman, whose ideas on literal meaning are criticized within the AI community itself. It would have been more useful if they gave a more balanced and comprehensive account of current research directions. It would have been more interesting to read a critique of Grosz's work on comprehension using the context of a discourse, or Cohen's on interpretation of utterances as elements of a joint plan between speaker and listener. These are better examples to illustrate the richness of theory that is now more the norm in computer models of natural language comprehension. Continuing in this vein, the authors treat the obvious failures of the reductionist account of meaning as proof of inherent weakness in the rest of the rationalistic tradition. While it is apparent that scientists build models that they use for prediction and that technologists build computer simulations for similiar purposes, it is not reasonable to claim that they always use them without cognizance of the limitations. When they dismiss the formation and testing of scientific hypotheses as being trivially and methodologically blind, they simply misunderstand the practice [1, 7]. We felt an anti-technological bias in their description of science and the major contributions of scientists.

Symbol blindness

At the base of this rhetoric there is a dispute about the limitations of the use of symbols to model reality. Winograd and Flores believe that the difficulties (or impossibilities) of creating intelligent machines turn on these limitations. They quote Heidegger as asserting that "cognition is not based on the systematic manipulation of representations." This assertion seems to be a confusion of levels, a confusion of function with structure, or a confusion of a result with an implementation that achieves the result. It is like saying that computation is not based on the propagation of electrical signals, or that life is not based on organic chemistry. Although they don't say this directly, perhaps the level confusion is their point and that from their perspective, Newell and Simon's physical symbol system hypothesis [5] is also a confusion of levels. Connectionists may or may not agree [11] given current accounts of symbols distributed among the neurons. The point deserves further discussion, but that won't be found in the book.

Another example of similar argumentation is in the description of Maturana's work. Maturana develops a vocabulary to describe coordinated activity that is independent of the use of any symbols (structural coupling is the key concept). As such, it provides a domain of explanation that is different than the symbolic descriptions of artificial intelligence. They rightly point out that it is unlikely that a baby uses a symbolic representation of its mother's goals and plans in deciding when to turn its head for milk or to cry. However, this does not preclude a symbolic representation at another level of description: one could describe the rooting reflex—where a baby turns towards a touch on its cheek—in terms of information flow. Even a phenomenon as complicated, and "biological" as color perception [4], may be usefully described as a symbolic process, at rather early stages of processing including color recognition [3, 6].

Ultimate limits

The authors' attitude about computers seems to be that computers are valuable, even though they will never be intelligent. Symbol blindness (that is, the necessity to interpret the world within an impoverished set of concepts) is essential to their argument that computers can never be intelligent. They say:

> The program is forever limited to working within the world predetermined by the programmer's explicit articulation of objects, properties, and relations among them.

For intelligence, computers would either have to be programmed with a complete set of concepts (which is manifestly impossible), or they must be able to learn and evolve. And evolution just takes too long.

This story is rightfully discouraging, but it isn't air tight. We simply don't understand very much yet about learning programs. Nor is it reasonable to assume that "evolution" would need to go back to the beginning, whatever that might mean. In addition, a computer linked to the world, with the possibility of effective action and feedback, has the opportunity to learn its own new sets of concepts based on its structural coupling with the world. In this sense, computers could "grow up" in a world. Thus, although Winograd's SHRDLU never grew up, newer computer systems connected more intimately to the world might acquire background that we humans bring to bear to understand the world and to interact with each other. Of course, this is beyond the current state of the art.

A new basis?

The subtitle of the book promises a new basis for design. It does not deliver any formal framework—that would probably be antithetical to the spirit of book. However, it provides some aphorisms and warnings, worded in the somewhat stilted style of Heidegger. "In creating tools we are designing new conversations and connections." (Computer tools shape the possible communications in an organization. Sometimes they are too rigid.) "Domains of anticipation are incomplete." (You can't predict everything. Design should proceed in a cycle with feedback from users.) "Breakdown is an interpretation—everything exists as interpretation within a background." (The requirements of success for computer systems are perceived differently by different members of an organization.)

Winograd and Flores provide an example of a new system built with the new premises in mind: a specialized electronic mail system. It categorizes messages in one of a small number of speech acts (request/promise, offer/acceptance, report/acknowledgement), and has required entries for each. Their claim is that using this will help productivity in organizations.

The design is surprising in several ways. First, it uses vocabulary associated with rich and complex human interactions (e.g. promises) with very specific technical meaning. Although they acknowledge this explicitly, it seems to violate the spirit of their use of vocabulary. Secondly, although breakdowns are a crucial part of their way of thinking about systems, there is no notion described for the coordinator of how to deal with breakdown. Handling this in the redesign cycle for the system (as suggested later) is not very satisfying. They conclude with an admonishment that we be aware of what our design process is, and how a system can change our way of working. That is of course very good advice.

Computers aren't people, and vice versa

In the last part of the book, the authors come to their fundamental observations about why we should always treat and understand computers as different from people. They assert that computers cannot make commitments or accept responsibility. As in their discussion of intelligence, they make the jump from reasoned arguments to rhetoric. They simply state that computers cannot make commitments, have responsibility, or be intelligent. In this they ignore the lesson they preach in the rest of the book. Terms like promise, commitment, and responsibility are mutually defined and used by people in different ways depending on circumstances. The appropriateness of the terms with respect to people and computers must be examined in the particular contexts. We saw previously how the common notion of promise was narrowed through the use of the coordinator system. Let us consider how the term commitment may have an application that usefully includes a computer.

Consider the scenario of buying an airline ticket from a vending machine at the airport, only later to discover that the flight was overbooked. The question is, did the ticket machine make a commitment? Presumably Winograd and Flores would say no because only people make commitments. These reviewers suspect that this would not hold up as a defense in a court of law. It is useful to say the ticket machine did make a commitment, just as we would for a human clerk in such a role; the commitment was done for the airline. We wouldn't sue a ticket machine for overbooking, nor the human ticket clerk. We'd sue the airline.

This airline example might make Winograd and Flores uneasy, as an example of the loss of "sense of responsibility in modern society." A more complete consideration of the situation would show that such legal practice balances several different notions of justice. Corporate law may seem to make it possible for the rascals to get away with it in some cases, but it also provides stable accountability through changes of management. The point is that commitment and responsibility are complex notions with social and legal dimensions. The treatment of them in this book dismisses them without any substantial consideration of their fundamental properties.

Given an extended discussion of commitment, is it reasonable to expect that we will ever want to think of computers as making commitments in the same way that people do? Asimov's R. Daneel Olivaw is a robot of the future that must delicately balance his actions with the goals and needs of the people around him (it?). One can ask whether such robots are possible; to be useful such robots would need to be able to give an account of their actions and to act as if they make human-like commitments. Would it still be useful to distinguish between their commitments and those of humans?

Conclusion

These reviewers agree with the warnings posted by Winograd and Flores that it is important to better understand the uses and limits of computer technology. Their examples from Heidegger point out that computers are embedded in the world and must act as well as reflect. However, the authors fail to give effective prescriptions for the future. They also fail to characterize the ultimate shortcomings of technology in terms of fundamentals.

For example, in their analysis of the futility of artificial intelligence, it is never clear exactly where symbols, search, and sufficient computational power must ultimately fail. Any single example of a computer acting appropriately is not proof of intelligence; but neither is any single example of creative action by humans proof that something is beyond machines. AI has nothing analogous to Hilbert's famous problems. Perhaps we shall one day develop classes of complexity for computational beings that will relate in natural ways to Piaget's stages of development, or to some other measure of knowledge, familiarity with environment, and maturity.

In conclusion, is the book worth reading? It is odd that a book can be so annoyingly flawed, and yet contain many worthwhile insights. On pondering this, these reviewers recommend that the book be read twice. The first reading is to react to all of the half-arguments and rhetoric, to get over being provoked by them and the somewhat anti-technology stance, and to accept that the book is strictly about the near future. The second reading is to skip or discount those sections and pay attention to the rest.

REFERENCES

1. Dobzhansky, T., Ayala, F.J., Stebbins, G.L. and Valentine, J.W., *Evolution* (Freeman, San Francisco, CA, 1977).
2. Drexler, K.E., *Engines of Creation* (Anchor Press/Doubleday, New York, 1986).
3. Horn, B.K.P., *Robot Vision* (MIT Press, Cambridge, MA, 1986).
4. Nathans, J., Thomas, T. and Hogness, D.S., Molecular genetics of human color vision: The genes encoding blue, green, and red pigments, *Science* **232** (1986) 193–210.
5. Newell, A. and Simon, H.A., Computer science as empirical enquiry: Symbols and search, *Commun. ACM* **19** (1976) 113–126.
6. Pentland, A. (Ed.), *From Pixels to Predicates: Inference of World Knowledge from Visual Data* (Ablex, Norwood, NJ, 1986).
7. Platt, J.R., Strong inference, *Science* **146** (1964) 347–353.
8. Stefik, M., Strategic computing at DARPA: An assessment, *Commun*. ACM **28** (1985) 690–704.
9. Stefik, M., The next knowledge medium, *AI Magazine* **7** (1) (1986) 34–46.
10. Stefik, M., Foster, G., Bobrow, D.G., Kahn, K., Lanning, S. and Suchman, L., Beyond the chalkboard: Using computers to support collaboration and problem-solving in meetings, *Commun. ACM* (1987).
11. Touretzky, T.S. and Hinton, G.E., Symbols among the neurons: Details of a connectionist inference architecture, in: *Proceedings IJCAI-85*, Los Angeles, CA (1985) 238–243.

T. Winograd and F. Flores, *Understanding Computers and Cognition*: *A New Foundation for Design* **(Ablex, Norwood, NJ, 1986); 207 pages, $24.95.**

Reviewed by: Lucy A. Suchman

            Xerox Palo Alto Research Center, Palo Alto, CA 94304, U.S.A.

There are two kinds of books in the world. On the one hand, there are those books that fall neatly into a particular intellectual tradition, to which they contribute some development, clarification, or revision of received ideas. For such books, the critical question is what is their thesis, and how well do they succeed in its exposition. On the other hand, there are those books, which tend to come along less often, that aim to challenge the basic soundness of received ideas, and to propose radical alternatives. *Understanding Computers and Cognition* aims to be this second kind; namely, a radical book, which should be read as such.

Taken as a radical book, the question to ask about *Understanding Computers and Cognition*, beyond how well it succeeds in its arguments, is whether those arguments are about something important. The answer to that question, I believe, is an unequivocal yes. Winograd and Flores start with the premise that any theorizing about how the world works, or how some part of it works, will be embedded in a particualr intellectual tradition. Both because tradition provides us with ways of seeing, and because it constrains our view, tradition shapes our understanding. To go beyond the limits of a tradition, or to effect radical changes in our view, requires that we explicate and reconsider the tradition's underlying assumptions. With respect to computers and cognition, this means reconsidering the assumptions that underlie ·what Winograd and Flores call the "rationalistic" tradition. The authors provide various examples of what the tradition assumes, including the following ideas about problem solving, meaning, mind, rational action, and cognition:

– Problem solving requires the representation of a situation in terms of identifiable objects with well-defined properties, and the logical application of general rules to situations so represented (p. 15).

– Meaning can be analyzed in terms of the correspondence between sentences in a natural language, and interpretations in a formal language for which the rules of reasoning are well defined (pp. 17–19).

– Mind is the logical manipulation of mental representations, treated as sentences in an "internal language" (p. 20).

– Rational behavior is a consequence of selecting among alternative courses of action, according to a comparative evaluation of outcomes (p. 20).

– Cognitive systems are symbol systems. A theory of cognition can be couched as a program in an appropriate symbolic formalism such that the program, when run in the appropriate environment, will produce the appropriate behavior (p. 25).

To characterize something as "the rationalistic tradition," by Winograd and Flores' own admission, is inevitably to accept a measure of glibness. Important distinctions are glossed, important subtleties missed, and while everyone is included, justice is done to no one. The only excuse for such gross generalization is the possibility that what is common is more important, for certain purposes, than what is distinct. The purposes in this case are to take off one set of eyeglasses and to try on another: to imagine what other way we might look not at the cognitive sciences, but at the phenomena of cognition that we are all trying to understand.

Those phenomena, on Winograd and Flores' account, are language, thought, and action. For the rationalistic tradition, they argue, and consequently for cognitive science, the machinery of mind has taken precedence in theory building, insofar as mental representations and logical operations are taken as the wellspring for cognition. In trying to imagine how it could be otherwise, Winograd and Flores take their inspiration from the biological theories of Maturana, and the philosophies of Gadamer and Heidegger, who suggest that what comes first, the basis for cognition, is an essentially unarticulated "background" of environment and experience. That background is not explicable in terms like "commonsense knowledge," or "world knowledge," or any other form of represented knowledge. Instead, thought and action are organized by what Maturana calls "structural coupling" and Heidegger "being-in-the-world," that is, an experientially based, physically embodied, and largely unarticulated relationship to one's material and social environment. The organism's knowledge of how to get around in that environment is nowhere explicitly represented, either in the organism or out in the world. It is rather a function of the interaction of structures of action, with structures of the environment, including the social and material environment that actions themselves produce.

The unarticulated background of cognition, according to this view, underlies our representational machinery, but also remains outside of its grasp. This is true whether we are engaged unreflectively in some routine activity, or deliberately in the analytic construction of scientific theory. It is only when some "breakdown" occurs, causing us to want to articulate some aspect of our situation or practice and reconstruct or repair it, that the unarticulated background can be represented, and is in innumerable ways. But whatever is represented is thereby transformed into something else; namely, an articulated object, that itself relies upon and takes for granted its unarticulated circumstances. What we need in the way of cognitive theory, therefore, is an account of the process whereby articulations of situations and actions interact with their unrepresented background. And this process clearly cannot be reduced to operations over a representation.

This alternative view of cognition has serious consequences both for artificial intelligence, and for the design of useful computer systems. In the second part of the book, Winograd and Flores turn to consider those consequences. Their summary conclusions are "that one cannot program computers to be intelligent and that we need to look in different directions for the design of powerful computer technology" (p. 93). It is worth considering each of these conclusions in turn. First, with respect to intelligence, Winograd and Flores appear to believe that research in AI is so deeply misguided about the nature of intelligence, that it can contribute little to our understanding. In their concern with the hegemony of received perspectives, Winograd and Flores come close to agreeing with the old adage that AI as presently constituted is equivalent to the tree-climber who believes that by that route he is moving closer to the moon. But the adage assumes that the only measure of success is actually getting to the moon; that there are not important lessons to be learned along the way, or from attempts to move closer that fail. Insofar as the climber masks the failures, or ignores the dead ends, there surely is nothing to be learned. But the failures of AI, in principle at least, can be as valuable as its successes. That is to say, while research in AI may not get us to an artificial intelligence soon, or even ever, in principle it can still contribute to our understanding of human intelligence, through its efforts to get closer.

Pushing a particular approach to the limit, like the application of logic to the control of situated action, or the stipulation of commonsense knowledge, can clarify what remains outside of that approach's grasp. But for such encounters with the limit to be instructive rather than destructive requires two things. First, an intellectual honesty on the part of researchers regarding the frustrations and downright failures of their efforts, as well as their successes. And in the case of AI, a clear distinction between the basis for evaluating technology, and the basis for evaluating long-term research. With respect to technology, we need to question whether or not, given the state of the art, AI holds the best hope for appropriate and useful technologies in a given domain. With respect to long-term research, we need to consider that it is the exploration that is the payoff, including understanding what isn't working and why, rather than any foreseeable applications. What is crucial in the latter case is not so much that the current research direction should be right, but that it should be elucidating, tentative, and open always to radical redirection based not only on advances but, more importantly, on obstacles discovered in its path.

Winograd and Flores' second conclusion concerns the consequences of their view for computer systems design. Winograd and Flores view computers as tools not for theory building, but to support human activities, while transforming them for the better. They suggest that while the tradition on which current discourse about computers is based "provides a fertile background for developing new technology, it does not support an adequate understanding of what computer devices do in a context of human practice" (p. 4). Their goal is to provide an alternative orientation, one that can serve as a basis for the design of technology rooted in that more adequate understanding.

What they offer as an exemplary case is a system called the Coordinator, intended to support communication within organizations. The idea behind the Coordinator is that organizations are held together by commitments: acts of communication that establish more and less temporary relations of interdependency among organization members. The goal of the Coordinator is not only to act as a tool with which people can make their commitments to each other, but also to reify those commitments, in the form of traces of the relevant communication that can be called up, consulted, cited, renegotiated, or whatever. The design rationale is an assertion that explicit commitments are better than implicit ones; that vagueness and ambiguity in communication over commitments is a source of organizational trouble, and that if people were to make their commitments (or their unwillingness to commit) explicit, organizational operations would be improved.

Like most computer systems, the design of the Coordinator appears to be based on a combination of intuitions and received theoretical commitments. The intuitions, presumably (though we are not actually told this), come out of Fernando Flores' personal and professional experience in management and management consulting. The received theory is a variation on speech act theory, which Winograd and Flores claim "challenges the rationalistic tradition by suggesting that language, and therefore thought, is ultimately based on social interaction" (p. 11). Unfortunately, the challenge is not that easy to mount. In fact, far from challenging the view that language use can be reduced to logical operations, speech act theory can be seen to extend that view, by making communication just another form of rational action [5]. The Coordinator reifies speech act theory, on the claim that "[m]uch of the work that managers do is concerned with initiating, monitoring, and above all coordinating the networks of speech acts that constitute social action" (p.12). But we see no evidence in support of the claim that speech act theory captures what managers do, or that the Coordinator, in reifying that theory, constitutes a useful managerial tool.

The concern with making things explicit, moreover, seems in some ways to contradict Winograd and Flores' commitment to understanding things in terms of their relation to an unarticulated background of community and practice. If this contradiction is deliberate, and intended to be therapeutic—"unconcealing" the commitments implicit in a communication makes better communication—we need to be convinced both that implicit commitments constitute a problem, and that their explication is the appropriate solution.

What Winograd and Flores, and the rest of us, really need in sum is less a prototype system, than a prototype process for new technology design. The complaint here is not so much that Winograd and Flores do not provide us with an articulation of that process themselves, as that they fail to recognize its importance, or even to indicate what its nature might be. While arguing for a concern with the sociological foundations of design, they offer neither a rich sociological theory, nor a strong method with which to uncover or build those foundations. The tools required are by no means ready for purchase off the shelf. Interestingly, however, the last 20 years have seen the emergence of a field of social studies based in a critique of traditional sociology that has much in common with Winograd and Flores' critique of the logical positivist tradition in philosophy, linguistics, and psychology. Ethnomethodology, as this field is called, takes its name from a concern not with methods for doing sociology, but with the methods by which members of the society produce mutually intelligible action in the course of their everyday lives. (For an introduction, see [3].) Like Heidegger, ethnomethodological studies start from the premise that socially organized activities are not adequately explained with reference to some body of rules that members of the society obey. Rather, the orderliness of the social world is based in the structures of everyday, practical activities. Those structures are not the reflection of underlying rules or norms, but are the product of methodical, systematic ways of organizing actions, however unique or idiosyncratic, so as to render them interpretable by other members of the community. What traditional social science takes to be the social facts that constrain appropriate behavior, ethnomethodology views as the emergent product of situated practices. And what traditional behavioral science takes to be essentially cognitive phenomena, are taken by ethnomethodology to have an essential relationship to a publicly available, socially organized world of material artifacts and situated actions.

In order to believe in the appropriateness of a new technology to what people do, we need more than an assertion of the fit. We need to know what the setting is, how the activities of that particular setting are organized at present, what in the present organization of activities is troublesome and what of that seems amenable to computerization, how the design of technology can be informed by such an understanding of the setting and its activities, and what actually happens when the new technology comes into use. And we need to know these things through systematic analyses. To get the latter, we need a sound methodology for the study and description of situated human practices, and the application of such descriptions to the design of tools; a need that itself delineates a major interdisciplinary research programme. Because those social scientists involved in studies of situated activities (see, for example, [1, 2, 4, 6]) have not by and large been concerned with technology, their studies tend to be published by presses not often read by those involved in technology design, and to have no clear relation to design problems. While not concerned with technology design, however, they do offer a model for the systematic analysis of what people do, including the relation of what they do to their technologies.

Understanding Computers and Cognition is an extremely important book, not because it provides a ready-made set of answers, but because it raises hard questions about the current premises and practices of cognitive science and computer design. It is not a textbook, but a book to argue with and talk about. If the discussions reduce to complaints about the particular characterizations offered, the book's value to the community will be minimized. But if the discussions are about not only this book, but what this book is about, then we may in fact gain new orientations toward cognitive science and computer design. And if Winograd and Flores manage to stir up those winds of change, they will have made a contribution indeed.

ACKNOWLEDGMENT

Thanks to Susan Newman, Debbie Tatar, and Randy Trigg of the Intelligent Systems Lab, Xerox PARC, for helping to clarify these reactions.

REFERENCES

1. Atkinson, J.M. and Drew, P., *Order in Court: The Organization of Verbal Interaction in Judicial Settings* (Macmillan, London, 1979).
2. Garfinkel, H., *Studies in Ethnomethodology* (Prentice-Hall, Englewood Cliffs, 1967).
3. Heritage, J., *Garfinkel and Ethnomethodology* (Polity Press, Cambridge, U.K., 1984).
4. Lynch, M., *Art and Artefacts in Laboratory Science* (Routledge & Kegan Paul, London, 1985).
5. Suchman, L., *Plans and Situated Actions: The Problem of Human-Machine Communication* (Cambridge University Press, Cambridge, U.K., 1987).
6. Zimmerman, D., The practicalities of rule use, in: J. Douglas (Ed.), *Understanding Every Life* (Routledge & Kegan Paul, London, 1971).

T. Winograd and F. Flores, *Understanding Computers and Cognition*: A New Foundation for Design (Ablex, Norwood, NJ, 1986); 207 pages, $24.95.

Reviewed by: William J. Clancey
Stanford Knowledge Systems Laboratory, Palo Alto, CA 94304, U.S.A.

1. Introduction

Every triumphant theory passes through three stages: first it is dismissed as untrue; then it is rejected as contrary to religion; finally, it is accepted as dogma and each scientist claims that he had long appreciated the truth. (Gould [6] quoting embryologist von Baer)

AI researchers and cognitive scientists commonly believe that thinking involves manipulating representations. For example, when we speak our thoughts are translated into words. We don't know what the mental operations are, but we assume that they are analogous to computer models of reasoning. There are hierarchical networks in the brain and stored associational links between concepts. There are propositions, implication rules, control processes, and so on. Thinking involves search, inference, and making choices. This is how we model reasoning, and what goes on in the brain is similar.

Winograd and Flores present a radically different view. In a nutshell, intelligence of the kind exhibited by people isn't possible by manipulating representations alone. In fact, they claim that our knowledge is not represented in the brain at all, at least not as stored facts and procedures. Many readers will reject this argument as obviously wrong, so obviously wrong they won't have to read the book to be convinced that it is just some variant of an Eastern religion or simply anti-scientific and not worth their time.

After reading the book twice and much consideration, I believe that Winograd and Flores are mostly right. We have the stuff here of Copernicus, Darwin, and Freud: At its heart, the human world is not what we thought. However, I believe that Winograd and Flores significantly understate the role of representation in mediating intelligent behavior, specifically in the process of reflection, when representations are generated prior to physical action. Furthermore, while the book convincingly describes the limitations of formal reasoning in the extreme, the practical extent of what can be accomplished is uncertain.

In understanding a book like this, it is useful to start with the problem that the authors are trying to address, that is, what they believe needs to be fixed. Winograd and Flores object to how computers are described in the popular literature, how AI researchers talk about intelligence, and the kinds of programs AI researchers, particularly in the area of natural language, are trying to develop. Winograd and Flores reject the commonly accepted beliefs that expert systems or any program could be intelligent, that representations can be used to model intelligent behavior, and that developing autonomous agents is an effective use for computers.

The book is based on the idea that understanding the nature of human cognition and what computers can do will enable us to use them more effectively. While many examples are given to illustrate limitations of current computer programs and to raise new possibilities, it is important to keep in mind that the authors have little interest in establishing what lies within practical bounds, that is, what the representational paradigm will allow. Rather they are trying to define the limit of what is possible. This makes the book of strong theoretical interest, but the practical implications, for example, what expert systems might ultimately be able to do not clear. The authors' philosophical stance places more value "in asking meaningful questions—ones that evoke an openness to new ways of being" not "in finding the 'right answers'" (p. 13). Without a doubt, this book raises good questions.

Any attempt to summarize the arguments of this book in a few paragraphs is sure to raise many more questions than it answers. I will only present a few of the important terms and describe the general structure of the argument. In subsequent sections, I describe what I learned by reading the book and the problems that I perceive.

In general, Winograd and Flores approach cognition and computation in terms of what it means to "understand language in the way people do." Their analysis leads them to conclude that computers cannot understand natural language—not just now, never. This is because all programs—all representations, abstractions and primitives alike—are based on preselected objects and properties. The background that motivates representations, the experience behind the designer's analysis, has been cut out. Thus, when breakdowns occur, that is, when an inability to cope occurs because the demands for action placed upon the program are different from expected, there will be no basis for moving beyond the initial formalization. Yes, the designer can anticipate typical breakdowns and provide for representational change, but these will themselves be limited and prone to breakdown. The only way out is to generate new representations from outside the representational realm.

The key to this argument is that new representations spring from a shared, *unformalized background*. Coping with a breakdown involves articulating the basis of a representation. If you don't have this background, you can't speak with commitment, that is, with an implicit promise to clarify your meaning if questioned. Since you can't negotiate meaning, you can't engage in language.

According to Winograd and Flores, the view that we codify and store experiences in representations that exist is the brain is naive. Rather, representation is a post-hoc interpretation of history. What we articulate has meaning within a context, and what we say has been shaped historically by that context. But it is only formalized (represented) when we speak. We are not translating what we have already formalized.

The question naturally arises, just what are we storing in the brain? Perhaps we do not *store* anything? What is memory anyway? What are experiences? Surely we retain something. But perhaps we are not carrying around things in our heads? Consider how much we take for granted, in particular how our conception of objects and space shapes our conception of the mind, and how little we understand.

This book is anti-illusion, not anti-technology. It is not about what computers can't do (see [3]) or shouldn't do (see [12]), but what they can do and how we should use them. It is primarily a positive statement, an insider's attempt to articulate AI practice, to understand what an AI researcher is doing when he writes a program. The goal is to understand how programs relate to life, what they capture of our nature, and what they leave out.

While the stated objective of the book is "how to design computer tools suited to human use and purposes," the authors are most interested in understanding what it means to be human (p. 12). They believe that the rationalistic tradition, based on ideas such as internal representation, search, and choice among a set of alternatives, must be replaced if we are to understand human thought.

2. What the book is like

Understanding Computers and Cognition is intelligent, measured, and instructive. It deliberately avoids "philosophic scholarship" in order to focus on central points critical to developing a new understanding. In four introductory chapters, the authors describe the rationalistic tradition, hermeneutics, consensual domains, and speech act theory. The discussion is admirably crisp. In just fifty pages, the book relates subtle, unfamiliar philosophical, biological, and linguistic ideas to what AI researchers do everyday as programmers.

While a cursory scan shows the book to be full of jargon—thrownness, readiness-to-hand, shared background, blindness, breakdown, commitment—these words turn out to be useful for retaining the message. Like Freud's jargon (e.g., ego, subconscious), these terms introduce a new language for thinking about familiar things (p. 40).

The book is also remarkable for sharp, definite statements that seem so contrary to common belief: "One cannot construct machines that either exhibit or successfully model intelligent behavior." Amazingly, this comes from someone who gave us another book entitled, *Understanding Natural Language*. A "born again" conviction might lie behind the book's bold remarks.

An AI researcher who reads only the section on expert systems and does not take the time to seriously study the arguments is likely to be greatly alarmed by the inflammatory language: "Calling it intelligent might be useful for those trying to get research funding. . . ." "The designers themselves are blind to the limits. . ." (p. 93). In a few places the polemic becomes obscure and is easily dismissed: "World as the background of obviousness is manifest in our everyday dealings as the familiarity that pervades our situation, and every possible utterance presupposes this" (p. 58). But with rare exception, the jargon and original point of view combine in clear and thought-provoking observations: "In trying to understand a tradition, the first thing we must become aware of is how it is concealed by its obviousness" (p. 7). Almost every page has an idea worth underlining.

Sometimes the book has a poetic, mystical tone: ". . . [We] present the main points, listening for their relevance to our own concerns." The authors evoke reverence for their ideas, reflected by the book's final sentence: "The transformation we are concerned with is not a technical one, but a continuing evolution of how we understand our surroundings and ourselves—of how we continue becoming the beings that we are" (p. 179). This is a book of religious philosophy, an inquiry into the origin of beliefs, values, and practices, of their nature, why they work, why they fail, and how they change. To quickly dismiss this book on technical grounds is to miss much more than the authors' conclusions about cognition.

If you are committed to understanding the book, I encourage reading the introduction (Chapter 1), then skipping around in whatever order appeals to you. Chapters 6 and 8 are excellent reviews; you could start there and then go forwards for the detailed discussion. Or if you prefer to start with the familiar, work backwards from the final chapter (which gives a good example of program design) to Chapter 10 (on current directions in AI) and the discussion in Chapters 7, 8 and 9 (on representation and language). However, I think that the book must be read completely to be accepted, and I found that reading it twice, separated by more than a year, was valuable.

3. Important ideas

Well into my second reading, I realized that somebody was wrong in a big way and I kept stopping in amazement at the possibilities. Could it be that Winograd and Flores are mostly wrong? What a grand embarrassment! From the other perspective, it's equally amazing how many researchers will respond with staunch certainty, "That's not right. Computers will do whatever we program them to do." Now I've accepted the main argument and have settled down to musing over details. I still think people will just shake their heads and go about their business.

On first reading, the idea that seemed most important was that the computer should be thought of as a medium for communication, rather than an autonomous agent. A computer does not understand, it is exhibiting my commitments remotely. It is not the computer that makes requests or promises, but the programmer. The computer shows my patterns, my associations, my preferences.

This view increases my sense of responsibility and gratification. It is my work after all, not somebody else printing things on the screen. This also leads to an interesting question: How should I project myself? What should I put on the screen to reflect my choices? But after a year, I don't think the "computer as a medium" idea has changed what I do, just my theoretical understanding of what I am doing. After all, I always felt embarrassed or proud about my programs. I always knew that the computer was just showing my own constructions (or that of fellow programmers).

On second reading, a completely different message hit me. I realized that I don't have any patterns, associations, or preferences stored in my mind. This is a somewhat depressing and confusing thought. As Winograd and Flores indicate, the implications are more than technical, relating to our image of what a person is, and this can influence our response to the argument. But the new conception is useful, and after awhile it starts to make sense. To illustrate this, in the following sections I summarize the ideas that I find particularly exciting by quoting from and paraphrasing the book. I amplify these ideas by discussing other connections and research implications.

3.1. *All behavior proceeds from the subconscious*

> To exist historically means that knowledge of oneself can never be complete (p. 33).

Language is necessarily blind to its context because it involves a formalization based on the *historical* structure of interactions. "As carriers of a tradition, we cannot be objective observers of it. Continuing work to revealing a tradition is at the same time a source of concealment" (p. 179). Language crystallizes what we are, but it is always partial, biased, and momentary. The power of language is to articulate recurrence, to identify patterns, to claim structure, to explain. But it is always post-hoc and apart from our being.

While these ideas may sound strange, most people are familiar with the idea that some behavior (at least) proceeds subconsciously, that is, not from articulated beliefs. This is the Freudian view of the subconscious: We act without knowing our own motivations. We do not always act rationally, by choice. Winograd and Flores take this to the extreme: All behavior is direct, without intervening representation.

In the popular understanding of psychiatric problems, subconsciously-directed behavior is associated with illness. We associate the subconscious with unusual, unhealthy behavior because the subconscious only becomes important to us when a breakdown occurs: a failure of a commitment, a violated expectation, a frustrated desire. When we perceive that we are apart from the world or when our actions are confused, this is when we use language to articulate what lies behind our behavior and our discomfort. We try to spell out what is not obvious, the assumed background that is affecting our behavior or our emotions.

In the "talking cure" of psychotherapy, a person articulates the recurrent structure in his behavior, naming situations and responses to them. Thus, he may become aware of the structural coupling in his life, allowing a new interpretation and new behavior. In this way, Freudian psychology has been reinterpreted as a form of hermeneutics: "The mental self is a story whose meaning is only interpretable in my life's history" [13, p. 276].

3.2. *We are always already interpreting*

In one of the most powerful ideas in the book, Winograd and Flores tell us that we are always attending, always selecting. To understand the value of this conception, consider the problem of explaining how we happen to attend to something. Suppose that I walk into a museum and see something interesting and walk over to study it. How did I know that it was interesting? What little clue made me decide to attend to it and to realize that it was interesting? What littler clue made me notice the first clue? Maybe the frame showed me where to look, but when did I decide to decide to notice that frame? In the museum I am always attending, always making interpretations. I am not matching preconceptions and recognizing value, as if they pre-existed as symbols in my head.

Following our practice in naming objects and properties around us, we place things in the mind: memories, symbols, patterns. We say: "Something gets recognized." There is an objective something in the world; there is a pattern being searched for in the brain; there is a matching process. Instead, Winograd and Flores tell us, there are just interpretations. There are no preconceived representations, no matching process. Instead, there is a "pre-orientation." "We are always already oriented to a certain direction of possibilities" (p. 147).

Similarly, in psychiatric analysis, the idea of a symbol is used as if it were something that resides in the head. But to say that "X symbolizes Y for person P" is only to say that P responds to X as if it were Y. In a historical interpretation of behavior, we note a pattern and explain it by this association. There need be no translation, no "symbol mapping rules."

The point is more stark than it might first appear. The argument leaves no room for saying that representations are perhaps "compiled," and this is why we have no conscious awareness of translating from representations to words. Rather we are not making decisions at all: *We have no choice, we are simply acting.* There are no "things stored in the brain" that we are searching or selecting between: ". . . the breakdown of a representation and jump to a new one happens independently of our will, as part of our coupling to the world we inhabit" (p. 99).

3.3. *All reasoning involves reinterpretation*

Another perspective on "direct action," or what Winograd and Flores following Heidegger call "readiness-to-hand," is that all intelligent reasoning is reinterpretation. This is far more advantageous than acting according to pre-conceived representations, and only finding out later that they are wrong. Yes, we make mistakes because we act inappropriately, but we are not following "plans." There is extreme plasticity in our behavior. Every action is an interpretation of the current situation, based on the entire history of our interactions. In some sense every action is automatically an inductive, adjusted process.

As an example of this phenomenon, close your eyes and consider how many windows are in your bedroom. Did you visualize the process of moving around your room? Possibly we are reactivating a motoric sequence, simulating that we are actually in the room and moving about. We replay the history and articulate what we would see. But we are not necessarily remembering a particular walk through the room. We are constructing a coherent story, which is implicitly a generalization of our experience because it is based on all of our experience. We chain together a sequence of impressions and pretend that they occurred together. In this way, the chains of association are constructed freshly each time, as a reinterpretation of the unformalized background.

A functional simulation of the cognitive system in terms of manipulated representations cannot generate the range of reinterpretation an unformalized background allows. Winograd and Flores conclude, following Searle, that manipulating a representation formally is not understanding. Certainly there are formal games which we understand how to play. We can even accomplish our goals by playing formal games. But as soon as the interaction changes from the previous history, breakdown occurs, and a reinterpretation in language is required. We engage in a dialogue that articulates the basis of a representation and adjusts it to a new situation. To understand is to be able to make the commitment to do this reinterpretation.

3.4. *We assume commitment in other people*

As Weizenbaum pointed out about ELIZA, it is amazing that we are so convinced by so little and that we assume so much. Even when you are told how little ELIZA, SHRDLU, and MYCIN know, it still strains the imagination to appreciate the magnitude of their ignorance. We are all like children pre-ferring to believe that the fantasy is real. Indeed, we don't have to "suspend disbelief" (in the theatrical sense), this is how cognition normally works: Attributing meaningfulness and assuming commitment go hand in hand. The situation is insidiousness: We don't normally articulate shared background, and computers don't have any. It plays right into our assumptions. If you use my words, I assume that you know what I mean. If you say you believe something, I assume that you are ready to convince me.

Weizenbaum stressed the lack of responsibility of computers because they are not part of the social fabric. The argument here is stronger: Computers cannot be responsible because they cannot even form commitments. When I speak with commitment I do more than just mouth words. I do not pretend. I am ready to defend what I say. I am committed. To speak the truth means to be willing and able to articulate why you believe it.

In providing explanations, we must determine why breakdown occurred. What is not obvious, not part of the shared background? What must be articulated? In constructing explanation programs, I have often concluded that we have not placed enough of the burden on the person asking the question. Unless there are systematic surprises that the explainer might guess, the questioner must articulate the nature of his surprise. The explainer must then be ready to form an interpretation that is contrary to his point of view.

However, we cannot completely model how a system's activity will perturb the interaction between user and machine. We can't anticipate every user's interpretations of what the machine is doing (p. 53). Given these limitations, we might focus instead on opening up the program's representations so they are easily browsed, making it easy for the questioner to figure out what he needs to know on his own.

Winograd and Flores provide an intriguing discussion of how computers might be best suited as coordinators of commitments, "the essential dimension of collective work." Following from their analysis of language, they propose that a program keep track of what we have to do, recording the status of our active commitments. Their proposal broadens our awareness from that of the individual working alone at a personal workstation to the social dimension of what is being written, computed, or recorded (p. 158). This idea is likely to have widespread appeal and could significantly enhance how we use computers.

3.5. *People do not carry models around in their heads*

Cognitive models explain patterns of behavior; they are developed by scientists. It is a strange and tremendous leap to say that these models actually exist in the heads of the people being modeled. While we commonly say that a person has knowledge, knowledge is not something that you can possess like an object. Knowledge is always an individual interpretation within a shared background. It is neither subjective, nor objective (p. 75). To say that someone knows something is not to say that he is in a certain state, but to explain his behavior over a sequence of interactions and to claim that he is predisposed to act in a similar way in similar situations (p. 47).

Few people believe that when we ride a bicycle we are manipulating internal representations of the handlebars and pedals, modeling their location internally, and computing trajectories. According to Winograd and Flores, speech is the same, a kind of skill coupled to the environment. While we may symbolize our utterances on paper in some calculus or written notation, there is nothing corresponding to these notations in the brain.

This has significant implications for understanding expert behavior. We are not modeling objects that exist inside an expert's head. This explains what is so patently obvious when you work with experts, namely that they have so much difficulty laying out consistent networks and describing relations among concepts in a principled way. If experts knew causal and subsumption networks as discrete concepts and relations, why would we find it so difficult to extract these statements from them? The concepts are often not defined, let alone related in a fixed, systematic way to one another. Experts know how to behave and they know formalizations that model how they behave.

The evidence in student modeling research is similar. Brown and VanLehn [1] found that student errors in subtraction, modeled as bugs in the procedure followed by students, changed over time. They called this "bug migration" and sought a systematic explanation for why the bugs changed. The key is that there never was a bug in the student's head. When you realize this, you realize that you don't have to explain why the students *decided* that one procedure was wrong and another was better. This does not mean that there is no pattern to be found. Winograd and Flores would say that there is a mechanistic argument, it just isn't based on manipulating a representation.

This analysis might lead to an entirely different teaching method: not isolating the bug, but establishing an appropriate coupling and forcing breakdown. However, we still need to understand what articulation does to behavior. For example, in physical skills, such as playing the piano, attending directly to a faulty action—actually feeling that you are making it happen—allows you to get a grasp on the behavior and change it. The role of language in isolating where an undesirable action occurs automatically is perhaps similar, again, the possible value of psychoanalysis.

By this model, the most effective training occurs on the job site, hence the instructional strategy of getting the students to the workplace and minimizing the classroom blabber. Winograd and Flores' analysis provides a subtler understanding: Teaching involves establishing the history of interaction that constitutes a background that will lead to useful interpretations. Establishing a "structural coupling" means experiencing this history of interactions, not just being told what you would do if you had gone through the process. The problem is familiar: You don't understand me because you don't know where I've been. If all intelligent behavior flows from the unformalized background, teaching how to behave by saying what to do can only provide patterns to follow by rote. You have to try it yourself and get the feel of it. Thus, the repeated teacher's fallback, "You'll know better what I mean when you get out there."

While the implications for instructional computing are not clear, it seems at least theoretically important to realize that there is a difference between solving a problem and articulating a model (rationalizing the solution sequence). We knew this already, but Winograd and Flores provide a theoretical foundation for building up a new understanding, so we can view the inability to articulate a model as not a lack of self-knowledge, but the normal state of affairs.

3.6. *Engineering develops from recurrent breakdown*

Understanding and anticipating failure (breakdown) is at the heart of engineering. Essentially, Winograd and Flores have provided a theoretical background for understanding how programming, especially knowledge engineering, is like structural engineering. Programs don't always do what we expect because the designer did not anticipate how users would interact with the program and interpret its actions. A large part of this book concerns how programmers must anticipate the demands of the environment and prepare programs to cope with breakdown.

As in structural engineering, what makes knowledge engineering possible is that breakdowns recur. These patterns lead the engineer to formulate "objective distinctions." Essentially what we take to be objective truth is what many people have articulated over a long period of time and we as observers expect to continue in the future.

However, constructing an autonomous agent is much more difficult than typical engineering problems. It is like building a bridge that will change its own structure as its interaction with the environment changes. This is the idea of an autopoietic system: It maintains its functions. This theory was developed in biology, and living organisms are the best examples we have. The idea now arises in computer systems engineering and plays an important role in the design of satellites and planetary probes.

A crucial point is that the organism adapts to meet the demands of its interactions. But this is not a process of representing the world: "The demands of continued autopoiesis shape this structure in a way that can be viewed as a reflection of an external world. But the correspondence is not one in which the form of the world is somehow mapped onto the structure of the organism" (p. 62).

3.7. *Systematic domains admit to formal representation*

Systematic domains are those in which there is a great regularity in relations over time and among people, so that there appears to be objective knowledge (p. 172). In modeling intelligent behavior within a systematic domain, we don't and needn't necessarily (indeed, can't) represent the meaning of terms. Rather we represent their systematic role within a network of requests and promises. Indeed, the operation of a program does not require that it represents anything at all. It's all in the eye of the beholder, who interprets input and output in terms of a systematic mapping in his world (p. 86). When MYCIN says the word "culture," you interpret it as something objective that you know about.

This analysis provides a fascinating handle on the nature of language, models, and formalization. It helps us understand why programs work as well as they do and what can go wrong. Thus, we can better understand what we are doing and perhaps how to go about it more systematically.

A surprising conclusion is that the Winograd and Flores analysis motivates a formal approach to knowledge representation. In short, the very nature of modeling is crystallizing our observations, the world as we know it, in terms of objects and properties. Formal representation methods are designed to attack this problem systematically.

The idea of systematic domains may also encourage us to adopt a less mystical view of knowledge acquisition. The task is to get at what's regular, recurrent. For example, in an interactive dialogue system, say a teaching program like GUIDON, we formalize the recurrent conversations that occur between a student and teacher. The idea of recurrence is very powerful for understanding what representation is all about.

Perhaps most important, Winograd and Flores lead us to see objects, properties, and relations as the essence of what a representation is, not just the present-day state of the art in AI research. We can never represent the meaning of terms. And because representation is a formalization process, we should use a logic-based approach, not because it's the solution to modeling intelligent behavior, but because it's precisely what we can do with computers. Formalization is what we're doing anyway, so we might as well be rigorous about it.

The idea that language arises in the need to action also fits very well with our experience in constructing programs. The relevant properties of a representation change as it is interpreted for different purposes such as problem solving, explanation, and cognitive modeling. For example, converting MYCIN to a hypothesize-and-test program required distinguishing between data and hypothesis "parameters" and classifying them. Similarly, an explanation program requires propositions in control rules to be classified as static and dynamic. A student modeling program needs to have control rules classified according to the constraints they satisfy. Thus, we build up representational structures according to the distinctions that are important for operating upon them. "Grounding of descriptions in action pervades all linguistic structure of objects, properties, and events" (p. 171).

The ideas of systematic domains and recurrent background have tremendous importance for knowledge engineering. For example, as we move from representing high-level patterns to representing generative theories for why these patterns occur, we must realize that this might not be possible in all cases.

For example, generating NEOMYCIN's control rules for diagnosis from more primitive concepts is probably impossible because they are based on a huge social context. Certainly, we could always generate a limited set of rules from more primitive concepts, and this might be worthwhile if the diagnostic procedure is relatively stable. But we must keep in mind that the primitives we choose are in an important sense ad hoc. The game can continue for several levels, but we can never get below the representation to something fixed and final. We will always have to assume a set of axioms. Of course, mathematicians have had to face this, and we should not have expected the formalization of medicine or other domains to be any different.

4. Unanswered questions

> One cannot construct machines that either exhibit or successfully model intelligent behavior (p. 11).

Winograd and Flores have chosen an uncompromising point of view about the nature of intelligence. Their definition contradicts the commonly accepted view that computer programs "which exhibit behavior we call 'intelligent behavior' when we observe it in human beings" are intelligent [4]. Even if a computer program consistently wins games of chess, Winograd and Flores would say that this is not intelligence. This restrictive view is unfortunate, because it greatly complicates the problem of understanding this book.

All models are approximate and selective. Engineering models are successful within some practical setting. Rather than insisting that "computers cannot diagnose diseases," for example, which violates common sense, it would be more useful to carefully articulate when the models will fail. Little is gained by saying that such programs are not models of intelligent behavior.

While the book has clear implications for research in natural language and instructional research, as I have described, it is unclear just how well computer models might eventually perform in systematic domains. That is, how well can we circumscribe domains to construct useful and effective representations? Is it of any practical value to say that commitment and hence language cannot exist in a systematic domain (where the importance of unformalized background is minimized)? Is the shared background of people as great as Winograd and Flores suggest when they exclude computers from participating in language? When breakdown occurs, just how well do people resolve it? In this section I consider ways in which the arguments in the book appear to be incomplete and perhaps distort the nature of cognition.

4.1. What is the mechanism of memory?

To recapitulate, conceptual structures are not stored in the brain; the concepts of our language do not organize our memory. There are no stored associations, no conceptual network. Instead, we act: We speak, we associate. We don't do this by interpreting a network that mirrors the conceptual structure in what we say. Rather, the history of our behavior may exhibit recurrence that we can represent as such a network.

We are left with the image of some amorphous blob that speaks. How can we explain recurrence, if there is no structural predisposition to associate concepts in some way? Winograd and Flores believe that there is some mechanism behind jumps to new representations, but they provide no description of what it might be. They make no attempt to reinterpret models of memory and learning according to their theory.

For example, what accounts for our tendency to remember exceptions (as described by Schank [11])? Winograd and Flores acknowledge that Schank's work and ideas like "default reasoning" are closer to the nature of cognition, but they insist that these approaches are still limited by the need to distinguish the relevant objects and properties before doing any representation (p. 116).

Is there any evidence of a mechanism that generates the recurrence in our behavior? What about timing experiments involving discrimination and recall? Winograd and Flores claim that these experiments do not deal with "meaningful material" (p. 114). But aren't hierarchical relations meaningful? Couldn't systematicity in abstraction, for example the patterns in levels of "natural kinds," be explained by structural properties of memory? The problem is that any admission of structure in the brain corresponding to conceptual relations undermines the argument that representations do not exist in the brain.

It appears obvious that the way the brain works favors categorization and association of certain kinds. From here it is but a short step to hierarchical search. Perhaps Winograd and Flores (and Maturana) have got the main idea right, that we aren't *examining* representations internally, but they have woefully ignored the problem of explaining recurrence in memory. It would have been helpful if the book included an appendix that at least acknowledged opposing arguments (such as Fodor's [5]).

4.2. *How much background is shared?*

> If a lion could talk, we could not understand him (Wittgenstein [15]).

According to Winograd and Flores, language requires being able to commit to articulating a shared background. If no common ground is found, then breakdown is not resolved. But the book seems to understate the difficulty of resolving breakdown. Isn't the normal state of affairs one in which individuals (and countries) frequently do not understand each other? We get by normally by making many assumptions and by ignoring differences. Perhaps resolving specific differences is not as important as sharing the goal to "work something out."

A few social rules (part of shared background) for coping with unresolved breakdown may be more important than having the shared background to resolve specific differences. Obviously, not much communication could occur on the basis of just agreeing to disagree. However, the book seems to adopt the opposite stance of idealizing language, suggesting that most breakdowns are resolved in the specific elements of shared background. The general agreement to adapt and cope with ambiguity and unresolved differences could be more important.

The book's idealized description of language is clear when we consider our interactions with animals and children. Shared background is minimized here, but communication is possible. It isn't necessary to be "fully human" to engage in language. Even if computers are programmed to be part of the social structure, even if they are our slaves, interaction with them can be consensual. Their speech acts can create commitment, just as much as a dog can request to play and then become engaged in a game of mock attack or chasing. Certainly there will be practical limitations, as we may not always understand a chimpanzee, and the differences between a dog's bark to play, to eat, or to warn may be too subtle for anyone but his master to discern. However, of what practical value is it to so narrowly define language and intelligence as to rule out the behavior of animals because they are not "fully human"? It is good to make people more aware of the social dimensions of language, but Winograd and Flores have adopted an almost religious point of view that may overstate the requirements of shared background and the extent to which breakdown is typically resolved.

4.3. What are the practical limits of formalization?

The book states that we are "now witnessing a major breakdown in the design of computer technology" (p. 78). No evidence for this observation is given; just the inverse seems to be true. We are witnessing a major recognition of how much human knowledge is regular and can be usefully formalized. In the rapid growth of expert systems applications, engineers in particular are realizing the value of qualitative modeling techniques for describing recurrent objects, properties, and relations. Possibly there has been a misinterpretation of what computers are doing and the nature of intelligence, but the payoff is on the upswing and the limits appear to be years away, at least.

The book provides very little basis for determining the practical limits of formalization, particularly for applications of Artificial Intelligence to science and engineering. Perhaps by continuing to find structure within structure we can get programs that are very good, and even fool most people. Yes, they will fail sometimes, but so do people. There is little evidence that the practical limitations of formal reasoning are as serious as the book suggests.

Practical implications of the argument tend to return to conclusions we already knew, as I indicated in briefly considering explanation, teaching, and knowledge acquisition. However, the book gives us an improved understanding of what is difficult and why we might not succeed. The most important change might be a better understanding of what we are doing.

4.4. Isn't reflection an essential part of reasoning?

> Human cognition includes the use of representations, but is not based on representation. Experts do not need to have formalized representations in order to act. They may at times manipulate representations as one part of successful activity, but it is fruitless to search for a full formalization of the pre-understanding that under-lies all thought and action (p. 99).

> The essence of our intelligence is our thrownness, not our re-flection.

I believe that this book significantly understates the importance of reflection, to the point of distorting the nature of cognition. In reflection, we articulate our background in order to compare possible behaviors, anticipate consequences, and plan, rather than acting impulsively. Even granting the nature of unformalized background, readiness-to-hand, and the immediate nature of reflection (we don't decide to reflect), the valued action in a consensual domain is one that anticipates ramifications. Human reasoning is immensely more successful by our ability to simulate what might happen, to visualize possible outcomes and prepare for them. We do this by reflecting, saying what we expect, and responding to what we say. (An excellent description of this imagination process appears in Jaynes' [7].)

We create representations by language, by acting. We make interpretations by what we say. Every representation is an interpretation. But isn't every representation therefore potentially crucial in our action? Granted that representations are not "inside" and that they are blind, once articulated don't they play a central role in intelligent behavior? We are always reinterpreting old representations. We are not just speaking like birds singing. The articulation is essential, it can change our behavior. Winograd and Flores fail to properly emphasize the loop: We are always listening to ourselves. Even if representations are not directly generated from representations, they are generated *in response to* representations. In particular, imagery and silent utterances are a form of "mental representation" which is part of the cognitive system. While these representations may be unnecessary for behavior, much behavior is mediated by them.

The weakness of the argument minimizing the centrality of representation is most clear in the example of the chairman who is always directly acting (p. 34). Winograd and Flores greatly understate the importance of making observations, forming hypotheses, and consciously choosing a course of action. In chairing a meeting, I attend, stop myself from saying something (anticipating a reaction), plan things to say, arrange a list of people to call upon, attempt to weigh alternative topics, watch the time, and suggest a revised agenda. The book seems to overgeneralize the nature of physical skills—as provided by the example of a hammer and how we attend to it—in suggesting that cognitive behavior generally has the same degree of automaticity and lack of reflection. Granted behavior must be immediate; there is no homunculus inside interpreting representations. But forming representations and reinterpreting them is where all of the action is! Cognitive behavior is strongly coupled to the representations it creates; as visualizations and silent utterances, they are "inside" the system as much as anything else.

Most of my day involves an inner conversation. Most of my awake activity is a long sequence of telling and asking statements to myself. Granted, I don't know where the questions come from (I don't have to work at firing neurons). Granted, I don't know where the answers come from. I just keep making requests and promises to myself. "What are all of the projects I'm working on now? I have to call Jan. What will I do when I finish this? I'll work on the review tomorrow. Where is my yellow pad?" Most of my life seems to involve responding to my own language, the representations I generate.

Winograd and Flores appear to have got the emphasis wrong. In emphasizing that TELL and ASK actions do not come from interpreted representations, they ignore the crucial point that thinking involves the generation of representations and attending to them. We are constantly observers to our own thinking behavior. We are constantly responding to representations. Most important, we tell ourselves what we *might do*. Then we react to this. And in our reaction we promise ourselves that we will do something different or make a request. We do not just simply act. We are engaged in a loop of imagining action and visualizing consequences. Yes, our words and motoric actions always proceed directly, but often not before intervening representational actions and sometimes not at all without them.

How then do we get to the state of reflecting? What, after all, changes us? Perhaps reflection is built in? Being able to place ourselves in a situation so we can know how we might behave is incredibly powerful. It means being able to simulate a structural coupling, to know what we are apt to do. This is much more than articulating a background; it is articulating the behavior that the background will elicit. By projecting forward in this way, admittedly with uncertainty, we can anticipate the consequences of behavior. This anticipation then has the potential of changing our background and resultant behavior.

By overemphasizing the direct, ready-to-hand, unreflective core of all behavior (including reflection itself), Winograd and Flores understate the importance of representation in intelligent behavior. That an expert can act without a representation is not very interesting in comparison to how impoverished his behavior would be if representations were not available for solving the difficult problems.

5. Recommendations

This book should make AI researchers more cautious about what they are doing, more aware of the nature of formalization, and more open to alternative views. By addressing the nature of representation and reasoning with examples familiar to most AI researchers, the book has the potential of being more influential than other criticisms of the field.

A scientific enterprise requires openness to blindness of all kinds. This book explains why blindness is inevitable and elevates our awareness of the origin of language and how breakdowns occur. When the Chenobyls and Challengers of AI occur, we can look back at this book to better understand why our programs failed. The book provides an important theoretical basis for the analysis of failure in knowledge engineering. Indirectly it tells us how to analyze domains: What are the recurrent dialogues? What breakdowns occur? What are the expert's methods for coping with breakdown? What are the shared sources of experience? Who can talk to whom and why?

Every AI researcher should read this book. Designers of interactive programs interested in theoretical aspects of language and improving their understanding of what they are doing will find this book to be fascinating, engrossing, and obstinately provocative. The title is apt: If you are interested in understanding what computers can do, for example how you might use them in your business, and have a philosophical bent, you should definitely read this book. However, be forewarned that it points the way, rather than providing answers.

The authors state that the book is not intended to be a scholarly treatise, and it was probably a good idea to simplify the presentation in this way. However, I think the book will mostly appeal to researchers and academicians, and these readers should be aware that there are other books that adopt similar points of view. For example, I learned about "readiness-to-hand" from reading Polanyi [8], who calls the idea "tacit knowledge" (using the same hammer example). Yet, Winograd and Flores do not cite Polanyi, and Polanyi does not cite Heidegger. The intellectual development of the ideas is therefore obscure. I believe that Richard Rorty's [10] *Philosophy and the Mirror of Nature* (not cited by Winograd and Flores) is a good reference for readers who want a more complete understanding of the argument against the idea of internal representation. *Understanding Computers and Cognition* goes a long way towards making philosophical works like this more accessible to AI researchers.

In conclusion, even though the book is extremely well written, its arguments are so counterintuitive many readers are likely to remain confused and unconvinced. The book helps resolve foundational issues of AI, but the practical implications are unclear.

One goal for writing the book was to prevent a false view of computers from distorting our understanding of people. Ironically, the book's new view of cognition is a little scary, making reasoning seem limited and out of our personal control. The earth is not in the center; man is not in the center, and neither is his conscious mind. The relation of responsibility to reflection needs to be better developed and balanced against the core of automaticity that lies behind behavior. On the other hand, the book supports a humanist position, emphasizing our commonality, that what we are is mostly what we do together.

Certainly, this book might change how you think about the world. As I squashed a huge mosquito the other night, I thought, "So much for another structural coupling."

REFERENCES

1. Brown, J.S. and VanLehn, K., Repair theory: A generative theory of bugs in procedural skills, *Cognitive Sci.* **4** (4) (1980) 379–415.
2. Clancey, W.J., From Guidon to Neomycin and Heracles, *AI Magazine* **7** (3) (1986) 40–60.
3. Dreyfus, H.L., *What Computers Can't Do: A Critique of Artificial Reason* (Harper and Row, New York, 1972).
4. Feigenbaum, E.A. and Feldman, J., *Computers and Thought* (Robert E. Krieger, Malabar, 1963).
5. Fodor, J.A., *The Language of Thought* (Harvard University Press, Cambridge, MA, 1975).
6. Gould, S.J., *Ever Since Darwin* (Norton, New York, 1977).
7. Jaynes, J., *The Origins of Consciousness in the Breakdown of the Bicameral Mind* (Houghton-Mifflin, Boston, MA, 1976).

8. Polanyi, M., *The Tacit Dimension* (Anchor Books, Garden City, NY, 1967).
9. Pribram, K.H., *Languages of the Brain* (Wadsworth, Monterey, CA, 1977).
10. Rorty, R., *Philosophy and the Mirror of Nature* (Princeton University Press, Princeton, NJ, 1979).
11. Schank, R.C., Failure-driven memory, *Cognition and Brain Theory* **4** (1) (1981) 41–60.
12. Weizenbaum, J., *Computer Power and Human Reason: From Judgment to Calculation* (Freeman, San Francisco, CA, 1976).
13. Wilber, K.W. (Ed.), *The Holographic Paradigm and Other Paradoxes* (Shambhala, Boulder, CO, 1982).
14. Winograd, T., *Understanding Natural Language* (Academic Press, New York, 1972).
15. Wittgenstein L., *Philosophical Investigations* (Macmillan, New York, 1958).

On *Understanding Computers and Cognition*: A New Foundation for Design

A response to the reviews

Terry Winograd
Computer Science Department, Stanford University, Stanford, CA 94305, U.S.A.

Fernando Flores
Logonet, Inc., Berkeley, CA 94704, U.S.A.

1. A theory of language

In *Understanding Computers and Cognition*, we presented a theory of language, on which we base our understanding of cognition and of computers. It includes some basic assertions about how language works:

(1) Language does not convey information. It evokes an understanding, or "listening," which is an interaction between what was said and the pre-understanding already present in the listener.

(2) An utterance produces different understanding for different listeners, since each person has a background of pre-understanding generated by a particular history. This background does not determine interpretation in a rigid way, but generates the domain of possibilities for how what is heard will be interpreted.

(3) The background that is relevant to understanding grows out of concerns, practices, and breakdowns in those practices. People interpret language in a way that makes sense for what they do.

(4) The background of concerns and practices is not purely individual, but is generated within a tradition. Each person is unique, sharing background to varying extents with other people. Some amount is universally human; more is shared with members of the same culture; more yet with those in the same line of work; and still more with partners in frequent conversation.

The reviews collected here offer a striking validation of this theory. The same piece of language (in this case, our book) produced four widely different understandings, each generated within the background of a particular listener. The important issue is not that different reviewers "liked" the book more or less, but that they heard it as addresing different concerns in different ongoing conversations. We will begin our response by examining their interpretations and the backgrounds in which they arose.

2. Four traditions

In the book, we use "tradition" in a relatively broad sense, discussing at some length the "rationalistic tradition," which has developed over the course of centuries in Western society (see Chapter 2). In this response, we will focus on more narrowly delineated traditions, associated with a particular academic discipline or even a "school" within a discipline. At this scale the differences of background among the reviewers become most visible.

In identifying each of the reviews with a tradition, we do not imply that an individual can be taken purely as a representative. Each of us is a product of a unique history and has individual concerns. However, all too often in our culture, people focus on individuality without recognizing the degree to which thought and language are shaped by a history shared with others. In characterizing these four responses as representing traditions, we deliberately de-emphasize the personal aspects, in order to bring out the generality—to show how these authors reflect a much wider circle of potential readers.

Vellino

Vellino responds in the tradition of academic analytic philosophy: his primary concern is the articulation of "ideas" and logical arguments supporting them. The abstractions take on a life of their own, and the discourse centers on their logic, rather than on trying to make sense of them with respect to some world of practical concerns. In his entire review, he does not consider any of the questions we take as primary: how our theory makes sense in the practice of work and what it offers for design. Instead, he enters into a debate about the arguments, focussing on identifying "... mistaken belief that the language of the analytic tradition is not sufficient to express ideas that are critical of its own presuppositions . . . [and that] analytic theories cannot handle context dependency in natural language."

What is most revealing in these comments is the unquestioned assumption that the appropriate domain for discussion is that of "beliefs," "ideas," "presuppositions," "analysis," "theory," and so on. One of the major directions of our book is precisely to question this assumption—to show how language works in terms that do not postulate such objects of thought (see Chapter 5). Of course, Vellino is not alone in using this language and the form of argumentation that goes with it. It is a central thread in the rationalistic tradition, in which all of us are immersed. The style reflected in his comments is so pervasive in academic discourse that it is hard to recognize it for what it is: an extremely useful, but also limited way of understanding.

We see the same concern in Stefik and Bobrow's review. For example, they assert that "Projections of the ultimate scope of a technology should be argued from carefully defined assumptions and sources of fundamental limits," adopting the popular model of the physical sciences and assuming that it is the only appropriate mode of discourse. They adopt the same narrow focus on definition in trying to understand the rationalistic tradition:

> Search for a definition leads to puzzlement about the rationalistic tradition: It is a strange composite that includes one rendition of the scientific method, some out-of-favor notions about how sentences convey meaning, the physical symbol system hypothesis in AI, and various kinds of reductionism . . . . It is not clear to whom they ascribe this mess.

There is a basic failure here to recognize how traditions are manifested. They are not coherent bodies of carefully articulated theory, of the kind that might be ascribed to individual authors and defended in a debate. In talking of a tradition, we are not identifying and labelling a thing—a "school" or "stance" or "position." We speak of tradition to point out how our history of conversations (both individual and in a society) shapes our language and thought, by providing the ground on which we work. As an analogy, consider the tradition of "free-market economics" that is prevalent in present-day America. One might say:

> Search for a definition leads to puzzlement about free-market economics: It is a strange composite that includes one rendition of the functioning of pure competition, some out-of-favor notions about how government monetary policy can guide the economy, the welfare ideas of the New Deal, and various kinds of anticommunism and social Darwinism. . . . It is not clear to whom they ascribe this mess.

The answer is, of course "To nobody—and to all of us." We participate in a tradition and it changes through our participation. But we do not choose it or design it. It would be foolish to ignore the power of this particular tradition (as distinct from a European Social-Democratic, or a Chinese Communist one, each of which would be equally complex) because it cannot be precisely defined.

Special effort is required to recognize one's own tradition and to question what is taken for granted within it. We have attempted to do that with the rationalistic tradition. In its attempt to reduce everything to logical arguments among competing ideas and beliefs, there is a constant danger of ungrounded abstraction and a kind of "blindness." Rather than listening to language for what it might mean or do, one jumps eagerly into the game of "making points," "defending positions," and searching for "mistaken beliefs." Stefik and Bobrow complain that we "make little attempt to present a balanced or representative account of the relevant ideas." Indeed, that is not what we were trying to do. The very idea of a "balanced or representative account" takes for granted a broad consensus as to what constitutes the domain of "relevant" discourse. Our book aims to move outside of the conventional discourse—to stimulate new thinking about computer design, not to set up and defend a position (or what Vellino calls a "conceptual scheme.")

Stefik and Bobrow

Stefik and Bobrow are researchers who create programming techniques for use in artificial intelligence. Their concern for the logic of arguments is in service of their concern with inventing new theories and mechanisms. They find it disturbing that we criticize current research without offering alternative ways to proceed in their enterprise. If we argue that current techniques cannot do what AI researchers have claimed they will, then what other techniques do we advocate? Instead of answering that directly, let us examine the research paradigm that they represent, which we characterize at length in our book (see Chapters 7–9).

Put in a simple slogan, AI research is the quest to capture the essence of thought and language in the form of explicit symbolic representations. The statement by Stefik and Bobrow quoted above about "carefully defined assumptions" is indicative of the implicit assumption that everything worth saying or thinking can be so defined. Further, Stefik and Bobrow belong to a predominant tradition within AI that sees little value in foundational (called "philosophical") questions. Shortcomings of current techniques and systems are seen as a transient failure to cover the right details and to invent the right clever mechanisms, rather than as anything more basic. Instead of a radical challenge to foundations, they would rather see arguments over the technical details: "It would have been more interesting to read a critique of Grosz's work on comprehension using the context of a discourse, or Cohen's. . . . It would have been more useful if they gave a more balanced and comprehensive account of current research directions."

They imply that if we focus on the details of the technology, somehow it will all work out. They indulge in science-fiction speculations, such as ". . . newer computer systems . . . might acquire background that we humans bring to bear to understand the world . . ." and "Perhaps we shall one day develop classes of complexity for computational beings that relate in natural ways to Piaget's stages . . . ," and they evoke images of robots from the novels of Isaac Asimov. This kind of innocent optimism about technological achievement has been common among AI researchers since the beginning of the discipline. We hope that a major result of our book will be to call it into question and to open conversation about it. In doing this, we are not trying to halt or slow the development of computer technology. We accept technology as a basic fact of human activity, not inherently good or bad. We are concerned with its direction and its grounding, and we want to increase our collective capacity of thinking about it. Stefik and Bobrow state that in our book they ". . . felt an anti-technological bias." Clancey was listening to us more clearly when he said "This book is anti-illusion, not anti-technology." It is dangerous to fall into naive optimism, believing that local successes at satisfying particular technological objectives (such as building a micro-chip or a successful chess playing program) indicate a more global success at understanding what we are doing and where it is leading. In the face of technological illusions with negative practical consequences, it is necessary to be anti-illusion (and anti-*de*lusion).

Suchman

Suchman [3] has examined practical situations of computer use, applying her training in the methods of the social sciences, particularly anthropology. Within that discipline there has been an ongoing foundational debate about what it means for a person from one tradition to understand or describe the practices and languages of a different one. The Western anthropologist entering a remote native village presents an extreme case of different backgrounds leading to different understandings and interpretations. As Suchman points out, the "ethnomethodologists" recognize that the same problem arises in every attempt to articulate a description of human culture and behavior. We need to become aware of what we take for granted in our own tradition, in order not to project it blindly onto what we observe.

The conversation called "ethnomethodology" is akin to the one that has gone on under the label "hermeneutics," and is much closer to our own theories of language than to those of the rationalistic tradition. It is no surprise that Suchman is more open to our critique and more able to recognize the ways we use language. After noting, as Stefik and Bobrow did, that there is no simple definition of the rationalistic tradition, she says (with apparent approval) "The only excuse for such gross generalization is the possibility that what is common is more important, for certain purposes than what is distinct. The purposes in this case are to take off one set of eyeglasses and try on another: to imagine what other way we might look . . . at the phenomena of cognition that we are all trying to understand."

She sees our work as providing an "alternative view"—a way to alter our stance as an observer, and thereby to escape from previous blindness and to situate our understanding of computer technology in a context of human practices. This is appropriate and it is also misleading. In a way, the ethnomethodologists are trapped in the domain they criticize. Their critique is solid, but the response is to search for better methodologies—to create precise structures (or "views") which can provide a systematic method for dealing with background. Suchman says:

> We need to know all these things [what the setting is, how activities are organized, etc.] through systematic analyses. To get the latter, we need a sound methodology for the study of situated human practices, and the application of such study to the question of designing tools; a need that itself delineates a major interdisciplinary research programme . . . . [Winograd and Flores] offer neither a strong theory, nor a strong method with which to uncover or build [the sociological foundations of design.]

While we concur with her plea that questions of computer design not be approached from a purely technical orientation, we do not share the appeal to methodologies—the creation of a systematic "study" that can be applied to questions of design. As we will discuss below, we are very concerned with developing practices for design, and in this we will use systematic methodologies (and even analytic logic). But taking the methodologies as an end in themselves is ultimately limiting in the same sense as the analytic tendency to take the arguments as an end in themselves. We want to expand our ability as observers, within a context in which we are not detached but are engaged in the practices we ourselves observe.

The difference between detached methodology and concerned involvement is apparent in Suchman's defense of current AI research:

> While research in AI may not get us to an artificial intelligence soon, or even ever, in principle it can still contribute to our understanding of human intelligence, through its efforts to get closer. Pushing an approach to the limit, like the application of logic to the control of situated action, or the stipulation of common-sense knowledge, can clarify what remains outside of the approach's grasp.

This statement is carefully hedged ("in principle"), and as an abstract principle of scientific methodology, it sounds fine. But what is it saying in this context? It appears as justification for the continuation of AI research along its present lines, even if the stated goal is not to build intelligent robots (as implicit for Stefik and Bobrow), but to "contribute to our understanding." We reject the implicit argument. If the basic concern is the design of technologies that are appropriate to human settings, then we need to look for possibilities that go outside the old directions, not spend our efforts on more sophisticated "studies" within the existing framework.

Clancey

Clancey is clearly the reviewer most affected by the book. He tells of transformations in his own thought and language, as he allowed himself to enter seriously into our discourse. It seems strange in light of all the negative characterizations in the first two reviews that he describes the book as "intelligent, measured, and instructive," and urges others to read it, as ". . . it might change how you think about the world." It is too easy to dismiss this in terms of personal preference or to make psychological speculations. The relevant question isn't whether he *likes* the book, but what background he brought to it, and how he listened within that background.

Clancey has been primarily concerned with the practical design of expert systems and of educational techniques associated with them [1]. He has worked with "experts" in various subject domains, trying to apply the methods of artificial intelligence to codifying their work. Our theory fits his experience:

> . . . this [our theory] explains what is so patently obvious when you work with experts, namely that they have so much difficulty laying out consistent networks and describing relations among concepts in a principled way . . .

In reading the book he was looking for new possibilities, not for arguments: ". . . This analysis might lead to an entirely different teaching method. . . ." When he encountered our unfamiliar use of language (what Vellino called the "obtuse use of English"), he saw it not as a source of confusion, but as a potential for new interpretations:

> While a cursory scan shows the book to be full of jargon—thrownness, readiness-to-hand, shared background, blindness, breakdown, commitment—these words turn out to be useful for retaining the message. Like Freud's jargon (e.g. ego, subconscious) these terms introduce a new language for thinking about familiar things. . . . This gives meaning to "things only exist through language." Do thrownness, readiness-to-hand, shared background, blindness, breakdown, and commitment exist? For that matter, do the ego and the subconscious?

Although phrases such as "retaining the message" show his grounding in the old tradition, his use of new language throughout the review demonstrates the degree to which it has taken root in his own understanding. The problems he has encountered in his own attempts to apply AI to real situations are the ones we address in our book: What are we doing with computers? How do we teach people? How are we affected by technology? Clancey demonstrates from personal experience that our discourse is relevant to these questions.

3. Listening to the critiques

What about our own background for listening? How do we hear the language of the reviews for our own concerns? As suggested in various sections above, we did not set out to create and defend a position. We do not pretend to have produced a definitive treatise in which one can find the "correct" synthesis. Our concern is to participate in the generation of a theoretical basis that works for design. As the "computer revolution" unfolds, new domains of human action are being created and old practices are being changed. We share with most of the reviewers a basic concern with developing "cognitive technology"—a computer technology that is grounded in an understanding of what people do and how they think. But we do not share the assumption that the background for this development is adequately grounded in the existing academic disciplines of philosophy, linguistics and artificial intelligence. We see the need for a radical shift, not just better accounts within the prevalent tradition. At the same time, answers will not be provided by jumping to hermeneutics or speech act theory as a replacement. It is just as limiting to take these as the "right conceptual scheme." Our goal is to evoke openness to a new discourse that will guide the technology of the future.

Much of what we say is already implicit in other parts of the larger tradition of our society, and for that matter in some of the computer system design that is already done. Devices such as automatic teller machines grew out of an implicit understanding of tools for conversation, graphic user interfaces provide "readiness-to-hand," and elements of this understanding are visible even in programs such as operating systems. We want to design computer technology in a more principled way. Before the theory of thermodynamics, people built steam engines with a fair degree of success. Good designers did it well, without explicit articulation of a theory. But with explicit theory we can do more than improve the old designs—we can create new possibilities.

With this as our concern, we need to recognize what happens when our writing is interpreted. We will look at three ways in which these reviews indicate something that is potentially wrong or missing.

Failure to evoke an openness to the discourse

The first condition for language to work is that the hearer be open to enter into a conversation with the speaker. No amount of logical or beautiful or stirring language makes sense if it is not listened to. There is no use talking if the backgrounds of speaker and hearer are too different to create open and serious listening—even if the words are read, they will be too distantly reinterpreted.

Clancey says, "Ironically, the book's new view of cognition is a little scary, making reasoning seem limited and out of our personal control." He points out that many potential readers will react by not giving the book an open and serious reading. It is clear from the reviews that his concern is valid. For Vellino, at least, it is apparent that we did not evoke a commitment to go beyond making arguments in order to understand what we were about. He says of one section, for example, "Frankly, I do not understand what this passage says that cannot be stated more simply by the following sentence: 'meaning depends on a set of background beliefs, desires, and dispositions.'" We could enter into a discourse on why "set of background beliefs. . ." is a totally distorting way of characterizing the background we discuss. In fact, we do so any number of times in the book. But Vellino's pre-understanding is not sufficiently close to take that discourse seriously. Serious listening means something different from endorsing or criticizing the logic:

> . . . look first for the apparent absurdities in the text and ask yourself how a sensible person could have written them. When you find an answer, I continue, when those passages make sense, then you may find that more central passages, ones you previously thought you understood, have changed their meaning. [2, p. xii]

Stefik and Bobrow are more confusing. On the one hand, their explicit characterizations indicate a reading that rejects what we say:

> [The book is] disappointing both for those who expect a carefully reasoned position, and those who seek an articulate account of the way things should be. . . . What they have to say about limits . . . has little enduring value. . . . [They] fail to characterize the ultimate shortcomings of technology in terms of fundamentals.

At the same time, as Editor-in-Chief and Book Review Editor of the most important theoretical journal in artificial intelligence, they have given the book the unprecedented prominence of this set of reviews. Their actions reveal another kind of listening, in which they too are affected in deep ways by what we say, but cannot deal with it in terms of the rational arguments and critical judgments they feel compelled to offer. As researchers in artificial intelligence techniques, they sense the frustration and dissatisfaction that have beset the field. Having seen the limitations of what they call "the current technology" and opened themselves to deeper questions, they cannot return to the innocent optimism of the early days. But at the same time, from their positions as senior representatives for the field, they are called upon to defend the received position and to pass judgment on those who cast doubts.

One senses a mood of anger in their repeated criticisms that we have not made things sufficiently "clear" or given sufficient arguments. They experience the disorientation that comes from questioning the grounds on which current discourse stands, and there is a natural reaction of disagreement and defense. Their characterizations of our writing (such as "confusing fragments of argument and rhetoric for substance") show that we did not succeed with them in establishing the groundwork of trust that turns disorientation into an openness to new possibilities. But they have reached the first stage of what Clancey describes in the process of reading the book. Fundamental concerns are touched, and although their assessments are primarily negative, the sense of confusion (and frustration) shows that the book has evoked serious concern.

Suchman and Clancey were more evidently open in their listening. This is not to say we agree with everything they write, or that they have an openness that transcends their own background. They like all of us, are always moving in the tumultuous space between the traditions they embody and a new understanding that is emerging. Their response is neither an argument nor a judgment, but a participation in a conversation. Overall, the people that will do something about our central concerns are people, like them, who work with designing computer systems for real settings.

Generation of wrong interpretation

Even for a serious and open reader, a text can be written in a way that generates a wrong interpretation. In saying that an interpretation is "wrong" we are not appealing to some objective standard of truth, but recognizing that the interpretation would lead to different grounding and consequences for action than we anticipate. There are clearly some parts of our book that have not been uniformly effective in creating an understanding close to ours.

One example we discussed earlier was the misunderstanding of "tradition" that led Stefik and Bobrow to treat it as something that can be defined and justified. A more troubling example (because it was misunderstood by several of the reviewers) is our discussion of the Coordinator[1], and the treatment of commitment within it as a systematic domain.

> The design [of the Coordinator] is surprising in several ways. First, it uses vocabulary associated with rich and complex human interactions (e.g., promises) with very specific technical meaning . . . [this] seems to violate the spirit of their use of vocabulary. . . . They ignore the lesson they preach in the rest of the book. Terms like promise, commitment and responsibility are mutually defined and used by people in different ways depending on circumstances.

Suchman also interprets what we say as contradictory:

> The concern with making things explicit, moreover, seems in some ways to contradict Winograd and Flores' commitment to understanding things in terms of their relation to an unarticulated background of community and practice.

What has been missed is the difference between an observational account of a domain of practices, and a space of distinctions that generates the domain. Indeed, as Stefik and Bobrow assert, ". . . commitment and responsibility are complex notions with social and legal dimensions." One cannot give precise definitions for them or reduce them to any mechanical algorithm or implementation, and it was not our intention to do so. We made no claim of writing

---

[1] The Coordinator is a trademark of Action Technologies, Inc.

about the question of responsibility, and in writing about "commitment," we are not trying to define how the word has been used, but to create a domain of possibilities in which it is a distinction (see Chapters 11 and 12).

As an analogy, consider commerce and finance. An arbitrary formalized construct like "I owe the bank $4,000" in no way captures the meaning of property, debt or value. But the systematic structure of money, expressed as standardized conversations about finances, gives us a mutually recognized basis on which to structure our transactions. The point of making things explicit in the Coordinator is to generate such a mutually recognized base. When we label a particular utterance as a "request," we make no pretense of dealing with the full human context of requesting. We are providing the utterer and listener with a simple way to make an explicit declaration within a mutually understood context of practices. When someone sends a "request," everyone involved can anticipate that it will be followed by certain potentials for further action and breakdown, just as we can recognize that a price tag of $1.59 signals a potential for certain business transactions.

In claiming that the distinctions embodied in the Coordinator are universal, we are not implying a uniformity of cultural interpretation. We are identifying a universal constitutive feature of human social activity. People ascribe to themselves and others the capacity to make commitments—to use language in a way that allows others to anticipate their future actions. There will be very different cultural interpretations of who is able to make and recognize what kinds of commitments, and how to interpret the consequences of breakdowns when the promised action is not carried out. But there is always the basic relation, in which one person can take seriously another's language about "I will do. . . ."

From the standpoint of design, the issue is how to provide tools for operating in this domain. As Clancey discusses in his Section 3.7, computers are especially suited to dealing with the formalized structure that provides a space in which to make explicit acts. The Coordinator is just one example. Automatic Teller Machines, mundane as they may seem, are another application. They implement a network of possible conversational acts in which the customer and bank employees can participate, making particular recurring patterns explicit and "ready-to-hand" (see Chapter 12).

Missing possibilities for action

In looking for what is wrong with the book, we are at least as concerned with what is *not* there as with what *is* there. Clancey notes that the book is "of strong theoretical interest, but the practical implications, for example, what expert systems might ultimately be able to do, are not clear." Suchman urges the development of a "prototype process for design." They are not playing the role of critic, but are inviting us (and the readers) to go further. We are at an early stage of a new conversation, and are just beginning to reveal its consequences. The links have not yet been made that will carry our overall theoretical orientation into the specific practices of designer. That is the task for the coming years.

In particular, there is a body of practice based on theories of representation that pervades computer system building. We would be foolish to argue that it should be ignored or rejected, and as Clancey points out in his Section 4.4, there is much work to be done in reinterpreting and reintegrating it. As a next step in this process, we are now beginning a theoretical study of current practice in building "expert systems," and have begun to elaborate a theory of representation based on the emergence of distinctions in a linguistic domain, in response to recurrent patterns of breakdown. Much more theoretical work needs to be done here, in conjunction with the practical applications.

In a similar vein, we are developing a design methodology that will aid in creating systems that are consistent with our theories of human action and technology. A methodology is a kind of "coaching"—not a formula for producing a result, but a set of practices that can lead to appropriate questioning and to appropriate change. We want to shift concern away from the computer-technology focus of the standard "system development" methods towards a concern with the design of work and language, using computer tools (see [4] for a first step in this research).

Finally, we are engaged in the direct development of the theory through practice. We are gaining a great deal of experience with The Coordinator as a commercial product with thousands of users, and are designing computer systems that go beyond both its simple facilities and the simplistic logic of "expert systems." As with all inventions, whether they are "right" is not a matter for abstract debate, but of seeing how they work and what new ways of working emerge in using them. This is true of the theory as well. Success is not the result of fending off competing arguments, but of generating a new ground on which argument is carried out. This kind of shift cannot be immediate—it will be measured in decades and proceed in unpredictable ways. The coming years of experience will be our teacher and our most exigent reviewer.

REFERENCES

1. Clancey, W.J., From Guidon to Neomycin and Heracles in twenty short lessons, *AI Magazine* 7 (3) (1986) 40–60.
2. Kuhn, T., *The Essential Tension: Selected Studies in Scientific Tradition and Change* (University of Chicago Press, Chicago, IL, 1977).
3. Suchman, L., *Plans and Situated Actions: The Problem of Human-Machine Communication* (Cambridge University Press, Cambridge, U.K., 1986).
4. Winograd, T., A language/action perspective on the design of cooperative work, in: *Proceedings Conference on Computer-Supported Cooperative Work*, Austin, TX, 1986.

Lucy A. Suchman, *Plans and Situated Actions*: *The Problem of Human-Machine Communication* (Cambridge University Press, Cambridge, 1987); 203 + xii pages, $37.50 (hardback), $11.95 (paperback).

Reviewed by: Philip E. Agre
               Department of Computer Science, The University of Chicago,
               1100 East 58th Street, Chicago, IL 60637, USA

Lucy Suchman is an anthropologist at Xerox PARC. Her book, *Plans and Situated Actions*, is an ambitious attempt to build a bridge between the cultures of anthropology and AI by comparing the views that prevail in each of them concerning the nature of action. The sensibilities and backgrounds of these two fields are far enough apart that the bridge is necessarily long and occasionally tenuous. Even so, *Plans and Situated Actions* is clear and compelling enough to be of use to anyone who would like a look at what is available on the other side. It is also a book that repays several readings, such is the depth of the challenges and alternatives it offers to our ideas and practices in AI.

1. Planning Research

Suchman's book is topical given the great ferment currently under way in AI research on action. I think it is fair to say that until around 1985 the AI community used words like "plan," "planning," and "execution" in consistent ways, as part of what we might refer to as "classical planning." Since then, though, at least four factors have combined to drive research in a number of interestingly divergent directions:

(1) attempts to apply computational ideas about planning to actual industrial settings (for example, Fox and Smith [17], Wilkins [72]);
(2) renewed interest in the theoretical and practical problems involved in building autonomous agents (for example, Brooks [9], Payton [50], Rosenschein and Kaelbling [54], Simmons and Mitchell [61]);
(3) dissatisfaction with the theoretical limitations of classical planning techniques (for example, Chapman [11]);
(4) projects that make organized domain knowledge central to the process of deciding what to do (for example, Hammond [30]).

Proposed alternatives or extensions to classical planning are often described

Artificial Intelligence **43** (1990) 369–384
0004-3702/90/$03.50 © 1990 — Elsevier Science Publishers B.V. (North-Holland)

using the adjective "reactive" (Firby [16], Fox and Smith [17], Georgeff and Lansky [22], Schoppers [60]). Various authors understand the relationship between "reactive systems" and "planners" in different ways. (For an attempt to sort out some of the issues see Agre and Chapman [3].) In each case, though, the point is that an autonomous agent needs some capacity to respond flexibly to the moment-to-moment contingencies of its environment. A question now receiving considerable attention is what role, if any, plans might have in this process.

Though part of an extremely different intellectual tradition, Suchman's book is relevant in important ways to these current issues. In it, she offers novel proposals about the nature of action and the role of plans. Her thesis, briefly put, is that plans are resources in situated action. Let us anticipate the more detailed discussions by sorting out some of what this does and does not mean. It does mean:

(1) Action is social in that we understand its practicalities in ways that we have formed in the course of our interactions with other people.
(2) Actions are influenced by many and varied aspects of the situations in which they are performed.
(3) The availability of a plan is only one of these aspects.
(4) Using a plan requires finding a way to interpret the plan and the situation as being relevant to one another.

It does *not* mean:

(1) Plans are like computer programs, from which action can result through a process of execution.
(2) Action is a matter of reacting to immediate circumstances without any understanding of the past or anticipation of the future.

Thus Suchman's thesis suggests that the classical planning approach and the reactive approach, at least on certain interpretations of them, are both based on incorrect views of action. Her alternative goes by the name of "situated action," which is roughly the idea that all action is improvised within a field of socially organized meanings. This is a difficult idea. Let us now start over and consider Suchman's ideas in her own terms.

2. Suchman's Ideas

Suchman's argument contrasts two views of action. On the *planning view*, action derives from the execution of plans that are constructed ahead of time.[1]

---

[1] For some of the classical AI work on plans and their automatic synthesis, see Allen and Koomen [4], Chapman [11], Fikes and Nilsson [14], Giralt, Chatila, and Vaisset [23], Lozano-Perez, Mason, and Taylor [44], McDermott [46], Sacerdoti [55], Stefik [62], Tate [66], Waldinger [67], Warren [68], Wilkins [71]. For some of the work specifically concerned with models of the construction and use of plans by human beings, see Hayes-Roth and Hayes-Roth [31], Miller, Galanter, and Pribram [47], Sussman [64], Wilensky.

She opposes this to the view that all actions are *situated*, meaning that they take place in particular situations and, moreover, that the nature of action is deeply affected by the difficulty of a sufficient a priori specification of the relevant details of these situations. Plans might play a role in an agent's situated action, as resources in deciding what is happening and what to do next, but they do not control it. In particular, plans are not responsible for the orderly nature of action. As she puts it,

> ... the organization of situated action is an emergent property of moment-to-moment interactions between actors, and between actors and the environments of their action. (p. 179)

Suchman believes in the latter, situated-action view.

Her book falls into two roughly equal halves. The first half presents and compares on a theoretical level these two views of action. The second half uses this theoretical material in a very interesting case study. In the early 1980s, the Xerox Corporation, upset by complaints that its photocopiers were unreasonably difficult to use, set out to understand the problem and to do something about it. To this end, Richard Fikes built a computer system to help a person use a Xerox copier. Given a description of the user's photocopying goal, the system first constructed a representation of the plan the user ought to be following to achieve that goal and then attempted to guide the user through the execution of this plan (Fikes and Henderson [15]).

It is plain that Richard Fikes knows what he is doing, so that any difficulties this system ran up against had no shallow causes. As it happened, though, communication often broke down between the system and its users. Why? Suchman's thesis is that the system's problems reflected the view of human action it embodied, the planning view, and that the nature of these problems counted as evidence in favor of a view of action as situated. She argues for this conclusion in a novel way, through detailed analyses of videotapes of people trying to use the machine. Her argument is clear despite its theoretical sophistication because she sticks so closely to the data on these tapes.

Technical people with no previous exposure to the social sciences will definitely be disoriented at first when reading Suchman's book. One likely problem derives from the fact that computational and social theory employ contrasting prototypes of action. In the AI literature, it is natural to think of action as organized through the construction and execution of plans because the domains and examples tend to involve a solitary agent taking discrete actions in a highly regulated world, be it blocks world or a factory floor. For Suchman, though, the prototype of all action is conversational interaction, the face-to-face work of living in a shared world. On this view, the central problem of action is not the achievement of a goal as such but rather the maintenance of mutual intelligibility in the collaborative pursuit of a goal. In other words, the big question is not "What should I do?" but simply "What is going on?" Just as computational research has brought the essence of the planning view to a wide variety of activities, Suchman wishes to view all action as social action. This does not mean that nobody ever acts alone. Instead, it means that all action is organized through an improvisatory process of making sense of the ongoing situation through socially defined categories. This perspective is likely to be new to an AI audience. Let us, then, consider the intellectual background that lies behind Suchman's study.

3. Background

Suchman practices a variety of social inquiry known as *ethnomethodology* (Garfinkel [19], Sacks [56]). While principally resident in sociology departments, ethnomethodology originated in a reaction *against* traditional sociology. The question in each case is the central question of the social sciences: What is the nature of the social order? It has been the practice throughout the social sciences to offer particular sorts of answers to this question, taking the common-sense categories of everyday social talk—rules, institutions, classes, generations, genders, jobs, families, crimes, professions, and all the rest—and remaking these into a scientific vocabulary within which hypotheses might be framed and tested, whether through experiments or surveys or archival research or direct observation of one sort or another.

For the founders of ethnomethodology, Harold Garfinkel and Harvey Sacks, this sort of theorizing precisely begged the question. As they put it, common-sense talk about rules and institutions and the rest is not a *resource* for sociological theory. Instead, it is the *phenomenon* that sociology ought to be studying [20]. Things like rules and institutions are not objectively existing entities which sit still in a Platonic social universe while sociologists talk about them. Instead, they are things that people *make*. The making, or "construction," of rules and institutions, moreover, is not something one does once and gets over with. Instead it is, as they put it, a "continual accomplishment" of the members of any given social setting. The members' success in their accomplishment of a common understanding of their shared situation is forever contingent, subject to a boundless variety of disruptions, confusions, mismatching interpretations, and other troubles which forever need to be averted, repaired, or explained away (Jordan and Fuller [36]).

The organization of human activities, on this view, is not imposed from the outside by objective structures. Instead, it is a local kind of organization, an organization continually made afresh by the situated, collaborative work of particular individuals. If the rules and institutions to which people appeal *seem* like objective, external things in the world, that too is an accomplishment of a setting's members. These are, as one might expect, highly controversial propositions. In defending them, ethnomethodological research offers detailed dissections of the methods whereby people accomplish these things and thus construct social reality in particular settings. Garfinkel, Sacks, et al. have pursued these themes in investigating such activities as legal trials (Atkinson and Drew [5], Pollner [51]), laboratory science (Lynch [45]), mathematical theorem-proving (Livingston [43]), office work (Suchman [63]), and medical examinations (Heath [32]).

Although I cannot offer, in this space, a satisfactory summary of what is by now a substantial body of work (see [33]), the connections to the case at hand are clear enough. As Suchman explains, the ethnomethodological view of social action recommends focusing on the ways in which the photocopier advisor and its user work together to maintain a shared understanding of what is going on between the two of them and the copier. Given this focus, it then suggests that, insofar as the interaction between the machine and its users is social action, any attempt to run this interaction by means of an a priori plotting out of its course will bring danger as soon as anything starts to go wrong—which it will, of course, and in any of innumerable ways. When trouble does arise the user will presumably employ all the skills of a competent social actor to set it right. But since the machine, certain that it knows what is going on, will not be pulling its weight, and since most of the rationale behind its actions will not be available to the user, this may not be enough to get things back on track.

In defending this analysis, Suchman relies on the analytic tools developed by a particular group of ethnomethodologists, those concerned with *conversation analysis*.[2] For an ethnomethodologist, conversation is where the social world is made. Consequently, a detailed understanding of the workings of conversations plays a foundational role in ethnomethodological studies of the social world. Research into conversation analysis typically takes the form of an extended study of the fine structure of the interactions recorded in a relatively short audio or video tape of some naturally occurring conversation among ordinary people.

Everyday conversations, it seems, are immensely complicated. Conversation analysis has a highly evolved vocabulary for talking about the structure and significance of such phenomena as turn-taking, pauses, gestures, *ums* and *ahs* and *uh-huhs*, false starts, and interruptions. It also has a notational system for transcribing these conversations, one devised by Gail Jefferson in the course of the original studies of conversations, begun by Harvey Sacks and Emmanuel Schegloff in the 1960s [58]. The analysis by Sacks [57] of the activity of "doing 'being ordinary' " in the recounting of an everyday event, along with the whole volume in which it appears [6], makes an excellent introduction to the field.[3]

---

[2] For introductions to conversation analysis see Heritage [33, Chapter 8] and Levinson [42, Chapter 6]. For some other views on conversational structure see Goffman [26] and the papers in [37]. For a contrasting perspective on the organization of face-to-face interaction see [13]. For some cross-cultural views of conversation see [29].

[3] Several more volumes of work in conversation analysis are also currently available. See for example Atkinson and Drew [5], Goodwin [27], Moerman [48], Psathas [52], Schenkein [59].

4. Suchman's Analysis

In Suchman's tapes, pairs of people work together in attempting to perform some middlingly complex photocopying tasks. (Having them work in pairs is a natural way to encourage them to talk.) It is impossible here to provide a thorough account of the use Suchman makes of conversation analysis in interpreting her observations, so a few brief examples will have to suffice. The premise, of course, is that the machine tells the people what to do and the people do it. As with just about any instance of instruction giving, though, it is not always obvious to the people what exactly the machine is asking them to do. They can ask for help, but the system's repertoire of explanations will often fail to anticipate the users' particular concern. For example, they might be uncertain why the machine has offered them an unexpected instruction, only to receive help in interpreting the instruction itself.

Further difficulties arise from the interactional significance of the actions themselves. When the users take some action and the machine responds by telling them what the next step is, the users take this as a ratification of the interpretations they have made and thus continue to act on them, even if these interpretations and the actions that resulted from them were incorrect. On the other hand, if the machine happens to offer the same instruction twice in a row, the users interpret this as an indication that their first enactment of the instruction was faulty and stands in need of repair, instead of as an instruction to do the same thing again.

These are all phenomena that conversation analysts observe in their data. Each of them, and the several other kinds of difficulty that Suchman observed, poses its own challenge to the engineering of AI systems. The various individual difficulties may not be insurmountable, but at a minimum they call for some serious rethinking of computational ideas about action and about the role of plans. Avoiding and overcoming these kinds of troubles, Suchman argues, requires an improvisatory style of action that is not readily reconciled with the planning view. Far from executing a fully operational plan for effecting a fixed goal, the photocopier users continually reinterpreted their situation and based their various actions on their evolving interpretations.

One consequence of this view of action is a notion of what plans are: plans are representations of action that serve as resources for situated action. Someone might use a plan in deciding what to do, but people do not "execute" plans and plans do not "control" behavior. Reasoning about action must take many aspects of the current situation into account, so it takes work to determine whether and how one might make use of a plan's advice. People regularly use other resources besides plans in deciding what to do. These resources include the states and arrangements of the objects they are working with, appeals to general principles, and the actions of others.

The difficulties Suchman observed are thus not simply the effects of a faulty user interface. Instead, they are evidence that the system embodied a mistaken notion of what plans are and what purpose they serve in organizing activity. The machine assumed that the sense, the force, and the reference of its instructions would automatically be clear, subject at most to a short list of prespecifiable misinterpretations. The evidence, though, suggests that the relationship between a plan and the circumstances of its use—what things in the environment a given plan step is referring to, what attributes of them it intends to make salient, and what actions it prescribes toward them—is open to a potentially unbounded process of negotiated interpretation. As Suchman puts it,

> ... while instructions answer questions about objects and actions, they also pose problems of interpretation that are solved in and through the objects and actions to which the instructions refer. (p. 142)

This process of reciprocal interpretation—using the instructions to figure out the environment and the environment to figure out the instructions—takes work. This work is not always easy. Indeed, troubles in the course of interpretive work account for a significant portion of the activity Suchman recorded. It is in the context of this work that the case for a situated view of action comes out most clearly.

A plan serves as a resource, then, when it plays a heuristic or mnemonic or advisory role in someone's activity. Suchman's ideas, though, run deeper than that. She has further elaborated the view of plans as resources by studying the roles that plans play in real social settings. In one project [63], she investigated the organization of activity in offices where workers are *required* to act according to some plan. She discovered, though, that the actual role of the prescribed office procedures was *not* to specify how the worker should proceed. Instead, the procedures provided a criterion for judging how their work should turn out at the end of the day. The office workers used the official procedures as resources in figuring out what their work should come to, but they based their decisions about how to achieve this end on the particulars of each next case that came along. If they had tried to follow the procedures literally, they would not have been doing their jobs well.

Suchman's ideas about plans have been discussed widely in the AI community. One rebuttal to them that I have often encountered in conversation goes as follows:

> The gist of Suchman's argument is that human action is marked by a striking flexibility that could not be predetermined by a plan. She wants to conclude from this that the nature of human action implies strong constraints on the design of artifacts. But this seems like a contradiction. If people are flexible enough to navigate in the social world, why are they not flexible enough to interact with whatever computer interfaces they are given?

The answer is that the flexibility of human interaction is not unilateral. In their dealings in the social world, people rely on one another to work together in continually constructing that world. Someone who fails to do their share of this work is regarded as crazy or rude (see [33, Chapter 4]). Since the photocopier advisor failed to do *its* share of the collaborative work of constructing the social world of photocopying, it was regarded as frustrating.

5. AI and the Social Sciences

The growing importance of computers in the everyday world is causing the subject matter of computer science and the social sciences to draw ever closer. This is a good thing. It reminds us that a computer, like all the artifacts that engineers design, is an object in the world, and not just the physical world but the social world as well (see Latour [40]). An understanding of the small- and large-scale dynamics of the social world can help us do good engineering, both in the sense of making devices that serve useful purposes and in the sense of shaping technology so as to help make the world a better place.

The changing roles of computers are bringing changes in the engineering behind them. Designing computers that are to operate in isolation is one thing, but designing computers that are to occupy an important place in the lives of real people is something else. A mainframe is a box in a computer room with only a simple and stereotyped interface to the outside world. Since the action goes on inside the box, the designer can plot its course in detail and then figure out the fastest way for the machine to run that course. If a machine is for someone to use, however, its purpose is not to run but to dance. The dance must somehow synthesize the ways of the machine with the ways of its user. If we are going to engineer machines that dance, we ought to understand something about dancing. What forms does the dance take? What forms *can* it take?

Much is known about the social world. As a long tradition in the social sciences has learned, the study of the social world brings special problems and special opportunities. The social world is not an enigmatic quasar or neuron but rather the sea in which we all swim all day while we're busy being scientists and lovers and parents and grocery shoppers. The problem of knowing things about the social world is the fish's problem in knowing about the sea. As a consequence, the project of putting words to the many aspects of the social world that do not normally become articulated is inevitably a matter of participant-observation.

The phrase "participant-observation" aptly expresses the position and methods of any social scientist, and most particularly the anthropologist or sociologist engaged in fieldwork. Fieldwork means going and looking at the social world. The looking, though, is not from outside this world but from inside it. The anthropologist herself, in her involvements with other people, serves as a sort of scientific instrument. By continually pooling their experiences as participant-observers, checking these experiences against theory, and then taking their shared insights back out to the field for another look, fieldworkers develop an ever-deeper understanding of the social world. At its best, this understanding is portable, in the sense that it can be brought home and used to make the familiar seem strange and the taken-for-granted seem contingent.

AI research is a fieldwork discipline too, at least sometimes. Where the anthropologist might study the way in which a pastoral people understand the passing of the seasons or the ways in which the members of some tribe use their culture's symbols in conducting disputes, the AI person who wishes to understand and model some human activity might study, though usually more informally, the way in which mechanical engineers understand the dynamics of physical devices or the ways in which city dwellers use landmarks in learning how to get around. Where the anthropologist asks questions of native informants, the builder of expert systems asks questions of domain experts. Each inquiry involves passages back and forth between sensations of strangeness and familiarity. While things seem strange it is hard to know even what questions to ask. While things seem familiar it is easy to come to an understanding that makes internal sense and accords with all of one's existing ideas but then proves, with time and testing, not simply to be mistaken but to miss the whole point.

In the end, though, both the anthropologist and the AI person are confident of coming through the other side of this process with some kind of understanding, incomplete certainly but useful nonetheless. In each case, this understanding has two levels, the specific and the general. On the specific level, one wishes to describe how a particular culture reckons its calendar or drafts its blueprints. On the general level, one wishes to contribute to a broader understanding of the awareness of time or the practice of design. This is the role of each discipline's portable knowledge. The anthropologist expects the anthropological vocabulary of symbols, lineages, practices, and social constructions to be useful in describing the specifics of each next culture and in formulating some new insight about culture in general for others to use. Likewise, the AI person expects to be able to use the computational vocabulary of representations, architectures, processes, and protocols, not only in describing the specifics of some activity but in contributing novel ideas about cognition and activity generally.

In both anthropology and AI, the hoped-for result is not just a simple description or a rote simulation but rather an explanation of what human activity is like, why it is that way, and what else it could be instead. One might have many motives for seeking such an understanding. Doing engineering, adding to human wisdom, and changing the world are three fine ones, each of which tends to be bound up with the others. It is for these reasons that a convergence between social and computational thought is something to be hoped for. Suchman's book contributes to this goal by permitting principled comparisons to be drawn between certain aspects of social and computational views of action. By pursuing its pointers into the literature of sociology and anthropology, we can begin to compare—and contrast, and possibly synthesize—social and computational ideas about representation and learning and language as well.

6. Discussion

One can come at Suchman's argument from a number of angles. One might regard the photocopier advisor as a sort of probe in a novel kind of sociology experiment: studying human activity by perturbing it and seeing how it breaks down. One might also derive from her analysis some novel rules of thumb to use in designing new computer-based tools (see Tang [65]); after all, just as knowledge of the way wind interacts with physical structures ought to inform the design of bridges, knowledge of the way people interact with complex artifacts ought to inform the design of computers. Finally, one might view Suchman's study as an instance of experimental AI. If we build an artifact that embodies some computational theory of action (or representation or diagnosis or design or whatever) and place it into some real situation in the world, what happens? By looking closely at the ways in which our artifacts fit—or fail to fit—into the world, we can learn about the strengths and weaknesses of the theories they embody.

The limits of Suchman's kind of argument are still poorly understood. She makes a strong case that the photocopier advisor does not participate in meaningful interactions in the same way that people do. But what about other kinds of AI systems? As our machines move out of machine rooms and begin to engage the world in complex ways, the sociology of computation will certainly grow more important in the design process. But it is still hard to say what an argument like Suchman's can really demonstrate about the fundamentals of engineering—about what can and cannot be gotten to work. The project of bringing together ideas and methods of AI with those of the social sciences, promising as it is, has hardly begun.

Suchman's ideas have influenced my own work. I first encountered them in 1985 when I was looking around for new ways of thinking about the things I saw in my informal studies of everyday routine activity. My computational ideas certainly do not fully capture the insights of ethnomethodology, but Suchman's work did introduce me to the idea that cognition might be something that takes place in the world.[4] This idea seems paradoxical at first if we follow the Cartesian tradition in starting from a strict separation between the

---

[4] For some other versions of this idea see Brown, Collins, and Duguid [40], Greeno [28], Lave [41], Rogoff and Lave [53], Wertsch [69].

mind and the world and in defining cognition as something that goes on entirely in the mind. I have tried to make computational sense of these non-Cartesian ideas in my dissertation work [1] and David Chapman and I drew considerable inspiration from them in the design and implementation of the Pengi program [2]. We would not claim that ours are the only mechanisms that are compatible with Suchman's arguments or with ethnomethodology or the social sciences in general. Too many profound technical questions are still open. We do, however, expect research on the nature of the social world to exert an increasing influence on work in AI.

All of this having been said, though, Suchman's book does have a few minor shortcomings as a work of social theory; I will mention these briefly as occasions to point at some issues that ought to concern AI researchers as well. One of them is that she does not do a very thorough job of placing computational ideas about action into social and historical context. She states, for instance, that "[t]he view, that purposeful action is determined by plans, is deeply rooted in the Western human sciences as *the* correct model of the rational actor" (p. ix, italics in the original). This is too simple. The idea of deliberative action goes back at least to Kant, and a bureaucratic discourse of rational planning goes back roughly a hundred years, but the scientific idea of human action as determined by plans first gained currency thirty years ago with Miller, Galanter, and Pribram [47], though Lashley's "serial order" paper [39] was an important but less programmatic statement of similar ideas. Suchman cannot be blamed too strongly for this oversimplification, though, given the poorly developed state of critical studies of computational ideas and their place in society. More research is needed.

Suchman rests her argument in part on the premise that "[e]very human tool relies upon, and reifies, some underlying conception of the activity that it is designed to support" (p. 3). This proposition is reasonably clear in the case of the photocopier advisor, but it is not immediately clear what it would mean in the case of a hammer, a lamp, or a beer bottle, to mention some artifacts that, at least in their most common and prosaic instances, are not so much designed as evolved.[5] Designers are often negligent or confused in ways that admit of useful theoretical elucidation (Norman [49]), but Suchman's claim is much stronger. It is also much stronger than she requires, given that her case study concerns a system that was built within a community whose views about action were clearly articulated.

Another, somewhat peculiar difficulty is that Suchman opens her book with a passage from a work of anthropology that seems to me to needlessly

---

[5] But see Bakhurst [7] for a new approach to the question based on "activity theory," a school of social psychology that originated in the Soviet Union.

undermine her own point in a way that is liable to mislead an AI audience. It reads:

> Thomas Gladwin [24] has written a brilliant article contrasting the method by which the Trukese navigate the open sea, with that by which Europeans navigate. He points out that the European navigator begins with a plan—a course—which he has charted according to certain universal principles, and he carries out his voyage by relating his every move to that plan. His effort throughout his voyage is directed to remaining "on course." If unexpected events occur, he must first alter the plan, then respond accordingly. The Trukese navigator begins with an objective rather than a plan. He sets off toward the objective and responds to conditions as they arise in an ad hoc fashion. He utilizes information provided by the wind, the waves, the tide and current, the fauna, the stars, the clouds, the sound of the water on the side of the boat, and he steers accordingly. His effort is directed to doing whatever is necessary to reach the objective. If asked, he can point to his objective at any moment, but he cannot describe his course (Berreman [8, p. 347]).

This passage suggests, falsely, that the Trukese navigators operate in a planless manner that AI researchers might characterize as "reactive." Gladwin, though, soon realized his mistake and adopted a view much more in line with Suchman's actual thesis:

> A final few words need to be said about planning. As initially conceived this study was expected to discover in planning a principal basis for distinguishing the thinking processes of Puluwat [the particular island where Gladwin did his fieldwork] navigators from Western navigators and Western thinking in general (Gladwin [24]). It seemed likely that the plans of Western navigators were prepared in advance, whereas on Puluwat plans were made up and changed continually as the person using them went along. This does not appear as a valid distinction. The Puluwat navigator also has advance plans which cover the entire voyage. These are the sailing directions he has learned and they are quite as complete as those of any Western skipper. The difference is rather that the Puluwat navigator has his plans available before the voyage is even prepared. He has had them ever since he learned navigation. The Western navigator in contrast makes up a new one for each trip. Thus we come again to the matter of innovation. Yet by the time both the Western and the Puluwat navigators are ready to get under way their plans are remarkably similar. They are based on somewhat different maps, both cognitive and on paper, and the process

as a whole seems superficially very different, but they cover the same things for the same reasons. Probably they could not do otherwise. However diverse the intellectual traditions of the navigator, the sea is a demanding master. No style of thinking will survive which cannot produce a usable product when survival is at stake [25, p. 232].[6]

Suchman's argument gets at the issue precisely. A plan can be a valuable resource in conducting a complex activity. But using a navigational plan, or any other kind of plan, is hard work. Action in complex environments is situated because one must take a great deal about each next situation into account in deciding what to do. Plans are therefore not responsible for the organization of action. Instead, this organization is an emergent property of a complex interaction whose rationality is a local accomplishment of the individuals involved.

Finally, I should discuss an aspect of Suchman's presentation that might get in the way for a reader in AI. Bridging the gap between two such disparate cultures as ethnomethodology and AI is an excellent public service, but it has the price of the occasional necessary oversimplification. Technical readers are likely to be either bored or annoyed by Chapter 2 on interactive artifacts and Chapter 3 on plans, neither of which is long enough to review the issues in detail. These two chapters might thus be skipped on a first reading. The temptation might be strong to skip directly to the technical substance of the case study in Chapter 7, but in order to appreciate the nature of the argument being made I would strongly recommend taking the time to understand the clear exposition of the theoretical material in Chapters 1 and 4–6 first.

A more serious issue is Suchman's black-and-white opposition between a "planning view" and the idea of "situated action." Those who actually reside in the AI community are likely to regard planning research, with some justification, as covering too much ground to deserve being lumped into a "planning view." Moreover, recent computational work has begun to address certain aspects of the problem of situated action (Agre and Chapman [2], Brooks [9], Connell [12], Firby [16], Fox and Smith [17], Georgeff and Lansky [22], Horswill and Brooks [34], Kaelbling [38], Rosenschein and Kaelbling [54], Schoppers [60]). The point, though, is much broader. The perspective on action into which Suchman offers a point of entry is truly very, very different from anything that has heretofore motivated computational research. It is a perspective evolved by intelligent people through a great deal of going and looking. It is worth a look from us as well.

---

[6] Gladwin's study of Micronesian navigation, together with that of Hutchins [35] and related studies of navigation by Frake [18] and Gell [21], could provide a critical resource for computational research on mobile robot navigation.

ACKNOWLEDGEMENT

John Batali, Danny Bobrow, David Chapman, Jim Davis, Walter Hamscher, Beth Preston, Mark Stefik, and Randy Trigg offered useful comments on drafts of this review.

REFERENCES

1. P.E. Agre, *The Dynamic Structure of Everyday Life* (Cambridge University Press, Cambridge, forthcoming).
2. P.E. Agre and D. Chapman, Pengi: An implementation of a theory of activity, in: *Proceedings AAAI-87*, Seattle, WA (1987) 196–201.
3. P.E. Agre and D. Chapman, What are plans for?, in: P. Maes, ed., *New Architectures for Autonomous Agents: Task-level Decomposition and Emergent Functionality* (MIT Press, Cambridge, MA, 1990).
4. J.F. Allen and J.A. Koomen, Planning using a temporal world model, in: *Proceedings IJCAI-83*, Karlsruhe, FRG (1983) 741–747.
5. J.M. Atkinson and P. Drew, *Order in Court: The Organization of Verbal Interaction in Judicial Settings* (Humanities Press, 1979).
6. J.M. Atkinson and J. Heritage, eds., *Structures of Social Action: Studies in Conversation Analysis* (Cambridge University Press, Cambridge, 1984).
7. D. Bakhurst, In the beginning was the deed: Ilyenkov on activity and the ideal, Presented at Conference on Work and Communication, University of California at San Diego (1988).
8. G. Berreman, Anemic and emetic analyses in social anthropology, *Am. Anthropologist* **68** (1966) 346–354.
9. R.A. Brooks, A robust layered control system for a mobile robot, *IEEE J. Rob. Autom.* **2** (1) (1986) 14–23.
10. J.S. Brown, A. Collins and P. Duguid, Situated cognition and the culture of learning, *Educ. Researcher* **18** (1) (1989) 32–42.
11. D. Chapman, Planning for conjunctive goals, *Artificial Intelligence* **32** (1987) 333–377.
12. J.H. Connell, Creature design with the subsumption architecture, in: *Proceedings IJCAI-87*, Milan, Italy (1987) 1124–1126.
13. S. Duncan Jr and D.W. Fiske, *Interaction Structure and Strategy* (Cambridge University Press, Cambridge, 1985).
14. R.E. Fikes and N.J. Nilsson, STRIPS: A new approach to the application of theorem proving to problem solving, *Artificial Intelligence* **2** (1971) 189–208.
15. R.E. Fikes and D.A. Henderson, On supporting the use of procedures in office work, in: *Proceedings AAAI-80*, Stanford, CA (1980) 202–207.
16. R.J. Firby, An investigation into reactive planning in complex domains, in: *Proceedings AAAI-87*, Seattle, WA (1987) 202–206.
17. M.S. Fox and S. Smith, ISIS: A knowledge-based system for factory scheduling, *Expert Syst.* **1** (1) (1984) 25–49.
18. C.O. Frake, Cognitive maps of time and tide among medieval seafarers, *Man* (*new series*) **20** (1985) 254–270.
19. H. Garfinkel, *Studies in Ethnomethodology* (Prentice-Hall, Englewood Cliffs, NJ 1967).
20. H. Garfinkel and H. Sacks, On formal structures of practical actions, in: J. McKinney and E. Tiryakian, eds, *Theoretical Sociology* (Appleton-Century-Crofts, 1970).
21. A. Gell, How to read a map: Remarks on the practical logic of navigation, *Man* (*new series*) **20** (1985) 271–286.
22. M.P. Georgeff and A.L. Lansky, Reactive reasoning and planning, in: *Proceedings AAAI-87*, Seattle, WA (1987) 677–682.
23. G. Giralt, R. Chatila and M. Vaisset, An integrated navigation and motion control system for autonomous multisensory mobile robots, in: M. Brady and R. Paul, eds., *Proceedings First*

Symposium on Robotics Research, Bretton Woods, NH (MIT Press, Cambridge, MA, 1984) 191–214.

24. T. Gladwin, Culture and logical processes, in: W.H. Goodenough, ed., *Explorations in Cultural Anthropology: Essays Presented to George Peter Murdock* (McGraw-Hill, New York, 1964).

25. T. Gladwin, *East is a Big Bird* (Harvard University Press, Cambridge, MA, 1970).

26. E. Goffman, *Forms of Talk* (Basil Blackwell, Oxford, 1981).

27. C. Goodwin, *Conversational Organization: Interaction Between Speakers and Hearers* (Academic Press, New York, 1981).

28. J.G. Greeno, Situations, mental models, and generative knowledge, in: D. Klahr and K. Kotovsky, eds., *Complex Information Processing: The Impact of Herbert A. Simon* (Erlbaum, Hillsdale, NJ, 1989).

29. J.J. Gumperz and D. Hymes, eds., *Directions in Sociolinguistics: The Ethnography of Communication* (Basil Blackwell, Oxford, 1986).

30. K.J. Hammond, *Case-Based Planning: Viewing Planning as a Memory Task* (Academic Press, New York, 1989).

31. B. Hayes-Roth and F. Hayes-Roth, A cognitive model of planning, *Cogn. Sci* **3** (1979) 275–310.

32. C. Heath, *Body Movement and Speech in Medical Interaction* (Cambridge University Press, Cambridge, 1986).

33. J. Heritage, *Garfinkel and Ethnomethodology* (Polity Press, 1984).

34. I. Horswill and R.A. Brooks, Situated vision in a dynamic world: Chasing objects, in: *Proceedings AAAI-88*, St. Paul, MN (1988) 796–800.

35. E. Hutchins, Understanding Micronesian navigation, in: D. Gentner and A.L. Stevens, eds., *Mental Models* (Erlbaum, Hillsdale, NJ, 1983).

36. B. Jordan and N. Fuller, On the non-fatal nature of trouble: Sense-making and trouble-managing in Lingua Franca talk, *Semiotica* **13** (1) (1975) 1–31.

37. A.K. Joshi, B.L. Webber and I.A. Sag, eds., *Elements of Discourse Understanding* (Cambridge University Press, Cambridge, 1981).

38. L.P. Kaelbling, Goals as parallel program specifications, in: *Proceedings AAAI-88*, St. Paul MN (1988) 60–65.

39. K.S. Lashley, The problem of serial order in behavior, in: L.A. Jeffress, *Cerebral Mechanisms in Behavior: The Hixon Symposium* (Wiley, New York, 1951).

40. B. Latour, *Science in Action: How to Follow Engineers and Scientists Through Society* (Harvard University Press, Cambridge, MA, 1987).

41. J. Lave, *Cognition in Practice: Mind, Mathematics and Culture in Everyday Life* (Cambridge University Press, Cambridge, 1988).

42. S. Levinson, *Pragmatics* (Cambridge University Press, Cambridge, 1983).

43. E. Livingston, *The Ethnomethodological Foundations of Mathematics* (Routledge and Kegan Paul, London, 1986).

44. T. Lozano-Perez, M.T. Mason and R.H. Taylor, Automatic synthesis of fine-motion strategies for robots, *Int. J. Rob. Res.* **3** (1) (1984) 3–24.

45. M. Lynch, *Art and Artifact in Laboratory Science: A Study of Shop Work and Shop Talk in a Research Laboratory* (Routledge and Kegan Paul, London, 1985).

46. D.V. McDermott, Planning and acting, *Cogn. Sci.* **2** (1978) 71–109.

47. G.A. Miller, E. Galanter and K.H. Pribram, *Plans and the Structure of Behavior* (Holt, New York, 1960).

48. M. Moerman, *Talking Culture: Ethnography and Conversation Analysis* (University of Pennsylvania Press, Philadelphia, PA, 1988).

49. D.A. Norman, *The Psychology of Everyday Things* (Basic Books, New York, 1980).

50. D.W. Payton, Internalized plans: A representation for action resources, in: P. Maes, ed., *New*

Architectures for Autonomous Agents: Task-level Decomposition and Emergent Functionality (MIT Press, Cambridge, MA, 1990).

51. M. Pollner, *Mundane Reason: Reality in Everyday and Sociological Discourse* (Cambridge University Press, Cambridge, 1987).

52. G. Psathas, ed., *Everyday Language: Studies in Ethnomethodology* (Irvington, 1979).

53. B. Rogoff and J. Lave, eds., *Everyday Cognition: Its Development in Social Context* (Harvard University Press, Cambridge, MA 1984).

54. S.J. Rosenschein and L.P. Kaelbling, The synthesis of digital machines with provable epistemic properties, in: J. Halpern, ed., *Proceedings Conference on Theoretical Aspects of Reasoning About Knowledge*, Monterey, CA (1986).

55. E.D. Sacerdoti, *A Structure for Plans and Behavior* (Elsevier, Amsterdam, 1977).

56. H. Sacks, Unpublished transcribed lectures, University of California, Irvine, CA (1964–72); Transcribed and indexed by Gail Jefferson.

57. H. Sacks, On doing 'being ordinary', in: J.M. Atkinson and J. Heritage, eds., *Structures of Social Action: Studies in Conversation Analysis* (Cambridge University Press, Cambridge, 1984) 413–429.

58. H. Sacks, E. Schegloff and G. Jefferson, A simplest systematics for the organization of turn-taking in conversation, in: J. Schenkein, ed., *Studies in the Organization of Conversational Interaction* (Academic Press, New York, 1978).

59. J. Schenkein, ed., *Studies in the Organization of Conversational Interaction* (Academic Press, New York, 1978).

60. M. Schoppers, Universal plans for reactive robots in unpredictable environments, in: *Proceedings IJCAI-87*, Milan, Italy (1987) 1039–1046.

61. R. Simmons and T. Mitchell, A task control architecture for mobile robots, in: *Proceedings AAAI Spring Symposium in Artificial Intelligence: Robot Navigation*, Stanford, CA (1989).

62. M. Stefik, Planning and meta-planning, MOLGEN: Part 2, *Artifical Intelligence* **12** (1981) 141–169.

63. L. Suchman, Office Procedures as practical action: Models of work and system design, *ACM Trans. Office Inf. Syst.* **1** (1983) 320–328.

64. G.J. Sussman, *A Computer Model of Skill Acquisition* (Elsevier, Amsterdam, 1975).

65. J. Tang, Listing, gesturing, and drawing in design: A study of the use of shared workspaces by design teams, Ph.D. Thesis, Stanford University Mechanical Engineering Department, Xerox PARC Tech. Rept. SSL-89-3, Palo Alto, CA (1989).

66. A. Tate, Interacting goals and their use, *Advance Papers IJCAI-75*, Tbilsi USSR (1975) 215–218.

67. R. Waldinger, Achieving several goals simultaneously, Tech. Note 107, SRI Artificial Intelligence Center, Menlo Park, CA (1975).

68. D. Warren, Warplan: A system for generating plans, Memo No. 76, Department of Computational Logic, University of Edinburgh, Edinburgh, Scotland (1974).

69. J.W. Wertsch, *Vygotsky and the Social Formation of Mind* (Harvard University Press, Cambridge, MA, 1985).

70. R. Wilensky, *Planning and Understanding: A Computational Approach to Human Reasoning* (Addison-Wesley, Reading, MA, 1983).

71. D.E. Wilkins, *Practical Planning: Extending the Classical AI Planning Paradigm* (Morgan Kauffman, Los Altos, CA, 1988).

72. D.E. Wilkins, Can AI planners solve practical problems?, Tech. Rep. 468, SRI International Artificial Intelligence Center, Menlo Park, CA (1989).

H.A. Simon, *The Sciences of the Artificial*. Second Edition (The MIT Press, Cambridge, Massachusetts, 1981); 247 pages, $4.95.

Reviewed by: Mark Stefik
        Xerox Palo Alto Research Center, 3333 Coyote Hill Road,
        Palo Alto, CA 94304, U.S.A.

My first encounter with *Sciences of the Artificial* was as a graduate student when one of my advisors remarked "It's a delightful small book and an easy evening read. You'll enjoy it." I followed his advice and afterwards noticed that the book was quite frequently cited in books far removed from AI. Since then the 1969 edition has become increasingly difficult to find, but now Simon and the MIT Press have provided us with a second edition even broader in scope.

Readers of the first edition will re-encounter some of their old friends. Simon's simple ant on the beach, and the old clock makers Tempus and Horus are still there, ready to provide us with insights on the nature of complexity. For new readers, the moral of the ant example is that the complexity of the ant's walk results from the environment, not the complexity of the ant. The moral of the clock makers story is the centrality of modularity (or 'near decomposability') for constructing, designing, or even evolving complex systems. These stories are so evocative and have been read by so many people that they have become famous parables in AI. The original essays on "Understanding the Natural and Artificial Worlds", "The Psychology of Thinking", "The Science of Design", and "The Architecture of Complexity" are essentially unchanged. To these Simon has added three new essays substantially expanding the discussion of the artificial sciences. They are "Economic Rationality", "Remembering and Learning", and "Social Planning".

Several themes are woven throughout the book. One is the notion that man-made things (call them artifacts) operate at the boundary between an inner and outer environment. Simon's first example of this is a mechanical ship's clock that keeps accurate time in spite of the pitching and rolling of a ship in a storm. Getting the relationships right between the inner environment (the clock's mechanism) and the outer environment (the ship) is essential to the proper operation of the clock.

A second theme of the book is that human cognition can be usefully

Artificial Intelligence **22** (1984) 95–97
0004-3702/84/$03.00 © 1984, Elsevier Science Publishers B.V. (North-Holland)

understood in terms of 'bounded rationality'. This is reflected in models of how memory works (e.g. 'chunking'), models of how social institutions like a free market really work (e.g., by distributing information to agents of bounded rationality), and models of reasoning that account for the problems of complexity (e.g., satisficing *versus* optimizing).

Simon uses the word *artificial* in a specific sense to mean "things that are man-made and for a particular function". They are adapted to fit into an environment and there are particular goals for their use. His exploration of this notion is sweeping in its scope, but to my thinking somewhat uneven in quality. His strong suit is his discussion of complexity, design, and bounded rationality. I learned a lot from his chapter on economics and enjoyed the anecdotes from his chapter on social planning. On the other hand his discussion about processing natural language completely overlooks the work on speech acts in the past few years. Examples abound of utterances whose meaning can be understood in terms of their intended effect on a particular listener. This does not contradict his view of language as an artificial creation, but it does make his characterization of discourse seem somewhat naive.

A more puzzling thesis is his contention that

> A man, viewed as a behaving system, is quite simple. The apparent complexity of his behavior over time is largely a reflection of the complexity of the environment in which he finds himself.

Here Simon extends his notion of artificiality to include man himself, and in so doing defines the 'somewhat arbitrary' boundary between the inner and outer environments so that a man's memory is part of the *outer* environment. What he has in mind for the inner environment is a *physical symbol system*. A symbol system possesses a number of simple processes that operate on symbol structures—creating, copying, and destroying symbols. The hypothesis that he developed with Allen Newell in their Turing Award lecture [1] is that a physical symbol system has the necessary and sufficient means for intelligent action. A system like this is apparently what is left of the mind of a man, after we have exiled his memory to the outer environment.

My first complaint is that this line of thought is misguided in its restriction to a single level of analysis. From the evidence that Simon cites, the interesting part of a man's behavior derives from what he knows. (As the knowledge engineering community would say, "in the knowledge lies the power".) Simon's characterizations of semantically rich domains provide evidence for this source of power. So by placing memory on the outside he excludes essential architecture from his analysis. If the techniques for reasoning, learning, abstraction, and what have you all reside in the memory, then the hypothesis about necessary and sufficient conditions for intelligence is about as interesting as saying that "information can be encoded in bits" or "computers can be built out of logic switches". Given that so much of the book is about the organization of complexity and the science of design, I find it annoying that his hypotheses about man and intelligent systems provide no important guide for designing an intelligent artifact, and they are presented as if they did.

My second complaint is that even if the hypothesis about the simple core of the physical symbol system in man is true, it does not matter much for the design of intelligent machines. In Simon's model, the simple physical symbol system *merely* interprets a (perhaps complicated) memory structure. Whether this is true seems at most a curious quirk of one possible implementation; a matter of no great concern. A somewhat different implementation might have completely different partitionings. For example, if the memory were part of the inner environment, we could consider the structure of *active memories* with substantial parallel processing capabilities. Simon's 'no parallel processing' position is one that he has defended on other occasions [2]. This stance was unexpected from someone who writes so convincingly about the utility of parallel processing of a free market. In addition, I find it odd that someone familiar with biological evolution would propose this line of thought. Rather one would expect a parallel processing brain to be the natural end result from brain structures that evolved from simple neural nets connecting sensors.

These complaints aside, I have asked myself how the book stands up when revisited three years later. I find that overall, my advice is the same as my advisor's. It's a delightful small book and an easy weekend read. You'll enjoy it.

REFERENCES

1. Newell, A., and Simon, H.A., Computer science as impirical enquiry: symbols and search, *Communications of the ACM* **19**(3) (1976).
2. Simon, H.A., Cognitive science: the newest science of the artificial, *Cognitive Science* **4**(1) (1980) 33–46.

April 2, 1984

Dear Mark,

Thank you for your cordial review of *The Sciences of the Artificial*. Of course, I don't agree with what you say about memory or parallelism, but I don't think you expected me to.

The treatment of memory is, of course, in many ways a rhetorical device, but it has the serious purpose of emphasizing that, except for the control and perceptual end of the machinery, what is stored in memory and even the way in which it is stored, is not a built-in characteristic of the mechanism, but almost entirely determined by interaction with the external environment—the memory mirrors the outside world more closely than it mirrors built-in features of the mechanism. Search in the memory is not very different from search of the external environment.

On the parallelism issue, I try to make a clear distinction between the obvious parallelism of the sensory/perceptual system, and the obvious serial character of thought requiring conscious attention. The former system has been evolving about 400 million years, and has had lots of time for fine tuning. The latter system has been evolving for about a million years, and hasn't even been locally optimized—even assuming that there aren't deep reasons for serial organization.

Ed Feigenbaum and I are publishing in *Cognitive Science* (the last issue of 1984) a reply to criticisms of the seriality of EPAM that were published by Barsalou and Bower in the first issue of 1984 of the same journal. The reply incorporates some comparison of serial with proposed parallel recognition systems.

Cordially yours,

Herbert A. Simon

Artificial Intelligence **26** (1985) 231
0004-3702/85/$3.30 © 1985, Elsevier Science Publishers B.V. (North-Holland)

Donald A. Norman, *The Psychology of Everyday Things* (Basic Books, New York, 1988); 257 pages, $19.95.

Reviewed by: Daniel S. Weld
Computer Science Department, University of Washington, Seattle, WA 98195, USA

Donald Norman's *The Psychology of Everyday Things* (POET) is perfect bedtime reading for the AI researcher. Packed with amusing anecdotes, the book sparks a number of insights into the dynamics of human interactions with the environment.

By developing a model of routine human activity, Norman explains why so many familiar devices are hard to use, and provides guidelines to avoid these problems. POET should be required reading for all people engaged in design, whether the artifact is a nuclear power plant, computer software, or the handle on a door. Norman's book speaks to everyone frustrated by perverse designs: if you can't program your VCR or put a caller on hold with the new office phone system, it's the designer's fault, not your own. And for the AI audience, POET carries a deeper message about the nature of cognition.

The touch that makes POET both provocative and fun is Norman's numerous examples of wayward devices. The controls to Norman's refrigerator are a case in point. The two dials and instructions are shown in Fig. 1. Your objective is to raise the temperature in the freezer without changing the temperature of the fresh food compartment.

As the controls seem so straightforward, you might not even bother reading the instructions. This would be a mistake. Look carefully at the sample settings. Do they make sense? The labels clearly suggest that the respective dials independently control the two compartments. The natural conceptual model dictates that the refrigerator has two cooling units and two thermostats to match the dials. Alas, it's not that simple. In fact, there is only one cooling unit and only one thermostat; the other dial controls the relative temperature of the two compartments. But knowing the correct model is of limited help:

> . . . I still cannot accurately adjust the temperatures because the refrigerator design makes it impossible for me to discover which

Artificial Intelligence **41** (1989/90) 111–114

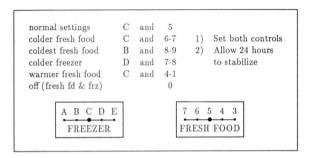

Fig. 1. Controls to a refrigerator (adapted from Fig. 18, p. 14).

control is for the thermostat, which control is for the relative proportion of cold air, and in which compartment the thermostat is located. The lack of immediate feedback for the actions does not help: with a delay of twenty-four hours, who can remember what was tried? (p. 17)

Of course, these refrigerator controls are a pathological example. In most cases designers don't actively suggest a false conceptual model, they simply neglect to induce the correct one. Whose fault is it if a harried cook cannot remember which knob in the row of identical controls corresponds to the burner in the upper right corner? If the placement of the controls was in clear spatial correspondence with the burner layout, they would be much easier to use.

A third example raises more subtle cognitive issues:

> ... Mr. Tanaka, had difficulty remembering how to use the turn-signal switch on his motorcycle's left handlebar. Moving the switch forward signaled a right turn, backward a left turn. The meaning of the switch was clear and unambiguous, but the direction in which it should be moved was not. Tanaka kept thinking that because the switch was on the left handlebar, pushing it forward should signal a left turn. That is, he was trying to map the action "push the left switch forward" to the intention "turn left", which was wrong. As a result, he had trouble remembering which switch direction should be used for which turning direction. ... Mr. Tanaka solved the problem by reinterpreting the action. Consider the way the handlebars of the motorcycle turn. For a left turn, the left handlebar moves backward. For a right turn the left handlebar moves forward. The required switch movements exactly paralleled the handlebar movements. (p. 69)

This phenomenon is probably familiar to many readers. The amount of information to be remembered is small in this case, but unless the information can be explained in some way, it is almost impossible to recall. Why does the explanation help? After all, there are two competing explanations, so the problem has not been simplified by recursing. How does one remember which explanation to use?

This anecdote illuminates an interesting feature of people's cognitive architecture. However, the real question is why does explanation facilitate memory? In particular is it an accident that humans find memory difficult without an explanation, or is there a sound computational reason? In the case of Mr. Tanaka, the answer is far from clear, but the following story about an Audi car suggests that intelligent machines (even with the potential for flawless memories) may find it useful to explain their environment:

> Supposedly, if the ignition is not on, the sunroof cannot be operated. However, a mechanic explained that you could close the sunroof even without the ignition key if you turned on the head-lights and then (1) pulled back on the turn-signal stalk (which normally switches the headlights to high beam), and (2) pushed the close control for the sunroof.
>
> My friend said that it was thoughtful of Audi to provide this override of the ignition key in the case that the sunroof was open when it started raining. You could close it even if you didn't have your key. But we both wondered why the sequence was so peculiar. (p. 71)

Obviously, an intelligent machine could have the memory to simply record this peculiar mode of operation and use it in the future. But consider the explanation: imagine a keyless person parked on the side of a dark road. The Audi designers saw this as a dangerous situation and designed a mechanism to allow emergency flashing of the headlights: pulling back on the high-beam stalk. Their implementation of the safety feature connects the whole electrical system when the stalk is pulled—enabling movement of the sunroof.

For many people, this explanation facilitates remembering the mechanism for keyless sunroof operation, but it does considerably more as well. It predicts, for example, that the radio and fan can be operated by the same technique. In short, the explanation fleshes out a conceptual model for the system that generalizes the current behavior. The result can be used to predict the results of novel events. This ability has obvious utility for machines, regardless of memory size.

Although these examples convey the excitement of Norman's book, they understate the importance of the themes raised by POET. In one sense the evidence bolsters the case of the situated-action (or reactive systems) community: Norman implies that people continually rely on the environment for cues to direct their actions and asserts that many problems (e.g., turning on the wrong stove burner) can be attributed to a faulty design that foils the necessary cues. On the other hand, the refrigerator and many other examples suggest that people use complex mental models when reasoning about devices. This view lauds designs that facilitate correspondence between a user's model and the actual state of the device. Norman's attempt to unify these views is reason enough to buy the book, but there is an even simpler reason you should read POET. The book is fun.

George Lakoff, *Women, Fire, and Dangerous Things* (University of Chicago Press, Chicago, IL, 1987); 614 pages, $29.95.

Reviewed by: Daniel S. Weld
MIT AI Lab, Cambridge, MA 02139; and
Xerox PARC, Palo Alto, CA 94304, U.S.A.

Few things are more central to thought than categorization. As Lakoff says:

> Every time we see something as a *kind* of thing, for example, a tree, we are categorizing. Whenever we reason about *kinds* of things—chairs, nations, illnesses, emotions, any kind of thing at all—we are employing categories. (p. 5)

It is an understatement to say that the book is ambitious. It attempts a comprehensive discussion of categorization, and in addition, it details a broad argument against a philosophical position underlying certain research in cognitive science, the so-called *objectivist* paradigm which holds that there is one correct way to view reality. With a scope this broad, any book will have flaws, but these are minor compared to the panorama of exciting ideas Lakoff presents:

– A summary of relevant and surprising experiments in linguistics and psychology that will probably change the way you view human thought.

– A critique of the "classical" representation of categories. Lakoff convincingly argues the inadequacy of defining categories as a set of objects with common attributes (e.g., satisfying some logical combination of predicates).

– The beginnings of a fascinating new theory of concepts, Idealized Cognitive Models, which agrees with empirical evidence.

– A series of case studies demonstrating the adequacy of the new framework on a range of categorical phenomena.

– A comprehensive argument attacking the philosophical, objectivist, world-view.

Women, Fire, and Dangerous Things is well worth reading for any one of these topics. However a bit of work may be required to locate the topic given the division of the book into three parts. Book I, Part I contains the first three

Artificial Intelligence **35** (1988) 137–141
0004-3702/88/$3.50 © 1988, Elsevier Science Publishers B.V. (North-Holland)

points: psychological evidence, criticism of the classical theory of categories, and discussion of the new framework. Book I, Part II is primarily the fifth point, the philosophical attack, but chapter seventeen contains important details on the semantic structure of Lakoff's theory of Idealized Cognitive Models. Book II contains three detailed case studies. Lakoff organizes the book this way because his main motivation for studying categories seems to be the philosophical attack on objectivism. As I found the constructive aspects of the book far more exciting, I discuss these first and address philosophical issues at the end.

What's wrong with classical categories

In the classical view,

> Things were assumed to be in the same category if and only if they had certain properties in common. And the properties they had in common were taken as defining the category. (p. 6)

Lakoff summarizes the fascinating research of a dozen psychologists and linguists and concludes that this definition is woefully inadequate to express the categories that people actually use. Prototype effects are the phenomena which motivate him; if a category were defined solely in terms of necessary properties, then every member of the category would seem equally good. This is clearly not the case, for example, a bachelor is commonly defined as an adult, single, man, but is the Pope a bachelor?

Strongly influenced by Eleanor Rosch's work on prototype theory, Lakoff supports her recent admission that while prototypes constrain the nature of category representation, they probably do not mirror it directly (p. 43). Lakoff claims that prototype phenomena are surface effects induced by a multitude of causes. The fact that the Pope seems not to be a bachelor is due to implicit background assumptions about society. This is an example of what Lakoff calls *embodiment*; when a concept is motivated by societal or bodily experiences it becomes impossible to define independent of those experiences.

Different categories display prototype effects for different reasons. Try defining the category of mothers in terms of common properties. Does it include stepmothers, adoptive mothers, and women who supply eggs to be implanted in the wombs of others? Lakoff concludes that some categories are structured *radially*; the stereotypical mother is at the center of a number of overlapping subcategories. No properties are shared by all outlying mothers (p. 83). Lakoff presents a wealth of evidence in tasteful detail for these and other limitations of classical categories. His arguments are both persuasive and fun to read; although the title isn't fully explained until page 92, it's worth the wait.

Idealized Cognitive Models

Lakoff proposes the theory of Idealized Cognitive Models (ICMs) not to predict the extension of all categories, but to understand them after the fact. For example, while it is impossible to predict that the use of the word "mother" is reasonable in the sentence "He wants his girlfriend to mother him." (p. 76), it is possible to make sense of it.

Lakoff distinguishes four types of ICMs:

– Propositional models are like classical categories. Lakoff does not dispute the utility of classical theory; he just claims that alone it is inadequate.

– Metonymic models state that a part may stand for the whole. Suppose the existence of a propositional model for an institution states that all institutions have a physical location. A metonymic model could link to that relation and say that the location of an institution can stand for the institution itself. This kind of ICM explains the sentence "Paris is introducing shorter skirts this year" (p. 77).

– Metaphoric models state that one model may be thought of as another. Lakoff discusses metaphor only briefly, directing readers to his excellent book with Mark Johnson, *Metaphors We Live By*.

– Image-schematic models are directly understood kinesthetic concepts such as container and center-periphery. These ICMs are abstracted from perceptual input (e.g., container is an idealization of the body). Because image schemas are derived directly from human perceptual facilities, their meaning is grounded.

The issue of concept meaning is important to Lakoff; his attack on objectivism (see next section) is motivated by the rejection of absolute truth. In addition to image schemas, he suggests that certain *basic-level* propositional models are directly understood. For example, the category "maple" is basic but "leaf-bearing-tree" is not. As usual, he supports this distinction with convincing arguments and evidence (pp. 31–38). Complex concepts are motivated using the other types of ICMs. Furthermore, Lakoff claims that the very structure of categories is a result of the metaphoric projection of image schemas. Thus a radial concept like "mother" results from the mapping of many container and center-periphery schemas.

There is tremendous appeal in the tight, almost recursive manner in which ICMs can be seen to structure all categories, even the category of categories. Unfortunately, Lakoff is distressingly vague about the details. His examples and distinctions are extremely exciting, yet only partially worked out. For example, the description of radial structure sounds less racy when the word "set" is substituted for "container image schema". Most disappointing is his evasion of any firm description of what the four ICM types really are; he introduces them with less explanation than I present above, then rushes into examples. This weakness would be less bothersome were it not for his strong attack on people who *do* try to precisely define their terms. Even if one accepts his dislike for model theory, a more thorough and rigorous description is warranted.

Partial redemption comes in Book II, Case Studies. He tackles three interestingly different examples: anger, the word "over", and the set of grammatical "there"-constructions. His analysis is comprehensive, shows the power of Idealized Cognitive Models, and throws new light on the subjects at hand. However, one could still ask for a clearer account of this "theory", independent of examples.

Anti-objectivism

Lakoff's motivation for studying categories appears to be philosophical.

> Are concepts and reason 'transcendental,' that is, independent of the nature and bodies of the reasoning beings? Is reason just the mechanical manipulation of abstract symbols that are meaningless in themselves, but get their meaning through conventional correspondences to things in the world—and only in that way? Do concepts provide 'internal representations of external reality'? (p. 154)

Lakoff persuasively answers no to all these questions, but his style will offend many. He starts by defining the objectivist paradigm, a philosophical strawman which happens to answer these questions yes, then destroys it. Since no one is likely to believe in objectivism exactly as he describes it, the attack becomes frustratingly methodical.

Lakoff's aims are reasonable. He is irritated by researchers who blindly assume the yes answer to these questions:

> No doubt, defenses of objectivism will be forthcoming. What is important is that objectivist views can no longer be taken for granted as being obviously true and beyond question. (p. 373)

Unfortunately, Lakoff gets carried away with his polemic. For example, while one might grant him Putnam's result that semantics based on model theory cannot satisfy a strong (but reasonable) criterion for a theory of meaning (Ch. 15), this does not amount to his implicit conclusion that formalist research is devoid of value. Model theory may still be a useful tool in the hands of those who know its limitations, and alternate approaches to rigorous definitions may indeed be possible.

Given this exaggerated style of argument, I was somewhat skeptical of his claim that "understanding and meaningful thought goes beyond what any machine can do" (p. xvii). Yet when he approaches this issue (Ch. 19), he does so with carefully enumerated assumptions and considerable restraint. The result is more likely to interest philosophers than computer scientists. Lakoff agrees:

> Most practitioners of artificial intelligence and cognitive psychology will most likely not care about this. On the whole, they could not care less whether the computational models they come up with really count as 'representations of the external world' of a sort that would satisfy objectivist philosophy. (p. 343)

Of course, some AI types will disagree with Lakoff's claims, and Part II will be of special interest to them. But current trends in AI (e.g., situated action) seem in agreement with Lakoff's call for meaning through embodiment.

Conclusion

There is so much in Lakoff's book, that it is easy to recommend. The philosophic-faint-of-heart should not fear; just skip Part II except Chapter 17. Lakoff's sketch of a new theory of categories is an inspirational summary of the work of many people. And the motivating summary of psychological results is by itself enough reason to read the book. The surprising results of these experiments show categories to be much more subtle than assumed by most AI researchers. For example, what would the KL-ONE classifier say about the Pope? Definitely, a bachelor.

III *Architectures of Interaction*

Introduction

In *Unified Theories of Cognition*, Allen Newell's proposal for a "human cognitive architecture" begins at the neural level with what he calls the "biological band." As Newell put it, "We have to start someplace." It has only been recently, however, that biological studies have begun to address the physical relationships between mind and brain. A major consequence of these studies has been a shift away from viewing "mind" as some sort of substance or entity. Rather, the brain is studied for its capacity to implement a collection of mental processes.

The brain abounds in processes, and these processes are manifested at many different levels of granularity. Summarizing this situation in his introduction to *Scientific American*'s special issue on mind and brain (September 1992), Gerald Fischbach wrote that "one must consider how nerve cells, or neurons, work; how they communicate with one another; how they are organized into local or distributed networks, and how the connections between neurons change with experience." Given such a vast array of processes, however, can we really sort out those that are mental and isolate them for study?

This is one of the fundamental questions that lies behind Marvin Minsky's book *The Society of Mind*. In Minsky's own words, "Any brain, machine, or other thing that has a mind must be composed of smaller things that cannot think at all." In other words, any device that exhibits mental processes must be composed of other devices whose processes are not mental. From where, then, does the mental nature of a process emerge? The argument in *The Society of Mind* is that a mental process is not a simple engineering construct that may be reduced to component processes; rather, the interactions among those components will have more to do with mind than the nature of the components themselves. To paraphrase an old saw (which happened to be a favorite of Newell's), God is not so much in the details as in how those details interact.

The idea that a process is more than just the sum of its component processes—that it can be understood only in terms of the interactions of its components—is not a new one. The entire discipline of systems analysis is concerned with how the behaviors of complex systems arise from the behaviors of simpler components. Computation itself provides many examples in which complex processes do not readily decompose into individual components (often called modules) that may be analyzed in isolation; rather, the understanding of complexity can be founded only on the patterns of interactions among those modules.

"Modular programming" may seek to minimize the number and nature of those interactions, but however small their numbers may be, those interactions are still responsible for the arising complexity.

Whereas the tradition of software engineering has long sought to tame complexity by trying to reduce systems to simple, modular elements, the collection of papers assembled by Bernardo Huberman in *The Ecology of Computation* emphasizes that the complexity inherent in interactions must be confronted for what it is. One cannot approach complex systems as problems in engineering that differ from simple problems only in the number of elements involved. Instead, one must resort to thinking in terms of other complex systems as models for behavior. The sorts of systems explored in Huberman's book as models include not only the ecological but also the bureaucratic and the economic. Michael Wellman's review surveys the roles of all three of these types of models as specified in the contributions to Huberman's book. The bureaucratic model is addressed through Carl Hewitt's argument that offices are open systems. Evolution lies at the heart of the study of ecological models, not only in terms of specific phenomena that may emerge from population diversity but also in terms of the dynamics of emergence, particularly in light of questions involving the stability of those dynamics. As Wellman demonstrates, however, economic models tend to carry more impact than do the other two. Wellman discusses the significance of principles such as negotiation, price setting, welfare, and market design, thus providing a host of unorthodox but enlightening views of software structure. Through these natural and social metaphors, computation reveals itself to be not just complex but inevitably complex. In the face of such complexity, it no longer seems quite so pejorative to argue that mind may be "just another form of computation." Rather, we may wish to move from the techniques that Huberman's book offers for the study of complex computations to the question of whether mental processes are fundamentally similarly complex computations.

Why, then, should we try to associate those mental processes with a "thing" that we wish to call "mind?" According to Minsky, this association is basically a mental construct for coping with complexity. Minsky calls it "thing-ifying." The color photographs in a book such as James Gleick's *Chaos* are appealing because we see patterns in them, but often those patterns cannot be reduced to specific constructs in the equations that generate them. Rather, we say that they are emergent properties of the systems defined by those equations. The patterns we perceive are our "thing-ifications" of those emergent properties.

Emergence is thus the manifestation of some behavior in a process that cannot be readily attributed to the individual behaviors of the components of that process. Perhaps, then, if we want to talk about "mind" at all, our best approach may be to view it as an emergent property of mental processes and, as originally proposed, to concentrate our attention on achieving a better understanding of such processes. Nevertheless, the nature of emergence itself was important enough to be explored at the Ninth Annual International Conference of the Center for Nonlinear Studies on Self-Organizing, Collective, and Cooperative Phenomena in Natural and Artificial Computing Networks, held in Los Alamos, New Mexico, in May of 1989. The proceedings of this conference were published in the volume *Emergent Computation,* which provides a collection of companion papers for those in Huberman's collection. Again, the focus is on the search for suitable models for the understanding of complexity. Some of these models are ecological, others are biological, and yet others draw on the technology of connectionism. This last approach figures significantly in the work of our reviewer, Peter Todd, who has been concerned with connectionist models of cognitive psychology. Todd offers us a broad perspective that accounts for both biological and other mathematical models as bases for a better understanding of the question of how emergent properties may be understood in terms of the complex systems from which they emerge.

Where, then, are the symbols that are so important to the symbolic theories of mind addressed in part I? The "emergent" point of view may be that questions concerned with whether or not there are really symbols in the head, or even the question of what is or is not a symbol, are actually red herrings. The real issue has to do with characterizing symbol-processing behavior. When one looks at a low-level stimulus-response system, an individual neuron, or even an abstract neuron in a connectionist network, one does not see symbols. Nevertheless, when one observes large collections of such elements interacting, one perceives the emergence of symbol-processing behavior. What is important is that emergence of this behavior does not necessarily imply that the symbols are there in any concrete manifestation.

Such an emergent view of symbol-processing behavior, however, remains quite controversial. Many of the key issues of this controversy were captured in a special issue of the journal *Cognition,* which was subsequently reprinted by The MIT Press under the title *Connections and Symbols.* This controversy has continued long since these articles first appeared, and the arguments articulated in those articles continue to be cited. Unfortunately, there is a tendency to try to reduce such debates to winners and losers. In reviewing these articles, Mark Derthick has tried, instead, to cultivate an appreciation for each published position, assessing each article in terms of both its most forceful arguments and its most critical vulnerabilities. Even those who have been deeply embroiled in this debate are likely to benefit from the perspective Derthick offers, which is concerned less with whether or not the debate has yet been resolved than with the sources of the key grounds for argument.

What makes *The Society of Mind* particularly important is the way in which it relates to the themes that have been explored by these other volumes. Much of Minsky's own interest in interaction had its origins in his early study of the biology of the nervous system. Thus, though Minsky has tended to distance himself from the study of emergence as a scientific discipline, his focus of attention on the behaviors of complex systems is very much in sympathy with the attitudes we find reflected by the contributors to *The Ecology of Computation* and *Emergent Computation*. Furthermore, though Minsky has also distanced himself from most of the connectionists, those connectionists share with him a skepticism about the power of formal reasoning systems based on symbol manipulation. Thus, Minsky's own position on formal reasoning serves as an excellent preface to the articles reprinted in *Connections and Symbols*.

The Society of Mind is thus both the keystone of this part of our forum and the first book to be considered. We present a set of reviews by representatives from four parts of the research communities of AI and cognitive science. Michael Dyer's work has focused on connectionist models and their relation to high-level cognitive tasks. His interests include natural language understanding, conceptual dependency theory, neural networks, and artificial life. Matthew Ginsberg's research has focused on formal methods in AI, particularly multi-valued and nonmonotonic logics, modal operators, and applications to planning and automated design. George Reeke works on brain and neural models. He is interested in how natural intelligence arises, and to that end he constructs computer models of neural systems and tests them on tasks relating to categorization in perception and motor control. Stephen Smoliar has been engaged in the development of expert systems and automatic programming. He has also worked in the areas of software engineering, computer processing of dance notation, and computer applications to music theory, an interest that he shares with Minsky and which was actually responsible for some of Minsky's initial thoughts on a society of mind. These four perspectives are then followed by a response from Minsky. In the period of time between the publication of *The Society of Mind* and the initial publication of these reviews, however, Minsky reflected further on both the ideas in his book and their presentation. In his contribution he uses the reviews as an opportunity not only to respond to criticisms but also to explain further and advance his thinking. He thus concludes the discussion of his own book leaving the reader well prepared to proceed to the reviews of the other three books addressed in this part.

Artificial Intelligence 48 (1991) 321–334
Elsevier

A society of ideas on cognition: review of Marvin Minsky's *The Society of Mind**

Michael G. Dyer

Computer Science Department, UCLA, Los Angeles, CA 90024, USA

Received January 1990

1. Introduction

It is unfortunate that cognitive scientists have, for the most part, reacted to Minsky's book as though it were light reading or a minor conversation piece, to be relegated to a coffee table. Minsky himself is partly to blame here, since he has written the book in a style as though it were intended only for those uninitiated to the cognitive sciences. The book consists of a set of discrete observations, each limited to a page in length, and there are no citations in the text. There is no separate bibliography at the end and what bibliography there is is embedded within the glossary.

In spite of this informal organizational style, *The Society of Mind* is well worth reading by cognitive scientists, whether coming from linguistics, psychology, connectionism, neuroscience, or AI. Minsky's discrete observations are organized into thirty chapters, covering a wide range of topics (e.g. consciousness, emotions, development, language, jokes, space, reasoning, memory, individuality) and the book is somewhat reminiscent of Wittgenstein's *Philosophical Investigations*, where the intent is more to stimulate novel questions and ideas in the mind of the reader than to actually inform the reader

*(Simon & Schuster, New York, 1986); 339 pages, $10.95 (paperback).

0004-3702/91/$03.50 © 1991 — Elsevier Science Publishers B.V.

of what has been accomplished in AI (as with textbook) or pursue one theory or technology in depth (as with a research monograph).

The Society of Mind should be useful both for "symbol-pushing" AI researchers, since it contains a strongly connectionist perspective, and for connectionist researchers, since it addresses high-level cognitive tasks and sketches out the kinds of architectural entities and relationships that are needed to support such tasks. Minsky's book is seminal and evocative, like a series of parables, aphorisms, or koans. It can have the effect of making one re-evaluate one's own knowledge, methods, and approaches to cognitive science research. From this point of view, the more one brings to the book, the more one will get out of it. To some, the book may seem vague and sketchy, but if read by researchers who augment it with their own imagination, the book can provide templates for generating new research directions, much in the same way that Minsky's original frames paper did [20].

In what follows, I refer to quoted segments by section number, rather than by page number, since each section in the book is just one page in length. As a reviewer I have selected a small subset of just some of the issues and ideas Minsky raises, that I found particularly central and/or intriguing. These are: the notion of self, K-lines, conceptual relationships, the development of cognitive abilities, a vocabulary for describing aspects of thinking, and the role of logic in systems with common sense.

2. The notion of self

Minsky maintains that intelligence is not a unary entity, but results from the interaction of many distinct "agents" in the mind. This view leaves as problematic the fact that we each experience our "self" as a unity. Rather than explain exactly how this subjective unity arises from our internal mental diversity, Minsky puts forth arguments for why something like the sense of "self" had to come about.

> ... If we changed our minds too recklessly, we could never know what we might want next. We'd never get much done because we could never depend on ourselves. (Section 4.4)

I have noticed on many occasions that small children have great difficulty in relinquishing control of an object when being asked by adults to share it with other children. Selfishness or greediness explains only a small part of this behavior. My own observations have lead me to believe that, often, a very young child cannot rely on himself to remember later to regain control of, or to even want to use the object again. Since the child cannot yet rely on himself to want to regain possession at a later date, he prefers to use the object exclusively while he has both an interest in and control over it.

Minsky examines similar kinds of situations to explore the nature of the self. He discusses how the notion of the self helps us to remain stable over time and allows us to predict ourselves, and why this self-prediction is important. He explores how and when the self changes, and why we cannot control ourselves in any direct fashion. Minsky examines a scenario in which a professor motivates himself to continuing working on a problem, even though the professor is getting bored and sleepy, by imagining that another researcher, i.e. Professor Challenger, is about to solve the problem first. Minsky points out that this self-motivation scheme can work, even in the case when the professor knows that the real Professor Challenger is not actually interested in that class of problems! So what we have is one agent in the mind attempting to activate another, where each agent has limited spheres of influence and knowledge.

> What makes us use such roundabout techniques to influence ourselves? Why be so indirect, inventing such misrepresentations, fantasies and outright lies? Why can't we simply tell ourselves to do the things we want to do? (Section 4.4)

Minsky argues that we must create methods for constraining the effects that our own changes will have on our future behavior.

> Extinction would be swift indeed for species that could simply switch off hunger or pain. Instead, there must be checks and balances. We'd never get through one full day if any agency could seize and hold control over all the rest. This is why our agencies, in order to exploit each other's skills, have to discover such roundabout pathways. All direct connections must have been removed in the course of our evolution.
>
> This must be one reason why we use fantasies: to provide missing paths. You may not be able to make yourself angry simply by deciding to be angry, but you can imagine objects or situations that make your angry . . . . (Section 4.5)
>
> Most of our self-control methods proceed unconsciously, but we sometimes resort to conscious schemes in which we offer rewards to ourselves: "If I can get this project done, I'll have more time for other things." However, it is not such a simple thing to be able to bribe yourself. To do it successfuly, you have to discover what mental incentives will actually work on yourself. This means that you—or rather, your agencies—have to learn something about one another's dispositions . . . . (Section 4.5)

With the Professor Challenger scenario, Minsky raises a host of issues, including the role of fantasy, emotions, and dispositions. These issues are explored throughout the book. For instance, in the chapter on emotions,

Minsky states,

> ... The question is not whether intelligent machines can have any
> emotions, but whether machines can be intelligent without any
> emotions. I suspect that once we give machines the ability to alter
> their own abilities we'll have to provide them with all sorts of
> complex checks and balances. (Section 16.1)

Minsky argues that what we call emotions are manifestations of these needed
checks and balances. In general, the role of emotions has been ignored in AI.
However, in our own investigations of the role of emotions in natural language
comprehension and planning [5, 6, 24], we have arrived at conclusions similar
to those of Minsky. For instance, a student of mine, Mueller [23], has
constructed a hypothetical scenario generator, called Daydreamer, whose
memory retrieval, fantasies, planning and learning behavior are influenced by
emotional states. Mueller argues that emotions are an efficient way of switching control to alternate goals in a system with many competing goals.

3. The K-line theory of memory

A major theory proposed in *The Society of Mind* is that of K-lines (Chapter
8). Like Minsky's earlier frame theory, K-line theory (consisting of "knowledge lines", first described in [21]) is really more a general framework for
generating models than a detailed theory in itself. K-line theory is highly
connectionist in orientation and includes weighted connections, inhibition,
gated connections and microfeatures. Basically, whenever a number of agents
are discovered to be useful in solving a given problem, a K-line attaches to
them. The next time a similar problem arises, that K-line will reactivate those
agents. In K-line theory, old agents and new agents compete with one another,
censor one another, learn to cooperate, and so on, through the use of different
K-line configurations and forms of organization. K-lines are especially useful in
setting up distributed memories, in reconstructing memories from partial input,
and in implementing non-propositional forms of information, such as attitudes
and dispositions.

Unlike concepts that can be articulated, and represented in terms of symbols
and their relationships, dispositions are difficult to describe.

> Suppose a certain sentiment or disposition involved the activities of
> many different agents. It would be easy to construct a huge K-line
> with which we could, later, make ourselves approximately reex-
> perience that complicated state—simply by arousing the same ac-
> tivities. But this would not automatically enable us to describe
> those feelings, which is another matter entirely, because it would
> require us to summarize that huge, dispersed activity in terms of

some much more compact arrangement of verbal expressions. (Section 8.3)

In the last few years there has been a great interest in connectionist models, partly because many cognitive scientists sense that purely symbolic structures and logical operations are too brittle in attempting to represent many of the kinds of knowledge that people (and animals) exhibit. The use of spreading activation, weighted connections, and distributed representations allows the representation of implicit "dispositions to action", versus the more explicit representations of knowledge that are easily articulable in terms of rules and symbolic structures.

Most likely, connectionist researchers will find K-line theory very vague and incomplete, in comparison to the recent explosion of more detailed localist and distributed connectionist models of memory and learning. In the K-line theory presented in *The Society of Mind*, there are no detailed algorithms, mathematical analysis, or computer simulations of how particular configurations perform, or how learning and self-organization might occur using K-lines. K-line theory is not specified at the same level of detail as, e.g., backpropagation [26], self-organizing feature maps [14], tensor manipulation networks [3, 4], structured connectionist networks [11, 28], adaptive resonance theory [12] or symbol formation and structuring through recurrent methods [9, 25]. However, K-line theory has the advantage of being at a generally higher level of abstraction than current connectionist literature.

Connectionists (whether using distributed or localist approaches) tend to operate at the level of simple, activation-passing units formed into layers. In K-line theory, a K-line becomes attached to agents (entire networks that perform a basic cognitive task), not just to simple processing units. As a result, K-line theory is more concerned with the broader architectural issues facing connectionist approaches, than with the details of learning or processing within a single network.

Although the book lacks detailed algorithms and analysis, it still contains a number of useful ideas for local connectionist processing. For example, Minsky discusses the problem of building connectionist networks that can compare and contrast related thoughts. The problem that arises is the need to represent two similar thoughts simultaneously, in order to perform the comparison. This need results in a proliferation of temporary memory structures. As an alternative, Minsky proposes what he calls "time blinking":

> ... we can compare two descriptions simply by presenting them to the same agency at different times. This is easily done if the agency is equipped with a pair of high-speed, temporary K-line memories. Then we need only load the two descriptions into those memories and compare them by activating first one and then the other. (Section 23.3)

This description suggests using the temporal dimension to propagate and compare information. Such an approach has recently been explored by Lange, Vidal and Dyer [17] and by Ajjanagadde and Shastri [1].

For connectionists to get the most out of this book, they must read, not just K-line theory, but also examine the architectural and cognitive issues (throughout the rest of the book) that are motivating Minsky in forming his theory of K-lines. Connectionists should not forget that Minsky's careful analysis of perceptrons [22] revealed fundamental weaknesses in simple associative and adaptive learning architectures when facing higher-level cognitive tasks. So when someone like Minsky examines human cognition and cognitive development from a connectionist perspective, it is a worthwhile reading what he has to say.

4. Concepts and their relationships

One of Minsky's major concerns is the formation of representations that capture the relationships between concepts. In Chapter 19, Minsky describes how processing units that weigh evidence on their inputs can be used to recognize objects. However, such evidence-weighing units lack the ability to recognize relationships among the features whose evidence they are weighing. This observation led to the downfall of perceptrons.

> Failure to verify relationships is the basis of a certain type of nonsense joke:
> What has eight legs and flies?
> —A string quartet on a foreign tour. (Section 19.6)

In order to represent relationships, Minsky reintroduces his notion of frames (Chapters 24–26) and shows how they can be used to handle natural language input. These chapters cover familiar ground for AI researchers, but should be of interest to many connectionists, who tend to dismiss the need for structure and combinatorial processes. So far, it has been my own experience that natural language cannot be successfully processed by training a single multilayer feedforward (or even a simple recurrent) backpropagation network. Instead, one needs a great many of such networks, and they must be organized to approximate relationships among frames [7, 29].

Our own attempts at learning scripts [27] automatically from input (and reimplementing script-based inferences and script-based paraphrase generation in recurrent PDP networks [19]) also has required the use of a number of networks communicating among each other through a global lexical memory, where the representations of the lexical entries are changing as the system learns its various mapping tasks [18]. In our more direct attempt to implement general Minsky-style frames and bindings [16] via spreading activation, various units end up gating others, thus requiring higher-order connections, and bindings are encoded by passing special forms of activation along highly structured pathways.

In general, my own research experiences lead me to predict that frame theory will not be superseded by connectionism, but that connectionist researchers will have to learn how to implement useful approximations of frames, in order to handle the syntactic and conceptual relationships (and associated structure-manipulating processes) necessary in natural language comprehension and other high-level cognitive tasks.

5. Cognitive development

Minsky is also concerned throughout the book with the development of cognitive abilities. In Chapter 10, he introduces us to Papert's Principle:

> ... Some of the most crucial steps in mental growth are based not simply on acquiring new skills, but on acquiring new administrative ways to use what one already knows. (Section 10.4)

Minsky attempts to explain the results of Piaget's experiment—in which children state that there is more water in a tall thin glass than in a low flat glass, even after seeing both filled from glasses holding the same amount of water—in terms of the development and interaction of separate agents for reasoning about "more", with one agent reasoning from height knowledge and another from knowledge about widths.

In observing my own daughter (now 4 years old), I have been struck by how often knowledge is compartmentalized and how much time is required to integrate it. For example, at the age of 3, my daughter knew that certain objects were "hers", that she could take them with her on outings, that people would bring her presents, that these presents became "hers", etc. One day we were at her grandmother's house and her grandmother gave her a present. She now knew it was "hers", but she still asked if she could take it home. Her grandmother, somewhat bemused, answered "of course". She then became very excited, and ran up to me, exclaiming, "Guess what! I can take it home! I can take it home!" Clearly, at that point she had not yet established (or better yet, disestablished) the relationship between receiving, owning, and location.

All parents have such stories to tell, usually for their entertainment value, but Minsky is trying to explain such behavior in a systematic way, through modeling the communication among agents. He proposes that such apparently "universal" structures, such as the grammars of natural languages, are actually manifestations of deeper, conceptual relationships, and that central to the formation of such relationships is the ability of one agent to "read" the descriptions that other agents manipulate.

Many scientists have asked, indeed, why so many human languages use similar structures as nouns, adjectives, verbs, clauses, and sentences. It is likely that some of these reflect what is genetically built into our language-agencies. But it seems to me even more likely that most of these nearly universal language-forms scarcely depend on language at all—but reflect how descriptions are formed in other agencies. The most common forms of phrases could arise . . . from machinery used by other agencies for representing objects, actions, differences and purposes . . . . (Section 26.7)

In Minsky's theory, an important form of communication is that of censorship (i.e., inhibition or gating of one set of agents by another). Minsky uses his theory of censorship to explain the role of certain classes of jokes, laughter and humor. Basically, derisive jokes involve the recognition of ineffectual forms of reasoning and derisive laughter acts to disrupt socially ineffectual reasoning and initiate the construction of a new censor.

Many people seem genuinely surprised when shown that humor is so concerned with unpleasant, painful, and disgusting subjects. In a certain sense, there is nothing humorous about most jokes . . . frequently, the thought itself is little more than "See what happened to someone else; now, aren't you glad it wasn't you?" In this sense most jokes are not actually frivolous at all but reflect the most serious of concerns. Why, by the way, are jokes usually less funny when heard again? Because the censors learn some more each time and prepare to act more quickly and effectively. (Section 27.8)

We have developed symbolic models to recognize situations that contain humorous elements, e.g., ironic situations [10], but our models lack the temporal effects and memory modifications (postulated by Minsky) that would explain why we fail to laugh at jokes that we already know. I believe that humor is crucial to high-level intelligence, since it involves both inventing forms of nonsense (i.e. errors in reasoning) and spotting such errors when they occur.

6. A vocabulary for thinking about thinking

Minsky argues that part of our problem in addressing the mind is that we lack a vocabulary for thinking about thinking. Throughout the book Minsky coins new words in an attempt to establish this needed vocabulary. For example, a "neme" is an agent "whose output represents a fragment of an idea or state of mind" (Glossary, p. 330). There are a number of different types of nemes, depending on their roles. For example, a "microneme" is a K-line that reaches

> ... into many agencies with widespread effects on the arousal and suppression of other agents—including other micronemes ... for example, the activity of your microneme for "outdoors" makes a small contribution to arousing your "hunting" microneme". (Section 20.5)

A "polyneme" is a type of K-line that sends

> ... the same, simple signal to many different agencies: each of those agencies must learn, for itself, what to do when it receives that signal. When you hear the word "apple," a certain polyneme is aroused, and the signal from this polyneme will put your Color agency into a state that represents redness. The same signal will set your Shape agency into a state that represents roundness, and so forth. (Section 19.3)

Polynemes are permanent K-lines and hold long-term memories.

A "nome" is "an agent whose outputs affect an agency in some predetermined manner" (Glossary, p. 330). There are several types of nomes. For example, "pronomes" are "pronounlike devices" that act as temporary "handles" for exploiting

> ... whatever mental activities have already been aroused, to interlink thoughts already active in the mind. (Section 21.1)

Unlike polynemes, pronomes are temporary K-lines and hold short-term memories. Pronomes play the roles of semantic cases (e.g. actor, recipient, source, destination, instrument) as used in case-frame systems for language processing. Certain pronomes operate in different domains at the same time. Minsky calls these "paranomes".

> Many of our higher level conceptual-frames are really parallel arrays of analogous frames, each active in different realm. (Section 29.3)

For example, paranomes support our ability to manipulate abstract concepts in terms of spatial relations, as when we talk about problems as obstacles to "go around".

"Isonomes" are a kind of opposite of polynemes. While a polyneme sends a signal that causes different effects in each of its recipients, an isonome sends a signal that causes the same effect in each recipient.

> Both isonomes and polynemes are involved with memories—but polynemes are essentially the memories themselves; while isonomes

control how memories are used . . . the power of polynemes stems from how they learn to arouse many different processes at once, while isonomes draw their power from exploiting abilities that are already common to many agencies. Pronomes are a particular type of isonome . . . .

Minksy describes the use of isonomes to control the instantiation of frames. He uses as an example a TRANS-frame (analogous to Schank's PTRANS conceptual dependency structure, used to represent concepts involving movement of an object from one location to another). To instantiate a TRANS-frame, the case roles (pronomes) have K-lines to terminal nodes that represent their values (e.g., the actor pronome has a K-line, k1, connecting to the terminal representing John). A frame-agent then has a K-line that gates k1 by an AND node. The particular frame-agent sends out as many gating K-lines as there are case-roles (pronomes).

This method seems very localist to me, since each distinct frame instance requires a separate, gated K-line from a pronome to a terminal node. I believe that there are several alternative methods for instantiating multiple instances of frames. One is the use of tensors, which was first proposed by Smolensky and then implemented by a student of mine in terms of tensor manipulation networks [3]. Dolan uses tensor manipulation networks for storing and retrieving distributed representations of Aesops fables in a natural language understanding system. Tensors are nice because they allow one to associate pairs of vectors while storing many pairs in the same tensor. Another method is that of Parallel Distributed Semantic (PDS) networks [29]. PDS networks look, at the macroscopic level of organization, like semantic networks implementing frame templates. However, each macro-level semantic node actually consists of an ensemble of PDP units and a pattern over those units represents a particular instance. The parallel, weighted connections between semantic nodes act to reconstruct other instances in the ensembles that play the role of case-role nodes. A third method is to represent instances and temporary bindings in terms of particular activation values. For example, when the case-role node of actor has the same activation value as that of the node(s) representing John, then the actor role is (virtually) bound to John. These kinds of virtual bindings can be implemented as distributed patterns in space or as phase-locked oscillations in time [1, 17].

While I applaud Minsky's attempt at coining new terms for describing aspects of mental function, in general, I do not believe that his attempt is particulary successful in *Society of Mind*. Without sufficient concrete examples his terms are too vague—sometimes appearing to be implementational in nature, other times appearing to be psychological in nature. To make these terms more solid would require the existence of one or more actual systems.

7. Logic and common sense

One message of the book is that systems with "common sense" are very complex and behave through the interaction of many distinct agents, each at different levels of learning and/or development. As a result, one should not look for a single mechanism to explain all higher cognitive functions.

> Human thought is not based on any single and uniform kind of "logic," but upon myriad processes, scripts, stereotypes, critics and censors, analogies and metaphors. (Section 17.11)

> What magical trick makes us intelligent? The trick is that there is no trick. The power of intelligence stems from our vast diversity, not from any single, perfect principle. Our species has evolved many effective although imperfect methods, and each of us individually develops more on our own. Eventually, very few of our actions and decisions come to depend on any single mechanism. Instead, they emerge from conflicts and negotiations among societies of processes that constantly challenge one another. (Section 30.8)

I suspect that the brain makes use of all of the methods (e.g. tensors, phase locking, PDS networks, etc.), including the AND-gating and "time blinking" methods proposed by Minsky. Like Minsky, I do not believe that there is one nice clean mechanism or theory that will be discovered to explain all of higher mental function. At the knowledge level, there are many different types of tasks to be performed (e.g. binding pronouns, handling embedded clauses, inferring unstated facts, generating expectations, forming instantiations, generalizing, etc.) while at the brain level, there are many structures, including gated connections, tensor structures, trees structures, recurrent cycles, competitive organizations, short-term binding structures, columnar formations, layered structures, and so on, that all have developed within neural populations as the result of competition and other selectional pressures.

While we must always search for what is most fundamental and systematic in mind/brain; unfortunately, mechanisms at lower levels rarely solve research problems at higher levels. Whether or not memories are implemented in the brain as "energy minima", "strange attractors" or "property lists", we are still left with specifying how specific memories evoke specific processing strategies and how these strategies come about and how they learn to interact. For instance, after we know how the brain retrieves an episode (given cues A, B, and C), we must still face the problem of how a planner, given those cues, finds instead a counterexample (as during argumentation).

One mechanism for explaining mental function is that of logic, which Minsky argues has very little to do with what actually goes on in the mind/brain.

When do we actually use logic in real life? We use it to simplify and summarize our thoughts. We use it to explain arguments to other people and to persuade them that those arguments are right. We use it to formulate our own ideas. But I doubt if we use logic actually to solve problems or to "get" new ideas. Instead, we formulate our arguments and conclusions in logical terms after we have constructed or discovered them in other ways . . . . (Section 18.1)

Unfortunately there are no simple, foolproof ways to get around the inconsistencies of common sense. Accordingly, we each must learn specific ways to keep from various mistakes. Why can't we do that logically? The answer is that perfect logic rarely works. One difficulty is finding foolproof rules for reasoning. But the more serious problem is that of finding foolproof bases for our arguments. It is virtually impossible to state any facts about the real world that actually are always true . . .

Exceptions are a fact of life because few "facts" are always true. Logic fails because it tries to find exceptions to this rule. (Section 27.4)

In our own research in modeling argumentation [2], logic plays a very small role, with the major processing tasks involving the retrieval and application of memory structures.

8. Conclusions

8.1. Society of Mind's niche

One can view the society of cognitive science researchers as an "ecology", in which different founders of AI and their colleagues have "invaded" and gained control of different "niches". For example, McCarthy and his colleagues at Stanford, e.g., Genesereth and Nilsson [13] hold the "mind-is-logic" niche; Rumelhart, McClelland and their colleagues hold the "mind-is-a-connectionist-network" niche; Schank and his colleagues hold the "mind-is-conceptual-dependencies" niche; Newell and his colleagues [15] hold the "mind-is-rule-chunking" niche. Within this ecology, Minsky's book has most affinity to connectionism and conceptual dependency theory. However, a comparison to others is somewhat unfair, since *Society of Mind* follows its own inclinations and presents it own, unique observations.

8.2. Using Society of Mind in an academic setting

Society of Mind is best used as recommended reading in a cognitive science course. Graduate students have to be warned, however, that the book is *not* intended to serve as a format for how survey articles, term papers, or dissertations should be written, since the book itself is written in what I call the "Grand Old Man" style. One should only attempt writing such a book after one has directed research in the field for many years and has been a founding member of the field (in terms of the influence of one's ideas on the research of others). At that point one can write a book of general observations and give indications of directions that researchers might take. From this perspective, I view the book as a success.

The Society of Mind should be read by anyone interested in cognitive science. It contains numerous seminal ideas and interesting observations, making it impossible to summarize, and that's rather nice. One cannot get away with just reading reviewers' commentaries.

References

[1] V. Ajjanagadde and L. Shastri, Efficient inference with multi-place predicates and variables in a connectionist system, in: *Proceedings Eleventh Annual Conference of the Cognitive Science Society*, Ann Arbor, MI (1989).

[2] S. Alvarado, M.G. Dyer and M. Flowers, Natural language processing: computer comprehension of editorial text, in: H. Adeli, ed., *Knowledge Engineering* 1. *Fundamentals* (McGraw-Hill, New York, 1990).

[3] C.P. Dolan, Tensor manipulation networks: connectionist and symbolic approaches to comprehension, learning, and planning, Ph. D. Thesis, Computer Science Department, University of California, Los Angeles, CA (1989).

[4] C.P. Dolan and P. Smolensky, Tensor product production system: a modular architecture and representation, *Connection Sci.* 1 (1) (1989) 53–68.

[5] M.G. Dyer, The role of affect in narratives, *Cogn. Sci.* 7 (1983) 211–242.

[6] M.G. Dyer, Emotions and their computations: three computer models, *Cogn. Emotion* 1 (1987) 323–347.

[7] M.G. Dyer, Symbolic neuroengineering for natural language processing: a multilevel research approach, in: J. Barnden and J. Pollack, eds., *Advances in Connectionist and Neural Computation Theory* 1 (Ablex, Norwood, NJ, 1991).

[8] M.G. Dyer, Symbol processing techniques in connectionist networks and their application to high-level cognitive tasks, in: W. Brauer and C. Freksa, eds., *Wissenbasierte Systeme* (Springer, Berlin, 1989).

[9] M.G. Dyer, M. Flowers and Y.A. Wang, Distributed symbol discovery through symbol recirculation: toward natural language processing in distributed connectionist networks, in: R. Reilly and N. Sharkey, eds., *Connectionist Approaches to Natural Language Understanding* (Erlbaum, Hillsdale, NJ, 1991).

[10] M.G. Dyer, J. Reeves and M. Flowers, A computer model of irony recognition in narrative understanding, in: E. Nissan, ed., *Advances in Computing and the Humanities* 1 (JAI Press, CT, 1991).

[11] J.A. Feldman and D.H. Ballard, Connectionist models and their properties, *Cogn. Sci.* 6 (1982).

[12] S. Grossberg, Competitive learning: from interactive activation to adaptive resonance, *Cogn. Sci.* 11 (1) (1987).

[13] M.R. Genesereth and N.J. Nilsson, *Logical Foundation of Artificial Intelligence* (Morgan Kaufmann, Los Altos, CA, 1987).

[14] T. Kohonen, *Self-Organization and Associative Memory* (Springer, Berlin, 2nd ed., 1988).

[15] J.E. Laird, A. Newell and P.S. Rosenbloom, SOAR: an architecture for general intelligence, *Artif. Intell.* **33** (1987) 1–64.

[16] T.E. Lange and M.G. Dyer, High-Level inferencing in a connectionist network, *Connection Sci.* **1** (2) (1989).

[17] T.E. Lange, J.J. Vidal and M.G. Dyer, Artificial neural oscillators for inferencing, in: V.I. Kryukov, ed., *Neurocomputers & Attention* (Manchester University Press, Manchester, 1990).

[18] R. Miikkulainen and M.G. Dyer, Encoding input/output representations in connectionist cognitive systems, in: D. Touretzky, G.E. Hinton and T. Sejnowski, eds., *Proceedings 1988 Connectionist Models Summerschool* (Morgan Kaufmann, San Mateo, CA, 1989).

[19] R. Miikkulainen and M.G. Dyer, A modular neural network architecture for sequential paraphrasing of script-based stories, in: *Proceedings International Joint Conference on Neural Networks (IJCNN-89)*, Washington, DC (1989).

[20] M. Minsky, A framework for representing knowledge, in: P.H. Winston, ed., *Psychology of Computer Vision* (McGraw-Hill, New York, 1975).

[21] M. Minsky, K-lines: a theory of memory, *Cogn. Sci.* **4** (2) (1980).

[22] M. Minsky and S. Papert, *Perceptrons* (MIT Press, Cambridge, MA, expanded ed., 1988).

[23] E.T. Mueller, *Daydreaming in Humans and Machines: A Computer Model of the Stream of Thought* (Ablex, Norwood, NJ, 1989).

[24] E.T. Mueller and M.G. Dyer, Toward a computational theory of human daydreaming, in: *Proceedings Seventh Annual Conference of the Cognitive Science Society*, Irvine, CA (1985).

[25] J. Pollack, Recursive auto-associative memory: devising compositional distributed representations, in: *Proceedings Tenth Annual Conference of the Cognitive Science Society*, Montreal, Que. (1988).

[26] D.E. Rumelhart, G.E. Hinton and R.J. Williams, Learning internal representations by error propagations, in: D.E. Rumelhart and J.L. McClelland and the PDP Research Group, eds., *Parallel Distributed Processing: Explorations in the Microstructure of Cognition* (MIT Press/ Bradford Books, Cambridge, MA, 1986).

[27] R.C. Schank and R. Abelson, *Scripts, Plans, Goals and Understanding* (LEA Press, Hillsdale, NJ, 1977).

[28] L. Shastri, *Semantic Networks: An Evidential Formalization and Its Connectionist Realization* (Morgan Kaufmann, San Mateo, CA, 1988).

[29] R.A. Sumida and M.G. Dyer, Storing and generalizing multiple instances while maintaining knowledge-level parallelism, in: *Proceedings IJCAI-89*, Detroit, MI (1989).

Artificial Intelligence 48 (1991) 335–339
Elsevier

Marvin Minsky, *The Society of Mind**

Matthew Ginsberg

*Department of Computer Science, Stanford University, Margaret Jacks Hall, Stanford,
CA 94305, USA*

Revised January 1990

Abstract

Artificial intelligence is fundamentally an engineering discipline; our collective goal of
constructing an intelligent artifact is fundamentally an engineering one. Good engineering
builds on good science. Good science, quite frequently, builds on good mathematics.
   The Society of Mind does not pretend to be good engineering or good mathematics. My
aim in this review is to discuss the question of whether or not it is good science.
   I will do this by examining two separate but related issues. The first involves Minsky's
abandonment of the usual methods of scientific inquiry and a discussion of the problems to
which this leads; the second is an analysis of Minsky's criticisms of formal logic and its role
in AI.

1. Falsifiable claims

Consider Newton's observation that the acceleration imparted to objects in a
gravitational field is independent of their mass. If I can find two objects for
which this rule fails, Newton is wrong and his theory needs to be revised. I do
not need to seek him out and discuss the matter; he has no choice. The theory
of gravitation allows us to make precise claims about observations to be made
in the future, and we evaluate the theory by testing the validity of these claims.

   In *The Society of Mind*, Minsky makes no such precise claims (about gravity
or anything else). Instead, he builds up a loose framework in which the
behavior of a single conscious entity is analyzed in terms of the collective

---

* (Simon & Schuster, New York, 1986); 339 pages, $10.95 (paperback).

behavior of a host of individual "agents" that comprise it. Minsky goes on to argue that this approach can address a wide variety of longstanding issues in philosophy and psychology—everything from autism to the fact that postpubescents can't learn to speak a new language without an accent.

How are we to evaluate views that are so vaguely formalized? The hallmark of good science is that it forces us to stick our necks out by requiring that we make falsifiable claims, but Minsky has no inclination to do this—indeed, the foundation from which he writes is too vague to allow it. Instead, the book rambles and ends up being a collection of interesting but fundamentally *ad hoc* speculations about how intelligence might work.

In fairness, I should point out that Minsky is aware that he is turning his back on conventional scientific methodology. In Essay 25.6, he writes that a good theory should not be specified in too much detail, because that encourages other scientists to "'test' it, instead of contributing their own ideas."

Unfortunately this "testing" is the cornerstone of modern science. And what makes AI interesting as a discipline is that it allows us to apply the tools of science, engineering and mathematics to questions that have previously been in the realm of philosophy and psychology. In abandoning these tools, Minsky also abandons exactly those things that make our field unique and support our expectations that AI will make substantial contributions to these far-flung disciplines.

Again, I am saying nothing of which Minsky is unaware. In the postscript, he writes that, "This book should be read less as a text of scientific scholarship and more as an adventure story for the imagination." I suppose that Minsky's stature as a founder of our discipline sanctions such flights of speculation, but he should be more candid throughout about his intentions.

2. Formal logic

At the other end of the scientific spectrum from Minsky's work is the work by some researchers on applying formal mathematics to the understanding of intelligence. Most commonly, some generalization of first-order logic is used; the falsifiable claims made typically revolve around the question of whether some particular knowledge representation scheme can efficiently encode our understanding of some commonsense domain.

Minsky seems at special pains to dismiss these efforts. In Essay 24.5 he tells us, "What appears to be a matter of 'logic' is usually not logical at all and frequently turns out to be wrong." In Essay 27.4, "Logic fails because it tries to find exceptions to [the rule that] exceptions are a fact of life."

The problem is that Minsky is viewing "logic" far too narrowly. Witness his description in Essay 18.4:

> The difference [between logic and ordinary thinking] is that in logic there's no middle ground; a logic link is either there or not. Because of this, a logical argument cannot have any "weakest link."

One way to view the work on nonmonotonic reasoning is as discovering what default assumptions underlie a particular conclusion; as such, this work is concerned *exactly* with the problem of identifying the "weakest link" in a deductive argument. Minsky's 1985 copyright gives him no excuse to ignore this large body of material.

I will return to the role of nonmonotonic reasoning in a moment, but before doing so, let me point out that one of Minsky's other criticisms of logic is even further from the mark. In Essay 18.1, he says that logic "can serve as a test to keep us from coming to invalid conclusions, but it cannot tell us which ideas to generate, or which processes and memories to use. Logic [cannot] explain how we think. ...." Underlying this suggestion is the idea that logic can be used to solve classification problems (is the conclusion valid or not?) but not synthesis problems (what plan would achieve the given goal?).

This is simply wrong; it is well known that logic can be used to solve planning problems (for example) by proving that there exists a plan to achieve a particular goal. If the proof is constructive (and most proofs found in logic programming are), then the details will contain a specification of the plan that should be used. This idea dates back to Green's work in 1969 [2]; more recently, Finger [1] and others have shown that synthesis problems can be solved using truth maintenance techniques as well.

But let me return to nonmonotonic reasoning and issues arising from it. When I look at the progress that has been made since the realization around 1980 that commonsense reasoning had nonmonotonic properties, I am struck not by how *much* progress has been made, but by how *little*. Nonmonotonic reasoning has turned out to be far more difficult than any of us expected. The fundamental advantage of working with formal methods—the advantage of making falsifiable claims—is that we are forced to address these difficulties, to confront the nasty surprises that lie between speculation and practice.

As an example, consider inheritance reasoning, which deals with things such as the fact that birds fly but ostriches don't. This example is due to Minsky himself, and he discusses it at various points in the book. The suggestions made aren't any different from the basic idea, well known in the nonmonotonic community, that subclasses should inherit by default the properties possessed by the superclasses that contain them. Thus canaries can fly because birds do, and ostriches are an exception to this sort of a rule.

The surprise is that inheritance reasoning is hard; this simple idea is not enough. In fact, inheritance reasoning is *very* hard—the nonmonotonic community has seen a flurry of recent papers concerned with finding a satisfactory formalization of it. The problem is that for any particular property (e.g., "rich") and object (e.g., a particular public-defence attorney), there is likely to be conflicting default information (lawyers tend to be rich but public servants tend not to be). The fact that Minsky has no answer to this problem doesn't trouble me (I don't have one either); what troubles me is that he manages to discuss inheritance without even mentioning the issue.

The need to select among competing default rules appears to be completely ubiquitous in commonsense reasoning. Most of the recent formal work on nonmonotonic methods, whether concerned with inheritance or not, has been aimed at addressing this issue. If this is where all the "action" is from a scientific point of view, how is it that Minsky leaves the topic completely unaddressed?

Just as the nonmonotonic work on conflicting defaults is not limited to inheritance reasoning, the problem also has a general analog in Minsky's setting. When different agents disagree about a particular issue, how is their difference to be settled? Perhaps Minsky would introduce new agents to mediate the conflict, but that completely misses the point. How, *exactly*, is this mediation to be accomplished? Without an answer to this, the concept of an agent is an idea with no practical value; it is so general that it might encompass anything. The science, the engineering, the *value* of ideas lie in specifications and the associated falsifiable claims that Minsky chooses not to make.

It is all well and good to invent interesting theories and speculate about their consequences, but such an approach almost inevitably leads to an examination of the strengths of these theories and not of their weaknesses—and Minsky's inability to choose between conflicting agents is indeed a weakness of his theory. A formal approach would have forced him to focus on this weakness until some resolution was obtained; his informality allows him to deal with it by sticking his head in the sand.

3. Concluding remarks

The Society of Mind is a fascinating and provocative book. But in abandoning the standard methods of scientific inquiry, Minsky has allowed himself to fall into the classic trap of speculative science, highlighting the strengths of his approach and ignoring its shortcomings. His failure to either discuss difficult issues or to make sharp claims concerning the applicability and limitations of his approach makes it difficult to evaluate the work; it is a sign of AI's maturation as a discipline that scientific validation is now expected.

Where Minsky does make sharp claims regarding the inapplicability of first-order logic to AI, he has taken too myopic a view. The shortcomings of the formal work on AI are apparent, but they are not as dire as Minsky suggests. In fact, the focus they provide to the formal community can be viewed as much as a strength as as a weakness.

All told, *The Society of Mind* is as Minsky describes it: an adventure in speculation, and not substantive science. It is well worth reading, but only in that light.

References

[1] J.J. Finger, Exploiting constraints in design synthesis, Ph.D. Thesis, Stanford University, Stanford, CA (1987).

[2] C.C. Green, Theorem proving by resolution as a basis for question-answering systems, in: B. Meltzer and D. Michie, eds., *Machine Intelligence* **4** (American Elsevier, New York, 1969) 183–205.

Artificial Intelligence 48 (1991) 341–348
Elsevier

Marvin Minsky, *The Society of Mind*[*]

George N. Reeke Jr

The Neurosciences Institute and The Rockefeller University New York, NY 10021, USA

Received January 1990

Connectionist societies in functionalist minds

The Society of Mind (*SOM*) represents Marvin Minsky's brave attempt to reconcile traditional artificial intelligence (AI) with connectionist approaches that eschew explicit programming in favor of self-organizing systems of simple processors connected by weighted links. In *SOM*, Minsky deals, often implicitly rather than explicitly, with fundamental issues in the philosophy of mind that are at the heart of current debate on the theoretical possibility of achieving AI and on the relative merits of various approaches to AI. In this review, I shall try to indicate the nature of some of these issues, then give a few vignettes from *SOM* that illustrate Minsky's approach. Finally, I will point out some difficulties that this approach appears to share with conventional AI and suggest that careful attention to the biology of organisms that display adaptive behavior may be well rewarded.

Minsky is well aware of the pitfalls in seeking a reduction of intelligence to mechanism. He is careful to avoid the so-called "homunculus problem", which plagues most attempts to break down intelligent behavior into simple components. This problem arises when the output of a particular unit being studied turns out to require intelligent interpretation elsewhere in order to play its role in the overall behavior of a system. An infinite regress ensues in which intelligence can never be localized to any of the units studied. Minsky deals with this problem by assuming that tasks can be subdivided into simpler and simpler subtasks until the agents required to carry out the subtasks are

---

[*] (Simon & Schuster, New York, 1986); 339 pages, $10.95 (paperback).

0004-3702/91/$03.50 © 1991 — Elsevier Science Publishers B.V.

manifestly unintelligent (these agents form the Society of his title). Similar ideas have been discussed extensively by Hofstadter [9] and by Dennett [3], in both cases with the same notion that intelligent behavior can be understood in terms of "dumb" elements if the total system is just divided finely enough. Of course, some sort of reduction to elementary units and processes must be possible if the homunculus (or his dualist cousin, the immaterial mind) is to be avoided; the real questions have to do with the nature of the elementary units and the tasks they perform, the meaning of the signals they exchange, and how they become organized. In addressing these questions, Minsky generally takes the view that intelligence is no special thing—in the glossary at the end of the book, he dismisses it as "the myth that some single entity or element is responsible for the quality of a person's ability to reason." He believes that behavior is determined by algorithms, and therefore, that free will is an illusion (Section 30.6). He thus places himself squarely in the camp of those who consider that the brain is a kind of computer. "Let's try" he says at one point (Section 2.6), "to understand what the vast, unknown mechanisms of the brain may do. Then we'll find more self-respect in knowing what wonderful machines we are."

This view is one form of the philosophical theory known as "functionalism", [1] which holds that the relevant level of description for mental states is not that of physical processes going on in the brain (or in a computer), but rather that of so-called "functional states". Functional states correspond to computations and thus are purely formal constructs. Their significance is fundamentally independent of the way in which they are physically realized. Functionalist systems may operate upon information expressed in symbolic form (arguments strongly supporting the need for symbolic representations are given in [14]) or in some other manner [19].

Throughout the book, Minsky finesses the critical question of whether his mental machines, or indeed real brains, are symbol processors. However, he is unambiguous in maintaining the strong functionalist position that thought can be understood independently of the nature of the substance that instantiates it. When he discusses the familiar problem that it is difficult to make computers do well what people do easily, he fails to notice that perhaps the reason for this problem is the very assumption that minds are computers.

Nonetheless, some human elements remain in this generally mechanical picture. Although logic is often considered to be the quintessential trademark of mechanical thinking, Minsky recognizes that humans often use logic only as a technique to formalize thought that has already occurred by some other mechanism, and that analogy and metaphor play major roles in thought. He notes that "grammar is the servant of language, not the master" (Section 26.6) thus implicitly attacking Chomsky's and Fodor's theories of language. It is interesting to see how this can be done from an unabashedly functionalist position as Minsky attempts to graft human qualities onto mechanical thinking.

Minsky's basic procedure for combining AI with connectionism is to imagine a society of simple agents, operating algorithmically but communicating in a connectionist manner. This kind of architecture is obviously ideal for implementation on a distributed-memory MIMD computer, and we may take it that this is the metaphor for the brain that is in Minsky's mind as he writes.

A major part of Minsky's scheme for building agents is the use of "frames" as a way to reason about everyday situations. Thus, in one sense *SOM* may be considered an update of the frame concept which shows explicitly how it may be made compatible with connectionism. The two ideas fit together well—network connections can be attached to the terminals of frames, permitting ambiguous or conflicting responses to be dealt with by network relaxation processes involving both excitatory and inhibitory connections.

Minsky, however, does not forget that he was one of the authors of *Perceptrons: An Introduction to Computational Geometry* [12], a volume which did much to discourage the connectionist models of its time. Thus, he reminds us that forming a weighted sum of evidence is inadequate to solve many classification problems (see also [2] and below). *En passant*, he updates his critique, pointing out a number of difficulties that are implicit in the modern connectionist approach, as it has been presented, for example, by Rumelhart, McClelland, and their colleagues [11, 16]. These include the need to add hierarchical or top-down control mechanisms to such systems. Minsky notes that brain structures are not all constrained to operate by a single rule as most connectionist models do; evolution provides a variety of structural types which are relatively resistant to change even as their functions change across the phylogenetic scale.

Minsky's thought experiments

Minsky largely tackles these large philosophical questions by presenting a *gedanken* implementation of his Society of Mind. This presentation provides more insight into his thinking. Some of the problems that he considers show plainly that he conceives of the mind as a parallel computer:

- In a Society of Mind, one agent may need to call upon another as one function calls another in a traditional computer program. To do so, Minsky proposes that it could create an appropriate collection of input signals to the called agent that would simulate an environment recognized by that agent (Section 16.7). So far, no problem.
- Time is relative in parallel computers and there is a problem defining synchronicity, as there is in our Einsteinian Universe at large. Two agents may disagree about which of two events elsewhere in the system occurred first (Section 6.6). While solutions to this problem have been devised by

computer architects, the brain does not seem to have the necessary mechanisms.
– An agent may invoke itself, generating the equivalent of a recursive call. When this happens, or when a task is interrupted, Minsky notes that all the nested environments of the agents involved must be saved, just as a computer program saves invocation frames or contexts (Section 15.9). However, the brain seems to have no mechanisms to do this, again suggesting that the underlying computational analogy needs revision.

Minsky also reflects on some implications of his theory for human psychology. I mention two of these observations very briefly to give the reader a sense of the kind of arguments Minsky is making:

– He suggests that the loss of the ability to learn new speech sounds which generally occurs in humans around the time of puberty is a mechanism for stabilizing language, which would rapidly drift if parents imitated the new constructions of their children (Section 23.5).
– Humor exists to help censor agents learn their tasks. The function of laughter (he is referring here particularly to scorn) is to disrupt normal thought processes in another person so that censors may be constructed against the behavior being ridiculed (Section 27.7).

Organization and style

The book is organized in an unusual manner reflecting, as Minsky puts it in his prologue, a society of many small ideas. It consists of a series of short articles, none longer than a single page, that present various aspects of Minsky's thinking in a manner that builds toward an overall idea but with numerous excursions along the way. This style is perhaps ideal for the reader brought up in the age of television, but it comes across to this reviewer as somewhat of a hodge-podge. Some promising lines of argument are developed only minimally, particularly in the sections dealing with consciousness and the meaning of "self". Many of the classical problems of the philosophy of mind are simply defined away: "Intelligence is our name for whichever of those [mental] processes we don't yet understand" (Section 7.1); "What magical trick makes us intelligent? The trick is that there is no trick" (Section 30.8); "The principal activities of brains are making changes in themselves" (Section 28.6).

Another problem for many readers is likely to be the collection of idiosyncratic terms Minsky has invented to describe components of his model. Many of these can in fact be identified with familiar concepts in computer science. It is not clear whether the new terms are deliberately introduced to prod the reader into seeing well-known concepts in a new light, or whether Minsky has

Table 1
A comparison of Minsky's terminology with standard terminology.

Minsky term	Computer science term
Agent	Function; subroutine; module
B-brain	Operating system; supervisory program
Exploit an agent	Call a subroutine
Isonome	Variable symbol implemented as a process
K-line	Interrupt vector; branch table
Level bands	"Ports" that restrict communications, e.g. between address spaces
Microneme	Microinstruction
Neme	Process that builds a record within a data structure or binds a value to a variable
Nome	Function returning a coded value
Paranome	A nome which returns a value that, when transmitted to multiple recipients, has the same effect on each of them
Polyneme	A process which returns a value that, when transmitted to multiple recipients, has different effects on each of them
Pronome	Local variable to which a value has been bound; short term memory
Script	Procedure; algorithm
Short term memory agent	Register file implemented as a process
Simulus	Argument list
Transframing	Linking by communicating; metaphor
Uniframing	Set intersection

simply used them in his own thinking for so long that he is no longer aware of the need to point out their relationships to more familiar terms; in either case, a guide may be helpful to the reader, and I have attempted to provide one in Table 1. If you are put off by terms like "paranome" and "isoneme", then consider yourself fairly warned.

The trouble with societies

More important than these structural defects are some serious difficulties with Minsky's approach to a theory of mind. These difficulties can be traced directly to the attempt to treat thinking as computation upon encoded information, and they occur in all such theories. These problems range from the treatment of simple recognition and categorization all the way to the remarks on the possible nature of consciousness itself. Taken together, they demand, in my opinion, a fundamental reexamination of the basic postulates of the dominant computationalist (i.e. functionalist) paradigm in all its forms, but particularly in the strict form advocated by Minsky.

This paradigm treats concepts, like categories, in the classical manner as sets defined by necessary and sufficient conditions. Thus, in Section 12.1 we have an arch described by an hypothetical child as:

> Two standing blocks and something else. The standing blocks must not touch. They must support the other thing. The other thing must be A WEDGE OR A BLOCK. (Minsky's emphasis)

This view of categories, however, has been known for some time to be untenable except in special cases [20]. The evidence, which includes primacy effects, typicality effects, and failures of superordination, has been extensively discussed by Smith and Medin [18]. In addition, the possibility that linguistic categories, which are presumably based upon prelinguistic mental categories, could be classical in nature has been totally demolished by Lakoff [10]. Minsky does understand and discuss the need for rule-based descriptions of categories to be accompanied by collections of exceptions, but he doesn't provide any way for an individual to acquire these lists as a result of its individual history in a particular environment. Indeed, it is not clear that it is possible to construct any such list if it is required that the exceptions be enumerated in symbolic representations. Minsky seems at times to be working away from such representations, as in his description of "K-lines" (Section 8.1) but comes back to them because they are necessary for his central "frames" concept to work. Paradoxically, frames provide a mechanism for context to influence categorization, but this mechanism is not easily used by "K-lines", which are more like simple perceptrons in their categorizing abilities.

Minsky goes beyond categorization and frame-based reasoning to consider matters of intentionality and consciousness. As part of his general program of mechanizing thought processes, he considers intention to be nothing more than having a goal and persisting in its achievement. He considers the difference-engine scheme developed by Newell, Shaw, and Simon [13] to be "the most useful conception of goal, purpose, or intention yet discovered" (Section 7.9). He thus seems to take the position that the everyday meaning of the word "intention" in sufficient for his purposes, and to reject the position, advocated by Searle [17] and others, that consciousness involves a special form of intentionality, namely, the notion that thoughts and words must be "about" something [4]. (For example, an idea can be "about" a rock, but a rock is not "about" anything. This "aboutness" must be a property of the thoughts themselves, not of some conscious entity interpreting them, for otherwise we should have a particularly vicious circular version of the homunculus problem. *Symbolic representations* of thoughts, however, can have by definition only the meaning assigned to them by a conscious observer, and no meaning of their own. Such symbols can indeed carry out control functions in an automaton

(Section 19.1) but perforce cannot have intentionality.) The interpretation that Minsky rejects this view is supported by his statement in this context (Section 19.1) that "It is the underlying emptiness of words that gives them their potential versatility." In fact, I would argue that it is the underlying emptiness of symbol systems, i.e., their lack of intentionality, that makes computers incapable of intelligence or common sense, and the intentionality, that is, the non-emptiness, of thought that makes intelligence possible.

Minsky, however, perseveres in his program, culminating in a treatment of consciousness as a society of individually unintelligent agents busily sending messages to each other and occasionally to other such societies. Certainly it is the case, if any scientific explanation of consciousness is possible at all, that one must eliminate the indivisible "self" at the center (the homunculus again) and replace it with some sort of material mechanism. The question is whether Minsky has replaced in with the right thing. This question is too complex and uncertain to resolve here, but its proper answer surely must be based on a detailed consideration of the physiology, development, and evolution of the brain. However, Minsky is not a biologist and his proposals seem to have been largely uninfluenced by biological constraints. Thus, he has largely ignored the apparent lack of repeating patterns in neuronal firings that could be interpreted as codes. He has ignored the extreme variability in the developmental mechanisms by which collections of neurons form and establish communications with one another. And he has ignored the total absence of any known genetic mechanism that would permit the transmission between generations of the information needed to specify the properties of the agents in his *SOM*. These data would tend to suggest the predominance of a lower level of organization than is proposed by Minsky, that is, a level of neuronal groups that have neither purpose nor codes for representing information. At this level, function is not likely to be separated across purposeful agents, but to be overlapped opportunistically across bits of circuitry that happen to have the required responses. This alternative view has been extensively developed elsewhere [5, 6, 15] and has recently been extended to provide a theory of consciousness [7] that is consistent with the biological data. The two views agree, however, on one point: both postulate that the ability to recognize events within the brain itself was a critical element in the development of consciousness.

Concluding remarks

In summary, *The Society of Mind* is a wide-ranging and sometimes entertaining exploration of some critical questions that beset the scientific study of intelligent behavior. Despite its defects, I recommend reading it for at least two reasons: Minsky's presentation may be read as an implicit critique of connectionism from the AI perspective that complements the criticism raised by others from the biological side. This critique should prove useful in evaluating connectionist research. (It also complements some of the criticisms of AI raised by connectionists, as in [8].) Most important, the gymnastics Minsky must go through to get his Society of Mind to work, even in principle, reveals the grave difficulties that are inherent in the functionalist position.

References

[1] W. Bechtel, *Philosophy of Mind: An Overview for Cognitive Science* (Erlbaum, Hillsdale, NJ, 1988).

[2] M. Bongard, *Pattern Recognition* (Spartan, Washington, DC, 1970).

[3] D.C. Dennett, *Brainstorms: Philosophical Essays on Mind and Psychology* (MIT Press, Cambridge, MA, 1981).

[4] D.C. Dennett and J.C. Haugland, Intentionality, in: R.L. Gregory, ed., *The Oxford Companion to the Mind* (Oxford University, Oxford, 1987).

[5] G.M. Edelman, Group selection and phasic reentrant signaling: a theory of higher brain function, in: G.M. Edelman and V.B. Mountcastle, eds., *The Mindful Brain: Cortical Organization and the Group-Selective Theory of Higher Brain Function* (MIT Press, Cambridge, MA, 1978).

[6] G.M. Edelman, *Neutral Darwinism: The Theory of Neuronal Group Selection* (Basic Books, New York, 1987).

[7] G.M. Edelman, *The Remembered Present: A Biological Theory of Consciousness* (Basic Books, New York, 1989).

[8] S.R. Graubard, ed., *The Artificial Intelligence Debate: False Starts, Real Foundations* (MIT Press, Cambridge, MA, 1988).

[9] D.R. Hofstadter, *Gödel, Escher, Bach: An External Golden Braid* (Basic Books, New York, 1979).

[10] G. Lakoff, *Women, Fire, and Dangerous Things: What Categories Reveal about the Mind* (University of Chicago, Chicago, IL, 1987).

[11] J.L. McClelland, D.E. Rumelhart and the PDP Research Group, eds., *Parallel Distributed Processing: Explorations in the Microstructure of Cognition* 2: *Psychological and Biological Models* (MIT Press, Cambridge, MA, 1986).

[12] M. Minsky and S. Papert, *Perceptrons: An Introduction to Computational Geometry* (MIT Press, Cambridge, MA, 1969).

[13] A. Newell, J.C. Shaw and H.A. Simon, Elements of a theory of human problem solving, *Psych. Rev.* **65** (1958) 151–166.

[14] Z.W. Pylyshyn, *Computation and Cognition: Toward a Foundation for Cognitive Science* (MIT Press, Cambridge, MA, 1984).

[15] G.N. Reeke Jr and G.M. Edelman, Real brains and artificial intelligence, *Daedalus, Proc. Am. Acad. Arts and Sciences* **117** (1988) 143–173; also in: S.R. Graubard, ed., *The Artificial Intelligence Debate: False Starts. Real Foundations* (MIT Press, Cambridge, MA, 1988).

[16] D.E. Rumelhart, J.L. McClelland and the PDP Research Group, eds., *Parallel Distributed Processing: Explorations in the Microstructure of Cognition* 1: *Foundations* (MIT Press, Cambridge, MA, 1986).

[17] J. Searle, Minds, brains, and programs, *Behav. Brain Sci.* **3** (1980) 417–457.

[18] E.E. Smith and D.L. Medin, *Categories and Concepts* (Harvard University, Cambridge, MA, 1981).

[19] P. Smolensky, On the proper treatment of connectionism, *Behav. Brain Sci.* **11** (1988) 1–74.

[20] L. Wittgenstein, *Philosophical Investigations* (Macmillan, New York, 1973).

Artificial Intelligence 48 (1991) 349–370
Elsevier

Marvin Minsky, *The Society of Mind**

Stephen W. Smoliar

*USC Information Sciences Institute, 4676 Admiralty Way Suite 1001, Marina del Rey,
CA 90292-6695, USA*

Received June 1989
Revised January 1990

1. What is this book about?

The year 1950 saw the publication of "Computing Machinery and Intelligence" [12], an extensive discussion by Alan Turing of the fundamental principles of a subject which would come to be known as "artificial intelligence". In retrospect, the value of this essay lies not in any specific technical insights or even in the suggestion that artificial intelligence might be possible, but in the *breadth* of its view of intelligence and the observation that, for all that breadth, what we call "intelligence" might *still* lie within the power of a machine. This breadth is admirably captured in the following list of capabilities which Turing anticipated [12]:

> Be kind, resourceful, beautiful, friendly, have initiative, have a
> sense of humour, tell right from wrong, make mistakes, fall in love,
> enjoy strawberries and cream, make some one fall in love with it,
> learn from experience, use words properly, be the subject of its
> own thought, have as much diversity of behaviour as a man, do
> something really new.

When artificial intelligence began to emerge as a discipline, its scope narrowed considerably in the interest of performing experiments which would yield concrete results under the limitations of existing technology. Since that

---

* (Simon & Schuster, New York, 1986); 339 pages, $10.95 (paperback).

0004-3702/91/$03.50 © 1991 — Elsevier Science Publishers B.V.

time, artificial intelligence has pursued a wide variety of activities in areas such as perception, problem solving, planning, and the use of language. Nevertheless, the *literature* of artificial intelligence remains narrow: reports of individual efforts confined to a limited domain with little consideration to the many issues which occupied Turing's imagination.

Marvin Minsky's *The Society of Mind* is perhaps the first written attempt to confront seriously the breadth of machine intelligence first imagined by Turing. This is not to say that Minsky has implemented all of Turing's capabilities. Indeed, it would be foolish to attempt to predict just *when* those capabilities might actually be realized. Nevertheless, what is important is that *The Society of Mind* is a book which tries to pull us away from the narrow focus of past individual accomplishments so that we may consider a broader, more realistic sense of intelligence. In our lust for specific achievement, we tend to be intimidated by that broader sense and push it off to the side. Minsky would have us eschew that intimidation and begin devoting some time to speculating about the future. However distant that future may be, it is only through our imaginations that we may begin to approach it. Minsky is daring enough to imagine boldly; and if one accepts that spirit as a foundation of the book, such boldness can be contagious.

There are many ways to regard this book. First and foremost, it is a hypothesis about the nature of intelligence. This hypothesis is developed through the exploration of two major metaphors. The first lies in Minsky's title: "society" as a metaphor for mind. The second involves physical metaphors for thought. These basic themes will now be reviewed, after which the principal arguments will be considered in terms of several key questions which introduce the text. Finally, the book will be addressed in light of some other relevant achievements.

1.1. The nature of intelligence

A key theme in *The Society of Mind* is that the study of mind is misguided by confused assumptions about what is simple and what is complicated. Minsky summarizes this argument as follows:[1]

> This book assumes that any brain, machine, or other thing that has a mind must be composed of smaller things that cannot think at all. The structure of the book itself reflects this view: each page explores a theory or idea that exploits what other pages do. Some readers might prefer a more usual form of story plot. I tried to do that several times, but it never seemed to work; each way I tried to line things up left too many thoughts that would not fit. A mind is

---

[1] All quotations are from *The Society of Mind* unless otherwise indicated. Square brackets indicate the location of each quotation.

too complex to fit the mold of narratives that start out *here* and end up *there*; a human intellect depends upon the connections in a tangled web—which simply wouldn't work at all if it were neatly straightened out.

Many psychologists dream of describing minds so economically that psychology would become as simple and precise as physics. But one must not confuse reality with dreams. It was not the ambitions of the physicists that made it possible to describe so much of the world in terms of so few and simple principles; that was because of the nature of our universe. But the operations of our minds do not depend on similarly few and simple laws, because our brains have accumulated many different mechanisms over aeons of evolution. This means that psychology can never be as simple as physics, and any simple theory of mind would be bound to miss most of the "big picture." The science of psychology will be handicapped until we develop an overview with room for a great many smaller theories. [Postscript]

Our sense of simplicity has been distorted by the very words we use. We take refuge in a single word, assuming that it embodies something within our grasp. Minsky regards "intelligence" as such a word:

A term frequently used to express the myth that some single entity or element is responsible for the quality of a person's ability to reason. I prefer to think of this word as representing not any particular power or phenomenon, but simply all the mental skills that, at any particular moment, we admire but don't yet understand. [Glossary: "Intelligence"]

Equally deceptive is the word, "memory":

An omnibus term for a great many structures and processes that have ill-defined boundaries in both everyday and technical psychology; these include what we call "re-membering," "re-collecting," "re-minding," and "re-cognizing." This book suggests that what these share in common is their involvement with how we reproduce our former *partial mental states*. [Glossary: "Memory"]

Thus, if we go about our work under the assumption that words like "intelligence" and "memory" are simple summaries of our objectives, we are likely to make very little progress. One might read this as a very pessimistic statement on Minsky's part—an argument that a theory of mind may always be too complex to be within our grasp. However, the true tone of this argument is realism, rather than pessimism: we should respect complexity rather than deluding ourselves into attempts to falsely simplify it. Simplicity lies in the lowest-order devices from which machines, such as computers, are built; and the complexity of "mental skills" emerges from the ways in which these devices may interact. How, then, are we to talk about such complexity? This is the essence of Minsky's use of "society" as a metaphor for mind.

1.2. Society as a metaphor for mind

A good way to try to develop some intuition for this metaphor is to observe an example:

> To start to see how minds are like societies, try this: *pick up a cup of tea!*
>> *Your GRASPING agents want to keep hold of the cup.*
>> *Your BALANCING agents want to keep the tea from spilling out.*
>> *Your THIRST agents want you to drink the tea.*
>> *Your MOVING agents want to get the cup to your lips.*
> Yet none of these consume your mind as you roam about the room talking to your friends. You scarcely think at all about *Balance*; *Balance* has no concern with *Grasp*; *Grasp* has no interest in *Thirst*; and *Thirst* is not involved with your social problems. Why not? Because they can depend on one another. If each does its own little job, the really big job will get done by all of them together: drinking tea. [1.3]

Thus, the metaphor itself is relatively straightforward. However, as Minsky observes, its pursuit raises many questions:

Function:	*How do agents work?*
Embodiment:	*What are they made of?*
Interaction:	*How do they communicate?*
Origins:	*Where do the first agents come from?*
Heredity:	*Are we all born with the same agents?*
Learning:	*How do we make new agents and change old ones?*
Character:	*What are the most important kinds of agents?*
Authority:	*What happens when agents disagree?*
Intention:	*How could such networks want or wish?*
Competence:	*How can groups of agents do what separate agents cannot do?*
Selfness:	*What gives them unity or personality?*
Meaning:	*How could they understand anything?*
Sensibility:	*How could they have feelings and emotions?*
Awareness:	*How could they be conscious or self-aware?* [1.1]

These are the questions we should ask if we wish to consider how the complexity of intelligent behavior may emerge from interactions among simple components. As such, they constitute a general plan of discussion for *The Society of Mind*. Nevertheless, it is important to remember the disclaimer from the book's Postscript: These questions cannot be answered by straightforward narrative, and one should not expect to come away with fourteen answers to fourteen questions. What one *will* come away with, if one applies oneself, is a better appreciation for the questions themselves, accompanied by a healthy sense of how to think about them.

1.3. Physical metaphors for thought

The societal metaphor is not the only one to be pursued in *The Society of Mind*. There is also considerable attention given to the discussion of thoughts, memories, and inferences as if they were physical objects. Minsky introduces this metaphor through a question:

> But why do we feel we have to think of what we learn as *things* or *concepts*? Why must we "thing-ify" everything? [10.7]

Minsky draws upon the practice of traditional mnemonic techiques to hypothesize an explanation for such behavior:

> Indeed, for many centuries our memory-training arts have been dominated by two techniques. One is based on similarities of sounds, exploiting the capacities of our language-agencies to make connections between words. The other method is based on imagining the items we want to remember as placed in some familiar space, such as a road or room one knows particularly well. This way, we can apply our thing-location skills to keeping track of our ideas.
>
> Our ability to treat ideas as though they were objects goes together with our abilities to reuse our brain-machinery over and over again. Whenever an agency becomes overburdened by a large and complicated structure, we may be able to treat that structure as a simple, single unit by thing-ifying—or, as we usually say, "*conceptualizing*"—it. Then, once we replace a larger structure by representing it with a compact symbol-sign, that overloaded agency may be able to continue its work. This way, we can build grand structures of ideas—much as we can build great towers from smaller parts.
>
> I suspect that, *as they're represented in the mind*, there's little difference between a physical object and an idea. Worldly things are useful to us because they are "substantial"—that is, because their properties are relatively permanent. Now we don't usually

think of ideas as substantial, because they don't have the usual properties of wordly things—such as color, shape, and weight. Yet "good ideas" must also have substantially, albeit of a different sort:

> *No conception or idea could have much use unless it could remain unchanged—and stay in some kind of mental "place"— for long enough for us to find it when we need it. Nor could we ever achieve a goal unless it could persist for long enough. In short, no mind can work without some stable states or memories.* [22.6]

Physical metaphors facilitate Minsky's exposition of his K-line model of memory (see Section 2.2 of this review). Control is considered in terms of level-bands, which are discussed as if they were objects with well-defined locations, rather than simply relationships among K-lines; and relationships among the level-bands are frequently described using the vertical prepositions "below" and "above". Thus, it would appear that one cannot escape the physical, no matter how non-physical may be the issues of the discussion! Consequently, while the passages from Minsky's Glossary quoted above in Section 1.1 criticize the ways in which we use words like "intelligence" and "memory", such words may be recognized as further evidence of "thing-ification". As has been observed, these words are not simple summaries of a research agenda; rather, we should recognize that they are merely products of attempts of the mind to deal with its own complexity.

2. The principal arguments

It should be clear from Section 1 that there is quite a lot to *The Society of Mind*. By returning to the breadth of intelligence as it was first considered by Turing, the book cannot help but cover a lot of ground; and the nature of the material is such that it does so in a rather sprawling manner. Any attempt to consider all of the questions cited above in Section 1.2 would probably be as sprawling as the book itself, so this review will focus attention on those questions which reveal some of Minsky's most striking insights.

2.1. How do agents work?

The essential answer to this question is that agents work like very simple computer programs. However, once one starts thinking in terms of computer programs, one cannot avoid some fundamental programming language baggage. In Minsky's case probably the most important piece of such baggage which must be confronted is the issue of parameter passing:[2]

---

[2] Note the notational convention that agents are represented in capitalized italics.

Suppose *Thirst* knows that water can be found in cups—but does not know how to find or reach for a cup; these are things only *Find* and *Get* can do. Then *Thirst* must have some way to exploit the abilities of those other agents. *Builder*, too, has a similar problem because most of its subagents cannot communicate directly with one another. It would be easy for *Thirst* or *Builder* simply to turn on other agents like *Find* and *Get*. But how will those subordinates know *what* to find or get? Must *Thirst* transmit to *Find* a picture of a cup? Must *Builder* send a picture of a brick? The trouble is that neither *Builder* nor *Thirst* is the sort of agent to contain the kind of knowledge required by *Find*—namely, the visual appearances of things. That kind of knowledge lies inside the memory-machinery of *See*. However, *Thirst* can achieve its drinking goal by activating *two* connections: one to cause *See* to "hallucinate" a cup and another connection to activate *Find*. *Find* itself can activate *Get* later. This should suffice for *Thirst* to locate and obtain a cup—if there is one in sight. [16.7]

Thus, agent behavior is determined by *mental states*; and "parameters are passed" through the imposition of such states. This amounts to a rather elaborate generalization of conventional computation, where machine states are imposed by writing data into registers. Mental states which support such "parameter passing" are called "short-term memories"; and they are induced by the mechanism of "temporary K-lines" (see Section 2.2 below). These temporary K-lines usually draw upon connections to more "permanent" K-lines, which induce "long-term memories". For example, the "hallucination" of a cup which allows *Find* to serve *Thirst* is a short-term memory whose lifetime is basically that of the *Thirst* agent. On the other hand, that hallucination is based on long-term memories about what cups look like.

Agents which induce long-term memories are also called *polynemes*. Minsky uses the word *neme* for an agent which reproduces a former partial mental state (his basis for memory as cited above in Section 1.1). So a polyneme is an agent that induces a memory which will elicit many different behaviors from a variety of other agents:

When you hear the word "apple," a certain polyneme is aroused, and the signal from this polyneme will put your *Color* agency into a state that represents redness. The same signal will set your *Shape* agency into a state that represents roundness, and so forth. Thus, the polyneme for "apple" is really very simple; it knows nothing whatever about apples, colors, shapes, or anything else. It is merely a switch that turns on processes in other agencies, each of which has learned to respond in its own way. [19.3]

Short-term memories are called *pronomes*, since they embody associations similar to those of pronouns. Pronomes are a special case of *isonomes*, so-called because each isonome elicits the same behavior from each agent which receives it. In the case of pronomes, the behavior is that of associating the short-term memory with a long-term memory. One might say that pronomes are like the variable symbols of a procedural programming language, and polynemes are like the values which are bound to those variables when a program written in such a language is actually executed. This view is admittedly somewhat distorted: polynemes and pronomes are defined in terms of *behaviors of agents*, rather than *properties of entities*. Nevertheless, it may still provide a useful initial intuition.

2.2. How do agents communicate?

Let us now consider the K-line mechanism which induces mental states:

> Whenever you "get a good idea," solve a problem, or have a memorable experience, you activate a K-line to "represent" it. A K-line is a wirelike structure that attaches itself to whichever mental agents are active when you solve a problem or have a good idea. When you activate that K-line later, the agents attached to it are aroused, putting you into a "mental state" much like the one you were in when you solved that problem or got that idea. This should make it relatively easy for you to solve new, similar problems! [8.1]

Thus, agents communicate by activating K-lines.

Of course, there is a danger of "communication overload" here. One agent activates a K-line, inducing a mental state to which many other agents respond by activating other K-lines, and so on. Unless there is some way to limit the "repercussions" of an agent's activity, there would always be a danger that a single agent could ultimately arouse all other agents. In order to impose such necessary limitations, Minsky introduces the idea of the "level-band". While the mechanism of the level-band is not discussed as much as the K-line, one can establish that limitation is based on a notion of "proximity" between the agent which activates the K-line and agents which are aroused; but no actual proximity metric is ever offered.

It is clear from Minsky's discussion, however, that agent proximity is no simple matter. First, there is a "central level-band" which is associated with the activation of a K-line. However, this level-band has "lower" and "upper" "fringes", which are meant to embody more "distant" associations. It is never quite clear how all these pieces fit together or are appropriately controlled; but Minsky offers a vivid description of how they are expected to perform:

> Both fringing effects serve to make our memories more relevant to our present purposes. The central level-band helps us find general

resemblances between remembered events and present circumstances. The lower fringe supplies additional details but does not force them upon us. We use them only "by default" when actual details are not supplied. Similarly, the upper fringe recalls to mind some memories of previous goals, but again, we're not forced to use them except by default, when present circumstances do not impose more compelling goals. Seen this way, we can think of the lower fringe as concerned with the *structures* of things, and we can think of the upper fringe as involved with the *functions* of things. The lower levels represent "objective" details of reality; the upper levels represent our "subjective" concerns with goals and intentions.

How could the fringes of the same K-line lie in two such different realms? Because in order to think, we need intimate connections between things and goals—between structures and their functions. What use would *thinking* be at all, unless we could relate each thing's details to our plans and intentions? Consider how often the English language employs the selfsame words for things and for their purposes. What tools would you use, when building your house, to saw and clamp and glue your wood? That's obvious: you'd use a *saw* and a *clamp* and some *glue*! Behold the wondrous force of those "meanings": no sooner do we hear the noun form of a word than our agents strain to perform the acts that correspond to it as a verb. This phenomenon of connecting *means* with *ends* is not confined to language—we'll see many other instances of it in other kinds of agencies—but language may allow such linking with the least constraint. [8.7]

It is particularly important that communication among agents is an *indirect* process. When he is first considering the sorts of agents which guide our behavior, Minsky postulates a *Work* agent which tends to conflict with a *Sleep* agent for command of our bodies. He then postulates that we may engage an *Anger* agent as "motivation" to keep working even if we are tired. Thus, the *Anger* agent prevents *Sleep* from "taking control," so that *Work* may proceed without conflict. Why is *Anger* necessary? Why could not *Work* simply disengage *Sleep* directly? Minsky's answer is both practical and simple:

> To see why we have to be so indirect, consider some alternatives. If *Work* could simply turn off *Sleep*, we'd quickly wear our bodies out. If *Work* could simply switch *Anger* on, we'd be fighting all the time. Directness is too dangerous. We'd die. [4.5]

2.3. How do we make new agents and change old ones?

Learning is one of the most important topics in *The Society of Mind*; and, as is the case with other fundamental issues in this book, Minsky takes on the deceptive simplicity of the word "learning", itself:

> The problem is that we use the single word "learning" to cover too diverse a society of ideas. Such a word can be useful in the title of a book, or in the name of an institution. But when it comes to studying the subject itself, we need more distinctive terms for important, different ways to learn. Even [a simple example involving building arches from blocks] reveals at least four different ways to learn. We'll give them these new names:

> **Uniframing** combining several descriptions into one, for example, by observing that all the arches have certain common parts.
>
> **Accumulating** collecting incompatible descriptions, for example, by forming the phrase "block or wedge."
>
> **Reforming** modifying a description's character, for example, by describing the separate blocks rather than the overall shape.
>
> **Trans-framing** bridging between structures and functions or actions, for example, by relating the concept of arch to the act of changing hands [while trying to move something *through* the arch].

> . . . It seems to me that the older words used in psychology—such as *generalizing*, *practicing*, *conditioning*, *memorizing*, or *associating*—are either too vague to be useful or have become connected to theories that simply aren't sound. In the meantime, the revolutions of computer science and Artificial Intelligence have led to new ideas about how various kinds of learning might work, and these new ideas deserve new names. [12.2]

Each of these different ways to learn is discussed extensively in *The Society of Mind*. Indeed, once introduced, they tend to dominate the book. However, breaking down the concept of learning into many different ways to learn is only part of the issue. There remains the question of how these more specialized learning activities *interact*, both with other agents in the Society of Mind and among themselves. If one can draw on a variety of different approaches to learning, which approach is taken under what circumstances?

Minsky confronts this question with the thesis that learning is based on learning ways to learn. It is not just a matter of "mastering" uniframing or accumulating; nor is it a matter of "acquiring knowledge". What is more important is the ability to know what knowledge to draw upon and how to manipulate it. Unfortunately, no philosophers' stone will resolve this issue:

But how can we judge which facts are useful? *On what basis can we decide which features are essential and which are merely accidents?* Such questions can't be answered as they stand. They make no sense apart from how we want to use their answers. There is no single secret, magic trick to learning; we simply have to learn a large society of different ways to learn! [12.3]

2.4. What are the most important kinds of agents?

This question never receives a direct answer. Indeed, given that Minsky lays far more stress on *interactions* among agents, as opposed to the behavior of *individual* agents, it was a little bit surprising to see that he should have raised it at all. Nevertheless, there are certain agents which figure heavily in a variety of different arguments in the book; so it would be fair to assume that Minsky assigns some level of importance to these agents.

Of course, K-lines are, themselves, agents; and their effect on mental states makes them fundamental to Minsky's theory. Equally important, however, is the process of *recall*, which involves a more elaborate interaction of agents called "Closing the Ring" (the title of Section 19.10) and seems at least partially inspired by David Hume [3]. The best way to describe this "ring" is to summarize the different classes of agents which are involved:

(1) *Sensors* are those agents which pass stimuli from the "outside world" to the "agents of the mind". We can associate them with the physical senses of sight, smell, hearing, taste, and touch.

(2) *Memorizers* are the polynemes, each of which registers a particular confluence of sensations which may then be "processed" by different agents as described in Section 2.1 of this review.

(3) *Recognizers* are agents which respond to a variety of messages from the different agents which respond to polynemes and integrate that variety into a single *neme*, i.e. memory agent.

(4) An *ascending neme* is a "recognized neme" which induces a "state of recall" in memory. That state of recall then activates other K-lines.

(5) A *descending neme* is a K-line activated by this "state of recall" which "descends" to interact with the memorizers to "flesh out" the recollection. The connection from descending nemes to memorizers "closes the ring" of this process of recall.

Minsky also considers the importance of being able to explicitly *disable*, as well as *enable*, certain agents. Such tasks are performed by classes of agents which he calls *suppressors* and *censors*:

> **Suppressor-agents** wait until you get a certain "bad idea." Then they prevent your taking the corresponding action, and make you

wait until you think of some alternative. If a suppressor could speak, it would say, "Stop thinking that!" [27.2]

Censor-agents need not wait until a certain bad idea occurs; instead, they intercept the states of mind that usually *precede* that thought. If a censor could speak, it would say, "Don't even begin to think that!" [27.2]

2.5. What happens when agents disagree?

Minsky considers a variety of approaches to the need to resolve conflicts among agents. The most fundamental of these approaches is to postulate that conflict-resolution is yet another task which the mind must perform. This task is then assigned to what Minsky calls the "*B*-brain".

The theory behind the *B*-brain is that there is some "primary" part of the brain, called the *A*-brain, which is connected to sensors and effectors and is basically responsible for getting on in the world. The *B*-brain, on the other hand, is connected *only* to the *A*-brain and serves rather like a manager:

Like a manager, a *B*-brain can supervise an *A*-brain without understanding either how the *A*-brain works or the problems with which the *A*-brain is involved—for example, by recognizing patterns of activity that indicate the *A*-brain is confused, wasting time in repetitive activity, or focused on an unproductive level of detail. [Glossary: "*B*-brain"]

Feasibility of the *B*-brain's task requires some organization in the *A*-brain; and Minsky argues that such an organization should be hierarchical, providing an example in terms of agents which might be involved in the behavior of a child:

In several sections of this book, I will assume that conflicts between agents tend to migrate upward to higher levels. For example, any prolonged conflict between *Builder* [an agent which builds towers of blocks] and *Wrecker* [an agent which knocks such towers down] will tend to weaken their mutual superior, *Play-with-Blocks*. In turn, this will reduce *Play-with-Blocks'* ability to suppress *its* rivals, *Play-with-Dolls* and *Play-with-Animals*. Next, if *that* conflict isn't settled soon, it will weaken the agent *Play* at the next-higher level. Then *Eat* or *Sleep* might seize control. [3.1]

In addition to hierarchical structure, Minsky suggests an "economics of priority" to assist in conflict resolution:

This way, for better or for worse, we often assign some magnitude or price to each alternative. That tactic helps to simplify our lives so much that virtually every social community works out its own communal measure-schemes—let's call them *currencies*—that let its people work and trade in harmony, even though each individual has somewhat different personal goals. The establishment of a currency can foster both competition and cooperation by providing us with peaceful ways to divide and apportion the things we have to share.

But who can set prices on things like time or measure the values of comfort and love? What makes our mental marketplaces work so well when emotional states seem so hard to compare? One reason is that no matter how different those mental conditions seem, they must all compete for certain limited resources—such as space, time, and energy—and these, to a rather large extent, are virtually interchangeable. For example, you'd end up with essentially the same result whether you measure things in terms of food or time—because it takes time to find food, and each amount of food helps you survive for some amount of time. Thus the value we place on each commodity constrains, to some extent, the values we'll assign to many other kinds of goods. Because there are so many such constraints, once a community sets up a currency, that currency takes on a life of its own, and soon we start to treat our "wealth" as though it were a genuine commodity, a real substance that we can use, save, lend, or waste. [28.2]

Lest this "economic" metaphor seem too appealing, however, Minsky is quick to remind us that resolving conflicts among agents is not necessarily in the same class as thought:

Whenever we turn to measurements, we forfeit some uses of intellect. Currencies and magnitudes help us make comparisons only be concealing the differences among what they purport to represent. [28.3]

Thus, should we become too enamoured of quantitative approaches to decision making [11], we must be careful not to allow our own mental skills to succumb to an approach which is more suitable to the meager capabilities of an agent in the *B*-brain.

2.6. How could networks of agents want or wish?

Much of the behavior which Minsky considers is basically "goal-driven". Following the approach of Allen Newell and Herbert Simon [9], a "goal" is regarded as a state to be achieved; and actions are taken to bring the existing state into conformity with the goal state. These actions are based on a "difference-engine", which can detect how a given state differs from a goal state. Information from that difference-engine may then be processed by agents which can take actions to reduce the detected differences.

Is such activity intentional? Minsky addresses the question as follows:

> Do difference-engines "really" want? It is futile to ask that kind of question because it seeks a distinction where none exists—except in some observer's mind. We can think of a ball as a perfectly passive object that merely reacts to external forces. But the eighteenth-century physicist Jean Le Rond d'Alembert showed that one can also perfectly predict the behavior of a rolling ball by describing it as a difference-engine whose goal is to reduce its own energy. We need not force ourselves to decide questions like whether machines can have goals or not. Words should be our servants, not our masters. The notion of goal makes it easy to describe certain aspects of what people and machines can do; it offers us the opportunity to use simple descriptions in terms of active purposes instead of using unmanageably cumbersome descriptions of machinery. [7.9]

Nevertheless, phenomena such as "drives" do exist. However, Minsky would prefer to view them as "engineering decisions" which facilitate the operation of agents, rather than intentions or desires:

> In order for hunger to keep us fed, it must engage some agency that gives priority to food-acquiring goals. But unless such signals came before our fuel reserves were entirely gone, they'd arrive too late to have any use. This is why feeling hungry or tired is not the same as being genuinely starved or exhausted. To serve as useful "warning signs," feelings like pain and hunger must be engineered not simply to indicate dangerous conditions, but to *anticipate* them and warn us *before* too much damage is done. [28.4]

Thus, there is nothing special about "wanting" or "wishing" which obliges them to be treated as peculiarly non-mechanical. Intention is simply a behavior, like other forms of behavior considered in *The Society of Mind*, which may be exhibited through the interaction of Minsky's agents.

2.7. What is the source of understanding?

Minsky argues that the source of understanding lies in an ability to identify differences:

> Much of ordinary thought is based on recognizing differences. This is because it is generally useless to do anything that has no discernible effect. To ask if something is significant is virtually to ask, *"What difference does it make?"* Indeed, whenever we talk

about "cause and effect" we're referring to imaginary links that connect the differences we sense. What, indeed, are goals themselves, but ways in which we represent the kinds of changes we might like to make? [23.1]

Note, however, that by placing the emphasis on difference, Minsky removes the idea of any entity having a meaning unto itself; meaning becomes a relative relation among all the entities of the world around us:

> We'll take the view that nothing can have meaning by itself, but only in relation to whatever other meanings we already know. [6.9]

The ability to recognize differences is applicable not only to the entities we perceive but also to the differences we discern in perceiving them:

> The ability to consider differences between differences is important because it lies at the heart of our abilities to solve new problems. This is because these "second-order-differences" are what we use to remind ourselves of other problems we already know how to solve. Sometimes this is called "reasoning by analogy" and is considered to be an exotic or unusual way to solve problems. But in my view, it's our most ordinary way of doing things. [23.1]

Indeed, as far as Minsky is concerned, analogy lies at the heart of understanding:

> How do we ever understand anything? Almost always, I think, by using one or another kind of analogy—that is, by representing each new thing as though it resembles something we already know. Whenever a new thing's internal workings are too strange or complicated to deal with directly, we represent whatever parts of it we can in terms of more familiar signs. This way, we make each novelty seem similar to some more ordinary thing. [6.2]

The significance of this approach is that it is just as important to keep track of what *doesn't* change as what *does*. If we were overwhelmed by differences, we would not be able to sort out the complexity to arrive at understanding. Differences can only be appreciated to the extent that they contrast with an expected uniformity:

> However, I suspect that if we had to start seeing all over again from every moment to the next, we'd scarcely be able to see at all. This is because our higher-level agents don't "see" the outputs of the sensors in our eyes at all. *Instead, they "watch" the states of middle-level agencies that don't change state so frequently.* What keeps those "inner models" of the world from changing all the time? This is the function of our frame-arrays: to store what we

learn about the world at terminals that stay unchanged when we move our heads and bodies around. This explains a wonderful pseudoparadox: objects in the world seem to change only when the pictures they project into our eyes *don't* change—that is, don't change according to our expectations. [25.3]

3. Comparison with other approaches

One cannot come away from *The Society of Mind* without the impression that Minsky is extremely well read. It is clear that a variety of sources—both distant and near past, both fiction and non-fiction—have served as inspiration for material in this book. To attempt to track all the many connections to the literature would require another entire book. Nevertheless, three which have not been explicitly acknowledged deserve some mention.

3.1. Wittgenstein

The *Philosophical Investigations* of Ludwig Wittgenstein [13] was a major attempt to confront the shortcomings of strictly logical definitions. Ultimately, Wittgenstein abandoned definition in terms of formal conditions which were necessary and sufficient in favor of what he called "family resemblance", citing, as an example, the difficulty of defining "game". Minsky, too, considers the definition of "game" in his discussion of meaning in Chapter 12 of *The Society of Mind*. One might say he has responded to Wittgenstein with the argument that it is a mistake to try to view "game" as an "object-thing". Ultimately, Minsky's stand is that meanings are apprehended not through things but through processes in the mind. Thus, he sympathizes with Wittgenstein's frustrations and responds with the suggestion that Wittgenstein was barking up the wrong tree.

3.2. Laban

One of the more interesting innovations in *The Society of Mind* is the introduction of the "interaction-square" concept:

> The idea of representing the interaction between two processes by linking pairs of examples to *direction-nemes*. We can use this same technique not only for representing spatial relationships, but for causal, temporal, and many other kinds of interactions. This makes the interaction-square idea a powerful scheme for representing *cross-realm correspondences*. [Glossary: "Interaction-Square"]

The systematic breakdown of spatial relationships which forms the interaction-square is very reminiscent of Rudolf Laban's approach to the development of a notation for human movement [4]. Indeed, some of Minsky's remarks recall Laban's own approach:

> If square-arrays can represent how *pairs* of causes interact, could similar schemes be used with three or more causes? That might need too many "directions" to be practical. We'd need twenty-seven directions to represent three interacting causes this way, and eighty-one to represent four. Only rarely, it seems, do people deal with more than two causes at a time: instead, we either find ways to reformulate such situations or we accumulate disorderly societies of partially filled interaction-squares that cover only the most commonly encountered combinations. [14.9]

While Laban's own notation was based on an "interaction-cube" of 27 directions, he nevertheless appreciated the need to limit the number of interactions which could be represented by a single piece of notation. He also became very interested in using his notation to record other forms of relationships—the same metaphorical approach to the spatial which forms the crux of Minsky's argument.

As another application of spatial relationships, in Appendix 3 of *The Society of Mind*, Minsky considers the use of trajectories of movement as a cue to recognizing a person's mental state. This role of movement was also of great interest to Laban, initially from the point of view of how a performer could use movement to portray a particular personality type. Ultimately, Laban extended his notation for describing such trajectories beyond the concerns of recording directions and into the recording of movement *qualities*. Laban called such qualities "efforts"; and he developed a taxonomy of these efforts which supplemented his notation of spatial directions.

3.3. *SOAR*

Another approach to the modeling of general intelligence is the work on SOAR initiated by Allen Newell and his students, John Laird and Paul Rosenbloom [5]. Two of the more significant elements of the SOAR architecture address issues raised in *The Society of Mind*. One of these concerns the issue of conflict-resolution considered in Section 2.5 of this review. Minsky's approach is that disagreements between agents should be resolved by other agents. This is called the "noncompromise principle":

> The idea that when two agencies conflict it may be better to ignore them both and yield control to yet another, independent agency. [Glossary: "Noncompromise Principle"]

This is essentially the same as SOAR's "automatic subgoaling". In SOAR a conflict takes the form of an "impasse"; and impasses are handled by introducing new goals to resolve them. Thus, both Minsky and SOAR agree that conflict should be handled by a shift of attention, either to other agents in Minsky's Society or through the introduction of new goals for SOAR to satisfy.

The other area of shared interest is SOAR's approach to skill acquisition through "chunking". Minsky makes the following observation about expertise:

> The people we call "experts" seem to exercise their special skills with scarcely any thought at all—as though they were simply reading preassembled scripts. Perhaps when we "practice" to improve our skills, we're mainly building simpler scripts that don't engage so many agencies. This lets us do old things with much less "thought" and gives us more time to think of other things. [13.5]

Such "scripts" bear a strong resemblance to SOAR chunks, each of which is a single production summarizing a collection of productions used to solve a problem.

4. Conclusion

4.1. Many books in one

Section 2 began with the observation that *The Society of Mind* covers a lot of ground. Any reader of this review who has progressed this far is probably convinced of this point by now. However, in addition to the bulk of the material which is necessary to address Minsky's basic societal metaphor, the covers of *The Society of Mind* have managed to embrace several "auxiliary books"—extended discussions of supplementary topics which are clearly of great importance to Minsky. Two of these auxiliary books are critiques of formal logic and linguistics, respectively; and they deserve a brief acknowledgement.

4.1.1. Assessing formal logic

Minsky feels it is very important to develop an argument that there is more to epistemology than formal logic. This view is actually shared by the philosopher Alvin Goldman in his book *Epistemology and Cognition* [2], but Minsky's approach is to again exploit the metaphor of the physical. Reasoning is a matter of constructing chains. These metaphorical chains represent associations such as "causes, similarities, and dependencies" [18.2]. Such associations have a directionality, so they can be thought of as embodying a *trajectory*. Thus, the *physical* trajectory, say of a car from Boston to New York, serves as a model for "trajectories of inference", like the connection between a switch being flipped and a light turning on. A single "link" of such a trajectory is embodied in an entity which Minsky calls a *Trans*-frame, the name being a generalization of Roger Schank's "primitive actions" PTRANS, ATRANS, and MTRANS [10]. Inference then becomes a matter of "fitting together *Trans*-frames into chains" [22.5].

How does this approach advance epistemology beyond the limitations of formal logic? There appear to be two fundamental sources of difference:

(1) *Trans*-frames provide connections which are more general and flexible than the deductive connections of formal logic. Such flexibility allows us to consider inferential mechanisms in which *robustness* is more important than *precision*.

(2) The entities connected by *Trans*-frames are not the propositions of formal logic. Rather, they are those "partial mental states" which are associated with memory (as quoted from Minsky's Glossary in Section 1.1). These entities are the K-lines, discussed in Section 2.2 of this review; and they are based on *dispositions*, rather than *propositions* [8].

4.1.2. Language

Minsky's approach to language has some of the same iconoclasm one finds in his view of formalization:

> If we're to understand how language works, we must discard the usual view that words *denote*, or *represent*, or *designate*; instead, their function is *control*: each word makes various agents change what various other agents do. [19.1]

This stance gives rise to a variety of interesting (and perhaps provocative) observations about the words we use and how we use them:

> A word can only serve to indicate that someone else may have a valuable idea—that is, some useful structure to be built inside the mind. Each new word only plants a seed: to make it grow, a listener's mind must find a way to build inside itself some structure that appears to work like the one in the mind from which it was "learned." [26.10]

This is very similar to the position of Humberto Maturana [7]:

> Language must arise as a result of something ... that does not require denotation for its establishment, but that gives rise to language with all its implications as a trivial necessary result. This fundamental process is ontogenic structural coupling, which results in the establishment of a consensual domain.

Minsky's ultimate view of language is best summarized in what he calls the "re-duplication theory of speech":

My conjecture about what happens when a speaker explains an idea to a listener. A difference-engine-like process tries to construct a second copy of the idea's representation *inside the speaker's mind.* Each mental operation used in the course of that duplication process activates a corresponding *grammar-tactic* in the language agency, and these lead to a stream of speech. This will result in communication to the extent that suitably matched "inverse grammar-tactics" construct, inside the listener's mind, an equivalent representation. [Glossary: Re-duplication Theory of Speech]

Thus, communication through language amounts to a process of reconciling the differences in the mental states (as discussed in Section 2.6) of the two parties who are communicating.

4.2. Approaching the book

The Society of Mind should be required reading for anyone interested in artificial intelligence. However, this is no ordinary book; and it should not be read under the assumption that the reader is going to be gently led down the path of a narrative exposition. If the book has a "stylistic spiritual ancestor", it is Wittgenstein's *Philosophical Investigations,* with its numbered paragraphs offered as individual atoms of insight and little guidance as to how these atoms join together to form molecules. Looking for such molecules can often become frustrating, but it can also distract attention from the atoms themselves and thus from the observations Wittgenstein most wanted to make. So it is with Minsky. The reader must approach him with the good sense to discern what it is he is saying, unencumbered by expectations of how such a book is *supposed* to be written.

Thus, one should first put aside anticipation of a straightforward narrative laid out in a simple structure. Indeed, because the material, as Minsky observed, *defies* the linear nature of the printed book, one should consider the possibility of reading it non-linearly. Such a reading is actually facilitated by the Glossary at the end of the book. All of the key terms of Minsky's exposition are laid out here, each with a brief definition and many with an accompanying discussion. Along with each term, Minsky also gives a "pointer" to that section of the text which discusses the term at greater length. Indeed, one can use this glossary somewhat the way one might use the "browsers" in a Smalltalk environment [1].

4.3. Questions rather than answers

The reader should next accept the fact that this book is more a source of *questions* than of *answers*. In *Philosophy in a New Key*, Susanne Langer wrote [6]:

The way a question is asked limits and disposes the ways in which any answer to it—right or wrong—may be given.

Many of the questions which Turing first raised in 1950 became side-tracked with the pursuit of artificial intelligence as a "concrete" discipline. One gets the impression from reading *The Society of Mind* that Minsky is not particularly content with the narrow focus of attention which such concrete concerns has spawned. Nevertheless, it is clear that the breadth of Turing's initial inquiry involves a complexity which must be treated with great respect. What would Minsky have us do? Ultimately, *The Society of Mind* sets an example to encourage us to *speculate*, viewing those concrete results which have been achieved thus far not as ends in themselves but as potential tools in negotiating the many issues which must be confronted if we are going to think about mind.

Because the emphasis is on questions, rather than answers, the reader should also approach some of the more flamboyant declarations of this book with caution. Often their intent is more to provoke than to inform. (Maturana [7] calls such sentences "triggering perturbations".) For example, Minsky's theory about split brains, as articulated in Section 11.8, is at odds with certain results in the published literature.[3] Unfortunately, Minsky does not provide citations to either support or rebut his own point of view. For better or for worse, he seems to have assumed that the interested reader will pursue such references on his own.

Nevertheless, taken on its own terms, this is a very exciting book—perhaps the most exciting book ever to have been published on the subject of mind. It is provocative in the questions it raises and challenging because it does not provide cut-and-dried answers to those questions. Ultimately, it serves the most important function which any book may serve: *It inspires the reader to think about these matters on his own.* Such books are rare in *any* subject. We should all be thankful that Marvin Minsky has been able to serve the discipline of artificial intelligence so well.

References

[1] A.I. Goldberg, *Smalltalk-80: The Interactive Programming Environment* (Addison-Wesley, Reading, MA, 1984).
[2] A.I. Goldman, *Epistemology and Cognition* (Harvard University Press, Cambridge, MA, 1986).
[3] D. Hume, *A Treatise of Human Nature* (Dent, London, England, 1911); Introduction by A. D. Lindsay.
[4] R. Laban, *The Mastery of Movement* (Plays, Inc., Boston, MA, 1971); Revised and enlarged by L. Ullmann.
[5] J.E. Laird, A. Newell and P.S. Rosenbloom, SOAR: an architecture for general intelligence, *Artif. Intell.* **33** (1987) 1–64.

[3] I wish to thank Bob Kohout for pointing this out to me.

[6] S.K. Langer, *Philosophy in a New Key: A Study in the Symbolism of Reason, Rite, and Art* (New American Library, New York, 1951).

[7] H.R. Maturana, Biology of language: the epistemology of reality, in: G. A. Miller and E. Lenneberg, eds., *Psychology and Biology of Language and Thought: Essays in Honor of Eric Lenneberg* (Academic Press, New York, 1978) 27–63, Chapter 2.

[8] M. Minsky, K-lines: a theory of memory, *Cogn. Sci.* **4** (1980) 117–133.

[9] A. Newell and H.A. Simon, *Human Problem Solving* (Prentice-Hall, Englewood Cliffs, NJ, 1972).

[10] R.C. Schank, *Conceptual Information Processing* (North-Holland, Amsterdam, Netherlands, 1975).

[11] H.A. Simon, *The Sciences of the Artificial* (MIT Press, Cambridge, MA, 1969).

[12] A.M. Turing, Computing machinery and intelligence, in: E.A. Feigenbaum and J. Feldman, eds., *Computers and Thought* (McGraw-Hill, New York, 1963) 11–35.

[13] L. Wittgenstein, *Philosophical Investigations* (Basil Blackwell, Oxford, England, 1974); Translated by G.E.M. Anscombe.

Artificial Intelligence 48 (1991) 371–396
Elsevier

Society of Mind:
a response to four reviews

Marvin Minsky

MIT, Media Lab, 545 Technology Square, Cambridge, MA 02139, USA

Received September 1990

1. Introduction

The goal of this book was to introduce a large-scale model of the mind. The thesis is that the human brain performs its great variety of functions by exploiting the advantages of many different knowledge representations, reasoning methods, and other mechanisms. It is this diversity that enables us, when any part fails, to manage to do things in other ways. What was the basis for that idea? A wide variety of biological, developmental, behavioral, and psychological observations. We now know that the brain itself is composed of hundreds of different regions and nuclei, each with significantly different architectural elements and arrangements, and that many of them are involved with demonstrably different aspects of our mental activities. This modern mass of knowledge shows that many phenomena traditionally described by commonsense terms like "intelligence" or "understanding" actually involve complex assemblies of machinery.

Dyer and Smoliar are generally enthusiastic about the new ideas, while Ginsberg and Reeke seem distressed about my rejection of older ideas. For example, consider how differently Dyer and Reeke interpret my aphoristic summary:

> What magical trick makes us intelligent? The trick is that there is no trick. {30.8}[1]

---

[1] Numbers in curly brackets { } mark quotations from *The Society of Mind*. Numbers in angle brackets ⟨ ⟩ mark references to the reviews.

Reeke treats this as evidence that I am simply trying to duck a "classical problem in the philosophy of mind", whereas Dyer interprets it as saying not to look for any single, simple cause for such complex phenomena. Most philosophers still attempt to discuss such things in terms of obsolete ideas. I'll demonstrate later that it isn't me, but Reeke and his philosophers, who are doing the ducking of problems today.

My responses to Dyer and Smoliar are brief, because I found few reasons to disagree; my replies to the others need much more space. But first I want to answer the review editor of this journal, who asked how the overall thesis of *The Society of Mind* could be wrong. Do we really need to postulate so many types of agencies and architectures—or could the whole range of human thought emerge from fewer principles? The history of psychology is paved with attempts to discover schemes through which an entire adult mind might grow from simple origins—for example, from the repeated "association of ideas", from the chainings of "conditionings", or from the iterated reinforcements of behavioral "operants", etc. But none of those theories bore much fruit, and psychology grew in complexity. However, in more recent years, newer computational theories have offered surprisingly simple procedures that really do in fact produce behaviors of unlimited complexity. These include, for example:

- Post "production" systems,
- Turing machines and general-purpose computers,
- iterative cellular arrays,
- chaotic differential or iterative algorithms,
- recursive logical inference engines,
- induction based on algorithmic probability,
- recursive schema-building procedures,
- large re-entrant connectionist networks,
- evolutionary mutation-selection schemes.

Surely our brains employ some of these, in various places and various ways. But we've also learned that these systems, too, always appear to be fatally slow, unless they have been pre-equipped with suitably clever heuristic techniques. So, in view of the speed at which infants learn, none of them yet seem plausible as self-contained sources of mental growth. Nevertheless, for the goals of AI, it is entirely conceivable that some such machine might rival a brain—given a proper environment and a long enough interval of time. Ginsberg hopes that this could come from suitably engineered logic machines— nor do I believe we can rule that out. Reeke seems convinced that that cannot be, because no computer could ever embody a missing link, between mind and matter, that he calls "intentionality".

However, so far as the brain is concerned, this issue is moot because we known that brains are *not* based on some few simple schemes—because we can actually demonstrate that they are composed of hundreds of anatomically different architectures that are involved with demonstrably different, special-ized functions. To be sure, it was widely supposed, in the first half of this century, that the brain functions depended on generally unlocalized, holistic, mechanisms. But although that belief still persists in the popular literature, there are now fifty years of accumulated evidence against it, and now it would seem perverse to doubt that human mental function and growth depend on a great many agencies.

Several of the reviewers suggest that my book does not look very technical. But I'd argue that it really is—or, in any case, its subject is—soon to become a new and important scientific specialty: the presently unexplored domain con-cerned with communication between systems that use different representations. Such systems cannot communicate in the ways that we're accustomed to—that is, by using common languages—hence much of the book is occupied with other ways to enable such systems to interact.

2. Dyer's review

Dyer ⟨Section 6⟩ doubts that my attempt at coining new terms for describing aspects of mental function will be successful—if only because I did not provide enough concrete examples. This is not the first time I made that mistake: there were too few examples in my 1979 K-line paper, and those ideas have received little notice.

Nevertheless, it is vital for both AI researchers and cognitive scientists to evolve a new vocabulary for thinking about thinking, for both technical reasons and philosophical reasons. I suspect it is because of defects in our com-monsense vocabulary that so many of our students and peers seem unable to deal with those recent debates about thinking machines. Consider the following composite of the sorts of arguments presented by Penrose, Searle, or Reeke.

> It is obvious that people not only respond behaviorally to language, but also understand it. However, although we have no trouble making computers respond behaviorally, no one can conceive of how to enable computers to "understand" the "meanings", "inten-tions", or "ideas" that words bring to mind—because this involves non-algorithmic processes.

Most such discussions make no sense at all, because the terms they employ are too coarse for their subject. In commonsense philosophy, the quoted terms above are regarded as so simple, direct, and immediate that even young children know what they mean; therefore if an adult philosopher can find no simple explanations for them—then, assume that they can't be explained at all! But *The Society of Mind* [2] takes the opposite view, that many things that seem obvious to us are actually vastly intricate!

If common sense is so diverse and intricate, what makes it seem so obvious and natural? This illusion of simplicity comes from losing touch with what happened during infancy, when we formed our first abilities. As each new group of skills matures, we build more layers on top of them. As time goes on, the layers below become increasingly remote until, when we try to speak of them in later life, we find ourselves with little more to say than "I don't know." {1.6}

Thousands and, perhaps, millions of little processes must be involved in how we anticipate, imagine, plan, predict, and prevent—and yet it all proceeds so automatically that we regard it all as "ordinary common sense." But if thinking is so complicated, what makes it all seem so simple? [Because] in general, we're least aware of what our minds do best. It's mainly when our other systems start to fail that we engage the special agencies involved with what we call "consciousness." Accordingly, we're more aware of simple processes that don't work well than of complex ones that work flawlessly. This means that we cannot trust our off-hand judgments about which of the things that we do are simple, and which of them require complicated machinery. Most times, each portion of the mind can only sense how quietly the other portions do their jobs. {2.5}

The secret of what something means lies in how it connects to other things we know. That's why it's almost always wrong to seek the "real meaning" of anything. A thing with just one meaning has scarcely any meaning at all. An idea with a single sense can lead you only along one track. Then, if anything goes wrong, it just gets stuck: a thought that sits there in your mind with nowhere to go. That's why, when someone learns something "by rote"—that is, with no sensible connections—we say that they "don't really understand." Rich meaning-networks, however, give you many different ways to go: if you can't solve a problem one way, you can try another. True, too many indiscriminate connections will turn a mind to mush. But well-connected meaning-structures let you turn ideas around in your mind, to consider alternatives and envision things from many perspectives until you find one that works. And that's what we mean by thinking! {6.9}

We need new terms for psychology because, both as scientists and as children, our infancies were centered in a geocentric spatial world and an egocentric single self. Physics made its Copernican move a full four centuries ago—but psychology and philosophy are still attached to Ptolemy.

Dyer objects, in his Section 6, that instantiating frames by using ANDs

{24.3} would surely be too localist. I quite agree. I used that example mainly to make it easy to understand three other ideas—first to explain the idea of an isonome, then to show how to make terminals for frames in the frame-construction problem, and later {in 24.8} to show how to instantiate a frame-array. Dyer proposes three more versatile implementations, which each appears to have advantages. As Dyer himself points out in his Section 7, the brain may well use many such schemes, even including the simple AND scheme. I would further emphasize that we should not dismiss highly-localized mechanisms for doctrinaire reasons. There may not exist any "grandmother cells" but there very likely do indeed exist "grandmother cell assemblies", from which emerge "grandmother micronemes"—that is, bundles of connections that are more or less specifically involved with activating other grandmother-related agents. A common objection to this is that localized structures would be too vulnerable to be dependable. But what if each such "concept" were realized, redundantly in, say, ten separate locations. Then, even if half of the brain were destroyed, there would be but one chance in a thousand of losing all ten representatives. A common fault of "distributionists" is to leap from concern about the fragility of localized structures to proposing too widely distributed representations—a sort of "1, 2, 3, . . . infinity" disposition. But fragility can be warded off with surprisingly small redundancies, while avoiding the serious (but rarely recognized) expenses and opacities of more "holistic" strategies.

Just as humor has never been taken seriously enough in our field, neither has the phenomenon of daydreaming, or wishful thinking. So I would like to further endorse Dyer's citation of Mueller's ideas, which seem to be to indicate an important direction of research.

3. Smoliar's review

My reply to Smoliar is brief because he summarized my views so well, and my answers to most of the questions he raised fit into the texts of my other replies. Smoliar describes my attempt to widen the scope of AI as daring and bold. But in some ways I see it, instead, as conservative—for it seems to me more daring—indeed reckless—to try to explain commonsense reasoning on the basis of deductive logic—rather than, say, on the basis of the sorts of chains {18.2} that children link ⟨Section 4.1.1⟩. A logician might correctly complain that such informal linkages may lead to improper scoping and binding of variables—but that's often just what adults do, while yet outperforming logic machines. Similarly it seems more rash to base language research so much on syntactic forms, rather than developing theories of how those forms are produced and understood. This is why, in {22.10}, I proposed instead the "copy-duplication" theory, summarized in Smoliar's Section 4.1.2, which tries to account for syntactic forms as reflections of cognitive strategies.

Let me elaborate here more of that idea about what happens, say, when Mary wants to tell something *S* to Jack. Assume that somewhere inside Mary's brain exists a certain representation *S*—and Mary's language agency's job is to utter a sequence of sounds that will direct the language agency in Jack's brain to construct its own copy of *S*. *I conjecture that this is usually done by a process that first makes a copy of S inside Mary herself*—by using a version of GPS. Mary's language agency repeatedly compares *S* with the growing copy *T* and each significant difference engages a (cognitive) process that augments *T* accordingly. As this proceeds, the resulting stream of copy-making operations also drives the machinery for overt speech, through various intermediate mechanisms whose regularities are seen as syntax and morphology.

I agree with Smoliar's reference to Wittgenstein ⟨Section 3.1⟩, and would like to amplify what I said in my book. Wittgenstein's analyses revealed many deficiencies of logically precise descriptions, and he tried to deal with some of these by introducing informal ideas about "family resemblances". But I feel that he gave up the game too soon, because, although single descriptions usually fail to capture commonsense concepts, it appears that we can often do much better at capturing ideas by surrounding them with two or more *different types* of descriptions. For example, one can't capture much of the concept of "chair" by simply describing a structure like this:

STRUCTURE: a thing with legs and back and seat.

For each of those parts can be changed in so many ways that it is hard to make a definition to catch them all. Another way would be to explain a chair's purpose or intended use:

FUNCTION: to keep one's bottom about 14 inches off the floor, to support one's back comfortably, and to provide space to bend the knees.

Now, this describes what chairs are "for" but provides no clue about how to build or recognize them. Thus, on one side we can provide structural descriptions, while on the other side we can give functional descriptions. But, while neither type of definitions is much good by itself, {12.5} suggests how to get much more by interweaving both together, to describe how the parts of a chair serve its purposes: the chair-seat support the sitter's weight, while the chair-legs serve as sub-goals for supporting the seat at the proper height. Traditional structural definitions are inadequate because they don't accommodate purposes. When, for example, is a toy chair a chair? That depends less on what it "is" than on what you want to use it for. Thus I felt, as Smoliar says, that Wittgenstein was off the mark because, although he quite properly rejected set-theoretic definitions, his family resemblance idea did not accommodate enough procedure or teleology. Because of this, I feel that Reeke's citation of Wittgenstein, in his review, was misdirected in not recognizing that I was augmenting, rather than ignoring, Wittgenstein's objections to conventional definitions.

Smoliar points out that my space-frame idea resembles some of Laban's work. In fact, that idea may have come from Smoliar himself, because in retrospect I now recall his urging me to consider using Laban's representations of motions and gestures in our robotics project at MIT.

In regard to SOAR ⟨Smoliar, Section 3.3⟩, I did not follow that project while working on *The Society of Mind*. But the importance of the "chunk" idea was already weighty in my mind, and my 1979 paper on K-lines was motivated by the need for a way to make chunks from the traces or records of the agents employed in solving a problem. My thinking in that area was also influenced by a related concept of "cauldron" proposed by Kenneth Haase, as well as by Chunk Rieger's earlier conception of "bypassing".

4. Ginsberg's review

Ginsberg disputes the value of my work, and offers as alternative the "substantial contributions" he expects to emerge from augmenting non-monotonic logic with truth maintenance. But he provides little reason to support this view and seems aware of this himself, as shown by his bleak remark:

> When I look at the progress that has been made since the realiza-
> tion around 1980 that commonsense reasoning had nonmonotonic
> properties, I am struck not by how much progress has been made
> but how little. ⟨Ginsberg⟩

A principal goal of [2] was to try both to account for this stagnation and to suggest ways to deal with it. Ginsberg objects that my suggestions are unfalsifiable—hence scientifically useless. Here I think he confuses two things, specific conjectures, and conceptual tools.

Ginsberg says that my theories are untestable because their claims are imprecise. But lack of specificity is not untestability; it only means, as Dyer says, that my ideas "require more effort on the part of the reader to fill in the implied details." For example, one might object that my copy-duplication {22.10} language idea, as mentioned in Section 3 above, is not specific enough to test, without making more assumptions about the underlying cognitive operations. (Each such assumption might then lead to a prediction about "universal" constraints on syntax.) But that objection would be wrong, because the theory is specific enough to be verified by direct observations of brain activities—once we develop suitably non-invasive instruments for observing the micro-structure of brain activity, together with software proficient at recognizing GPS-like activities. Such tools are still beyond our reach, but the present state of technology should not constrain our hypotheses; on the contrary, such theories are needed to stimulate the advancement of technique. It is absurd for Ginsberg to fear that my speculations might discredit an already mature science. Both AI and cognitive psychology are still in early stages, both technically and conceptually.

As for falsifiability, that idea simply makes no sense when applied to conceptual tools. One can only try to assess their heuristic value in helping to formulate useful ideas. My associate Kenneth Haase put it this way, in an e-mail note to me:

> Refutability is central in science only when it is clear that the language of our claims corresponds to the phenomena they purport to describe. The discussions in [2] suggest that the ways in which present-day AI often casts its claims are in fact inadequate to the phenomena they describe. In particular, their single-self, consistency-demanding criteria are inappropriate to what we know of the commonsense reasoning that any child can do and which only intensive schooling can bring us to forget. Approaches like nonmonotonic reasoning (which emerged out of Minsky's own invention of "default reasoning" in the mid-1970s) attempt to address the phenomena of common sense with tools that are inappropriate to the endeavor. The efforts of a virtural army of brilliant and talented researchers in nonmonotonic logics have yet to capture adequately the observations and inferences made by a child of five.

Ginsberg suggests that my stature as a founder of AI might "sanction such flights of speculation" as are found in [2]. So it is irony enough that my similarly speculative 1974 paper on frames [1] was the very one that first named the "monotonic" character of traditional logic and identified it as making logic unsuitable for commonsense reasoning. And given his involvement in the area, it is even more ironic for Ginsberg to complain that my suggestions about including default reasoning in frames

> aren't any different from the basic idea, well known in the nonmonotonic community, that subclasses should inherit by default the properties possessed by the superclasses that contain them. . . . The surprise is that inheritance reasoning is hard; this simple idea is not enough. ⟨Ginsberg⟩

But that community did not yet exist when I first made those suggestions, and to see how deeply those problems were understood at that time the interested reader can review the section by Scott Fahlman in the original edition of [1]. For the frame idea was intended, in the first place, to reduce the need for inheritance by dealing with entities in terms of the extents to which descriptions might need to be changed in order to match appropriate frames. It seems even stranger for Ginsberg to say that I "leave completely unaddressed" the problem in which "all the 'action' is from a scientific point of view"—namely, of how to choose among competing default rules. Heavens, the *whole book* is about ways to treat conflicting fragments of knowledge. Chapters 8 and 10 are especially concerned with deferring such decisions to managers—who may, in turn, conflict, and Smoliar reviews my other such schemes in his Section 2.5. Perhaps, when Ginsberg says that I offer no answer to this problem, he means that I offer no *single*, universal way to decide between conflicting agents. But I doubt that any such scheme could exist; not all questions have answers, nor do all dilemmas have resolutions, and we are forced to live our lives with many conflicts unresolved.

Here is a joke that might help to explain. You might conclude from these reviews that the score is even—two against two. Then you would not know what to think. But you could resolve the conflict another way: consider what those four agents say:

> Reeke maintains my theory is too logical.
> Ginsberg contends it's not logical enough.
> Dyer and Smoliar say it's just right

Now apply to this the Principle of Non-Compromise:

> The longer an internal conflict persists among an agent's subordinates, the weaker becomes that agent's status among its own competitors. If such internal problems aren't settled soon, then other agents will take control and the agents formerly involved will be dismissed. {3.2}

According to this principle or, more precisely, to the modification of it called "Papert's Principle" in {10.4}, Reeke's and Ginsberg's views conflict, hence tend to cancel each other out. So when we look down from the top, approval seems unanimous.

In any case, monotonicity is only one of logic's limitations. Another fundamental problem is that the inexpressiveness of its basic connectives and quantifiers confine it, in heuristic effect, to expressing only universal statements like "For all X, $P(X)$". Such statements work well in formal realms—but only because those realms, themselves, are *based* on expressions of such kinds. (Universal axioms work only in those formal domains where what we label "inference" is actually tautology. As I explain in {6.10} this works just fine for the worlds which we make (namely, what we call mathematical models)—but not in the world that we're actually in.) But when it comes to real life, such expressions can serve only as shorthand for ideas like this:

For things like X in the current context, the assertion $P(X)$ should be useful for achieving goals like G, when used with heuristically appropriate procedures.

In the commonsense world, for which we have no axioms, we have no choice except to build systems that grow through experience, by generating, justifying, modifying, and developing "evidence" for new hypotheses—as well as new ways to think and reason. But the latter is antithetical to the very conception of logic itself—which has as its basic strategy, the policy of trying to dissociate its axioms from its deductive rules—in other words, *to separate its knowledge from its knowledge about how to use knowledge*. This makes logic incapable of learning which kinds of reasoning are useful in different circumstances. That constraint is especially strong in the "first-order" systems in vogue today. I am amazed at how few students think of rejecting this strange restriction!

Thus logic is designed from the start to make it difficult to learn. The outcomes of its axioms must be always produced and forever maintained. But in the growth of a child's thought, one has to learn when one should use various styles of reasoning. We can lessen logic's rigidity by making it less monotonic, but in real life it is not enough merely to take some assumptions back. We sometimes must reject the form of deduction itself—as when a humor-laughter-censor-agent works to make you realize that a logical-seeming argument need not be taken seriously {21.6}.

Ginsberg agrees that formal AI has had shortcomings, but maintains that these are "not as dire" as I suggest. Yet it seems to me that the remarks in [1] still apply today: (These paragraphs may be new to some readers because the section on logic in the original version of *A Framework for Representing Knowledge* was not reproduced in most subsequent reprints.)

Why then do workers try to make Logistic systems do the job? A valid reason is that the systems have an attractive simple elegance; if they worked this would be fine. An invalid reason is [that such systems] can imply no contradictions. For I don't believe that consistency is necessary or even desirable in a developing intelligent system. No one is ever completely consistent. What is important is how one handles paradox or conflict, how one learns from mistakes, how one turns aside from suspected inconsistencies.... "Logical" reasoning is not flexible enough to serve as a basis for thinking; I prefer to think of it as a collection of heuristic methods, effective only when applied to starkly simplified schematic plans; it cannot discuss at all what *ought* to be deduced under ordinary circumstances.... At the popular level it has produced a weird conception of the potential capabilities of machines in general. At the "logical" level it has blocked efforts to represent ordinary knowledge, by presenting an unreachable image of a corpus of context-free "truths" that can stand almost by themselves. And at the intellect-modelling level it has blocked the fundamental realization that thinking begins first with suggestive but defective plans and images, that are slowly (if ever) refined and replaced by better ones. [1]

We both agree that there has been little progress toward simulating commonsense reasoning. But this is not simply because, as Ginsberg says, "inheritance reasoning is hard"; it is also because commonsense thinking involves many other kinds of knowledge and types of reasoning. This too is argued at length in my book, but was said more compactly in [1].

A typical attempt to simulate common-sense-thinking by logistic systems begins in a "microworld" of limited complication. At one end are high-level goals such as "I want to get from my house to the Airport." At the other end we start with many small axioms like "the car is in the garage," "one does not go outside undressed," "to get to a place one should move in its direction," etc. To make the system work one designs heuristic search procedures to "prove" the desired goal, or to produce a list of actions that will achieve it. But the problem of finding suitable axioms—the problem of "stating the facts" in terms of always-correct, logical, assumptions—is very much harder than is generally believed. Just constructing a knowledge base is a major intellectual research problem. Whether one's goal is logistic or not, we still know far too little about the contents and structure of commonsense knowledge. A "minimal" commonsense system must "know" something about cause and effect, time, purpose, locality, process, and many other types of knowledge. It also needs ways to acquire, represent, and use such knowledge.

Ginsberg complains that [2] is a collection of interesting but *ad hoc* speculations about how intelligence might work. He would like to see something more orderly. But human minds—the work of our brains—are not the products of planful designs, but of the accumulation over a half-billion years of accidental generation and selection, of thousands on thousands of intricate genes—the result of which is too intricate to be explained by simple tricks. Furthermore, each human individual must personally evolve and, as Piaget showed, a child's ability to make logically correct deductions develops slowly for more than a decade—and few of us ever learn to use it well. (Roughly a third of [2] is concerned with child development—yet neither Ginsberg's nor Reeke's would give readers any hint of this.)

Ginsberg starts by saying that good science frequently builds on good mathematics. But the systems that he advocates seems clearly less than adequate to found the science that he seeks. That illustrates the other side—that misdirected mathematics leads to bad science. Ginsberg concludes his review by reproaching me for "abandoning the standard methods of scientific inquiry", and complaining that my unsharp claims are "difficult to evaluate". My answer is as Dyer says: "To some, the book may seem vague and sketchy, but the more one brings to the book, the more one will get out of it."

5. Reeke's review

This critique says little of what *The Society of Mind* is about, and much about how Reeke categorizes theories. He begins by describing my book as an "*attempt to reconcile traditional artificial intelligence with connectionist approaches*" and he depicts the book as having the goal of describing the mind in terms of conventional symbols, algorithms, and computer architectures. Reeke says, in one nice bit of rhetoric, that

> throughout the book, Minsky finesses the critical question of whether his mental machines, or indeed real brains, are symbol processors.

My word-search finds only six pertinent occurrences of "symbol" in the book—yet this is made into evidence that I camouflaged that interest. But it was less an attempt at "finesse" than of treating that issue as out of date. I do not consider symbolic descriptions to be categorically different from other representations, but regard symbol-ness as merely a matter of comparative compactness, and see traditional arguments about symbols and their referents to be relics of what will someday be seen as an early, childish stage in our progress toward understanding how what happens in the human brain relates to what happens in the rest of the world. But Reeke insists that in my book, "*many of the classical problems of philosophy are simply defined away.*"

> Our minds contain processes which enable us to solve problems that we consider difficult. Intelligence is our name for whichever of those processes we don't yet understand. {7.1}

Defined away, my foot. That would ignore a hundred pages that show why traditional terms like "intelligence" are too coarse to be technically useful today—and need to be improved or replaced. Granted, one might dislike this interpretation of "intelligence" because it dooms that word's meaning to undergo change when we understand more of psychology—but that's just the way it ought to be. For, it seems to me, the traditional view of intelligence is like "the unexplored parts of Africa"—which disappear as soon as we discover them. Reeke similarly misses the point of my query, "*What magical trick makes us intelligent? The trick is that there is no trick.*" Fortunately, the reader can see the full context in Dyer's Section 7, where its serious content can be seen.

5.1. Concepts and symbols

I was amazed that Reeke could say that I *treat "concepts, like categories, in the classical manner as sets defined by necessary and sufficient conditions."* He bases this entirely on my one-page summary {12.1} of Winston's method for learning descriptions from examples, which was meant to illustrate only one of many different possible ways to represent a wooden Arch. In this and the next two chapters are a dozen other alternatives, and all of this should be read in the context of {Chapter 10}, which explains why many concepts usually regarded as elementary must be replaced by larger molecules. This is exemplified by discussing the concept of "quantity" in Piaget's scenario of child development, which Papert and I propose to replace by what we call "the Society of More"—a system that replaces declarative definitions by management organizations.

5.2. Functionalism

Reeke names me a "functionalist"—which he defines as one who believes that *"the relevant level of description for mental states is not that of physical processes, but rather that of constructs that correspond to purely formal computations."* This description makes me angry, because I cannot see how anyone could interpret *The Society of Mind* as supporting *any* particular level of description, given its emphasis on the need to shift among different types and styles of descriptions, depending upon one's purposes, *both when describing the brain and when using it*. The entire book is concerned with different ways to move between the agent and agency views; with schemes for building memories, goals, and processes that can focus on different level bands; with machinery for switching and sliding among members of frame-arrays; and with methods for using several types of representations at once, by exploiting cross-realm correspondences. (Now, suddenly I share Ginsberg's view. It really is a slippery book—yet Reeke thinks it's too logical!)

Let me amplify my annoyance. Reeke seems to treat so many terms as co-extensive—e.g., *mechanical, functional, computational, formal, symbolic, algorithmic, deterministic*—that I can't discern what he regards as common to them all—except to suggest that they all are bad. And the label "functionalist" seems especially muddled to me, because function itself is so relative. It would miss the whole point of the book to ask, "Which kind of description is best to use—formal, computational, or connectionist?" For different levels and types of descriptions have different uses, depending on our problems, contexts, and circumstances. Which sort of description is "relevant", to use Reeke's word, depends upon our current goals—what we're trying to do, which problem to solve, what types of theories we need to make. What I tried to explain throughout that book was the importance of discovering how to tailor our descriptions to our purposes.

It is a simple matter of common sense that our description must suit what we're trying to do. Suppose that you wanted to explain why a certain person gave a particular answer to a simple question. Normally it would be enough to know a little about that person and the previous conversation, and there would be less than nothing to gain by descending to the level of discussing that person's brain-cells' biochemistry. However, in the case that the respondent were near some point of exhaustion, it might indeed be "relevant" to ask about the metabolic states of the most intensely-activated neurons because, under these circumstances, such conditions might well have unusual effects on the progression from one mental state to another. Perhaps we could, in principle, imagine a brain so non-modular that the answer to *every* psychological question would critically depend on enormously many such small-scale details. However, I'll argue in Section 6 below that this isn't the case for human minds, because of how our brains evolved. What is my point in saying that? It is simply to emphasize that choosing the "relevant" level of description here is a matter of *natural history* and not one of philosophy. *Until one knows how the system works*, one cannot deduce, on purely ideological grounds, what depth-detail or description-type will be useful to use.

5.3. Neuronal firing patterns

> Minsky is not a biologist and his proposals seem to have been largely uninfluenced by biological constraints. Thus he has largely ignored the apparent lack of repeated patterns of neuronal firings that could be interpreted as codes. ⟨Reeke⟩

Reeke could have scarcely hit further from the mark. A major section of my 1954 thesis includes a theorem which proves that under conditions which apply to most neurons, the output pattern of a circular buffer-ring quickly converges to simply periodic. This convinced me that it would be hard for repetitive patterns of neuronal firings to carry much information. (I was unaware, before Reeke's review, that repeated patterns are rarely found, so I appreciate confirmation of this old hypothesis!) What preconception led Reeke to suppose that my agents depended on serial codes? The repeated conjecture in my book is that most agents cannot transmit elaborate messages, but can only signal their levels of activation. This theorem suggested that inter-agent communications would more likely take the forms of synchronous patterns on parallel nerve bundles, and I expect many of such signals to use the extraordinarily simple "superimposed random coding" schemes {20.8} invented long ago by Calvin E. Mooers [3].

These codes easily can be given enough redundancy to compensate for the variability of individual neural events. But there is also a deeper reason to expect the brain to use such "almost-local" bussing schemes. I argue in {20.9} that the greater the extent to which the individual elements of our representations come to have independent significance, the easier it will be to mutate, vary, and perturb them in heuristically useful ways—and also, the easier it would be to make knowledge represented in one agency available for use by other agencies. This is why it is important for different agencies to share the use of the same common "micronemes", "coding components", or "hidden units". Do we have any evidence, in brains, for these Zato-coded messages? None yet, I presume, because biologists would tend not to discover them before being asked to look for them. It would be hard to find the nerves involved with any particular microneme, because one might have to monitor millions of brain cells while inducing the subject to entertain the corresponding concept, word, or partial mental state. No biologist is yet equipped to insert enough probes to discover such things. But this is only a matter of time.

In {20.9} I briefly consider how these patterns might be learned, and Dyer suggests some other ways. Reeke ignores that whole discussion of micronemes, and maintains instead that at low levels of organization "the neuronal groups have neither purposes nor codes for representing information." He adds that this is "consistent with the biological data", but so is virtually any other theory today, including the Pollack–Waltz concept of micronemes.

5.4. Genetics

> [Minsky] has ignored the total absence of any known genetic mechanisms that would . . . specify the properties of the agents. ⟨Reeke⟩

I actually did discuss this in {11.4} and several other places, under the index title "predestined learning". And {31.3} describes a theory of how an infant could be genetically predisposed to learn to recognize, and sympathize (!) with its caretaker. The non-biologist reader could be misled by the phrase "*any known genetic mechanisms*". Scientists know a good deal about the chemistry of genes—but scarcely yet know anything about how genes determine neuronal architectures. If even a few of my theories are right, they might assist biologists to develop this immature area.

> [He] ignored the extreme variability in the developmental mechanisms by which collections of neurons form and establish communications with one another. ⟨Reeke⟩

The Society of Mind considers many kinds of learning through which agents can both exploit and protect themselves against various kinds of variability. And those who know the past of AI and neural network research will smile at Reeke's hint that what he proposes is wholly new—that "level of neuronal groups [in which] function is not likely to be separated across purposeful agents, but to be overlapped opportunistically across bits of circuitry that happen to have the required responses." That image goes back to the earliest days of experiments on neural nets, in my own thesis, in the earliest simulations of cell-assemblies, and in the myriad of AI systems that learn by variation and selection. But I cannot respond to Reeke's idea except to wonder about the power of a selection scheme that includes no mechanism for duplicating agents that are fortunate enough to be selected. Sections 22.10 and 22.11 of *The Society of Mind* does suggest schematically how a brain might construct approximate copies of useful structures and adapt them to new, creative purposes.

5.5. Computationalism versus humanism

Reeke's critique discounts my work by assuming that what I try to do is clearly something that can't be done. He says that "logic is often considered to be the quintessential trademark of mechanical thinking", as though such gossip's popularity endowed it with validity. He asserts that I am attempting to "graft human qualities onto mechanical thinking"—as though these were known to be two different things. He even wrongly reads my mind when, after observing that my theory is "ideal for implementation on a distributed-memory MIMD computer", he adds, *"we may take it that this is the metaphor for the brain that is in Minsky's mind."* Granted that one could implement most *anything* on such a machine, it simply doesn't make any sense to summarize that way the architecture that my book described; the memory schemes are not particularly distributed, nor is the control structure particularly MIMD. Not much of the rudimentary vocabulary of present-day computer science is of much help in describing the hypothetical brain-like structures sketched throughout the book, most explicitly in {8.2, 8.8, 15.8, 19.8, 20.8, 24.3, 24.9, 29.3, 31.3 and 31.4}.

In the specific context of {15.9}, I said that *to the extent that our agencies can resume their work after interruptions*, they will need mechanisms for restoring their previous states, and that would imply some sort of stack-like mechanism. Reeke perhaps misinterpreted this as asserting that humans have extensive such abilities, and objected that *"the brain seems to have no mechanism to do this, again suggesting that [Minsky's] underlying computational analogy needs revision."* On the contrary, I argue in {15.10} and elsewhere that infants scarcely can do this at all; then, as we grow, we manage to improve our skills in this regard—but even when mature adults, "we simply aren't very good at dealing with the kinds of situations that need such memory stacks." We do succeed to some extent, and I later guess in {22} that the brain uses pronomes (temporary K-lines) for such functions. In any case, *most* brain mechanisms are still unknown, and will remain so until the right conjectures are made. Neurological experiments are hard to make until we know what we're looking for. Here we should seek evidence for a small number of very extensive temporary K-line mechanisms. If these are as large as my theory suggests, they ought not be terribly hard to find.

5.6. Insulationism

Reeke claims that my views are too logical to be in tune with biology. But the compact, non-distributed representations that we call "symbols" are not mere artifacts of modern computers; they are vital, as well, in biology! We all know how crucial this was in making evolution, as we know it, possible—by expressing our inheritance in discretely transmissible codes. It is not so often recognized how the sharpening of boundaries were critical in how brains evolved. Here are some of those "insulations".

(1) The appearance of individually separate nerve cells with sharp input thresholds and long axons carrying constant-amplitude spikes. These "standardizations" of signals enabled nerve cells first to simplify and summarize their input environments and then to transmit the results over long distances, without being distorted by other interactions along the way.

(2) The emergence of many anatomical arrangements with lateral-inhibition functionality. These served further to simplify and summarize selections among the results of lower-level weighted-evidence schemes.

(3) The evolution of highly specific bus-oriented architectures, based on genetically determined connection specifications. These are selected first by positive tropisms of long-distance nerve-bundle migrations, followed by the destruction of connections that reach histologically unacceptable destinations.

(4) The formation, on many sizes and scales, of distinct sub-assemblies, each functionally insulated from all but a few others. On a small scale, these include specialized cell-groups arranged in many forms of clusters, clumps, and regions with laminar and columnar boundaries. The larger-scale groupings include hundreds of specialized "brain centers", each relatively bounded in space. And the overall form is based on the initial differentiation of an axially segmented architecture.

(5) The interconnection of many specific pairs of brain centers, on several scales of sizes, usually by topology-preserving bundles of fibres. These spatially coherent data-paths tend further to preserve the information represented over smaller scale localizations inside each brain center.

(6) The evolution of many other kinds of insulation mechanisms, e.g., the blood brain barrier, that functionally isolate our neural computation mechanisms from most other kinds of chemical changes in other parts of the body.

(7) The development of temporal insulation mechanisms, e.g., brain waves. Many of these large-scale synchronies will turn out to be involved in enabling the same brain center to operate on new rounds of data without excessive interaction with traces of its earlier states. And when we find exceptions to this, we should also discover that many of these support

specific schemes for allowing certain controlled types of interactions, e.g., for computing successive differences of temporarily preserved traces of previous states.

(8) We should be prepared to discover even higher-level signal-simplifying mechanisms. For example, Michison and Crick have conjectured that a major function of REM sleep in the removal of interactions among representations being constructed in long-term memory.

The overall effect of each of these developments was to make the brain more "computer-like" (at several levels of organization) by protecting activities at each level, from being disrupted by irrelevant disturbances from the chemical, electrical, and informational side-effects of other activities at other levels. I suppose Reeke might object to terms like "irrelevant" and "side-effect", because they conflict with his idea that "neuronal groups have neither purposes nor codes for representing information." But perhaps there is no real conflict here except (as explained in {7.8}) about the uses of words like "purposes" and "goal".

These evolutionary steps resemble claims in patents for computer designs, each one a move toward computations that are in various ways more localized, and each with substantial survival advantages—the properties that enable our brains to think.

5.7. Intentionality

> An idea can be "about" a rock, but a rock cannot be about anything. This "about-ness" must be a property of the thoughts themselves, and not of some conscious entity interpreting them—for otherwise we should have a particularly vicious circular version of the homunculus problem. ⟨Reeke⟩

Hmmph. Despite its nonsensical character, this kind of argument has attracted so much attention lately that I feel impelled to deal with it, though I find it strange to have to defend my new ideas against such an old monstrosity—Brentano's 1874 irreducibility hypothesis. The idea of a unicorn, is that about a unicorn? And what of the idea of a square? (There aren't "really" any squares.) What is "the idea of what an idea is about" about? Would it not make equal sense to say, "A book can be 'about' a book, but a book cannot be about anything." And what to say of Reeke's last clause, about that "vicious circularity". Doesn't it just make everything worse to suppose that every separate "thought" has a separate meaning and significance? A zillion different homunculoids, each entertaining its own belief!

I wouldn't take space for discussing this, were it not that so many students, colleagues, and journalists seem unable to digest this sort of word salad. According to Brentano and his followers, notably, John Searle and—apparently, George Reeke—there is a certain intimate relation between an idea (say, the concept of Plymouth Rock) and what that idea is "about" (namely, Plymouth Rock itself). This relationship is asserted to be so basic and immediate, that it cannot be "reduced" to smaller parts, nor in any other conceivable way be explained in terms of other things.

But what could such an assertion mean? When Brentano, or Searle, or anyone else, asserts that some relation X is irreducible—that tells you nothing at all about X. It merely testifies to the speaker's incapacity to imagine a suitable theory of that relationship. It simply reports, to Brentano's shame, that he has nothing more to say about the relations of thoughts with things. Now suppose, in the nineteenth century, you asked why animals' muscles contract. The explanations you would have heard might well have said that motility is an irreducible property of living things. But today we know a great deal more, and can talk about the ratcheting effect on actin of a myriad of myosin heads. And even that we can further explain, by "reducing" it to a great network of interrelations among more than a thousand different species of molecules. Contrary to common belief, "reductionism" is the opposite of oversimplification—and no one today would pay much heed to assertions like *"muscles are 'about' contracting, and that's all there is to say about it."*

I certainly don't mean that there is anything shameful about Brentano's (or Reeke's) inability to explain ideas. For the background of pre-computational philosphers reflects a scientific era too early to provide either the inclination or the conceptual technology needed to try to figure out the operations of a trillion component computer. But it does seem shameful to further claim that no future thinker could ever succeed. In much the same way, the "vitalism" theory of biology reigned until biochemistry was able to exorcise that ghost by using the theory of molecules to explain hitherto inexplicable phenomena like reproduction and metabolism. Today, I claim, we're on the verge of a similar change in psychology, by using agents and agencies to explain what has been inexplicable in the era of the "single-self" theory of mind. I hope the reader therefore can appreciate my annoyance, after investing many years at constructing a new explanation of the nature of ideas, to have it dismissed in a book review, on the grounds that no such theory is possible.

Why do we like the strange idea, that thoughts are like things with properties? In {10.7}, I argue that this is a useful way to start to think in early childhood. But while commonsense psychology serves well in everyday life, its concepts are unsuitable for the realm of words like "mean" and "know"—which children incorrectly see as naming close relationships. We must learn, as scientists, to disregard those illusions of simplicity, and recognize that such terms disguise large networks of intermediate relationships. A simple-seeming word like "rock" engages a huge society of systems in a brain including, for example, many kinds of visual, tactile, and haptic representations—which each in turn activate other networks of relationships among other structures, processes, and memories. But none of that is directly sensed by our agencies involved with goals, plans, speech, and "consciousness", which—just because of being more "articulate"—can only deal with summaries. Paradoxically, it is *because* our higher-level systems know so little of how their massive infra-structures work that we feel free, in everyday life, to use enveloping terms like "understand". It's just *because* such terms "make sense" that they impair all our attempts to penetrate the systems that they envelope. But Reeke persists in that pursuit:

> It is their lack of intentionality that makes computers incapable of intelligence or common sense, and the intentionality of [brains or thought] that makes intelligence possible. ⟨Reeke⟩

No such pronouncement is of use, unless it offers to explain *what* it is, and *how* it works, and *why* intentionality makes any such thing possible. Otherwise, it is as vacuous as saying that the rain-god's presence makes it rain, and that its absence causes drought. As I said in {2.3},

> Sometimes giving names to things can help by leading us to focus on some mystery. It's harmful, though, when naming leads the mind to think that names alone bring meaning close.

Brentano–Searle intentions are unscientific myths. Despite their seeming im-manence, they simply don't exist.

5.8. Reeke's glossary

Reeke objects to the "collection of idiosyncratic terms I have invented", and wrongly asserts that "*many of these can in fact be identified with familiar concepts in computer science.*" He then amplifies this aspersion by XOR-ing two different insults.

> It is not clear whether the new terms are introduced deliberately to prod the reader into seeing well-known concepts in a new light, or whether Minsky has deliberately used them in his own thinking for so long that he is no longer aware of the need to point out their relationships to more familiar terms.

In fact I introduced only a dozen new terms, each after deliberate, conscienti-ous consultations with colleagues. Good new terms are pivotal to scientific progress—but bad ones are monstrosities. Only time will tell if my new terms will help as much as I hope they will. But mistranslations like those of Reeke's could stop that process in its tracks. It is not clear whether Reeke's definitions are introduced deliberately to deceive the reader into believing that my book offers no new concepts, or whether Reeke himself has used such crude computational notions in his thinking for so long that he is no longer aware of their deficiencies. Here are my responses to Reeke's attempts to redefine my glossary.

Simulus ⇒ Argument list.

Response. I defined a simulus {16.8} to be "An illusion that a certain thing is present, caused by a process that evokes, at higher levels of the mind, a state resembling the state of mind that would be caused by that thing's actual presence." There is simply no equivalent term in English, and we need one.

Agent ⇒ Function; subroutine; module.

Response. Sciences grow by making good distinctions. Instead of applauding a valuable one, Reeke prefers to muddle three others! I recycled the old words "agent" and "agency" because English lacks any standardized way to distinguish between viewing the activity of an "agent" or piece of machinery as a single process as seen from outside, and analyzing how that behavior functions inside the structure or "agency" that produces it. The distinction is explained in detail in {1.6}.

Level bands ⇒ Ports that restrict communication,
        e.g., between address spaces.

Response. Reeke appears to refer to what computerists call "segmentation" but that was not my intention at all; we also need a distinctive term for zones of knowledge that overlap, to help us escape from the traditional conceptualization of machinery in terms of hard-edged compartments. The fringes (not edges!) of my level bands are not rigid and sharp, but soft and fuzzy, as described in detail in {8.7}. Reeke's definition better matches the sketchy entry in my glossary, but not the section to which it refers.

Script ⇒ Procedure; algorithm.

Response. Perhaps Reeke was unaware of the established use of this Schank–Abelson idea: that we frequently behave in accord with pre-assembled plans, and also often employ such scripts in perceiving and explaining. We need such a term as distinct from "algorithm" because the latter is used to refer to rigidly self-contained procedures, and cannot be applied to plans that are tentative, heuristic, and adaptable.

Transframing ⇒ Linking by communicating; metaphor.

Response. Reeke must be confusing this very highly specific type of knowledge representation and generalization with something else. A Trans-frame is "a particular type of frame which is centered around the trajectory between two situations, one for "before" and the other for "after". This important idea deserves a name so, because it combines three ideas of Roger Schank, I "thing-ified" the suffix he applied to all of them.

Uniframing ⇒ Set intersection.

Response. A "uniframe" is a description constructed to apply to several different things at once. When all of those things share common parts, then intersection plays a role but, as I explain in {12.12}, intersection is not enough because uniframes need additional ways to choose which features and relationships to enforce, suppress, or disregard.

Microneme ⇒ microinstruction.

Response. Entirely wrong. Micronemes are agents whose outputs are summed as preconditions for the arousals of many other agents. The "context" within which a typical agent is activated is largely determined by which micronemes are presently active. (Micronemes are exactly the same as the "microfeatures" of David Waltz and Jordan Pollack [4], and I renamed them, perhaps unnecessarily, for reasons of uniformity.)

K-line ⇒ Interrupt vector; branch table.

Response. Evidently Reeke misunderstood K-lines to be perceptual classifiers, which must be why he likens them to "simple perceptrons in their categorizing abilities". However, perceptrons fan in, but K-lines fan out. This is an easy mistake to have made, for Reeke must have correctly recognized that K-lines would indeed be hard to use without some good way to activate them. And although K-lines are introduced in {8.1} this problem is not addressed in detail until much later in {19, 20} which suggest using the sort of "ring-closing" mechanism that Smoliar describes in his Section 2.4. Section 3 of Dyer's review suggests some possibly better ways.

B-brain ⇒ Operating system; supervisory program.

Response. Close, except that the *A*-brain works autonomously, while the *B*-brain only occasionally intervenes—whereas Reeke's terminology would seem to put the *B*-brain in charge. This is an area that needs many more kinds of distinctions.

Isonome ⇒ Variable symbol interpreted as a process.

Response. This is not too far from the mark, but what I meant is better explained in Smoliar's Section 2.1.

By changing the meanings of each of my words, Reeke can see me as saying whatever he wants. Virtually every one of these suggestions shows a failure to comprehend some very important distinction. Contrast them to Dyer's remarks ⟨Section 7⟩, which clarify and amplify. To be sure, Dyer also is concerned that some of my terms may not succeed because they "sometimes appear to be implementational in character, other times psychological in nature." Dyer is right: that's just what I did—and I did not do it unwittingly. For I maintain that that's just what we need, in order to make it easy to switch between agency and agent views, just as in Smoliar's quotation ⟨Section 2.2⟩ which observes how, in ordinary language, we find it useful to employ the same word "glue", as both noun and verb, to represent both the object itself and its intended function. The same technique can also help in psychology.

6. ENVOI

In writing *The Society of Mind* I was not simply trying, as Reeke suggests, "to reconcile traditional artificial intelligence with connectionist approaches." A quite different issue came first in my mind: how to organize the awesome structural complexities uncovered by such discoverers as Tinbergen, Freud, and Piaget. The central thesis of my book is that common sense does not emerge from any particular programming trick, nor from any magic property of sub-neuronal chemistry, nor from any logically universal computational mechanism. Instead, what we casually call intelligence—the range of abilities most people share—stems from the great diversity of the many structures in human brains. But there are two problems in making a theory about this: we do not yet know either what components to include in such a system, nor how to organize those ingredients. So it seemed to me that our theorists got stuck, each waiting for a breakthrough on one side or the other. However, no breakthrough came on either side, because of a double-edged deadlock: without a suitable overview, it is hard to decide what components to use— while, without such a set of components it is hard to envision an overview. So the basic purpose of my book was to propose enough ideas about *both* sides to imagine how such a system might work—and thus lay out a prospective map of what future mind-scientists might try to do.

Did I succeed in doing that? Dyer ends with the remark that *The Society of Mind* contains too many ideas to summarize. Ginsberg's review suggests that it contains too many ideas to be useful at all. In either case, I fully agree that, from a literary point of view, *The Society of Mind* may seem too fragmented. It is indeed a complex book, and I wish it had come out more easy to read:

popular stories have straightforward plots. But if the hundreds of already identified brain centers are each involved in importantly different aspects of mind, then perhaps no simple, linear tale would help us to understand much of it.

In any case, I decided to present my theory in terms of its many parts and interrelationships, without providing a simplified plot. In retrospect, I think that this was a bad decision, because most of my colleagues perceived the book as too disarrayed to understand. And if a book is badly received, this is as much the fault of the author as of the audience. In retrospect, I wish I had proceeded more in accord with what I said on the book's first page!

> What can we do when things are hard to describe? We start by sketching out the roughest shapes to serve as scaffolds for the rest; it doesn't matter very much if some of those forms turn out partially wrong. Next, draw details to give these skeletons more lifelike flesh. Last, in the final filling-in, discard whichever first ideas no longer fit. {1.1}

So let me attempt an overview. In the early days of AI, students would ask, "What is the best way to represent knowledge" and I usually answered that we didn't yet know. But now I would give a different reply:

> To solve all but the simplest problems, we'll need to use several different representations. This is because each particular kind of data-structure has its own virtues and deficiencies, and none by itself can be adequate for all the different functions involved with what we call 'common sense".

What happens when you entertain a typical concept, thought, or idea? Suppose I said that "Romeo kissed Juliet". What's going on now, inside your brain? The answer: a great many kinds of activities, involving many kinds of representations, for example,

- sequential scripts for such physical scenes {21.3},
- picture-frames for visual representations {24.8},
- before–after Trans-frame representations {22.7},
- default-scripts for changing emotions {13.5},
- remembering the actors' roles in Shakespeare's play {26.12},
- default descriptions of their personalities {19.5},
- emotional networks for love-affairs {31.3}.

Presumably, different parts of the brain are architecturally specialized to support different types of such representations—and each of those agencies also must be able to learn its own ways to modify, combine, and apply those structures. Having that diversity is what enables us to think about the same real-world situation in different ways—physical, social, emotional, possession-al, and even mathematical. Whatever situation one finds oneself in, we always have more than one way to represent, and to deal with it. When any particular method breaks down, we can quickly switch to other realms that may be able to carry on.

However, it would not suffice merely to maintain separate processes in separate agencies. Whenever some agencies become disorganized, some of the others should always be able quickly to "take over"—not simply to "start over". But in order to accomplish that, the human brain must contain some machinery that tends to constrain all those different processes to proceed along analogous tracks, despite their doing things different ways—e.g., the way a mathematician often coherently represents different aspects of the same problem in terms of geometry, algebra, arithmetic, logic, and topology. How could an AI or brain maintain such different, yet analogous activities? That is the subject of the final parts of *The Society of Mind*. The key idea is that while different representations of something may use different structures and procedures, they will also tend to share in common many analogous elements or "slots"—the way that the legs, seat, and back of a physical chair correspond, in various useful ways, to the legs, "seat" and back of the person using that chair. How could all that come about? By forcing all those representations to coherently grow, from early in our infancy, by being subject, simultaneously, to the same higher-level "control-scripts" or reasoning procedures. But this, in turn, requires some special hardware, and those final chapters sketch out some ways by which certain large-scale neuronal connection-bundles (my hypothetical micronemes, polynemes, isonomes, pronomes, and paranomes) could be used to generate—and later exploit—the analogies embodied in those correspondences. On the knowledge side, the "nemes" bias different agencies to activate analogous fragments of knowledge, while on the procedural side, the "nomes" simultaneously apply analogous operations to the structures in the short-term memories of those agencies. Section {29.3} gives some more details of how I imagine all that machinery to work, but this is only roughly sketched—and leaves plenty of room for researchers looking for something new to do.

My ideas have developed a good deal further since the publication of *The Society of Mind* and—unless others proceed along those lines—I'll probably publish a new version in a few years, with more theories about paranomes, goals and level bands. I hope this won't be necessary because there are other things I want to do. In the meantime, I plan to distribute a hypertext version, containing roughly twice as much material; that would seem a more natural way to present such nonlinear material. And before that, I expect to publish a more linear exposition of these theories, embedded within the format of an exciting adventure-mystery techno-thriller about the state of AI, robotics, and immortality in the year 2023, *When Tomorrow Comes*, co-authored with Harry Harrison.

References

[1] M. Minsky, A framework for representing knowledge, in: J. Haugeland, ed., *Mind Design* (MIT Press, Cambridge, MA, 1981) 95–128; originally: Memo 306, Artificial Intelligence Laboratory, MIT, Cambridge, MA (1974); excepts reprinted in: P.H. Winston, ed., *The Psychology of Computer Vision* (McGraw-Hill, New York, 1975); also reprinted in: R. Brachman and H.J. Levesque, eds., *Readings in Knowledge Representation* (Morgan Kaufmann, Los Altos, CA, 1985).
[2] M. Minsky, *The Society of Mind* (Simon and Schuster, New York, 1986).
[3] C.R. Mooers, Zatocoding and developments in information retrieval, *ASLIB Proc.* **8** (1) (1956) 3–22.
[4] D.L. Waltz and J. Pollack, Massively parallel parsing, *Cogn. Sci.* 9 (1) (1985).

Artificial Intelligence 52 (1991) 205–218
Elsevier

B.A. Huberman, ed.,
*The Ecology of Computation** *

Michael P. Wellman

AI Technology Office, USAF Wright Laboratory,
WL/AAA-1, Wright-Patterson AFB, OH 45433, USA

Received September 1990
Revised March 1991

1. Overview

The Ecology of Computation (*EoC*) is a book of metaphors. Bernardo
Huberman and most of the contributors to this collection believe[1] that adopting a social or ecological perspective on distributed computation offers distinct
advantages over the prevalent centralized individualistic viewpoint. Although
this attitude is shared by many researchers in Distributed Artificial Intelligence
(DAI) [2, 3, 8], the realization of a societal perspective rarely proceeds beyond
the metaphorical. The articles collected here push further, developing analytical techniques and architectural foundations based directly on concepts from
biology and the social sciences.

The computational environments under investigation are *open systems*,
defined by Huberman as "distributed computational systems without global
controls". The characteristics of open systems enumerated by Hewitt—concur-
rency, asynchrony, incrementality, incompleteness and inconsistency of central

---

* (North-Holland, Amsterdam, 1988); 342 pages, $84.25 (hardback), $39.50 (paperback).

[1] In reviewing a compilation such as this, it seems impossible to simultaneously provide an
overall sense of the book, maintain accuracy, and avoid hedging universal statements about what
the authors believe. Henceforth I shall omit these tedious qualifiers, with the understanding that
assertions about the volume as a whole do not always represent a unanimous consensus among its
various authors. Generally speaking, these views are most reliably attributed to the "mainstream",
Xerox PARC contributors, whose chapters comprise the bulk of *EoC* and almost all of those
papers written originally for this collection.

Elsevier Science Publishers B.V.

information, and some others—suggest why they resist attempts at global supervision. These same factors indicate that analysis of open systems from a centralized or global perspective would be intractable and produce inaccurate results at an inappropriate level of description.

The alternative approach is inspired by an analogy between the semi-autonomous computational modules of open systems and organisms and agents in ecologies and societies. Its appeal lies in the fact that these natural systems are often able to achieve complex and globally desirable behaviors without central direction and little or no explicit coordination of any sort. For example, the ability of evolution by natural selection to produce intricate organisms of seemingly purposeful design has been justly celebrated [5]. Equally admired is the "invisible hand" of Adam Smith, which in some circumstances can guide collections of completely self-interested agents to produce economic results of maximal social good, all without centralized design or calculation. In this context, "perfect competition" substitutes for "perfect computation".[2]

Researchers adopting this approach would like to harness the awesome power of mechanisms like the Invisible Hand and the Blind Watchmaker for the task of distributed computation. Achieving this will require some understanding of their principles of operation, and how they relate to features peculiar to the computational environment. A methodological premise is that the concepts and tools developed by biologists and social scientists for analyzing their systems provide the most appropriate starting point for modeling and designing distributed computational systems. Although computational ecologies and societies might be quite different from their organic counterparts, the mathematical theories of the latter represent the only *existing* analytical machinery designed expressly for studying collections of decentralized, interacting agents.

As Huberman notes in his introduction, the book's chapters span the range of general issues and concepts, comparative studies, implementation, and language design. Although "ecology" takes the title role, the individual contributions introduce an array of distinct social metaphors for the analysis and design of distributed computation. Because the conceptual core of the book lies in its analogical framework, the detailed review below is organized according to the central social metaphors—bureaucracy, ecology, and economy—applied by the various articles.

2. Bureaucracy

It is common for pedagogues to draw the analogy between complex computer systems and bureaucracies. Distinct functions are delegated to modular

---

[2] This phrase is borrowed from Weitzman [22].

"departments", organized in a hierarchy and controlled in a top–down fashion. This view of bureaucracy is of course grossly idealized [19]. In real organizations, the lines of communication do not correspond exactly to the chain of command, directives can be only imperfectly implemented, and the separate agencies have their own interests and information states that may be incompatible with each other and those of the bureaucracy as a whole.

Hewitt cites these features and others to support his titular assertion that "offices are open systems". Rather than lament their departure from the bureaucratic ideal, however, he proposes that mechanisms employed by human organizations for coordination and cooperative problem solving provide a suitable model for achieving competence in distributed computer systems. In fact, Hewitt argues that the model is necessary for computer systems supporting organizations that are themselves open systems.

In lieu of a globally consistent view of the problem-solving domain, the distributed system is composed of a collection of locally coherent models of circumscribed subdomains, called *microtheories*. Deductive reasoning is performed exclusively within microtheories, which form in effect the "closed" components of open systems. Interactions between microtheories are mediated by a set of protocols, conventions, and procedures collectively referred to as *due process*. Due process influences the establishment and development of microtheories, and is the ultimate arbiter of conflicts among them.

Hewitt suggests a number of models for due process, based on human organizational activity (e.g., litigation processes, parliamentary procedure, peer review in scientific communities, negotiation processes). We can enlarge this set by including mechanisms based on the other social metaphors considered in *EoC*: ecosystems and economies. But even for processes with a decidedly non-bureaucratic flavor, the concept of microtheory as the basic unit of self-consistent behavior serves to bound the realms of decentralized control. Because it defines the fundamental granularity of a distributed environment, the specification of microtheories plays a central role in the design of open systems.

3. Ecology

In their article on *Comparative Ecology*, Miller and Drexler (M&D) define an ecosystem to be "any set of evolving, interacting entities operating within a framework of rules". By substituting "entities" for "organisms" and "framework of rules" for "natural environment", they are intentionally broadening the original biological concept to encompass computational ecologies as well. To facilitate comparison of different ecological structures, they parameterize the space of ecosystems in terms of evolutionary mechanisms, the capabilities of entities, and the types of interactions among entities and with their environment.

For example, collections of entities that interact through voluntary trades are called *market ecosystems*. M&D contrast the negative-sum relationship between predator and prey characteristic of biologic ecosystems with the positive-sum, symbiotic interactions prevalent in markets. Of course, mutual benefit and hence positive sum is a prerequisite for voluntary trading, so markets can survive only in environments where these opportunities are sufficiently numerous.

Ecological analysis attempts to relate the structural features of ecosystems to their behavioral properties. The special case of market ecosystems is distinct enough (and sufficiently important in human society) to have earned its own branch of study, economics. As such it merits treatment as a separate metaphor in the classification of ecological perspectives. But first I examine some of the non-market computational ecosystems discussed in *EoC*.

3.1. Evolution

An *evolutionary ecosystem* (again according to M&D) is one where the population is altered over time by the variation and selection of replicators. Selection serves to bias the population's development toward entities which are most "fit" for the environment. The idea of mimicking natural selection computationally occurred early on to machine learning researchers, and the evolutionary metaphor continues to exert a strong influence, evidenced, for example, by work on genetic algorithms. M&D classify evolutionary ecosystems according to their units of replication, their methods of variation across generations, and the criteria for selection. One example they discuss is Lenat's EURISKO, whose replicators are heuristics which are syntactically mutated and selected by a set of special metaheuristics. The aim of EURISKO is to evolve sets of heuristics that are increasingly competent for a given task, ultimately exceeding the performance of any solution that could be implemented directly.

In an article reprinted from this journal, Lenat and Brown provide a retrospective account of the secret of EURISKO's success (or lack thereof) in various tasks. The conclusion of their analysis is that viability of the syntactic mutation approach depends on a correspondence between the structural encoding of heuristics and the semantic structure of the domain. EURISKO's predecessor AM discovered interesting set-theoretic concepts thanks to the direct structural analogy between the mathematical domain and its representation in LISP code. Apparently, even a master craftsman like the Blind Watchmaker needs appropriate tools and components to avoid being buried by junk before producing a workable timepiece.

3.2. Dynamics

Given the necessary structural correspondence, under what conditions will

EURISKO or similar programs ultimately evolve useful ecosystems? How do features of the architecture and environment influence the course of evolution? And what patterns of behavior over time are possible or likely based on alternate selection strategies? These questions of dynamics are central to the design and analysis of computational ecosystems.

Because it is a hill-climbing procedure, evolution by natural selection is not guaranteed to produce a global optimum with respect to the selection criterion. And because this evaluation function is defined over the entire ecosystem, the fitness of particular entity types depends on the composition of the rest of the population. Considering that the entities are evolving in parallel, the prospect clearly exists for complex dynamic behavior.

Islands of constancy amidst the general fluctuation are the *evolutionarily stable strategies* (ESSs). Strategies (classes of entities with similar interactive policies) are evolutionarily stable if their dominance of an ecosystem inhibits replacement by competing strategies. An example adduced by M&D is the ecosystem of Axelrod's iterated Prisoner's Dilemma tournament [1]. In this environment, the ESSs tend to cooperate in general but retaliate against defectors. Strategies that always cooperate ("suckers") are unstable because they can be exploited by "con man" strategies. Con men are ultimately unstable because they will use up their prey and be outstripped by groups of retaliatory cooperators. In a generalized version of this ecosystem, the ESSs gain further protection from invasion by forming coalitions of cooperation among themselves [7].

The existence of stable strategies is one of the properties investigated by Huberman and Hogg ·from the perspective of dynamic systems. This study is based on a mathematical model of a simple "game ecology", where the computational agents choose from a set of alternative strategies at each time point. The payoff for selecting a strategy may depend on what the other agents are doing; for example, the return on a strategy that requires a scarce resource diminishes as the number choosing it increases. The model reflects incomplete knowledge by making payoffs probabilistic, and accounts for information delays by imposing a lag in the feedback to each agent regarding the selection profile for previous time periods. Huberman and Hogg proceed to examine the population of strategies over time, assuming the entities attempt to maximize expected payoffs with respect to their available information.

Analysis and simulation of their model reveals that a wide range of dynamic behaviors are possible, including asymptotic convergence to stable equilibria, damped or persistent oscillations, and chaos. Oscillations are attributable to the time delays, and chaotic behavior to the nonlinear dependence of payoffs on strategy selection profiles. These basic patterns have proven robust to changes in parameters as well as some incremental variations in the model's structure [11].

One feature of the model deserving of some scrutiny is the information upon which agents base their choice of strategies. In the basic setup, agents maximize expected payoff under the assumption that the latest report on the allocation of strategies reflects the current situation. This reliance on dated information leads to oscillation, as the strategy-switching agents repeatedly overshoot and undershoot the optimal proportions. A more rational selection policy would take the time delay into account, and in subsequent work [11], the authors consider "smart" agents that attempt to anticipate the oscillations. The problem with this approach is that the smart agents' predictions neglect the possibility that others are playing the same game, resulting in chaotic oscillation and reduced overall performance in ecologies where such agents are prevalent.

There are at least two potential antidotes to chaos from this source. In what economists might call a "rational expectations" model, each agent would take into account the other agents' beliefs and preferences in computing its own expectations about the current state. In principle, the information about other agents could be provided or inferred from their previous actions. Although it represents a truer maximization of expected payoffs, Kephart, Hogg and Huberman [11] point out that this approach might not be computationally tractable, or even decidable. It is irrational to expect perfect decision making in an ecology composed of real computational agents.

The second measure promoting stability is to increase uncertainty in the model. The authors lament that the price of avoiding chaos this way is a degradation of information and therefore overall performance. But in these instances, the "information" being degraded is based on false premises—that there are no time delays or other smart agents—so that actually, the increased uncertainty represents a more rational expectation than does the original heuristic. We could probably improve performance even further by allocating the uncertainty systematically to counteract the known biases of the heuristic's underlying assumptions.

The main lessons of this work are that a variety of dynamic behaviors are possible, that dynamic properties significantly influence overall performance, and that analyses of this sort can identify structural features determining dynamic behavior. The ultimate objective, pursued in continuing work by these authors [10], is to exploit the results of dynamical analysis in the design of well-behaved distributed systems.

4. Economy

In complex ecologies with heterogeneous entities and nonuniform distribution of types and quantities of resources, entities can often improve their situation by engaging in trades of mutual benefit. When such trades constitute a primary mode of interaction among entities, we apply the term *economy* or *market* to the ecosystem.

Advocates of the economic model for distributed computation point to a series of attractive properties. First, trading is a local activity that can be carried out asynchronously with minimal global coordination. Second, the decentralization of authority is justified by the assumption that agents are best positioned to know their own values and options. Third, the combination of local behaviors can lead to an efficient allocation of resources for the system as a whole. Finally, economic theory provides analytic models relating configurations of agents and resources to aggregate properties of the economy. M&D suggest that we can exploit these models to design computational economies achieving globally desired behaviors as an "emergent property" of the local trading interactions.

The success of this approach depends on the faithfulness of the economic analogy with respect to these issues, and perhaps some others. Although we are not yet in a position to realize or evaluate the full potential of computational economies, the articles in *EoC* examine many of the relevant factors. The economic approach to distributed computation must address a range of topics, including individual trades, large-scale market systems, aggregate behavior, and computational mechanisms. We attend to each of these in turn.

4.1. Deal-making agents

A necessary step in building a computational economy is to define the mechanisms whereby the agents arrange and execute trades, or make "deals". Beginning with the work of Smith and Davis on the contract net [4], considerable effort in DAI has been devoted to "negotiation" models of distributed computation. This line of research has primarily focused on communication and coordination protocols rather than on economic analysis of the transactions involved.

Protocols address the procedural issues of *how* deals can be negotiated in a distributed environment. An equally important topic is *what* deals should or would be made by a set of agents as a function of their circumstances. Rosenschein and Genesereth consider questions of this sort from the perspective of game theory and rational agency. In their framework the set of admissible deals is characterized in terms of the given situation and a collection of rationality postulates. Not surprisingly, under reasonable conditions the set of admissible deals is highly underconstrained. Game theorists often restrict the set of solutions by imposing additional equilibrium conditions, although the normative and descriptive validity of this practice is somewhat controversial. In the computational case (as Huberman notes), stronger results may be obtainable by virtue of rationality properties built into the synthetic agents during their design.

4.2. Markets and prices

When a large pool of deal-making agents interact in a *market*, they generally have to compete with each other to secure trading partners. Malone et al. explicitly appeal to the metaphor of competitive enterprise in describing their "market-like" distributed task scheduling protocol. Allocation of processors to tasks is accomplished via a competitive bidding process, where the highest priority tasks get assigned to those processors declaring the shortest estimated completion times. As M&D point out, however, the flexibility of this scheme is limited by its lack of a common currency for expressing tradeoffs among combinations of priorities and processing times.

To qualify as a full-fledged computational economy, a distributed system requires a critical mass of trading agents, some homogeneity in the goods and services supplied and demanded by its agents, and a system of prices dictating the terms on which these items are exchanged in a common currency. Because barter mechanisms impose a severe communication overhead in a large market, a price system is necessary to achieve the computational benefits of market decentralization.

The value of prices lies in their ability to summarize a large body of information relevant to resource allocation decisions [12]. Whether a particular resource should be deployed in production of a particular good depends in general on the alternative uses of the resource, its own means of production, the potential uses of the good, and the alternative means by which it might be produced. The potential producer, however, need consider only whether the manufacture would result in a profit, given the respective prices of resource and good. In a "perfect market", these prices fully reflect the situation as shaped by the more fundamental factors. Decision making in the overall economy is a highly distributed endeavor, with individual agents communicating solely by means of price "signals".

The metaphor of markets effectively performing distributed computation is invoked repeatedly by M&D to motivate the use of market-based computational architectures. This interpretation of markets is not at all foreign to economists. The invisible hand, after all, is central in economic lore, described in introductory textbooks [18] as a mechanism determining the solution to economic problems of production and consumption distributions. Samuelson [17] has referred to the market as an "analogue calculating machine", producing a result that might be computed in principle by a globally omniscient authority solving a set of equilibrium equations.

The computational view of markets figures prominently in the writings of Hayek [9], an apparently significant influence on M&D. Much of Hayek's discussion is in the context of a debate on the problem of "calculation" in socialist or command economies. To support his position, he quotes an observation of Pareto that, even if all the data on production technologies and consumption preferences were available, determining an equilibrium for the smallest of economies would require solution of an enormous number of simultaneous equations. While it is doubtful that Pareto considered the possibility of electronic computers, their existence does negligible damage to his argument—at least with respect to human markets, where the relevant question is whether central planning can match the "analog computation" of the aggregate economy. For a computational economy, we would need to establish that the centralized solution of equilibrium equations is inferior to the result producible by the *same* computational resources distributed in a market arrangement. Although such a demonstration might be possible (and would be very interesting), a more compelling argument for decentralization is the infeasibility of gathering information to set up the global equations in the first place. Hayek stresses this difficulty and contends that a competitive market is necessary to reveal the knowledge about values required for central planning. These distinct "cognitive" roles of markets are discussed by Lavoie [14], who also notes the historic irony in the current proposal that markets be exploited as computational mechanisms within computer systems.

4.3. Welfare economics

Before we conclude that market architectures are a panacea for distributed computation, we need to understand the conditions under which they can be expected to work. In economics, this issue is addressed by *General Equilibrium Theory* (see [18, 20], for some textbook treatments). The central results of this field include a pair of welfare theorems dictating that (1) all market equilibria are *Pareto optimal* (no agent can be improved without harming some other), and (2) *any* Pareto optimum can be achieved by some initial distribution of resources to the economy. These properties seem to offer exactly what we need: a guarantee that the solution will be reasonable in some sense, plus the prospect that we can achieve the most desired behavior by careful engineering of the initial configuration of the computational market. Moreover, in an efficient equilibrium, the market-clearing prices reflect exactly the information needed for distributed agents to optimally evaluate perturbations in their behavior without resorting to communication or reconsideration of their full set of possibilities.

The welfare results are subject to some severe restrictions, however. Economists have identified a host of exceptional features, which fall in three primary categories:

- *externalities*, where an agent's preferences or production possibilities depend on the production and consumption of others,
- *imperfect competition*, where the actions of a single agent have a non-negligible impact on prices, and
- *economies of scale*, where the output of production grows more than proportionately with an increase in inputs (or similarly, utility and consumption).

There are some other caveats as well—particularly in relation to uncertainty and information—but I need not provide an exhaustive list here. The point is that the conditions for potential market failure are common in human economies, and we need to consider these pitfalls in the computational context as well. For example, the most commonly cited externality is pollution emitted as a by-product of production. While our computational markets are unlikely to suffer from pollution in the literal sense, care must be exerted to prevent analogous problems, such as "garbage" dumped in a common storage area as a by-product of one agent's computational activities. M&D claim that this kind of externality is avoidable in computational economies, by maintaining a working market in storage, communication channels, and the like (just as they can be "internalized" in human economies, for example by charging proper prices for environmental usage).

M&D cite a variety of other reasons that markets in computational economies should be expected to work *better* than human market systems. They even go so far as to label computational markets "direct", because the rewards of economic success can be channeled directly to the responsible ideas, in contrast to the "indirect" markets observed in human society, where benefits of successful ideas are enjoyed by their "hosts". In indirect markets, humanitarian concern for these hosts requires attention to complicating issues of distributive justice that may interfere with the efficiency of the market mechanism. In contrast, we need not lose sleep over the suffering or even the demise of agents that fail to earn a subsistence income in the computational economy.

We can exploit the computational nature of the environment in other ways as well. For example, M&D suggest that violations of the market such as fraud and theft can be enforced by "physical laws" of the software and hardware. And because the individual agents are simpler and better-understood (because we designed them), applications of "incentive engineering" to the computational economy are likely to be more effective than similar attempts on human economies.

I think that these reasons are generally valid, and would not be surprised if computational markets turn out to be more amenable to economic analysis than are "real" economies. However, I am not very confident that there are not other issues that present unique problems for computational economies. For example, *public goods* represent an extreme form of externality where the available quantity of the good to an individual is not diminished by another's consumption [17]. Standard examples include national defense and medical research. M&D believe that many public goods can be privatized, and in any case are not aware of any particularly serious public goods problem in the computational realm. However, in an enterprise of distributed problem solving (e.g., as envisioned by Davis and Smith [4]), agents are continually producing intermediate results and pieces of information that are generally useful to the entire community of problem solvers. Consumption of this information by one agent does not preclude its use by others. While not technically a public good (because it is often feasible to restrict access), information is a notoriously difficult commodity to produce and distribute efficiently via a market mechanism. Moreover, generation of information could plausibly involve economies of scale over a broad range. Until such issues as these are sorted out, any categorical conclusions about the welfare properties of computational economies would be premature.

4.4. Market design

Having identified some general properties of interest, we can now consider the nitty-gritty task of designing computational market architectures. One of the first issues that must be tackled is how the computational economy is to arrive at the market-clearing prices that balance supply and demand. For this purpose, *auctions* offer the advantages of simple, orderly procedures that have been well-studied in economics [15]. M&D consider a variety of auction setups, and draw on economic models to assess their suitability for implementing the basic substrate of computational markets. Their analysis illustrates an interesting balance that must be struck in the design of auction algorithms between the desired economic properties and computational concerns such as communication overhead.

M&D also propose high-level market configurations for specific resource-allocation tasks. In their treatment of storage management, analogy is a driving force: caching policies are "business location decisions", objects sharing memory pages are "carpooling", and garbage collection is "eviction". Their comprehensive scheme is quite sophisticated and presents a variety of interesting issues. Objects are required to pay "rent" for the privilege of occupying memory, with more desirable (i.e., faster access) memory locations naturally commanding higher rents at auction. These payments are drawn from income derived from "clients": the other objects referencing this object, which have an interest in its retention in memory. Ultimately, the retainer fees can be traced back to a set of primitive funding sources, for example the original human sponsors of the computational task.

Objects that cannot collect sufficient fees from clients to pay their rent are evicted by an algorithm M&D call "market sweep". Because rent is zero unless there is excess demand, referenced objects will be garbage-collected only when there are competing objects able to pay for the space. However, to ensure that the most valuable objects always prevail at auction, M&D must address a significant problem inherent in the client–object payment scheme. The difficulty is that the persistence of an object in memory is a public good in that it can be enjoyed by one prospective client without diminishing its value to others. In consequence, each client has an incentive to ride free and let others pay the retainer. As a solution, M&D propose a scheme called the *dividend algorithm*, where, in return for their investment, clients obtain a share of the future earnings of the object. This equity provides an incentive to contribute toward the rent, as long as the object is expected to have future value to paying customers. In fact, there is no reason these capitalists have to be identical with the clients; perhaps maintaining separate investor objects would avoid some of the conflict-of-interest issues complicating the dividend algorithm.

Note also that this scheme presumes that objects can effectively charge clients on a per-use basis. The dividend algorithm addresses the public-goods problem of *retention*, but serious difficulty remains if the object itself is a public good. That is, if *usage* of the object does not diminish its value to others, then charging an access fee results in a socially suboptimal allocation, since marginal cost is zero. To efficiently recover the production and retention costs, some sort of taxation scheme appears to be necessary.

My objective in this discussion is not to shoot holes in this particular procedure. Rather, it is to illustrate the richness of issues that arise in designing market architectures, and to demonstrate the importance of economic concepts in elucidating and resolving them. M&D's contribution represents the deepest investigation of computational economies to date, and is the only one of which I am aware that can be analyzed meaningfully at the economic level.[3] Conclusive analysis, however, must await further development of these ideas and broader experience with actual computational economies. The SPAWN effort underway at Xerox PARC [21] provides one experimental vehicle; others must be constructed to explore the full potential of market architectures for decentralized computation.

5. Institutional infrastructure

Developers of computational ecosystems must devote some attention to the implementation of the infrastructure realizing the environment and mediating the agents' interactions. In elucidating their approach to computational markets, M&D argue that system-level issues such as operating systems and languages are critical because they provide the means to enforce market regulations via physical laws of the software. For example, encapsulation mechanisms can be applied to guarantee property rights. My first impression was that this heavy emphasis on security issues was excessive, for it should be possible for the designers of computational marketplaces to simply mandate that the agents behave legally and ethically. However, M&D make a strong case that this is ultimately inadequate, especially in an evolutionary ecosystem

---

[3] Others (e.g., Kurose, Schwartz and Yemini [13]) have made significant use of economic concepts to solve particular problems in distributed computation. The architecture of M&D is unique in its comprehensive scope and uniform application of the direct market approach.

where illegal behavior may evolve through selection, even in the absence of any malicious intent.

EoC includes three articles specifically devoted to operating systems and languages. Despite their relevance, however, the contributions by Rashid and Liskov and Scheifler are clearly not motivated by the "ecological" issues of computation, and are generally out of tune with the main chorus of *EoC*. The article by Kahn and Miller more explicitly addresses itself to open systems, and provides further argument for the importance of programming language issues in the development of computational ecosystems.

"The Next Knowledge Medium" proposed by Stefik can be viewed as a piece of computational infrastructure for the evolutionary ecosystem of human knowledge and ideas. The replicators in this system are *knowledge memes*: the basic units of knowledge and culture present in a society. Knowledge media are the means by which these memes are transferred (perhaps with some variation) across individuals. Stefik argues that an important role for AI technology should be to facilitate transfer of knowledge memes, thus serving to accelerate the development and broaden the exploitation of society's collective knowledge. Current (non-human) knowledge media are either passive (e.g., books, data transmission networks) or lack the flexibility to interact meaningfully with other knowledge media (e.g., expert systems). The next knowledge medium, according to Stefik, will emphasize collaboration and interoperability among a variety of knowledge sources and processes.

6. Discussion

EoC is rich in both inspirational and applicable technical material on the behavior of computational ecosystems. Readers will find their analogical faculties stretched more than usual, but this exercise will pay off in an expanded repertoire of concepts for thinking about decentralized computation. The perspective of the biological and social sciences is so entirely different from that typical of computer science that we should not be surprised if the former offers a more appropriate view (perhaps even direct solution) for some of the problems in their common domain.[4]

The most significant reasons to pick up this book are the contributions by Huberman and Hogg and the trio of articles by Miller and Drexler (most of the other chapters are reprinted from other publications). In fact, I would not hesitate to designate the M&D papers as required reading for prospective designers of computational marketplaces. This burden should be quite tolerable, as there is currently little else to read on the subject—at least in the computer science section of your library.

---

[4] This suggestion has been made previously by others advocating a social perspective on computing, notably Minsky in his *Society of Mind* [16]. For a specific example, see Doyle and Wellman's application of social choice theory to problems in default reasoning [6].

Acknowledgement

This review benefited from suggestions by Jon Doyle, Marty Weitzman, and the Book Review editors.

References

[1] R. Axelrod, *The Evolution of Cooperation* (Basic Books, New York, 1984).
[2] A. Bond and L. Gasser, eds., *Readings in Distributed Artificial Intelligence* (Morgan Kaufmann, San Mateo, CA, 1988).
[3] A. Bond and L. Gasser, An analysis of problems and research in DAI, in: A. Bond and L. Gasser, eds., *Readings in Distributed Artificial Intelligence* (Morgan Kaufmann, San Mateo, CA, 1988).
[4] R. Davis and R.G. Smith, Negotiation as a metaphor for distributed problem solving, *Artif. Intell.* **20** (1983) 63–109; reprinted in: A. Bond and L. Gasser, eds., *Readings in Distributed Artificial Intelligence* (Morgan Kaufmann, San Mateo, CA, 1988).
[5] R. Dawkins, *The Blind Watchmaker: Why the Evidence of Evolution Reveals a Universe without Design* (Norton, New York, 1986).
[6] J. Doyle and M.P. Wellman, Impediments to universal preference-based default theories, *Artif. Intell.* **49** (1991) 97–128.
[7] P.S. Fader and J.R. Hauser, Implicit coalitions in a generalized prisoner's dilemma, *J. Conflict Resolution* **32** (1988) 553–582.
[8] L. Gasser, Social conceptions of knowledge and action: DAI foundations and open systems semantics, *Artif. Intell.* **47** (1991) 107–138.
[9] F.A. Hayek, *Individualism and Economic Order* (University of Chicago Press, Chicago, IL, 1948).
[10] T. Hogg and B. Huberman, Controlling chaos in distributed systems, Tech. Report P90-0013, Xerox PARC, Palo Alto, CA (1990).
[11] J.O. Kephart, T. Hogg and B.A. Huberman, Dynamics of computational ecosystems, *Phys. Rev. A* **40** (1989) 404–421.
[12] T.C. Koopmans, Uses of prices, in: *Scientific Papers of Tjalling C. Koopmans* (Springer, Berlin, 1970) 243–257; originally in: *Proceedings Conference on Operations Research in Production and Inventory Control* (1954).
[13] J.F. Kurose, M. Schwartz and Y. Yemini, A microeconomic approach to decentralized optimization of channel access policies in multiaccess networks, in: *Proceedings Fifth International Conference on Distributed Computing Systems* (1985) 70–77.
[14] D. Lavoie, Computation, incentives, and discovery: the cognitive function of markets in market socialism, *Ann. Am. Acad. Political Soc. Sci.* **507** (1990) 72–79.
[15] P.R. Milgrom and R.J. Weber, A theory of auctions and competitive bidding, *Econometrica* **50** (1982) 1089–1122.
[16] M. Minsky, *The Society of Mind* (Simon and Schuster, New York, 1986).
[17] P.A. Samuelson, The pure theory of public expenditure, *Rev. Econ. Stat.* **37** (1954) 387–389.
[18] P.A. Samuelson and W.D. Nordhaus, *Economics* (McGraw-Hill, New York, 12th ed., 1985).
[19] H.A. Simon, *Administrative Behavior* (MacMillan, New York, 2nd ed., 1957).
[20] H.R. Varian, *Microeconomic Analysis* (Norton, New York, 2nd ed., 1984).
[21] P. Wayner, Time and money, *Byte* **15** (1990) 252–258.
[22] M.L. Weitzman, Economic choice in production, Unpublished Class Notes, MIT, Cambridge, MA.

Artificial Intelligence 60 (1993) 171–183
Elsevier

ARTINT 1041

Stephanie Forrest, ed., *Emergent Computation: Self-Organizing, Collective, and Cooperative Phenomena in Natural and Artificial Computing Networks* *

Peter M. Todd

The Rowland Institute for Science, 100 Edwin H. Land Boulevard, Cambridge, MA 02142, USA

Received November 1992

Emergent Computation is a collection of 31 papers from the Ninth Annual Interdisciplinary Conference of the Center for Nonlinear Studies held at Los Alamos National Laboratory in 1989. As the subtitle indicates, it presents a broad look at the ways that emergent behavior can be employed to process information in natural and artificial systems. This proceedings volume does a better job than most at conveying a coherent picture of a dynamic field. While there are certainly a few papers that will be of interest mainly to specialists, there are also several clear threads that wind through the book and tie together individual papers. Happily, these threads form a web of concepts in a mutually-supporting network. In reading several papers together, emergent phenomena themselves thus come into play: ideas are linked, connections and analogies made, and greater understanding is afforded than in reading these papers in isolation. This is a mark of good editing and selection, for which Forrest is to be commended. In this review, we will cover two of the main threads in this book. The first concerns the

---

Correspondence to: P.M. Todd, The Rowland Institute for Science, 100 Edwin H. Land Boulevard, Cambridge, MA 02142, USA. E-mail: ptodd@spo.rowland.org.
* (MIT Press, Cambridge, MA, 1991); 452 pages, $32.50.

nature of systems in which emergent computation is possible, and how to get such systems to perform more efficiently. The second thread considers the multiple levels of adaptation necessary to produce adaptive, responsive agents. Each thread has tendrils leading off, further afield, into other papers throughout the volume, as will be indicated.

Forrest begins the volume by introducing the concept of emergent computation, defined as an emergent pattern of behavior that is interpretable as processing information. Such behavior can emerge when a number of agents designed to behave in a pre-determined way engage in myriad local interactions with each other, forming global information-processing patterns at a macroscopically higher level. From the collective low-level explicitly defined behavior of individuals, the higher-level implicit behavior of the system emerges. Parallel computation processes that take advantage of such emergence can be more efficient, flexible, and natural than those that struggle to impose a top-down hierarchical organization on the individual processing agents and their communications. Furthermore, emergent computation may be the *only* feasible way to achieve certain goals, such as modeling intelligent adaptive behavior. But because the components and interactions of emergent computation systems are typically nonlinear, their behavior can be very difficult to control and predict. It is these problems that the papers in this volume set out to address.

Central themes in the realm of emergent computation include:

- self-organization, with no central authority to control the overall flow of computation;
- collective phenomena emerging from the interactions of locally-communicating autonomous agents;
- global cooperation among agents, to solve a common goal or share a common resource, being balanced against competition between them to create a more efficient overall system;
- learning and adaptation replacing direct programming for building working systems; and
- dynamic system behavior taking precedence over traditional AI static data structures.

In all of these ideas, emergent computation dovetails with the "animat path" to simulating adaptive behavior (Wilson [14]) and the behavior-based approach to AI (Maes [8]). The papers in this volume, though, are not solely addressed toward simulating intelligent behavior for autonomous agents. Many of the authors are striving for greater understanding of natural parallel-processing systems such as the brain or the immune system, or for better designs for computer networks. (Forrest divides the papers into the categories of artificial networks, learning, and biological networks.)

1. The emergence of computation on the edge of chaos

Langton asks a more fundamental question: What are the necessary foundations for the emergence of computational abilities themselves? That is, what characteristics does a system need in order to support information transmission, storage, and modification? Langton investigates this problem within the context of cellular automata (CAs), discrete deterministic spatial collections of cells that update their states over time based on the states of their neighbors at the previous point in time. Conway's game of Life (see Gardner [5]) is the archetypal example of a CA system. Langton believes that as abstractions of physical systems, CAs can provide a medium for characterizing the requirements of computation in any system. In the context of CAs, such computational abilities take the form of very long chains of CA states. This is because CA patterns that extend over a long range in time and space can store and transmit information, and the complex interactions these transients exhibit can modify that information. These three abilities make up the necessary components of computation.

After giving a brief clear description of CA systems, Langton presents a method for describing a wide range of CAs with a single parameter that represents the bias of the CA's rules toward a particular (arbitrary) state. This parameter can range from a maximum amount of single-state bias (causing the most homogeneous set of CA rules) to a minimum level (causing the most heterogeneous rules). In his studies, Langton varied the parameter over this range and recorded the dynamics of CAs randomly generated with these values. The results were very interesting. Langton discovered an important relationship between this single parameter and the length of transients (and hence support of computation) in the corresponding CAs. Very homogeneous rules created static behavior (the CA settled quickly into a fixed state), while very heterogeneous rules generated random behavior (the CA changed states chaotically). But at a crucial point in between these two extremes, a small range of parameter values yielded CAs with very long transients. Langton likens this crucial parameter range to a phase-transition between the solid (static) CA phase and the fluid (chaotic) phase, and concludes that computation is best supported at just such a transitional point. (Conway's Life turns out to be poised at just this point, which accounts for the long dynamic behavior that makes it so interesting.)

This is illustrated very well in the qualitative figures Langton includes in his paper, showing the evolution of states for the different types of CAs. The quantitative analysis of this phase-transition effect is a bit harder to follow (and some terms are left undefined, such as site-percolation). But this analysis, adapted in part from information theory and thermodynamics, presents some useful measures of the complexity and information content inherent in these systems. This exciting work provides strong support for the notion that "[c]omplex behavior involves a mix of order and disorder" (p. 32), the type of mix that happens when systems are poised "at the edge of chaos" between the solid and fluid phases. It has wide implications for the nature of computation—for instance, simulated annealing techniques, as discussed in Greene's paper in this volume, can be seen as a way of achieving useful computations by keeping the system "near freezing". However, the important work of developing ways to *control* (and communicate with) these long complex transients, so that they can be harnessed to do the computing that users want rather than just computing *something*, remains to be addressed. Finally, even more generally, this work speaks perhaps to the evolution of life itself, via a self-selecting process maintaining itself near a phase-transition point.

2. Fitness landscapes and the requirements for evolvability

In his paper later in this volume, Kauffman addresses a very similar issue from a different perspective, exploring the characteristics necessary for a system to evolve. The process of evolution can create complex structures in a quest for greater and greater fitness in some environment. But in order for evolution to work in a given system, that system must have the property of evolvability, which Kauffman defines as the ability to accumulate successive small improvements in the changing structures. One of the main criteria of evolvability is that the fitness landscape occupied by the evolving structures must be at least partially correlated. This partial correlation makes for a fairly smooth landscape, so that small changes in the structures will typically result in small changes in their fitness. In other words, nearby points in the fitness landscape will have similar fitness values. If this is not the case—if the fitness landscape is completely uncorrelated and rugged—then the small mutations that evolution typically capitalizes on will cause wildly varying changes in the fitness of structures, and no successive set of mutually beneficial mutations will be able to accumulate: evolution will be impossible.

Most systems in nature that exhibit this sort of evolutionary adaptability (including learning and immune responses) are networks of simple processing agents acting in parallel. Following the lead of this observation, Kauffman investigates the property of evolvability in the artificial setting of Boolean networks. These networks consist of a set of interconnected binary elements, each of which computes a Boolean function of all its inputs from other elements. When these networks are connected randomly and use random Boolean functions, their activity over time consists of a set of deterministic trajectories through binary-vector state space. These trajectories, since they are finite and deterministic, end up either going to a fixed point, or looping endlessly around a state cycle, with the pattern of unit activities (on or off) of the system as a whole recurring after some fixed length. Evolvability in such Boolean networks corresponds to small changes in the network (either changes in connectivity, or in the Boolean functions the units use) causing small changes in the behavior of the state cycles. That is, if changing one link in the network results in changing one or two states in one of the state cycles, the network exhibits high evolvability. If one different link causes the complete destruction of several state cycles, the network has low evolvability.

Kauffman has explored several ways of parameterizing the evolvability of Boolean networks. First of all, the connectivity of the network appears to be critical. Networks in which every unit has only two inputs from other units show high evolvability, while those with greater or lesser levels of connectivity show drastically lower evolvability. Another critical parameter is the bias of the Boolean rules used, that is, the percentage of states that map to 1 (or 0), analogous to Langton's rule-bias parameter. As in Langton's CAs, Kauffman has found that there is a critical level of this bias parameter that leads to high evolvability of the Boolean network. This parameter setting too seems to be associated with a phase transition, which shows up quite dramatically in the networks' behavior. For low bias levels, the networks exhibit extremely long state cycles, with each unit's activity essentially changing randomly from one time-step to the next. When visualized as lights (or pixels), the units all seem to "twinkle" on and off. For high bias levels, the majority of the units get stuck, "frozen" either on or off, so that very little activity is seen in the network. But right at the critical value, a web of frozen elements percolates through the network, separating a number of isolated still-active ("melted") areas. In this part-solid, part-liquid state, relatively few, short state cycles are created, each with large basins of attraction. This is what gives these networks their high evolvability: changes (mutations) made to the network can only have a limited local effect, and are stopped from spreading further at the frozen boundaries. All of these properties—small attractor cycles, homeostasis (large basins of attraction and hence resistance to state-changes), and evolvability (highly correlated landscapes)—are linked: "Self-organization for one, bootstraps all" (p. 148).

3. The emergence of symbols in classifier systems

Both Langton's and Kauffman's papers are very elegant, the sort of papers that fill one with excitement and further ideas while reading. The type of work to which these over-arching ideas about the nature of computation and adaptability can be put is well-illustrated in the paper by Forrest and Miller, on emergent behavior in classifier systems. Classifier systems are designed to model intelligent behavior through the action of a large set of condition/action rules. The actions of these rules post messages to a common list, and their conditions register the presence in that list of messages from other rules (see the papers by Holland and Farmer for a fuller description). The rules are constructed by a process akin to evolution (the genetic algorithm), and their strengths are modified by a credit-assigning learning algorithm (the bucket brigade). Forrest and Miller are interested in the emergence of symbol-processing behavior in classifier systems. What could symbols look like in the context of a classifier system? As the authors see it, symbols in a classifier system could take the form of co-adapted sets of rules, chained together by their messages to each other. Such linked rules can implement default hierarchies, where categorizations of inputs can activate other higher-level categories of greater abstraction. For instance, an input that signifies a "moving object" may turn on a general (default) rule whose output indicates "food", while two other inputs for "red" and "round" may trigger a more specific rule whose output also indicates "food". This second rule overrides the default of the first rule with the inclusion of more specific information (an exception to the default rule). But taken together, the two rules form a higher-level concept (a compound categorization) of "food". and the system should react in the same way no matter how the judgment of "food" was reached. These higher-level representations of concepts can be far removed from the lowest-level messages of the system's input/output interface by many intervening chained messages. Such a picture of symbols, complex entities distributed across several interacting rules, may not seem like the indivisible wholes we often associate with symbolic processing. But their behavioral effects in the system should make them familiar—symbols will be in the eye of the beholder. These compound concepts should allow the classifier system to achieve complex reasoning and efficient encodings of abstract knowledge that a simpler stimulus–response system (with very short rule-chains) could not. (This symbol-grounding problem is addressed in depth by Harnad in his paper, and briefly by Holland in his, as will be mentioned later.) An important question thus arises: Under what conditions will classifier systems exhibit the emergence of long chains of rule activation that may facilitate this type of symbolic processing?

Classifier systems, being complex combinations of several adaptive processes, have typically not been amenable to such inquiries. But through an insightful mapping from classifier systems to Boolean networks of the sort Kauffman has investigated, Forrest and Miller bring the methods of analysis possible in the latter to bear on the former. In this mapping, classifier system messages are converted into Boolean network units, so that looking for chains of message-passing classifiers now becomes looking for chains (or cycles) of unit activity in the Boolean network. While the results of this study were preliminary at the time, they did provide some interesting insights, indicating for instance the susceptibility of the system to freezing over a wide range of conditions. Freezing is to be avoided in this instance, since it means that messages are locked on or off, and hence are doing little useful work. The authors also found that learning classifier systems have difficulty in creating longer rule-chains (at least in one investigated application). But the importance of this work is in creating a bridge between one powerful, but hard-to-analyze, technique for emergent computation, and another paradigm in which analysis methods have been further developed. Forrest and Miller see benefits passing in both directions across this bridge, aiding the understanding of classifier systems, and spurring on the expansion of analytical results in Boolean networks and other easily quantifiable models of adaptation. Based on this lead, other similar bridges are likely to be built.

4. Speeding co-evolution with parasites

Kauffman is also interested in the dynamics and evolvability of higher-level systems, in particular ecosystems of co-evolving species. In such cases, there is no fixed fitness landscape, as the fitness of one species depends on, and in turn affects, the fitness of other species in the ecosystem. Co-evolutionary systems can show frozen components in the form of species that reach a fitness equilibrium with each other (a Nash equilibrium), being poised at a semi-stable local adaptive peak. These frozen regions will again separate more dynamic portions of the ecosystem in which species continue to evolve with and against one another.

Such ongoing co-evolutionary dynamics are addressed in Hillis' paper on the use of parasites to improve the efficiency of evolutionary search methods. Hillis considers the evolution of the shortest possible sorting networks, lists of test-and-swap actions applied to sequences of values to sort them, a topic of some interest in computer science. He found that by simply evolving the sorters with a fixed fitness function based on the percentage of all possible sorts they performed correctly, a very respectable short sorting network would emerge. (Only binary sequences need to be used to test these sorters, making testing straightforward.) For instance, for 16-number sorters, this scheme found ones that use 65 tests, compared to the current best-known sorter with 60 tests. Hillis used a spatially-organized genetic algorithm with local mating (the implications of which have been explored further more recently by researchers such as Collins and Jefferson [3]), in which different species of sorters could appear at different points on a two-dimensional grid. (He also uses a diploid gene representation and some other techniques that are confused a bit by a seemingly unrelated set of details in the first section.) However, he noticed that this simple first method included a large amount of wasted computation, for two reasons. First, the fixed fitness landscape induced by the testing method was somewhat rugged, and hence amenable to local optima; once a reasonably short sorter was discovered, it was hard to make small changes to it to produce a better sorter. Second, the majority of the sorting tests used to assess a sorter's fitness were unnecessary, since most of the sorters in the population got most of the tests right after just a few generations.

To help solve both of these inefficiencies, Hillis eliminated the fixed fitness function and instead introduced co-evolving parasites, consisting of 10 to 20 test-cases for the sorting networks. These parasites were also distributed over the two-dimensional grid. Their fitness was determined by the number of cases the spatially corresponding sorter failed to get, while the sorter's fitness was the number of cases it *did* solve. With this competitive fitness scheme in place, the test-case parasites evolved to be as hard for the sorters as possible, while the sorters evolved to do better and better at overcoming the hard cases. The "successive waves of epidemic and immunity" (p. 233) that resulted served to keep the fitness landscape in constant flux and prevent convergence to local optima, while the small size of the parasites avoided wasting computation on unnecessary tests. The sorters that evolved from this co-evolutionary contest were consistently better than those produced by the straight-evolution scheme, getting down to just 61 test-and-swap steps. Thus, the co-evolutionary process that emerged with the introduction of parasites made for the evolution of better sorters in less time. One of the interesting aspects Hillis sees in this work is that the quest for improved optimization techniques like this brings us closer to mechanisms we find in real biological systems.

In the following paper, Ikegami and Kaneko also investigate the nature of co-evolution, creating a model in which to explore the emergence of symbiotic behavior between two species. Their model consists of a set of differential equations specifying the growth relationships between a set of parasites and hosts, represented in an interesting manner as binary strings whose Hamming distance governs their positive or negative effect on one another. They hoped to find situations in which a host–parasite pair would emerge that are *beneficial* to each other (improving each others' fitness), rather than antagonistic. Such behavior did emerge in some circumstances; however, the fact that the authors build in pairs with such beneficial interactions seems to undermine a truly convincing emergence of symbiosis. Furthermore, the strictly periodic behavior their system exhibits does not seem overly natural. This interesting topic calls for more work.

5. A Rosetta Stone between disciplines

A second major thread begins with Farmer's paper, an effort to show the commonalities between many of the computational paradigms discussed throughout this book. Farmer's intent is to develop a common underlying language with which to describe connectionist techniques (including neural networks, classifier systems, immune systems, and autocatalytic sets), so that researchers in one field can see analogies in another, and mathematical analysis techniques can be shared across disciplines. The resulting paper is well-written, with straightforward mathematics, and would be a good place to begin reading this volume. Farmer starts by discussing the three time-scales of adaptation in "connectionist" systems (this may be a poor choice of a term for all the systems he intends, but we will use it here for consistency). These time-scales can combine synergistically in the creation and behavior of autonomous agents. From shortest time-scale to longest, we have state dynamics, affected by transition rules; parameter or weight values, affected by learning rules; and the structure or architecture of a system, altered by graph dynamics. (In more natural terms, these three would be information processing, learning, and evolution.) The presence of three separate adaptive processes, each operating on a distinct time-scale, distinguishes connectionist systems from other, typically simpler, dynamical systems with change on just a single time-scale, Farmer asserts.

Farmer then goes on to describe each of four different connectionist systems in these general terms, to show their similarities and differences. His discussion of neural network systems as prime examples of connectionism is quite clear, but that for classifier systems is rather too terse and dense, and may not reveal much to someone who doesn't already know about this area (again, Holland's paper presents a better introduction to classifier systems). Models of the immune system are covered next. This area, which has been receiving growing attention (see for example Perelson and Kauffman [10]), has interesting and distinct problems of its own. These include how to recognize self from non-self, how to implement a connectionist system in a fluid (like the bloodstream), which is not amenable to fixed patterns of connectivity, and how different forms of memory and information-processing functions can be implemented in a system of immune components (which may not have independently-variable connection strengths). With the rise of epidemics striking primarily at the immune system, this research may also offer insights about a topic of growing importance to autonomous human agents, and any progress that can be made by contact with other connectionist fields will be valuable. Finally, Farmer considers autocatalytic networks, that is, systems of polymers that stably reproduce themselves. However, these networks may be importantly different from the other systems discussed: while the first three can be seen as adapting *toward* some external state (i.e. learning the structure of the world, or adjusting to a mix of antigens), autocatalytic networks have their own existence as their only goal. This difference may make connectionist analogies to these systems difficult or misguided.

Farmer briefly mentions several other areas in which the connectionist language may be useful, including Boolean networks, ecologies, and economics and game theory. He raises a set of questions for further study; some of these have since been answered (for instance, Fahlmann and Lebiere [4] have developed a method for incrementally growing, rather than pruning, neural networks), but others remain important avenues for research. He concludes with a Rosetta Stone for translating various terms and concepts between the different connectionist paradigms, a concise and useful table.

One of the primary problems Farmer poses is the development of methods that can appropriately adapt connectionist systems at all three time-scales. The papers by Wilson, and Schaffer, Caruana, and Eshelman, address this problem. Wilson uses the genetic algorithm (a search method based on evolutionary principles) to evolve designs for learning perceptron systems. This approach combines architectural evolution with rule-strength learning and the system's usual state dynamics to adapt over the three time-scales. Wilson finds that the evolutionary search can design relatively complex problem-solving structures. But he also reconfirms that the non-specific credit assignment that evolution employs (basing feedback on total lifetime fitness or performance, rather than moment-by-moment success) makes for much slower emergence of efficient computational systems than do methods (like classifier systems or backpropagation neural networks) with more precise multi-level credit apportionment. This work points up the need to evolve not only connectionist structures, but other adaptation methods (e.g. at the level of learning) for finer-grained temporal adjustment of those structures as well, as some reseachers (Cecconi and Parisi [2]; Miller and Todd [9]) have begun to explore. Schaffer et al. look at a similar task, evolving neural networks with good generalization ability. They get interesting results, but with unclear computational efficiency and implementation methods (the details here are not as forthcoming as in Wilson's paper). Their work also seems to miss the point raised by Wilson's paper: it would probably prove more efficient for evolution to design learning methods that *themselves* generalize, rather than architectures that generalize with a given learning rule. Recent research has begun to elucidate just such network methods that promote generalization ability as they learn (see e.g. Weigend, Rumelhart, and Huberman [13]).

6. Adapting behavior by making predictions

Holland is similarly concerned with the problem of feedback: how can an agent improve its performance in some environment when it only receives very sparse information about how it's doing? One important approach is for the agent to develop an internal model of its world, that allows looka-head for behaviors that will lead eventually to rewards. Such models require the ability to form high-level symbolic conceptualizations of low-level input information dynamically, Holland states. This view links Holland's work with that of Mitchell and Hofstadter later in the volume on fluid symbol creation and manipulation in a model of analogy-making, and with Forrest and Miller's interest in the emergence of symbols in classifier systems. At the time, Holland believed that connectionist (that is, neural network model) systems were inadequate for this task, though since then connectionist im-plementations of lookahead and internal models have been developed. (See for example Jordan and Rumelhart [7]. Rumelhart has in fact developed a connectionist implementation of the original Samuel lookahead method for learning checkers that Holland mentions early on in his paper.) Instead, Holland chose to look at the emergence of lookahead and internal models in the classifier systems he developed.

Holland describes a method by which lookahead can be implemented in a classifier system, using messages to propagate virtual action forward in time in a world model formed of rules that capture causal relationships. Chains of triggered rules thus predict what possible rewards lie down different paths of action. By using these predicted rewards to adjust the virtual strength of possible competing current choices, an appropriate action can be taken. The messages used (or portions of messages, called tags) could become protosymbols "associated with external, manipulatable patterns (physical symbols)" (p. 194), leading to a natural symbol grounding (cf. Harnad's paper). These are the same kind of emergent symbols that Forrest and Miller seek in classifier systems, and should similarly be associated with complexes of rules that abstract and generalize from the basic input categories of the system to create new higher-level categories. (The question of what initial low-level categories should be supplied by the input/output interface to the external world is also an important one; Cariani [1] and Todd and Wilson [12] have begun to address this question in evolutionary systems.) Holland hoped that such symbol-based predictive models would emerge on their own in classifier systems, but did not himself achieve this goal. Riolo [11] has since developed a working system that uses an internal model and lookahead to choose its actions, but this area is still very open for further research.

One of the first papers in this volume bridges the two threads considered here: Kephart, Hogg, and Huberman's investigation of the behavior of a system of co-evolving predictive agents. This work comes out of the authors' study of computational ecosystems, in which a set of agents (like computer processes) choose among a collection of resources (like memory access or hardware accelerators) according to their perceived payoffs (like access time). These expected payoffs depend on what the other agents in the system are also doing, and may be erroneous; that is, individual agents may figure wrong about the resource with the best payoff, and thus make the wrong decision about which resource to choose. A primary source of expectation error is the time delay between assessing the current state of the system and making the move to use a particular resource: resource R may be free at time T, but by the time the agent decides to use it at time $T + 1$, it may be swamped with other competing agents. If agents simply choose to ignore this variable time delay, a variety of global behaviors can emerge in the system, including persistent oscillations and even chaos in the assignment of agents to resources (both of which seriously decrease the overall fitness of the system). Thus, some means of taking this information delay into account—that is, predicting the behavior of the system—should help the agents and their decisions.

Kephart et al. consider three types of predictive agents. The first, technical analysts, operate on knowledge of past system performance and use linear extrapolation or cyclical trend prediction to estimate future system performance. But such agents can push the system into even worse oscillations, or, if successful in small numbers, bring on chaos when they dominate the population. System analysts use a model of the preferences of other agents and how they can affect the system dynamics. If they begin with incorrect assumptions about the perceptions and utility judgments made by other agents, though, they can drive the system to an equilibrium far from optimal. The best performance was attained by combining these two approaches. This resulted in adaptive system analysts that were sensitive to the behavior of the system and changed their internal model in accordance with errors in their predictions. Thus, not taking the behavior of others into account (technical analysts) or making incorrect assumptions about that behavior (system analysts) can lead to poor system-wide performance. Adding prediction-correcting adaptation of this internal model, though, allows rapid system convergence to a nearly-optimal cooperative solution. As the authors have discussed elsewhere [6], these studies can reveal not only insights into the behavior of living biological agents, but also new methods for designing more responsive computer networks and systems.

7. Concluding remarks

Two other main threads that run through *Emergent Computation* are descriptions of various learning methods (including a stochastic delta rule, geometric learning algorithms, and parallel simulated annealing), and models of biological neural networks (including selectionist models, theories of visual processing, and computation within the cytoskeleton of individual neurons). Many of these papers are of a more specialized nature, and will appeal primarily to researchers in the particular fields involved. But overall, there is enough of a critical mass of papers with more general insights in this volume, and a high degree of coherence and connection between them, to recommend it to a wide audience interested in the nature of adaptive behavior and computation, and their emergence through low-level interactions in highly parallel systems.

References

[1] P. Cariani, Emergence and artificial life, in: C.G. Langton, C. Taylor, J.D. Farmer and S. Rasmussen, eds., *Artificial Life* II (Addison-Wesley, Reading, MA, 1992) 775–797.

[2] F. Cecconi and D. Parisi, Neural networks with motivational units, *Proceedings Second International Conference on Simulation of Adaptive Behavior* (Mit Press, 1993).

[3] R.J. Collins and D.R. Jefferson, The evolution of sexual selection and female choice, in: F.J. Varela and P. Bourgine, eds., *Toward a Practice of Autonomous Systems*: *Proceedings of the First European Conference on Artificial Life* (MIT Press/Bradford Books, Cambridge, MA, 1992) 327–336.

[4] S.E. Fahlman and C. Lebiere, The cascade-correlation learning architecture, in: D.S. Touretzky, ed., *Advances in Neural Information Processing* 2 (Morgan Kaufmann, San Mateo, CA, 1988) 524–532.

[5] M. Gardner, Mathematical games: the fantastic combinations of John Conway's new solitaire game 'Life', *Sci. Am.* **223** (1970) 120–123.

[6] B.A. Huberman, ed., *The Ecology of Computation* (North-Holland, Amsterdam, Netherlands, 1988).

[7] M.I. Jordan and D.E. Rumelhart, Forward models: supervised learning with a distal teacher, *Cogn. Sci.* **16** (1992) 307–354.

[8] P. Maes, Behavior-based artificial intelligence, *Proceedings Second International Conference on Simulation of Adaptive Behavior* (Mit Press, 1993).

[9] G.F. Miller and P.M. Todd, Exploring adaptive agency I: theory and methods for simulating the evolution of learning, in: D.S. Touretzky, J.L. Elman, T.J. Sejnowski and G.E. Hinton, eds., *Proceedings 1990 Connectionist Models Summer School* (Morgan Kaufmann, San Mateo, CA, 1990) 65–80.

[10] P.S. Perelson and S.A. Kauffman, *Molecular Evolution on Rugged Landscapes: Proteins, RNA and The Immune System* (Addison-Wesley, Reading, MA, 1991).

[11] R.L. Riolo, Lookahead planning and latent learning in a classifier system, in: J.-A. Meyer and S.W. Wilson, eds., *From Animals to Animats: Proceedings of the First International Conference on Simulation of Adaptive Behavior* (MIT Press/Bradford Books, Cambridge, MA, 1991) 316–326.

[12] P.M. Todd and S.W. Wilson, Environment structure and adaptive behavior from the ground up, in: *Proceedings Second International Conference on Simulation of Adaptive Behavior* (Mit Press, 1993).

[13] A.S. Weigend, D.E. Rumelhart and B.A. Huberman, Generalization by weight-elimination with application to forecasting, in: R.P. Lippmann, J.E. Moody and D.S. Touretzky, eds., *Advances in Neural Information Processing* 3 (Morgan Kaufmann, San Mateo, CA, 1991) 875–882.

[14] S.W. Wilson, The animat path to AI, in: J.-A. Meyer and S.W. Wilson, eds., *From Animals to Animats: Proceedings of the First International Conference on Simulation of Adaptive Behavior* (MIT Press/Bradford Books, Cambridge, MA, 1991) 15–21.

Steven Pinker and Jacques Mehler, eds., *Connections and Symbols* (The MIT Press, Cambridge, MA, 1988); 255 pages, $17.50. Reprinted from *Cognition: International Journal of Cognitive Science* **28** (1988).

Reviewed by: Mark Derthick
      MCC, 3500 West Balcones Center Drive, Austin, TX 78759, USA

1. Introduction

This collection of three articles is a reprint of a 1988 special issue of *Cognition* devoted to critical examinations of connectionist theories of cognition as compared with more traditional symbolic accounts. Over the past five years there has been tremendous growth in interest in connectionist theories for their claimed ability to learn automatically from an environment, generalize behavior to novel situations, gracefully degrade in the face of conflicting input or in the face of internal damage, and their superficial similarity to the organization and behavior of massively parallel networks of neurons. These properties are at best less central in traditional theories of cognitive science, which are based on manipulation of symbol structures. These papers are the first detailed published criticisms of connectionism from the symbolic point of view. The latter two, by Steven Pinker and Alan Prince, and by Joel Lachter and Thomas Bever, are from a linguistic perspective and use David Rumelhart and James McClelland's account of past tense formation in English [21] as the leading example of connectionist linguistic modeling. The first, by Jerry Fodor and Zenon Pylyshyn, is more philosophical and less concerned with specific systems. There has been heated debate on electronic bulletin boards among these authors, Rumelhart and McClelland and others. Consequently all three papers, as well as various unpublished and forthcoming replies (such as [18]), fit well together.

2. Overview of Connectionist Theories

All three papers review the differences between symbolic and connectionist

Artificial Intelligence **43** (1990) 251–265

theories of cognition.[1] The most important function of symbols is furnishing a compact access path to an arbitrary data structure. Symbols can be conveniently copied and used as building blocks in further data structures, giving rise to hierarchical structure. This naturally provides run-time flexibility and recursion. In contrast, connectionist network structures are not alterable at run-time. The only "data structures" are patterns of activity over the units in the network, each of which has an associated scalar state. Each unit is connected by weighted links to a subset of other units in the network. These connections, which may be excitatory or inhibitory, mediate the influence of one unit's state on its neighbors. Commonly some of the units will be inputs, whose states are set externally to represent the problem to be solved. Some units are outputs, whose states, after some time for propagation through the network, represent the solution. There may be other units, called hidden units, which develop internal representations to facilitate correct "inferences" between inputs and outputs.

Two types of network representations are often distinguished [12]. In a localist representation, each concept in the domain is assigned a unit. To represent "John loves Mary" the JOHN, LOVES, and MARY units would be active. (There are various ways to distinguish this from "Mary loves John" including having units connecting JOHN and SUBJECT, or having units for every pair of concept and role.) In a distributed representation, the units represent "micro-features" such as MALE and PERSON. Then John is represented by a pattern of activation over these units. If Mary were the subject, this would be represented by a slightly different pattern over the same units. Eliminating ambiguity when multiple concepts are simultaneously represented is even harder with distributed representations, but there is better generalization to similar concepts because inferences can be tied to shared feature units. Although widespread, the distinction is both fuzzy and subjective. Having units for binding concepts and roles introduces a degree of distributedness, for instance, and in any case one theory's concept is another's micro-feature.

Connectionists see many drawbacks to symbolic cognitive architectures [22]. They believe that (much of) high-level cognition is similar to low-level processing, for instance visual object recognition. This leads them to be most concerned with the fact that natural intelligence degrades gracefully in the face of incomplete or inconsistent information, and often generalizes correctly to novel inputs. They believe this is the result of fast parallel satisfaction of global constraints, rather than chains of local interaction. In particular, top-down and bottom-up influences mutually constrain one another. Rules (micro-inferences) interact arithmetically rather than all-or-none overriding. In contrast, symbolic theories are (fairly or unfairly) associated with discrete, serial, local rules.

---

[1] Those unfamiliar with connectionist theories might read the four introductory chapters of [23] before these papers. For an alternative, connectionist, perspective on the differences consult [6, 25].

Both camps agree that language use is a paradigmatic aspect of human cognition, and that their paradigm is particularly well suited to it. This fortunately allows the arguments to be grounded in particulars. All three papers refer to Rumelhart and McClelland's past tense formation net [21] (henceforth abbreviated RM). This is an excellent choice for discussion because it is widely known and highly regarded in the connectionist community, and is claimed to exhibit just the kinds of blending and subregularities connectionists believe are missing from rule-based accounts of cognition. In this network the input is a distributed phonological representation of present tense English verbs, and the output is a distributed phonological representation of the corresponding past tense verbs. For instance, the input for the verb *guard* is /gɑrd/, and the desired output is /gɑrd^d/. There are no hidden units. The weights of the network are initially set to zero. The training set of verbs is input to the network, and the outputs computed. By comparison to the desired outputs, a feedback procedure incrementally modifies the weights so that if the same input were presented again, the probability of the computed output matching the desired output would be slightly higher. Eventually the network learns to map from present to past not only for the training set, but also for some other English verbs. RM attribute this success to "micro-inferences," correlations between input micro-features and output micro-features.

All three papers discuss the relationship between connectionist and symbolic theories. Using the terminology of Pinker and Prince, there are three possibilities. In "implementational connectionism" the network level of organization is simply a lower system level than the symbolic level, much as a transistor level analysis of a logic circuit is at a lower system level than a logic gate analysis. In this case, research into symbolic theories of cognition could go on largely unaffected by connectionist theories. In "eliminative connectionism" there would be no exact mapping from the network level architecture to the symbolic level. That is, the components of the network could not be characterized in semantic terms, but only in physical terms. Hence exact psychological mechanisms could not be explained at the symbolic level. Pinker and Prince include in this case both the possibility that the input/output mapping is the same as it would be for a symbolic theory and the possibility that no symbolic theory has the same input/output mapping as the network. Eliminative connectionism would radically affect the future of symbolic psychological theorizing. "Revisionist-symbol-processing connectionism" is an intermediate position in which "[connectionist] theory could lead to fundamental new discoveries about the character of symbol-processing, rather than implying that there was no such thing" (p. 78). The authors of these three papers argue for the first alternative and are sometimes willing to accept the third, while they take most connectionists to uphold the second.

Actually, I think Rumelhart and McClelland advocate something slightly different. They do not go so far as to say units have no semantic interpretation, yet neither do they agree that the relationship is akin to that between logic gates and transistors. Rather they appeal to the relationship between quantum and classical physics. There is definitely a sense of higher and lower system levels, yet the higher level is not autonomous because it cannot provide an exact account of behavioral phenomenon. Using the above definitions of eliminative connectionism, Lachter and Bever and, to a lesser extent, Pinker and Prince, point to evidence of semantic interpretability of units in the RM model as evidence that it supports symbolic theories. To show that the RM model implicates implementational connectionism it must be demonstrated not only that all the units be semantically interpretable, but also that the dynamic relations between the units be modeled with rules. Fodor and Pylyshyn avoid this shortcoming by arguing that the only way a connectionist network can model linguistic behavior is by simulating a symbolic architecture exactly.

3. Fodor and Pylyshyn

3.1. Summary

Fodor and Pylyshyn (henceforth FP) acknowledge no contributions of connectionism to cognitive science. They see it as a revival of associationism, whose only new idea is hidden units: "[Connectionist psychology is] not readily distinguishable from the worst of Hume and Berkeley" (p. 64). To those who agree with FP, or to those who have not read propaganda from the other side [15], little will be gained from this essay. So skilled are the arguments that the uninformed reader will wonder what all the fuss is about. However, for someone (like me) who has taken connectionist arguments to heart, the polemic is a constant challenge. Fodor and Pylyshyn have undertaken a daunting task in arguing in principle against any contribution of connectionism to cognitive science, especially given the variety of connectionist theories to argue against. They cast a broad enough, and strong enough, net that I was forced to retreat several steps before settling on a counterargument I felt comfortable with. No staunch connectionist will reverse his research strategy as a result of these philosophical considerations but a reconsideration of the place of connectionism in a theory of the mind is bound to be healthy.

The most important section is the first, in which FP define their terms and distinguish "classical" from connectionist architectures. As is typical with philosophical papers, it is in the definitions that one finds the most to disagree with. The most important definition is that classical architectures are just those in which symbols have constituent structure, in the sense that "John" is a constituent of "John loves the girl" and contributes the same meaning as when it occurs in "The girl loves John." To say this another way, representations have combinatorial syntax and semantics. Because semantics maps in a regular way onto syntax, and because the inference processes are sensitive to the syntactic structure in an appropriate way, the system's behavior makes semantic sense for a very large (combinatorial) set of inputs. In contrast connectionist representations are (at the appropriate level of analysis) atomic. There is no syntactic relation between the representation for "John loves the girl" and that for "The girl loves John." The number of micro-features required is "of the order of magnitude of the *sentences* of natural language" (p. 24).

Surely by this time FP are flogging a dead horse. Connectionists are well aware of the implausibility of "grandmother cells," and do not doubt there is some regularity in mental representations. Yet a large fraction of the paper is devoted to four arguments for regularity, based on the productivity, systematicity, compositionality, and inferential coherence of language. Chomsky originated productivity arguments [2]: Under the assumption that people are competent to utter or understand an infinite number of sentences (albeit they are limited in performance by considerations such as memory), yet must have only a finite language organ, the knowledge of language must be in terms of recursive rules that can be applied over and over to distinct tokens of a given type. To allay doubts about whether human competence is really infinite, FP advance an argument from the weaker premise that language is systematic. You don't find minds that can think "John loves the girl" without being able to think "The girl loves John." There would be no reason for this if representations really were atomic and independent. The compositionality and inferential coherence arguments are similar; the reason these two example sentences are systematically related in the mind is because of their similarly structured combinatorial representations and common primitives. Due to the similar structure, and the syntax-sensitive nature of the inference processes, inferences that are of similar logical type are carried out by the same psychological mechanisms. Hence you don't find minds that can make some, but not all, inferences of a single logical type.

Atomicity is a fundamental problem which also stymied the Associationists. For Hume, too, learning is based on strengthening of associations between "Ideas" based on their frequency of co-occurrence in the environment. However association of whole gestalts, without some mechanism to generalize to similar gestalts, cannot model the productivity of natural intelligence.

In addition to characterizing the distinction between connectionism and symbolism, FP also point out a widespread but mistaken notion of what the distinction is. Paul Smolensky [25] has used "symbol level" to characterize those internal states whose referent is in the intuitive domain vocabulary, and "subsymbolic level" for states whose referent cuts the domain finer than this. FP point out that linguists' use of features predates the New Connectionism, so it certainly isn't the case that if the cognitive level is subsymbolic, it can't be classical. In fact this distinction is completely orthogonal to that between connectionist and classical architectures.

Both connectionists and classicists are "Representationalists," that is, the internal states of the system refer to things. It is at the level of these referential states that a theory is cognitive. Although a connectionist architecture could simulate a Turing machine, upon which a classical architecture ran, the nodes in the network would no longer refer to objects in the domain. Therefore a connectionist network *at the level of a cognitive theory* cannot be a classical theory.

FP then examine ten arguments for connectionism, and dismiss each either on the grounds that the phenomenon in question can be explained equally well by classical theories, or that the phenomenon is a result of implementation-level considerations, and is irrelevant to whether cognitive level architecture is classical or connectionist. In dismissing these arguments, FP allow that a classical architecture may have rule firings determined by noisy analog processes, firing may not always be all-or-none, the representations may be subsymbolic, the rules may fire in parallel, and the rules may not be explicit. This is accommodating connectionists a lot more than they are used to. Many of the arguments cited by FP for connectionism, which they say misunderstand classicism, are in fact opposed to Allen Newell's Physical Symbol System Hypothesis [17] (PSSH). This hypothesis is much stronger than the one FP try to defend, which only requires that connectionist representations not have constituent structure. The PSSH is widely regarded as correctly describing the intent of workers in artificial intelligence, as even Pylyshyn agrees [20, pp. 51, 54–55]. Three of the requirements of the PSSH not included in FP's definition of classical are that data be discrete, that data can be treated as program (that is, rules are explicit), and that the system be universal, in the sense of being able to simulate any other system. FP do not explicitly point out that the definition of classical they use here is weaker than the PSSH.

In light of their criticisms FP conclude by suggesting two worthwhile goals for connectionist theorizing:

(1) Treat connectionist theories as theories of implementation, below the cognitive level. This would still be an interesting topic to investigate, but would give up many of the hopes for connectionism.

(2) Allow that some mental processes have a classical explanation, while others (presumably those closer to perception and action) are best modeled with connectionist architectures

This naturally fits Fodor's modularity hypothesis [9] and Pylyshyn's notion of functional architecture [20].

3.2. Discussion

I found Section 2, where FP argue that connectionist representations are atomic, to be the most contentious and the most interesting. As a matter of fact connectionists are quite proud of network generalization—the fact that the networks generate correct outputs for novel inputs. Surely this can only happen if the internal representations are systematic. The reader must be careful to observe that FP lump localist and distributed networks together by defining "node" to be whatever single unit or pattern over units signifies a concept. A technical objection to equating patterns in a network using distributed representations with nodes in a higher-level localist network is that when this transformation is made, the nodes can no longer be modeled with simple activation functions [24], so the resulting network is not truly connectionist.

A second objection is that at first glance it seems calling patterns nodes and then saying nodes have no constituent structure is unfair. The explanation hinges on the definition of "constituent" in Section 2.1.4 of their paper. Consider the representation of CUP as the conjunction of micro-feature units such as HAS-A-HANDLE. According to FP, the relationship between CUP and HAS-A-HANDLE, subsuming predicates, just isn't the same as that between "John loves the girl" and "John." The latter, which FP call "real-constituency" corresponds to a part-of relationship between the representations, while HAS-A-HANDLE just isn't part of CUP. Now this seems a clear case of assuming their language of thought representation before judging what constitutes "real-constituency." Who is to say that the internal mental representation of CUP doesn't contain as a "real-constituent" HAS-A-HANDLE? Yet the relationship of subsuming predicates *is* confining. As they point out, if the representation of "John loves Mary and Ted hates Alice" is just a conjunction of all the features (another way of saying subsuming predicates), how can this fail to be ambiguous with respect to "John hates Mary and Ted loves Alice"? Using role-specific features is the beginnings of an approach, suggested by Geoffrey Hinton [11]. This at least overcomes the ambiguity between subject and object, if not that between multiple subjects. Yet FP disallow this move, saying it is just more subsuming predicates, now labeled JOHN-SUBJECT and MARY-OBJECT.

I believe they are right as long as JOHN-SUBJECT and JOHN-OBJECT don't have anything to do with one another, and in systems like Hinton's [11] they really don't. However a new generation of connectionist KR systems is emerging [1, 5, 7, 16, 27,] in which patterns representing an object really can be passed around, so there really is a notion of distinct tokens of a given type. Within one pattern, the combination rule for features is conjunction. But the combination rules among distinct patterns can be wired-in to be much more complicated. There is still a finite state flavor, since the architecture must be isomorphic to the structure of the particular proposition. So to represent a compound sentence like the one above requires two copies of a complete role-sensitive architecture. However by structuring networks isomorphic to frames or scripts rather than the less uniform structure of natural language sentences, there is hope that a predetermined architecture will be useful for a wide variety of objects of thought.

There is also progress being made in packing and unpacking recursive structures [11, 19]. Combined with sequential control, this opens the door to arbitrarily powerful inference, even where the structure of the problem cannot be immediately and all at once mapped onto the connectionist architecture [26]. Such hybrid systems would have a very powerful set of primitive operations, such as instantiating a frame or script, which a classical architecture could call on for routine problems. The diplomatic conclusion may be drawn that there aren't any in-principle differences between classical and connectionist architectures: both allow subsymbolic analog parallel combinatorial representations.

4. Pinker and Prince

In contrast to FP's philosophical perspective, Pinker and Prince (henceforth PP) offer a detailed critique of a specific connectionist implementation, the RM past tense model. Because the discussion centers on empirical comparison of network performance to human data rather than abstract in-principle arguments, it is of interest to anyone concerned with the psychology of language production in particular, and cognitive architectures in general, as well as those interested in the connectionist/symbolist melee for its own sake. Both sides should be congratulated for the care with which the known data are treated. PP display a thorough understanding of exactly what the RM model is doing, and offer penetrating insights into the reasons.

RM claim that correct performance on novel verbs confirms that the model has correctly captured the underlying regularities without recourse to explicit rules, and with a single mechanism to handle both regular and irregular verbs. The model passes through three stages during learning, just as children do:

(1) a rote learning stage in which the past tense of common irregular verbs (like "go") are used correctly,
(2) an overregularization stage in which the regular rule is applied indiscriminantly (producing incorrect forms for irregular verbs like "goed" or "wented"),
(3) the mature stage in which both regular and irregular verbs are treated correctly, as are novel verbs.

There are other parallels between errors the model makes and those observed in children as well.

PP believe the task is difficult and judge that no adequate theory, symbolic or otherwise, has been proposed. The RM model is to be credited for being mechanistic and testable, so that the exhaustive empirical inquiry PP present is even possible. This inquiry requires considerable, and at times tedious, analysis of the RM system and comparison with human data. PP begin with an overview of English verbal inflection, and symbolic theories of its acquisition. These theories posit a rule-inducer with built-in bias to account for the observed constancies across language. The rules learned are explicit, but inaccessible to conscious introspection.

PP admirably separate model-specific shortcomings from in-principle limitations of connectionism, and their explanations are carefully explained and convincing. RM's evolution through three stages during learning can as easily be attributed to the time course of the input corpus as to any emergent properties. For the first 10 iterations, 80% of the input verbs (the 10 most frequently occurring English verbs) were irregular, while for the remaining 190 iterations only 20% were (the 420 most frequently occurring English verbs). The intuitiveness of some of the other errors may be attributable to the peculiar "Wickelfeature" representation.[2] For instance the largest irregular class consists of no-change verbs that end in /t/ or /d/, such as "hit." This class is particularly easy for RM, possibly because the representation for "hitted" is very similar to that for the correct form. In addition, Wickelfeatures are inadequate to distinguish some pairs of words involving repeated phoneme sequences, such as *algal* and *algalgal* in the Australian language Oykangand.

The RM model forms the past tense directly from the phonological form of the root, dispensing with a separate morphological level and lexicon. PP list a number of subregularities in past tense formation that can be accounted for only by appeal to distinctions that are lost at the phonological level. A straightforward example is "break" (irregular) versus "brake" (regular). RM themselves have reservations about Wickelfeatures, and caution that it should not be taken too seriously in detail. Most of PP's criticisms apply to any scheme remotely resembling Wickelfeatures, however.

Looking beyond the past tense, PP give more data about English verbal inflection, showing that the same regular rules apply in forming the past participle, for instance, yet the irregulars are unique to each system. By doing away with the distinction between rule-following and exceptional behavior, RM force themselves to duplicate everything for each system. And in this case, the irregular regularities across systems have no explanation.

PP amass further evidence that the regular and irregular classes are functionally distinct. For instance in low frequency irregular forms, the past behaves as a distinct lexical item, which explains how "forgo" can come to have no usable past form. For regulars, this phenomenon is not observed no matter how rare the verb.

In a summary of empirical performance, PP rate the RM model as distinctly worse than conventional symbolic accounts of adult performance, and no

---

[2] Wickel*phones* are a way to represent inherently sequential data in parallel form. Each phoneme in a word is augmented with the previous and subsequent phoneme. The set of these triples usually contains enough context to reconstruct the word. The set for "guard" is /gɑrd/ → { $_\#g_\alpha$, $_g\alpha_r$, $_\alpha r_d$, $_r d_\#$ }. Wickel*features* are formed from Wickelphones by replacing the triples of phonemes with triples of features such as voiced, nasal, etc. There are further details given by RM.

better than symbolic accounts of development. Using RM's test data, PP point out that on 72 test verbs (which were not used for training), the model had a strong tendency to pick incorrect responses for 24, for a generalization rate of only 66%. Most of this ability can be traced to two factors, which can equally well be part of symbolic accounts: Type-frequency-sensitive strengths account for the U-shaped curve following the changing mix of regulars and irregulars in the training data. Competition between hypothesized forms in the output-decoding network enables alternative rules, such as a regularity and an exception, to override one another properly. One effect seen in RM that could not be explained so well on symbolic accounts is blending. Whether rule-blending occurs in children is very hard to test, however, and the evidence that can be brought to bear is negative.

The concluding section is the reward for plowing through so much data and detailed analysis of RM performance. PP broaden their scope from the RM model as published to any connectionist model of language use which uses a single level of surface-form representation. The argument for lexical items to distinguish "break" from "brake" carries over to any system based only on surface forms. Although adding semantic features can solve this problem, it gives the model too much power: no language encodes a wide variety of semantic features inflectionally. Further, there is still a need to distinguish distinct individuals with exactly the same properties, and to differentiate between seeing two similar individuals on two occasions from seeing the same individual after having undergone a change. The discussion of the type/token distinction, what variables are, and why they are needed is a very clear explanation of these slippery concepts. Their discussion of the difference between the abstractness of rules and the grounding in particulars of connectionist systems is also clear, if not clearly right. They offer a bit of hope that more powerful connectionist models may overcome some of the problems with RM. But multi-layer models with abstract internal representations are not so radical a departure from rule-based theories.

The conclusion also contains a nice discussion of the difference between a connectionist implementation of a rule-based system (implementational connectionism), and a connectionist system with an epiphenomenal rule-based description (eliminative connectionism). In the latter case the connectionist design principles must follow from strictly network level considerations, rather than requiring explanations referring to the rule-based analysis of the domain. As I mentioned above, however, I don't believe this is exactly the question that divides PP from RM. PP, like FP, allow that connectionist networks may end up implementing a micro-structure of cognition whose macro-structure is rule-based. But this would not vindicate eliminative connectionism as a theory of cognitive science since such a system would really be rule-based. If one takes it that the goal of psychology is to produce a knowledge level account of behavior, then the implementational/eliminative distinction might not be important to psychology. However the fervor surrounding these papers indicates otherwise.

5. Lachter and Bever

The book's last paper is a purported exposé of RM by Lachter and Bever (henceforth LB), concentrating on explaining why the model works rather than evaluating how well it works. In choosing input representations, decisions were made which are arbitrary from the connectionist level, but which seem well motivated from the point of view of rule-based theories. It is only in virtue of these TRICS (The Representations It Critically Supposes) that the past tense network achieves even 66% generalization. This is the form of argument PP advocate in order to differentiate implementational connectionism from eliminative connectionism. LB conclude that having such "rule-based representations" makes the theory rule-based: "[RM] actually confirms the existence of rules as the basis for natural language" (p. 208). This claim is indeed true given their broad definition of rule as "a function which maps one representation onto another" (p. 196). But as an exposé of Rumelhart and McClelland's TRICS, the paper fails because RM's claim that the model does not use rules is based on a different definition.

For the purposes of the debate between symbolic and connectionist models of language, a definition of "rule" which involves looking at what goes on inside the model, rather than a behavioral one involving only what the domain and range of the mapping is, seems more useful. Both FP and PP use such a definition, making the RM model fall on the other side of the fence from traditional theories.

To the extent that the representations and inference processes used by a connectionist network have a simple interpretation in the language of a rule-based theory, it is indeed implementational connectionism. Yet to show that this is all that can be claimed for RM, it is necessary to show that *all* of the behavior can be explained by the rule-based theory. LB's TRICS list shows merely that some aspects of the representations can be explained at the rule level. Their criticism implies a connectionist theory must regard *every* concept used in rule-based theories as inappropriate. Further, they make no claims that the internal processing can be modeled with high-level rules.

The TRICS themselves are interesting to note, and fall into two categories: building in representations sensitive to the right things and choosing training data to bring out the desired time-course of learning. For instance, choosing Wickelfeature dimensions where long vowels and voiced consonants are grouped together, in opposition to short vowels and unvoiced consonants, facilitates learning the regular rule for adding /d/, which is done for verbs ending with long vowels or voiced consonants. As noted above, providing appropriate primitives is a long way from building in specific rules.

The most worthwhile sections of the paper survey other connectionist linguistic models. LB show that the models of Dell [3], McClelland and Elman [13], McClelland and Kawamoto [14], Elman and Zipser [8], and Hanson and Kegl [10] also depend on TRICS. As with RM, the analysis offers valuable insights into the models, though not into the connectionist/symbolic debate. They even credit parallel top-down and bottom-up influence with generating the word-superiority effect in the TRACE model [13], and say a production system would have a hard time modeling this. Yet they never seem to realize that the debate between connectionists and symbolists is as much about internal processing as it is about the symbol level interpretability of the primitives.

It is also helpful to see examples of the sorts of rules forming rule-based theories of past tense formation, which, like RM, use features as primitives. For example one of the rules for the regular /ed/ rule is "Insert a neutral vowel, 'e', between two word-final consonants that have identical features, ignoring voicing" (p. 201).

They pose an interesting and ambitious test for any learning system: after training, it should be used as a "parent" to train a second generation system, which would then become a parent itself. The evolution of the language over generations should follow the same patterns as the evolution of real languages. They argue that RM would fail this test, quickly evolving toward uniform regularity.

They then cite some unconvincing evidence for rules in people: "Dialects differ by entire rule processes, not isolated cases" (p. 217). They also point out that people recognize the difference between their performance and the dictates of linguistic competence. In particular there are sentences recognized as grammatical but unusable, and those recognized as usable but ungrammatical. The first observation can be explained by any model which can generalize, and the second by any that has distinct representations of linguistic knowledge for performance and introspection.

LB seem not to have the detachment from their own paradigm that makes FP and PP so engaging to a connectionist. In addition to taking ambiguous evidence too easily as decisive, they repeatedly presuppose their overall conclusion that human language processing is rule-based: "Thus, none of these connectionist models succeed in explaining language behavior without containing linguistic representations, which in speakers are the result of linguistic rules" (p. 197).

In considering the question of whether a system is rule-based, I find the analogy to interpreted versus compiled programs helpful. Leaving aside execution speed, there is no important difference to the user until he wants to debug. (Imagine you're shown a video game and asked to figure out if it's running interpreted or compiled.) In compiled (i.e. connectionist) systems you can't debug the rules[3] because the efficient cause of the behavior isn't at that level.

Since rule-advocates say the rules are inaccessible, it's hard to test whether a system learns by modifying explicit rules. It seems the only way to probe the black box is to examine errorful behavior. If errors can be systematically attributed to typos in a postulated mentalese syntax, it's a pretty good reason to use that brand of mentalese in a theory of behavior [4]. For instance in the RM model the mentalese phonetic representation of words, Wickelfeatures, is potentially ambiguous. If people made errors attributable to incorrect reconstruction of ambiguous collections of Wickelfeatures it would be circumstantial evidence for that representation scheme. However LB, like PP, argue that there is no need to invoke such uniquely connectionist explanations for any of the errors modeled by the RM network.

6. Conclusion

It is unfortunate that definitions, particularly of "rule-based system," are not sufficiently pinned down to always prevent the connectionists and symbolists from talking past one another. Connectionists prefer Newell's PSSH definition because that puts all the contested theory-space on their side. LB especially, but to a degree FP and PP also, push the definition so far the other way that many connectionist theories end up being symbolic. Rigging the game so the other side is wrong isn't very useful. It *would* be interesting if someone like FP came out and said the PSSH is wrong. Universality is a key property in AI rule-based systems, and it's initially surprising that none of these essays mention the fact that their definition of rule-based does not require it. Perhaps given the wide acceptance of universal across-language constraints, linguists take it for granted that the PSSH is too strong when applied to linguistic behavior. Yet in the more philosophical passages dealing with general cognitive architectures this issue should be discussed.

Given the recent explosive growth in connectionist research, the first two essays in this book offer timely, well-written, thought-provoking reconsiderations of its goals, achievements, and standards. Because connectionist manifestos have been largely ignored by symbolists, ill-considered extravagant claims and arguments have gone unanswered and become truisms in that community. Even for those connectionists who aren't interested in the subtleties of philosophy, these papers are worth reading strictly for the asides pointing out some of these extravagancies. There are already attempts to modify the RM model in light of the criticisms presented here, and indications that some of the TRICS are not necessary [18].

FP provide a fun mental exercise for the philosophically minded advocate of

---

[3] A debugger may make it *look* like you are, but it's really accessing special data structures left around just for this purpose, which aren't causally involved in execution.

connectionism, and would be a good optional reading for a course on connectionism or philosophy of mind whose required reading includes a section on connectionism. PP is more down-to-earth and directly relates to issues of representation in connectionist networks. Both it and the Rumelhart and McClelland paper it discusses are worth emulating by anyone proposing or examining any computational model of language acquisition in terms of breadth and detail. PP provide sufficient introduction to be read independently by nonlinguists or nonconnectionists.

REFERENCES

1. P. Anandan, S. Letovsky and E. Mjolsness, Connectionist variable-binding by optimization, in: *Proceedings Eleventh Annual Conference of the Cognitive Science Society* (1989) 388–395.
2. N. Chomsky, *Language and Mind* (Harcourt, Brace, and World, New York, 1968).
3. G. Dell, A spreading activation theory of retrieval in sentence production, *Psychol. Rev.* **93** (1986) 283–321.
4. D. Dennett, When do representations explain? *Behav. Brain Sci.* **3** (1983) 406–407; Commentary on Edward Stabler, Jr. *How Are Grammars Represented?*, *Behav. Brain Sci.* **3** (1983) 391–402.
5. M. Derthick, Mundane reasoning by parallel constraint satisfaction, Ph.D. Thesis. Available as School of Computer Science Tech. Rept. CMU-CS-88-182, Carnegie-Mellon University, Pittsburgh, PA (1988).
6. M. Derthick and D.C. Plaut, Is distributed connectionism compatible with the physical symbol system hypothesis?, in: *Proceedings Eighth Annual Conference of the Cognitive Science Society*, Amherst, MA (1986) 639–644.
7. C.P. Dolan, Tensor manipulation networks: Connectionist and symbolic approaches to comprehension, learning, and planning, Ph.D. Thesis, Artificial Intelligence Laboratory Tech. Rept. UCLA-AI-89-06, University of California, Los Angeles, CA (1989).
8. J.L. Elman and D. Zipser, Learning the hidden structure of speech, Tech. Rept. 8701, Institute for Cognitive Science, University of California, San Diego, CA (1987).
9. J.A. Fodor, *The Modularity of Mind* (MIT Press, Cambridge, MA, 1983).
10. S. Hanson and J. Kegl, PARSNIP: A connectionist network that learns natural language grammar from exposure to natural language sentences, in: *Proceedings Ninth Annual Conference of the Cognitive Science Society*, Seattle, WA (1987).
11. G.E. Hinton, Representing part-whole hierarchies in connectionist networks, in: *Proceedings Tenth Annual Conference of the Cognitive Science Society*, Montreal, Que. (1988).
12. G.E. Hinton, J.L. McClelland and D.E. Rumelhart, Distributed representations, in: D.E. Rumelhart, J.L. McClelland and the PDP Research Group, eds., *Parallel Distributed Processing: Explorations in the Microstructure of Cognition*, I (Bradford Books, Cambridge, MA, 1986) Chapter 3, 77–109.
13. J.L. McClelland and J.L. Elman, The TRACE model of speech perception, in: J.L. McClelland, D.E. Rumelhart and the PDP Research Group, eds., *Parallel Distributed Processing: Explorations in the Microstructure of Cognition*, II (Bradford Books, Cambridge, MA, 1986).
14. J.L. McClelland and A.H. Kawamoto, Mechanisms of sentence processing: Assigning roles to constituents, in: J.L. McClelland, D.E. Rumelhart and the PDP Research Group, eds., *Parallel Distributed Processing: Explorations in the Microstructure of Cognition*, II (Bradford Books, Cambridge, MA, 1986) Chapter 19, 272–326.
15. J.L. McClelland, D.E. Rumelhart and G.E. Hinton, The appeal of parallel distributed processing, in: D.E. Rumelhart, J.L. McClelland and the PDP Research Group, eds., *Parallel Distributed Processing: Explorations in the Microstructure of Cognition*, I (Bradford Books, Cambridge, MA, 1986). Chapter 1.

16. R. Miikkulainen and M.G. Dyer, A modular neural network architecture for sequential paraphrasing of script-based stories, Tech. Rept. UCLA-AI-89-02, University of California, Los Angeles, CA (1989).

17. A. Newell, Physical symbol systems, *Cogn. Sci.* **4** (1980) 135–183.

18. K. Plunkett and V. Marchman, Pattern association in a back propagation network: Implications for child language acquisition, Tech. Rept. 8902, Center for Research in Language, University of California, San Diego, CA (1989).

19. J. Pollack, Recursive auto-associative memory: Devising compositional distributed representations, in: *Proceedings Tenth Annual Conference of the Cognitive Science Society*, Montreal, Que. (1988) 33–39.

20. Z.W. Pylyshyn, *Computation and Cognition: Toward a Foundation for Cognitive Science* (MIT Press, Cambridge, MA, 1984).

21. D.E. Rumelhart and J.L. McClelland, On learning the past tenses of English verbs, in: J.L. McClelland and D.E. Rumelhart, and the PDP Research Group, eds., *Parallel Distributed Processing: Explorations in the Microstructure of Cognition*, II (Bradford Books, Cambridge, MA, 1986) Chapter 18, 216–271.

22. D.E. Rumelhart and J.L. McClelland, PDP models and general issues in cognitive science, in: D.E. Rumelhart, J.L. McClelland and the PDP Research Group, eds., *Parallel Distributed Processing: Explorations in the Microstructure of Cognition*, I (Bradford Books, Cambridge, MA, 1986) Chapter 4, 110–146.

23. D.E. Rumelhart, J.L. McClelland and the PDP Research Group, *Parallel Distributed Processing: Explorations in the Microstructure of Cognition*, I (Bradford Books, Cambridge, MA, 1986).

24. P. Smolensky, Foundations of harmony theory: Cognitive dynamical systems and the subsymbolic theory of information processing, in: D.E. Rumelhart, J.L. McClelland and the PDP Research Group, eds., *Parallel Distributed Processing: Explorations in the Microstructure of Cognition*, I (Bradford Books, Cambridge, MA, 1986).

25. P. Smolensky, On the proper treatment of connectionism, *Behav. Brain Sci.* **11** (1988).

26. D.S. Touretzky, Representing and transforming recursive objects in a neural network, or, "Trees DO grow on Boltzmann Machines", in: *Proceedings IEEE International Conference on Systems, Man, and Cybernetics* (1986).

27. D.S. Touretzky and S. Geva, A distributed connectionist representation for concept structures, in: *Proceedings Ninth Annual Conference of the Cognitive Science Society*, Seattle, WA (1987) 155–164.

IV *Memory and Consciousness*

Introduction

The idea of a memory in which facts about the world and procedures for behaving are stored is central to all symbolic models of the mind. Indeed, in our everyday talk about thinking and remembering, we say we are filing away ideas, or searching for them. Forgetting is viewed as erasing ideas from memory, or being unable to access them. Learning is viewed as capturing and storing knowledge. To be more intelligent is to know more things.

Changing the storage idea of memory is like pulling the rug out from under most theories in cognitive science and AI. What is knowledge if it isn't something stored in memory? What does it mean for the brain to represent something if stable structures—physical things such as templates, facts, and rules—aren't stored inside? Our idea of memory is intricately tied to our idea of representation, meaning, and reasoning. What is reasoning if it is not retrieving and matching previously stored knowledge? How could behavior be goal directed without stored programs? What is comprehending text, if it isn't parsing and matching definitions and semantic graphs?

Laced through the discussion about symbols, plans, and interacting systems of our previous chapters are questions about the human brain. Behind the philosophical, social, and computational arguments about the limitations of the symbolic view of the mind—especially the idea of stored symbolic structures in memory—there are nagging, fundamental concerns that human experience is being ignored. Indeed, the success in modeling cognition in areas as diverse as physics problem solving, medical diagnosis, manufacturing design, scheduling, and the like highlights the learning deficiencies and lack of creativity of AI programs. These limitations prod researchers to reexamine human capability and experience.

Before there was such a thing as AI, Alan Turing suggested that, rather than asking whether or not a machine could think, we address the more limited question of whether or not it could convincingly imitate human behavior (Turing 1963). Although this is a challenging problem, researchers have tended to focus attention on specific areas of behavior, and such a limited focus determined what they expected computers to do and how they evaluated their success. Three notions of human capability have dominated AI research: (1) perception and movement (vision, speech, robotic maneuvering); (2) mathematical and logical games (chess, theorem proving); and (3) knowledge-based tasks (medical diagnosis, engineering, scientific modeling). This has led to some rather serious omissions in delimiting the nature of human behavior to be modeled. Real-time hand-eye coordination has been relegated to control theory (based on differential calculus). Emotion, psychiatric disorders, personality, and more general issues of human evolution and consciousness remain the province of psychology, biology, and philosophy, as if these are either details about human limitations or subjects not central to building a robot. And indeed these were reasonable simplifications for the AI field in the 1960s and 1970s. Researchers were amply satisfied by getting a computer program to diagnose and treat an infectious disease, understand a chemical spectrum, and schedule manufacturing processes.

More than a decade ago, John Haugeland eloquently reminded AI researchers who espoused the view that intelligence could be exclusively replicated by symbolic manipulation (whom he described as "Cognitivists") of the deficit between such machines and human capability:

Like their predecessors, Cognitivists have made undeniably important and lasting discoveries. But also as before, these discoveries are conspicuously narrow, even small, compared to the depth and scope of psychology's pretheoretic purview. The brilliance of what has been done can blind us to the darkness that surrounds it, and it is worth recalling how many shadows Cognitivism has not (yet) illuminated. How is it, for example, that we recognize familiar faces, let alone the lives reflected in them, or the greatness of Rembrandt's portrayals? How do we understand conversational English, let alone metaphors, jokes, Aristotle, or Albee? What is common sense, let alone creativity, wit, or good taste? What happens when we fall asleep, let alone fall under a spell, fall apart, or fall in love? What are personality and character, let alone identity crises, schizophrenia, the experience of enlightenment, or moral integrity? We turn to psychology if we think these questions have scientific answers; and if we shouldn't, why shouldn't we? Cognitivists are as vague and impressionistic on such issues as psychological theorists have always been. Of course, they too can buy time with the old refrain: "be patient, we're only just beginning (though so-and-so's preliminary results are already encouraging)." Promissory notes are legitimate currency in vigorous sciences, but too much deficit spending only fuels inflation. (Haugeland 1981)

As the reviews in this book have shown, the AI community's concern with such deficits is mounting. Although no one has been able to formulate the matter precisely, critics of Soar (Arbib, Purves), critics of models of human planning (Suchman, Agre), and critics of rational models of thought (Winograd, Flores), suggest that these programs are inherently limited relative to human capability. Of course, critics have been saying this since Hubert Dreyfus started saying it in the 1960s. The difference lies in having another approach to try. The ideas of connectionism and emergent computation, with their new computational architectures, produced for the first time in AI a rival method, a new way of thinking about representation, behavior, and computation. Not surprisingly, these new approaches are inspired by existing complex systems in the world: the neural networks of the brain, the diversity of species, the competitive-symbiotic interactions of social systems.

As always in AI, researchers are split into two groups: engineers taking inspiration from existing systems (for example, roboticists) and scientists committed to modeling empirical phenomena (for example, cognitive modelers). Perhaps the most striking difference in the empirically oriented branch of AI starting in the mid-1980s has been the attempt to relate theories of the mind not just to psychology but to neurobiology and neuropsychology. In this part, we present a strongly related set of reviews with just this emphasis, focusing on the nature of memory and consciousness. The work of Israel Rosenfield and Gerald M. Edelman in particular is fundamentally committed to broadening our understanding of human experience and its biological and social roots. Indeed, what distinguishes their endeavors from situated action, neural networks, genetic algorithms, and emergent computation is their central focus on the interpenetration of biological and social systems. This idea, which is new to many cognitive scientists with a psychology or computer science background, has a long history in biology and anthropology.

Unlike the other parts of this collection of reviews, which are anchored by a multiple review of a single book, this part offers a collection of reviews concerning a single broad topic, Edelman's model of the brain. Rosenfield's *Invention of Memory* provides a historical introduction, reexamining early studies of neural dysfunctions. The review extends Rosenfield's critique of symbolic models of memory to related work in cognitive psychology. William Clancey restates Rosenfield's ideas in anticipation of an AI reader's interpretations and objections. Edelman's theory of memory, learning, and consciousness is described in reviews of *Neural Darwinism, The Remembered Present,* and *Bright Air, Brilliant Fire* (a popularization and elaboration of the arguments against the symbolic approach). These reviews develop the links between biology and models of reasoning. Rosenfield's *The Strange, Familiar, and Forgotten: An Anatomy of Consciousness* frames the series, with a heartfelt rededication to human experience, prodding us to listen more carefully to how intelligence is manifested—not as solving a Tower of Hanoi puzzle, but as stories and interpretations of personal experiences.

The other reviews in this part also propose to explain consciousness, to tell us how it evolved, and to delineate arguments about it. Daniel Dennett's *Consciousness Explained* and Robert Ornstein's *Evolution of Consciousness* make the same commitment to biology and the brain that we find in the work of Rosenfield and Edelman. These authors, however, are less concerned than the former with describing the details of human experience and how the brain works, and more concerned with making sense of opposing theories of consciousness. Where Edelman prefers to wipe the slate clean and put forward his own theory, Dennett and Ornstein strive to understand how the folk psychology view of consciousness evolved, why it is useful, and how it is improved (for the sake of robot design) by alternative models.

The esoterica of William Seager's *Metaphysics of Consciousness* provides a good resting point for our book. We are reminded how scientists have struggled for centuries to make sense of something right under their very noses. Consciousness is part of every thought and theory, yet it defies the treatment science has brought to agriculture, space science, and data processing. Seager's work brings us far afield from the biology and everyday experience of Edelman and Rosenfield. But his distinctions remind us by contrast how theorizing can founder without revealing data to study, without alternative kinds of mechanisms to entertain, or without a grasp of what needs to be explained.

In these reviews the argument about the architecture of the mind—the focus of Newell's and Pylyshyn's work in part I—has fundamentally shifted to the search for the architecture of the brain that enables the memory, learning, and reasoning described in models such as Soar. Readers wanting to quickly grasp Edelman's theory of the brain might begin with the summaries in the reviews of *Neural Darwinism, The Remembered Present,* and *Bright Air, Brilliant Fire.* Readers wanting to understand this view of memory might begin with the reviews of Rosenfield's *Invention of Memory* and *The Strange, Familiar, and Forgotten.* For a philosophical approach, begin with the last reviews, starting with the discussion of "functionalism" in *Bright Air, Brilliant Fire.*

Finally, the reader might relate this part to other themes in this collection. Understanding the human mind becomes a multidisciplinary juggling act, as researchers go back to reconsider what Winograd, Suchman, Agre, and Lakoff say about human activity. How can computer programs replicate the fluid, improvisatory nature of intelligence that linguists and social scientists claim is so much distorted by our descriptions of behavior and representational models of knowledge? For example, can Lakoff's bodily grounded categories be related to Edelman's schema for higher-order consciousness? Engineers looking for design ideas wander over to emergent phenomena of the chaos theorists, the connectionists, and artificial life. Is the mechanism yet in hand to construct an artificial intelligence? Some engineers think they are getting closer: Forget the representations; connect up more layers of networks; start with insects. Many sociologists hesitate: Could it be that intelligence is not an isolated function like flying, but an interactive, temporally extended phenomenon, like migration, that makes sense only as a description of behaviors developing in a flock—a "community of practice"? Neurobiologists declare that this is the decade of the brain, but they caution us that the loops and interacting levels of control are more intricate than anything we have ever built before. And the philosophers, Dennett, Haugeland, and others—now maybe more collaborators than critics—help balance the enthusiasm and ignorance, reminding us of where we have wandered before.

Nobody knows how close we are to creating an AI machine with human capabilities. The day is not so close that many will hazard a prediction. But this forum for book reviews, and the attendant conferences, journals, and professional organizations, suggests that a new center is forming. New ideas are coming into play. Connections are found to the most vibrant thinkers of the first half of this (now almost completed) century: Dewey, Bateson, Piaget, Vygotsky, Wittgenstein, and Ryle. Old work is resurrected and given new interpretations, for better and for worse. Biologists and programmers work together. New models are built, and the next generation of robots rolls down the hall.

It is a good time to be contemplating minds.

References

Haugeland, J. 1981. The Nature and Plausibility of Cognitivism. In *Mind Design: Philosophy, Psychology, Artificial Intelligence,* edited by J. Haugeland. Cambridge, Mass.: The MIT Press.

Turing, A.M. 1963. Computing Machinery and Intelligence. In *Computers and Thought,* edited by E.A. Feigenbaum and J. Feldman. New York: McGraw-Hill.

Artificial Intelligence 50 (1991) 241–284
Elsevier

Israel Rosenfield, *The Invention of Memory: A New View of the Brain**

William J. Clancey

Institute for Research on Learning, 2550 Hanover Street, Palo Alto, CA 94304, USA

Received January 1990

1. Introduction

This short, thought-provoking book claims that both machine intelligence research and modern neurobiology are based on faulty interpretations of nineteenth-century clinical studies of human memory. Rosenfield argues against the commonplace view that human memory is a kind of filing cabinet or database, that memories are permanent records, that remembering is retrieving something, that practiced behavior is reexecuting a stored program, and that learning, perceiving, and behaving are separate processes in the brain. Rosenfield's heroes are Freud, Marr, and Edelman. The book is exciting exactly because of this juxtaposition of ideas: Freud's psychiatric interpretations that seek to formalize the origin and effects of emotions (non-symbolic organizers of behavior), Marr's constructivist model of vision (recognition without top-down matching of internal descriptions), and Edelman's developmental approach to connectionism (perception as category learning). Rosenfield challenges the AI researcher to understand the relation between Freud, Marr, and Edelman, arguing that their work supports a radically different, non-representational model of memory—memory for processes of perceiving and behaving rather than memory as descriptions of how the world or behavior appears.

The book is essentially a historical argument for Edelman's work [23]; it grew out of a series of essays originally written for *The New York Review of*

---

* (Basic Books, New York, 1988); x + 229 pages.

0004-3702/91/$03.50 © 1991 — Elsevier Science Publishers B.V.

Books. Edelman's book has already been reviewed here at length (Smoliar [54]), so I will focus on Rosenfield's historical synthesis:

- A reconsideration of nineteenth-century studies of brain-damaged patients suggests new explanations of reading, speaking, and writing dysfunctions, not based on stored memories.
- Freud's work suggests that emotion is not a secondary coloration of memory, but the basis of the constructive process by which we achieve a sense of continuity.
- Marr's work provides a pivotal link between the conventional AI claim that recognition is based on matching internal descriptions of the world and Edelman's neural model of bottom-up perception.

This cast of characters is made all the more interesting when, towards the end of the book, the PDP connectionist approach is lambasted as making the same mistakes as the rest of AI research in its failure to integrate perception, memory, and learning. This highly readable book should be studied by every AI and cognitive science researcher who wishes to understand alternative approaches for designing intelligent machines (e.g., situated automata [36, 59]) or for modeling human behavior (e.g., situated action [1, 56]).

1.1. The localization hypothesis

According to Rosenfield, nineteenth-century interpretations of reading and writing dysfunctions, often caused by brain lesions, assume that memories are fixed. That is, memory is a *place for storing things* where they remain unchanged until they are retrieved. Briefly put, to explain why a patient can speak, but not write, physicians of the day argued for a memory of "permanent traces"—specialized images of things in the world, for example, permanent records of sounds, shapes, colors, and movements. Thus, ability to speak the word "ship", but inability to write it, suggests that the necessary information for speaking and writing is stored separately in the brain. This is called the *localization hypothesis*. Rosenfield demonstrates through a historical survey of the evolution of research that the localization hypothesis has had a major, enduring influence on neurology. Using the work of Freud, Marr, and Edelman, supported by psychological research on perception, Rosenfield argues that this hypothesis is fundamentally wrong.

Rosenfield attacks the view that knowledge consists of stored representations, for example, that we can recognize a table because we retrieve a description of what tables generally look like. Most of AI research is based on this model of memory, epitomized by Quillian's semantic networks, Minsky's frames, and Schank's MOPS, as well as natural language grammars. Knowledge is assumed to consist of stored descriptions of how the world appears (e.g., disease hierarchies, device models) and descriptions of how an agent behaves (e.g., scripts, reasoning strategies). These descriptions are stored as labeled things in memory, so they can be selectively indexed and retrieved, reassembled, and then translated into outward behavior.

But if memory is not a storage place for descriptive structures, "How do I know I'm looking at a table?" In most machine learning research, perception is a peripheral process that feeds objective data to a cognitive matcher; learning involves fine-tuning, composing, and ordering prestored categories (e.g., Norman [42]). The standard AI view is that "There is no perception without prior 'learning'. . ." (p. 7).[1] Rosenfield (after Edelman) argues that perception is not matching internal descriptions of features against sensations. Instead, perceiving is itself a process of categorizing. Perception is not a peripheral process feeding data to an inferential process, but the very act of recognition or understanding itself.

1.2. Behaving is coordinating is learning

Rosenfield claims that the essential problem of categorization goes unaddressed in AI research: ". . . it is unexplained how the images during the initial encounter with information are recognized as worthy of storage" (p. 7). In conventional AI programs, the problem is circumvented by having a program designer build in primitive categories. Rosenfield is thus addressing the well-known problem of how categories get into the brain in the first place. His approach is to overturn the initial assumption that categories are stored *things*. In effect, he claims that categorization occurs at runtime.[2] Put simply, *every new perception or behavior is a generalization*, composed of past perceptions and behaviors (a claim associated with Vygotsky [58]). Current neural organizations are thus related to those constructed in the past, but without an indexing, retrieval, and matching process.

Rosenfield opens the book with a direct fusillade against the idea of stored descriptions, what he calls the Platonic approach:

> This book is about a myth. . . that we can accurately remember people, places, and things because images of them have been imprinted and permanently stored in our brains. (p. 3)

> Failure to recall could, therefore, be explained as the loss of a specific image (or center) or as the brain's inability to search its files. . . . (p. 5)

If memory is not a storage place for descriptive forms, then there can be no localization of function at the level of skills like reading and writing. For example, the word "cat" is not stored as a sequence of letter descriptions

---

[1] Except as noted, all page numbers refer to the book being reviewed.

[2] To be precise, we say "categorizing", not "forming categories", just as Bartlett wrote about "remembering", not "memories" [4].

(c-a-t), whether in one place or in some distributed network; a word, or a concept in general, is not a thing that is put away and retrieved. Reinterpreting the historical data of neurological deficits, Rosenfield postulates instead that functional losses are caused by an inability *to establish correlations*. For example, when attempting to read "cat" as something other than the letters "c-a-t" in sequence, we are correlating a sequence, perceiving, categorizing. To perceive is to compose is to categorize.

In general, "re-collection" involves *coordinated recombination of past processes of perceiving and behaving*. This coordination is organized by (and in some sense subsumes) what the person is currently perceiving and doing. The essence of Rosenfield's critique is that most neuro and cognitive scientists have ignored the nature and role of this ongoing *context* in perceptual categorization: Perception is not peripheral or antecedent to movement, but rather part of a single, coordinated process of behaving, of composing. This means that new processes arise so that they are constituted by processes already occurring. This view unifies intellectual and physical skills, so that at a base level a person is always like a dancer balancing her next steps against the inertia of past movements and her view of where she is going. Throughout the book, examples are given of the role of the ongoing context in correlating present and past behaviors and in coordinating a sequence of coherent movements for some skill (including especially reading and writing).

1.3. Similar claims in past research

Although Rosenfield's claims may first appear outrageous, they are hardly new. In fact, for decades many researchers have made the same claims, supported by psychological experiments. This places me in the ironic position of trying to explain to incredulous AI readers what has already been clearly presented in psychology books and journal articles. None of this work is cited by Rosenfield, except for Bartlett, suggesting that the fragmentation of neuro-cognitive research is an extensive and serious problem. For this reason, I will quote at some length from the original sources.

A proper historical review might begin with Frederic C. Bartlett's [4] famous work:

> Remembering is not the re-excitation of innumerable fixed, lifeless and fragmentary traces. It is an imaginative reconstruction, or construction, built out of the relation of our attitude towards a whole active mass of organised past reactions or experience, and to a little outstanding detail which commonly appears in image or in language form. [4, p. 213]

> Suppose I am making a stroke in a quick game, such as tennis or cricket. . . . I do not, as a matter fact produce something absolutely

new, and I never merely repeat something old. The stroke is literally manufactured out of the living visual and postural "schemata" of the moment and their interrelations. [4, p. 202]

> It is with remembering as it is with the stroke in a skilled game. We may fancy that we are repeating a series of movements learned a long time before from a text-book or from a teacher. But motion study shows that in fact we build up the stroke afresh on a basis of the immediately preceding balance of postures and the momentary needs of the game. Everytime we make it, it has its own characteristics.

> [T]here is no reason in the world for regarding these [traces/ schemata] as made complete at one moment, stored up somewhere, and then re-excited at some much later moment. [4, p. 211]

> I strongly dislike the term "schema". It is at once too definite and sketchy. . . . It suggests some persistent, but fragmentary, "form of arrangement", and it does not indicate what is very essential to the whole notion, that the organised mass results of past changes of position and posture are actively doing something all the time. . . . [4, p. 201]

> Everything in this book has been written from the point of view of a study of the conditions of organic and mental functions, rather than from that of an analysis of mental structure. It was, however, the latter standpoint which developed the traditional principles of associationism. The confusion of the two is responsible for very much unnecessary difficulty in psychological discussion. [4, p. 304]

William James also makes basic distinctions:

> Memory proper, or secondary memory as it might be styled, is. . . *knowledge of an event, or fact,* of which meantime we have not been thinking, *with the additional consciousness that we have thought or experienced it before.* . . . [P]sychical objects (sensations, for example) simply recurring in successive editions will remember each other *on that account* no more than clock-strokes do. No memory is involved in the mere fact of recurrence. [30, p. 252]

In the notes to this page, James wrote, "Faculty view. Ideas not *things* but processes | No reservoir" [30, p. 452].

In spite of this early work, the idea of memory as a storage place took hold and became the basis of the "knowledge is power" movement in AI and cognitive science since the 1960s; it continues in the belief today that common sense knowledge can be collected like so many butterflies. Contemporary psychologists in the past three decades have directly attacked this model:

James J. Gibson:

> The invariance of perception with varying samples of overlapping stimulation may be accounted for by invariant information and by an attunement of the whole retino-neuro-muscular system to invariant information. The development of this attunement, or the education of attention, depends on past experience, but not on the *storage* of past experiences. [25, p. 262]

Jean Piaget:

> I think that human knowledge is essentially active. . . . I find myself opposed to the view of knowledge as a copy, a passive copy of reality. [44, p. 15]

> [F]or the genetic epistemologist, knowledge results from continuous construction, since in each act of understanding, some degree of invention is involved. [44, p. 77]

James J. Jenkins:

> [T]he phenomena disclosed by these experiments pose formidable problems for storage theories of memory. [31, p. 792]

> [W]e should shun any notion that memory consists of a specific system that operates with one set of rules on one kind of unit. [31, p. 793]

> Apart from the belief that the construction of the mind is attributed to the past, he [William James] saw nothing to set memory apart from perception, imagination, comparison, and reasoning. Such a claim is unsettling because it says: *Memory is not a box in a flow diagram.* It is also threatening because it seems to demand an understanding of all "the higher mental processes" at once. Yet, that is what the data in our experiments suggest. To study memory without studying perception is. . . pushing all the difficult problems out of memory into the unknown perceptual domain for someone else to study. [31, p. 794]

John D. Bransford et al.:

> Our purpose is not to deny the importance of *remembering*. . . . But we question the fruitfulness of assuming that a concept of *memory* underlies these events. [C]urrent uses of the term memory involve tacit or explicit assumptions. . . that memory can be broken down into a set of *memories*, that these consist of relatively independent *traces* that are stored in some *location*, that these traces must be *searched for* and *retrieved* in order to produce remembering, and

that appropriate traces must be "contacted" in order for past experiences to have their effects on subsequent events. [9, p. 431]

[In associative models]... the problem of remembering begins where the parsers stop. [9, p. 444]

[W]e believe it unfruitful to separate problems of remembering from problems of comprehending and perceiving. [9, p. 454].

Even researchers sensitive to the complexities of cognition unquestioningly adopt the storage model, to the point of misrepresenting Bartlett:

As a theory of episodic memory, Bartlett's approach has the interesting implication that general attitudes, undifferentiated as to motor, perceptual, or symbolic content, are stored most faithfully in memory. (Miller and Johnson-Laird [38, p. 150])

Describing Bartlett's model, Miller and Johnson-Laird proceed to talk about "reinstatement" (instantiation of schemas) in every place that Bartlett emphasizes novel construction. This discussion appears in a section titled "memory locations and fields" under the topic of "The organization of memory".

Iran-Nejad writes persuasively about the dominance of the storage metaphor and general blindness to alternatives:

Counterintuitive as it may seem at first, it is entirely conceivable, however, that the patterning aspect of cognition is a transient functional-phenomenal, rather than a long-term memory structural, organization. [29, p. 115]

Iran-Nejad [28] characterizes cognitive science knowledge models as *intralevel* theories: "They assume that the holistic structures and their constitutive elements are both mental in nature" [28, p. 281]. Following Bartlett he argues that we need an *interlevel* theory to explain how the moment-by-moment group functioning of neural elements creates mental structures (transient, composed processes of correlating, attending, and resolving). Crucially, the causality goes in both directions: "... mental structures have a causal influence on the functioning of neuronal elements" [28, p. 283]. By analogy, cognitive science's intralevel theories are like models of a fountain of water that only describe its shape, as if the stable form is produced by an internal template and made out of a fixed set of unchanging parts [28, p. 285].

Bickhard and Richie [7], building on Gibson's theory of perception, outline an interlevel architecture in which mental structures are controlling, non-representational processes embodied as active neural elements ("material processes"):

From an interactive perspective, however, there is at least one level of emergence *between* the material and the representational: the level of interactive control structures. Representation, then, is an emergent functional property of certain forms of goal-directed interactive control structures, which in turn, are emergent properties of certain patterns of material processes. [7, p. 57]

In present-day information-processing or computational approaches. . . the level of interactive control structures and processes that is properly *between* the material level and the representational level has instead been moved *above* the level of encoded representations, leaving the level of encodings hanging in midair with no grounds for explication. [7, p. 57]

In summary, the idea of memory as stored structures has been criticized and experimentally questioned, but such studies are either ignored or misrepresented in AI and cognitive science research of the past two decades.

1.4. Relevance to AI research

Rosenfield's book is important because it provides an avenue for explaining the "situated cognition" perspective, which has become an important subfield in AI [1, 17, 36]. Situated cognition emphasizes the role of interaction and context in organizing behavior.[3] Rosenschein [47] motivates situated-automata robotics research by criticizing the storage model of memory:

Since logical sentences are used at the abstract level to express the *content* of knowledge, what could be more natural at the implementation level than to imitate their *form* as well and to think of each distinct fact known by the system as a symbolic assertion stored in the computer's memory?

I believe that the chief contribution of situated cognition research will be to help resolve the learning problem of artificial intelligence by forcing us to abandon the idea that representations are structures stored in memory. In effect, we will be forced to distinguish between representations as they are created and interpreted in perceivable form and the momentary, non-representational constructions that Bickhard and Richie [7] call "interactive control structures".

---

[3] Jenkins [31] describes the roots of the term in American pragmatism, in the work of William James, C.S. Pierce, and John Dewey. Jenkins calls it *contextualism*. "Contextualism holds that experience consists of events. Events have a quality as a whole. By quality is meant the total meaning of the event. The quality of the event is the resultant of the interaction of the experiencer and the world. . . . For the contextualist, no analysis is 'the complete analysis'." By contrast, "Associationism asserts that there is one correct and final analysis of any psychological event in terms of a set of basic units and their basic relations" [31, p. 787]. By the contextualist view, a knowledge-level description is inherently subjective, relative to the purposes of an observer (cf. Bordieu, [8]).

Simply put, the "perception as coordination" perspective helps us explain how representations are created and given meaning. The relation between knowledge and context is fundamentally changed: Although we may describe knowledge discretely, as a collection of representations that explain an agent's behavior, what we are modeling is a capacity to interact adaptively. This intricate linking of sensation and action cannot be reduced to (replaced by) statements about either the agent or the environment (cf. Winograd and Flores' [61] discussion of Maturana).

Representations, which AI and cognitive science have taken to be the very stuff of inner processing, are instead continuously created in perceptual activity, in an interaction of neural and environmental processes. (To speak is to represent is to perceive, not to translate from something already said privately inside.) Habits, ways of talking, and categories are stable behaviors, not generated from stored descriptions, but continuously reconstructed, albeit strongly biased by previous perceptual-motor compositions. What we have taken in AI to be the inner stuff of cognition—grammars, scripts, strategies— are observer-relative descriptions of patterns of behavior, stable interactions between the agent and his environment which develop over time. To behave according to a pattern is not to be following a template-thing. The pattern description, what we generally call a representation of the agent's knowledge, exists only in the statements, writing, and diagrams of the observer-theoretician [16, 17].

Although Rosenfield intends to make contact with the work of machine intelligence and contrasts it with Marr and Edelman at some length, I don't believe that he is sufficiently familiar with the context sensitivity of goal-driven and machine learning programs to be convincing to most AI readers. Many statements and turns of phrase may appear too loose or ungrounded. If you don't reject claims about context sensitivity outright, you are likely to say, "But that's just what program X can do!" If you believe that MOPS explains the mechanism of reminding (Schank, [51]), if you believe that Bartlett [4] supported the idea of schema-structures, or if you believe that connectionism (Rumelhart and McClelland [48]) shows how knowledge could be distributed in the brain, then you are likely to have trouble reading this book. But you also have a lot to gain.

1.5. Outline of this review

The objective of this review is to bridge the gap between Rosenfield's and the typical AI researcher's perspective. I begin by clarifying what kind of memory Rosenfield is arguing against, attempting to anticipate common misunderstandings. By placing these positive aspects of the discussion first, I am hoping the reader will become sympathetic to the not-stored-structures thesis, and even enthusiastic to learn about Rosenfield's historical analysis in the sections which follow:

- classical neuroscience explains deficiencies in terms of localizable memories (fixed traces), which Rosenfield argues against;
- Freud's work shows how *emotion, a non-representational context*, can organize behavior;
- perception research empirically demonstrates *the process of context coordination* in organizing stimuli;
- Marr's model of vision provides a primitive computational demonstration of *bottom-up categorization*;
- PDP devices misconstrue *the nature of information* as given, rather than perceptually created from stimuli; and finally,
- Edelman's model of *neural map selection* shows how a process memory might work.

At the end, I'll consider particular difficulties readers may have with Rosenfield's statements about learning, goals, and symbols, and provide interpretations that better delineate the opposing points of view.

2. What model of memory is Rosenfield arguing against?

Before considering Rosenfield's remarks about localization in more detail, we need to make clearer just what AI and cognitive science have claimed about memory and what specifically Rosenfield rejects. As we have already seen, one difficult idea is that Rosenfield argues that memory and perception constitute one integral process. As we delve further, Rosenfield requires us to alter our views about the nature of concepts, representations, and even information. The process is frustrating because so many related ideas that have been useful in AI research for decades start moving around like ill-defined pieces in a puzzle and merging with each other. The underlying difficult, I believe, is that if Rosenfield is right, we can't say what human memory is like because we have never built anything like it. All we have are bad or misleading metaphors deriving from our existing machines and designed processes (e.g., computer memory, tape recorders, holography).

2.1. Not grammars, not stored structures

To start with a simple idea, it is generally accepted that human memory is associative [2]. But we mustn't assume that because we observe someone associating "CAT" with "DOG" that these words are physically linked by neurological structures in the subject's brain (e.g., that pointers connect places in the brain where these concepts are stored). This is a common way of modeling associative behavior—the brain *appears to behave* as if it were an implementation of a semantic network. Rosenfield is saying that this isn't how the mechanism actually works. A better perspective is that the *process* of saying, seeing, and/or hearing "CAT" is physically related to the *process* of saying, seeing, and/or hearing "DOG". Semantic network models describe how the *perceived products* of these processes (e.g., spoken words) are related. Crucial to Rosenfield's argument, such mechanisms are fundamentally incapable of producing the range of behaviors that neurological processes accomplish.

The semantic network model of memory has been elaborated in the past few decades in what I will call the *grammatical model of cognition*. This approach assumes that knowledge consists of concepts linked in a "memory structure", which is accessed by programs for constructing mental models [42]. Much of knowledge representation research can be viewed in terms of making the grammatical nature of process models more explicit by separate domain models from the inference rules that operate upon them [19].[4] In knowledge engineering, this approach has led to generalization of modeling languages (e.g., causal representations) and inference procedures (e.g, "generic strategies" for diagnosis or design). An implicit claim of knowledge engineering is that human-equivalent intelligence can be produced from grammars.

Although Rosenfield doesn't speak in these terms, his book can be viewed as an argument against the grammatical model. First, programs based on grammars simply follow patterns, they can't break the mold and do something new (essentially the argument of Winograd and Flores [61] about the limitations of representations). We can represent any process by grammars, but if we *replace* the processes of human behavior by grammars we lose flexibility.

A second argument against the grammatical approach—following a quite different tack—is that grammatical models of cognition are based on the localization hypothesis. For example, knowledge engineering (and much of cognitive modeling) assumes that programs in the brain are retrieving and manipulating stored relational networks such as classifications and state-transition networks. Significantly, the argument against stored structures also argues against there being *stored programs* in the brain that are themselves retrieved and interpreted. This is not a distinction between compilation versus interpretation or declarative versus procedural. Rather, what's at stake is the

---

[4] Knowledge about processes in the real world (e.g., diseases) is represented in the memory structure by a basic set of relations and compositions of them. These relations correspond to links between categories: subtype, cause, part-of, location, time. Problem-solving processes (e.g., how to do diagnosis) can be modeled by rules that refer only to relations, rather than domain terms (e.g., NEOMYCIN's abstract strategy rules [15]). In effect, such rules make explicit the grammar that assembles the domain lexicon into behavioral sequences. For example, the ODYSSEUS student modeling program uses NEOMYCIN's diagnostic strategy as a kind of grammar for parsing a student's sequence of data requests [60]. The relation of discourse rules (e.g., GUIDON's case-method tutoring rules) to content matter (the topics represented by the domain model) is similar; that is, abstracted tutoring rules constitute a grammar for a case-method dialogue.

very idea that the brain *stores* any kind of structures that are selectively accessed and manipulated *as structures*. Once again, memory is not a place where *things* (whether representations or programs) are stored. Rosenfield would say that the compilation model is wrong because there is nothing stored that can be retrieved and compiled into something else.

Putting together the two arguments against grammatical models of cognition, the distinction is not between, say, a program interpreting an equation for a circle and a turtle program for drawing a circle. Both fail to account for novelty and both presuppose storage of structures. Instead, to put it simply, Rosenfield is asking, how do I manage to *trace a new line*, to coordinate what I see with my hand's movement? Again, by the model of memory presented here, every movement is a new coordination, not merely following instructions or executing a program.[5] In summary, grammatical models are rejected because they don't account for the novelty of every behavior and they require stored structures. From the AI research perspective, the novelty argument is of course more important, but the argument against stored structures is valuable because it alone forces rejection of the grammatical approach.

To recap, the conventional view of memory is based on the metaphor of storage. Storage involves putting some*thing* in some*place*. Arguing against localization is not saying that a thing is stored in many places (e.g., multiple copies of "CAT") or that it is distributed over several locations (e.g., "C" and "T" are in very different locations in the brain.) or that it is encoded at another level (e.g., a description of C as a set of curves is stored, not the image of "C" itself). Rather, arguing against localization is more like saying that *concepts are not things*, but processes of perceiving and processes of behaving.

To take a familiar example, human memory is not like a dictionary. Words are not written somewhere in the brain. Words do not have labels or addresses by which they can be "looked up". To be trying to define a word is not to be moving a name around the brain, matching it against other names or indexing the place where it is stored. There are no addresses, no pointers, no labeled networks in the brain. We cannot access and display brain structures and as observers say that they correspond to concepts. Brain structures are not stored away, retrieved, and interpreted as objects. This is the essence of Rosenfield's claim.

2.2. *Capacity to compose, cycles of perceiving*

Okay, so what is memory? To begin, we must shift from viewing memory as a place where descriptions are stored to a capacity to do and recompose what we have done before. To use a bad metaphor, contrast a CD as an encoding

---

[5] Even for so-called rote behavior the neural constructions are new because the external interactional context and the internal on-going context, within which behaviors are coordinated, are never identical on different occasions.

for producing sounds directly with a score representing the music, instruments, and orchestration in some notation. Human memory is more like the capacity to replay what was done before directly; it doesn't require (and indeed *never directly involves*) interpreting a description of what the behavior should look like (e.g., interpreting a score or grammar or following a script).

The CD metaphor is bad because it involves localized encodings of sounds. We don't store a description of how a word sounds or even instructions for generating it. Rather, our neurological structures are biased to reorganize themselves so we can say the word or write it or spell it out again. Human memory is a capability to organize neurological processes into a configuration which relates perceptions to movements similar to how they have been coordinated in the past. If this sounds too vague to implement, that's no surprise: we can't build anything like human memory. We don't know how to describe how it works, just what it *appears* to do.

In contrast with a single utterance, such as saying CAT, conversational speaking, as an ongoing activity, involves intervening use of representations. Conversational speaking involves *cycles* of perceiving, reorganizing neural processes, and behaving. We are "using representations" each time we utter a word or phrase and, reflecting on what it means, make a clarification or elaboration. In describing the process of remembering a word, for example, we must distinguish between the single memory-coordination process of generating a feature (e.g., "it starts with an S") and the overarching cycles of reflecting on feature descriptions—*perceiving them*—and thereby using representations to organize behavior. Structures have to be perceived to be treated as representations.[6]

Elaborating on Rosenfield's argument, we might say that AI and cognitive science have confused the representational manipulation that goes on in the outward behavior of our speaking and writing over time with what goes on *within a single cycle* of categorizing and creating a representation (for example, by uttering a sentence). We must distinguish the mechanism by which we perceive what someone just said and utter a reply from the process over time by which we carry on a conversation.

Donald Schön [52, 62] clarifies these levels of behavior in his analysis of the logic of inquiry, which might be paraphrased as follows:

- *Doing*: Words are used automatically, we are just actively talking (generating representations automatically, but not commenting on them).
- *Adapting*: We are caught short momentarily, but easily continue. We

---

[6] This means that perception includes interaction with internal constructions, as in visual imagination and silent speech, not just interacting with something outside. Vygotsky [58] considers how these two forms of perception differ, focussing on the development of shortcuts in inner speech.

"glitch" on something unexpected, but respond automatically (automatically commenting on representations).

- *Framing*: What are we talking about? What categorization fits our activity of speaking? We are transforming the conversation (deliberately attempting to generate appropriate representations).

- *History-telling*: We are articulating new theories, relating images to words, describing how we feel, reviewing what has been said so far (reflecting on a sequence of prior representations, composing past perceptions into a new way of seeing).

- *Designing*: We are deliberately guiding the conversation so it becomes an inquiry-project, resolving a problematic situation (defining what representation generation should be about; creating and carrying out an activity involving the above four components to some end; representing what we intend to compose and then managing that composition process).

This analysis makes clearer how representations build on one another. For example, one form of reflection, which I call history-telling (Schön's "reflection on knowing- and reflection-in-action"), involves commenting on a *sequence* of prior representations. Representations play a different *role* in organizing behavior, depending on how they relate to prior behavior. For example, at the base level—within a cycle of perceiving and behaving—*doing* does not involve commenting about representations at all.[7] Crucially, Schön's analysis suggests that representations are constructed compositionally, over time, as the context becomes more complex and subsumes previous observations and commentary. This nesting isn't arbitrary and isn't the same at each level, but has a logical form relating to automaticity, reference, sequence, and functional composition.

The result is a shift in perspective: We view representations as *created in our outward, conscious behavior*—in our imagining, speaking, writing, drawing, not manipulated in a hidden, unperceivable way inside our brains. In its primary manifestation, memory is the capacity for automatically composing processes of perceiving and behaving, including creating representations (doing, adapting). In cycles of such behavior, what James called the "secondary" aspect of remembering, we reflect on (represent) what we have said and done before (framing, history-telling, designing). Thus, memory is fundamentally indistinguishable from coordinated perception and movement—in both its primary and secondary manifestations, relating what we have done before to what we are doing now.

---

[7] By this analysis, we might say that grammatical models never go beyond "doing" and "adapting". One difficulty in AI research is that what appears to be framing, such as introducing a new topic of a conversation, can be modeled grammatically (e.g., turn-taking rules). Although we have represented these and similar patterns, we have never explained how they develop by interactions between people over time, except as grammatical modifications to grammars, which begs the issue.

2.3. Regular behavior without internal representation

One general implication, consistent with Winograd and Flores' [61] analysis, is that human reasoning involves the use of representations (such as this written review), but human behavior is not generated directly from representations. For example, when we speak we are not translating words from an internal description of what we are planning to say. When we do plan what to say, we generate such plans as words or diagrams that we can perceive (including when we talk to ourselves or visualize things). Such plans do not come from other plans directly, but like all speaking and representation creation, they come from our ability to directly sequence, compose, and substitute previous behaviors.

In effect, all speaking involves novel conceptualizations and compositions. There is no internal, grammatical description of sentences that we interpret and apply in some hidden way, just regular ways of behaving (patterns perceived by an observer—abstractions—expressed as representations). Similarly, there is no lexicon of defined words from which our concepts are selected and rotely applied. Indeed, to use a grammatical rule or a word definition, we must recite it first. No representation can be *used* in the sense of being given a meaningful interpretation without being perceived first.

Although this may seem strange to many AI researchers, it is an old idea and has much support in linguistics (Tyler [57]), anthropology (Suchman [56]), and sociology (Mead [37]). Consider for example these remarks by Collingwood from *The Principles of Art* [21]:

> We think that the grammarian, when he takes a discourse and divides in into parts, is finding out the truth about it, and that when he lays down rules for the relations between these parts he is telling us how people's minds work when they speak. This is very far from being the truth. A grammarian is not a kind of scientist studying the actual structure of language; he is a kind of butcher, converting it from organic tissue into marketable and edible joints. Language as it lives and grows no more consists of verbs, nouns, and so forth than animals as they live and grow consist of forehands, gammons, rump-steaks, and other joints. [21, p. 257]

> [A] coagulation of several words into a single whole, quite different from the sum of the words that compose it in their recognized grammatical relations to each other, is called an "idiom". . . . [A]ll the grammarian has done by calling them idioms is to admit that his own grammatical science cannot cope with them, and that people who use them have spoken intelligibly, when according to him, what they say should be meaningless. [21, p. 258]

> Language is an activity; it is expressing oneself, or speaking. But this activity is not what the grammarian analyses. He analyses a product of this activity, "speech" or "discourse" not in the sense of a speaking or a discoursing, but in the sense of something brought into existence by that activity. [21, p. 254]

From this perspective, a blackboard model of the mind, in which discourse plans and sentences are grammatically assembled and posted on many levels of detail before any speaking occurs (e.g., "speakers use the rules to determine how to say what they want to say" (Hovy [27]) is a fantastic reductio ad absurdum account of how speaking actually works. Of course, some AI researchers have realized the implausibility of current models. Minsky [39] suggests that we "put aside most of the old language theories":

> If we're to understand how language works, we must discard the usual view that words *denote*, or *represent*, or *designate.* . . . If we want to understand how language works, we must never forget that our thinking-in-words reveals only a fragment of the mind's activity. [39, p. 196]

The non-representational memory model raises many questions that we thought perhaps cognitive science had resolved, hindering change from old ways of thinking. For example, why does human speech appear to be regular if it is not produced by interpreting grammars? Why do we sense that we are reusing words, rather than forming new concepts? How do we represent and immediately follow rules when we are given explicit instructions (Hadley [26])?

Obviously, there are many stable reconstructions; apparently, the very business of perception is to view the world conservatively (noticing only what is different) in order to adopt previous successful ways of behaving. But although rote recall may be the paradigm of remembering, speaking grammatically and mimicking are hardly marks of high intelligence. Rather it is performances requiring subtle adaptations to apparently new situations, whether on the high trapeze or juggling a financial portfolio, that we view as perceptive and intelligent.

Indeed, even what we take to be a highly stable behavior, such as reciting a phone number, is highly contextual. Phone numbers and log-on passwords are not retrieved, but are speaking or typing or dialing behaviors that occur in the context of other perceptual and motor processes. You can establish this context (a composition of active neurological processes) by sitting in front of keyboard, by visualizing a phone, etc. Rosenfield's main claim is that building a human-like memory requires understanding the integral manner in which perceptions and movement processes are composed, reactivated, sequenced, and coordinated.

To summarize, according to Rosenfield human memory does not consist of addressable, localizable, retrievable structures (stored representations). Rather, memory gives us *the capability to produce structures*, which we call representations, that do have these properties (in our speaking, drawing, writing, gestures, visualizing, etc.). We do not store descriptions of what our behaviors should look like, but rather have the capacity to reorganize our perceptual/motor coordination in ways biased by previous organizations. We don't literally follow a script, though we can create one, perceive it, and organize our behaving accordingly.[8]

2.4. *Self-organizing on one level, reflective on the next*

The idea of self-organizing, emergent processes is central here, and sharply contrasts with a typical AI architecture for deliberately controlling complex activity. Winograd and Flores [61] describe a committee meeting as an example of a self-organizing process. The members of a committee don't retrieve a description of how to interact in a meeting, which is then executed. Nor is the chairperson determining what individuals say. But the group might have a written agenda, and individuals might speak to themselves, represent what is going on, and plan what to say. These representations are produced so they can be perceived, not manipulated, indexed, retrieved, etc. in some hidden way. First there must be a process of saying or writing something (directly creating a representation), then a perceptual process of commenting on what was represented (reflection).

To say that representations don't directly cause behavior is to claim that hidden interpretation of plans and scripts is not the mechanism that organizes behavior.[9] By analogy, the storage view of memory and representations is like modeling a camera's mechanism by describing the photographs it produces [29]. The dominant AI paradigm is based on the idea that all action follows from descriptions (grammars) that order behavior—as if descriptions of the photographs were inside before any pictures were taken. Cohen [20] had the same problem in designing AARON: How can we build a machine that creates new representations without building in descriptions of them? If the plans, statements, and behaviors in general are produced inside before the actual behavior, from what is this internal description produced? (Could AARON have another agent inside who draws pictures before they are drawn on paper?) To defeat the homunculus fallacy, we must realize that the compositional, modular nature of the mind is in the form of self-organizing processes, not as agents *speaking* to each other, using representations, in the form of

---

[8] When asked what I think of the CYC project [34], I respond in like vein: When we finally do create an intelligent machine, of which I have no doubt, it will enjoy reading Lenat's encyclopedia.

[9] Cf. Bickhard and Richie's reordering of levels, Section 1.3.

schedulers, message-passing, and agenda. Minsky's [39] society of mind metaphor generally adheres to this restriction.[10]

Progress in AI has been so much based on notions of search and control, we have essentially ignored natural examples of self-organizing processes and what kinds of complex behaviors they can produce. A traffic backup is a good example to start, because it is clearly not deliberately organized. A bottleneck may form where roads converge or narrow. The individual cars are not following a plan for "how to participate in a traffic back-up" or even "how to create today's traffic back-up". The organization that observers see in the lines of cars was not predescribed, but is a structure that emerges through the interaction of many parts. There is no scheduler deciding what car gets to move next. Observers will see patterns in the emergent behavior over time (e.g., as a bottleneck becomes released just beyond the scene of an accident, even hours after the area has been cleared away). But there is no "pattern"—some*thing*— that is being "followed" (interpreted) by the participants.[11]

In general, AI and cognitive science have confused grammatical models, which describe adapted patterns of interaction between individuals over time, with the mechanism that produce momentary individual behavior.[12] That is, we

---

[10] Minsky says, "Memories are processes that make some of our agents act in much the same ways they did at various times in the past" [39, p. 154]. But on the same page, he says "stores the traces of the past", adopting a storage of substance view, not a process view. In an interesting twist, Minsky suggests there may be two distinguished and specialized high-level agents (the *B* and *A* brains, popularly referred to as the Left–Right brain distinction) that react to the representations each produces, one focusing and articulating distinctions top-down, the other forming images bottom-up (see Minsky [39, p. 59; 43]).

[11] Bartlett uses the example of a game like Rugby football: "Nine-tenths of a swift game is as far as possible from the exploitation of a definite, thought-out plan, hatched beforehand, and carried out exactly as was intended. The members of the team go rapidly into positions which they did not foresee, plan, or even immediately envisage, any more than the bits of a glass in a kaleidoscope think out their relative positions in the patterns which they combine to make" [4, p. 277]. Bartlett goes on to say that if individuals have to think what another player is going to do, the team will be disconnected. In terms I have paraphrased from Schön, there is little place for framing and history-telling during a play. Again, this is not to say that we don't sometimes generate representations to change our behavior, but to underscore that behavior is often possible, indeed required, without them.

[12] Emergent descriptions are a characteristic and necessary aspect of *interlevel* theories. Stable organizations develop over time by interactions between individual parts which themselves can be described mechanistically (e.g., we can describe individual cars in the traffic jam, the goals and plans of the drivers, and how cars locally interact). However, the system as a whole develops patterns that no individual or isolated group could be said to control. As Bartlett explains, the role of individual actions can only be understood in terms of *ongoing trends* of the already organized mass: "We can put our finger upon this, that or the other thing and say: 'This comes from such and such an individual source.' But when we have done all that can be done in this way, there is much left over. It is left, not merely because the phenomena are too complicated, but because any constructive achievement of social organisation depends upon the form and trend of the group before the achievement is effected, as well as upon the efforts of innumerable individuals in the mass" [4, p. 278]. In contrast, *intralevel* descriptions explain behavior exclusively in terms of how individual, connected parts causally affect each other (e.g., how an automobile engine works). *Interlevel* theories relate individual components (e.g., car paths) to systemic patterns or trends
⟶

have described what adaptations occur, but not the local process of adapting. This is why I said that the promise of situated cognition research is to provide better explanations of human learning. The essence of Rosenfield's book is that perceiving, behaving, and learning are one process. We are not retrieving descriptions of what is true or what to do, but constructing (speaking, imaging, moving) behaviors directly from how we have perceived and moved before.

How we talk about reflection in terms of expectations, assumptions, and rationalizations exemplifies our confusion. As Schön [52] says, we engage in "historical revisionism" when we suppose that a "failed expectation" was necessarily represented prior to its articulation. Assumptions are similar. We say, "I did that because I must have assumed. . . ". Such rationalizations are relative to our current context, as we look back as theoreticians and perceive patterns and comment about relations in our behavior, not necessarily something we said before that caused us to act in some way. Winograd and Flores [61] use the term *breakdown* to characterize how representations describing behavior emerge when we seek to explain an interruption in our otherwise automatic flow of behavior ("doing" and "adapting"). Bartlett's experiments illustrate how remembering is a construction or rationalization that finds a way of working around an impasse. It is in framing, according to Schön, that expectations and assumptions are articulated. Such representations are about our activities, but their causal effect is towards the future, as perceptual organizations of behavior [3].

The difficulty in modeling people is that they do use representations and they do represent their own behavior. Every schoolboy knows something about the grammar of his native tongue, and this, we hope, affects his speaking behavior. But we always forget that children speak long before they know what nouns and verbs are. The Platonic view is that categories of speech are inborn ideal forms. Indeed, even modern linguists struggle to account for how the patterns they perceive as observers could possibly be "produced" by subjects without a stored, internal form [10]. They fail to distinguish emergent interactions from preconceived rules. Rather than asking how habits develop as an interaction of perceptions and movements, they continuously wonder how *descriptions of*

→

observed over time (e.g., bottlenecks) at the level above, not just to physically connected components at the same level (e.g., neighboring cars and roads). Moreover, recalling the fountain example of Section 1.3, emergent structures don't map onto fixed units in the level below (e.g., different cars are caught at the bottleneck at different times). Thermodynamics is a familiar interlevel theory, relating properties and interactions of individual molecules to the volume, pressure, and temperature of gas in a container. The key idea of emergence is that the observed system-wide properties cannot be explained just in terms of the component interactions at the level below—you must refer to the ongoing trends of the system (e.g., the way temperature, a property of a gas volume, affects individual molecules). In the interlevel theory of Bickhard and Richie, representations emerge from the interactions of neural structures in the level below. For Bartlett, the "society of mind" is not just a metaphor; his theory of social organizations closely parallels his theory of neural organizations—indeed, social-neuropsychology is the interlevel theory he strives for.

how the habits appear to an observer could be known at birth, encoded, or learned "tacitly". Popular views of instinct and talent as inborn behavior programs are similarly misconceived [5].

In summary, the idea of neurological self-organization is that neurological processes come together in ways that are coherent without a controlling program that assembles neurological structures. The construction is in the perceiving and behaving itself, not a separate process that creates something that is later "run". Again, we don't speak by constructing an internal description of what we are going to say, except of course when we actually do say something to ourselves and reflect on it. A schoolboy doesn't use a grammar representation until someone tells him the rules.

2.5. Implications of an alternative model

Okay, so what? Why should AI researchers care about human memory anyway? We can't build a bird either, but we can get to the moon. Planes don't need feathers. Even if Rosenfield is right, what are the implications for building intelligent machines?

First, Rosenfield argues that previous neurological data has been misinterpreted, distorting our view of memory and knowledge. The idea of modularity of function at the level of reading and writing still holds sway today, influencing both modern neurobiology and AI. Consider for example this remark from a recent book review of *From Neuropsychology to Mental Structure* [22]:

> Some patients whose reading of content words such as *elephant* and *chrysanthemum* is good cannot read even the commonest function words such as *the* or *and*. Examples of such selective deficits are now legion in cognitive neuropsychology. They show that cognition must be profoundly modular. Our semantic systems must have separate subsystems for animate and inanimate concepts; our knowledge of names must involve one subsystem for proper nouns and another for common nouns; and there must be separate lexical systems for content words and function words. These are claims about normal cognition; but they are made on the basis of studies of people with damaged cognitive systems.

Evidence that such interpretations are wrong could suggest new mechanisms to be incorporated in AI programs. Modular separation of data (memory) and programs (the grammatical approach) is surely a virtue for software design, but the very idea of indexing, matching, and assembling structures is the origin of combinatoric search. If the brain has a mechanism for self-organization that avoids the problems of search and matching that are legion in AI programs, we will want to know about it.

Second, as everyone knows, human intelligence grossly exceeds AI program capabilities. This is especially true regarding conceptualization, the creation of new representations. What if we have matters inside-out? What if speaking involves *constantly* creating representations and creating representations that interpret them, as Schön's analysis suggests? What if perception is when learning takes place, as Rosenfield and Edelman claim? By what self-organization architecture are neurological processes subsumed and composed? How is a previous organization reaccomplished more easily (the practice effect)? AI researchers know that adaptation is important. Learning is roundly acknowledged as our key unsolved problem. We might look more clearly at psychological data (e.g., [9, 31]) and realize what aspects of human flexibility are not captured by grammatical models, and then find alternative models for capturing the underlying processes (for example, see the interlevel architecture theories of Iran-Nejad [28] and Bickhard and Richie [7], mentioned briefly in Section 1.4).

Third, when we study knowledge bases such as NEOMYCIN's, we find that Collingwood's claims (Section 2.3) are not so foreign. In effect, situation-action rules model what experts most directly know—*how to behave*. But when we study and decompose these rules into conceptual and procedural abstractions (such as occurred in the transition from MYCIN to NEOMYCIN), we are stating a nodel that goes well beyond what experts state without our help [15]. If human memory is not a place where representations are stored, this new understanding could have a dramatic impact on how we view the knowledge acquisition bottleneck, as well as explanation and teaching using knowledge bases [18].

With this background, I now turn to the main sections of Rosenfield's book.

3. Classical memory research

Rosenfield's reinterpretations of seminal experiments and case studies of neuropsychology illustrate alternative—non-storage and non-representational—explanations for what we term recall, recognition, and skilled performance. His main claim is that failures to behave appropriately reveal much more about human memory than "failure to retrieve" or "failure to execute a plan". We will consider here some of the key researchers in Rosenfield's review.

3.1. Paul Broca

Paul Broca is perhaps most remembered for localizing speech capacity to an area in the brain. However, in 1861, Paul Broca argued "not (for) a memory of words, but a memory for the movements necessary for articulating words" (p. 20). Because of this emphasis on coordinating movements, Rosenfield views

Broca's work in a positive light. Unfortunately, Carl Wernicke in 1874 and Ludwig Lichtheim in 1885 took Broca's localization of speech to an extreme by emphasizing the idea of separate centers where visual, auditory, and motor "images" are recorded. In particular, they argued for stored records of individual words. Yet other studies by Armand Trousseau in 1865 had already indicated the importance of context. For example, a patient could not repeat a word like "student", but could repeat "all the students" This suggested that "student" was not represented in a single place as a single word in the brain.

3.2. Frederic Bateman

In 1882, C. Giraudeau described a case of *word deafness*, by which a patient could hear spoken words, but not recognize what they mean. In 1890, Frederic Bateman interpreted this problem in terms of "complete loss" of function (and hence dysfunction of a localized part of the brain). Rosenfield argues that the same data can be interpreted in terms of difficulty in establishing a context, that is, an inability to coordinate, to get a coherent process moving in the current situation, relative to what was done before. For example, rather than saying a patient can't understand speech, the patient apparently "has great difficulty establishing a context in which she can understand the questions being asked" (p. 29). For example, when asked her occupation, she describes her medications, as if she anticipates the logic of the inquiry, but is unable to coordinate her memory of the process with what is currently happening. She apparently has some sense of a familiar setting, but can't dynamically correlate her past experiences with what she is currently perceiving; she cannot construct a coherent new composition that is analogous to what she has done before. Given that she can speak and does after much repetition answer questions appropriately, explanations of her deficiency in terms of individual words would appear to be inadequate. Nevertheless, this is what Bateman concluded.

3.3. Jules Dejerine

By the time of Jules Dejerine's work in 1891, the localization of function was well accepted. Dejerine explained reading failures as disconnections between visual (right hemisphere) and language (left hemisphere) faculties. One patient could "recognize" only single letters or two-digit numbers (but not words or more complex numbers); he could recognize a signature but not the individual letters in it. The patient demonstrated an intriguing ability to state letters when he made the corresponding writing gestures. Dejerine concluded that "motor activity (writing) can organize stimuli, making recognition possible" (p. 58), which Rosenfield cites as a theoretical advance.

However, Dejerine's basic theory was that the patient couldn't write because he couldn't read, and this implied a *word blindness*, a retrieval or disconnect problem. According to Rosenfield, Dejerine makes a false distinction between drawings and symbols, as if the recognized forms were treated as pictures being matched in the brain. The very idea of word blindness wrongly suggests that the patient receives words as stimuli, and as such they are unrecognized wholes. Instead, the failure to read words reveals an inability to construct "an overall organization—in which identical stimuli, letters, are constantly changing in significance" (p. 49). This is not a breakdown of a specific linguistic function, but a general inability to organize stimuli, a coordination or composition problem. To summarize:

> If recognition depends on being able to organize similar stimuli in a variety of different ways, memory, too, must in some sense be based on this organizing capacity. When we recognize a face, we are organizing stimuli in ways that are similar (but not necessarily identical, since the person might have aged) to how we have organized related stimuli in the past. It is the similarity of organization that relates past and present. (p. 50)

3.4. Norman Geschwind

More recently, in 1965 the late Norman Geschwind refined the disconnection hypothesis by explaining capacities such as reading as composites of independent brain operations. Information from different brain centers is available for correlation, explaining why one sensory association may fail when another succeeds. For example "a man can see an object without recognizing it, and yet he can touch the same object and have no difficulty naming it" (p. 56). Such cross-modal associations and associations of associations are generally compatible with Edelman's models. But Rosenfield is always skeptical of claims that parts of the brain are working independently of each other and produce results that must be later assembled. Geschwind's cross-modal view was substantiated by Charcot's earlier experiment that showed one could read by tracing letters, suggesting a graphic-motor center. But Rosenfield emphasizes that Dejerine's later interpretation of his patient, Oscar, didn't require such a center to be postulated. Dejerine pointed out that one can write with different hands, which clearly aren't controlled by a single "writing center" (given that localization of left-right muscular control is accepted).

3.5. Appraisal and discussion of the historical view

With all the many historical cases and multiple interpretations, Rosenfield's survey would benefit from a table or time-line summary. The exposition is confusing at times because many of the researchers are inconsistent from Rosenfield's perspective. For example, Dejerine attacked the idea of a writing center, but still held to the idea of fixed visual images of words stored in different places.

We come away with a wide variety of interpretations of fascinating clinical cases. Although it's not the best scientific history, it is sufficient to make Rosenfield's point that there are alternate models of performance failure, and the fixed-trace/localization hypothesis is not only unnecessary, but obviously simplistic. Other explanations for dysfunctions are possible:

- a previous organization between sensations and movements can't be reaccomplished (visible objects can't be named);
- a process can still be accomplished at a high level, but it can't be integrated with ongoing processes in the present (the patient carries out a medical interview, but out of synch with her inquirer);
- a past neural organization was never retained at all.

To make this more concrete, contrast these views with a typical AI interpretation of Loftus' studies of confabulation on the witness stand [35]. According to the stored memory view, the witness has a permanent record of what she actually observed at the scene of the crime. If this record isn't manifested in a correct recall performance, it is because her internal description is transformed or distorted by the *pragmatics* of the courtroom situation. She actually knows what she saw, but her current biases lead her to produce a new story. Or perhaps resource problems (not having enough time to remember) prevent her from retrieving the truth, so she fill in the details. Hence, the AI model is RETRIEVE + FIX, rather than CONSTRUCT + FIX.

A good example of the RETRIEVE + FIX model is Repair Theory (Brown and VanLehn [12]), which postulates that subtraction bugs arise from impasses caused by omissions from an otherwise correct procedure. A student knows the ideal form of the subtraction procedure, but there are gaps in what he can retrieve, so he makes those parts up. One problem with this grammatical model (cf. Section 2.1) is that bugs change over time. Behavior isn't identical every time, as a rote view of memory would imply, so the notion of selective forgetting and "bug migration" must be introduced. Here we have the equivalent of epicycles in cognitive modeling.[13]

---

[13] In general, "pragmatics" is invoked to explain why behavior doesn't adhere to grammatical descriptions, or more generally, "why and how is it that we say the same thing in different ways to different people, or even to the same person in different circumstances" [27]. The general claim is that pragmatics take into account context, in the form of the agent's relation to his environment (e.g., conversational atmosphere, interpersonal relationships, goals to influence behavior). But if oral speech is fragmented because of the pressures of real-time interactions, why is written speech generated in pieces, scratched out, restated, reordered, and reconceptualized? Text isn't created whole and spit out in a single stream. We reflect, speak, reflect, revise. The idealized "text generation" of natural language programs never occurs in human experience: Speech is fragmented and written prose is revised. Why do we produce "inadequate" prose? Why can't we say it right the first time? Here is the essence of what representations do for us: *We don't know what we want to say until we say it.*

The primary difference between the retrieval and construction models is not in the cycles of reflection and commentary on the evolving story, which is essentially the level that most AI programs model, but where each utterance comes from. Rather than *retrieving* descriptions of what happened and translating them into words (or retrieving procedures to be executed), the constructivist view is that *speaking is conceiving*:

> When Dejerine stressed that writing could be carried out in a number of different ways and therefore is not localized, he, too, was suggesting that memory is procedure, but without seeing this fact as true of all motor acts, including speech. (p. 62)

In contrast, Bartlett [4] described an exclusively constructivist model based on his data of story recall experiments. Bartlett suggests that perception and speaking are a single process (the categories called *doing* and *adapting* in the discussion of Schön, Section 2.2). Impasses occur when automatic behavior is unable to continue forming a coherent composition (a story). Bartlett describes a process of resolving the gap by which a detail, usually an image, is perceived, an act that forms a new composition (corresponding to *framing* and *history-telling*, Section 2.2). Comments about the meaning of these perceptions—now treated as representations, that is meaningful forms—constitute categorizations that orient subsequent behavior.[14] Note that Bartlett's model of memory requires a different view of perception, concepts, and representation. The bundling of these ideas—which now become ill-defined and moving pieces of a puzzle—is what makes shifting from the memory-as-structures perspective so difficult.

Relating this back to the clinical studies, Rosenfield is attacking the view that drawing a letter is copying an internal description of it, or that speaking is translating an internal description of what we intend to say. By this grammatical view, there is always an internal representation (plan or image) that precedes and controls movements. Rosenfield takes a procedural (process) view: "The procedures of writing themselves create the 'images' we set on paper" (p. 61). Furthermore, this is not merely a form of knowledge that is "compiled" (because there are no structures to retrieve and compile), but must be the basis of all behavior, including declaring facts about the world. Nor are these procedures stored programs that are retrieved and applied to current information: They are *processes constructed on the spot* that correlate stimuli and movements. To develop the view that memory is inherently a capability to coordinate and construct such processes, Rosenfield turns to Freud, Marr, and Edelman.

---

[14] Again, "categorization" suggests a process; "category" suggests a static description. The emphasis is on recurrent processes of organizing behavior, not stored descriptions of the world or how behavior appears.

4. Freud

Rather than making emotions something secondary to an ideal memory, Freud viewed them as controlling behavior. Emotions play an integral role in setting up the context by which ongoing behavior is composed:

> Crucial to the Freudian view is the idea that emotions structure recollections and perceptions. (p. 6)

> Recollections without affect are not recollections. Emotions. . . establish a memory's relative importance in a sequence of events much as a sense of time and order is essential for a memory to be considered a memory, and not a thought or a vision at some particular instant, unrelated to past events. (p. 72)

Where does this leave memory theories like MOPS, which do not include emotion? Relative to the process of human memory, most cognitive science theories appear to be more akin to database maintenance, rather than human psychology. To treat emotion as a veneer—a coloration of something fundamentally concerned with storage and retrieval—is to adopt the Platonic view again of ideal forms that emotion only distorts, rather than processes that an emotional orientation creates and reconstructs. "Events that become emotionally charged are thereby categorized and 'understood'" (p. 73). Notice that the grammatical approach only allows emotions to be labeled and stored, just like concepts. It is probably because this is so intuitively disagreeable that emotions have been routinely omitted from AI models. The rationalist view is that emotions can only distort logical thought; real thinking only occurs when we don't allow emotions to get in the way.

Freud's work suggests that emotions are perceptions that make a kind of commentary on other perceptions. For example, Bartlett claimed that his subjects experienced an emotional attitude about their on-going story-telling, which was correlated with resolution of an impasse. The emotional attitude signified a "coming to terms" with a subject's overall state. According to Freud, in our ongoing sense-making an emotional experience leads a perception to be attended to, named, and thereby remembered. Put simply, emotions play a pivotal part in explaining how habits of seeing and doing are formed. Emotions are important in understanding cognition because they are evidence that non-representational "memories" can structure behavior.

But Freud still held to the idea of memory as a permanent record. Arguing against Freud's interpretation of dreams, Rosenfield says,

> [Dreams'] lack of sense is a lack of context, not disguise and displacement. The mechanism of condensation is an illusion created by a [later] interpretation in which one seeks a context that can give the image meaning and coherence. (pp. 75–76)

Thus, relative to the interpretation, the dream is condensed, but it was not *produced* from this interpretation, like an abridged or condensed book. Dreams, according to this view, are ambiguous fragmentary constructions, "because there are no constraints on the organization of these fragments" (p. 75). Whatever conscious control we exert in forming an ongoing, overarching composition from our perceptions while awake (what Rosenfield repeatedly refers to as coordination of sequences of perceptions and movements) is evidently not active while we are dreaming; in some sense, we are not paying attention to what we are doing. Interpreting a dream is supplying a context that resolves the ambiguities and unifies the fragments into a whole (p. 76).

Here Rosenfield summarizes the alternative to a fixed-trace memory:

> There are no specific recollections in our brains; there are only the means for organizing past impressions. . . . Memories are not fixed but are *constantly evolving generalizations*—recreations—of the past, which give us a sense of continuity, a sense of being, with a past, a present, and a future. They are not discrete units that are linked up over time but a dynamically evolving system. (p. 76, emphasis added)

Realizing the centrality of sense-making, Freud postulated the unconscious as an agent responsible for maintaining "the dynamics of the categorizations and recategorizations that give our mental life the sense of a whole. . ." (p. 77). But Rosenfield argues that specific unconscious memories, supposingly what the dream is dredging up, "would not account for our sense of continuity; continuity is a consequence of our ability to view things in larger relations given the present."

Indeed, Freud pursued this point of view early in his work, in *On Aphasia*, illustrated by his somewhat startling remark:

> "Perception" and "association" are terms by which we describe different aspects of the same process. But we know that the phenomena to which these terms refer are abstractions from a unitary and indivisible process. . . . Both arise from the same place and are nowhere static. [24, p. 57]

Cognitive science theories have not been built on this insight and the clinical studies from which it came. Similarly, structure-based models of memory ignore Bartlett's insistence that schemas are not fixed traces that are stored and retrieved, but always constructed during the remembering process. Modern theories view perception as a *peripheral* process that parses the world into discrete structures (called "symbols"), upon which association operates, manipulating and storing them away as other static structures, which remain unchanged until they are used again.

Although Freud believed there to be permanent traces, his mechanisms emphasize that memories are new creations. For example, the obsessional neurotic's "redoing" of unpleasant experiences, attempting to make them into pleasant experiences, is doomed to failure because they are driven by unpleasant feelings. Rosenfield points out that these attempts are often realized as physical acts in "a very real attempt to redo, to create, a memory" by making some ritual movement. Ritual *activity* of this sort underscores the connection between memory, perception, and movement. Rosenfield generalizes this:

> In fact, we are all "redoing" the past, and an act of repetition must be understood not as an act symbolizing a specific past event but rather as a whole history of attempts at recapturing the past, a history that is being put into a specific context at a given moment when the repetition is occurring. . . . Just as it would be misleading to say that a pianist's rendition of a sonata is a recollection of an earlier performance. Every performance is unique, though every performance does have a history; but the significance of that history depends on the present context. . . . [T]here is no recollection without context. And since context must, of necessity, constantly change, there can never be a fixed, or absolute memory. Memory without the present cannot exist. (p. 80)

"Context" here, like information and memory itself, becomes slippery and dialectic in nature. It simultaneously refers to "what you are currently doing", "what you perceive to be happening", and "the on-going internal construction of neural processes". Context is neither inside nor outside, past nor present. It constantly changes. Remembering does not exist apart from behavior in some context. Every performance coordinates what the person is currently doing with what has been done in the past. "Memory" is not something fixed or absolute; it is only manifested in the context of a performance and each manifestation is different by virtue of being adapted (cf. Bartlett's remarks about tennis. Section 1.4).

The nature and importance of context is supported by further reinterpretations of Freud and an appraisal of the work of A.A. Low, and A.R. Luria. Misinterpretations of Low and Luria's results on memory for nouns, verbs, and function words influenced modern ideas about modularity (as cited in Section 2.5). In fact, Low concluded that it is not the grammatical category that matters so much as the difficulty of establishing context.

> Words like *at* and *as* have a range of meanings (at home, at ease, at your service) and acquire a specific sense only in a given context. On the other hand, words like *beyond* and *above* have definite meanings of their own, regardless of context. (p. 86)

Of course, we can only say what "beyond" means by supplying a context for interpreting it; but the interpretations appear to be similar in different contexts. Context-generality could account for why patients can read "content words" like *elephant*, but not "the commonest function words such as *the*" [22]. Storage by category need not be invoked as an explanation. Rosenfield describes other, more contemporary work that ignores the effect of context (the lexical dictionary approach of John C. Marshall and Freda Newcombe) or still adopts a filing system model (the verb concept hierarchy of Elizabeth Warrington).

5. Perception research

As stated in the introduction, Rosenfield attacks the view that "there is no perception without prior 'learning'. . ." (p. 7).

> Nobody pretended to understand the mechanisms that created the fixed images. That is a physiological question; its resolution would tell us little or nothing about the nature of memory. (p. 15)

> Furthermore, a hidden and unquestioned assumption of the localizationist view is that there is some specific information in the environment that can become the fixed memory images. But if recognition depends on context, it is the *brain* that must organize *stimuli* into coherent pieces of information. . . . [F]unctional specializations, suggested by the study of clinical material must be illusory, for what is implied is not that the brain creates our perceptions out of ambiguous stimuli but that it *sorts* neatly packaged information coming from the environment. (p. 63)

From Rosenfield's point of view, you haven't explained memory at all unless you begin with perception of stimuli. Information is not given but created ("as categories, organizations, and orderings of stimuli" (p. 66)) (cf. [45]). This is the inherent flaw of cognitive science and most of connectionist research today. The world does not present itself as interpretable symbols. To predigest the world for your program by prelabeling things and events is to bypass the essential problem that memory must address.

The process of perception must begin at the level of stimuli; it must create the representations that reasoning operates upon (recall the *within* versus *sequence of cycles* distinction of Sections 2.2 and 2.4). This creation is inherently a process of categorizing in every situation, because perception is inherently contextual and the context—an ongoing, internal composition by which perceptions and movements are organized—is always new.

The book gives fascinating examples of experiments that establish that "sounds are categorized and therefore perceived differently depending on the presence or absence of other sounds". For example, there is a "trade-off between the length of the *sh* sound and the duration of the silence [between the words of "say shop"] in determining whether *sh* or *ch* is heard" (p. 106). In fact, "lengthening the silence *between* words can also alter the *preceding* word" (p. 107). For example, "if the cue for the *sh* in 'ship' is relatively long, increases in the duration of silence between the words ["gray ship"] cause the perception to change, not to 'gray chip' but to 'great ship'." Hence, phonemes are not *given* but constructed within an ongoing context of overlapping cues. "What brain mechanism is responsible for our perceptions of an /a/, if what we perceive also depends on what came before and after the /a/?" (p.110) In no sense does an /a/ exist somewhere in isolation in the brain.

The basic claim is that "the categorizations created by our brains are abstract and cannot be accounted for as combinations of 'elementary stimuli'." There are no innate or learned primitives like /a/ to be found in the brain; that is, there are no primitive stimuli *descriptions* in the brain that can be combined. There are just patterns of brain activity that correspond to *organizations of stimuli*. Our perception depends on past categorizations, not on some absolute, inherent features of stimuli (such as the frequencies of sounds) that are matched against inputs (p. 112).

But the memory-as-structures approach holds that:

> . . . acquired knowledge is stored as fixed images in specific centers, just as the nineteenth-century neurologists believed. . . . The world is knowable according to this view, only if it is already known: the recognition of a shape is possible only if there is a fixed image of that shape already stored in the brain. (p. 112)

> Seeing, they [AI researchers] argued, requires first knowing what one is looking for. (p. 115)

David Marr challenged this view. Rosenfield reexamines Marr's approach in order to contrast it with other AI research and illustrate how perception can be modeled computationally as a constructive, bottom-up process.

6. Marr

Elizabeth Warrington's work, which was briefly mentioned in Section 4, "suggested to Marr that the brain stores information about the use and function of objects separately from information about their shape, and that our visual system permits us to recognize objects even though we cannot name them or describe their function" (p. 117). This separation of function continues the "localizationist orthodoxy", but the idea of recognizing shapes without named, stored images is a dramatic departure. Marr's approach is to view the world from the organism's perspective, in terms of what stimuli it is given and what it must be able to accomplish for its goals. He showed how shape can be derived from intensity correlations, independent of a memory system describing what shapes might be present. But Rosenfield points out that Marr's programs "were carefully designed, rather than learned, suggesting that Marr had not fully solved the problem" (p. 122). Although Marr pointed a way out of requiring a fixed memory of images upon which perception operates, he didn't fully develop these ideas and indeed used them "to justify arguments for functional specialization, overlooking [the] radical implications".

In summary: "In its failure to free itself from fixed symbols, the computational approach ultimately stifles what could have been a new view of memory as procedure" (p. 128) (cf. Bickhard and Richie's "encodings hanging in mid air", Section 1.3). Even though Marr's programs could recognize a shape bottom-up, "the naming of the shape [e.g., as a cube] still relies on access to a fixed memory" (p. 126). Marr's view is that the recognition procedure is fixed at perception time (given) and information is objective (given, perceived by everyone); thus recognition is still a *match* between internal descriptions and external stimuli. More flexibility is required: Perception and learning are inseparable; one cannot be input to the other. Perceiving is learning. But how is experience (what procedures were used previously) part of perception? The key process to be explained is how context is established by building on what the organism perceived in the past, without requiring this experience to be stored as symbolically interpretable, fixed structures (including programs). Connectionist research attempts to address this issue.

7. PDP devices

Rosenfield rejects parallel-distributed processing (PDP) devices [48] as a solution to the memory problem because they hold to the idea of a fixed memory, manifested by static storage of weights: Every item is represented by a specific pattern of activity (p. 147). A PDP machine constitutes a clever hash-coding scheme, based on the same idea of conventional computation, in which memory is a place for storing things. The memory's distributed nature does not change this fundamental characteristic.

It might be objected that the contribution of connectionism is not at the level of how categories are stored, but of forming new categories. But according to Rosenfield, the generalization capability of PDP devices is "prefabricated" by the programmer's encoding of inputs. The machine's capability to associate a color with an unknown flower originates in the programmer's encoding of the flower in terms of codes similar to those already learned (e.g., supplying tokens for size and shape), not in the nature of flowers or colors as encountered in the world (p. 148).

In contrast, categorization depends on not just finding common subfeatures of stimuli and noting their contextual relations (p. 148), but on combining stimuli in a useful way (that is, related to motor activities, sense-making and emotions). Furthermore, what constitutes information for an organism cannot be given by a teacher, but must arise from the organism's own organizing processes in interaction with its environment:

> The generalizations in PDP devices are nothing more than overlapping patterns in *predetermined* codes. Real generalization creates *new* categories of information. . . from the organism's point of view, the consequence of unforseen elements in the environment. (p. 149)

For example, a PDP machine, unless preprogrammed to do so, cannot recognize a smudged letter as a symbol. A PDP researcher might claim that the preloading of the net in a teaching phase is just a way to get started, to show how perception occurs based on experience. But this begs several questions: Why does the organism attend to particular stimuli at all? How does past experience influence the perceptual process itself? "How do we create new ways of viewing the present, new *kinds* of generalizations?" (p.. 152) "How [do] patterns of activity acquire significance in a particular context?" (p. 153) For example, how do children acquire the idea of past tense? (p. 155) Edelman's work addresses these issues by suggesting how categorization is a perceptual process.

8. Edelman

One of the key ideas in Edelman's developmental approach is that "the nervous system can only approximate what it has already produced" (p. 220). In dismissing the idea of an ideal recording device, we must also change our idea of past and present: There is no time stamp in memory, only correlations and sequences of states (organizations) (p. 162). "What [the patient] lost was not time but the way events and objects were related. . . . There are no calendars in the brain". Rather, a sense of time depends on the ability to construct a context that composes the sense of what is happening now with previous behaviors. That is, placing the past in perspective requires a kind of coordination between past processes of behaving and current stimuli:

> Memories, then, are the procedures that are responsible for the organization of perceptions. They are themselves *generalizations* of previous experiences, ways of organizing sensory stimuli that permit them to be related to past experience. (p. 62)

Memory is a correlation and coordination process. In reinterpreting the clinical studies, Rosenfield finds that:

> [I]t is not that memories have been lost, but that the ability to establish correlations has been destroyed. Those utterances that require little or no such ability remain, giving the illusion that a few specific memories [such as recognizing individual letters or writing one's signature] have been spared destruction while all other words have been lost. (p. 71)

So how does this correlation process work, according to Edelman?

> [N]euronal groups are organized into sheets, called *maps*, and the interactions among the numerous maps—and the fact that all maps are connected to a motor output and to the initial sensory input—categorize information. *The past is restructured in terms of the present.* Perception and recognition, then, are part of the same unitary process. (p. 9, emphasis added)

Behavior isn't determined by single maps (between sensory and effector systems) but in the *relation* of maps to one another at a given time. Again, the cause of behavior is not localizable to specific structures that are permanently associated with that behavior. In a lucid description of Edelman's theory, Rosenfield raises the provocative possibility that neural transmissions are establishing boundaries between neural groups (structural sheets). They are not *communicating* anything via the electrical pulses (i.e., transmitting symbolically interpreted information), but rather are establishing demarcations that constrain further additions and modifications of boundaries. Thus, an organization of neural processes would be composed of a combination of (multi-dimensional?) boundaries. One can further speculatively imagine hierarchical mappings built up as sheets reorganize themselves within the spaces created by currently active sheets. Some key ideas are *reentrant maps* (those that feed back on themselves, allowing for their stimulation in the presence of later different, but similar inputs), *maps of maps* (secondary structure of neural groups), and *multisensory intersections* (correlating maps from different sensory systems for coordinating movements).

Edelman's model of the brain starts with an initial population of maps between sensors and effectors. These maps are then selectively reinforced by use, in direct analogy to the selection of antibodies in the immunosystem. The model has been developed in a series of computer programs; an example in an appendix illustrates how cross-correlation of mappings leads to generalization. Further details can be found in Smoliar's [54] review of Edelman's book.

Applying neural mapping ideas to situated automata [36], we might *model* neural selection in terms of finite-state automata that are selected (as opposed to assembled from abstract descriptions or schemas) by use. Layers of inhibitory and excitatory connections might emerge (each layer produced by a boundary?). Similarly, we might work backwards from models such as MOPS

to see what kind of composition of maps corresponds to the observed contextual aspects of reminding. For example, could the failure-driven nature of
memory observed by Schank be generalized in terms of perceptual impasses?[15]
In general, the book opens the door to reconceptualizing the patterns represented in cognitive science models, so they can be integrated better with the
psychology of memory and perception (cf., [41]).

Rosenfield concludes that "The brain is biological structure. Only in terms of
biological principles will be able to understand it" (p. 10). This remark is too
strong and probably wrong. Surely functional descriptions of intelligent behavior (for example, existing cognitive science descriptions of complex
problem-solving and discourse) and studies of the environment emphasizing
social structures (e.g., [32, 33]) will be useful for characterizing what the brain
accomplishes, and hence help us to comprehend what the neurons are doing.
Indeed, the notion of categorization so central to Edelman's theories is
arguably in the psychological domain, not biology alone. Rosenfield might
have better said, "Only by *incorporating* biological principles will we be able to
understand the brain". A social view of learning without neuroscience is like
attempting to explain family resemblance without molecular genetics. But the
chemistry of amino acids itself could neither predict nor explain population
dynamics or punctuated equilibria [13]. A balanced perspective will give proper
attention to each level of analysis (neural/genetic, representational/phenotype,
social/environment) and describe their interplay.

9. Criticisms of Rosenfield

To make Rosenfield's arguments about localization understandable for an AI
audience, I have focussed on the distinction between memory as stored
structures and self-organizing processes, which is what I believe Rosenfield
means when he says memory is procedural. Similar problems arise when we
consider Rosenfield's discussion of learning variability, goals, and symbols.

---

[15] By hypothesis, whatever is perceived is learned and hence "remembered" [49]. But most
perceptions, by the very process of construction from past organizations, are similar to past
experience (i.e., made analogous by subsumption and composition of maps). As James said
(Section 1.4), experience is full of recurrence that doesn't provoke a secondary experience of
remembering. To be distinguished, an experience must resist categorization. We remember our
failures because that is when coherence, our story-telling accomplishment, required deliberate
framing and history-telling to guide the categorization process. That is, as Bartlett, Winograd, and
Schön describe, it is at an impasse – an inability to act and adapt automatically – that we use
(generate and perceive) representations in order to behave. We later reconstruct (remember) the
representations that eased the original impasse. It remains to explain how horses and pigs get by
without this.

9.1. Variability from emergent behaviors

Rosenfield often makes strong statements intended to attack the grammatical approach of AI programs. But he is apparently unfamiliar with machine learning research and therefore fails to make clear the limitations of current programs. For example, he argues that AI programs are inflexible, identifying it with "genetic determinism", the idea that genes constitute *instructions* for assembling the body. He claims that this "strains credibility because it makes it difficult to account for the enormous variability of thought and action" (p. 171). Those familiar with the capabilities of AI programs to plan and assemble new action sequences may be tempted to respond, "but we have programs with such flexibility". Rosenfield says, "Accurate memory traces would hardly help us survive in an ever-changing world" (p. 79). At first glance, an AI researcher might conclude that Rosenfield doesn't understand how schemas can be composed and adapted to new circumstances.

Rosenfield's claims about variability are important, but they don't come to grips with the essential difference between stored-program and self-organizing systems, which he should have emphasized (recall the examples given in Section 2.4). In a stored-program system, a controlling process directs how structures and behaviors are organized according to template (schema, script, grammar) descriptions. In a self-organizing mechanism, global patterns of phenotypic structure (the physical appearance of the organism) and behavioral routines develop over time from local interactions between internal and environmental processes. Bateson [6] describes how stable organizations (physical and behavioral) can emerge through the interaction of two stochastic processes, one with a digital randomizer (genes, neurons), the other continuous (the environment). Such mechanisms are explored by "artificial life" research (e.g., [55]).

9.2. Goals as ongoing, constructed processes

Similarly, Rosenfield's claim that goals determine the kinds of information that the brain is capable of deriving from environmental cues (p. 121) at first glance appears consistent with AI views. Rosenfield doesn't realize the complex ways in which goals, focus of attention, and behavior interact in today's complex programs. He thinks he is laying out specifications that no program could approach, when in fact on the surface these are the very concerns of everyday AI research.

Rosenfield fails to emphasize that a goal, in his model of memory, isn't tied to a description of something to be matched in the world. A goal should be thought of as an active, organizing process (cf. Bickhard and Richie's, "interactive control structures" [7]). According to the composition idea, a goal is a perceptual categorization that orients the construction of a new perception and hence ongoing movements. (For example, see Schön's [52] description of how ways of talking subsume ways of seeing in the invention of a synthetic paint brush). A goal is not a label or a program, or even something different from a conceptual category, except for its status as active and dynamically orienting behavior. Observers (either theoreticians or subjects themselves) ascribe goals to activities in their framing, history-telling, and reflections on design. Talk about goals, like other representations, must be perceived to effect behavior (recall the discussion of grammars and plans in Section 2; see also [1, 56]).

Rosenfield goes on to say that physical attributes of the world are "a consequence not of any programs in the brain, but of our experience in the world" (p. 135). Readers familiar with machine learning programs might object that a program can change how the world is described by virtue of experience. What Rosenfield apparently means to say is that a program that is fixed (when perception begins), rather than constructed on the spot as part of an ongoing sense-making process, is insufficient. In particular, if a program is always required for perception, the stored-program approach begs the issue of where the first programs came from. Again, this is not the distinction between "declarative" and "procedural" knowledge as discussed in the AI literature. Both declarative and procedural views suppose that perception is carried out by structures that are fixed before the perceptual activity begins and only changed after the perceptual activity is complete. But if there is no protected place where this program could be stored (if memory is not a permanent record and functionality is not localized), procedures must be changed during the perceptual process itself.

Again, what is at stake here is the mechanism: stored-program versus self-organizing system. By analogy, the stored-program idea says that genes are predetermined, internal descriptions of how the organism will appear (declarative view) or they are predetermined, internal instructions for how to assemble structures (procedural view). Similarly, the stored-program idea says that behavioral routines are generated either by interpreting descriptions (e.g. scripts) or by running a stored, assembly program. The self-organizing view requires a kind of machine we haven't yet built (indeed, there is reason to believe that we must first change our idea of what a mechanism can be). The self-organizing view is highly relational, dynamic, and interactional. Information isn't given, it is created. It is the relations between stimuli and differences that are detected, not individual, objective things (something Bateson [5] constantly emphasized). What is "stored" is what neural maps have been active in the past in relation to other active maps.

9.3. Symbols in the brain

Rosenfield nicely summarizes the lesson from Edelman: "We perceive the world without labels, and we can label it only when we have decided how its features should be organized." However, he may go too far when he says,

"There are no symbols in the brain; there are patterns of activity, fragments, which acquire different meanings in different contexts" (p. 166). This is apparently a contradiction. For a pattern of activity (a perception) to acquire meaning is for it to be symbolic, to be treated as a representation. Hence, when I interpret something I have just imagined or perceived (e.g., silent speech)—an activity that clearly occurs in my brain—I am treating patterns of activity within my brain as symbols. What Rosenfield means to say is that representing (e.g., saying something), producing forms that can be perceived, occurs at a higher level, *in sequences of behavior.* In the case of silent speech, for example, we are not literally producing *sounds,* which is perhaps Rosenfield's point. But our experience is the same as if someone spoke (sound hallucinations). We "hear" the sounds, then interpret what they mean. Representations are thus created and interpreted in *cycles of perceiving* (recall the levels of reference in Schön's analysis of framing, history-telling, designing). Representations are not manipulated, stored, indexed, etc. *within* each perceptual act. Symbol structures—meaningfully interpretable forms—must be produced so we can perceive them, and this occurs in our writing and speech, as well as privately in the brain.

10. Common objections

In the process of preparing this review, I have been repeatedly asked a number of questions, which are summarized here.

Question 1. *You refer to AI of the past. Recent work in connectionism and parallel processing is addressing these issues.* There is indeed no reason to draw a boundary between AI, situated cognition, connectionism, etc., causing researchers to feel isolated or obsolete. It is important to build on the insights that arise from different fields with different motivations. For example, Ullman's architecture for bottom-up vision is exploited and extended in Chapman's [14] model of situated cognition. However, we must be clear that talk of "connectionist symbol mapping", "language of thought", and "parallel, distributed problem-solving" generally adopts the metaphor of memory as stored structures. These are not alternatives to the grammatical approach.

Question 2. *It's not new.* In part that's my point; the information-processing view of the mind has failed to take into account psychological and social theories developed over the past 70 years. Related claims that "we tried that and failed" (e.g., pattern recognition) miss the point that situated cognition research builds on cognitive science; it's not just rehashing old ideas. We want to integrate cognitive science, knowledge-level models (e.g., prototypes, novice/expert differences, misconceptions, strategies) with the psychology of perception, psychiatry, and the social sciences.

Question 3. *It's just an implementation issue.* In effect that's right: All we have ever done is describe what a process memory can do, we've never built one! Situated cognition reformulates the knowledge level versus symbol level distinction. The knowledge level is an observer's specification of an agent-in-an-environment (cf. [5, 16, 17, 46]). Symbols aren't stored in memory and manipulated as structures; they are generated and interpreted anew with each perception. How memory is implemented (as opposed to described) is the essential problem we face as engineers. Memory-as-structure-storage models human intelligence, but can't replicate its flexibility.

Question 4. *"Why is it, although everybody now admits the force of the criticism of associationism, the associationist principles still hold their ground and are constantly employed?"* [4, p. 307]

> First, it is because the force of the rejection of associationism depends mainly upon the adoption of a functional point of view; but the attitude of analytic description is just as important within its own sphere. . . .
>
> Secondly, it is demonstrable that every situation, in perceiving, in imaging, in remembering, and in all constructive effort, possesses outstanding detail, and that in many cases of association the outstanding detail of one situation is taken directly out of that, and organised together with the outstanding detail of a different situation. . . .
>
> Thirdly, we have seen how to some extent images, and to a great extent words, both of them expressions often of associative tendencies, slip readily into habit series and conventional formations. They do this mainly in the interest of intercommunication within the social group, and in doing it they inevitably take upon themselves common characteristics which render them amenable to the general descriptive phrases of the traditional doctrines of association.
>
> In various senses, therefore, associationism is likely to remain, though its outlook is foreign to the demands of modern psychological science. It tells us something about the characteristics of associated details, when they are associated, but it explains nothing whatever of the activity of the conditions by which they are brought together. [4, p. 308].

Question 5. *How do you model medical diagnosis strategies now?* Just as we always have. Classifications and production rules are fine for stating behavioral patterns (what Bartlett calls "analytic description" of "habit series and conventional formations"). It remains to explain how they *develop* ("the conditions by which they are brought together"). Most learning programs grammatically describe how representations accumulate within a fixed language. They don't explain how representations are created, or more generally, the evolution of new routines not described by the given grammar.

Question 6. *Could there be a universal grammar?* Yes, in the sense that simple operations such as sequence, composition, and subsumption might constitute the "grammar" out of which all categorizations and behaviors are constructed. But these are processes, not descriptions or templates.

Question 7. *How would you test these theories psychologically?* In part, it's been done. Situated cognition research claims that empirical studies contradict cognitive science models. For example, Bartlett's [4] data argues against "fixed trace", semantic network memories. Jenkins [31] and Bransford et al. [9] demonstrate contextual effects that contradict models of memory based on search and matching. Other facts are obvious: people don't speak like grammatical automatons; emotions organize behavior; knowledge engineers are creating models—new representations—not extracting precoded networks from expert brains; AI programs aren't capable of writing reviews like this. The challenge goes the other way: What does AI have to say about Freud's analyses? About dreams? About musical ability? To pick a more mundane example, how could I write a page-long biography of a person, yet not remember his name? Schema-based storage models offer no explanation: How could I have access to a dozen feature-slots, but have no handle on the most obvious label for indexing the frame itself? Concerning psychological testing, note that situated cognition research rejects the validity of laboratory experiments that subtract out the complex, interactive context of everyday cognition [33]. Predictive social-psychological experiments are more like manipulating the weather than running rats through a maze.

Question 8. *Who is Rosenfield?* The book's jacket states,

> Israel Rosenfield received his M.D. from New York University and his Ph.D from Princeton. He teaches at the City University of New York and is the author of *Freud: Character and Consciousness* and co-author (with Edward Ziff) of *DNA for Beginners*.

For those swayed by authority, Oliver Sacks states in a recent article, ". . . I have been assisted by discussions with Pietro Corsi, Otto Creutzfeld, Gerald Edelman, Ralph Siegel – and, most especially, Israel Rosenfield" [50]. Rosenfield himself thanks researchers from the MIT AI Laboratory (regarding Marr's work), James McClelland (regarding PDP models), and others whose work he analyzes (Edelman, Marshall, Warrington).

Question 9. *It's all mystical.* Every science must exclude phenomena that are viewed as too complicated for a given paradigm. In cognitive science, problem-solving research has generally excluded emotion, psychiatric disorders, religious behavior, and other matters relating to personal identity and motivation. But it is sloppy thinking to contrast scientific methods (e.g., using logic and representational models) with ill-understood or apparently non-productive behaviors, thus circularly defining what needs to be explained by what can be modeled. We have done this in AI to the extent that logic is contrasted with emotion and deliberate reasoning with intuition. The very notion of "judgment" has become something expressible as a rule, when our every day experience is that judgments arise from non-represented thought. The currently popular view that common sense knowledge can be reduced to representations similarly distorts what needs to be explained.

The result is a science that resembles Oliver Sacks' patient, Dr. P., "the man who mistook his wife for a hat". Dr. P. apprehends objects by matching features of categories. For example, he describes a glove as "a continuous surface. . . infolded on itself. . . . [with] five outpouchings. . ." [49, p. 114]. Sacks comments,

> Our cognitive sciences are themselves suffering from an agnosia essentially similar to Dr. P.'s. Dr. P. may therefore serve as a warning and parable—of what happens to a science which eschews the judgmental, the particular, the personal, and becomes entirely abstract and computational. [49, p. 20]

11. Conclusions

What is memory? What is retained from experience? Memory is a capability to recompose sequences of behaviors, to coordinate past maps between perceptions and movements within a constructed context of ongoing perceptions and behaviors. In short, memory is indistinguishable from our capability to make sense, to learn a new skill, to compose something new. It is not a place where descriptions of what we have done or said before are stored. In more detail, memory-based performances involve an intricate combination of reconstructed "feelings" and "attitudes" that orient composition of new sequences, and specific reconstructed images, sounds, and other sensations that constrain behavior from "below". This is essentially Bartlett's model of constructive memory [4]; Rosenfield might have given him more credit for integrating emotion and sensation in this way.[16]

[16] The citation of Bartlett's work on p. 193 appears to be an afterthought. George Mead published a book two years after Bartlett's *Remembering*, with a strikingly similar emphasis on social aspects of cognition. For Bartlett and Mead, social interactions structure perception and meaning attribution. In this respect, we can criticize Rosenfield for not breaking severely enough with the egocentric view he means to attack. A more recent statement in this tradition is Lave's [33] eloquent discussion of how cultural knowledge cannot be reduced to representations that describe it.

Rosenfield's analysis provides a point of view for critiquing both cognitive science of the 1970s and 1980s and connectionism, while laying down requirements for a different model of perception and memory. To put it more strongly, as Rosenfield clearly intends, this book provides one starting point for overthrowing the views of memory that dominate the cognitive science and neural net community. Rosenfield sees both communities as ignoring basic properties of human memory that could be exploited in designing an intelligent machine: The prevalent cognitive science view is that memories are stored structures; the prevalent neural net view is that the world is received by the organism as an array of meaningful inputs (e.g., words).

It is no coincidence that Rosenfield cites case studies of patients who cannot read words or multinumeral digits. The question is not how we recognize or generate *single forms* or movements. But rather, how do we *coordinate a sequence* of perceptions or movements? This emphasis on coordination, correlation, and composition into coherent ongoing processes is the essential capability that connectionist research by and large has not yet addressed (but see, for example, [40]). A wonderful example of what situated cognition could bring to robotics is Ghengis' ability to develop the coordinated, tripod gait after a few minutes [36].

Situated cognition calls our attention to the environment and importance of on-going context. Our study of Rosenfield suggests a significant reformulation of the nature of context:

- the social-physical environment is important because behavior is perceptually organized by an interaction of environmental and internal processes;
- representations are created perceptually and interpreted in cycles of perceptual categorizing; in this they become part of the context that organizes behavior; to speak is to perceive is to represent is to learn;
- context is not given (i.e., as objective data); the context that causally directs perception is an *internal* construction of processes (neural sensory-effector maps and maps of maps), an ongoing composition;
- neural and perceptual theories are essential; the social sciences alone cannot explain why habits develop, account for the effects of practice, or most basically, explain how perceptual categories are biased by experience.

Recent interest in relating cognitive science to neurobiology, in what is called *cognitive neuroscience*, requires serious consideration of Rosenfield's attack. Looking for knowledge and stored plans in brain tissue is almost certainly fundamentally confused. Instead, we should take cognitive science theories as an observer's descriptions of what the brain, in interaction with an environment, accomplishes. We should look for a mechanism, along the lines of Edelman's neuronal group selection, which could account for how strategies and plans are manifested as compositions of sensory-effector maps, and how these orient the selection of neural groups, are modified by them, and endure.

There is reason to be optimistic that we are about to make some breakthroughs in our understanding of the brain. But ironically, it will come at the expense of overturning nearly everything AI has assumed about the *physical mechanisms* of perception, learning, and memory. Indeed, we must stop and rethink the rubric of "information-processing" that still unites most parts of AI and cognitive science. Perhaps our field betrays too much its origins in the computer industry, with data supplied on cards and each job completed as a neat processing from input to output piles. More generally, what is at stake is our ideas about how models relate to mechanisms and what mechanisms can be built. The most important clues remind us of powerful ideas from physics and biology: frames of reference, dynamics, development, and emergent structure. Having invented a kind of memory that ignores these aspects of life, we must now try to invent another.

Acknowledgement

If memory serves me, extensive revisions of these representations were socially structured by Susan Chipman, Dan Russell, Steve Smoliar, Mark Stefik, and Kurt VanLehn. This work was supported in part by gifts from the Digital Equipment and Xerox Corporations.

References

[1] P.E. Agre, Book Review of *Plans and Situated Actions: The Problem of Human-Machine Communication* (L.A. Suchman), *Artif. Intell.* **43** (1990) 369–384.

[2] J.R. Anderson and G.H. Bower, *Human Associative Memory* (Winston, Washington, DC, 1973).

[3] J. Bamberger and D.A. Schön, Learning as reflective conversation with materials: notes from work in progress, *Art Educ.* (March 1983).

[4] F.C. Bartlett, *Remembering—A Study in Experimental and Social Psychology* (Cambridge University Press, Cambridge, 1932; reprint 1977).

[5] G. Bateson, *Steps to an Ecology of Mind* (Ballentine Books, New York, 1972).

[6] G. Bateson, *Mind and Nature: A Necessary Unity* (Bantam, New York, 1988).

[7] M.H. Bickhard and D.M. Richie, *On the Nature of Representation: A Case-Study of James Gibson's Theory of Perception* (Praeger, New York, 1983).

[8] P. Bordieu, *Outline of a Theory of Practice* (Cambridge University Press, Cambridge, 1932).

[9] J.D. Bransford, N.S. McCarrell, J.J. Franks and K.E. Nitsch, Toward unexplaining memory, in: R.E. Shaw and J.D. Bransford, eds., *Perceiving, Acting, and Knowing: Toward an Ecological Psychology* (Erlbaum, Hillsdale, NJ, 1977) 431–466.

[10] J. Bresnan and R.M. Kaplan, Grammars as mental representations of language, in: W. Kintsch, J.R. Miller and P. Polson, eds., *Method and Tactics in Cognitive Science* (Erlbaum, Hillsdale, NJ, 1984).

[11] R.A. Brooks, How to build complete creatures rather than isolated cognitive simulators, in: K. VanLehn, ed., *Architectures for Intelligence: The Twenty-Second Carnegie Symposium on Cognition* (Erlbaum, Hillsdale, NJ, 1991).

[12] J.S. Brown and K. VanLehn, Repair theory: a generative theory of bugs in procedural skills, *Cogn. Sci.* **4** (1980) 379–426.

[13] W.H. Calvin, *The River That Flows Uphill: A Journey from the Big Bang to the Big Brain* (Macmillan, New York, 1986).

[14] D. Chapman, Vision, instruction, and action, Ph.D. Thesis, AI Laboratory Tech. Report #1204, MIT, Cambridge, MA (1990).

[15] W.J. Clancey, Acquiring, representing, and evaluating a competence model of diagnosis, in: M.T.H. Chi, R. Claser and M.J. Farr, eds., *The Nature of Expertise* (Erlbaum, Hillsdale, NJ, 1988) 343–418.

[16] W.J. Clancey, The knowledge level reinterpreted: modeling how systems interact, *Mach. Learn.* **4** (1989) 287–293.

[17] W.J. Clancey, The frame of reference problem in the design of intelligent machines, in: K. VanLehn, ed., *Architectures for Intelligence* (Erlbaum, Hillsdale, 1991).

[18] W.J. Clancey, Why today's computers don't learn the way people do, in: P. Flasch and R. Meersman, eds., *Future Directions in Artificial Intelligence* (Elsevier, Amsterdam, 1991).

[19] W.J. Clancey, Model construction operators, *Artif. Intell.* (to appear).

[20] H. Cohen, How to draw three people in a botanical garden, in: *Proceedings AAAI-88*, St. Paul, MN (1988) 846–855.

[21] R.G. Collingwood, *The Principles of Art* (Oxford University Press, London, 1938).

[22] M. Cohtheart, Cognition and its disorders, review of *From Neuropsychology to Mental Structure*, *Science* **246** (1990) 827–828.

[23] G.M. Edelman, *Neural Darwinism: The Theory of Neuronal Group Selection* (Basic Books, New York, 1987).

[24] S. Freud, *On Aphasia* (International Universities Press, New York, 1953).

[25] J.J. Gibson, *The Senses Considered as Perceptual Systems* (Houghton Mifflin, Boston, MA, 1966).

[26] R.F. Hadley, Connectionism, rule following, and symbol manipulation, in: *Proceedings AAAI-90*, Boston, MA (1990) 579–586.

[27] E.H. Hovy, Pragmatics and natural language generation, *Artif. Intell.* **43** (1990) 153–197.

[28] A. Iran-Nejad, Affect: a functional perspective, *Mind Behav.* **5** (1984) 279–310.

[29] A. Iran-Nejad, The schema: a long-term memory structure or a transient functional pattern, in: R.J. Tierney, P.L. Anders and J.N. Mitchell, eds., *Understanding Readers' Understanding: Theory and Practice* (Erlbaum, Hillsdale, 1987).

[30] W. James, *Psychology: Briefer Course* (Harvard University Press, Cambridge, MA, 1892); reprinted, with annotations (1984).

[31] J.J. Jenkins, Remember that old theory of memory? *Well, forget it! Am. Psychol.* (November, 1974) 785–795.

[32] B. Latour and S. Woolgar, *Laboratory Life: The Social Construction of Scientific Facts* (Sage, London, 1979).

[33] J. Lave, *Cognition in Practice* (Cambridge University Press, Cambridge, 1988).

[34] D. Lenat and R. Guha, *Building Large Knowledge Bases* (Addison-Wesley, Reading MA, 1990).

[35] E.F. Loftus, Leading questions and the eyewitness report, *Cogn. Psychol.* **7** (1975) 560–572.

[36] P. Maes, ed., Designing autonomous agents, *Rob. Autonomous Syst.* **6** (1, 2) (1990) Special Issue.

[37] G.H. Mead, *On Social Psychology* (University of Chicago Press, Chicago, IL, 1964); first published (1934).

[38] G.A. Miller and P.N. Johnson-Laird, *Language and Perception* (Harvard University Press, Cambridge, MA, 1976).

[39] M. Minsky, *The Society of Mind* (Simon and Schuster, New York, 1986).

[40] Y. Miyata, Organization of action sequences in motor learning: a connectionist approach, in: *Proceedings Ninth Annual Conference of the Cognitive Science Society*, Seattle, WA (1987) 496–507.

[41] U. Neisser, *Cognition and Reality: Principles and Implications of Cognitive Psychology* (Freeman, New York, 1976).

[42] D.A. Norman, *Learning and Memory* (Freeman, New York, 1982).

[43] R.E. Ornstein, *The Psychology of Consciousness* (Penguin, New York, 1972).

[44] J. Piaget, *Genetic Epistemology* (Norton and Company, New York, 1970).

[45] G.N. Reeke and G.M. Edelman, Real brains and artificial intelligence, *Daedalus* **117** (1) (1988) "Artificial Intelligence" Issue.

[46] S.J. Rosenschein, Formal theories of knowledge in AI and robotics, Tech. Note 362, SRI, Menlo Park, CA (1985).

[47] S.J. Rosenschein, The logicist conception of knowledge is too narrow—but so is McDermott's, Tech. Note, SRI, Menlo Park, CA (1987).

[48] D.E. Rumelhart, J.L. McClelland and the PDP Research Group, eds., *Parallel Distributed Processing* (MIT Press, Cambridge, MA, 1986).

[49] O. Sacks, *The Man Who Mistook His Wife for a Hat* (Harper & Row, New York, 1987).

[50] O. Sacks, Neurology and the Soul, *The New York Review of Books* (November 22, 1990) 44–50.

[51] R.C. Schank, Failure-driven memory, *Cogn. Brain Theory* **4**(1) (1981) 41–60.

[52] D.A. Schön, Generative metaphor: a perspective on problem-setting in social policy, in: A. Ortony, ed., *Metaphor and Thought* (Cambridge University Press, Cambridge, 1979) 254–283.

[53] D.A. Schön, *Educating the Reflective Practitioner* (Jossey-Bass, San Francisco, CA, 1987).

[54] S.W. Smoliar, Book Review of *Neural Darwinism: The Theory of Neuronal Group Selection* (G.M. Edelman), *Artif. Intell.* **39** (1989) 121–136.

[55] L. Steels, Cooperation through self-organisation, in: Y. Demazeau and J.-P. Müller, eds., *Multi-agent Systems* (North-Holland, Amsterdam, 1989).

[56] L.A. Suchman, *Plans and Situated Actions: The Problem of Human-Machine Communication* (Cambridge University Press, Cambridge, 1987).

[57] S. Tyler, *The Said and the Unsaid: Mind, Meaning, and Culture* (Academic Press, New York, 1978).

[58] L. Vygotsky, *Thought and Language* (A. Kozulin, ed.) (MIT Press, Cambridge, MA, 1986); original published (1934).

[59] M.M. Waldrop, Fast, cheap, and out of control, Research News, *Science* **248** (1990) 959–961.

[60] D.C. Wilkins, W.J. Clancey and B.G. Buchanan, On using and evaluating differential modeling in intelligent tutoring and apprentice learning systems, in: J. Psotka, D. Massey and S. Mutter, eds., *Intelligent Tutoring Systems: Lessons Learned* (Erlbaum, Hillsdale, NJ, 1988).

[61] T. Winograd and F. Flores, *Understanding Computers and Cognition: A New Foundation for Design* (Ablex, Norwood, NJ, 1986).

[62] D.A. Schön, The theory of inquiry: Dewey's legacy to education, Presented at Annual Meeting of American Educational Research Association, San Francisco, CA (1990).

Gerald M. Edelman, *Neural Darwinism: The Theory of Neuronal Group Selection* (Basic Books; New York, 1987); xxii + 371 pages.

Reviewed by: Stephen W. Smoliar

USC Information Sciences Institute, 4676 Admiralty Way Suite 1001, Marina del Rey, CA 90292-6695, U.S.A.

1. What Is Neural Darwinism?

1.1. Basic ideas

The relevance of the study of the human brain to the study of artificial intelligence has long been an issue of debate. However, regardless of whether or not better knowledge of the brain will help us to build better expert systems, the fact remains that every human carries within his skull a lump of hardware whose behavior is the very inspiration for the study of artificial intelligence. Those who eschew the study of that biological hardware argue that it is too complex and too mysterious to yield useful guides for the construction of intelligent machines. However, others have been drawn to study that hardware for its own sake; and every so often, those studies yield insights which may ultimately prove to benefit artificial intelligence as well as biology. Gerald Edelman's theory of neuronal group selection, sometimes called "neural Darwinism," may prove to be such a source of insights.

I first encountered news of this research in an article in *The New York Review* by Israel Rosenfield [17], which has subsequently become the final chapter of Rosenfield's book, *The Invention of Memory* [19]. This article piqued my curiosity into investigating some of the technical literature, but it was the appearance of Edelman's own book which finally helped me to pull together my first understanding of some new and revolutionary ideas about what the mind is and how it comes to be. I think that these ideas have potentially significant repercussions with regard to the study of artificial intelligence; but before these repercussions can be considered, it is necessary to lay out an exposition of the ideas themselves.

This exposition must touch upon a variety of topics, each of which will be

Artificial Intelligence **39** (1989) 121–139

summarized in a separate section. First I shall consider those questions which provoked Edelman's research program. Then I shall summarize the three fundamental claims of neuronal group selection. This will be followed by four discussions of increasingly complex mental activity: perception, categorization, memory, and learning. Once these foundations are laid, it will be worthwhile to consider the source of their inspiration. With all this information as background, the theory may be considered in relation to questions of artificial intelligence.

After the specific achievements of neuronal group selection have been reviewed, the theory can be compared with other models which may claim to be related to neural activity. These include the "parallel distributed processing" (PDP) models [11], Marvin Minsky's "society of mind" [13], and the systems of John Holland [7]. Having made these comparisons, I shall attempt to provide an assessment of the contributions of neuronal group selection as they pertain to the study of mind, the practice of science, and the scientific literature.

1.1.1. The fundamental problem

The study of knowledge representation is very much a matter of laying out structural categories, attributes, and relationships in terms of which we may describe the world around us. However, Edelman feels it is very important to be aware that while such artifacts are important to any *representation* of knowledge, they should not be assumed to be *inherent* elements of the world being modeled:[1]

> While the world is not amorphous and the *properties* of objects are describable in terms of chemistry and physics [14], it is clear that, at the macroscopic level, objects do not come in predefined categories, are variable in time, occur as novelties, and are re- sponded to in terms of relative adaptive value to the organism rather than of veridical descriptions. (pp. 259–260)

This lack of predefined categories is a critical problem which Edelman feels must be addressed by any study of neural activity:

> One of the fundamental tasks of the nervous system is to carry on adaptive perceptual categorization in an "unlabeled" world—one in which the macroscopic order and arrangement of objects and events (and even their definition or discrimination) cannot be prefigured for an organism, despite the fact that such objects and events obey the laws of physics. (p. 7)

---

[1]All references in quotations are those of the author being cited.

Thus, neuronal group selection is a result of an attempt "to explain how perceptual categorization could occur without assuming that the world is prearranged in an informational fashion or that the brain contains a homunculus" (p. 4).[2]

Edelman associates these assumptions which he wishes to avoid with what he calls "information processing models" of mind. However, because there have been a variety of approaches to what is now called information processing psychology, it is useful to consider what Edelman regards as the most salient (and, therefore, most susceptible to criticism) features of such models:

> According to information processing models, neural signals from the periphery are *encoded* in a variety of ways and are subsequently transformed by various nuclei and way stations; finally, they are retransformed in a variety of ways by increasingly sophisticated relay systems culminating in cortical processing and output. Perforce, this view puts a very strong emphasis on strict rules for the generation of precise wiring during the development of the brain. Such models strongly rely on neural coding [1] and on the transfer of *information* from one particular neuron to another. This view also makes an assumption about the nature of memory which it considers to occur by representation of events through recording or replication of their informational details. The notion of information processing tends to put a strong emphasis on the ability of the central nervous system to *calculate* the relevant invariances of a physical world. This view culminates in discussions of algorithms and computations, on the assumption that the brain computes in an algorithmic manner [9]. Categories of natural objects in the physical world are implicitly assumed to fall into defined classes or typologies that are accessible to a program. Pushing the notion even further, proponents of certain versions of this model are disposed to consider that the rules and representations [2] that appear to emerge in the realization of syntactical structures and higher semantic functions of language arise from corresponding structures at the neural level. If statistical variation enters at all into such a view of the brain, it is considered in terms of noise in a signal, which in information processing models is taken to be the main manifestation of variation. (p. 38).

[2]From *The Oxford Companion to the Mind*: "The term 'homunculus fallacy' is often used to condemn accounts of psychological processes which are vacuous or circular, because they ascribe to some internal device the very psychological properties which were being investigated in the first place" [3]. In this case the problem is one of claiming that the brain can form categories by virtue of a component (whose specification is not given in any detail—the "homunculus") which "knows" how to form categories.

Edelman bases his rejection of such models on a wide variety of sources of physiological evidence; and that evidence, in turn, becomes a basis for the development of his own model of neuronal group selection.

1.1.2. The three claims

As its name implies, the fundamental principle of Edelman's model is that the brain acquires its abilities for mental activities as a result of *selections* from a vast population of structures which result from the development of the organism. This principle rests on three claims:

(1) This population is an *epigenetic* result of prenatal development. In other words, the neural structure (and, for that matter, the entire morphology) of an organism is not exclusively determined by its genetic repertoire. Instead, events *external* to strictly genetic activity contribute to the development of a diverse population of neural structures. Specific molecular agents, known as *adhesion molecules*, are responsible for determining the course of a morphology and, consequently, the resulting pattern of neural cells which are formed in the course of that morphology; and these molecules are responsible for the formation, during embryonic development, of the population from which selection will take place.

(2) After birth, the neural structure is basically "in place." The focus of development now turns to modifications in the strengths of connections (synapses) between neural cells. Actually, at the time of birth, these cells have already been arranged into the specific structures of "neuronal groups"; so the connections which are modified are between these groups, rather than between specific cells. (Some biologists, such as Young [23], would stress the importance of the roles of individual cells; but, as Rosenfield has observed [18], the experimental evidence which supports this view is questionable.) This initial source of groups is known as the *primary repertoire*, and selection is responsible for the creation of a *secondary repertoire* which will be involved in the subsequent behavior of the organism.

(3) Connections must be established between those groups which are created in the secondary repertoire and those elements of the nervous system which enable an organism to get around in its world, namely the so-called "sensory receptor sheets" and "motor ensembles." These connections are manifested as "maps," which are also products of selection.

We may now see the appropriateness of the name "neural Darwinism." From Edelman's point of view, "the brain is a selective system more akin in its working to evolution than to computation or information processing" (p. 25). This is pretty heady stuff, so it should be no surprise that he requires almost 400 pages of text to make this point. Nevertheless, his effort is an impressive one which offers many striking observations as the argument works its course.

1.1.3. *Perception and activity*

Edelman's book deals with his three claims in the order in which they are presented. However, it is the third claim which first takes the reader into major concerns of mind and intelligence. Once it is established that an appropriate population can be created and that there is a mechanism which will allow selection to take place, one can turn to the *real* question of *what* is going to be selected and for *what reasons*.

What is particularly interesting about Edelman's approach is that *both* sensors and effectors (i.e. motor ensembles) are involved in this process:

> According to the theory of neuronal group selection, the units of action are functional complexes for gestures and postures, the musculoskeletal components of which form a degenerate set. [*Degenerate* groups are fundamental to the theory. They are basically groups which are isofunctional without being isomorphic.] Matching between elements in this set and degenerate reentrant [i.e. interconnected] circuits is considered to be the main basis of patterned action. Gestures, the sets of all coordinated motions that produce a particular pattern, have to confront the same problems of specificity and range as those confronted by sensory signals. In this view, *action is fundamental to perception, and sensory sheets and motor ensembles must operate together to yield a sufficient basis for perceptual categorization* [reviewer's emphasis]. Discrimination of objects occurs (at least initially) by combining feature correlations arising from those sensory signals that are coupled to gestures with the feature extractions arising from the coordinated multimodal responses of sensory sheets. (p. 238)

This point is further elaborated as follows:

> The major and essential contribution of motor ensembles to perception is feature *correlation*, which arises out of the *continuity* properties of motion and the continual focusing of sensory signals by creating postural and gestural movements. As has been suggested by Liberman [10], the correlations of gestures provide essential bases for speech recognition, perhaps the most sophisticated form of perceptual categorization. (pp. 238–239).

This leads to the "phenomenological punch line" which characterizes what constitutes a perceived object:

> During perception, categorization of features correlated continuously by gestures serves to define an equivalent of an object, which is simultaneously related to features extracted by sensory sheets. (p. 239)

1.1.4. *Categorization*

We have now moved into what Edelman regards as the most significant of mental activities: categorization. This activity lies at the heart of the initial fundamental problem: how does the mind impose structure on a world which has no inherent labels? Categorization is primary to perception and the principal activity which all neuronal population selection is intended to support. As we shall see in Section 1.3, it is also the one activity for which Edelman's theory has been reinforced by an automaton model. In addition, categorization serves to bridge the concerns of perception with those of memory.

1.1.5. *Memory*

The role of categorization leads Edelman to an admittedly radical view of memory as "the enhanced *ability* to categorize or generalize associatively, not the storage of features or attributes of objects as a list" (p. 241). Here are his fundamental points:

(1) The term "memory" is used to designate an operation which is *repeated* in the course of categorization activities of neuronal groups.

(2) Because it is related to neuronal activity, it is also related to perceptual and motor acts.

(3) Categorization is *obligatory* to the occurrence of memory.

(4) Associations are the results of neural events separate from those entailed by this view of memory.

(5) Long-term storage, which is not to be confused with memory, is a result of rules which alter synaptic strengths of neuronal groups associated with maps.

While these views are as radical as Edelman claims them to be, they have also been demonstrated in an impressive computer model which Edelman developed with his colleague George Reeke. This model will be discussed in Section 1.3.

1.1.6. *Learning*

From memory one may proceed to learning. At this point Edelman admits that he is being more speculative than in earlier portions of his book. However, he is still willing to offer the following "minimal model:"

> In this model, learning alters the linkage of global mappings to hedonic centers through synaptic changes in classification couples [interconnected groups], some of which may be species-specific. Such changes yield a categorization of complexes of adaptive value under conditions of expectancy. (p. 293)

Thus, learning is basically categorization on a broader scale concerned with the higher-level (i.e. hedonic) needs of the organism and resulting in synaptic modifications which entail long-term storage.

This completes the summary of the basic ideas which *Neural Darwinism* has to offer. It is now possible to consider how these ideas may impact the study of artificial intelligence. However, that discussion will be preceded by a brief digression concerned with the background behind the theory of neuronal group selection.

1.2. Background

When one is confronted with a bold and revolutionary new view of a subject, it is natural to ask how such ideas came to be. In Edelman's case the ideas have their origin in a discipline which would not appear to be particularly related to any aspect of neuropsychology or neurophysiology. Rather, as reported by Rosenfield, the source of Edelman's ideas was immunology, an area in which he holds a Nobel Prize [17]:

> In 1969 Edelman and his colleagues worked out the complete chemical structure of the antibody molecule, providing the important clue to what structures within the molecule are varied to produce millions of different kinds of antibodies needed to protect the body against foreign organisms. For this work he won the Nobel Prize in 1972 along with the late Rodney Porter of England. Their studies confirmed a theory suggested in the 1950s by MacFarlane Burnet and Niels Jerne that all animals are born with a complete repertoire of antibodies and that intruding bacteria *select* those antibodies that can effectively combat their presence.

Thus, it was the observation that the immune system was operating as a *selective* system which led Edelman to consider that the brain might function in a similar manner. This led to the articulation of the three fundamental claims reviewed in Section 1.1.2. These claims had to address those questions which must be asked of any system whose operation is based on selection:

(1) What is the source of the population within which selection takes place?
(2) How is the operation of selection manifested?
(3) What is the relationship of external events to specific operations of selection?

The major substance of Edelman's book is concerned with the justification of these three claims. In each case he draws extensively on a vast literature of experimental results. Indeed, considering how great a mystery the nervous system is, this book is quite impressive in providing a guide to just how much has been learned, particularly over the last twenty years. In substantiating his own hypotheses, Edelman is obliged to escort his reader through much of the current substance of thought concerned with the mind, not to mention seemingly unrelated topics such as embryonic development. (The discussion of how adhesion molecules contribute to the development of a single feather in a chick embryo is particularly fascinating.)

Thus, Edelman cannot make a convincing argument for his case without spinning out a rather long and elaborate story. Because the story ultimately encompasses such a wide variety of disciplines, there is a danger that the reader might lose the basic path. However, Edelman is well aware of this danger; and, as a result, he does an excellent job of always relating each of his observations, no matter how apparently remote, back to his fundamental claims of neuronal group selection. The journey through this book is an arduous one. Nevertheless, Edelman begins with a clear description of where he is going; and at the end of the journey the reader can look back and see that he has been exactly where Edelman promised to take him.

1.3. Results related to artificial intelligence

From the beginning of this book, it is clear that Edelman takes a rather dim view of approaches to mind which are based on information processing. The main source of what he calls "the crises of information processing" (p. 43) is the problem of the homunculus cited in Section 1.1.1. Since the world is not based on some inherent system of labels, it is unreasonable to consider any model of thought which requires the imposition of such labels as a precondition, since then one has to ask how those labels are imposed. If the sourse of such labels can only be explained in terms of a component agent which ultimately must exhibit the very thought processes being modeled (i.e. a homunculus [3], composed, perhaps, of Daniel Dennett's "wonder tissue" [4]), then the original model of thought is evading the question rather than answering it.

Edelman also rejects what he calls "the computationalism of Marr: . . . the idea that the nervous system computes a function" (p. 235). His argument is basically one of recognizing that the cart belongs *behind*, rather than *before* the horse:

> The selective behavior of ensembles or neuronal groups may be *describable* by certain mathematical functions; it is clear, for example, that the physical properties of receptors can be so described. But it seems as unlikely that a collection of neurons carries out the computation of an algorithm as that interacting lions and antelopes compute Lotka-Volterra equations. (p. 235)

(Edelman is certainly to be praised for the selection of vivid examples as a means to make his points.) In other words, it is perfectly acceptable to view algorithms or mathematical functions as *post hoc* explanations of the behavior of the nervous system. The "computationalism" which Edelman rejects is the thesis that such functions serve as *propter hoc* specifications of the architecture of that system, just as the Lotka–Volterra equations are not specifications of interactions between lions and antelopes. Thus, Edelman's major concern is with those *casual factors* which give rise to neural behavior, as opposed to abstractions which facilitate the description of that behavior.

In spite of this basically negative attitude towards information processing, Edelman nevertheless has an appreciation for the value of automata as models. Thus, a key element of his exposition is the discussion of a "recognition automaton" (p. 8) which is capable of performing elementary tasks of categorization on a limited input of two-dimensional figures. (In spite of the aforementioned emphasis on the need to integrate both perceptual and motor functions with neuronal group selection, this automaton has no motor element. It is intended only as a first cut at an abstraction of how the process of selection may contribute to categorization.)

The automaton (which has been simulated in software) is called Darwin II; and it is built from two interconnected (what Edelman calls "reentrant") components. The first component, called Darwin, is concerned with explicit recall of images. In other words selection takes place in such a way that the repetition of an input stimulus will encourage the activity of the same neuronal groups. The second component, called Wallace, is concerned with recall of certain properties which may be shared by many different images (such as, for example, topological properties). The interconnection of these two components allows for the association of such properties with a specific stimulus.

The two components were initially tested separately. Thus, Darwin was first tested for its powers of exact recall. Each figure presented as an input would entail some initial pattern of neural activity. If the figure reappeared, the activity would also reappear and be reinforced. Wallace, on the other hand, was capable of exhibiting similar responses to figures which were similar without being identical, such as two versions of the letter A: one tall and thin, the other short and squat.

When Darwin and Wallace were interconnected, the resulting behavior became more interesting. The test figures used for this experiment were an × and a +. These characters were markedly different as far as Darwin was concerned but recognized as topologically similar by Wallace. As a result, presentation of an × would provoke the activity of a set of simulated neuronal groups. However, when the stimulus was removed, the decay of that activity would be accompanied by a rise in the activity of those groups associated with Darwin's "recall" of the +. The claim was that Darwin II had acquired the knowledge of a category which included both × and + through no influence other than the presentation of the stimuli and resulting activities of selection.

There are a variety of specific questions about Darwin II which are not addressed in this book, and they should not be overlooked. Most importantly, what is the basis for the generation of the population of neuronal groups within which selection took place? Darwin and Wallace are clearly endowed with "feature detecting" groups in their initial populations. However, there is no indication as to how broad these populations are or how they were created for the purposes of the experiments conducted. There is also the question of the generality of the possibilities for interconnection (reentry) in the experimental definition of Darwin II. It is always valuable to see the *positive* side of the behavior of an experiment, but it would also have been useful to get a sense of some of the *negative* influence of *rejection* resulting from the selective process. Otherwise, one might accuse Darwin II of being biased with regard to possible alternatives for either the features which may be detected or for the connections which may be established among those features, biases which would ultimately embody the very homunculus Edelman has been trying to avoid. Another issue of negative influence amounts to a null hypothesis: How would Darwin II behave if presented with an intentionally random set of stimuli? (I am thankful to Paul Mockapetris for this observation.) Would the general activity of all neuronal groups remain low; or would Darwin II begin to "hallucinate" associations among its stimuli?

One assumes that the details of Darwin II were omitted for lack of space. This book gives a broad view of a rather complex subject, and it is probably unreasonable to expect a discussion of all the details regarding the design and implementation of this one experiment. In spite of this omission, there is a general thoroughness in Edelman's approach to his subject matter which leaves one with a sense of confidence in his work. One is willing to assume that experimental detail would, in this case, reveal that the process of selection which is the basis of Edelman's theory was, indeed, being validly demonstrated by his experiments with Darwin II. For example, one of Edelman's earlier papers [5] addresses specific questions concerned with the population of neuronal groups and connections which are involved in the Darwin component.

While the scope of Darwin II is extremely modest—16×16 digitizations of a simple character set [15]—it is still sufficient to indicate the means by which selective neural mechanisms may serve as the *cause* of the formation of categories. It also supports the *dynamic* view of memory cited in Section 1.1.5. Much remains to be investigated, including a more realistic set of perceptual stimuli, the relationship of those stimuli to motor ensembles, and Edelman's "minimal model" of learning reviewed in Section 1.1.6. However, the apprehension of categories without presuming their a priori existence is fundamental to Edelman's approach to such investigations; and Darwin II has served to demonstrate how such apprehension can take place.

2. Relation to Other Areas in Artificial Intelligence

2.1. Parallel distributed processing

Edelman is certainly not alone in his experiments with Darwin II as an exploration of what might be called "neural computing." At present probably the major source of attention is the so-called "connectionist" work which has built on previous research on perceptrons [16] and has evolved into various networks of "parallel distributed processes" [11]. Edelman makes it clear that he is aware of this work, but his major criticism is that it has not confronted the problem of the homunculus. In particular the networks explored by such research are based on what Edelman calls "a priori semantic conventions or assumptions in establishing the categories that lead to adaptive or memorial responses" (p. 290).

2.2. Society of mind

Edelman does not seem to be aware of Marvin Minsky's "society of mind" research. His only citation of Minsky is that of his analysis of perceptrons with Seymour Papert [12] and then only to observe that reentry "vitiates the limitations described by Minsky and Papert" (p. 289) in their study. However, there would appear to be a basis for what Wittgenstein [22] probably would have called a "family resemblance" between Edelman's work and Minsky's more recent investigations. This should not be surprising when one recognizes that Minsky has been devoting more of his recent attention to results specifically concerned with the behavior of the brain.

At the heart of this family resemblance is Minsky's desire to give *dispositions* a higher priority than *propositions* [13]:

> In this modern era of "information processing psychology" it may seem quaint to talk of mental states; it is more fashionable to speak of representations, frames, scripts, or semantic networks. But while I find it lucid enough to speak in such terms about memories of things, sentences, or even faces, it is much harder so to deal with feelings, insights, and understandings—and all the attitudes, dispositions, and ways of seeing things that go with them. . . . We usually put such issues aside, saying that one must first understand simpler things. But what if feelings and viewpoints are the simpler things? If such dispositions are the elements of which the others are composed, then we must deal with them directly. So we shall view memories as entities that predispose the mind to deal with new situations in old, remembered ways—specifically, as entities that reset the states of parts of the nervous system. Then they can cause

that nervous system to be "disposed" to behave as though it remembers. This is why I put "dispositions" ahead of "propositions."

This emphasis on the creation and recall of dispositions is very similar to the outline Edelman provides in his initial discussion of what learning is and how it takes place (p. 293).

The major differences between Minsky and Edelman would appear to be over matters of specific mechanisms. For Minsky, dispositions are recalled as a result of the *creation* of "K-nodes" and the connections associated with respective "K-lines," while Edelman would reject the idea of any such agent being created. Rather, he argues that only an initial population of alternatives is created and that all subsequent activity is *selective*. Also, Minsky introduces his "Level-band principle" as a means of confining the influence of a given K-node. Edelman and Reeke, on the other hand, place more emphasis on the redundancy provided by degeneracy as a means to guard against any individual agent having too far-reaching an effect. In fairness to Minsky, however, it should be noted that, unlike Edelman, he has not tried to address the implementation of his theory at the neural level [13]:

> Not enough is known about the nervous system to justify proposing specific details. In our references to brains our intention is to suggest that it might be useful to consider architectural hypotheses compatible with the general ideas of the society of mind approach.

What is more important is that the general theme of Minsky's approach seems very much in sympathy with neural Darwinism, so that the study of mind might well benefit from a synthesis of these two viewpoints.

2.3. Holland's classifiers

Another approach to selection has been taken by John Holland in his work on classification systems [7]. Holland's work is based on an attempt to impose rules of "survival of the fittest" on an ensemble of simple productions. This ensemble is further enhanced by rules which "implement" processes of genetic crossover and mutation on the productions in the population. Thus, productions which survive a process of selection are not only applied but also used as "parents" in the synthesis of new productions.

Edelman does not acknowledge Holland's work. However, one suspects that he would accuse Holland of being as much a victim of the homunculus as are the connectionists. In Holland's case an external agent is still required to lay out the basic architecture of those productions upon which both selective and genetic operations are performed. Thus, while it would appear that Holland's classification systems do not require any explicit prior knowledge of the categories to be identified, closer inspection of their implementation reveals that this knowledge is very much implicit in the structure of the productions. In other words, the very "genes" of Holland's systems must be built with *a priori* categorical knowledge before they can exhibit any viable performance. Indeed, Holland's "genes" may be viewed as a possible approach to that neural level implementation of rules and representations which Edelman rejects (on the basis of physiological evidence) in information processing models (Section 1.1.1).

3. Lessons to Be Learned

3.1. Regarding the study of mind

Perhaps the most important lesson to be learned from this book is an appreciation of the problem of categorization and the breadth of the gulf which separates any results in artificial intelligence from the "real world:"

> When we consider the world, there is no given semantic order: an animal must not only identify and classify things but also decide what to do in the absence of prior detailed descriptive programs, with the exception, of course, of certain fixed programs [8] handed down by evolution. This point deserves emphasis, because it is central to all other considerations: in some sense, the problem of perception is initially a problem of taxonomy in which the individual animal must "classify" the things of its world. Whatever solutions to this problem are adopted by an individual organism, they must be framed within that organism's ecological niche and for its own adaptive advantage. In other words, the internal taxonomy of perception is adaptive but is not necessarily veridical in the sense that it is concordant with the descriptions of physics [21].
>
> From the standpoint of the adapting organism, the categorization of things is relative and depends upon cues, context, and salience [20]. Categories are not immutable but depend upon the present state of the organism, which in turn is a function of memory and behavioral "set." At the macroscopic level, such categories are not general in the sense that a quantum description of particles is general. Animals can nonetheless *generalize*; that is, an individual organism can encounter a few instances of a category under learning conditions and then recognize a very great number of related but novel instances [6]. This ability of individuals in a species to categorize novel objects in classes is a stunning reflection of what might be called the idiosyncratic (i.e., self-adaptive) generalizing power of neural networks. (pp. 26–27)

It is because of this situation that Edelman feels it is necessary to reject what he calls "information processing models" of mind, as summarized in Section 1.1.1:

> The context-driven character of perceptual categorization and the capacity to generalize from a few learned examples together strongly challenge any logic-based or "information-driven" explanation of the data. The very same object can be classified differently at different times, and an animal may use different means to classify that object at different times. (p. 30)

Neuronal group selection has been presented by Edelman as a means to confront these difficulties, and it thus provides us with a new way to view the mind.

Because the study of mind has often provoked rather fierce confrontations between the scientific community and those who have been more concerned with philosophical issues, it is also worth citing the following observation by Rosenfield [17]:

> Each person according to his [Edelman's] theory is unique: his or her perceptions are to some degree creations and his or her memories are part of an ongoing process of imagination. A mental life cannot be reduced to molecules. Human intelligence is not just knowing more, but reworking, recategorizing, and thus generalizing information in new and surprising ways. It could be that inappropriate categorizations from damaged maps may cause psychoses, just as the inability to correlate the succession of objects or events in time may be largely responsible for the loss of specific memories . . . .

> Of course, language is acquired in society, but our ability to use it, to constantly reconceive the world around us, is at least in part a reflection of the multiple mappings and remappings that appear to be central to brain function. Such a view reinforces the idea that no two brains can be, or ever will be, alike. Edelman's theory of neuronal group selection challenges those who claim that science views individual human beings and other animals as reproducible machines and that science is little concerned with the unqiue attributes of individuals and the sources of that uniqueness. Humanism never had a better defense.

3.2. Regarding scientific activity

In many ways this book may be regarded as a model account of scientific research. It has tackled an extremely hard problem and addressed means by which that problem can be broken down into separately manageable components. Each component is considered in the context of a thorough understanding of the existing scientific literature, and where such knowledge is not available it becomes a basis for the execution of new experiments.

However, after Edelman has completed the erection of his entire structure, he still knows enough to recognize that all he has built is a *theory*. He thus concludes with a discussion of what he feels are the most essential components of that theory. This final review is meant to emphasize the fact that if subsequent findings would lead to the falsification of any one of those components, then it would be necessary to call the entire theory into question. Such a combination of reality and humility tends to be rare in a scientific community which is often driven more by the quest for funding than the quest for knowledge. As such, it is good to be reminded that many of the ideals we like to entertain about scientific method can still be respected.

3.3. Regarding writing about science

Regardless of its scientific content, it is important to remember that *Neural Darwinism* is a book to be *read*. In this respect Edelman deserves as much praise as a scientific writer as he merits as a researcher. I must confess that this book was very hard going, due to my unfamiliarity with much of the "world view" of the study of the brain and nervous system. As a result I was significantly impressed with Edelman's efforts to make my journey through his book an endurable (if not always pleasant) one. The reader is constantly provided with valuable milestones: reminders of where one has been, where one is now heading, and why one is going there.

Above all, this book is a model of clear writing. One would like to assume that such clarity of communication is a consequence of clarity of understanding. Edelman has been occupied with this work for quite some time, so that he has built up his own internal vision of what he is doing and why he is doing it. This vision appears to be very well-formed and thought through in its many ramifications and repercussions. Such depth of understanding reveals itself in Edelman's ability to take all the complexity of this subject and offer it up in a book which can impart some sizable portion of that understanding to the reader. Such excellence does not come around very often, and it deserves to be appreciated by all who share this author's interest in his domain of investigation.

REFERENCES

1. Bullock, T.H., Signals and neuronal coding, in: G.C. Quarton, T. Melnechuk and F.O. Schmitt (Eds.), *The Neurosciences: A Study Program* (Rockefeller University Press, New York, 1967) 347–352.
2. Chomsky, N., *Rules and Representations* (Columbia University Press, New York, 1980).

3. Cottingham, J.G., Homunculus, in: R.L. Gregory (Ed.), *The Oxford Companion to the Mind* (Oxford University Press, New York, 1987) 313.
4. Dennett, D.C., Cognitive wheels: The frame problem of AI, in: Z.W. Pylyshyn (Ed.), *The Robot's Dilemma: The Frame Problem in Artificial Intelligence* (Ablex, Norwood, NJ, 1987) 41–64.
5. Edelman, G.M., Group selection as the basis for higher brain function, in: F.O. Schmitt et al. (Eds.), *Organization of the Cerebral Cortex* (MIT Press, Cambridge, MA, 1981) 536–563.
6. Herrnstein, R.J., Stimuli and the texture of experience, *Neurosci. Biobehavioral Rev.* **6** (1982) 105–117.
7. Holland, J. H. et al., *Induction: Processes of Inference, Learning, and Discovery* (MIT Press, Cambridge, MA, 1986).
8. Marler, P. and Terrace, H.S. (Eds.), *The Biology of Learning* (Springer, Berlin, 1984).
9. Marr, D., *Vision: A Computational Investigation into the Human Representation and Processing of Visual Information* (Freeman, San Francisco, CA, 1982).
10. Mattingly, I.G. and Liberman, A.M., Specialized perceiving systems for speech and other biologically significant sounds, in: G.M. Edelman, W.E. Gall and W.M. Cowan (Eds.), *Functions of the Auditory System* (Wiley, New York, 1987).
11. McClelland, J.L., Rumelhart, D.E. and Hinton, G.E., The appeal of parallel distributed processing, in: J.L. McClelland and D.E. Rumelhart (Eds.), *Parallel Distributed Processing: Explorations in the Microstructure of Cognition*, Computational Models of Cognition and Perception **1** (MIT Press, Cambridge, MA, 1986) 3–44.
12. Minsky, M. and Papert, S., *Perceptrons: An Introduction to Computational Geometry* (MIT Press, Cambridge, MA 1969).
13. Minsky, M., K-lines: A theory of memory, *Cognitive Sci.* **4** (1980) 117–133.
14. Pantin, C.F.A., *The Relations between the Sciences* (Cambridge University Press, Cambridge, England, 1968).
15. Reeke, G.N., Jr and Edelman, G.M., Selective networks and recognition automata, *Annals New York Academy of Sciences* **426** (1984) 181–201.
16. Rosenblatt, F., *Principles of Neurodynamics* (Spartan, New York, 1959).
17. Rosenfield, I., Neural Darwinism: A new approach to memory and perception, *The New York Rev.* **33** (15) (October 9, 1986) 21–27.
18. Rosenfield, I., Reply to letters to the editor, *The New York Rev.* **34** (4) (March 12, 1987) 45.
19. Rosenfield, I., *The Invention of Memory: A New View of the Brain* (Basic Books, New York, 1988).
20. Staddon, J.E.R., *Adaptive Behavior and Learning* (Cambridge University Press, Cambridge, England, 1983).
21. Vernon, M.D., *A Further Study of Visual Perception* (Hafner, Darien, CT, 1970).
22. Wittgenstein, L. *Philosophical Investigations* (Basil Blackwell, Oxford, England, 1974); Translated by G.E.M. Anscombe.
23. Young J.Z., Letter to the editors, *The New York Rev.* **34** (4) (March 12, 1987) 44.

Artificial Intelligence 52 (1991) 295–318
Elsevier

Gerald M. Edelman, *The Remembered Present: A Biological Theory of Consciousness**

Stephen W. Smoliar

5000 Centinela Avenue #129, Los Angeles, CA 90066, USA

Received March 1991

1. Background

In his pioneering essay on artificial intelligence [28], Alan Turing began by explicitly posing the question, "Can machines think?" Implicit in this question was the assumption that he was interested in a specific form of *behavior* and the issue of whether such behavior, normally associated with human beings, might also be associated with machines. Turing's original research was concerned with computation as a form of machine behavior [29], although the machine he considered in those studies was purely imaginary. Nevertheless, he felt compelled to consider the extent to which *computational* behavior might be broad enough to encompass *intelligent* behavior; and he was able to sketch out some initial steps concerned with how that goal might be achieved.

By beginning with the study of an imaginary machine, Turing could also assume that behavior did not necessarily require any *physical* basis. Thus, one could talk about the behavior of computing a sum without resorting to a need to account for such physical skills as making marks on a piece of paper or pressing buttons on a calculator. In extrapolating this assumption to the behavior of thought, Turing essentially embraced René Descartes's dualist assumption of the separation of mind and body [5]. As far as Turing was

---

* (Basic Books, New York, 1989); xxi + 346 pages.

concerned, one could study thought independently of any concerns for the body doing the thinking.

In his recent research on the brain, Gerald Edelman has chosen to reject this Cartesian position. His study of mind has been founded on the assumption that "all cognition and all consciousness must rest on orderings and processes in the physical world" (p. 10).[1] His initial arguments for making this assumption and supporting results were published in 1987 in his book *Neural Darwinism: The Theory of Neuronal Group Selection* [7].

The baseline for Edelman's investigations is a list of twelve cognitive science issues drawn up by Donald Norman [18]: belief systems, consciousness, development, emotion, interaction, language, learning, memory, primary perception, performance, skill, and thought. Edelman used this list as a basis for his introduction to *Neural Darwinism* [7]:

> The key list I shall consider is: development, perception (in particular, perceptual categorization), memory, and learning, and I will take up these subjects in that order. My hope is that once a constrained theory adequate to link these processes is built, it may become possible to construct a more comprehensive description, not just in terms of perceptual categorization but also in terms of perceptual experience.

This quotation not only summarizes *Neural Darwinism* but also serves as a forecast for *The Remembered Present*, Edelman's latest book and the subject of this review.

In order to consider Edelman's most recent work, it is first necessary to provide a context. Thus, this review will begin with a summary of Edelman's theory of neuronal group selection and a brief survey of the achievements documented in *Neural Darwinism*. This will provide a basis for Edelman's own characterization of his "unfinished business". The developments reported in *The Remembered Present* will be presented with respect to seven topics: memory, ordering, concepts, "presyntax", primary consciousness, language, and higher-order consciousness. This work will then be compared with related developments, concluding with some remarks on its relevance to the practice of artificial intelligence.

1.1. The theory of neuronal group selection and its promises

The operant word in the theory of neutonal group selection (TNGS) is "selection". Edelman's work may be viewed as a reaction to physiological studies which have attached too much importance to attempting to analyze behavior in terms of the activities of individual cells. Because the results of

---

[1] All page references are from the book under review.

these attempts have not been particularly promising, Edelman has explored the alternative of choosing cell *populations* as the proper object of study. According to this approach, we should not try to establish an analogy between brain and computer which descends to the point of assuming that each neural cell is like a transistor in some elaborate digital architecture. The secrets of the behavior of the brain lie not in trying to isolate functions of individual cells and determining their lines of communication through connections but in looking for generalities in the behavior of what Edelman calls "neuronal groups". The resulting theory is expressed in terms of proposals for three mechanisms known as *developmental selection, experiential selection,* and *reentrant mapping* [23].

The first proposal invokes selection as the mechanism which leads to the "wiring" of the neurons in the brain:

> During development, dynamic processes of morphogenesis lead selectively to the formation of anatomy specific for a species but *obligatorily* possessing enormous anatomical variation at its finest levels and ramifications. A population of groups of neurons in a given brain region, consisting of variant neural networks arising by such processes of somatic selection, is known as a primary repertoire. (p. 242)

In other words each individual organism arrives at a neural architecture as a result of selective processes which occur during the fetal development of its brain. Information in the genetic code does not provide a specific "wiring diagram" but simply allows for the creation of a space of options within which such selection will take place. Consequently, at the level of neurons, it is very unlikely that any two individuals will be identically wired, *even if they are clones of the same genetic code*.

While the first proposal is concerned with prenatal development, the second proposes another selective process which is engaged after birth:

> During behavior, and as a result of neural signaling, a second means of selection occurs—without alteration of anatomy, various synaptic connections are selectively strengthened or weakened to give a secondary repertoire consisting of variant functioning neural circuits. (p. 242)

Thus, while all connections are established before birth, the *strengths* of these connections are only determined by selective mechanisms which are engaged once the organism is born and starts behaving in its world. It is through this secondary repertoire that neural circuits are engaged to deal with managing the body's sensors and effectors.

The final proposal concerns the development of a "high-level architecture" built upon this secondary repertoire:

As a result of evolution and through interaction between sensory and motor systems, many of these repertoires are arranged in maps. Such maps are connected by parallel and reciprocal connections that provide the basis of the third tenet of the theory—the occurrence of reentrant signaling. As a result of input from the environment and phasic reentrant signaling during behavior, some groups in local maps are competitively selected over others. (pp. 242–243)

Maps are established through the strengths of connections between different groups of elements in the secondary repertoire. They are the basis for associations; and they, themselves, may be subject to complex patterns of interconnection (reentrant signaling).

The fundamental promise of the TNGS is that such strengthening of connections among these maps by selective means ultimately accounts for behavior at levels which we can observe. In other words these maps serve as a "bridge" between the *physiological* and the *psychological*. Given the scope of cognitive psychology, at least as outlined by Norman, that bridge is going to have to be rather complex. Consequently, within *Neural Darwinism* Edelman confined the bulk of his attention to perceptual categorization, offering some initial suggestions for how memory and learning might also be accommodated.

1.2. The achievements of Neural Darwinism

The investigation of perceptual categorization reported in *Neural Darwinism* is based on two premises: the lack of any a priori set of labels for categories and the lack of a unique "wiring diagram" for the brain doing the categorization. While the reference to Darwin is clearly meant to reflect an emphasis on selection, the actual *process* of selection is rather different from those mechanisms which have been considered in evolution:

> Experiential selection does not, like natural selection in evolution, occur as a result of differential *reproduction*, but rather as a result of differential *amplification* of certain synaptic populations. The rules that govern the pre- and postsynaptic changes in experiential selection do not, however, act to convey information from a single presynaptic neuron to a single postsynaptic neuron as in the Hebb rule [11]. Instead, they act heterosynaptically [9] on neuronal groups and thus act on *populations* of neurons. This activity involves statistical signal correlations rather than the carriage of coded messages. (p. 46)

To demonstrate how such selection may lead to perceptual categorization, Edelman and his colleagues have developed a series of "Darwin automata" which can perform such categorization. The most compelling presentation in *Neural Darwinism* is of their Darwin II automaton, whose neuronal groups are organized into three interconnected networks, labeled R, R of R, and R_M. This is illustrated in Fig. 1. R and R of R together constitute the "Darwin" network, while R_M and its inputs which pre-process the visual array form the "Wallace" network.

Each neuronal group in R consists of a set of local feature detectors responding to the "cells" in the input array. Thus, each group is somewhat like a miniature version of a single layer of one of Frank Rosenblatt's perceptrons [24]. However, while Rosenblatt's units were essentially modules of threshold logic with binary output, each neuronal group responds with a level of activation which varies over time.

Just as the neuronal groups of R respond to activity in the input array, the neuronal groups of R of R respond to samples of randomly selected combinations of monitored activity in R. As such, R of R may be said to represent "features of the feature detectors". This would correspond to a second "layer" in a Rosenblatt perceptron. R of R is also distinguished in that, while all connections in R are excitatory, R of R incorporates both excitatory and inhibitory connections [23].

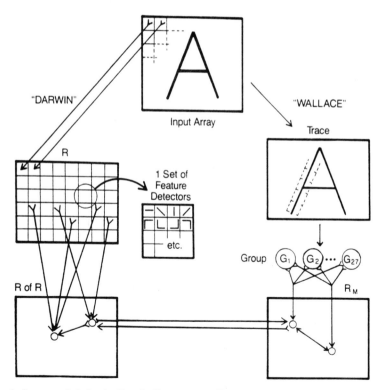

Fig. 1. Image analysis by the Darwin II automaton. (Reproduced, with permission, from [22].)

On the Wallace side the visual input is pre-processed by a computer program, called TRACE [23], which detects and traces contours. This program is thus capable of responding to a variety of topological properties which are encoded in twenty-seven "virtual" groups which provide the inputs to R_M. Edelman calls these groups "virtual" because "their input does not involve ordinary synaptic connections but is instead connected to a computer simulation of the scanning and tracing function" [7]. Thus, the number "27" has no physiological significance but is simply a consequence of a simulation which was required in order to implement Darwin II. Each neuronal group in R_M then responds to the activities of these "virtual" groups with its own activation pattern.

The primary distinction between this Darwin automaton and a perceptron is the cross-coupling between R of R and R_M. Thus, the activity of a neuronal group in R of R may be determined not only by the activities of feature detectors in R but also by the activities of groups in R_M; and the dual situation holds for those groups in R_M. This is an example of what Edelman calls reentry, and the result is an automaton which can respond to a synthesis of both local and global topological features of an input image.

The behavior of this automaton is studied by observing the variation in time of the levels of activation of its individual neuronal groups. *Neural Darwinism* illustrates this with graphs of these activation levels for twenty-two neuronal groups in R of R for sixteen cycles of operation of the automata. Two input stimuli are considered: an X and a +. In each case the stimulus is displayed for the first four cycles of the experiment and then removed. In both cases a pattern of activity which is established during those four cycles continues after the image has been taken away. Thus, this pattern of response may be said to constitute a *memory trace* of the stimulus. However, the reentrant connections between R of R and R_M provide additional behavior. Because X and + have similar topological properties, they tend to induce similar patterns of activation among the neuronal groups of R_M. These activation patterns in R_M are further reinforced by connections from the groups which are active in R of R. However, connections in the *opposite* direction (that is, based on activity in R_M) serve to *induce* activity in R of R. Thus, after the X stimulus is removed, the activity of the groups which responded to it is supplemented by emergent activity of some of the groups which respond to +. In other words *recognition* of the X leads to subsequent *recall* of the +. Thus, on the one hand, the X and the + are recognized as different input stimuli; but after the immediate response to the stimuli, subsequent processing reveals evidence that they are members of a common category.

Substantial progress has been made on the development of Darwin automata since the work reported in *Neural Darwinism*. Chapter 3 of *The Remembered Present* includes a discussion of Darwin III, which differs from Darwin II both by being able to move its eye and through control of a four-jointed arm which is used for both feeling and moving objects. Thus, the output of Darwin III involves the exhibition of *observable behavior* in the movements of both the eye and the arm. Unlike Darwin II, the success of Darwin III can be demonstrated by what it does, as opposed to what one observes in the activation levels of its component neuronal groups. However, like Darwin II, Darwin III exists only at the level of a computer simulation, a rather thorough discussion of which has just been published [23].

Such experiments with Darwin automata demonstrate the contribution of the secondary repertoire and reentrant connections to the task of perceptual categorization. One might claim that reentry is nothing more than the sort of feedback one encounters in control theory. Edelman and his colleagues have responded to this claim as follows:

> Reentry is inherently parallel and involves *populations* of inter-connected units, whereas feedback involves the recursion of a single scalar variable. Reentry is distributed, that is, each area simulta-neously reenters to many other areas (note that reentry can occur between areas at the *same* heterarchical level as well as between higher and lower levels in a system). Reentry has a statistical nature inasmuch as not all connections are used at all times. Finally . . . reentry can give rise to the construction of novel operations, and is used more for correlation than for error correction or gain control [23].

1.3. Unfinished business

An agent that performs perceptual categorization need not necessarily be said to have a mind. As far as Edelman is concerned, if we are going to try to take on this latter quality, we have to approach it through consciousness. Thus, consciousness is the focus of his new book; and in his Preface, he sets out his goals:

> To qualify as a scientific account, a theoretical analysis of con-sciousness must achieve four goals: (1) propose explicit *neural* models that explain how consciousness can arise; (2) relate these models to the emergence of consciousness during evolution and development; (3) relate these models to concept formation, mem-ory, and language; and (4) describe stringent tests for the models in terms of known neurobiological facts, at least in the form of gedankenexperiments, if not ones that can be carried out directly on known living organisms. (pp. xviii–xix)

These are ambitious goals, particularly in light of the lack of any accepted consensus regarding the meaning of the term "consciousness". Nevertheless, Edelman argues that he can tease out an acceptable meaning for this controversial term and meet his goals at the same time—all by building on his TNGS. Furthermore, he proposes to do all this through a three-stage process:

> The TNGS must . . . first be extended to account for temporal succession or sequence. An explicit model must then be built to show that consciousness is a special property emerging from systems of memory and ongoing perceptual categorization. Finally, to account for higher-order consciousness, a brain-based theory of concept formation must be tied to a similarly based account of language and its forerunners. (p. 11)

This proposal may then serve as the outline for the rest of the book.

Actually, Edelman is both more specific and more confident in preparing the reader for what is to come. In his second chapter he provides the following rather impressive list of how the TNGS must be extended, complete with a road map which associates each extension with appropriate subsequent reading:

> The extended theory must do the following:
> 1. account for consciousness both as a product of evolution and in terms of morphology (all chapters)
> 2. account for the various forms of consciousness as processes explainable in terms of certain activities of the brain (all chapters)
> 3. show how consciousness may emerge in the course of individual development, accounting for the transition from primary consciousness in biologically defined individuals to higher-order consciousness in individuals with a concept of self (chapters 9 through 11)
> 4. account for its individual character in animals or its subjective character in humans (chapters 9, 11, 12, and 15)
> 5. account for its continuity as well as its changeability (chapters 7 and 11 to 13)
> 6. account for its dealing with objects independent of itself (intentionality) (chapters 3 to 5, 8, and 12)
> 7. account for its role in the ordering of subjective experiences (chapters 7, 11, 12, and 14)
> 8. account for its selectivity and its relation to attention and salience (chapters 3, 4, and 12)
> 9. account for the efficacy of consciousness in regulating behavior and actions and for its capacity (in humans) to regulate itself in

terms of direct awareness ("metacognition") (chapters 11 and 12)

10. account for its dependency on the activities of multiple parallel brain regions, activities that themselves can never become accessible to conscious awareness (chapters 3, 4, 7, 8, 12, and 13)

11. account for the failure to be conscious of signals in specific modalities or of memory after certain brain lesions, even though tests of performance indicate successful processing of the same signals or of memory in these modalities (this chapter and chapter 13)

12. account for the existence of unconscious states that can be called up to awareness, as well as the dissociability of constructs of the self (hysteria, "multiple personalities", etc.) (chapters 12 and 13)

13. account for the various forms of consciousness—for example, those that emerge in relation to immediate perception, to images, and to the onset of linguistic capabilities (chapters 5, 6, and 9 through 11)

14. account for the discriminability of various kinds of phenomenal experience (qualia) (this chapter and chapters 9, 11, and 15)

15. relate certain diseases of consciousness, such as schizophrenia, to the theory (chapter 13)

16. relate the premises of the theory to those sciences that have no need for its explicit descriptions, as well as to scientific heuristics and to various philosophical concerns (chapters 14 and 15) (pp. 18–19)

This is the writing of a self-assured and organized man. When one gets to the end of the book, one may look back on this list; and while there may be several grounds for questioning Edelman's confidence on some of these points, he has certainly been true to his organization. Without that organization the reader is too likely to be drowned by the magnitude of all these issues. Thus, Edelman, himself, has managed to give the reader enough orientation to pull together any thoughts which may ultimately bear on questioning the conclusions of this book.

Pursuing the sixteen promises in the above list is thus a great adventure. Obviously, this review cannot share all of that adventure. Instead, it will focus on six key "islands" which Edelman employs to construct a causeway from the capabilities of his Darwin automata to the consciousness of intelligent beings. These islands are memory, ordering, concepts, "presyntax", primary consciousness, and language. This review will now visit each of these islands and finally bring the reader to Edelman's conclusions about higher-order consciousness.

2. The achievements of this book

2.1. Memory

Experiments with the Darwin automata revealed a form of behavior which could reasonably be called "memory traces". However, it is important to observe that these traces emerge from the *dynamics* of the automaton, rather than any *static* properties:

> According to the TNGS, memory in global mappings is not a store of fixed or coded attributes to be called up and assembled in a replicative fashion as in a computer [7]. Instead, memory results from a process of continual recategorization, which, by its nature, must be procedural and involve continual motor activity and repeated rehearsal. Because of new associations occurring in different contexts, changing inputs, and the degeneracy [redundancy] of the neuronal group selection, a given categorical response in memory can be achieved dynamically in various ways. (p. 56)

Thus, the memory of a Darwin automaton cannot be represented in terms of any static configuration of bits. The dynamics of recategorization should be sufficient to allow for any sort of introspection upon a recalled object, such as might be required in having to describe that object to another agent. However, such tasks require powers of consciousness which are only developed towards the end of Edelman's book. For example, introspection upon a recalled image is a major feature of what Edelman calls "primary consciousness", while the description of such an image is accommodated by his approach to language. What is important in understanding the initial contribution of the TNGS is the recognition that what a Darwin automaton "remembers" may only be studied with respect to *how it behaves*.

Viewing memory in terms of *re*categorization emphasizes the dynamics of the situation:

> Recall, under the influence of constantly changing contexts, changes the structure and dynamics of the neural populations that were involved in the original categorization. Recall is the activation of previously facilitated portions of particular global mappings. Such recall can result in a *response* similar to a previously given response ("a memory"), but generally it is one that has been altered or enriched by ongoing changes. (pp. 110–111)

In other words one can only model memory if one models the entire system within which it functions. Darwin II is a simple example of such a system, but it must be extended to encompass the flow of information through a broader range of both sensors and effectors. The first steps in this direction were taken in the development of Darwin III.

Where, then, does learning fit in this picture? Is it just a matter of altering system dynamics in such a way that an outside observer would say that memory has been increased? As far as Edelman is concerned, the situation is not quite that simplistic:

> Perceptual categorization and memory are therefore considered to be necessary for learning but obviously are not sufficient for it. The sufficient condition is provided by the synaptic linkage of particular global mappings to the activity of hedonic centers and to the limbic system in a fashion that will satisfy homeostatic, appetitive, and consummatory needs. (p. 57)

In other words learning is a consequence of interactions between the dynamics of memory and those of the pleasure–pain responses of the limbic system. Edelman summarizes the situation in a neat aphorism: "values constrain behavior, action modulates it, and memory alters it and is altered in turn" (p. 251). This recapitulates his emphasis on the need to study dynamic, rather than static, properties of mind.

2.2. Ordering

Any model of memory implicitly carries with it assumptions about time. One cannot reason about one's memories without recognizing that they are associated with a *past* which is distinct from the *present*. It is this relationship between memory and time-consciousness which has inspired the title of Edelman's new book:

> One of the capabilities essential to the emergence of consciousness is that of recategorical memory; equally important is the capability of temporal ordering and succession. It is on these properties that the continual temporal correlation of inner states and the categorization of outer objects rest. Indeed, metaphorically, one might say that the previous memories and current activities of the brain interact to yield primary consciousness as a form of "remembered present". (p. 105)

For Edelman consciousness of time has its origins in succession, and succession is an issue which is introduced when one considers *effectors* as well as *sensors*. In other words if one is to achieve perceptual categorization with respect to motor behavior such categorization must "depend very much upon the succession of joint and muscle responses and of gestures that are, in general, themselves smoothly linked and successive [2]" (p. 119). Such categorization is necessary because, as Edelman demonstrates is supported by biological evidence, the brain deals with *patterns* of movement (in the form of gestures), rather than individual movements.

Succession, in turn, has *its* origins in three "organs of succession": the cerebellum, the hippocampus, and the basal ganglia. The cerebellum essentially sees to it that motor events are smoothly executed, i.e., that present events are continuously connected to their predecessors. The hippocampus implements short-term memory of perceptual experience—the ability to recognize an association between the present and the recent past. Finally, the basal ganglia contribute to the foundations of motor planning, deciding on the selection of motor events to respond to present circumstances. Edelman admits that all these claims "contain some speculative components" (p. 120); but they are all based on known physiological properties.

2.3. Concepts

The next step along Edelman's path to modeling consciousness is that of *concepts*. In artificial intelligence there is a tendency to view concepts as building blocks of knowledge representation [3]. They are usually constructed from linguistic primitives; and it is the desire to employ linguistic primitives as a foundation for the representation of concepts which led Jerry Fodor to pursue his ideas on the "language of thought" [10]. Edelman, however, rejects any assumption of language as a prerequisite for concepts, citing chimpanzees as an example of animals which lack linguistic abilities but can have and acquire concepts (p. 140).

Edelman also rejects any view of concepts being embodied in concrete entities which may be analyzed in terms of their representational structure. Rather, concepts are yet another extension of the brain's ability to form generalizations. Perceptual categorization is the simplest form of such generalization; the fact that the two characters, X and +, can induce similar patterns of activity in a network of neuronal groups indicates that the activation pattern is a generalization of those "raw" stimuli. The dynamics of *re*categorization extend this capability for generalization, since recategorization enables associations to be formed among those activation patterns. Ordering extends these concerns to include motor activities, as well as perceptual ones. Thus, the power of generalization accommodates not only what is perceived but also what actions are taken and how actions interact with perceptions. These generalizations are embodied in relationships among patterns of activation in the cerebral cortex with those in the cerebellum, hippocampus, and basal ganglia.

Thus, by the time we have a device which is capable of dealing with ordering, we have a rather complex dynamic system with a broad spectrum of patterns of interaction. In the face of such complexity, a need for an ability to perform *categorization on those patterns of activation* becomes more and more apparent. This is where Edelman's concepts enter the picture; they are the categories which are formed when, by bootstrapping its mechanisms for categorization, "the brain categorizes its own activities" (p. 145). While such a point of view may lie far from the beaten path of current knowledge representation technology, it should be noted that the philosopher John Pollock has approached the problem of "how to build a person" with a similar emphasis on such introspective generalization [19].

2.4. "Presyntax"

Edelman's next step is to observe that the ability to form and manipulate concepts is not the same as thought. His grounds for distinction are actually based on a speculation:

> It is conceivable, in other words, that an animal can develop concepts but not be able explicitly to carry out analogy formation or similar activities over any length of time (of course, the converse, that such activity requires concept formation, is necessarily true). (p. 147)

In order to perform such activities, Edelman claims that it is necessary to have not only concepts but also *structures* in which they may be arranged. These structures form the basis for achieving tasks such as analogy formation, deduction, and induction.

At this point, it would appear that Edelman is nearing the threshold of the knowledge respesentation camp and the sorts of issues which have been concerned with structuring semantic networks [3]. However, it is important to recall that Edelman is trying very hard not to let his own notion of concepts be reduced to the status of nodes in such a network. This is why he has introduced the term "presyntax". He views the sorts of semantic networks which tend to be incorporated in AI knowledge bases [3] as being structured by rules which are fundamentally syntactic in nature and dependent on a need for symbolic primitives as a foundation. Thus, "presyntax" is introduced as a term which attempts to capture structural relationships among concepts which need not be expressed in terms of either symbolic primitives or rules of syntactic structure.

Edelman's determination to avoid the constraints of grammars which impose structures on symbols seems very much in the same league as Marvin Minsky's rejection of formal logic as a model of thought processes:

> For generations, scientists and philosophers have tried to explain ordinary reasoning in terms of logical principles—with virtually no success. I suspect this enterprise failed because it was looking in the wrong direction: common sense works so well not because it is an approximation of logic; logic is only a small part of our great accumulation of different, useful ways to chain things together. Many thinkers have assumed that *logical necessity* lies at the heart of our reasoning. But for the purposes of psychology, we'd do

better to set aside the dubious ideal of faultless deduction and try, instead, to understand how people actually deal with what is *usual* or *typical*. To do this, we often think in terms of causes, similarities, and dependencies. What do all these forms of thinking share? They all use different ways to make chains. [15]

Thus, for Edelman presyntax is the embodiment of the capacity to make the sorts of chains (i.e., associative connections) which lie at the heart of Minsky's model of reasoning.

The introduction of presyntax constitutes a definite departure from biological foundations, and Edelman does not attempt to hide this fact. While he was able to develop his model of ordering on observations of parts of the brain, he admits that he has neither anatomical nor synaptic evidence for the sort of structuring which presyntax requires. Nevertheless, he *does* discuss how structures which are consequences of both concept formation and presyntax are related to the mechanisms of motor and perceptual sequences, with his global mappings serving as the basis for those relations.

2.5. Primary consciousness

We have seen that memory, ordering, and concepts arise through successive bootstrapping of a fundamental mechanism for perceptual categorization. We have also introduced presyntax to account for the need to arrange the results of such operations into structures. However, we have not really discussed how either these operations or their structures are going to be involved in the behavior of an agent that must manage in the world around him. We have the pieces from which such behavior may be built, but they still must be properly assembled. If we ask how to do this with respect to a *single* agent that can manage in a world without necessarily having to communicate with other agents, then our result would be what Edelman has chosen to call "primary consciousness".

Edelman's model of primary consciousness may best be viewed as a network of devices, each of which performs categorization on a different set of input signals:

- At the lowest level, there is a device for perceptual categorization, C(W), which operates on signals from the World as perceived by the different sense organs.
- Similar to C(W), there is a device for *Introspective* categorization, C(I), which operates on interoceptive signals, such as those from the autonomic nervous system and the endocrine system.
- Categorization may then be performed on signals which embody the activation states of both C(W) and C(I) as the agent experiences the world. Such categorization may involve both comparison of the signals from the two sources and comparison of present signals with past signals,

which will reveal categories of interaction. Edelman calls this categorization device C(W)·C(I).

- A final level of categorization is applied to the output of C(W)·C(I). The device which performs recategorization of the signals received from C(W)·C(I) as time progresses is called C[C(W)·C(I)].
- In addition to performing recategorization on C(W)·C(I), C[C(W)·C(I)] also maintains a reentrant exchange of signals with C(W). *This* is the basis for primary consciousness in Edelman's model. Through this reentrant connection, the agent's perception of the world (i.e., the ability to perform perceptual categorization on signals from the world) is affected by not only perceptual experience but also relations between those experiences and introspections from which that agent may attach *values* to those experiences. Thus, we now have the makings of an agent that should stand some chance of actually managing in its world.

(Note that the above summary uses the notation which Edelman employs in his book. The reader should be warned that it does not respect the traditional conventions of mathematical notation. The "C" symbol indicates a categorization process; and its "argument" serves to indicate those signals which are being categorized. However, it would be a mistake to interpret "C" as if it were a single mathematical function, even when Edelman invokes the "functional composition" of categorizing the results of categorization. Similarly, Edelman's use of a "dot product" indicates an interaction between two categorization processes, as opposed to any sort of mathematical product operator.)

The reentrant connection between a categorization device which is essentially responsible for concept formation and one which performs perceptual categorization on sensory input may be regarded as a source of "mental images". In other words mental images may be viewed as states which are *induced* upon C(W), by virtue of signals exchanged with C[C(W)·C(I)]. Nevertheless, Edelman is quick to point out that he does not subscribe to views, such as those of Stephen Kosslyn [14], that the brain actually *has* such images:

> In the brain, there is, of course, no actual image or sketch (even if we consider visual input alone). Instead, primary consciousness arises as a discriminative comparison of previous "self-categories" (which include prior environmentally stimulated categories that were correlated with interoceptive signals) with the current or immediately categorized exteroceptive input. It is the actual physical interaction between the reentrant circuits we have mentioned and the spatiotemporal ordering of current signals from the niche that together determine the "image". An image is, in fact, a set of *correlations* of such interactions with prior memory states. (p. 154)

It is also important to observe that Edelman's model stands in clear opposition to the Physical Symbol System Hypothesis [17]. A physical symbol system is not required in order to realize this model. In all fairness, however, the speculative nature of Edelman's work should again be emphasized. This book does not provide firm grounds for rejecting the Physical Symbol System Hypothesis, but it *does* provide food for thought for anyone who has ever considered *questioning* it. Furthermore, since the publication of *The Remembered Present*, Edelman, together with his colleague George Reeke, has explicitly considered the rejection of the Physical Symbol System Hypothesis at much greater length [8]. Given how much of artificial intelligence is committed to this hypothesis, a bit of healthy sceptical inquiry can always be useful.

It should be emphasized that Edelman, himself, does not use the word "device" in presenting his model of primary consciousness. The word is somewhat dangerous, because it tends to overlook the fact that the entire model, like each categorizing component, can only be viewed as a *dynamic system*. At every level categorization is a consequence of system dynamics; and any use of the word "state" is simply an abstraction of the signals which one component receives from another at any moment of time. This emphasis on dynamics is important because without those dynamics there can be no consciousness. Thus, one cannot envisage a situation in which one agent's "$C[C(W) \cdot C(I)]$ device" is disconnected and used to replace the same device in another agent. One cannot "freeze" system state in such a way that this sort of "brain surgery" would be possible.

2.6. Language

It is important to observe that Edelman has not yet assumed a need for any linguistic capabilities. Thus, an agent with primary consciousness need not necessarily also have a command of language. However, *without* language, that agent will be rather like Georg Büchner's little orphan girl [4]; without any ability to communicate with other agents, this agent would be essentially alone in the world.

Edelman's argument is that if we are to consider how language emerged from a biological point of view, then all the capabilities he has discussed so far must first be present. The capability for language is now achieved through four premises which he presents:

(1) The capability for dealing with concepts provides a necessary, but not sufficient, basis for semantics.
(2) Phonology and syntax are essentially more sophisticated ordering capabilities: "As various phonological and syntactic mechanisms evolved, they exploited the already existent cortical apparatus related to the categorization of global mappings and presyntax, which provide the

brain bases for ordering of gestures in terms of concepts and vice versa . . ." (p. 174).

(3) Development of phonological capabilities leads to the acquisition of sufficient ordering ability to form words and sentences. Once these abilities are in place, a capability for syntax can emerge.

(4) Categorization and ordering may now be applied to these resulting abilities, leading to the ability to "process" the constructs of language at the levels of morphemes, words, and sentences. At this stage the agent now has the ability to *use* language.

In other words concepts serve as a foundation for language, rather than the other way around. Once we have concepts, we can start worrying about associating them with the sounds we hear and make. Like everything else in Edelman's system, those sounds are subject to categorization and ordering, whence emerge categories for phonemes, words, and sentences. Since categorization of sentences is ultimately a matter of how they are structured, syntax is also a product of categorization and ordering. Finally, there is a level of categorization and ordering which basically captures our ability to *reason* with these constructs, just as concepts were built upon the categorization and ordering of our memory capabilities; and that level of reasoning is our linguistic ability. Note that this development is also distinguished by a progression from a *perceptual* bootstrapping of the categorization mechanism to a *semantic* one.

2.7. Higher-order consciousness

Once we have language at our disposal, we also have the elements of language: symbols which may be utilized for representation. At this point we may take one last shot at bootstrapping our machinery with the observation that perceptual categorization may be applied to these symbols, just as it has been applied at all the lower levels of Edelman's design. We are now at a level which comes close to the sorts of intuitions we have about "planning"; and Edelman calls this the level of "higher-order consciousness". This is the ultimate refinement of our capacity for introspection:

> In its fully developed form, higher-order consciousness may be considered an ability to model internal states free of real time (and occasionally also of space)—so that past, present, and future are connected in terms of such plans. (p. 173)

Higher-order consciousness may thus be viewed as a development in which symbolic processing begins to take over from subsymbolic processing [6]. While this is an issue which has been of considerable recent interest in the artificial intelligence community, it is one which Edelman does not pursue to any great extent. Rather than focusing his attention on aspects of *intelligent* behavior,

Edelman uses his model to fuel speculations on new views of *pathological* behavior.

Edelman chooses to call such behavior "diseases of consciousness", justifying his terminology as follows:

> Instead of talking about psychoses and neuroses or about organic and functional disorders, one is invited by this view to talk about diseases of attention, diseases of motion, diseases of categorization, diseases of reentry, diseases of succession, and diseases of qualia and of self. A consideration of these disorders in terms of the framework of the TNGS may reveal common patterns and show connections between particular brain functions and the origins of consciousness. (p. 215)

With this as his premise, he then attempts to interpret the behavior associated with such disabilities in terms of his model. The pathological conditions he reviews are amnesia, short-term memory disorders, aphasia (motor and sensory), dissociation, obsessive–compulsive disorder, affective disorder, and three forms of schizophrenia.

Edelman admits that the use of his model can be, at best, heuristic. However, he argues, "The framework may nevertheless be useful in focusing our thoughts on the various levels at which brain areas subserving consciousness interact" (p. 218). He also makes a case for the value his model may contribute to issues of therapy:

> Since primary consciousness and higher-order consciousness are individual (and subjective) processes, therapeutic attempts to change particular synaptic efficacies in order to achieve particular states of behaviors must continue to include communication and verbal exchange. It is not likely that a particular drug or biochemical manipulation can change a particular combinatorial pattern of synaptic efficacies in even two different individuals and achieve the same results as a semantic exchange. (Obviously, if our theory is correct, these two individuals have different detailed neural arrangements. No known drug can be delivered across variant anatomy and synaptic patterns to yield an effective selection of isofunctional neuronal groups, resulting in identical inputs or outputs in different individuals.) (pp. 234–235)

3. Related work

Edelman is an impressively well-read author, and he goes to great pains to support each step of his argument with appropriate references to the literature. Readers interested in artificial intelligence should therefore appreciate those discussions which attempt to situate his work in the context of both symbolic AI and connectionism. These relationships will now be reviewed. However, it is also important to recognize that there are two significant lacunae in Edelman's appreciation of the literature. These are Minsky's recent work on a "society of mind" and John Holland's research on classification systems. This review will also attempt to relate Edelman's results to these efforts which he has failed to acknowledge.

3.1. Acknowledged work

3.1.1. Symbolic artificial intelligence

It is interesting to observe that Edelman has relatively little to say about any specific *achievements* in symbolic artificial intelligence. For example, there is never any mention of Allen Newell in this book, which is unfortunate given that Edelman's model of primary consciousness may be viewed as a challenge to Newell's Physical Symbol System Hypothesis. Edelman seems more inclined to take on cognitive scientists whose theories have been fueled by artificial intelligence results than he is to discuss the results themselves. Thus, one of his primary targets is that approach to cognitive science which has emerged from speculations articulated in Fodor's *The Language of Thought* [10]. Edelman summarizes his position as follows:

> The extended theory provides a strong basis for a noncircular connection between concepts and language. There is no "language of thought", for concepts have none of the properties of language .... There is thought and there is language. Language systems evolved through the development of phonology, which by reentrant means could allow semantic bootstrapping and syntactic development. The rich reentrant connectivity between phonological, syntactic, and semantic levels is not so different in its consequences from that which allows object "images" to form from functionally segregated areas in the visual system .... The resulting development of a rich lexical functional grammar involves the realization of syntax during language acquisition. (p. 267)

When Edelman chooses to take on the computer itself, he begins by turning to the writings of Hilary Putnam. The following passage from Putnam's *Representation and Reality* is useful in approaching Edelman's philosophical position:

> Many years ago, I published a series of papers in which I proposed a model of the mind which became widely known under the name "functionalism". According to this model, psychological states ("believing that *p*", "desiring that *p*", "considering whether *p*", etc.) are simply "computational states" of the brain. The proper

way to think of the brain is as a digital computer. Our psychology is to be described as the software of this computer—its "functional organization".

According to the version of functionalism that I originally proposed, mental states can be defined in terms of Turing machine states and loadings of the memory (the paper tape of the Turing machine). I later rejected this account [20] on the ground that such a literal Turing machine-ism would not give a perspicuous representation of the psychology of human beings and animals. That argument was only an argument against one particular type of computational model, but the arguments of the preceding chapters constitute a more general reason why computational models of the brain/mind will not suffice for cognitive psychology. We cannot individuate concepts and beliefs without reference to the *environment*. Meanings aren't "in the head". [21]

Unfortunately, while it is certainly the case that any abstract Turing machine lacks sensors and effectors, it is virtually impossible to imagine any *concrete* computer which lacks them. Thus, there is no reason to assume that any such computer has less of an ability to refer to its environment than we, as humans, do.

Functionalism, as just described, appears to be Edelman's favorite target in discussing symbolic artificial intelligence. Unfortunately, his primary support in this attack is John Searle [25]. Given the amount of controversy surrounding Searle's approach to this question, beginning with the many opposing points of view which were published when "Minds, Brains, and Programs" first appeared, Searle seems an unlikely source of support for any argument to be considered by members of the artificial intelligence community. This is not to say that Searle may not some day succeed in defeating the premise that "the appropriately programmed computer really *is* a mind" [25] but simply to observe that he has not been particularly successful in making convincing arguments among those who are intimately acquainted with computational behavior. This is probably due to his emphasis on exploiting weaknesses in symbol manipulation systems and overlooking the fundamental fact that Turing [29] introduced symbol manipulation as a *model* for such computational behavior, not necessarily intending that the model be confused with the behavior, itself.

It also seems to be the case that Edelman is not accepting one of Searle's fundamental premises concerning the role of behavior. Searle has argued strongly that we cannot attribute mental states to a computer simply on the basis of how it interacts with other agents [25]. Nevertheless, Edelman is ultimately approaching the issue of consciousness on the basis of the behavior it exhibits. He is rejecting *Turing's* assumption that such behavior may be achieved through a computational model of a mind which is independent of any body; but behavior still lies at the heart of Edelman's own model, even when the body is factored into that model. Thus, if Searle is arguing that the existence of mental states cannot be decided on the basis of behavior alone, it is unclear that he would be any more supportive of Edelman's position than he is of Turing's.

3.1.2. Connectionism

In relating his work to the connectionist approach to artificial intelligence, Edelman is more inclined to cite specific achievements. Unfortunately, his citations are restricted to two contributions to the published literature [1, 13]. His primary criticism of this work is that it is not based on biological foundations. This observation is fair enough; but it is important to remember that, while Edelman has been very concerned about biological support for his models, the computer models which he actually discusses are also, by his own admission, rather removed from *their* biological foundations.

3.2. Unacknowledged work

3.2.1. Minsky's society of mind

In *Neural Darwinism* Edelman's only acknowledgment of Minsky involved his work on perceptrons. In reviewing this book [26], I hinted that this might have been rather a sin of omission on Edelman's part. In *The Remembered Present* there is no acknowledgment of Minsky at all. Nevertheless, I am still inclined to place these two men in a common camp, at least for purposes of thinking about many questions of mind. Two commonalities seem particularly significant.

The first concerns Edelman's emphasis on dynamic, rather than, static properties, beginning with his view of memory as *re*categorization. The K-lines which form the foundation for Minsky's model of memory [15] are also best viewed in terms of their interactive dynamics, as opposed to devices with states whose snapshots may be collected together as a representation of what an agent "remembers". These dynamics are best illustrated in Minsky's discussion of those processes which he calls "closing the ring", since these are activities which involve the contributions of perception and memory to concept formation. From this point of view, it would appear that Edelman is approaching concepts from the same direction which Minsky has considered.

The second commonality involves the approach Edelman has taken to building his model of primary consciousness. As was emphasized in Section 2.5, it is misleading to view the components of this model as if they were "devices". On the other hand, it seems particularly appropriate to view them as *agents* in a Minsky-like "society of mind". Essentially, they capture the basic philosophy to building a mind which Minsky endorses. One must begin by identifying loci of (computational) activity, each of which has a relatively simple task and patterns of interaction with other loci of activity. Not only may each component of Edelman's model be viewed as an agent, but the underlying TNGS model indicates how these agents may be constructed from even *simpler* agents. Thus, it does not seem at all inappropriate to say that the model which Edelman has developed is very much a "society of mind" in Minsky's sense of the phrase. Indeed, Minsky's most recent work on "mind-sculpture" [16] seems particularly appropriate to the approach Edelman has been taking. Furthermore, to view the relation in the opposite direction, because Edelman has tried to base his own work on physiological evidence, the reader who is interested in studying the work of Minsky would probably benefit from the ways in which Edelman provides a relevant biological orientation for understanding Minsky's theories.

3.2.2. Holland's classification systems

One cannot consider the capabilities of selection as a computational mechanism without accounting for the genetic algorithms which form the basis for Holland's classification systems [12]. However, it is probably fair to say that Holland's major advance has been in the area of *assignment* to categories, rather than the *formation* of those categories. Thus, the selective capabilities of his genetic algorithms are good for determining how an input stimulus should be classified; but the categories themselves are essentially "hard-wired" into the architecture of the system's "genes".

In a recent opportunity to comment on Edelman's emphasis on the need to perform perceptual categorization in the absence of any a priori labels, Holland argued that retinal patterns are just as much "labels" as are nouns in a natural language [27]. This argument seems to be suggesting that category formation is not an issue, which may be a questionable claim. Nouns may be viewed as abstractions of retinal patterns (among other things); and there may not be much to be gained from calling those things labels which really do not impose *any* abstraction on the input stimuli. Edelman seems to be saying that not only do such abstractions exist (i.e., abstractions on "raw data" like retinal stimuli) but also they have a biological foundation.

4. Conclusion

4.1. Writing quality

While *Neural Darwinism* was certainly a challenging book, Edelman wrote it in such a way as to guide the reader through each of its challenges. He was most conscientious in providing the reader with guideposts to indicate where he was and where he was going; and he always remembered to supplement his explanation of "where" with a justification of *why* he was pursuing a particular path. He thus wrote himself a tough act to follow.

Unfortunately, the writing of *The Remembered Present* is not quite as satisfying as that of *Neural Darwinism*. Part of the problem may have to do with the footnotes. Edelman avoided them in *Neural Darwinism*, but they season this book most liberally. They can also be confusing in their abundance, since he uses them to provide both citations to the literature and clarifying comments. Unfortunately, this can lead to awkward moments when a footnote is used in both capacities. Thus, one finds an "Ibid" immediately following a very lengthy combination of both comments and references, leaving the reader more than a little baffled as to the target of that latter note!

These, however, are relatively minor points. There are some more specific problems in that some of the figures could have done with better labels. However, the body of Edelman's text remains sound, which means that these figures can still be readily understood. Most important is that Edelman continues to guide his reader through the steps of his argument. We may not agree with his conclusions, but we shall have no trouble following his trail.

4.2. Relevance to artificial intelligence

The obvious question which one is likely to hear "in the trenches" regarding the relevance of a biological theory of consciousness is whether or not the whole issue of consciousness is a bit too elevated for the current concerns of artificial intelligence. This may very well be the case as it applies to the sorts of systems which are currently being produced. However, artificial intelligence should not focus its attention on what we are currently doing to the extent that it loses sight of some fundamental questions which may guide future investigations. In this respect questions of consciousness may not be as far afield as we might think. Confronting the limitations of current expert systems will probably take us to the brink of those questions. Once we recognize that we are at this brink, we can decide, from a purely pragmatic point of view, whether any insights regarding consciousness which have emerged from outside our own community (be they from psychology, biology, or philosophy) might be of use to us. Thus, even if we choose to make this decision later, rather than sooner, we should become more sensitive to questions of consciousness; and *The Remembered Present* provides a valuable perspective on a subject which is notorious for its opacity.

References

[1] D.H. Ballard, G.E. Hinton and T.J. Sejnowski, Parallel visual computation, *Nature* **306** (1983) 21–26.

[2] N. Bernstein, *The Coordination and Regulation of Movements* (Pergamon, Oxford, 1967).

[3] R.J. Brachman, What's in a concept: structural foundations for semantic networks, *Int. J. Man-Mach. Stud.* **9** (1977) 127–152.

[4] G. Büchner, Woyzeck, in: *Georg Büchner: Complete Plays and Prose* (Hill and Wang, New York, 1963) 107–138; Translated and with an introduction by C.R. Mueller.

[5] R. Descartes, Meditations on first philosophy, in: *The Philosophical Writings of Descartes* (Cambridge University Press, New York, 1984) 1–62; Translated from the Latin by J. Cottingham.

[6] M.G. Dyer, Symbolic neuroengineering for natural language processing: a multilevel research approach, Tech. Report UCLA-AI-M-88-14, Computer Science Department, University of California Los Angeles, Los Angeles, CA (1988).

[7] G.M. Edelman, *Neural Darwinism: The Theory of Neuronal Group Selection* (Basic Books, New York, 1987).

[8] G.M. Edelman and G.N. Reeke Jr, Is it possible to construct a perception machine?, *Proc. Am. Philos. Soc.* **134** (1) (1990) 36–73.

[9] L.H. Finkel and G.M. Edelman, Population rules for synapses in networks, in: G.M. Edelman, W.E. Gall and W.M. Cowan, eds., *The Neurosciences Institute Publications: Synaptic Function* (Wiley, New York, 1987) 711–757 (Chapter 25).

[10] J.A. Fodor, *The Language of Thought* (Harvard University Press, Cambridge, MA, 1975).

[11] D.O. Hebb, *The Organization of Behavior* (Wiley, New York, 1949).

[12] J.H. Holland et al., *Induction: Processes of Inference, Learning, and Discovery* (MIT Press, Cambridge, MA, 1986).

[13] P.K. Kienker et al., Separating figure from ground with a parallel network, *Perception* **15** (1986) 197–216.

[14] S.M. Kosslyn, *Image and Mind* (Harvard University Press, Cambridge, MA, 1980).

[15] M. Minsky, *The Society of Mind* (Simon and Schuster, New York, 1986).

[16] M. Minsky, Logical vs. analogical or symbolic vs. connectionist or neat vs. scruffy, in: P.H. Winston and S.A. Shellard, eds., *Artificial Intelligence at MIT: Expanding Frontiers* (MIT Press, Cambridge, MA, 1990) 218–243.

[17] A. Newell and H.A. Simon, Computer science as empirical inquiry: symbols and search, *Commun. ACM* **19** (3) (1976) 113–126.

[18] D.A. Norman, Twelve issues for cognitive science, in: D.A. Norman, ed., *Perspectives on Cognitive Science* (Erlbaum, Hillsdale, NJ, 1981) 265–295.

[19] J.L. Pollock, *How to Build a Person: A Prolegomenon* (MIT Press, Cambridge, MA, 1989).

[20] H. Putnam, Philosophy and our mental life, in: *Philosophical Papers 2: Mind, Language and Reality* (Cambridge University Press, New York, 1975) 291–303 (Chapter 14).

[21] H. Putnam, *Representation and Reality* (MIT Press, Cambridge, MA, 1989).

[22] G.N. Reeke Jr and G.M. Edelman, Selective networks and recognition automata, *Ann. New York Acad. Sci.* **426** (1984) 181–201.

[23] G.N. Reeke Jr et al., Synthetic neural modeling: a multilevel approach to the analysis of brain complexity, in: G.M. Edelman, W.E. Gall and W.M. Cowan, eds., *The Neurosciences Institute Publications: Signal and Sense: Local and Global Order in Perceptual Maps* (Wiley, New York, 1990) 607–707 (Chapter 24).

[24] F. Rosenblatt, *Principles of Neurodynamics* (Spartan, New York, 1959).

[25] J.R. Searle, Minds, brains, and programs, in: D.R. Hofstadter and D.C. Dennett, eds., *The Mind's I: Fantasies and Reflections on Self and Soul* (Basic Books, New York, 1981) 353–382 (Chapter 22).

[26] S.W. Smoliar, Book Review of *Neural Darwinism: The Theory of Neuronal Group Selection* (G.M. Edelman), *Artif. Intell.* **39** (1) (1989) 121–136.

[27] S.W. Smoliar, The challenge of Neural Darwinism, in: *Proceedings IJCAI-89*, Detroit, MI (1989) 1669–1671.

[28] A.M. Turing, Computing machinery and intelligence, in: E.A. Feigenbaum and J. Feldman, eds., *Computers and Thought* (McGraw-Hill, New York, 1963) 11–35.

[29] A.M. Turing, On computable numbers, with an application to the Entscheidungsproblem, in: M. Davis, ed., *The Undecidable: Basic Papers on Undecidable Propositions, Unsolvable Problems and Computable Functions* (Raven Press, Hewlett, NY, 1965) 115–154.

Artificial Intelligence 60 (1993) 313–356
Elsevier

ARTINT 1056

The biology of consciousness: comparative review of Israel Rosenfield, *The Strange, Familiar, and Forgotten: An Anatomy of Consciousness** and Gerald M. Edelman, *Bright Air, Brilliant Fire: On the Matter of the Mind***

William J. Clancey

Institute for Research on Learning, 2550 Hanover Street, Palo Alto, CA 94304, USA

Revised January 1993

1. Relating cognition to biology

For many years, most AI researchers and cognitive scientists have reserved the topic of consciousness for after dinner conversation. Like "intuition", the idea of consciousness appeared to be too vague or general to be a good starting place for understanding cognition. Work on narrowly-defined problems in specialized domains such as medicine and manufacturing focused

---

* (Alfred A. Knopf, New York,1992); xi + 157 pages.
** (Basic Books, New York, 1992); xvi + 280 pages.
Correspondence to: W.J. Clancey, Institute for Research on Learning, 2550 Hanover Street, Palo Alto, CA 94304, USA. Telephone: (415) 496 7925. Fax: (415) 496 7957. E-mail: bill_clancey@irl.com.

our concerns on the nature of representation, memory, strategies for problem solving, and learning. Some writers, notably Ornstein [34] and Hofstadter [27], continued to explore the ideas, but implications for cognitive modeling were unclear, suggesting neither experiments, nor new computational mechanisms.

But the time has arrived for raising consciousness in cognitive science. Books by Edelman, Rosenfield, Dennett, Varela, and others have appeared almost simultaneously, with a strikingly common theme: Biological and psychological evidence suggests that better understanding of consciousness is not only possible, but necessary if we are to improve our understanding of cognition. This evidence varies considerably, ranging from how neurological structures develop, the effects of neural dysfunctions on human behavior, perceptual illusions, the evolution of the human species, and the philosophy of language. In this comparative review, I consider the work of Edelman and Rosenfield. Taken together, these books may stimulate a broader view of intelligence, give further credence to the situated cognition view of language, and provide a more biological basis for "neural net" approaches. Prior work by Putnam, Dreyfus, and Winograd, to name a few previous critics, may also appear less threatening or less nonsensical when argued in neurophysiological terms.

2. Overview of *The Strange, Familiar, and Forgotten*

Rosenfield's psychological analysis of human experience motivates Edelman's more detailed neurological models of the brain, so I will consider *The Strange, Familiar, and Forgotten* first. This book is a significant contribution to cognitive science literature, in the interpretive, historical style of Sacks [43] and Luria [31]. Like Sacks and Luria, Rosenfield is an MD with a historian's bent. With a PhD in "intellectual history", Rosenfield attempts to make sense of clinical neuropsychology research (which he often translates from French sources). Reinterpreting past work, he applies a developmental perspective that learning occurs with every human interaction.

Like Sacks and Luria, Rosenfield uses historically well-documented cases to illustrate and contrast theories of memory, learning, and consciousness. Like them, he provides an ethnographic perspective on the patient, not merely as a patient with a lesion but as *a person struggling to make sense of emotional, physical, and social experience*. He considers not only laboratory evidence of the patients' verbal and perceptual behavior, but the stories they tell about their social life and mental experience.

Building on simple observations and comparison across cases, Rosenfield provides a broad view of experiences that theories of memory especially must address. For example, Mr. March could move his left hand, but only when told to do so (p. 58), and otherwise seemed not to relate to it as his own. When a nurse made her hand appear to be his left hand, he casually made sense of the situation:

> Asked where his own ring was, he said, "It's been taken away from me."
> And why was he now wearing a bracelet? "It has been put on me."
> "But this hand is all white and not as hairy as your own."
> "It's like that because it is paralyzed." (p. 59)

Rosenfield summarizes his thesis that dysfunctions are usually exhibited in the context of ongoing sense-making behavior:

> The neurologists' attempts to derive brain function from clinical reports of brain-damaged patients have too often overlooked the fact that the verbal reports of these patients are *conscious* reports ... limited awareness causes not the "loss" of words but an inability to make a certain sense of them and thus to use them in conventional ways ... in a concentration on the idea that individual functions had been lost or damaged in brain lesions, important and subtle symptoms went unexplained. Yet these symptoms were part of the patients' *conscious* states, and they suggest a broader functional breakdown than the view of compartmentalized functions allows. (p. 140)

Rosenfield argues that we need to better understand the nature of consciousness as a process, an activity in its own right, not as a side-effect, but an ongoing accomplishment. Related work by Greenwald [26] argues for the need to "explain one particularly intriguing 'emergent' property of the self system—its tendency (in the normal case) to perceive itself as unitary and real". We need a global view of the dynamics of sense-making, of creating an integrating view—in our conscious behavior—of our self-image. This parallels the emphasis in situated cognition (e.g., Suchman's [50] study of the use of plans) on *representing* as occurring in sequences of interactive behavior over time, within some ongoing situation, as opposed to being disembodied manipulation of calculi, in some timeless hidden (and subconscious) place inside the brain. Rosenfield and Edelman help us understand *why all reasoning isn't subconscious*: Sense-making (telling causally-connected stories) involves relating what you are currently doing to what you have experienced in the past and what you expect will occur in the future. Significantly, "relating" occurs without necessarily representing such relations in words, but rather directly, via neural feedback loops that couple perception, past (non-linguistic) conceptualizations, and bodily movements.

What is a patient *doing* when he says that last Saturday he was in the city of La Rochelle, when he has no idea what day was yesterday and denies that he is still in La Rochelle today? Rosenfield closely examines such story-telling behaviors, revealing that patients are not merely retrieving facts from memory, but revealing how they make sense of experience. By examining what can go wrong—in maintaining a sense of continuous time, an integrated personality and body image, and abstract categorical relations—we can understand better how consciousness structures everyday experience.

Rosenfield's view of the brain is consistent with cognitive science descriptions of behavior patterns (scripts, grammars), in so far as he acknowledges that such patterns are real psychological phenomena that need to be explained. Yet, he insists on an alternative view of neurological mechanism, by which observed behavior patterns are the product of interactions at both social and neural levels. This idea of *dialectic organization* is important in biology and anthropology, but quite different from the mechanisms designed by most engineers, computer scientists, and cognitive modelers. Stephen Jay Gould provides a useful introduction:

> Thus, we cannot factor a complex social situation into so much biology on one side, and so much culture on the other. We must seek to understand the emergent and irreducible properties arising from an inextricable interpenetration of genes and environments. In short, we must use what so many great thinkers call, but American fashion dismisses as political rhetoric from the other side, a dialectical approach.
>
> ... the three classical laws of dialectics embody a holistic vision that views change as interaction among components of complete systems, and sees the components themselves not as a priori entities, but as both the products of and the inputs to the system. Thus the law of "interpenetrating opposites" records the inextricable interdependence of components; the "transformation of quantity to quality" defends a systems-based view of change that translates incremental inputs into alterations of state; and the "negation of negation" describes the direction given to history because complex systems cannot revert exactly to previous states. [25, pp. 153–154]

According to this dialectical perspective, neural processes activate and are generalized within larger neural and social coordinations which they constitute, yet which create them. Areas of the brain are specialized, but the degree of modularity and stability is different from the labeled memory structures and independently invokable subroutines of most cognitive models. Areas of the brain aren't merely accessed or activated, but *organize each other within complete circuits* (as emphasized in Dewey's 1896 criticism of stimulus–response theories [17]). According to Edelman's model of the brain, these circuits are themselves generalizations involving bi-directional recategorizations at perceptual, sequential, conceptual, and linguistic levels.

Like Edelman, Rosenfield emphasizes the "interpenetrating" multiple levels of individual development, species evolution, and the interaction of cultural and neural processes. But in the more narrow style of cognitive neuropsychology, he focuses on what abnormal behavior reveals about normal function. In order to explain dysfunctions, as well as the openness and subjectivity of categories in everyday life, Rosenfield argues for a brain that continuously and dynamically reorganizes how it responds to stimuli (p. 134). Rather than retrieving and matching discrete structures or procedures, the brain composes itself in-line, in the very process of coordinating sensation and motion (hence behavior is "situated"). By Dewey's analysis, perceptual and motor processes in the brain are configuring each other without intervening subconscious "deliberation" [13].

Most interpretations of patients with dysfunctions (e.g., an inability to speak certain kinds of words) have postulated isolated memory or knowledge centers for different kinds of subsystems: auditory, visual, motor. The "diagram makers", exemplified by Charcot in the mid-1800s, drew pictures of the brain with "centers", linking memory and parts of the body. Dysfunctions were explained as loss of memory, that is, loss of specific knowledge stored in the brain. Rosenfield claims instead that memory loss in a brain-damaged patient is not the loss of a "memory trace", but evidence of a restructuring of how the brain operates. That is, we are not observing a primary, isolated "loss", but a secondary *process of reorganization* for the sake of sustaining self-image:

> Memory loss in the brain-damaged patient is ... evidence of a restructuring of the patient's conscious knowledge, a restructuring of the patient's relation to his or her surroundings. The brain has mechanisms for establishing this relation—that is the ultimate significance of the pathological findings—and the most important significance of these mechanisms is consciousness. With brain damage, function is altered, certain brain processes are no longer possible, and consequently consciousness, too, is altered. (p. 22)

> Patients with brain damage are confused when they fail to recognize and remember, and it is this confused, altered awareness, as much as any specific failures of memory, that is symptomatic of their illness. (p. 34)

The kinds of *confusion* reveal the normal function of the brain in coordinating present awareness with previous experience. Being conscious is being engaged in the act of sense-making; brain-damaged patients exhibit "a breakdown in the mechanisms of consciousness. A patient's state of confusion is no more to be ignored than his failure to recognize, say, his home. Memory, recognition, and consciousness are all part of the same process." (p. 35) Self-reference is integral to sense-making, and it is grounded in bodily experience. In people, there can be no "normal" understanding of language, no sense of time, no personality without a sustained, coherent self-image. The cases of brain-damaged patients support this view, but ultimately Edelman's architectural arguments provide the needed implementation-level support.

The first section of the book recapitulates some of the analysis from Rosenfield's *Invention of Memory* [11,41], but elaborated from the perspective of conscious experience:

> Our perceptions are part of a "stream of consciousness," part of a continuity of experience that the neuroscientific models and descriptions fail to capture; their categories of color, say, or smell, or sound, or motion are discrete entities independent of time. ... a sense of consciousness comes precisely from the *flow* of perceptions, from the relations among them (both spatial and temporal), from the dynamic but constant relation to them as governed by one unique personal perspective sustained throughout a conscious life.... Compared to it, units of "knowledge" such as we can transmit or record in books or images are but instant snapshots taken in a dynamic flow of uncontainable, unrepeatable, and inexpressible experience. And it is an unwarranted mistake to associate these snapshots with material "stored" in the brain. (p. 6)

By suggesting that memory was a place or a capability physically separated and distinct from the function of the brain (in speaking, moving, reasoning), Wernicke and others may have "falsified our understanding of numerous clinical disorders and of brain function in general" (p. 22). Dennett [15] provides a similar analysis:

> The consensus of cognitive science ... is that *over there* we have the long-term memory ... and *over here* we have the workspace or working memory, where the thinking happens .... And yet there are no two places in the brain to house these two facilities. The only place in the brain that is a plausible home for either of these separate functions is the whole cortex—not two places side by side but one large place. (pp. 270–271)

Rosenfield's model, in which memory is integral to skills, resembles theories such as Schank's dynamic memory (MOPS) and case-based reasoning, in which experiences and generalizations are integrated. However, these models postulate that declarative facts are stored as discrete units, even if they are linked to how they have been "accessed" or "used" in the past. Rosenfield and Edelman consistently emphasize that the brain operates only procedurally, with no storage of semantic information, either declarative or programmatic, as discrete linguistic structures [11].

Unlike Edelman, Rosenfield makes no attempt to address the AI audience directly. His statements require some reformulation to bring home the insights. For example, Rosenfield says, "No machine is *troubled* by, or even *intrigued* by, feelings of certainty that appear contradictory" (p. 12). Yet, AI researchers cite examples of how a program detects contradictory conclusions and uses that information. Without further discussion, it is unclear how being troubled is an essential part of creating new goals and values.

Providing a convincing case requires understanding the reader's point of view well enough to anticipate rebuttals. To this end, I re-present Rosenfield's key cases and contrast his analysis with other cognitive science explanations. The central themes of his analysis are: non-localization of function, the nature and role of self-reference (subjectivity), the origin and sense of time in remembering, the relational nature of linguistic categories, and the problem of multiple personalities. I reorder these topics in order to more clearly convey the neural-architectural implications.

2.1. Multiple personalities

The process of *sustaining a self-image* is illustrated by people with multiple personalities. Rosenfield argues such experiences are caused by pathology that *limits* neural organizational processes.

For example, "Mary Reynolds could, at different times, call the same animal a 'black hog' or a 'bear'." This behavior was integrated with alternative personalities, one daring and cheerful, the other fearsome and melancholic. From the standpoint of cognitive modeling based on stored linguistic schemas, there would be two memories of facts and skills, two coherent subconscious sets of representational structures and procedures. Rosenfield argues instead:

> There cannot be unconscious "traces" of these conscious states, since they require a dynamic organization that, given the complexity of the processes (the immediate, the past, and self-reference), are not reproducible. But what *are* more or less reproducible are the ways in which the brain organizes itself; certain pathologies limit the organizational processes, not the accessibility or inaccessibility of memories. (p. 129)

Again, neural structures coordinating what we say, imagine, feel, and how we move are activated "in place", as we are in the process of speaking, feeling, moving. Saying that some memories are forgotten and others recalled suggests a process of search and matching for relevancy; instead, the brain directly reorganizes itself *on a global basis*, not merely filtering or "reinterpreting" sensations, but physically recoordinating how perception and conceptualization occur.

Referring to another multiple personality, Rosenfield says,

> So there is no "Ansel" organized as such in "Arthur's" brain, or vice versa. Rather the single brain organizes itself as if it were Ansel (and there had never been an Arthur), then vice versa, because under certain conditions this damaged brain is reorganizing its way of responding to stimuli, the nature of its relations to the world.... Knowledge is the brain's ability to organize itself in particular ways at particular times. (p. 123)

We sometimes experience such figure–ground switches in our own experience: "Yesterday's 'friend' is today's 'objectionable person'." In normal people recategorization is gradual. In the patient with multiple personalities, "None of his or her personalities fully 'fits' the dynamic experience of everyday life: one personality will recognize family and friends; another will treat them as strangers and enemies" (p. 123). There are "too few 'selves'" (p. 138), a confined repertoire of fixations. Each personality appears one-dimensional; the reorganizations are disjoint. There is no gradation of "somewhat remembering" or "somewhat being able to control" the other personalities. This clinical evidence supports the neurobiological model of modular co-determination provided by Edelman, which we will discuss later.

2.2. Self-reference

Rosenfield's analysis of Mr. March's left-side discoordination supports Lakoff's [29] view that understanding of the world is grounded in and emerges from the dynamics of body movements. Body movements serve as a frame of reference by which stimuli are organized, and upon which more complex coordinations and categorizations are built. For the infant, consciousness only develops after "genetically determined reflexes" (p. 61) provide initial experience upon which stimuli can be systematically experienced and organized. The relation between new and old (what Edelman calls "the remembered present") is experienced as a sense of self-familiarity during activity itself, forming the basis of self-awareness and ultimately personality.

The nature of self-reference is revealed by patients with loss of awareness of their limbs ("alien limbs"), as well as the changed experience of people who become blind. For example, Hull suggests that after becoming blind he has difficulty in recollecting prior experiences that involve seeing. Rosenfield's interpretation is that neurological structures involved in seeing are now difficult to coordinate with Hull's present experience. His memories are not lost, but his visual self-reference is limited. That is, remembering is a kind of coordination process. Hull's present self-image is *visually restricted*: "There is no extension of awareness into space ... I am dissolving. I am no longer concentrated in a particular location ..." (quoted by Rosenfield, p. 64). Without an *ongoing* visual frame of reference, he is unable to establish relations to his *prior* visual experience.

Again, recollecting isn't retrieving and reciting the contents of memory, but a dynamic process of establishing "relations to one's present self" (p. 66). "Establishing relations" means physically integrating previous neural activations with currently active neural processes. A stored linguistic schema model fits Hull's experience less well than a model of memory based on physical processes of bodily coordination.

The case of Oliver Sacks' [43] alien leg (paralyzed and without feeling because of an accident) also reveals self-referential aspects of awareness. Upon seeing his leg in his bed and not recognizing it, Sacks actually tossed it out of the bed, landing on the floor. Rosenfield emphasizes that "seeing is not by itself 'knowing' and that the lack of inner self-reference, together with the incontrovertible sight of the leg, therefore created a paradoxical relation to it" (p. 53). Sacks is not just *sensing* his leg, for he can clearly see it and recognizes that it is a leg. Instead, Sacks is relating his categorizations to his ongoing sense of himself and his surroundings. If we see a strange object in our bed (especially an unfamiliar leg), we move to throw it out. Rosenfield argues that *we cannot separate categorizing from this ongoing process of sustaining the self versus non-self relation*. Both Rosenfield and Edelman argue that most cognitive models and AI programs lack self-reference, or view it as a secondary reflection after behavior occurs. Edelman's models suggest that self-reference involves neurological feedback between levels of categorization, including feedforward relations between higher-level coordinating and lower-level perceptual categorizations.

Another patient studied by Charcot, Monsieur A, lost his ability to recognize shapes and colors. He could no longer draw or visualize images (both of which he previously did extraordinarily well) or even recognize his family. As often occurs in these cases, Monsieur A was now, in his words, "less susceptible to sorrow or psychological pain". This *diminished sense of pleasure and pain indicates a change in self-reference*, of awareness of the self. Oddly, Monsieur A could speak and answer questions and continued his work and everyday life in a somewhat disjointed way. But he was unable to establish a relation between words and his sensory experience. He understood words only in their abstract relations. As in Hull's case, this inability to perceive now impaired his ability to remember; as Monsieur A put it, "Today I can remember things only if I say them to myself, while in the past I had only to photograph them with my sight" (p. 93). This suggests again that remembering is integrated with sensory experience, that *remembering is a form of perceiving.*

Early work by the "diagram makers" viewed neural lesions in terms of cutting off areas of the brain, such that stored images, word definitions, or the like are inaccessible. Contradicting Charcot, Rosenfield claims that Monsieur A had not lost specific visual memories, but his ability to integrate *present* visual experience—to establish a present sense of himself—that included immediate and practical relation with colors and shapes. Semantic content doesn't reside in a store of linguistic categorizations, but in the relation of categorizations to each other. Indeed, *every categorization is a dynamic relation between neural processes.* Edelman's model suggests that in Monsieur A neural maps that ordinarily relate different subsystems in the brain are unable to actively coordinate his visual sensory stimuli with ongoing conceptualization of experience. Experiments show that sensory categorization may still be occurring (e.g., some patients unable to recognize friends and family may exhibit galvanic skin responses) (p. 123). But conscious awareness of sensation requires establishing a *relation* with the current conceptualization of the self.

The process of sustaining self-coherence has a holistic aspect, such that loss of any one sensory modality has global effects on memory and personality. Again, this argues for consciousness not as a side-effect of a discrete assembly of components, but as the business of the brain as it coordinates past activation relations with ongoing perception and movement.

2.3. Time

A sense of time is inherently relational. Time is another manifestation of self-reference, awareness that present experience bears a relation to what we experienced before. Rosenfield argues that such feedback is inherently part of ongoing conscious awareness. When it is impaired, not only is memory impaired, but also our ability to learn, to coordinate complex concepts, and to sustain a coherent personality. Again, dysfunction reveals processes that we take for granted in everyday experience and inadequately credit in our theories of cognition.

Mabille and Pitres' patient in 1913, Mr. Baud, provides a good example. When asked if he knows the town of La Rochelle, he replies that he went there some time ago to find a pretty woman. He remembers where he stayed, and says that he never went back. Yet he has been in a hospital in La Rochelle for thirteen years. He also says he has a mistress whom he sees every Saturday. Asked when he last saw her, he responds, "last Saturday".

But again he hasn't left the hospital in all this time (p. 80). Contradicting Mabille and Pitres, Rosenfield tells us that we have no idea what the patient meant by "last Saturday". It could not possibly be a specific Saturday since he has no idea what day today is; Mr. Baud has no specific memory beyond the past twenty seconds.

Oddly, Mr. Baud is a bit like a stored linguistic schema program. He knows how to use words in a conversation, but he has no ongoing, connected experience. He is like a program that has only been living for twenty seconds, but has a stored repertoire of definitions and scripts. He knows the patterns of what he typically does and answers questions logically on this basis: Since he goes every Saturday, he must have gone last Saturday. But from the observer's perspective, which transcends Mr. Baud's twenty-second life span, he lacks a sense of time. Interpreting his case is tricky, because Mr. Baud can't be recalling La Rochelle as we know it if he doesn't acknowledge that he's currently in that town. How in fact, could he be recalling any *place* at all or any *time* at all in the sense that we make sense of our location and temporal experience?

Rosenfield argues that our normal "relation to the world is not sometimes abstract and sometimes immediate, but rather *always both*" (p. 80). To say that Mr. Baud has abstract, long-term memory, but lacks immediate, short-term memory ignores how our attention shifts in normal experience as we relate recollections to what we are experiencing now. "Distant experiences become specific—refer to a specific event in our past—when we can relate them to our present world" (pp. 75–76). Without this ability to coordinate his reminiscences with his present experience, Mr. Baud exhibits a breakdown in an aspect of sense-making, not merely a loss of memory or inability to store recent experiences. His recollections are "odd abstractions, devoid of temporal meaning" (p. 77). That is, a sense of time involves a kind of self-reference that Mr. Baud cannot experience.

Strikingly, this view of meaning goes beyond the idea of "indexicality", previously emphasized in situated cognition (e.g., [1]). Understanding is not just establishing the relation of words like "last Saturday" to the present situation. Knowing the present situation involves having a dynamic sense of self. Without being able to relate my experiences (either past or present) back to *me* (p. 87), my awareness of the past, of history, of memory, and the present situation will be impaired. Put another way, understanding, as well as remembering and reasoning, involve orienting my *self*. If I am confused about who I am, I can't understand what "here" and "now" mean.

Consciousness as a mechanism sustains a relation between our recollections and our ongoing sense of self. Naming, history-telling, and theorizing—integral aspects of sense-making [45]—are ways of establishing relationships in our experience (p. 98). Mr. Baud, lacking an "immediate" relation to his surroundings, can't have an abstract relation either. His recollections are *timeless* in lacking a relation to the present (p. 80). The view that there are isolated functions, such as short and long-term memory, and that one is simply missing, is inadequate. It is Mr. Baud's ability to coordinate neural processes, not access stored facts, that is impaired. This illustrates the thematic contention of Rosenfield and Edelman that cognitive science benefits from a biological re-examination of the nature of memory. In effect, prevalent functional models and computational engines assume a separability of activation and processing that the brain does not employ.

Rosenfield cites studies that suggest that dysfunctions like Mr. Baud's appear to be caused by damage to the hippocampus and associated structures in the limbic system (p. 85), which is "essential for establishing the correlations between the body image and external stimuli that are the basis of consciousness" (p. 86). Edelman's analysis goes further to relate such "primary consciousness" to conceptual categorization by the cortex.

2.4. Language

Rosenfield's discussion of language provides a good introduction to Edelman's model. Both authors claim that the nature of the brain's development, coupled with the evolution of language, suggest that grammars are neither innate nor stored as discrete structures in the brain. Speaking a language involves continual recategorization of both the sounds and meanings of words. A stored-rule view of static information is not sufficient to explain how we dynamically understand "different speakers [who] pronounce words differently, and a given speaker may pronounce the same word in a number of different ways" (p. 37). Rosenfield and Edelman argue that we are re-structuring previous neural activations directly, not reasoning about features of sounds or using an intermediate, descriptive representation. Crucially, *the same in-place adjustments occur as we conceptualize and understand meanings.*

As an example, Rosenfield describes brain-damaged patients unable to use terms like "red" abstractly, but who can nevertheless perceive and sort objects by color. Again, Rosenfield argues against a "disconnection model" in which concepts like "red" are assumed to be innate categories. This model is still current in cognitive neuropsychology, with claims that different kinds of words such as proper nouns, verbs, prepositions, etc. are stored in different parts of the brain that are genetically functionally specialized. An alternative explanation is that the mechanism by which *relations* are constructed and differences generalized is impaired: The patient "finds puzzling Gelb and Goldstein's insistence that all the variant shades are 'red'" (p. 103). The patient has difficulty forming kinds of *conceptual* categorizations (i.e., coordinating perceptual categorizations), not retrieving facts about colors.

Using examples from infant learning, Rosenfield argues, "Learning a language might well be described as the acquisition of the skill of generalization or categorization" (p. 105). That is, *naming is a sense-making activity*, and processes of categorization build on each other. So, for example, "children first learn the words for size and only later the words for colors" (p. 105).

Crucially, categories are *relations*, as Rosenfield says repeatedly. Edelman calls coherent responses to stimuli "perceptual categorization". But according to Rosenfield, this fails to emphasize that each categorization is a relation to other coherent coordinations (ongoing and previously activated) (p. 83). That is, the meaning of a concept is embodied in the functional relation of ongoing neural processes, themselves constructed from prior coordinations. Bartlett made this same point in 1932:

> It is with remembering as it is with the stroke in a skilled game. We may fancy that we are repeating a series of movements learned a long time before from a text-book or from a teacher. But motion study shows that in fact we build up the stroke afresh on a basis of the immediately preceding balance of postures and the momentary needs of the game. Every time we make it, it has its own characteristics.
>
> [T]here is no reason in the world for regarding these [traces/schemata] as made complete at one moment, stored up somewhere, and then re-excited at some much later moment. [5, p. 211]

Rosenfield provides a useful analogy:

> How categorization of a stimulus is achieved might be best understood by an analogy. Imagine, for example, a group of musicians, let us say a string quartet. As each member of the quartet plays his individual instrument, he both sends to and receives from his fellow musicians "signals" about the sound, volume, rhythm, accent, and tone quality of the music. Each player is carrying on an individual dialogue with the other players, together creating a sound at any given moment. There is no conductor, no central command. So, too, in the brain, local interactions among the brain's maps, their "speaking" back and forth to each other by an exchange of signals, creates a coherent response to a stimulus. The response to the stimulus is not predetermined; local interactions among different parts of the brain give the response its coherence. Just as the shape and overall sound of the quartet's performance is created by the various sounds from moment to moment, so, too, categorizations emerge from the brain's relating one coherent response to another and another. (p. 83)

Instead of a score, the brain's "players" are reenacting their previous roles, improvising their relations to each other in a new composition. Chaos or "oscillation" models of the brain [23] suggest that both local interactions and global effects may be accommodated simultaneously, in real time. Edelman's "maps of maps" provide another top-down organizing mechanism. The key ideas involved in dialectical control and organization are: (1) composition in place (as opposed to use of buffers, copying, or a central place where conceptions are assembled; in terms of the analogy, the musical effect arises and exists only in actual playing), and (2) no intermediate linguistic descriptions in the forms of grammars, scripts, or word definitions (except in so far as the person interactively engages in such representing behavior in cycles of perceiving and acting over time; taking our analogy literally, musical scores are only interpreted in playing over time, not stored and executed internally). Finally, for the ensemble of musicians, as well as the brain, coherence arises because of the *relation* between local and global constraints.

Possible relations are constrained by the available mechanisms in the brain, the evolution of human language as a social process, and the development of the individual. Rosenfield illustrates the generalization process of creating new languages with examples of sign language and Creole. Note that the issue is *how a new language develops*, not how people learn an existing language. In this case, linguists observe a two-generation process by which the first generation of children and adults develops gestures or pidgin, with only a simple grammar if any at all. The younger children of the second generation "abstract (categorize) the gestures of older students, creating from them symbols and more abstract categories of relations among these symbols—a true grammar. An older child may point (gesture) to a rabbit to indicate his subject; a younger one will categorize the pointing gesture as 'rabbit,' and the gesture becomes a symbol" (pp. 110–111). The need for a second generation suggests that neural mechanisms alone are not sufficient, in the individual, for developing a new grammatical language.

In effect, the experience of many different gestures present in the environment becomes categorized into a repeated experience of "gesturing", with an associated typology and ordering of gestures as symbols. A similar analysis is demonstrated by Bamberger's [4] studies of children learning to perceive and use musical tones, not just as integrated parts of a melody, but as named and ordered objects that can be manipulated to produce meaningful sequences. This developmental process illustrates the "brain's constant reworking of its own generalizations" (p. 111).

The patterns between sign language and Creole language development suggest the importance of social sharing of language, as well as neurological constraints that limit an older child's ability to abstract a language beyond its immediate and practical relations. We are reminded of brain-damaged patients who lack a sense of abstract time, color, shape, etc., but can handle particulars in the "here and now". (Again, without a possible concomitant abstract meaning, the particulars have a different sense than experienced by people with abstraction capabilities.)

Rosenfield and Edelman both argue against the existence of specific innate categories or grammar rules, and emphasize the overwhelming importance of cultural influences on what can be accomplished by individuals. However, they agree that the mechanism that enables *grammatical* language to develop involves neurological structures that evolved in the human species and are not found in other animals. Nevertheless, these are "new areas of the brain … not new principles of mental function" (p. 119). This is supported by Edelman's model, which shows new relations between existing processes of categorization, not a new kind of compositional activation process. Similar arguments are made by Head and Bartlett; more recently, Calvin [9] claims that sequencing control processes for physical movements such as throwing are involved in speech and complex conceptualization. That is, the same kinds of neurological processes may occur in different areas of the brain, becoming specialized for different functions through use. Rosenfield calls this the "holistic" view, in which parts are "not independently specialized, but interdependent" (p. 24). Categorizing areas of the brain establish dynamic, time-sensitive relations to other areas, as opposed to storing discrete representations of words, sounds, meanings, etc. in isolation. This is also what Rosenfield means when he says that functions are not predetermined, either inborn in the infant or as pre-stored responses in the adult.

The primary repertoire of neural interactions, within which categorization and coordination occurs, is not determined by genes, but develops in adolescence through a complex process involving topological constraints, redundant connections, and experiential strengthening. Even the brains of identical twins are wired differently (p. 82). This is of course strong evidence against the idea that specific linguistic rules or categories could be inherent in the brain. Rather the existence of commonalities in human language, known as universal grammar, is evidence of common *transformational* principles by which categories are formed.

Specifically, language adds a new kind of self-reference (p. 119), in which we become explicitly conscious of ourselves, by naming of phenomenological experience, historical accounts, and causal rationalizations [45]. This self-reference required the evolution of a special memory system that "categorized the vocal cord's gestural patterns":

> The brain, *linking these gestures to its nonlinguistic categorizations of its own activities,* and categorizing these linked signals in another special memory system, created the basis for a gestural system that can refer to objects and actions. A developed gestural

language became a stimulus [internally] and was recategorized into symbols and a true syntax. After sufficient lexical experience, the language was in turn treated as a stimulus by the categorical centers and recategorized; thus language became an independent means of thought, creating the notion of time past, present, and future. (pp. 112–113; emphasis added)

As we will now see, Edelman's models of the brain specify what areas of the brain are involved and their relations to each other.

3. Overview of *Bright Air, Brilliant Fire*

AI researchers may struggle to find implications for program design in Rosenfield's book, so I have explained his ideas at some length. Edelman's argument is more accessible to AI researchers because he draws on some familiar sources, referring to Lakoff throughout the book, and explicitly discussing models of representation and learning. Nevertheless, the neurobiological argument is intricate and is by and large unfamiliar to AI researchers. Although the theory of Neural Darwinism has been reviewed for this audience [48,49], I present the ideas again to provide an alternative synthesis that includes Edelman's earlier work on topobiology and makes connections to the broader themes of cognitive science that Edelman now wishes to emphasize.

The title *Bright Air, Brilliant Fire* comes from Empedocles, "a physician, poet, and an early materialist philosopher of mind" (p. xvi) in the sixth century B.C., who suggested that perception can be understood in terms of material entities. Edelman believes that understanding the particular material properties of the actual "matter underlying our minds—neurons, their connections, and their patterns" (p. 1) is essential for understanding consciousness and building intelligent machines, because the brain works unlike any machine we have ever built. Of special interest is how Edelman relates his understanding of sensorimotor coordination to Lakoff's analysis of concepts as embodied processes.

The book is organized into four parts: (1) "Problems" with current models of the mind; (2) "Origins" of new approaches based on evolution and developmental biology; (3) "Proposals" for neurobiological models of memory, consciousness, and language; and (4) "Harmonies" or "fruitful interactions that a science of mind must have with philosophy, medicine, and physics" (p. 153). The book concludes with a forty-page postscript, "Mind without Biology", criticizing objectivism, mechanical functionalism, and formal approaches to language. I will cover these ideas in the same order: (1) biological mechanisms that are potentially relevant, and perhaps crucial, to producing artificial intelligence; (2) a summary of the theory of Neural Darwinism; (3) how consciousness arises through these mechanisms; and (4) the synthesis of these ideas in the Darwin III robot. In Section 4, I elaborate on the idea of pre-linguistic coordination, which reveals the limitations of stored linguistic schema mechanisms. In Section 5, I argue for preserving functionalism as a modeling technique, while accepting Edelman's view that it be rejected as a theory of the mind.

3.1. The matter of the mind: biological mechanisms

> If you consider these extraordinary brain properties in conjunction with the dilemmas created by the machine or the computer view of the mind, it is fair to say that we have a scientific crisis …. For a possible way out, let us look to biology itself, rather than to physics, mathematics, or computer science. (p. 69)

Edelman believes that neuroscience now allows us to begin "connecting up what we know about our minds to what we are beginning to know about our brains" (p. 5). His analysis combines an alternative epistemology, which he calls "anti-cognitivist", with biological mechanisms he calls "value-based selectionism" and "Neural Darwinism".

Cognitivism is the view that reasoning is based solely on manipulation of semantic representations. Cognitivism is based on *objectivism* ("that an unequivocal description of reality can be given by science") and *classical categories* (that objects and events can be "defined by sets of singly necessary and jointly sufficient conditions") (p. 14). This conception is manifest in expert systems, for example, or any cognitive model that supposes that human memory consists only of stored linguistic descriptions (e.g., scripts, frames, rules, grammars). Echoing many similar analyses (e.g., [15,29,54]), Edelman characterizes these computer programs as "axiomatic systems" because they contain the designer's symbolic categories and rules of combination, from which all the program's subsequent world models and sensorimotor procedures will be derived. Paralleling the claims of many other theorists, from Collingwood and Dewey to Garfinkel and Bateson, he asserts that such linguistic models "… are social constructions that are the *results* of thought, not the basis of thought" (p. 153). He draws a basic distinction between what people do or experience and their linguistic descriptions (names, laws, scripts):

> Laws do not and cannot exhaust experience or replace history or the events that occur in the actual courses of individual lives. Events are denser than any possible scientific description. They are also microscopically indeterminate, and, given our theory, they are even to some extent macroscopically so. (pp. 162–163)

This distinction between practice and theory dominates anthropological theory [51].

Although science cannot exhaustively describe particular, individual experiences, it can properly study the *constraints* on experience. Edelman focuses on biological constraints. He claims that the *biological organization of matter in the brain produces kinds of physical processes that have not been replicated in computers.* "By taking the position of a biologically-based epistemology, we are in some sense realists" (recognizing the inherent "density" of objects and events) "and also sophisticated materialists" (p. 161) (holding that thought, will, etc. are produced by physical systems, but emphasizing that not all mechanisms have the same capabilities).

Edelman believes that cognitivism produced "a scientific deviation as great as that of the behaviorism it attempted to supplant" (p. 14) in assuming that neurobiological processes have no properties that computers don't already replicate (e.g., assembling, matching, and storing symbol structures). This assumption limits what current computers can do, as manifest in: the symbol grounding problem, combinatorial search, inflexibilities of a rule-bound mechanism, and inefficient real-time coordination. The most "egregious" category mistake is "the notion that the whole enterprise [of AI] can proceed by studying behavior, mental performance and competence, and language under the assumptions of functionalism without first understanding the underlying biology" (p. 15). By this account, Newell's [32] attempts to relate psychological data to biological constraints (not cited by Edelman) are inadequate because the "bands" of *Unified Theories of Cognition* misconstrue the interpenetration of neural and environmental processes (Section 2). Putting "mind back into nature" requires considering "how it got there in the first place.... [We] must heed what we have learned from the theory of evolution".

Edelman proceeds to summarize the basic developmental neurobiology of the brain, "the most complicated material object in the known universe" (p. 17). Development is epigenetic, meaning that the network and topology of neural connections is not prespecified genetically in detail, but develops in the embryo through competitive neural activity. Surprisingly, cells move and interact: "in some regions of the developing nervous system up to 70 percent of the neurons die before the structure of that region is completed!" (p. 25).[1] The brain is not organized like conventionally manufactured hardware: the wiring is highly variable and borders of neural maps change

---

[1] Formation of primary connections between cells may continue in the development of the immature organism, intermixed with formation of secondary repertoires (neuronal groups). The nature of synaptic and neuronal group selection changes after adolescence, affecting acquisition of new languages in adults (explaining Rosenfield's analysis of language evolution over multiple generations).

over time. Individual neurons cannot carry information in the sense that electronic devices carry information, because there is no predetermination of what specific connections and maps mean:

> Nervous system behavior is to some extent self-generated in loops; brain activity leads to movement, which leads to further sensation and perception and still further movement. The layers and loops ... are dynamic; they continually change. (p. 29)

As previously mentioned, Dewey [17] emphasized that neural activations arise as complete *circuits*, within already existing coordinations (sequences of neural activations over time), not isolated paths between peripheral subsystems. Carrying the idea further, Edelman states that "there is no such thing as software involved in the operations of brains" (p. 30). As we will discuss later (Sections 3.2 and 4), this means that each new perceptual categorization, conceptualization, and sensory-motor coordination brings "hardware" components together in new ways, modifying the population of physical elements available for future activation and recombination. Crucially, this physical rearrangement of the brain is not produced by a software compilation process (translating from linguistic descriptions) or isomorphic to linguistic names and semantic manipulations (our conventional idea of software). Different structures can produce the same result, so "there is macroscopic indeterminacy ... the strong psychological determinism proposed by Freud does not hold" (pp. 169–170).

Edelman observes that only biological entities have intentions, and asks, what kind of morphology provides a minimum basis for mental processes, and "when did it emerge in evolutionary time"? (p. 33) . How did the brain arise by natural selection? By better understanding the development of hominid behavior in groups and the development of language, we can better characterize the function and development of mental processes, and hence understand how morphology was selected. Given the 99% genetic similarity between humans and chimpanzees, we would do well to understand the nature, function, and evolution of the differences. Edelman seeks to uncover the distinct *physical capabilities* that separate animals from other life and humans from other primates. What hardware organizations make language and consciousness possible?

3.2. Neural Darwinism: *the sciences of recognition*

Edelman received the Nobel Prize in 1972 for his model of the recognition processes of the immune system. Recognition of bacteria is based on competitive selection in a population of antibodies. This process has several intriguing properties (p. 78):

(1) there is more than one way to recognize successfully any particular shape;
(2) no two people have identical antibodies;
(3) the system exhibits a form of memory at the cellular level (prior to antibody reproduction).

Edelman extends this theory to a more general "science of recognition":

> By "recognition," I mean the continual adaptive matching or fitting of elements in one physical domain to novelty occurring in elements of another, more or less independent physical domain, a matching that occurs without prior instruction. ... [T]here is no explicit information transfer between the environment and organisms that causes the population to change and increase its fitness. (p. 74)[2]

By analogy, mental categories, coordinations, and conceptualizations are like a population of neural maps constituting a "species". There is a common *selectional mechanism* by which the organism "recognizes" an offending bacteria, as well as "recognizes" an experienced situation:

> Memory is a process that emerged only when life and evolution occurred and gave rise to the systems described by the sciences of recognition.... [I]t describes aspects of heredity, immune responses, reflex learning, true learning following perceptual categorization, and the various forms of consciousness.... What they have in common is *relative stability of structure under selective mapping events.* (pp. 203–204)

> The species concept arising from ... population thinking is central to all ideas of categorization. Species are not 'natural kinds'; their definition is relative, they are not homogeneous, they have no prior necessary condition for their establishment, and they have no clear boundaries. (p. 239)

The theory explains "how multiple maps lead to integrated responses, and how they lead to generalizations of perceptual responses, *even in the absence of language*" (p. 82, emphasis added).

Edelman's theory of neuronal group selection (TNGS) has several components:

---

[2]Here Edelman follows von Foerster's [53] usage, suggesting that the term "information" be reserved for categories constructed by an organism in segmenting and classifying signals. Maturana goes a step further, insisting that in labeling phenomena as "signals" an observer is partitioning a single interactive process into "inside" and "outside" components and events. This is an important aspect of scientific study, but should not suggest that the analytic categories have existence apart from the observer's ontology and purposes (for discussion, see [14,54]).

(1) how the structure of the brain develops in the embryo and during early life (topobiology);
(2) a theory of recognition and memory rooted in "population thinking" (Darwinism); and
(3) a detailed model of classification and neural map selection (Neural Darwinism).

Topobiology "refers to the fact that many of the transactions between one cell and another leading to shape are place dependent" (p. 57). This theory partially accounts for the nature and evolution of three-dimensional functional forms in the brain. Movement of cells in epigenesis is a statistical matter (p. 60), leading identical twins to have different brain structures. Special signaling processes account for formation of sensory maps during infancy (and in some respects through adolescence). The intricacy of timing and placement of forms helps explain how great functional variation can occur; this diversity is "one of the most important features of morphology that gives rise to mind" (p. 64). Diversity is important because it lays the foundation for recognition and coordination based exclusively on selection within a population of (sometimes redundant) connections.

Population thinking is a characteristically biological mode of thought "not present or even required in other sciences" (p. 73). It emphasizes the importance of diversity—not merely evolutionary change, but selection from a wide variety of options. "Population thinking states that evolution produces classes of living forms from the bottom up by gradual selective processes over eons of time" (p. 73). Applied to populations of neuronal groups, there are three tenets:

- *developmental selection*, through epigenetic processes already mentioned,
- *experiential selection*, the creation of a secondary level repertoire, called neuronal groups, through selective strengthening and weakening of the neural connections, and
- *reentry*, which links two maps bi-directionally through "parallel selection and correlation of the maps' neuronal groups" (p. 84).

The levels of nested components involved in categorization are: neural cells, neuronal groups, neural maps, classification couples, and global maps. I summarize these components in the following two subsections.

3.2.1. Neuronal groups and classification

Neuronal groups are collections of neural cells that fire and oscillate together (p. 95). Neuronal groups are the units of selection in the development of new functioning circuits (pp. 85–86). By analogy to organisms in a species and lymphocytes, neuronal groups are individuals (Table 1). Reactivation of a neuronal group corresponds to selection of individuals in

Table 1
Neuronal group selection viewed according evolutionary Darwinism.

Species	Functionally segregated map, responding to local features and participating in classification couples with other maps.
Population	Map composed of neuronal groups.
Individual	Neuronal group.

a species.[3] Although one might suppose individual synapses or neurons to correspond to individuals in a population, individual neurons are in general always selected within a group and only influence other neurons through groups: Each neural cell "receives inputs from cells in its own group, from cells in other groups, and from extrinsic sources" (p. 88).[4] The existence of neuronal groups is controversial, but has been experimentally demonstrated (pp. 94–95).

A *neural map* is composed of neuronal groups. Two functionally different neural maps connected by reentry form a *classification couple*:

> Each map *independently* receives signals from other brain maps or from the world.... [F]unctions and activities in one map are connected and correlated with those in another map.... One set of inputs could be, for example, from vision, and the other from touch. (p. 87)

Edelman doesn't relate neuronal selection as clearly to species evolution as we might expect for a popularized treatment. I attempt here and in Table 1 to make the connections more explicit. First, a significant number of non-identical neuronal groups can function similarly within maps (responding to the same inputs), a fundamental property of TNGS called *degeneracy* [21, p. 6]. This roughly corresponds to different individuals in a species having different genotypes, but selected within an environment for similar functional characteristics. Apparently, a population of neuronal

---

[3]Note that the ideas of "mating" and "reproduction" are not essential parts of the more general ideas of population thinking and recognition. Apparently, the reactivation of a neuronal group corresponds to reproduction of a new individual with "inherited" relations from its activation within previous maps. Changes in genotype of individuals in a species correspond to changes in strength of synaptic connections of neuronal groups within a map (p. 94). A simple evolutionary analogy might suggest viewing an individual as an *instance* of a species. Instead, we view a species as a coherent collection of *interacting* individuals (here a map of neuronal groups). Thus, the connections define the population. Furthermore, selection occurs on multiple levels of form—neuronal groups, maps, and maps of maps.

[4]Formation of synaptic connections (primary repertoire) and neuronal groups (secondary repertoire) can be intermixed (p. 85). The extraordinary, three-fold increase in human brain size after birth [30, p. 159] may be related to the formation of reentrant loops between the conceptual cortex and perceptual categorization, enabling primary consciousness (Fig. 1).

groups becomes a "species" when it becomes functionally distinct from other populations. This occurs when maps interact during the organism's behavior. In effect, the "environment" for a map consists of other active maps. Excitatory and inhibitory interactions between maps correspond to interspecies interactions at the level of competitive and symbiotic relations in the environment. Neural maps effectively define each other's populations by activation relations between their neuronal groups. Reentry (bi-directional activation between *populations* of neuronal groups)[5] provides the means for map interaction and reactivation during organism behavior. Reentry explains how "brain areas that emerge in evolution coordinate with each other to yield new functions" (p. 85) during an individual organism's lifetime. Specifically, local maps can be *reused without copying* by selection of additional reentry links to form new classification couples (with specialized interactions between their neuronal groups). Edelman concludes that reentry thus provides "the main basis for a bridge between physiology and psychology" (p. 85).

3.2.2. Coordinating categorizations by global maps: sequences and concepts

Another level of organization is required to dynamically coordinate categorizations to ongoing sensorimotor behavior: "A global mapping is a dynamic structure containing multiple reentrant local maps (both motor and sensory) that are able to interact with non-mapped parts of the brain" (p. 89). Selection continually occurs within local maps of a global map, making connections to motor behavior, new sensory samplings, and successive reentry events, allowing new categorizations to emerge:

> Categorization does not occur according to a computerlike program in a sensory area which then executes a program to give a particular motor output. Instead, sensorimotor activity over the whole mapping *selects* neuronal groups that give appropriate output or behavior, resulting in categorization. (pp. 89–90)

Appropriateness is determined by internal criteria of value that constrain the domains in which categorization occurs, exhibited most fundamentally in regulation of bodily functions (respiratory, feeding, sex, etc.):

> The thalamocortical system ... evolved to receive signals from sensory receptor sheets and to give signals to voluntary muscles. ... [I]ts main structure, the cerebral cortex is arranged in a set of maps ... as highly connected, layered local structures with massively reentrant connections.... [T]he cortex is concerned with the categorization of the world and the limbic-brain system

---

[5]See Reeke et al. [40] for further comparison of reentry to recursion.

is concerned with value. ... [L]earning may be seen as the means by which categorization occurs on a background of value ... (pp. 117–118)

Categorization is therefore relational, occurring within, and in some sense bound to, an active, *ongoing coordinated sequence* of sensory and motor behavior: "The physical movements of an animal drive its perceptual categorization ... " (p. 167). Crucially, global maps themselves rearrange, collapse, or are replaced through perturbations at different levels (p. 91).

Memory "results from a process of continual *recategorization*. By its nature, memory is procedural and involves continual motor activity" (p. 102). Hence, memory is not a place or identified with the low-level mechanisms of synaptic reactivation; and certainly memory is not a coded representation of objects in the world (p. 238). Rather, "memory is a system property" (p. 102) involving not only categorization of sensory-motor activations, but categorizations of *sequences* of neural activations:

> The brain contains structures such as the cerebellum, the basal ganglia, and the hippocampus that are concerned with timing, succession in movement, and the establishment of memory. They are closely connected with the cerebral cortex as it carries out categorization and correlation of the kind performed by global mappings.... (p. 105)

> The brain ... has no replicative memory. It is historical and value driven. It forms categories by internal criteria and by constraints acting at many scales. (p. 152)

Following Lakoff's analysis, Edelman distinguishes between concepts and linguistic symbols. *Concept* refers "to a capability that appears in evolution prior to the acquisition of linguistic primitives.... Unlike elements of speech, however, concepts are *not* conventional or arbitrary, do *not* require linkage to a speech community to develop, and do *not* depend on sequential presentation" (p. 108). Concepts are categorizations of internal categorizing:

> [I]n forming concepts, the brain constructs maps of its *own* activities.... [These maps] categorize parts of past global mappings according to modality, the presence or absence of movement, and the presence or absence of relationships between perceptual categorizations.... They must represent *a mapping of types of maps.* Instead, they must be able to activate or reconstruct portions of *past* activities of global mappings of different types.... They must also be able to recombine or compare them. This means that special reentrant connections from these higher-order cortical areas

> to other cortical areas and to the hippocampus and basal ganglia
> must exist to carry out concepts. (p. 109)

Thus, *intentional behavior* involves sensory-motor sequencing influenced in a top-down manner by conceptual reactivation and construction: "because concept formation is based on the central triad of perceptual categorization, memory, and learning, it is, by its very nature, intentional" (p. 110).

3.3. Consciousness

This brings us to consciousness, which Edelman characterizes on two levels: *primary consciousness*, found in some animals such as dogs, and *higher-order consciousness*, found in humans and to some degree in other primates:

> Primary consciousness is the state of being mentally aware of things in the world—of having mental images in the present. But it is not accompanied by any sense of a person with a past and a future.... In contrast, higher-order consciousness involves the recognition by a thinking subject of his or her own acts or affections. It embodies a model of the personal, and of the past and the future as well as the present. It exhibits direct awareness—the noninferential or immediate awareness of mental episodes without the involvement of sense organs or receptors. It is what we humans have in addition to primary consciousness. We are conscious of being conscious. (p. 112)

In effect, Edelman claims that a special kind of physical link between conceptual and perceptual categorization enables being tacitly aware of ourselves in relation to what we have done before or imagined will occur. This self-reference, the dynamic coordination of action and attention described by Rosenfield, involves conceptualization of internal experience in a manner that is "direct", rather than mediated by deliberation. Nevertheless, linguistic naming and inference in our previous activity over time plays a key role in self-conceptualization. For example, according to this theory, comprehending a set of instructions involves conceptualization that enables oriented action in the future, without consulting the instructions. Of course, linguistic representation (naming, telling stories, giving explanations) is essential for dealing with an inability to coordinate activity by primary consciousness alone ("impasses" described by Bartlett [5] and "breakdowns" described by Winograd and Flores [54]). For example, in following through a previously comprehended plan, we may become aware that we don't know what to do next because we sense that a situation is unfamiliar.

3.3.1. Primary consciousness: categorizing qualia into a scene

Paralleling Dennett's [15] analysis, Edelman suggests that reports of subjective experience can be correlated and used as a basis for the scientific study of consciousness.

> Qualia constitute the collection of personal or subjective experiences, feelings, and sensations that accompany awareness.... For example, the "redness" of a red object is a quale. (p. 114)

> [Q]ualia may be usefully viewed as forms of higher-order categorization, as relations reportable to the self.... (p. 116)

> [I]n some animal species with cortical systems, the categorizations of separate causally unconnected parts of the world can be correlated and bound into a *scene* ... a spatiotemporally ordered set of categorizations of familiar and unfamiliar events. ... [T]he ability to create a scene ... led to the emergence of primary consciousness. (p. 118)

Three evolved functions are sufficient for primary consciousness:

- a cortical system linking conceptual functions to the limbic system;
- a "value-category" memory, allowing "conceptual responses to occur in terms of the *mutual* interactions of the thalamocortical and limbic-brain stem systems" (p. 119); and
- "continual reentrant signaling between the value-category memory and the ongoing global mappings that are concerned with perceptual categorization in real time".

Linking perceptual events into a *scene* constitutes "a conceptual categorization of concurrent perceptions". This occurs *before* the independent perceptual signals contribute to independent memory of each modality (p. 119). As an adaptive way of directing attention, this mechanism accounts for *how a sense of similarity arises* prior to articulation of categorical features in metaphorical reasoning [44]. Current value-free perceptual categorization is interacting with the value-dominated conceptual memory before perceptual events and subsequent linguistic theorizing modify conceptual memory. Edelman calls this effect "the remembered present" (p. 120):

> An animal with primary consciousness sees the room the way a beam of light illuminates it. ... In all likelihood, most animals and some birds may have it .... [W]e can be fairly sure that animals without a cortex or its equivalent lack it .... (pp. 122–123)

Primary consciousness in itself does not constitute *awareness of having a long-term memory* or ability to plan based on it:

> Perceptual categorization ... is nonconscious and can be carried out by classification couples.... It treats *signals from the outside world*. By contrast, conceptual categorization works from within the brain, requires perceptual categorization and memory, and treats *the activities of portions of global mappings* as its substrate. Connecting the two kinds of categorization with an additional reentrant path for each sensory modality (that is, in addition to the path that allows conceptual learning to take place) gives rise in primary consciousness to a correlated scene, or "image." [A]n animal with primary consciousness alone is strongly tied to the succession of events in real time. (p. 125)

An animal with only primary consciousness can have long-term memories and act upon them, but "cannot, in general, be aware of that memory or plan an extended future for itself based on that memory" (p. 122). Additional categorization loops tied to linguistic actions enable us to transcend the immediacy of primary consciousness. As Bartlett put it:

> If only the organism could hit upon a way of turning round upon its own 'schemata' and making them the objects of its reactions .... It would be the case that the organism would say, if it were able to express itself: "This and this and this must have occurred, in order that my present state should be what it is". And, in fact, I believe this is precisely and accurately just what does happen in by far the greatest number of instances of remembering .... [5, p. 202]

Primary consciousness involves *internal* criteria to "determine the salience of patterns". Higher-order consciousness "adds socially constructed selfhood", further freeing the individual from "the constraints of an immediate present" (p. 133).

3.3.2. Higher-order consciousness: linguistically modeling past and future

Higher-order consciousness involves language for modeling the relation of the self to the world and interactions with other members of the species. But "a model of self–nonself interaction probably had to emerge prior to a true speech", as is indicated by chimpanzee behavior (p. 126). By such conceptualization, an animal can experience higher-order consciousness without language, but not represent what it means or employ it to reason *about* problems. Language involves naming, telling stories about the past, constructing causal theories, modeling designs for new artifacts, and comparing plans for future actions. In humans, "consciousness of being conscious" involves linguistically representing "a true self (or social self) acting on an environ-

Table 2
Relation of primary and higher-order consciousness.

Consciousness	Morphological requirements	Who experiences it?	Key features
Primary	Cortex reentrant loop connecting value-category memory to current perceptual categorization.	Chimpanzees, probably most mammals and birds	Awareness of directed attention in activity (awareness of intention; basic self-reference).
Higher-order	Broca's and Wernicke's areas; bootstrapping perceptual categorization through linguistic symbolization.	Humans	Awareness of having previous experiences, imagining experiences; conceptualization of self, others, world (awareness of self-reference).

ment and vice versa" (p. 131).[6] Individuals with impaired linguistic ability may have a self-concept that is historically and socially distorted from the perspective of other members of the group (cf. the case of Monsieur A).

Creation of language in the human species required the evolution of (1) cortical areas (named after Broca and Wernicke) to finely coordinate "acoustic, motor, and conceptual areas of the brain by reentrant connections ... [serving] to coordinate the production and categorization of speech" and (2) another layering of categorization, on top of conceptualization, to provide "the more sophisticated sensorimotor ordering that is the basis of true syntax" (p. 127). See Table 2 and Fig. 1.[7]

In a process called "semantic bootstrapping", "the brain must have reentrant structures that allow semantics to emerge *first* (prior to syntax) by relating phonological symbols to concepts" (p. 130). By "phonological sym-

[6]Edelman presents only abstract descriptions of "discriminating qualia", "delaying responses", and "inner events that are recalled". A psychologist or anthropologist would have given at least one example. Is higher-order consciousness necessary to buy groceries? To stalk game? To plant a crop? The evolutionary interactions of language, culture, and consciousness remain obscure. What happens when we comprehend a written plan? Diagnose a patient? Edelman hasn't even begun to relate his model of the brain to existing models of reading, problem solving, and understanding.

[7]Recalling Rosenfield's remark that Edelman should emphasize relations instead of categories, we might remain alert to misleading aspects of such diagrams. In particular, "correlation" occurs as areas of the brain configure each other; particular kinds of categories or memories are not *located* in particular boxes. If we treat boxes uniformly as structural areas of the brain and the lines as reentrant activation links, then classification occurs as a coupled reconfiguration of maps (composed of neuronal groups) within two or more boxes. That is, categorizing physically exists only as a process of co-configuring *multiple areas*, not as stuff stored in some place.

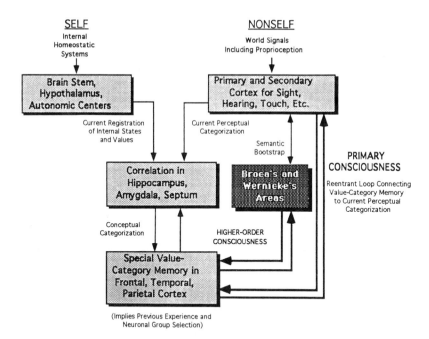

Fig. 1. A scheme for higher-order consciousness. (From Edelman's *Bright Air, Brilliant Fire*, p. 132.)

bols" Edelman apparently means words, viewed as acoustic categorizations. He goes on to say, "When a sufficiently large lexicon is collected, the conceptual areas of the brain categorize the *order* of speech elements". Thus, syntactic correspondences are generated, "not from preexisting rules, but by treating rules *developing in memory* as objects for conceptual manipulation". This is a memory for actual speaking coordinations, not a memory of stored grammar expressions. Edelman doesn't clearly say what he means by conceptual manipulation, but it presumably involves recategorization of previous symbol sequences, as well as categorization of the relation of concepts to symbol sequences:

> The addition of a special symbolic memory [the lexicon of words and phrases] connected to preexisting conceptual centers results in the ability to elaborate, refine, connect, create, and remember great numbers of new concepts.... Meaning arises from the interaction of value-category memory with the *combined* activity of the conceptual areas and speech areas. (p. 130)

Thus, there are stages of intention, reference, awareness, and control: Conceptualization enables an animal to exhibit intention. Primary consciousness involves *awareness of intention*, relating the self to ongoing events. Through categorizations of scenes involving intentional acts of self and others, animals with primary consciousness can exhibit an understanding of *reference* (e.g., a dog seeing a ball knowing that a game is beginning). Intentional acts are imagined, modeled, and controlled through linguistic actions over time in higher-order consciousness. With language, reference becomes symbolic. *Self-reference* begins as value-oriented categorization. When concepts of the self, the past, and the future relate conceptual-symbolic models produced in speech to ongoing perceptual experience, we become aware of self-reference and consciously direct it (e.g., Monsieur A's statement about the need to say things to himself in order to remember them). Reentrant loops give us the ability to project visual, verbal, and emotional experiences; we can attentively enact previously imagined actions—"as if one piece of spacetime could slip and map onto another piece" (p. 169). The problem of coordinating awareness of doing, talking, and visualizing so as to be "consciously unconscious" is a well-known problem in sports [24]. "We live on several levels at once" (p. 150).

> [I]n human beings, primary consciousness and higher-order consciousness coexist, and they each have different relations to time. The sense of "time past" in higher-order consciousness is a *conceptual* matter, having to do with previous orderings of categories in relation to an immediate present driven by primary consciousness. Higher-order consciousness is based not on ongoing experience, as is primary consciousness, but on the ability to model the past and the future. (pp. 167–168)

Once a socially-constructed self arises as a result of higher consciousness, the self becomes necessary "to link one mental image to the next in order to appreciate the workings of primary consciousness" (p. 124).

> Qualia, individual to each of us, are recategorizations by higher-order consciousness of value-laden perceptual relations in each sensory modality or their conceptual combinations with each other .... [They] are increasingly refined by language ... [A] world is developed that requires naming and intending. (p. 136)

Thus, reentrancy and bootstrapping from symbolic and conceptual memories becomes a necessary part of ongoing perceptual categorization. "Consciousness appeared as a result of natural selection. The mind depends on consciousness for its existence and functioning" (p. 149).

Edelman extends his model to broadly explain how neural dysfunctions lead to the kinds of behavior discussed by Rosenfield. He underscores that "All mental diseases are based on physical changes" (p. 178). In particular, he believes that Freud's explanations are limited by inadequately characterizing biological processes:

"Neurological disease" refers to disruptions of sight, movement, and so forth, and is the result of alterations in the regions of the brain involved in these functions. "Psychiatric disease" refers to alterations in categorization, mental activity, qualia, and so forth, in which responses are symbolically deviant or in which "reality testing" is compromised. (p. 181)

For example, schizophrenia may be a "disease of reentry" produced by a "disabling of communications between reentrant maps ..." (p. 184) resulting in overdomination of a perceptual mode (e.g., producing hallucinations), difficulty coordinating the organs of succession, or discoordination between "the lexicon, conceptual centers, and those that mediate imagery" (p. 185). Although not as dramatic as the effects of psychosis, the discomfort experienced by the patients discussed by Rosenfield apparently follows from their impaired ability to reestablish such relationships within a conscious "scene": "the patient's overall response is still an attempt at adaptation, at reintegration" (p. 185).

3.4. Design of Darwin III: synthetic neural systems

Thanks to Reeke et al. [40], Edelman's theories are being tested by development of computer models. Edelman strongly supports the constructive approach of AI: "the only way we may be able to integrate our knowledge of the brain effectively, given all its levels, is by synthesizing artifacts" (p. 188). He proposes the term "noetics" for devices that "act on their environment by selectional means and by categorization on value" (p. 192), in contrast with devices that adapt only within fixed, predesigned constraints (cybernetics) or programmed devices (robotics).

Darwin III [8] is a "recognition automata that performs as a global mapping" (p. 92) that coordinates vision with a simulated tactile arm in a simulated environment. It is capable of "correlating a scene" by reentry between value-category memory and perceptual categorizations. Values are built in (e.g., light is better than darkness), but the resulting categorizations are all internally developed. The system consists of 50 maps, containing 50,000 cells and over 620,000 synaptic junctions [40, p. 608]. This system rests on the model of "reentrant cortical integration" (RCI) which has been tested with much larger networks (129 maps, 220,000 cells, and 8.5 million connections) that simulate visual illusions and the detection of structure from motion in the monkey's visual cortex.

The statistical, stochastic nature of selection is common to many connectionism models. It was mentioned by Bateson [6] in his own discussion of

---

[8]This program shouldn't be confused with Calvin's "Darwin Machine" [9, p. 372], which was proposed five years after the initial work by Reeke and Edelman.

parallels between the evolution of biological phenotypes and the development of ideas. Edelman's model probes deeper by specifying how neural nets are *grown*, not merely selected, and how learning is based on internal value. Neural Darwinism can be contrasted with other connectionist approaches in these aspects:

- the influence of epigenetic and infant development as the source of variability;
- degenerate (redundant) populations of preferred maps for recognition;
- selection that is not merely eliminative (the rich get richer), but maintains variability;
- details concerning global mapping, reentrancy, sensorimotor maps, generalization, classification couples.

We can also apply Pagels' criteria [35, pp. 140–141] for comparing connectionists' models. First, like connectionist models, Darwin III is *not neurally realistic* and arguably lacks massive parallelism. But unlike most connectionist models, Darwin III is *not constructed by building in words* referring to concepts and things in the world that it will learn about [39]. Finally, Darwin III is *based on a series of principles* involving evolution, selectionism, development, non-encoding nature of representations, and a distinction between concepts and symbols.

NOMAD is a robotic implementation of Darwin III, claimed to be "the first nonliving thing capable of 'learning' in the biological sense of the word" (p. 193). But Edelman demurs of replicating the capabilities of the brain. Building a device capable of primary consciousness will require simulating

> ... a brain system capable of concepts and thus of the *reconstruction* of portions of global mappings.... [A]rtifacts with higher-order consciousness would have to have language and the equivalent of behavior in a speech community.... [T]he practical problems ... are so far out of reach that we needn't concern ourselves with them now. (p. 194)

4. Pre-linguistic coordination

Edelman's and Rosenfield's discussions of non-linguistic coordinations provide a way of understanding the claim that knowledge doesn't consist of stored representations and linguistic programs. Even if the reader doesn't buy their argument that there are no stored linguistic structures, the discussion of coordination reveals the adaptability they believe that programs lack.

To understand why stored linguistic schema models poorly capture the flexibility of human behavior, Rosenfield makes an analogy between posture and speech:

> [There is no] dictionary of all the words I know stored in my brain, waiting for me to use them. I create my language, and my sense of myself, more dynamically, just as I move around bodily in space. My sense of "posture" is not stored in my brain, but, rather, the ability to create one posture from another is, the ability to establish relations. And the senses of self and speech, like posture, are constantly evolving structures; what I just said determines, in part, what I will say. Just as one posture gives rise to another and one sentence gives rise to another, one expression of my personality gives rise to another.
>
> Memory, too, comprises the acquired habits and abilities for organizing postures and sentences—for establishing relations. (p. 122)

Head, an English neurologist working in the early part of this century and a teacher of Bartlett, introduced the term "schema" in this context. In 1920, he wrote:

> Every recognizable change enters into consciousness already charged with its relation to something that has gone before.... For this combined standard, ... we propose the word "schema" .... Every new posture of movement is recorded on this plastic schema, and the activity of the cortex brings every fresh group of sensations evoked by altered posture into relation with it. (pp. 48–49, quoted by Rosenfield)

Head's notion of a schema is not a linguistic description, but neural and sensory activations, similar to the meaning adopted by Bartlett [5] and more recently Arbib [2].[9] Furthermore, what is organized are the continuous series of dispositions, the changes over time, the relation to what has gone before. As stated by Head, "The unit of consciousness, as far as these factors in sensation are concerned, is not a moment of time, but a 'happening'" (p. 49).[10] Rosenfield nicely summarizes this:

> [A]wareness is change, not the direct perception of stimuli. Conscious images are dynamic relations among a flow of constantly evolving coherent responses, at once different and yet derived from previous responses that are part of an individual's past. (p. 85)

---

[9]Arbib's work (which isn't cited by Edelman) forms a bridge between neurological models like Neural Darwinism and cognitive theories of vision, planning, and learning. Arbib does an especially good job of reconciling the points of view, where Edelman tends to be dismissive.

[10]History does not record whether Head's "happening", so far in advance of the 1960's American theatrical form by the same name, bears any relation to the "be-in" experienced by Heidegger.

To understand this non-symbolic notion of a schema, consider the movement of limbs in space. The places and orientations of our limbs, eyes, fingers are infinite. Yet, we can symbolically model these relations. We can define points and parameterize space as a coordinate system, thus categorizing the locations of sensory surfaces. By doing this, we can effectively describe human motions, mimic motions in animated simulations, and effectively control robotic behavior. We do all this linguistically, in terms of objects, places, and angles we have defined in our modeling endeavor. The resulting parameterization has some degree of precision determined by the categories and scales we have chosen. The possible space of descriptions, learned behaviors, and control will be bound by the grain size of these representational primitives. For a stable environment with specified goals, a given model may fit satisfactorily. But more refined coordination descriptions will require finer distinctions—changing the representational language. As engineers, we can iterate in this way until we reach a satisfactory model for the purposes at hand.

Now, the claim implicit in Edelman's and Rosenfield's argument about biological function (and indeed, implied by Dewey [17]) is that the human sensorimotor system achieves increasing precision in real time, as part of its activity. Learning to be more precise occurs internally, within an active coordination. Animal behavior clearly shows that such adaptations don't require language. Indeed, there is a higher order of learning in people, involving a sequence of behaviors, in which we represent the world, reflect on the history of what we have done, and plan future actions. In this case, exemplified by the engineer redesigning the robot, the representational language develops in conscious behavior, over time, in cycles of perceiving and acting. Newell and Simon [33, p. 7] called this kind of learning a "second-order effect".

Rosenfield and Edelman insist that learning is also primary and is at this level not limited by linguistic representational primitives. Certainly, a scientist looking inside will see that adaptations are bound by the repertoire of neural maps available for selection and the history of prior activations. But first, the learning does not require *reasoning* about programs, either before or after activity. The bounding is in terms of prior coordinations, not *descriptions* of those coordinations, either in terms of the agent's body parts or places in the world. The claim is that this direct recomposition of prior sensorimotor coordinations, in the form of selection of maps and maps of maps, provides a "run-time" flexibility that executing linguistic circumscriptions of the world does not allow.

Indeed, reflection on prior behavior, learning from failures, and representing the world provide another kind of flexibility that this primary, non-linguistic learning does not allow. Chimps are still in trees; men walk on the moon. But understanding the role of linguistic models requires understanding what can be done without them. Indeed, understanding how models are created and used—how they reorient non-linguistic neurological components (how speaking changes what I will do)—requires acknowledging the existence and nature of this nonlinguistic mechanism that drives animal behavior and still operates inside the human. For example, it is obvious that the dynamic restructuring of posture and speech at a certain grain size bear, for certain kinds of knowledgeable performances, a strong isomorphic mapping to linguistic descriptions, as for example piano playing is directed by a musical score. But in the details, we will find non-linguistically controlled improvisation, bound not by our prior descriptions, but by our prior coordinations. For example, the piano player must sometimes play an error through again slowly to discover what finger is going awry, thus representing the behavior and using this description as a means of controlling future coordinations. How that talk influences new neurological compositions, at a level of neural map selection that was not consciously influenced before, becomes a central issue of neuropsychology.

The machine learning idea of "compiled knowledge" suggests that subconscious processes are merely the execution of previously conscious steps, now compiled into automatic coordinations. Edelman and Rosenfield emphasize that such models ignore the novel, improvised aspect of every behavior. Certainly the model of knowledge compilation has value as an abstract simplification. But it ignores the dynamic mechanism by which sensorimotor systems are structured at run-time with fine relational adjustments that exceed our prior verbal parameterizations. And for animals, such models of learning fail to explain how an animal learns to run through a forest and recognize prey without language at all.

In learning to ski, for example, there is a complex interplay of comprehending an instructor's suggestions, automatically recomposing previous coordinations, and recomposing (recalling) previous ways of describing what is happening. Behavior is coordinated on multiple levels, both linguistic and nonlinguistic, with prior ways of talking, imagined future actions, and attention to new details guiding automatic processes. The important claim is that representing what is happening, as talk to ourselves and others, occurs in our conscious behavior, that it is a manifestation of consciousness, and that it must necessarily be conscious in order to have deliberate, goal-directed effect. Dewey and Ryle's claim that deliberation occurs in our behavior, and not in a hidden way inside, is another way of framing Edelman and Rosenfield's claim that we must understand the structure of consciousness, the progressive flow of making sense of experience, if we wish to understand human cognition.

5. Edelman's view of functionalism

In the appendix to this book, "Mind without Biology: A Critical Post-script", Edelman removes his gloves, and tells us that it is necessary to engage "in a bit of bashing" (p. 211). Evidently, most AI researchers and cognitive scientists have "unknowingly subjected themselves to an intellectual swindle" (p. 229). Despite the many accomplishments of these fields, "an extraordinary misconception of the nature of thought, reasoning, meaning, and of their relationship to perception has developed that threatens to undermine the whole enterprise" (p. 228). What follows is an analysis of "one of the most remarkable misunderstandings in the history of science". Perhaps understandably, some readers have been incensed by this treatment:

> Edelman [22] is one theorist who has tried to put it all to-gether, from the details of neuroanatomy to cognitive psychology to computational models to the most abstruse philosophical con-troversies. The result is an instructive failure. It shows in great detail just how many different sorts of question must be answered before we can claim to have secured a complete theory of con-sciousness, but it also shows that no one theorist can appreciate all of the subtleties of the problems addressed by the different fields. Edelman has misconstrued, and then abruptly dismissed, the work of his potential allies, so he has isolated his theory from the sort of sympathetic and informed attention it needs if it is to be saved from its errors and shortcomings. (Dennett, [15, p. 268])

Edelman may go astray in viewing some disciplines outside his own in a stereotyped, monolithic way. Although he would never say "biology believes" or "physics believes" he presents AI and cognitive science as if they were points of view or dogmas, rather than disciplines of study. This error, pointed out by Sloman [47], treats a theory as if it were a field, dismissing the field instead of competing theories within it—a category error. Edelman's position is ironic, given his belief that constructing artificial intelligence systems is possibly the only way to integrate our knowledge of how the brain works.

Edelman's narrow conception of computer science is manifested in his use of the terms "software", "instruction", "computation", "information", "machine", and "computer" itself. For example, he says that it is not mean-ingful to describe his simulations of artifacts "*as a whole* as a computer (or Turing machine)" (p. 191). Thus, he identifies "computer" with "prespeci-fied effective procedure". This is silly, given that his own system, NOMAD, is built from an N-cube supercomputer. The useful distinctions are the dif-fering architectures, not whether a computer is involved. It is a category error to identify a particular software–hardware architecture as "acting like a computer". Here Edelman speaks like a layperson, as if "the computer" is a theory of cognition.

Unfortunately, this misunderstanding leads Edelman to reject all functional approaches to cognitive modeling. He believes that functionalism characterizes psychological processes in terms of software algorithms, implying that the hardware ("the tissue organization and composition of the brain", p. 220) is irrelevant. From this perspective, functionalism involves promoting a particular kind of hardware architecture, namely that of today's computers, as well as a particular kind of computational model, namely algorithms.

Part of the difficulty is that "functionalism" in cognitive science refers to the idea that principles of operation can be abstractly described and then implemented or emulated in different physical systems (e.g., mental processes are not restricted to systems of organic molecules), as well as the more specific view that *existing computer programs* are isomorphic to the processes and capabilities of human thought (recently stated clearly by Vera and Simon [52]). Within this strong view of Functionalism proper (capital F), proponents vary from claiming that the brain is equivalent to a Turing machine (e.g., Putnam [37]), to saying that "some computer" (not yet designed) with some "computational process" (probably more complex than Soar) will suffice. Johnson–Laird states a version of Functionalism, which Edelman is attacking:

> All theories are abstractions, of course, but there is a more intimate relation between a program modeling the mind and the process that is modeled. Functionalism implies that our understanding of the mind will not be further improved by going beyond the level of mental processes. The functional organization of mental processes can be characterized in terms of effective procedures, since the mind's ability to construct working models is a computational process. If functionalism is correct, it follows not only that scientific theories of mentality can be simulated by computer programs, but also that in principle mentality can be embodied within an appropriately programmed computer: computers can think because thinking is a computational process. [28, pp. 8–9]

This view, sometimes called *mentalism*, is also attacked by Lakoff, the later Putnam [38], Bruner [8], Searle, and many others whom Edelman cites. Some computer scientists find it hard to believe that anybody ever believed in Functionalism, even though it was the everyday working hypothesis that drove the invention of expert systems and cognitive modeling in the 1970s (see [12] for an extended discussion with other quotes from the AI literature).

On the other hand, it is obvious that Edelman accepts the weaker idea of functional descriptions, for he bases his distinction between perceptual, conceptual, and symbolic categorization on Lakoff's analysis of linguistic expressions [29]. Furthermore, Edelman explicitly acknowledges that in focusing on biology, he does not mean that artifacts must be made of organic molecules. When he says that "the close imitation of uniquely biological structures *will* be required" (p. 195), he means that developing artificial intelligence requires understanding the properties of mechanisms that today only exist on earth as biological structures. In this respect, Edelman is just as much a functionalist as Dennett. What he means to say is that certain capabilities may be practically impossible on particular hardware. For example, Pagels [35] argues that it is practically impossible to simulate the brain using a Turing machine, even if it could be so described in principle. AI is a kind of engineering, an effort of practical construction, not of mathematical possibility. Without functional abstractions to guide us, we'd be limited to bottom-up assembling of components to see what develops.

Models of "universal grammar" exemplify how functionalist theories can be reformulated within the biological domain. Arguing against Chomsky's analysis, Edelman claims that Neural Darwinism doesn't postulate "innate genetically specified rules for a universal grammar" (p. 131). But he doesn't consider the possibility that universal grammar may usefully describe (and simplify) the *transformations* that occur as conceptual and symbolic *re-categorizations*. Functional descriptions, as expressed in today's cognitive models, can provide heuristic guidance for interpreting and exploring brain biology.

Contrasting with Edelman's critique, Pagels [35] offers a more accessible analysis of the limitations of cognitive science. Pagels states that "the result of thirty years' work ... [is] brilliantly correct in part, but overall a failure. ... The study of actual brains and actual computers interacting with the world ... is the future of cognitive science" [35, pp. 190–191]. Pagels helps us realize the irony that the quest for a *physical* symbol system so often assumed that the *material processes* of interaction with the world are inconsequential (the Functionalist stance). Thus, mind is disembodied and a timeless, ungrounded mentalism remains.

According to the Physical Symbol System Hypothesis, the material processes of cognition are the data structures, memories, comparators, and read–write operations by which symbols are stored and manipulated. At its heart, Edelman's appeal to biology is a claim that *other kinds of structures* need to be created and recombined, upon which sensorimotor coordination, conceptualization, language, and consciousness will be based. This idea is certainly not new. Dewey [19] argued for biologically-based theories of mind (by which he meant a functional analysis of life experience, akin to

Rosenfield's level of description). Dewey also anticipated problems with exclusively linguistic models of the mind [20].

In conclusion, we might forgive Edelman's "bashing", in view of the fragmentation of views and varying formality of AI research. Edelman can hardly be criticized for adopting the most obvious meanings of the terms prevalent in the literature. In participating in our debate, we can't fault Edelman if he becomes bewildered when we respond, "Not that kind of computer (but one we have yet to invent)" or "Not that kind of memory (but rather one more like what a connectionist hopes to build)". We somehow expect newcomers to be not too critical of what's already on the table, and to sign up instead to the dream.

6. Research conclusions

Despite the different levels of analysis, Rosenfield's and Edelman's books are highly consistent and complementary. Both underscore that perceiving is a form of restructuring previous neural activations, as opposed to matching stored linguistic representations. Both emphasize that developmental stages are grounded in body experience. Both view consciousness as a primary human experience that requires explanation if we are to understand memory and reasoning (but neither cites Dennett). Both believe that theories of cognition must be based on biological arguments about development (but neither cites Dewey or Maturana). Differences lie in the level of discussion: Rosenfield focuses on the nature of consciousness, revealed by clinical data; Edelman provides a broad framework for constructing artificial intelligence, inspired by detailed models of neurological processes. Rosenfield extends the perimeter and depth of a theory of mind; Edelman fills it in.

When studied in detail, Rosenfield's and Edelman's books provide a wealth of new starting points for AI. For example, recently there has been more interest in modeling emotions in AI. These books suggest moving beyond static taxonomies (which are useful early in a scientific effort) to viewing emotions as dynamic, functional, relational experiences. Could the phenomenology of emotional experience be modeled as integral *steps* in sense-making, as Bartlett's model of reminding suggests?

The oddity of Rosenfield's patients, coupled with an evolving architectural model of the brain, often brings to mind questions for further investigation. For example, how did Mr. Baud's inability to remember experience past twenty seconds impair learning new skills or concepts? Cognitive scientists today could easily suggest interesting problems to give Mr. Baud. Similarly, could Gelb and Goldstein's patient, who couldn't understand proverbs or comparisons, make up a story at all? Did she understand causal explanations? Could she describe and rationalize her own behavior? As Rosenfield's book suggests, cognitive neuropsychology is changing. It is time to seek synergy between our disparate models and evidence. As some reviewers of Newell's *Unified Theory of Cognition* suggest, this also entails reconceptualizing what models like Soar describe in relation to the brain (Arbib [3], Pollack [36]).

6.1. Why isn't all reasoning subconscious?

As an example of how cognitive models might be reconceived, consider why a problem solver is aware of intermediate reasoning steps. Nothing in the stored-schema view requires that inference is *consciously* monitored. In Soar, for example, "working memory", where intermediate results come together, corresponds to an agent's awareness, but nothing in the model explains why reasoning is experienced as "phenomenally subjective" [32, p. 434]. Indeed, why isn't all verbal inference subconscious? When we ask a problem solver to think out loud, are we just, like our subject, witnessing ideas spilling over from their more usual, hidden source, like water splashing over a glass? Could verbal thoughts otherwise occur without anyone knowing?

Rosenfield's analysis provides a partial explanation: Representing and inquiry go on *in activity*, that is, in cycles of perceiving and expressing (talking, gesturing, writing) over time. By conjecture, sense-making is necessarily conscious because it involves action and *comprehension of what our acts mean* occurring together. For example, speaking is not just outputting prefabricated linguistic expressions, but a dual process of creating representations in action and comprehending what we are saying. We are "making sense" as we speak—perceiving appropriateness, adjusting, and restating in our activity itself. The process is "dual" because perception, awareness of what we are doing, is integral to every statement. Conscious awareness is not just passive watching, but an active process of sustaining a certain kind of attention that changes the results of inquiry. This analysis suggests specifically that we reconsider "remindings" and other commentary of the subject in experimental problem solving protocols as revealing the *perceptual work* of creating and using representations.

Following Edelman, the rest of the matter, what is going on behind the scenes, is non-linguistic coordination. Conscious acts of fitting—dealing with breakdowns [54]—occur precisely because there is no other place for linguistic representations to be expressed and reflected on, but in our experience itself. This is why we write things down or "talk through" an experience to clarify meanings and implications for future action. Protracted, conscious experience—as in writing a paragraph—is not merely an awareness of elements placed in "working memory", but an active process of recoordinating and recomprehending (reperceiving) what we are doing. In the words of Bartlett, "turning around on our own schemata" is possible precisely because we can recoordinate non-linguistic schemata *in our activity of representing*.

According to Edelman, the articulation process of "building a scene" is reflective at a higher order because of reentrant links between Broca and Wernicke's areas and perceptual categorization (the "semantic bootstrap" of Fig. 1): Our perceptual sense of similarity (reminding) and articulation (naming, history-telling, theorizing) are bound together, so symbolizing actions are driving subsequent perceptions. A sequence of such activity is coordinated by composing a story that accumulates observations and conceptual categories into a coherent sense of what we are trying to do (the scene). In other words, being able to create a story (e.g., the sense-making of a medical diagnostician) is precisely what higher-order consciousness allows. Crucially, human stories are not merely instantiated and assembled from grammars, but are coupled to non-linguistic coordinations grounded in perceptual and motor experience [29]. Hence, consciously-created stories can have an aspect of improvisation and novelty that stored linguistic schema mechanisms do not allow.

This analysis provides an alternative, biologically-grounded perspective on recent arguments about planning and situated action [1,50]. The key idea is that perceiving and acting co-determine each other through reentrant links. Representing occurs in activity, as a means of stepping outside the otherwise automatic process by which neural maps (schemata) are reactivated, composed, and sequenced. Goal-directed, attentive behavior of primary consciousness involves holding active a higher-order organization (global maps) and coordinating the relation to ongoing perceptions (i.e., directed attention). In higher-order consciousness, these global maps are coupled to linguistic descriptions of objects, events, goals, and causal stories.

Robot designers may be impatient with the vagueness of such descriptive theorizing. But it is clear that the clinical evidence and neurobiological mechanisms of Rosenfield and Edelman are adequate to promote further reconsideration of our models of explanation, remembering, and story-telling, including the seminal work of Bartlett.

6.2. Prospective

These two books suggest that subfields within cognitive science are changing and then coming together in new ways. New understanding of neural development and anatomy suggests radical reinterpretation of classic cases of psychological dysfunction. Cognitive neuropsychology is moving away from the stored linguistic schema model of memory. Selectionist models of learning suggest that functional processes can be constructed "in-line", without mediating linguistic descriptions of what the processes do or how the parts fit together. Studies of language and human learning place new primacy on the representations that people see, hear, and manipulate interactively, relegating internal subconscious structures and processes to another level of operation. Interest in modeling animal behavior leads us to reexamine the capabilities of agents without language, and the evolution of consciousness within a social system.

It is tempting to predict that the development of global map architectures, as in Darwin III, will become a dominant approach for neural network research, effectively building on situated cognition critiques of the symbolic approach [13]. However, if it becomes essential to understand the chaotic processes of the brain, as Freeman [23], Pollack [36], and others argue, it is less clear how the researchers who brought us Pengi and Soar will participate in building the next generation of AI machines.

All told, there are probably more pieces here than most researchers can follow or integrate in their work. A good bet is that progress in AI will now depend on more multidisciplinary teams and efforts to bridge these diverse fields. Rosenfield and Edelman make a big leap forwards, showing consciousness to be an evolved activity, grounded in and sustaining an individual's participation in the world as a physical and social personality. With theories like self-reference, population thinking, and selectionism, we pick up Bateson's challenge in *Mind and Nature: A Necessary Unity*, finding the patterns that connect the human world to nature and all of the sciences to each other.

Acknowledgments

The book review editors, Mark Stefik and Steve Smoliar, provided, as usual, a great number of insightful suggestions for clarification and elaboration of my remarks. Funding has been provided in part by a gift from the Xerox Foundation and the National Science Foundation.

References

[1] P.E. Agre, The dynamic structure of everyday life, Ph.D. Dissertation, MIT, Cambridge, MA (1988).
[2] M.A. Arbib, Schema theory, in: S.C. Shapiro, ed., *The Encyclopedia of Artificial Intelligence* (Wiley, New York, 1992).
[3] M.A. Arbib, Book Review of *Unified Theories of Cognition* (Allen Newell), *Artif. Intell.* **59** (1993) 265–283.
[4] J. Bamberger, *The Mind behind the Musical Ear* (Harvard University Press, Cambridge, MA, 1991).
[5] F.C. Bartlett [1932], *Remembering—A Study in Experimental and Social Psychology* (Cambridge University Press, Cambridge, England, 1977).
[6] G. Bateson, *Mind and Nature: A Necessary Unity* (Bantam Books, New York, 1979).
[7] P.L. Berger and T. Luckmann, *The Social Construction of Reality: A Treatise in the Sociology of Knowledge* (Anchor Books, Garden City, NY, 1967).
[8] J. Bruner, *Acts of Meaning* (Harvard University Press, Cambridge, MA, 1990).

[9] W.H. Calvin, *The Cerebral Symphony: Seashore Reflections on the Structure of Consciousness* (Bantam Books, New York, 1990).

[10] W.H. Calvin, Islands in the mind: dynamic subdivisions of association cortex and the emergence of the Darwin Machine, *Neurosci.* **3** (1991) 423–433.

[11] W.J. Clancey, Book Review of *The Invention of Memory* (Israel Rosenfield) *Artif. Intell.* **50** (2) (1991) 241–284.

[12] W.J. Clancey, Representations of knowing: in defense of cognitive apprenticeship, *J. Artif. Intell. Educ.* **3** (2) (1992) 139–168.

[13] W.J. Clancey, Situated action: a neuropsychological interpretation: response to Vera and Simon, *Cogn. Sci.* **17** (1993) 87–116.

[14] P.F. Dell, Understanding Bateson and Maturana: toward a biological foundation for the social sciences, *J. Marital and Family Therapy* **11** (1) (1985) 1–20.

[15] D.C Dennett, *Consciousness Explained* (Little, Brown and Company, Boston, MA, 1992).

[16] D.C. Dennett, Revolution on the mind: reviews of *The Embodied Mind* and *Bright Air, Brilliant Fire, New Scientist* (June 13, 1992) 48–49.

[17] J. Dewey [1896], The reflex arc concept in psychology, *Psychol. Rev.* **3** (1981) 357–370; Reprinted in: J.J. McDermott, ed., *The Philosophy of John Dewey* (University of Chicago Press, Chicago, IL, 1981) 136–148.

[18] J. Dewey, *The Child and the Curriculum* (University of Chicago Press, Chicago, IL, 1902); Reprinted in: J.J. McDermott, ed., *The Philosophy of John Dewey* (University of Chicago Press, Chicago, IL, 1981) 511–523.

[19] J. Dewey, *Logic: The Theory of Inquiry* (Henry Holt & Company, New York, 1938).

[20] J. Dewey and A.F. Bentley, *Knowing and the Known* (Beacon Press, Boston, MA, 1949).

[21] G.M. Edelman, *Neural Darwinism: The Theory of Neuronal Group Selection* (Basic Books, New York, 1987).

[22] G.M. Edelman, *The Remembered Present: A Biological Theory of Consciousness* (Basic Books, New York, 1989).

[23] W.J. Freeman, The physiology of perception, *Sci. Am.* (February 1991) 78–85.

[24] W.T. Gallwey, *The Inner Game of Tennis* (Bantam Books, New York, 1974).

[25] S.J. Gould, Nurturing Nature, in: *An Urchin in the Storm: Essays about Books and Ideas* (W.W. Norton and Company, New York, 1987) 145–154.

[26] A.G. Greenwald, Self and memory, in: G.H. Bower, ed., *The Psychology of Learning and Motivation* **15** (Academic Press, New York, 1981) 201–236.

[27] D.R. Hofstadter, *Gödel, Escher, Bach: An Eternal Golden Braid* (Basic Books, New York, 1979).

[28] P.N. Johnson-Laird, *Mental Models: Towards a Cognitive Science of Language, Inference, and Consciousness* (Harvard University Press, Cambridge, MA, 1983).

[29] G. Lakoff, *Women, Fire, and Dangerous Things: What Categories Reveal about the Mind* (University of Chicago Press, Chicago, IL, 1987).

[30] R. Leakey and R. Lewin, *Origins Reconsidered: In Search of What Makes Us Human* (Doubleday, New York, 1992).

[31] A.R. Luria, *The Mind of a Mnemonist* (Harvard University Press, Cambridge, MA, 1968).

[32] A. Newell, *Unified Theories of Cognition* (Harvard University Press, Cambridge, MA, 1990).

[33] A. Newell and H.A. Simon, *Human Problem Solving* (Prentice Hall, Englewood Cliffs, NJ, 1972).

[34] R.E. Ornstein, *The Psychology of Consciousness* (Penguin Books, New York, 1972).

[35] H.R. Pagels, *The Dreams of Reason: The Computer and the Rise of the Sciences of Complexity* (Bantam Books, New York, 1988).

[36] J.B. Pollack, On wings of knowledge: a review of Allen Newell's *Unified Theories of Cognition, Artif. Intell.* **59** (1993) 355–369.

[37] H. Putnam, Philosophy and our mental life, in: *Philosophical Papers* **2**: *Mind, Language and Reality* (Cambridge University Press, New York, 1975) 291–303.

[38] H. Putnam, *Representation and Reality* (MIT Press, Cambridge, MA, 1988).

[39] G.N. Reeke and G.M. Edelman, Real brains and artificial intelligence, *Daedalus* **117** (1) (1988) "Artificial Intelligence" issue.

[40] G.N. Reeke, L.H. Finkel, O. Sporns and G.M. Edelman, Synthetic neural modeling: a multilevel approach to the analysis of brain complexity, in: G.M. Edelman, W.E. Gall and W.M. Cowan, eds., *The Neurosciences Institute Publications: Signal and Sense: Local and Global Order in Perceptual Maps* (Wiley, New York, 1990) 607–707 (Chapter 24).

[41] I. Rosenfield, *The Invention of Memory: A New View of the Brain* (Basic Books, New York, 1988).

[42] G. Ryle, *The Concept of Mind* (Barnes & Noble, Inc., New York, 1949).

[43] O. Sacks, *A Leg to Stand On* (Harper Collins Publishers, New York, 1984).

[44] D.A. Schön, Generative metaphor: a perspective on problem-setting in social policy, in: A. Ortony, ed., *Metaphor and Thought* (Cambridge University Press, Cambridge, England, 1979) 254–283.

[45] D.A. Schön, The theory of inquiry: Dewey's legacy to education, presented at the Annual Meeting of the American Educational Association, Boston, MA (1990).

[46] R. Sheldrake, *The Presence of the Past: Morphic Resonance and the Habits of Nature* (Vintage Books, New York, 1988).

[47] A. Sloman, The emperor's real mind: review of Roger Penrose's *The Emperor's New Mind: Concerning Computers, Minds, and the Laws of Physics*, *Artif. Intell.* **56** (2–3) (1992) 355–396.

[48] S.W. Smoliar, Book Review of *Neural Darwinism: The Theory of Neuronal Group Selection* (Gerald M. Edelman), *Artif. Intell.* **39** (1) (1989) 121–136.

[49] S.W. Smoliar, Book Review of *The Remembered Present: A Biological Theory of Consciousness* (Gerald M. Edelman), *Artif. Intell.* **52** (3) (1991) 295–318.

[50] L.A. Suchman, *Plans and Situated Actions: The Problem of Human-Machine Communication* (Cambridge University Press, Cambridge, England, 1987).

[51] S. Tyler, *The Said and the Unsaid: Mind, Meaning, and Culture* (Academic Press, New York, 1978).

[52] A. Vera and H.A. Simon. Situated action: a symbolic interpretation, *Cogn. Sci.* **17** (1993) 7–48.

[53] H. von Foerster, Epistemology of communication, in: K. Woodward, ed., *The Myths of Information: Technology and Postindustrial Culture* (Coda Press, Madison, WI, 1980).

[54] T. Winograd and F. Flores, *Understanding Computers and Cognition: A New Foundation for Design* (Ablex, Norwood, NJ, 1986).

Artificial Intelligence 60 (1993) 303–312
Elsevier

ARTINT 1052

Daniel C. Dennett, *Consciousness Explained**

Robert Ornstein, *The Evolution of Consciousness: Of Darwin, Freud, and Cranial Fire: The Origins of the Way We Think***

William Seager, *Metaphysics of Consciousness****

Joseph O'Rourke

Department of Computer Science, Smith College, Northampton, MA 01063, USA

Received October 1992

1. Introduction

"The problem of consciousness, also known as the mind–body problem, is probably the largest outstanding obstacle in our quest to scien-

---

* (Little Brown; Canada, 1991); xiii+511 pages, ISBN 0-316-18065-3.
** (Prentice Hall; New York, 1991); xiv+305 pages, ISBN 0-13-587569-2.
*** (Routledge; London, 1991); viii+262 pages, ISBN 0-415-06357-4.
Correspondence to: J. O'Rourke, Department of Computer Science, Smith College,
Northampton, MA 01063, USA. E-mail: orourke@sophia.smith.edu.

tifically understand reality" [1]. That this opinion is prevalent among philosophers, cognitive psychologists, and neurobiologists may come as a surprise to researchers in artificial intelligence (AI), who perhaps take their cue from Minsky's opinion: "as far as I'm concerned, the so-called problem of body and mind does not hold any mystery: Minds are simply what brains do" [12, p. 287]. This assertion does not dispel the mystery for many, and an understanding of consciousness is under hot pursuit from several quarters, resulting in a spate of recent books on the topic. Here I will discuss three, covering the spectrum from psychology to philosophy. Along the way I hope to dislodge any smug attitudes that the mind–body problem is nonexistent or trivial or irrelevant.

The three books under review could hardly be more different. Ornstein's *The Evolution of Consciousness: Of Darwin, Freud, and Cranial Fire: The Origins of the Way We Think* can be classified as popular psychology. Although Dennett is a philosopher, his *Consciousness Explained* draws on psychology, neurophysiology, and computer science, and is aimed at an audience much wider than professional philosophers. Seager's *Metaphysics of Consciousness* is written by a philosopher for philosophers and is the most academic of the three. The central concern of all three is to "explain" consciousness, although their senses of explanation are disparate.

The term "consciousness" is notoriously variegated. The *Oxford English Dictionary (OED)* lists six distinct meanings, and none of the three authors bothers to define it precisely. This lack of precision is not as serious an obstruction to understanding as it might seem, as discussion usually focuses on particular more well-defined mental states. And besides, as Seager puts it, "the most notable feature of the mind–body relation remains our ignorance of it" [p. 4], so understanding any aspect of consciousness is an achievement.

I suspect that many AI researchers subscribe to the mind–body theory known as "functionalism", which claims (roughly) that if the functional roles of aspects of mentality are reproduced, consciousness necessarily emerges. Although most in AI are neither familiar with this term nor aware of the philosophical debates surrounding it, research in AI influences these debates. As AI systems become more complex, I believe the influence will increasingly run in both directions.

I will start with a brief sketch of the three books to provide orientation on their views, but I will make no attempt to summarize their complete contents. Next I will indicate what is problematic about consciousness, and then turn to several specific aspects of the problem on which the three authors express opinions. I will focus especially on functionalism, hoping at the least to transform any unexamined functionalist into an examined functionalist.

2. Characterizations

2.1. Ornstein

Ornstein's book is the least structured of the three, partitioned into twenty-six loosely connected chapters, festooned with fifty cartoonish drawings that I found only distracting. He emphasizes the evolutionary development of the brain and mind, and the implications of our evolutionary inheritance on the way our brains function today. He views most higher mental facilities as almost accidental, serendipitous use of surplus brain cells evolved to protect the brain against heat loss. He calls the unconscious talents of our brain "simpletons" and imagines squadrons of them rapidly shifting in and out of control. Here his theory is akin to Minsky's "Society of Mind" [12] (which he does not cite). Ornstein believes we can modify our behavior by deeper understanding of this shifting process, effecting a "conscious evolution".

2.2. Dennett

Dennett's book is more substantial and written in a delightfully fluid style, a happy medium between Ornstein's discursiveness and Seager's rigidity. His aim is clear from his audacious title: to explain consciousness. I think he falls short of this lofty goal, although the attempt is enthralling. His argument is long and complex, and I cannot do it justice here.

One focus of his energy is exposing what he believes are confusions in the philosophical literature. In particular, he debunks the "Cartesian Theater", the notion that there is some centered locus in the brain where information comes together to form consciousness. He proposes to replace this metaphor with his own "Multiple Drafts" model in which all mental activity consists of intertwining parallel skeins of processes of interpretation and elaboration. His claim is that there is no need to re-represent the data, no need to move it to a center, despite the search by neuroscientists such as Crick for neural correlates of visual awareness [3].

A second focus is less successful: his attempt to "disqualify" qualia. Qualia are the raw phenomenal subjective "feels" of mental experiences, the locus of considerable philosophical scrutiny. I will have more to say on this topic below, but roughly, his explanation of this aspect of consciousness is to deny that there is anything to explain!

2.3. Seager

Seager writes directly to philosophers of mind; and some sections are epitomes of the "angels on the head of a pin" donnish philosophy debate that many find so pointless. Nevertheless his highly structured organization permits the resolute to plunge into the philosophical thicket and return with a greater appreciation of its complexity. He critically examines a variety of mind–body theories, finding arguments for and against each, none conclusive either way. His search for a minimal theory resistant to attacks results in one that has only narrow applicability: to intentional states (beliefs, desires, and so on). The more intrinsic, ineffable mental phenomena (pains, visual awareness, and so on), remain for him mysterious: he feels this type of conscious experience fits no known paradigm, and ultimately may be inexplicable.

3. Varieties of consciousness

"Consciousness" is a word with many meanings. Indeed, Natsoulas wrote a series of papers on the six concepts of consciousness in the *OED*, and used his analysis to explicate James' stream of consciousness [14]. Some debates are confused by unwitting conflation of these meanings. The opposite extreme is to choose such a narrow definition that the mystery disappears. Minsky restricts his attention (in [11]) to the ability to sense what is happening "within and outside ourselves", and concludes that humans "do not possess much consciousness" and that "machines are already potentially more conscious than are people". This may be true for his restricted definition but hardly illuminates consciousness in its full variety.

Its full variety is usefully partitioned by Seager into intentional, contentful mental states (beliefs, desires), and more private, intrinsic properties (pains, color qualia). The former states require a more global, third-person perspective and seem closest to accurate capture by existing mind–brain theories. The latter "ineffable" states demand a first-person perspective and remain the sticking point of most theories. The main "problem of consciousness", then, is to *explain* consciousness: how do physical events in the brain engender these most private conscious experiences?

4. Evolution

Part of the answer might be found in the evolution of the brain. As Ornstein's title indicates, he focuses on evolution; but he concentrates his speculations on the growth of the brain and on the development of mental habits aimed at survival. Seager hovers one abstraction above the details of evolutionary development, which I consider a weakness of his argument. Dennett seems to strike the happiest balance, including a thorough discussion of evolutionary development and mechanisms, moving the discussion a significant step into cultural evolution.

Dennett suggests that a mechanism known as the "Baldwin effect" could have moved the evolutionarily advantageous skill of language into the genotype. This effect favors phenotypic plasticity, which permits individuals to quickly discover especially useful behavioral talents [7]. But he believes that consciousness, unlike our language facility, is not hardwired into the genotype: rather it is implemented in "software" and therefore invisible to neuroanatomy. This software is a product of "cultural evolution", an attractive notion proposed by Dawkins in *The Selfish Gene* [5]. Dennett suggests that the benefit of silently talking to oneself eventually led to the consciousness software. He views this software as effectively implementing a virtual sequential "Joycean machine" in the parallel architecture of the brain, and it is this machine that leads to the experience of a stream of consciousness.

The unit of cultural evolution is Dawkins' "meme": units of self-replicating cultural traits, such as catchy tunes, religious faith, education, and computer viruses. Thus Dennett sees consciousness as a huge complex of memes, a view I find compelling, albeit somewhat vague. Neither Ornstein nor Seager mentions memes. Nor do they mention Jaynes' theory of the recent rise of consciousness [9], which supports Dennett's view of consciousness as a late development. [1]

5. Mind–body theories

Knowing why consciousness emerged from evolution does not constitute an explanation of how the physical activities of the brain evoke our experience of consciousness, how the mind is related to the body. The three authors are unanimous in their rejection of dualism, which postulates that mind is a non-material substance. [2] They are equally disdainful of epiphenomenalism, a near-dualism that holds that mental events can have no effects in the physical world whatever, although physical events do cause mental events. What remains after rejecting dualism is materialism or physicalism, which claims the brain is exclusively physical and all its causal powers derive from the causal powers of its physical parts.

Seager analyzes five versions of physicalism, and finds all wanting but none refuted. I will sketch each tersely to give a sense for the variety and then follow with a more detailed analysis of functionalism.

(1) *Type-identity theory* is the strongest version of physicalism: it identifies psychological states with certain exactly specified brain states, claiming an eventual reduction of psychology to neurophysiology.

---

[1] Dennett does not endorse the specifics of Jaynes' theory, however.
[2] Despite the unpopularity of this view, a version is held by Popper and Eccles [15].

(2) *Functionalism* does not claim that psychological terms refer to definite brain states; but rather they refer to these indirectly via their function in an abstract system realized physically. It is the functional structure of the cognitive system that creates the mental.

(3) *Token-identity theory* (Davidson [4]) claims that there is an irreconcilable opposition between mental state ascriptions and physical state descriptions; rather they are parallel descriptions of one world, in which every item has a physical description. It weakens the identity claim of type-identity theory to representative or "token" mental and physical events.

(4) *Instrumentalism* (Dennett [6]) denies that there is a set of physical states that even approximately mirrors psychological states. Rather the brain behaves "instrumentally" according to folk psychology,[3] largely because evolutionary pressure leads to creatures describable this way.

(5) *Eliminative materialism* (Churchland [2]) goes even further, claiming that folk psychology will disappear with advances in neuroscience. Whereas instrumentalism maintains the truth of psychological characterizations, eliminative materialism claims folk psychology is a false theory.

Seager labels his minimal theory "constitutive global supervenience". Supervenience is a complex technical term that plays a key role in Seager's book; that it is not even mentioned by Dennett or Ornstein is indicative of a conceptual chasm. S-properties *supervene* on B-properties (base properties) if any two systems that agree on the B-properties necessarily possess the S-properties. Global supervenience permits the properties to depend on more than an individual's brain: including, e.g., culturally-determined language conventions. Constitutive supervenience demands more than mere correlation: for example, causal efficacy in the supervening relation à la Searle's "special causal powers" of neurons [18]. One can see from these subtleties how carefully nuanced is Seager's position.

Dennett strenuously resists any single label, but defends a version of functionalism throughout his book. He calls it "teleofunctionalism" to emphasize its grounding in evolutionarily advantageous functions.[4] We will see below how he skirts the problems of standard functionalism.

Ornstein does not delve into the philosophical issues enough to earn a label.

---

[3]"Folk psychology" is our shared, commonsense theory of human behavior that successfully explains, e.g., that we carry umbrellas because of our belief in their efficacy in keeping us dry.
[4]"Teleology" is the study of evidence for design in nature.

6. Functionalism

Functionalism claims that any system that realizes the functional structure of the brain will automatically possess all the mental properties of the mind—so intelligent machines will be conscious. Functionalism is uncontroversial for many phenomena: any system that cools its contents is a type of refrigerator. Somewhat more controversial is a functionalist theory of life: any system that adapts to its environment, metabolizes energy, and reproduces, is a form of life. [5] But is it the case that a state that results from bodily trauma, and elicits wincing, retraction of the afflicted body part, and in general plays the functional role of pain, must feel like pain, in fact *is* pain? Since functionalism is widely accepted in the AI community, it should be instructive to examine some of the reasons why philosophers find this position problematical.

Making precise the phrase "realizes the functional structure" is the first difficulty. Interpreted too loosely, functionalism slides into behaviorism. Suppose intelligent behavior were achieved with an extremely large (but finite) static lookup table. [6] Does the table enjoy a mental life? Most would say no. This leads to attempts to dig deeper than I/O behavior, and demand a similar functional organization.

Putnam

Putnam, the original functionalist [16], explored formalizing the definition of "functionally realize" in terms of finite state automata (FSA). But in recent work [17] he finds these definitions can lead to the absurd conclusion that any sufficiently complex system (e.g., the economy of Peru) can realize any FSA. This conclusion is reached by gerrymandering the states of the system to map to the FSA so that all "functional" transitions are preserved. The danger of tightening the definition of functional realization too much is that one can exclude the possibility of mentality in robots or extraterrestrials, for at a low level, their states and transitions would surely be rather different.

Putnam now believes the theory is unworkable for several reasons [17]. Meanings are not "in the head", so beliefs and other intentional states must incorporate references to the environment. "Sociofunctionalists" respond by including the environment in the purview of the mind–body relation (this is Seager's global supervenience relation). But Putnam feels the theory runs aground on the shoals of synonymy, possible world counterfactuals, and other hazards of the philosophical sea.

---

[5]This example is due to David Chalmers.
[6]Seager points out that this idea is present (in essence) in Leibnitz's work [10] in 1702!

Shifted spectra

No doubt the most vexing aspect of consciousness for functionalism is sensory qualia: our internal, subjective experiences of color, pain, pitch, and so on. Seager invites us to consider how functionalism can handle color qualia: the way it seems to you when you look at colors. Imagine a person's color spectrum shifted by a sudden surreptitious replacement of their cones with ones tuned to ultraviolet reflectances. Surely (Seager says) the nature of the color qualia would not change, but they are not functionally isomorphic. A functionalist could respond by redrawing the boundary so that what is crucial is the functional architecture of the color vision system, not the functional behavior of the sensors. But now the functionalist can be backed into admitting that two behaviorally-equivalent beings with mildly different functional architectures do not experience the same qualia.

Blindsight

"Blindsight" is often offered as a disproof of functionalism. Blindsight is a phenomenon observed in patients who have suffered partial damage to their visual cortex resulting in a distinct blindspot in one hemisphere. These patients nevertheless can "guess" when a visual stimulus is present in their blindspot, despite having no conscious experience of visual perception there. This seems to indicate that the function of vision can be present without the attendant mental experience; both Ornstein and Seager interpret it this way (Seager more cautiously). Dennett, however, uses this phenomenon as grist for his Multiple Drafts mill. He emphasizes how the experimenter's questions act as probes into the patient's stream of consciousness, eliciting not facts but rather answers more akin to fictional narratives. He suggests that time and training could change what a blindsighter considers conscious.

Searle

Functionalism implies that a suitably programmed silicon-based computer brain would be conscious, a claim vigorously challenged by Searle's notorious "Chinese Room" argument [18]. Neither Seager nor Dennett find force in Searle's argument; Ornstein doesn't mention it. Dennett sides with the "systems reply" [8], claiming that Searle fails to imagine the full complexity of the Chinese Room system: understanding *can* emerge (contra Searle) "from lots of distributed quasi-understanding in a large system" [p. 439]. Seager focuses on Searle's claim that neurons possess special causal powers. He argues that these speculative powers explain nothing, for "if one asked *why* such and such neuronal structure gave rise to ... conscious experience ... Searle would have no answer" [p. 181]. Seager is not objecting to the lack of a detailed account of how consciousness arises, but contends "we have no account at all" [p. 181].

7. Qualia

Is the subjective experience of pain something over and above a complex of "dispositions to react" in certain ways? Seager says yes; Dennett says no. This appears to be the crux of their difference, which I will illustrate with two final examples on color qualia.

Inverted spectra

Imagine another neurological Gedanken experiment: your cone cells are rewired to invert your color spectrum, so that grass is red and so on. There is evidence (mentioned by Ornstein and Dennett) that gradual behavioral adaptation would occur. Suppose it would; after complete adaptation of your "reactive dispositions", are your color qualia inverted? Dennett says no, because your qualia *are* your reactive dispositions. Seager's position is more cautious and complex. He concludes there is a nomological (lawlike) link between the physical properties of the brain and qualia, a view incompatible with Dennett's.

Tetrachromates

Pigeons are tetrachromates:[7] they have four different color receptors, and so their subjective color space is four-dimensional. Seager feels that our extensive neurological knowledge "does not afford us the least idea of what these extra 'hues' look like" [p. 151]: "the particularities of ... modes of consciousness are not exhausted by the constituting structure of the conscious being" [p. 219]. Dennett's position on Nagel's famous paper "What is it like to be a bat?" [13] implies that he would claim that pigeon qualia *are* accessible to us (with great effort): "the structure of a bat's mind is just as accessible as the structure of a bat's digestive system" [p. 447].

8. Conclusion

Ornstein's book is easy reading, informative, but ultimately unsatisfying: he risks few clear claims, and even those are not well supported. Seager is not for the philosophically timid, but his book is a model of careful reasoning that clarifies significantly while deepening the complexity of the issues. Although I remain unconvinced by Dennett, his theory is the most tantalizing. He is one of the few philosophers to take AI seriously, and those in AI should consider returning the favor.

---

[7]They might even be pentachromates.

Acknowledgements

I have benefited from discussions with David Chalmers and Jeff Dalton, and from the editors' comments.

References

[1] D.J. Chalmers, Consciousness and cognition, Center of Research on Concepts and Cognition, Indiana University, Bloomington, IN (1991).

[2] P.M. Churchland, *A Neurocomputational Perspective: The Nature of Mind and the Structure of Science*, MIT Press, (1989), Chapter 1.

[3] F. Crick and C. Koch, The problem of consciousness, *Sci. Am.* **267** (3) (1992) 153–159.

[4] D. Davidson, *Essays on Actions and Events* (Oxford University Press, Oxford, 1980).

[5] R. Dawkins, *The Selfish Gene* (Oxford University Press, Oxford, 1976).

[6] D.C. Dennett, *The Intensional Stance* (MIT Press, Cambridge, MA, 1987).

[7] G.E. Hinton and S.J. Nowland, How learning can guide evolution, Tech. Rept. CMU-CS-86-128, Carnegie Mellon University, Pittsburgh, PA (1987).

[8] D.R. Hofstadter and D.C. Dennett, *The Mind's I: Fantasies and Reflections on Self and Soul* (Basic Books, New York, 1981).

[9] J. Jaynes, *The Origin of Consciousness in the Breakdown of the Bicameral Mind* (Houghton Mifflin, Boston, MA, 1976).

[10] G.W. Leibnitz, Reply to the thoughts on the system of preestablished harmony..., in: *Gottfried Wilhelm Leibnitz: Philosophical Papers and Letters* (Reidel, Dordrecht, 1969).

[11] M. Minsky, Machinery of consciousness, in: *75th Anniversary Symposium on Science in Society* (National Research Council of Canada, to appear).

[12] M. Minsky, *Society of Mind* (Simon and Schuster, New York, 1986).

[13] T. Nagel, What is it like to be a bat? *Philos. Rev.* **83** (1974) 435–450.

[14] T. Natsoulas, Concepts of consciousness, *J. Mind Behav.* **4** (1983) 13–59.

[15] K. Popper and J. Eccles, *The Self and the Brain* (Springer, New York, 1977).

[16] H. Putnam, *Mind, Language and Reality: Philosophical Papers* (Cambridge University Press, Cambridge, 1975).

[17] H. Putnam, *Representation and Reality* (MIT Press, Cambridge, MA, 1988).

[18] J.R. Searle, Minds, brains and programs, *Behav. Brain Sci.* **3** (1980) 417–457.

Contributors

Philip E. Agre is Assistant Professor in the Department of Communication at the University of California, San Diego. His book, *Computation and Human Experience,* is in preparation for publication.

Michael A. Arbib is Director of the Center for Neural Engineering at the University of Southern California, where he is Professor of Computer Science, Neurobiology, and Physiology, as well as of Biomedical Engineering, Electrical Engineering, and Psychology. Arbib's current research focuses on mechanisms underlying the coordination of perception and action in human, monkey, frog, and robot. An overview of this work is given in *The Metaphorical Brain 2: Neural Networks and Beyond.* Philosophical implications are explored in his Gifford Lectures, *The Construction of Reality,* with Mary Hesse.

Daniel G. Bobrow is Research Fellow in the Systems and Practices Laboratory at Xerox Palo Alto Research Center. He is known for his work on collaborative systems with Mark Stefik, knowledge representation with Terry Winograd, and various topics in programming languages. A recent book, with Gregor Kiczales and Jim des Rivieres, is *The Art of the Metaobject Protocol.*

William J. Clancey is Senior Research Scientist at the Institute for Research on Learning. He is best known for knowledge-level analyses of expert systems and pioneering work in grounding AI research in scientific and engineering modeling. His current research includes developing simulations of work practice for work systems design. His books include *Knowledge-Based Tutoring* and *Artificial Intelligence and Education.*

Daniel Dennett is Distinguished Professor of Arts and Sciences and Director of the Center for Cognitive Studies at Tufts University in Medford, Massachusetts. Dennett is the author of several books dealing in part with AI, as well as of articles on specific issues and problems in the field. His most recent book, *Consciousness Explained,* includes a discussion of Newell's influence on cognitive science.

Mark Derthick is Member of the Technical Staff at Microelectronics and Computer Technology Corporation in Austin, Texas, where he builds knowledge entry tools and information retrieval applications for Cyc, the large-scale commonsense knowledge base.

Michael G. Dyer is Professor in the Computer Science Department of the University of California at Los Angeles and Director of the UCLA Artificial Intelligence Laboratory. He is best known for his work in symbolic and connectionist models of human language comprehension. He is author of the book *In-Depth Understanding*.

Michael Fehling is Director of the Laboratory for Intelligent Systems in the Department of Engineering–Economic Systems at Stanford University. Fehling is best known in AI for his work on knowledge-based system architectures for use in real-time, distributed problem-solving applications. His current research focuses on the nature of organizational problem solving and development of technology to coordinate and enhance organizational performance. Fehling is also working extensively on theories of limited rationality as a foundation for unified theories of cognition.

Fernando Flores is the founder and Chairman of the Board of Business Design Associates, Inc. and also founded Action Technologies, which developed software for supporting human communication. He is internationally known for his work in management, leadership, education, and computer science. In his native Chile, Dr. Flores served as Minister of Finance and led the largest applied cybernetics project ever undertaken, CYBERSYN. His interests are in the areas of language, human communication, management, and computer science. With Terry Winograd, he coauthored the book *Understanding Computers and Cognition,* which is reviewed in this volume.

Matthew L. Ginsberg is Director of CIRL, the computational intelligence research laboratory at the University of Oregon. His research interests include real-time planning and problem solving, multivalued logics, and scheduling. He is the author of numerous publications in these areas, the editor of *Readings in Nonmonotonic Reasoning,* and the author of the recent *Essentials of Artificial Intelligence.*

Barbara Hayes-Roth is Senior Research Scientist in the Computer Science Department at Stanford University. She is best known for her work on intelligent control and its embodiment in the BB1 software architecture. Her current research interests concern adaptive intelligent systems, which integrate perception, reasoning, and action to achieve multiple goals in dynamic environments.

Menachem Jona is Research Associate at The Institute for Learning Sciences at Northwestern University where he is working on building knowledge-based tools and interfaces for creating educational and training software. His graduate work focused on the representation of knowledge about teaching for use in building educational software.

John Laird is Associate Professor in the Electrical Engineering and Computer Science Department at the University of Michigan. He is best known for his work on integrated intelligent systems and the Soar architecture. His most recent book is *The Soar Papers,* coauthored with Paul Rosenbloom and Allen Newell.

Alan Mackworth is Professor of Computer Science at the University of British Columbia and the Shell Canada Fellow of the Artificial Intelligence and Robotics Program of the Canadian Institute for Advanced Research. He currently serves as Director of the UBC Laboratory for Computational Intelligence. He is known for his work on constraint satisfaction and its applications in perception, reasoning, and situated robots. He recently coedited a book with Eugene Freuder on constraint-based reasoning.

Marvin Minsky is Toshiba Professor at Massachusetts Institute of Technology in the EECS Department, the MIT AI Laboratory, and the MIT Media Laboratory. Minsky is well known for research on knowledge representation, machine vision, robotics, computational complexity, and confocal microscopy. He is currently working on the use of multiple representations, and his most recent books are *The Society of Mind* and *The Turing Option,* a novel about the future of AI (with Harry Harrison).

Joseph O'Rourke is the Olin Professor of Computer Science and chair of the department at Smith College. He is best known for his work in computational geometry, especially the monograph *Art Gallery Theorems and Algorithms* and the textbook *Computational Geometry in C.*

Jordan B. Pollack is on the Computer Science faculty at the Ohio State University, affiliated with both the Laboratory for AI Research and the Center for Cognitive Science. Pollack is known for his work at the boundary between the biological and symbolic approaches to language, learning, and representation. His current research interests are in the area of learning and complex behavior in recurrent neural networks, nonlinear dynamical systems, and evolutionary algorithms.

Dale Purves is George Barth Geller Professor for Research in Neurobiology and Chairman of the Neurobiology Department at Duke University. He is best known for his work on the formation and maintenance of synaptic connections in the developing nervous system. Recent books include *Body and Brain* and *Neural Activity and the Growth of the Brain.*

Zenon Pylyshyn is Professor of Psychology and of Computer Science at the University of Western Ontario in London, where he is Director of the Centre for Cognitive Science. His research interests have ranged from performance of human operators in control systems to topics in psycholinguistics. His current research is about mechanisms for human perception of visual displays. His book, *Computation and Cognition: Toward a Foundation for Cognitive Science,* is reviewed in this volume.

George Reeke is Associate Professor and Head of the Laboratory of Biological Modelling at The Rockefeller University. He is known for contributions to protein crystallography and is the principal developer of the Cortical Network Simulator software for neural modeling. Current interests include pattern recognition, perceptual categorization, and motor control.

Paul Rosenbloom is Associate Professor in the Computer Science Department, and Acting Deputy Director of the Intelligent Systems Division of the Information Sciences Institute, at the University of Southern California. His areas of interest include integrated architectures for intelligence, learning, problem solving and planning, models of memory (and their implementation), autonomous agents in simulation environments, expert systems, neural networks, and cognitive modeling. He is best known for his work on speed-up learning and the Soar integrated architecture. Recent books include *Universal Subgoaling and Chunking: The Automatic Generation and Learning of Goal Hierarchies* and *The Soar Papers: Research on Integrated Intelligence* (two volumes, with John Laird and Allen Newell).

Roger C. Schank is John Evans Professor of Electrical Engineering and Computer Science, Professor of Education and Social Policy, and Professor of Psychology at Northwestern University. He is the founder and director of the Institute for the Learning Sciences. He is best known for his work on natural language processing, story understanding, models of learning and memory, and case-based reasoning. His current research interests are in the area of developing innovative computer-based learning environments based on cognitive theories of learning, memory, and reasoning. His most recent books are *Tell Me a Story* and *The Connoisseur's Guide to the Mind.*

Herbert A. Simon is Richard King Mellon University Professor of Computer Science and Psychology at Carnegie Mellon University. He has worked in artificial intelligence and cognitive science since 1955 and is author of *Models of Discovery, Human Problem Solving* with Allen Newell, *Models of Thought* (two volumes), and numerous other books and articles.

Stephen W. Smoliar is Member of the Research Staff of the Institute of Systems Science at the National University of Singapore. His current research interests are in multimedia content understanding and computer-assisted piano pedagogy, and he is managing the Video Classification Project. He is best known for his papers on computer applications to music theory.

Mark J. Stefik is Principal Scientist at the Xerox Palo Alto Research Center. He is best known for his research on planning with constraints, computer support for collaboration, and object-oriented programming. His current research interests are in computer systems for managing intellectual property rights. His forthcoming textbook is *Introduction to Knowledge Systems.*

Lucy Suchman is Principal Scientist and heads the Work Practice and Technology area at Xerox Palo Alto Research Center. Suchman's research concerns the application of studies of work practice to computer systems design. Her book, *Plans and Situated Actions: The Problem of Human-Machine Communication,* is reviewed in this volume.

Peter M. Todd is Research Scientist in the Adaptive Animat Research Group (AARG) at the Rowland Institute for Science, Cambridge, Massachusetts. His research interests include evolutionary psychology and the exploration of adaptive behavior, particularly through computer models of evolving artificial creatures, and models of human musical cognition and composition; in the latter area he has edited a book, with D. Gareth Loy, entitled *Music and Connectionism.*

André Vellino is a logician for the Computing Research Lab at Bell-Northern Research and Adjunct Professor in the Department of Systems and Computer Engineering at Carleton University. His research has centered on the complexity of automated theorem proving and, more recently, constraint logic programming. He is coauthor of *Prolog Programming in Depth.*

Daniel S. Weld is Associate Professor in the Department of Computer Science and Engineering at the University of Washington. Although he is best known for his work on modeling and model-based reasoning, his current research interests center around planning algorithms, agent architectures, and intelligent information services. Recent books include *Readings in Qualitative Reasoning about Physical Systems* (edited with J. de Kleer) and *Theories of Comparative Analysis.*

Michael P. Wellman is Assistant Professor in the Department of Electrical Engineering and Computer Science at the University of Michigan. His research centers on computational decision making, including techniques for qualitative probabilistic reasoning and decision-theoretic planning. Currently, he is investigating market-oriented approaches to the design of distributed decision-making systems. He is the author of *Formulation of Tradeoffs in Planning under Uncertainty,* and coauthor (with Thomas L. Dean) of *Planning and Control.*

Terry Winograd is Professor of Computer Science at Stanford University. He directs the Project on People, Computers, and Design at Stanford, where he is developing a program on Human-Computer Interaction Design. Winograd has done extensive research and writing on the design of human-computer interaction. His early research on natural language understanding by computers was a milestone in artificial intelligence, and he has written two books and numerous articles on that topic. His book *Understanding Computers and Cognition: A New Foundation for Design* (with Fernando Flores) is reviewed in this volume. His most recent book, coedited with Paul Adler, is *Usability: Turning Technologies into Tools.*

Index

Artificial Intelligence (selected titles)

Patrick Henry Winston, founding editor

J. Michael Brady, Daniel G. Bobrow, and Randall Davis, current editors

Artificial Intelligence: An MIT Perspective, Volumes I and II, edited by Patrick Henry Winston and Richard Henry Brown, 1979

NETL: A System for Representing and Using Real-World Knowledge, Scott Fahlman, 1979

The Interpretation of Visual Motion, Shimon Ullman, 1979

Turtle Geometry: The Computer as a Medium for Exploring Mathematics, Harold Abelson and Andrea di Sessa, 1981

Robot Manipulators: Mathematics, Programming, and Control, Richard P. Paul, 1981

Computational Models of Discourse, edited by Michael Brady and Robert C. Berwick, 1982

Robot Motion: Planning and Control, edited by Michael Brady, John M. Hollerbach, Timothy Johnson, Tomás Lozano-Pérez, and Matthew T. Mason, 1982

Robot Hands and the Mechanics of Manipulation, Matthew T. Mason and J. Kenneth Salisbury, Jr., 1985

The Acquisition of Syntactic Knowledge, Robert C. Berwick, 1985

The Connection Machine, W. Daniel Hillis, 1985

Legged Robots that Balance, Marc H. Raibert, 1986

ACTORS: A Model of Concurrent Computation in Distributed Systems, Gul A. Agha, 1986

Knowledge-Based Tutoring: The GUIDON Program, William Clancey, 1987

AI in the 1980s and Beyond: An MIT Survey, edited by W. Eric L. Grimson and Ramesh S. Patil, 1987

Visual Reconstruction, Andrew Blake and Andrew Zisserman, 1987

Reasoning about Change: Time and Causation from the Standpoint of Artificial Intelligence, Yoav Shoham, 1988

Model-Based Control of a Robot Manipulator, Chae H. An, Christopher G. Atkeson, and John M. Hollerbach, 1988

A Robot Ping-Pong Player: Experiment in Real-Time Intelligent Control, Russell L. Andersson, 1988

The Paralation Model: Architecture-Independent Parallel Programming, Gary Sabot, 1988

Automated Deduction in Nonclassical Logics: Efficient Matrix Proof Methods for Modal and Intuitionistic Logics, Lincoln Wallen, 1989

Shape from Shading, edited by Berthold K.P. Horn and Michael J. Brooks, 1989

Ontic: A Knowledge Representation System for Mathematics, David A. McAllester, 1989

Solid Shape, Jan J. Koenderink, 1990

Theories of Comparative Analysis, Daniel S. Weld, 1990